Child Psychology and Development

Child Psychology and Development

S.K. Mangal
Formerly Principal, Professor and Head
Department of Post Graduate Studies & Research
C.R. College of Education, Rohtak

Shubhra Mangal
Principal, Professor and Head
Department of Post Graduate Studies
C.R.S. College of Education, Noida

STERLING⊒

STERLING PUBLISHERS (P) LTD.
Regd. Office: A1/256 Safdarjung Enclave,
New Delhi-110029. CIN: U22110DL1964PTC211907
Tel: 26387070, 26386209; Fax: 91-11-26383788
E-mail: mail@sterlingpublishers.in
www.sterlingpublishers.in

Child Psychology and Development
© 2019, S.K. Mangal and Shubhra Mangal
ISBN 978 93 86245 54 0
First Edition: April 2019

Printed and Published in India by

Sterling Publishers Pvt. Ltd.,
Plot No. 13, Ecotech-III, Greater Noida - 201306, U. P. India

Preface

Children are important as they are the real asset and future of any society, nation or civilisation in which they grow, develop and function. They are valuable to their parents and family, teachers and community members who have immense interest in seeing them grow and develop, adjust and behave in a useful way in the available environment for the good of the children themselves, as well as the family and society. But to achieve all this, the cooperation, help, proper guidance and well-intended efforts of the parents, family members, elders, teachers and community members are also needed to the children for beginning their life's journey, achieving their growth and developmental potential in a proper way as well as learning the needed behaviour to adjust, progress and performing their role as a responsible member of society. The task performed or the responsibilities to be shared on this account on the part of all the stakeholders of the children's interest and welfare, thus, are quite challenging not only in terms of their nature but also on account of the stakes involved in seeking such welfare of the growing children. A child's rearing and educating, in fact, is not as simple as it looks. It needs a lot of art and skills that need to be learned on their part for this purpose. They must be well acquainted with each and every aspect of the what, how and why of a child's growth and development, and the behavioural change that occurs at each stage and aspects of their development. Moreover, children are different and unique in the sense that (i) they show a remarkable resemblance in terms of the developmental path followed, milestones achieved and behavioural changes demonstrated at one or the other stage of their development in a variety of ways describable through general characteristics of the one or the other developmental stage, and (ii) they have their own uniqueness and specificities in reference to the development level achieved and behaviour demonstrated by them at one or the other environmental situation

In addition, it is also seen that a number of problems arise during rearing, imparting education and looking after the interest of developing children during one or the other stage of their development. Many of them are related with their psychological andlbehavioural functioning and maladjustment suffered on account of the many socio-cultural practice, and global changes occurring in societies across the world. The knowledge and understanding of all these aspects and issues are verydessential on the part of the parents, family members, teachers, well wishers and helpers of children for their proper development and welfare. The responsibility on this behalf can be very well executed by the literature available particularly the texts written on the subject of Child Psychology and Child Development. The present work entitled"*Child psychology and Developmen* is specifically designed and developed for serving this exact purpose but in its own way. For meeting its objectives, the contents or subject material of the text have been organized and divided into thirty chapters. A beginning in this direction has been made to provide an introductory description of the meaning, nature and scope of the parent subject Psychology and its off shoot Child Psychology in Chapter 1 and 2 of the text. Chapter 3 is then aimed at providing an introductory description of the concepts child growth and development along with the knowledge of the underlying principles and needs of their study.dThis is then followed by a description in Chapter 4 about the various methods, techniques and designs employed for investigating and knowing about the developmental pattern andlbehavioural changes occurring in developing children. Later a number of chapters ranging from Chapter 5 to Chaptere21 have been specifically written to provide quite a detailed and comprehensive account of the processes and mechanism of different aspects of a child's growth and development from the time of their conception till the attainment of maturity. In this concern a beginningnis made in Chapter 5 to provide a detailed description of the theories and perspectives related to child development such as biological and hereditary theories,lbehavioural and environmental theories, psychoanalytic theories of Freud and Adler, ecological perspective involving Lorenz's theory of Imprinting and Bronfenbrenner's Bio-Ecological theory. The rest of these theories, deal specifically with the description and explanation of the development of children in specific areas such as cognitive, moral and socio-cultural in the name of Piaget and Bruner's theory of cognitive development, Piaget and Kohlberg's theory of moral development, Erickson's theory of psycho-social development , Vygotsky's theory of socio-cultural developmen, and the theories of language development have been discussed in the subsequent chapters of the text. Chapter 6 then describes the mechanism and role of genetics (heredity) and environment in the development of a child. It is followed by a detailed description of the development of a child in its prenatal period, the process of his birth, possible birth complications, methods of delivery, after birth car, and the factors affecting the pre-natal development of the child. Chapter 8 provides the description about the development of a child related to his physical aspect including the development of essential physiological habits related to his sleeping and eatingrbehaviour, toilet training and handedness. Chapters 9,n10,n11,e12, 13 ,n1 and 16 of the text then provids the necessary account of a child's development carried out in the name of moral, sensory, mental or cognitive, language, moral or character development. Chapter 15 deals with quite a unique characteristic distinctly visible in the period of infancy, named as attachment and temperament with all necessary details about their concept, underlying theories and mechanism of development.

The role of the self is unmatchable in seeking one's own development in all its dimensions. Therefore, it is quite essential toebe familiar with the concept of one's self along with all its necessary aspects such as self–awareness, self-concept, self-esteem, self-efficacy and self-regulation. It has been usefully carried out in Chapter 17 of the text. Chapter 18 provides a useful description of the characteristics of various stages of development ranging from the period of infancy to adolescence. Here the description about the development going on in the period of adolescence in the various areas and aspects have beentexplained along with the discussion of the age-related needs and problems as well as stress-generating issues of modern age such as increasing loneliness, changing family structure and rising permissiveness. Chapter 19 provides the description of developmental tasks — those tasks that are carried out at the various developmental stages by the developing children. It is followed by Chapter 20 which throws light on the role of maturation in the development and learning on the part of children. The discussion about the development going on in the various areas and aspects at the various ages and stages of their development ends in chapter 2 with a useful discussion carried out in the formation or development of an integrated personality.

The subsequent chapters ranging fromeChapter 21 to Chapter 25, then present a direct application of the principles of child psychology in the name of acquainting the parents, care givers, teacher, andscounsellors with (i) the different styles or practices of child rearing, (ii) schooling of the developing children in relation to issues such as peer influencs, school culture, relationship with teachers, teacher expectations and school achievement, being out of schoo, and overage learners, (iii)lbehavioural problems of the growing children such as aggression, bullying and drug addiction, (iv)gcounselling of children in specific stressful conditions such as separation or divorce of the parents, loss of parents in armed conflicts, and victims or survivors of child abuse.

The developmental process of the children including the subsequentlbehavioural changes among them ishto a large extent influenced, controlled and shaped by a number of socio-cultural factors and forces playing their roles in a variety of shapes and forms. Deprivation and its impact on children, marginalization and the stereotyping prevalent in society and cultures, the impacs of growing urbanization, globalization and the impact of media all may be found to play a great role in shaping and influencing therbehaviour and development of the growing children in quite a mentionable way. The what, why and how of such impacts and influences have been properly discussed respectively in Chaptersx26,n27,t2, ande29 of the text. The last chapter of the text Chapter 3t is exclusively devoted to the discussion of quite a useful and essential aspect related to the safety, protection and overall well-being of the children in the name of 'Protection of Child Rights'.

In this way, the text in its organzsed format clearly stands for providing the needed information, knowledge and skill to the concerned persons for getting them adequately equipped to help and assist children on the path of their wholesome development, progress and overall well-being. The book has been adequately illustrated with examples, diagrams and tables for assisting the readers in their understanding of the topics discussed. For arriving at a proper and adequate understanding and getting a quick glance and a comprehensive view of what has been discussed in a given chapter, each chapter has been provided with a chapter summary. In addition, with an aim to help the readers delve deep into the subject, all the related references have been given at the tail end of each chapter as well at the end of the text in the form of a detailed bibliography.

Although at present as a text this work is purposely designed and developed for meeting the needs of students and faculty of B.A. and M.A. (Psychology), B.A. and M.A. (Education), Teacher Training courses, Diploma in Child education, caring and welfare, Nursing, Guidance andgCounsellingH however, with its wide coverage and useful discussion on the various aspects and issues related to child development, child caring, welfare and protection it can also prove quite useful to all those who are entrusted with the responsibilities of growing children as well as who are interested in assisting and seeking welfare of developing children.

The Authors are indebted to the various scholars, researcher, and experts in dealing with the what, how and why of the issues related to the developmental processes andlbehavioural changes occurring in growing children, the views and opinions of whom have been freely incorporated in the text. The special mention in this concern may be made to the experiences gathered and knowledge gained as a result of visits to USA in the past three years as a part of interactions and also the availability of lin+ facility of the US library. The authors are indebted to all of them for their direct and indirect impacts in setting the direction and evolution of the ideas for the text material. Authors also intend to thank the publisher, Sterling Publishers, New Delhi, especially the editorial and production team, for their praiseworthy efforts in presenting this text in such a useful form.

With the above submission, it is earnestly hoped that the text will be widely read and appreciated by all those for whose benefit it has been written. However, nothing is ever perfect and complete and therefore, the suggestions for bringing improvement in the book will be highly appreciated and thankfully acknowledged by the authors and publisher.

S.K. Mangal
Shubhra Mangal

Contents

Demerits of Interview • Case Study Method • Purposes or Objectives of the Case Study Method • Subjects of the Case Study • How to Make Use of the Case Study Method • Case Study of a Problem Adolescent • Remedial Work and Suggestions • Conclusion • Reflective Journals about Children • Structure of Reflective Journal • How to Proceed for Reflective Writing • Maintaining Anecdotal Records • Observed Event and Behaviours • Benefits and Purposes of Anecdotal Records • How to Write an Anecdotal Record • Taking Help from the Narratives • How to Carry out the Task in a Proper Way • Distinction Between Narratives and Anecdotal Records • Advantages of Narratives • Disadvantages of Narratives • Research Designs Used in Developmental Studies • The Longitudinal Design • The Cross-sectional Design • Summary • References and Suggested Readings

5. Theories and Perspectives in Child Development   79

What is Meant by the Term Theory of Child Development? • Biological or Hereditary Theories • The Merits and Good Points • The Limitations and Fallacy • Behaviourist or Environmentalist Theories • Psychoanalytic Theories or Perspective • Freud's Psycho-Sexual Theory of Child development • Alfred Adler's Perspective About the Development of Children • Ethological Perspective or Theories • Lorenz's Theory of Imprinting • Bronfenbrenner's Bio-Ecological Theory of Child Development • Bronfenbrenner's Ecological Systems and their Role in Child Development • The **Microsystem** • The Mesosystem • The Exosystem • The Macrosystem • The Chronosystem • Evaluation of the Role of Bronfenbrenner's Theory or Model of Child Development • Summary • References and Suggesting Readings

6. Genetics (Heredity) and Environment   99

What is Genetics? • What is Heredity? • Determination of Gender — Boy Or Girl • Heredity and Variations • Twins and Heredity • Laws of Heredity Governing Transfer of Heredity Characteristics • Law of Similarity (like begets like) • Law of Variation • Law of Regression • What is Environment • Boring, Langfield and Weld • Wordsworth and Marquis • Measures For Studying the Role of Heredity And Environment • Twins and Family Studies • What Is Then Contributed By Heredity And What By Environment • Genetics and Child Development • Implications of the knowledge related to the mechanism of heredity and environment • Summary • References and Suggested Readings

7. Pre-natal Development, Birth and Care of Newborns   115

Introduction • Conception of the Child and Beginning of Life • The Developmental Journey After Conception • The Period of Zygote • The Period of Embryo • The Period of Foetus • Three Trimesters of a Mother's Pregnancy • Labour and Delivery of Babies • The Stages of Labour • The Screening of the Baby in the Mother • Birthing Options and Techniques • The Decision About the Place of Delivery • The Decision About the Procedure or Technique Used For Delivery • Birth Complications • The Occurrence of Events Immediately After Birth • The Apgar Scale and Its Use for The Assessment of a Newborn • Weighing and Screening of the Baby • Factors Affecting the Prenatal Development of a Child • Summary • References and Suggested Readings

of Employing Attachment Q-Set • The Procedure or Steps Involved in the Use of AQS method: • What is Temperament? • Role of Heredity and Environment in Temperament Development • The Stability and Modification in Temperament • The Concept of 'Goodness of fit' and Child Rearing • Theories or Models of Temperament • Thomas and Chess's Theory or Model of Temperament • EAS Theory or Model of Temperament • Rothbart's Theory or Model of Temperament • Measuring Temperament • Critical Questions Indicating a Particular Type of Temperamental Dimension: • Summary • References and Suggested Readings

29. Impact of Media on Growing Children and Adolescents   500
The Meaning of the Term Media or Mass-Media • Impact of Mass Media on Growing Children and Adolescents • Deconstruction of Significant Events that Media Highlights and Creates • Summary • References and Suggested Readings

30. Protection of Child Rights   506
Introduction • Role and Contribution of UNICEF • Role and Contribution of WHO • Role and Contribution of National Commission for Protection of Child Rights • Role and Contribution of National Human Rights Commission • Functions and activities carried out by NHRC • Role and Contribution of Child Helplines • What is a Child Helpline? • The Field of its Operation • Objectives Served by the Child Helpline • Functioning of a Child Helpline • Role and Contribution of NGOs • Non-Governmental Organisations Operating at the International Level • Amnesty International • Children's Defense Fund • Human Rights Action Center • Human Rights Watch • Human Rights Without Frontiers • Non-Governmental Organisations Working at the National Level • Summary • References and Suggested Readings

List of Figures

List of Tables

1

Psychology — Meaning, Nature and Scope

Introduction

The subject psychology is nowadays becoming more and more popular. In comparison to other subjects a larger number of students are opting for it at the senior secondary and degree levels. Even in the most prestigious competitive examinations like the IAS and the allied examinations or the Provincial Civil Service examinations, the number of students opting for psychology, for the preliminary and mains, is increasing every year. The reason for its popularity lies with its body of knowledge, which is quite interesting, and its wide use and applications in almost all the walks and spheres of life.

However, there was a time when there was no such subject as psychology. The 'study of mind' was covered as a separate branch of philosophy called *Mental Philosophy*. Hence psychology is a legitimate child of philosophy. The breakaway of psychology from philosophy is said to be due to the fact that it gave up sheer speculation in favour of scientific procedure. This drift of psychology from philosophy to science took a long course, swaying one way or the other. Such a movement has been responsible for the change in the meaning and definitions of psychology from time to time as can be observed from the following discussion.

Defining Psychology

Etymological derivation of the word 'Psychology' indicates that it has its origin from two Greek words — psyche and logos. The word 'logos' conveys the process of the rational discourse of a study. However, the meaning and interpretation of the word 'psyche' has been in a state of change from time to time, leading to subsequent changes in the ways of defining the term 'psychology' as may be evident from the following four stages of its evolution.

- **First Stage.** By taking the meaning of the word 'psyche' as soul, psychology was first defined as the "study of soul". The subject philosophy almost dominated and influenced the views of the scholars including psychologists. Consequently, a philosophical meaning and interpretation was given to the word 'psyche'. However, soon such interpretation faced criticism when critics asked what is soul? How can it be studied? And so on. The inability to answer such questions led to the search for a new meaning of the word 'psyche'.

- **Second Stage.** At this stage, the philosopher cum psychologists tried to define psychology as the "study of the mind" by giving a new meaning and interpretation to the word 'psyche' in the form of 'mind'. Although the word 'mind' was less vague and mysterious than soul, it faced the same criticism with questions like — what is mind? How can it be studied? And so on.

- **Third Stage.** The criticism and unacceptability of the meaning of the word psyche as soul or mind led the psychologists to a new search of its proper meaning. The initiative was taken by famous psychologists like William James (1890), Wilhelm Wundt and Edward Bradford Titchener (1894) who, while interpreting psyche as consciousness, defined psychology as a study of consciousness. According to these psychologists the description and explanation of the states of consciousness is the task of psychology which is usually done by introspection (the process of looking within). In the state of consciousness, we remain aware of the situation, conscious or alive to the task we are doing and the process of thinking and feeling which is growing in our mind.

  This definition too was rejected on the ground that it had a very narrow vision as it did not include the sub-conscious and the unconscious activities of the mind, and also due to the most subjective nature of the method of introspection which the definition had taken into account.

- **Fourth Stage.** This stage in the evolution of the definition of the subject of psychology reflects the advent of the modern era of science and technology. Consequently, in the definition of psychology the word 'study' was replaced by 'science'. The first psychologist who, besides using the word science in place of study, replaced consciousness with total behaviour (conscious as well as unconscious), was the famous William McDougall. In the book *Physiological Psychology* published in 1905, he wrote: "Psychology may be best and most comprehensively defined as the positive Science of the conduct of living creatures." Later in 1908, in his book Introduction to Social Psychology, he added the word 'behaviour' to his definition and finally in An Outline of Psychology, gave the following meaningful definition: "Psychology is a Science which aims to give us better understanding and control of the behaviour of the organism as a whole." (1949, p. 38)

  In the same period, an American Professor Walter Bowers Pillsbury in his book Essentials of Psychology published in 1911 gave the same behavioural definition of the term psychology in these words, "Psychology may be most satisfactorily defined as the Science of human behaviour."

  However, later in 1913, J.B. Watson, the father of behaviourism, proposed to elaborate the concept of the term behaviour by including in it both human and animal behaviours and consequently he defined psychology as *"The science of behaviour"* (taking into account the human as well as animal behaviour).

  In the subsequent years of the 20th century, the scholars and psychologists tried to similarly define psychology as a science of behaviour.

  Let us cite a few important definitions for the purpose of illustration. First definition of this nature may be cited from the famous authors and psychologists, Woodworth and Marquis, who wrote:

"Psychology is the scientific study of the activities of the individual in relation to his environment." (1948, p. 20)

Going further on similar lines, the famous writer on psychology N.L. Munn summarised it in one of his books as follows:

"Psychology today concerns itself with the scientific investigation of behaviour." (1967, p. 4)

Analysis of Definitions

A close analysis of the definitions of the subject psychology discussed earlier clearly reveals that starting from their vague and mysterious concepts having a philosophical base, the definitions of psychology have now concentrated on the scientific investigation of behaviour. Commenting upon the history of evolution of these definitions, Woodworth (1948) writes, *"First psychology lost its soul, then its mind, then it lost its consciousness, it still has behaviour of sort."*

Hence, as per the latest definition, psychology is a science of behaviour, or a scientific study of the behavioural activities and experiences. Here the main emphasis is on the term 'behaviour' whose scientific study or investigation is clearly aimed through the theoretical and practical activities to be organised under psychology.

However, the issues which remain unanswered, even at this stage may be discussed as follows:

1. What should be clearly inferred from the term 'behaviour' whose study we aim at in psychology?

2. We aim to organise a scientific investigation of behaviour through psychology. It implies that psychology is a science quite capable of organising a proper scientific investigation or study of the behaviour. Is it true, therefore, that psychology is a science? If yes, then what kind of science is it?

Let us try to discuss and look for some answers to these issues.

Behaviour: Meaning and nature

The latest concept of the term behaviour has a very wide and comprehensive meaning revealed as follows:

(a) "Any manifestation of life is activity," says Woodworth (1948) and behaviour is a collective name for all these activities. Therefore, the term 'behaviour' includes not only motor (conative) activities like walking, swimming, dancing and so on, but also activities like thinking, reasoning, imagining (cognitive activities) and feeling happy, sad, angry (affective activities), etc.

(b) It concerns all the segments of human mind — conscious, sub-conscious and unconscious, and, therefore, covers not only the overt behaviour but also inner experiences and mental processes i.e., covert behaviour.

(c) In psychology, we study the behaviour of all living organisms. Therefore, it includes the behaviour of human beings as well as that of birds, insects, plants and animals, of normals as well as of abnormals, and of children as well as of adults.

Therefore, the term behaviour is too comprehensive to cover all the life activities and experiences of all the living organisms.

Nature of Psychology

Should Psychology be Considered a Science or Not

After a long discussion among scholars and psychologists on the acceptance of psychology as a science and its nature as scientific, the verdict has been in favour of giving it the status of science. The observation and concluding remarks of the famous authority N.L. Munn may be cited as a solid evidence for this purpose. He writes — "*Psychology is a science and a properly trained psychologist is a scientist, or at least a practitioner who uses scientific methods and information resulting from scientific investigation.*" (1967, p. 4)

Besides such assertions and observations of the various authorities, we can put the following arguments to justify its status as a science:

• Much like sciences, it has an organised and systematic body of knowledge, facts, principles and theories which are subject to change on the discovery of new facts and emergence of new principles and theories.

• Similar to sciences, it believes in the cause and effect relationship. It declares that each of the behaviour has at its roots, the factor of its causes and development.

• Like sciences, it emphasizes the search for truth. It studies facts of behaviour and describes the laws governing them.

• It adopts the method of systematic inquiry and scientific approach as used by sciences.

• Like other sciences, psychology too has its pure and applied aspects.

With all such evidences, it can be safely concluded that it is an accepted reality that psychology is a science.

Psychology as a Science

Science can be divided into two broad categories — Normative and Positive. The question arises as to which category should psychology be included in. Psychology studies facts and describes 'what is'. It does not concern with 'ought to be' as emphasized by Normative Sciences like Ethics, Logic, Philosophy, etc. Therefore, it is quite proper to describe it as a positive science.

What kind of positive science is psychology?

(i) It is not as perfect a science as physics, chemistry or mathematics. It is a behavioural science which deals with the behaviour of an organism.

(ii) This behaviour is quite dynamic and unpredictable. We are not consistent in our behaviour. On the other hand, physical reactions which are studied by the natural sciences are always predictable. This makes the study in natural sciences more exact, accurate and objective. Psychology has not yet attained the status of these sciences although it is trying hard to be more objective, exact and accurate. Therefore, it is better to name it as a developing positive science.

In the end, we can conclude that psychology although termed as positive science, is not yet much developed as the natural sciences and therefore can be defined as:

Psychology is a developing positive science which enables us to study the behaviour of a living organism in relation to his environment.

Scope of Psychology

What do we mean by the scope of a subject? The scope of a subject can usually be discussed in the following two heads:

A. Branches and the Fields of its Study
B. The limits and boundaries of its operation and applications

Let us discuss the scope of psychology in relation to these two heads.

A. Branches and the Fields of its Study

General psychology

It is relatively a large area or field of psychology which deals with the fundamental rules, principles and theories of the subject in relation to the study of the behaviour of normal adult human beings.

Abnormal psychology

It is that branch or field of psychology which describes and explains the behaviour of abnormal people in relation to their own environment. The causes, symptoms and syndromes, description and treatment of the abnormalities of behaviour form the subject matter of this branch.

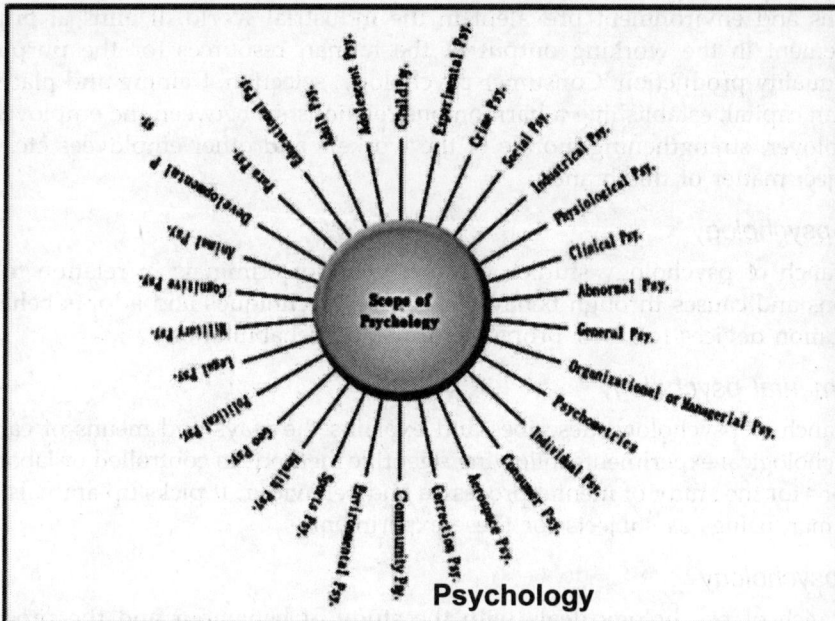

Fig. 1.1 Scope of Psychology in terms of its branches of study

Clinical psychology

Clinical psychology comes at the forefront after the work and operations of the knowledge and activities connected with abnormal psychology have been done. The knowledge about abnormality of behaviour and the underlying causes, symptoms, etc., provide necessary framework to the subject matter and skills required for the study of clinical psychology. The abnormality and maladaptation of the behaviour leads to mental illness and diseases. A proper diagnosis of such illness and diseases is then the work of clinical psychology. It analyses the causes of such maladaptation and mental illness and then suggests ways and means for the proper treatment and rehabilitation of the patient. The experts, who provide such treatment to the patients attending the clinic or hospital, are known as clinical psychologists.

Physiological psychology

This branch of psychology describes and explains the biological and psychological basis of behaviour. The study of the internal environment and psychological structure of the body, particularly brain, nervous system and functioning of the glands in relation to the conative, cognitive and affective behaviour of the human being, form part of the subject matter of this branch.

Social psychology

This branch of psychology studies human behaviour in relation to its social environment — one's behaviour as a member of the group, the process of communication and inter-personal relationship, group dynamics, social relationship, etc.

Industrial psychology

It is that branch of psychology which studies human behaviour in relation to the situations and environment prevalent in the industrial world. It aims at bringing improvement in the working output of the human resources for the purpose of raising quality production. Consumer psychology, selection, training and placement of human capital, establishing a harmonious relationship between the employee and the employer, strengthening morale of the workers and other employees etc., form the subject matter of this branch.

Crime psychology

This branch of psychology studies the behaviour of criminals in relation to their situations and causes through behaviour analysis techniques and adopts behaviour modification devices for their proper reforms and rehabilitation.

Experimental psychology

This branch of psychology describes and explains the ways and means of carrying out psychological experiments following scientific methods in controlled or laboratory situations for the study of mental processes and behaviour. It picks up animals, birds and human beings as subjects for these experiments.

Child psychology

This branch of psychology deals with the study of behaviour and the process of growth and development of children from conception to the period of adolescence.

Adolescent psychology

In this branch of psychology, we study the process of growth and development during the adolescence period, along with the personality characteristics, behavioural and adjustment problems faced by adolescents. It helps elders understand adolescents in their proper perspectives and also aids in their proper adjustment as well as personal and social welfare.

Adult psychology

This branch of psychology deals with the study of the behaviour of adults. The characteristics of growth and development in various dimensions of their personality, their interests, aptitudes and attitudes, the typical behavioural and adjustment problems especially related to the period etc., are studied under this branch. The knowledge of adult psychology proves helpful to teachers of adult education, workers and counsellors in teaching and guiding their subjects properly for their individual and social progress.

Educational psychology

In this branch of psychology, we try to study the behaviour of the learner, with respect to educational environment. As a science of education, the subject matter of this branch helps in improving all the processes and products of education. The teachers can teach well and the students can learn well with the help of the knowledge and skills gained through the study of this subject. It also helps the teachers in acquiring proper insight for bringing desirable modification in the behaviour and an all-round harmonious personality development of the students.

Para psychology

It is a relatively new branch of psychology. There are instances where people have sensed that somebody is in trouble despite being at a faraway place, have foretold the coming events or have given an account of their previous births. Parapsychology tries to go into the depth of such behaviour related to telepathy, extra-sensory perceptions, rebirth, etc.

Development psychology

This branch of psychology deals with the processes and products of the growth and development of human beings at all stages of life — from conception till death — and in all the aspects of their personality. The study of this branch equips us well with the knowledge of expected behaviour patterns and personality characteristics at various stages of growth and development.

Animal psychology

This branch of psychology deals with the study of animal behaviour in controlled situations. The study of the behaviour patterns of animals, carried out through various types of experiments and observations, constitute the subject matter of this branch. Citable in this connection are the studies related to the behaviour of cats by Thorndike, dogs by Pavlov, rats and pigeons by Skinner and that of chimpanzees by Kohlar and Koffaka. Such studies help in understanding the behaviour of these animals in some or the other type of controlled situation. The other major benefit that can be derived from these studies is of a comparative and inferential nature. We can derive a comparative analysis of the behaviour of different types of animals in a particular situation or environment. The results of these studies can then be generalised in dealing with behavioural adjustment and development problems of human beings.

Cognitive psychology

This branch of psychology deals mainly with the study of the processes and products of growth and development of cognitive abilities and capabilities of human beings. It studies the behaviour of the individuals in relation to the development of his cognitive strengths and their use in challenging circumstances. It emphasizes the role of one's cognitive abilities such as reasoning and thinking, analysis and synthesis, inferring and generalising, intelligence, insight, and so on, in the process of learning, problem solving, creative output, adjustment, etc. The experts dealing with the study of this branch are referred to as cognitive psychologists.

Military psychology

This branch of psychology studies the use of psychological principles and techniques in the world of military science. How to keep the morale of the soldiers and citizens high during war, how to fight a war of propaganda and intelligence services, how to secure better recruitment of the armed forces personnel, how to improve the fighting skills and organisational climate and leadership, etc., are the various topics that are dealt with in this branch of psychology.

Legal psychology

It is that branch of applied psychology which tries to study the behaviour of persons such as clients, criminals, witnesses and so on in their respective surroundings with the help of the application of psychological principles and techniques. The subject matter of this branch deals with improving the ways and means of detecting crimes, false witnesses and other complex phenomena. The root causes of a crime, offence, dispute or any legal case can be properly understood with the help of this branch of psychology, and proper reformatory and rehabilitation measures may be employed.

Political psychology

This branch of psychology relates itself with the use of psychological principles and techniques in studying politics and deriving political gains. The knowledge of the dynamics of group behaviour, judgement of the public opinion, leadership qualities, psychology of a propaganda and suggestions, the art of diplomacy, etc., are some of the key concepts that find place in the subject matter of political psychology.

Experimental psychology

This branch of psychology describes and explains the ways and means of carrying out psychological experiments following scientific methods in controlled or laboratory situations for the study of mental processes and behaviour. It picks up animals, birds and human beings as subjects for these experiments.

Geo-psychology

This branch of psychology describes and analyses the relationship between physical environment, particularly weather, climate, soil and landscape, with behaviour.

Health psychology

In this branch, the facts, principles and theories of psychology are used in the task of preservation of the physical and mental health of individuals. Since many of our physical ailments are said to be due to our anxieties, worries, stress, conflicts and frustrations, psychological handling of the affected individuals may help in the prevention and treatment of various physical and mental disorders, ailments and diseases.

Sports psychology

This branch of psychology deals with the study of the behaviour of players and sports personnel vis-a-vis the activities, experiences, situations and environment prevalent in the world of sports. Today, this branch of psychology is playing quite an effective role in bringing desirable improvement in the processes and persons connected to the sports world. This includes bringing improvement in the mental and physical health of the players, inculcating in them true sportsmanship through suitable behaviour modification and group dynamics techniques, providing sufficient motivation and raising their morale at the time of competition, devising training and coaching techniques so that the players excel in individual as well as in group activities.

Environmental psychology

Environment plays a key role in affecting and influencing the process of growth and development, evolution of behaviour patterns, learning of specific personality characteristics, disorders, behaviour problems, etc. The description and analysis of the process and the ways and the steps we can take for modifying and structuring environment for the social well-being — all these constitute the subject matter of environmental psychology. An environmental psychologist thus gives more emphasis and weightage to the environmental setting and facilities for moulding the behaviour of the individuals in the desired direction, solving their personal and social problems and working towards their individual and social progress.

Community psychology

A particular community, society or group is known to possess its own psychology of thinking, feeling and doing. Those belonging to this community have a unique style of living and behaving, coping with one's self and the environment, and maintaining intra-personal and interpersonal relations. The study of such behaviour patterns and styles may thus help in understanding the individual and studying group behaviour of the members of this community, the merits and limitations of the community resources as facilitator or barrier in their progress and so on. Such knowledge and understanding of community psychology may then help students, researchers and social workers devise means and ways for the welfare and progress of the community.

Correctional psychology

This branch of psychology is concerned with the corrective measures and activities designed for modifying the undesirable, abnormal and maladaptive behaviour of affected individuals. It discusses, explains and suggests the ways and means of diagnosis, prevention as well as treatment of the deviant behaviour, so that it is brought back to the right channel.

Aerospace psychology

It is relatively a new development of psychology and studies the behaviour of aeronauts and astronauts, who venture to travel in space. They face the challenges of a new environment quite different from that on Earth. As soon as they go higher and higher in space, there is tremendous change in their physiological functioning. Their mental functioning, emotional setup, etc., also get affected. The new challenges faced on account of weightlessness, changed equations of gravitational powers, and other special situations and difficulties created by the space-related environment demand from them quite a lot in terms of adapting behaviour and sound mental health. Aerospace psychology tries to focus on these issues in order to research the ways and means of providing adequate behavioural training to all those who plan to become astronauts or inhabitants of space colonies in the coming future.

Consumer psychology

This branch of psychology is concerned with the study of the behaviour of the consumers in relation to their present economic and social status and consumption-related environment. The study is quite valuable for manufacturers, advertisers, shopkeepers and salesman who wish to reach the mind and heart of their consumers for the sale of their products. What do the consumers need? What are their expectations from the products they wish to buy? What kind of behaviour do they expect from the shopkeepers and sales persons? How can they be approached, influenced or motivated to purchase a particular brand? And so on. A number of such questions can be successfully answered through the study of consumer psychology.

Individual psychology

There are differences among individuals with respect to each and every aspect of human behaviour and personality traits. The nature and causes of such differences are studied under individual psychology.

Psychometrics

This branch of psychology is concerned with the construction and use of different tests and techniques meant for the measurement or assessment of the various types of human abilities and capacities, the processes and products of human behaviour and nature of relationships and adjustment, etc. Thus, the task of construction and standardisation of various intelligence tests, interest and aptitude tests, attitude scales, inventories and other techniques meant for the assessment of personality traits, behavioural characteristics and adjustment, etc., are carried out through the study of this branch. Since statistical methods and techniques are very much needed in the construction, standardisation and application of these measures, these are also included in the subject matter of this branch of psychology.

Organisational or managerial psychology

The popularity of this branch of psychology is on a continuous rise on account of its utility in bringing desired efficiency in the organisational climate and managerial capacities. With the help of the knowledge and skills acquired through the study of this branch, we can properly study the behaviour of human resources related to the organisational climate of an establishment or institution. In the light of this study, we can devise suitable means and measures for maintaining proper co-ordination and inter-relationship among personnel holding different positions in an establishment. We can help them in maintaining their zeal and enthusiasm for exercising their duties properly and co-operatively by seeking proper job satisfaction and adjustment in their work environment.

In this way, we can try to provide an account of the scope of the subject psychology by dividing it into various branches on the basis of their fields of operation, nature of the subject matter included, and experiences gained and advantages derived from their use. However, by this division, it should not be assumed that all these branches of psychology are highly independent, autonomous and unrelated to each other. On the contrary, all being the offshoot of the subject psychology are quite interdependent and related to each other. We divide them into different branches only for the sake of our convenience with regard to their specialised study and application.

B. The limits and boundaries of its operation and applications

The field of operations and applications of the subject of psychology is too vast. It studies, describes and explains the behaviour of living organisms. Here the terms 'behaviour' and 'living organism' carry quite comprehensive and wide meanings.

*   Behaviour includes all types of life activities and experiences of a living organism — whether conative, cognitive or affective, implicit or explicit, conscious, unconscious or subconscious.

*   Besides this, the term living organism is to be applied to all living creatures created by the Almighty irrespective of their species, caste, colour, age, gender, mental or physical state. Thus normal, abnormal, children, adolescents, youth, adults, old, criminals, patients, workers, officials, students, teachers, parents, consumers and producers belonging to different stock, spheres and walks of human life are all studied under psychology.

*   Moreover, as a subject psychology does not limit itself to the study of human behaviour only but also tries to study the behaviour of animals, insects, birds and even plant life.

Summing up in this way, we may easily witness that where there seems some life and we have living organisms, psychology may be needed for the study of the activities and experiences of these living organisms. We know that living organisms as well as their life activities are countless and, therefore, no limit can be imposed upon the fields of its operation and application of the subject psychology. Consequently, we can hereby state the scope of the subject psychology as 'unlimited' — having no rigid boundaries for its study and applications.

Summary

Historically, studied in the name of 'Mental Philosophy' as a separate branch of philosophy, psychology has gradually emerged into a separate discipline claiming the status of science. In doing so, its meaning has changed from time to time as the study of soul, study of mind, study of consciousness and finally as the study of behaviour. Today it is well defined as the science of behaviour by equating the term 'behaviour' with all life activities and experiences of all living organisms.

On account of its scientific nature and characteristics, like its belief in cause and effect relationship, use of scientific methods in investigation and study of behaviour, it has been given the status of a science. However, it has not yet been developed, on account of its limitation, to study the behaviour as exactly as is possible in other natural and applied sciences. Thereby it is designated as a developing science and not as a developed science.

The scope of psychology is quite extensive and wide. It covers the study of all types of behaviour of all living organisms. As living organisms and their life activities are so diverse, no limit can be imposed upon the scope of this subject. It has many branches and fields for the study of all types of their behaviour in its theoretical and applied aspects like general psychology, abnormal psychology, industrial psychology, crime psychology, para-psychology, legal psychology, experimental psychology, animal psychology, military psychology, educational psychology and sports psychology. Equipped with the knowledge, understanding and skills of its so many branches and fields of study, psychology has gained quite wide and diversified applications in all the spheres and walks of life.

References and Suggested Readings

Guilford, J.B. (Ed.), *Fields of Psychology*, Van Nostrand, New York, 1966.

James, W., *Principles of Psychology*, (2 Vols), Henry Holt, New York, 1890.

– – –, *Psychology* (Briefer course), Collier, New York, 1962.

Keller, F.S., *The Definitions of Psychology*, Appleton Century, New York, 1937.

McDougall, W., *Psychology – the Study of Behaviour*, Henry Holt, New York, 1912.

– – –, *An Outline of Psychology*, 13th ed., Methuen, London, 1949.

Munn, N.L., *Introduction to Psychology*, (Indian ed.), Oxford & IBH, Delhi, 1967.

Pilsbury, W.B., *Essentials of Psychology*, Macmillan, New York, 1911.

Watson, J.B., *Psychology as a Behaviourist Views It*, Psycho. rev. Vol. 20, 1913.

– – –, *Psychology from the Standpoint of a Behaviourist*, J.B. Lippincott, Philadelphia, 1919.

– – –, *Behaviourism*, Kegan Paul, London, 1930.

Woodworth, R.S., *Psychology*, Methuen, London, 1945.

– – –, R.S., *Contemporary Schools of Psychology*, Methuen, London, 1948.

Woodworth, R.S. and Marquis, D.G., *Psychology*, 5th ed., Henry Holt, New York, 1948.

2

Child Psychology — Meaning, Nature and Scope

Child Psychology: Meaning and Definition

The subject psychology like other natural sciences has two aspects — Pure and Applied. As pure psychology, it formulates broad principles, brings out theories and suggests techniques for the study of human behaviour which finds the practical shape in its applied aspect, i.e., branches of applied psychology like occupational psychology, clinical psychology, crime psychology, industrial psychology, educational psychology, child psychology and so on.

In its pictorial form, these pure and applied aspects of the subject psychology, along with their branches, can be represented as shown in Figure 2.1.

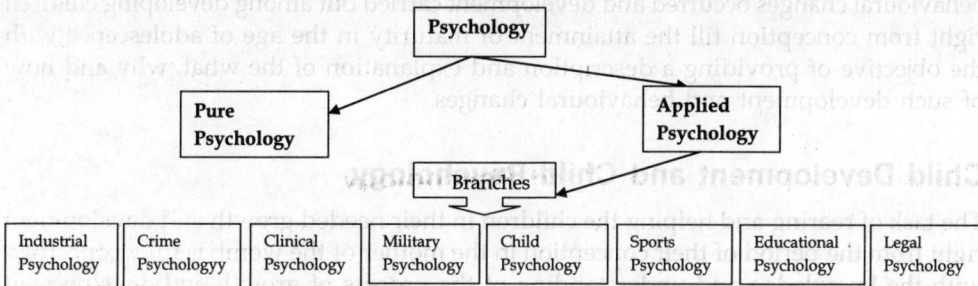

Fig. 2.1: Psychology and its Branches

In this way, child psychology may be seen to represent one of the branches of applied psychology and thus it may be known and identified as a well-intended attempt to apply the knowledge, principles, methods and techniques of psychology to study and know about the development and behaviour of the child specifically in reference to the environment and situations in which he or she is born, brought up and allowed to play their various role in the capacity of a child.

From time to time, scholars and psychologists have tried to define the term Child psychology in their own ways. Some of these definitions are as follows:

Hetherington and Parke (1986:1): Child psychology involves both the description and explanation of changes in children's behaviour and development right from their conception till the attainment of maturity at the adolescent stage.

Schaffer (2004:4): Child psychology is the scientific study of children's behaviour and development.

Vasta, Miller and Ellis (2004:3): Child psychologists in their study and research often resort to developmental studies. Developmental research has two basic goals. One is description to identify children's behaviour at each point in their development and the other is explanation, determining the causes and processes that produce changes in behaviour from one point to the next.

The analysis of the earlier-cited definitions and views about child psychology and child psychologist's task may help us reveal the following things regarding the meaning and characteristics of child psychology.

- Child psychology as a branch of psychology is concerned only with the studying of the behaviour and development of children
- Here the behaviour and development of the children is studied during their entire developmental period (i.e., from the conception till the attainment of maturity at the adolescence age)
- The study of behaviour and development of children is carried out in quite a scientific way with the use of appropriate methods and techniques for this purpose.
- For such study, child psychologists generally get engaged in developmental studies so that they can properly provide description and explanation of what, why and how of the development that occurred as well as the behavioural changes that accompanied the developmental periods.

In this way, as a matter of conclusion, we can define the subject and discipline of child psychology as a branch of psychology helpful in the scientific study of the behavioural changes occurred and development carried out among developing children right from conception till the attainment of maturity in the age of adolescence with the objective of providing a description and explanation of the what, why and how of such development and behavioural changes.

Child Development and Child Psychology

The task of rearing and helping the children in their needed growth and development right from the period of their conception in the mother of the womb is fully concerned with the knowledge and understanding of the process of growth and development in all the dimensions of their personality and demonstrated behaviour. It aims to produce desirable changes in them for the all-round development of their personalities and behavioural functioning in their present and future life.

The essential knowledge and skill to do this job satisfactorily is supplied by the knowledge and applications of the know-how pointed in the subject child psychology. In all its ways and means, Child Psychology helps us to understand the behaviour and development of our children, the range and limits of their capacities, the processes by which they learn, develop and behave in the manner they do in one or the other age or stages of their development.

In this way, the job of a child psychologist resembles that of an engineer, who is a technical expert and supplies all the knowledge and skills essential for the satisfactory accomplishment of a job like the construction of a bridge. In the same way, a child psychologist, who is a technical expert in the field of child behaviour and development, supplies all the information, principles and techniques essential for the growth and development of the children and their effective functioning and behaviour in their present and future (with a full understanding of their genetic foundation, biological and psychological makeup, and environmental facilities needed for erecting the solid structure of their personality).

• In this way, it is quite reasonable to address child psychology as a scientific study of children's behaviour and development. For substantiating the claim of the subject psychology further in this direction, let us now discuss the nature of Child Psychology.

Nature of Child Psychology

One question, that is often put forward, is "what is the nature of child psychology"? The answer that is more generally and readily available in this concern is also quite straight and that is: "The nature of the subject child psychology is sufficiently scientific". The arguments provided by the thinkers in this concern may be summarised as follows:

1. Child psychology is an applied branch of the subject psychology. By applying the principles and techniques of psychology, it tries to study the behaviour and experiences of children. The work and functioning of the subject child psychology is quite similar to its parent subject psychology. The only difference is that while in psychology we deal with the behaviour and development of all individuals in all walks of life, child psychology limits its study to the behaviour and development of children in relation to the environment available to them for their development and functioning. Hence, in their functioning and purposes both may be seen to carry out the functioning of a similar nature — the study of behaviour. There is no secret that psychology is defined and accepted as a science of behaviour and as a behavioural science its nature is also regarded as sufficiently scientific. If it is so, then how can we deny the acceptance of child psychology (one of the major components of the subject psychology) as a science and its nature as scientific.

2. Generally we accept and include a subject in the category of sciences if it is found (i) to employ scientific method and approach for its study, (ii) to be capable of describing and explaining the what, why and how of objects or events studied by it, (iii) to predict the future of things or the events on the basis of their present status and functioning.

Let us try and weigh the nature of child psychology on this criterion.

• Child psychology employs scientific methods and adopts a scientific approach to study the behaviour of children in the environment available to them in their developmental period. Throwing light on the nature of child psychology on this issue Schaffer (2004:4) writes:

• Note that the emphasis on the word 'scientific', for it is this which distinguishes child psychology from other, more subjective ways of looking at children. Here, Psychologists attempt to describe and explain children's behaviour and the way it changes over age, and do so in ways that do not depend on vague impressions, guesswork or armchair theorising but on the careful, systematic collection of empirical data.

- Child psychology tries to describe and explain the what, when, where, how and why of the developmental and behavioural characteristics of children as they pass through various ages and stages of their development.
- Its ability to carry out the study in experimental conditions by controlling the involved variable, and search for the common features or general trend of behaving and developing on the part of developing children helps it predict the future behaviour of the developing children in a satisfactory way.

In spite of all this, however, we can't term Child Psychology a perfect science. It falls in the category of behavioural sciences and hence has its own limitations. Human (as well as animal) behaviour is unpredictable. It is more variable and less reliable. Therefore, child psychology, the applied behavioural science, cannot claim objectivity, exactness and validity as claimed by natural sciences or even applied sciences like medicine and engineering.

The Scope of Child Psychology

The scope of a subject in general may be stated and described by pointing out (i) What is studied or what type of topics and contents are included in the study of that subject, (ii) what is its field of operation and application or for what use its study can be put to its users and (iii) what is its future in terms of its expansion and utilisation. Let us try to analyze and discuss the scope of child psychology from the earlier-cited angles one by one.

What is included in the study of the subject Child Psychology?

Child psychology as defined and understood earlier stands for a subject of study in which we try to describe and explain the changes in the behaviour and development of the growing children right from their conception till maturity at the age of adolescence. As a result, thus, its study must include the study of the topics helpful in detailing about the what, how and why of the changes occurred in the behaviour and the development going on among them in all its aspects and dimensions during their ages and stages of developmental years. In addition in its study, we also have to look after the interests of the different caregivers and service providers for helping the children in their growing and developing, behaving and functioning in a proper way especially under the developing socio-cultural scenario and arising problems. In view of all these considerations, the content material provided in the texts related to the subject Child Psychology generally may be found to be necessarily rich in answering questions such as the following:

1. What type of changes in the behaviour and development occur among the children since their conception till the attainment of maturity in the age of adolescence?
2. How do these changes take place or what is the underlying process and mechanism behind the occurrence of such changes in the behaviour and development of the children?

3. What are the possible factors or things responsible for bringing changes in the behaviour and development of children across various developmental stages and present state of functioning and behaving?

4. What can be expected from the caregivers and well wishers such as parents, family members, teachers, guidance personnel, etc., for helping children in their essential wholesome development and performance of appropriate behaviour on their part?

5. How can children be helped in getting rid of their behavioural problems, adjustment and developmental difficulties in the day-to-day scenario of fast changing social and cultural influences?

In search of the answers of these and other similar queries, the subject of child psychology is needed to include the following types of topics and sub-topics in its study in its quite usual and general form:

- Meaning of the term growth and development including the distinction between these two; the naming and categorising of various stages (such as pre-natal, infancy, childhood, adolescence) and dimensions (such as physical, motor, cognitive or mental social, emotional, linguistic etc.) of children growth and development.

- Description and explanation of the mechanism of how life begins for human babies in the form of their conception in the womb of the mother, what happens to them regarding their growth and development and behavioural characteristics in the womb of the mother, and how they are cared for in the womb in the prenatal period, at the time of their delivery, as well as newborns.

- Description about the various methods and techniques used, and modes and designs employed for study as well as the investigation carried out in the behavioural changes and development of children.

- Description and explanation of what goes to the children in terms of the changes brought about in their behaviour and development after their birth. It can be carried out in two different ways. In one way, it can be discussed in consideration of the various stages of growth and development such as development in infancy, early childhood (or pre-school period), later childhood (schooling years), adolescence, etc. In the second mode of its description, we can describe it in terms of its various aspects or dimensions such as physical, motor, sensory, mental or cognitive, social, emotional, moral and linguistic development, etc., in the form of essential details and needed explanations.

- Description of a number of theories and approaches helpful in providing explanation for the what, how and why of the changes occurring in the behaviour and development of children — psychoanalytical, behavioural, cognitive-developmental, biological, ethological in a generalised as well as a specific form such as cognitive, moral, socio-cultural and linguistic.

- Descriptions of the factors and forces responsible for guiding, controlling and influencing the process of growth and development of children, right from the period of their conception onward. It can start with the description of the mechanisms and relative roles of genetic (hereditary forces), biological structure and environmental factors in the growth and development of children. Afterward it can be supplemented and enriched by the inclusion of topics and material related to the discussion of the role of maturation, social and cultural forces, such as family, community, schooling of children, friends and peer influences, media, globalisation and urbanisation, deprivation, marginalisation and stereotyping visible in the society for influencing and affecting the behaviour and developmental processes of children in a variety of ways.

- Description of the types and varieties of individual differences visible in the behaviour and development of children in terms of their personality and behavioural traits such as the development of physiological habits, attachment and temperament, interests and attitudes, intelligence and aptitudes, self-concept, self-esteem, self-efficacy and self-regulation, cognitive skills and problem solving abilities, development of an integrated or well-balanced personality, etc.

- Description and explanation about a number of adjustment needs and behavioural problems (including their possible remedy) visible among the developing children arising in connection with their adjustment at home, school, peer relationships and interaction in community surroundings related to their delinquent, problematic and socially undesirable behaviour such as aggression, bullying, drug addiction, etc.

- The description of the generation of a number of adjustment and welfare problems arising out of the changing scenario and development in the family structure and community along with the possible remedy and needed counselling such as separation of the children from their parents, divorce and conflicts between the parents, loss of parents in armed conflicts/terrorist activities, victims or survivors of child abuse including sexual abuse.

- The description of a number of parenting or child-rearing practices involved in the care and bringing up of children by the parents and caregivers with their merits and demerits for helping in making use of appropriate practice for the proper development and progress of the children in one or the other situation.

The Uses and Applications of Child Psychology on the Part Of Stakeholders

Child Psychology is best defined as science of studying and knowing about the development and behaviour of growing children. In its simple meaning, therefore, it should stand for supplying all the essential knowledge, skills and other related art and techniques to all the persons associated with the development and welfare of children for exercising their roles as effectively as possible. On the other hand, as we know, in all its shapes and dimensions we all want to help our children grow and develop as effectively and appropriately as possible. The knowledge of the facts, principles and theories concerning such development may surely help all of us in the capacity of parents and family members; professionals working as child psychologists, social workers, counsellors and child development specialists; and people who create and carry out policies and programs that affect children and their families. Let us see how it can work:

1. **Helping the children:** With the help of their getting engaged in the task of self-study, growing children can have proper access to the literature, texts and other

useful reading material available on the subject child psychology. In addition, the children may be exposed to the knowledge, facts, principles of child psychology through other means such as direct instruction, audio-video recording, movies, mass media means made available to them in one or the other ways. These can help them a lot in understanding what is needed and desired from them at one or stage of their growth and development in terms of the behaviour demonstrated and developmental level or milestones reached in one or the areas or dimension of development. Accordingly, they may do their best (by their own as well as in guidance and cooperation of their well wishers) in remaining on track in terms of their behaving well and seeking all-round growth and development of their personality.

2. **Helping the family members, parents and caregivers:** The knowledge related to the subject psychology may prove helpful to the family members, parents and caregivers in the ways stated as follows:

   • The elders of the family can take charge of caring for the mother in her pregnancy well in tune with what is needed for her in terms of her diet, and looking after the welfare of the child growing in the womb of the mother.

   • The mothers at their own can do well for taking care of themselves and the child in their womb especially by keeping away from the consumption of harmful substances and engaging in the activities that can be detrimental for the child growing in the womb.

   • It can help the mothers and family members to take decision about the birth options and precautions needed on their part at the time of delivery and immediately after the birth of the child.

   • After birth, it can help the parents, elders and caregivers for engaging in the task of proper rearing and good parenting by getting acquainted with (i) the process of development and developmental milestones reached at one or the other stages in one or the other dimensions of their personality, (ii) the type of behaviour expected from them according to the age and stage of their development, (iii) the mode and methods to be adopted for the rearing of their child in a most suitable way, (iv) the techniques and ways of dealing with the problematic behaviour of the children and (v) helping and assisting their children at the time of their needs such as facing failure and frustrations, victim of bullying and child abuse, etc.

3. **Helping the teachers:** The knowledge and understanding about a number of facts and principles related to child psychology helps the teachers well in their task of teaching and performing other duties for the development and welfare of the children in the following ways:

   • With the application of the knowledge and understanding of the methods and techniques of collecting information about the behaviour of children, teachers find themselves in a position to gauge the strengths and limitations of their students. This knowledge can help them plan strategies for the learning and development of the children in a suitable way.

- Teachers with the help of getting equipped with the knowledge and skills of child psychology are made capable of providing the children with what is needed for them in terms of better schooling and the type of influences and impacts left on their minds through the interaction and behaviour of teachers, peer influences, teacher expectations, school achievements, etc.

- Teachers with the assistance of their learning in child psychology can render valuable help, assistance and guidance to the children for picking up the right ways of their learning and development, behaving and adjusting to the environmental needs, coming out of their failures and frustrations, and leading them towards creativity, construction and independence in their life.

    It can help the teacher to get equipped with the ways and methods of behaviour modification of their students, dealing with the problematic and irresponsible behaviour of their children and helping them at the time of need in a proper way.

4. **Helping all other professionals associated with the welfare of children**: With a lot of information, knowledge and skills lying in its armour, the subject child psychology is fully capable of rendering assistance and help to a number of professionals who may be found to help and assist children on their developmental path. Such professionals can guide and intervene when they are confronted with one or the other types of problems and promote positive thinking and desirable behaviour for the needed development and progress of the children. These professionals may include psychologists, therapists, guidance and counselling professionals, educational planners, social workers and others whose training is specifically geared toward issues related to children functioning at their homes, in the school and community life. Accordingly, it may be found to help and assist:

   - The guidance and counselling personnel working in the field of Child Development, Child Education, Child Rearing, Child and Parent counselling, Family Counselling, etc., for planning and implementing better guidance and counselling strategies for the welfare and development of children.

   - To help educational authorities and administrators, like educational planners, policy makers, curriculum framers, evaluators, educational administrators, etc., for exercising their roles as effectively as possible towards developing children by providing proper and organised education for them.

   - To help Social workers, Nurses, Caregivers, and Service providers for the rearing, safety and health maintenance of children in a more appropriate way.

   - To help researchers in carrying out their tasks effectively for the improvement of the processes and product of the children's behaviour and development.

Future of Child Psychology in Terms of its Expansion and Utilisation

The scope of subject is also well linked with its capability and strength of future expansion and possible utilisation in a number of ways. Child Psychology in the capacity of a developing subject has a bright future in terms of its wide expansion and capacity for being applied and utilised in the varying day-to-day life and professional services. The several emerging trends in this concern may be summarised as follows:

1. The research work in the field of child psychology and development is going at a good speed all over the globe especially in the advanced and developed countries in the field of education and research. In the near future its study and research will be more sophisticated and specialised giving birth to a number of specialised and utility centred areas of study and perspectives, helping the cause of children in a more specific and specialised way.

2. On the global basis at present sufficient attention is in progress towards collecting more and more information about the functioning of genes, their mysteries and contribution towards the development and behavioural functioning of children and adults. Its findings and conclusions will surely affect the direction and growth of the subject Child Psychology and its development in a desired way. There is a great possibility of the emergence of the quite handsome interdisciplinary links and sub-merging of the boundaries across the existing like-minded disciplines such as biology, anthropology, ethnology, sociology, child psychology, etc.

3. As a great impact of the phenomenon of globalisation, scientific and technical revolution, computerisation and development in the field of Information and Communication Technology, and adoption of the philosophy of inclusion in the field of education and business, the study and research in the field of child psychology and development will involve the task of addressing issues and concerns related to the diversities and differentiations found in the population in the shape of caste and racial discrimination, ethnicity differences, language and cultural variations, economic gulfs, gender differences, etc.

4. The study and research in the subject child psychology will be expanded a lot in terms of its applications and utilisation in a variety of fields and areas, services and professions such as education, health and medicine, games and sports, recreation and entertainment, insurance and public funding, etc that will be using the results and findings of child psychology and development for their benefit. As a result, child psychology and development will be developing as a subject of hot pursuit on the part of a number of professionals and manufacturers such as educators, social workers, nurses and other healthcare providers, genetic counsellors, guidance and counselling providers, child caregivers, material manufacturers such as toy makers, children's food, clothes and other bearings, children's movies, computer games, etc.

5. Besides this, the study and research carried out in child psychology and development will be casting their desirable impact over addressing a number of the issues arising on account of rapid globalisation, industrialisation, urbanisation, economic changes and poverty; change in the family structure and ways of living; deprivation and marginalisation of the children and their communities; increasing cases of violence including terrorism, child abuse and sexual exploitation of children; discrimination and differentiation between children on the basis of gender, caste, ethnicity, region or nationality; diversities and differentiation in social living; equity, equality and inclusive issues concerning education, and adjustment in living of the diverse and differently abled children, etc.

Consequently, as the trend is visible, the knowledge and study material that has been developed and expanded in the subject of child psychology as well as the research work done by the future child psychologists and researchers are going to make valuable contributions in the coming days of the present century in helping the subject child psychology to grow and develop in its scope in quite mentionable ways.

Summary

Child psychology stands for a branch of psychology helpful in the scientific study of the behavioural changes that occur in children and the development carried out among the developing children right from their conception to the attainment of maturity in the age of adolescence with the objective of providing description and explanation of what, why, and how of such development and behavioural changes.

Regarding, the nature of the subject child psychology, it is well claimed that its nature is quite scientific. It is supported on the solid grounds by the following: (i) it employs scientific methods and adopts scientific approach to study the behaviour of children in the environment available for them in their developmental period, (ii) it is quite capable of providing sufficiently objective and reliable description and explanation of the what, why and how of objects or events studied by it, (iii) like sciences, it is quite capable of predicting the future of the things or the events on the basis of their present status and functioning.

The scope of the subject child psychology is quite wide and extensive. We are in a position to access it on three grounds. (i) The content material provided in the texts related to the subject Child Psychology generally is quite rich in answering the questions related to what, why and how of the behavioural changes and development occurred in the children from conception till adolescence. (ii) It is quite wide and extensive in terms of its applications and uses and is helpful for a number of stake holders such as children themselves and their parents as well as family members, professionals working as child psychologists, social workers, counsellors and child development specialists, and people who create and carry out policies and programs that affect children and their families. (iii) Its future is quite bright as is visible through the ongoing research work and increasing expansion of its body of knowledge day by day.

References and Suggested Readings

Hetherington, E Mavis, and Parke, Ross D, (1986), *Child Psychology: A Contemporary Viewpoint*, New York: Mc Grow Hill

Schaffer, H.R. (2004), *Introducing Child Psychology*, U.K.: Blackwell

Vasta, Ross, Miller, Scott A. and Ellis, Shari, (2014), *Child Psychology* (4th edition), New York: John Willey & Sons, Inc.

3

Child Development — Concept, Principles, Factors and Need of its Study

Introduction

In the study of children, the study about the process of growth and development of children occupies a quite important and significant place. It is really quite interesting to know what makes a child take his or her birth from the womb of the mother, get nourished and developed before and after birth in all the dimensions of his or her personality and play its role in a particular way as a child during the entire period of the developmental age. The knowledge about all such aspects of a developing child is quite essential for the persons and agencies associated directly or indirectly with the proper development and welfare of children. A beginning in this direction may be made to get acquainted with the meaning and concept of the term child development, the underlying principles and factors helpful in the development of children along with the significance of its study to the stakeholders. Let us do all this in the present chapter. But first let us try to define the term Child development.

What is Child Development?

Child development in its word meaning stands for the development of a child, the journey of which is travelled by him right from his conception in the womb of the mother till his attainment of maturity in the adolescence. It is in this sense, that the term child development has been defined by the renowned author Feldman, Robert S. (2016:2) in the following words.

"Child development is the scientific study of the patterns of growth, change, and stability (in the human beings) that occur from conception through adolescence".

The analysis of the above definition given by Feldman may help us to reveal the following things related to its meaning, nature and characteristics.

- Child development refers to a process of carrying out a study for knowing about the type of growth and changes in one's appearance and behaviour occurring right from the time of conception in the womb of the mother.

- Besides, focusing on the ways children change and grow during the developmental period, the term child development also takes into consideration the factor related to stability in children's and adolescents lives. The researchers, on this account may be seen to work for finding out in which areas in what periods the developing children show change and growth and when and how their behaviour reveals consistency and continuity with prior behaviours.
- For engaging in such a useful developmental study a scientific approach is usually adopted by researchers.
- In all its ways and means, the study carried out for the purpose always focuses on human development well during the developmental period ranging from the time of conception till the end of adolescence.
- It helps us to get acquainted with the nature and types of changes or stability visualised in one's appearance and ways of behaving at one or the other stages or life span during the developmental period.

In the above discussion, we have just mentioned about the term growth and changes etc., for deriving the meaning of the term child development. For proper understanding to be reached on this account we earnestly need to know more about the concepts like growth and development accompanying changes in one's appearances and behaviour. Let us concentrate over this aspect now.

Growth and Development: Meaning and Distinction

Mostly, these two terms are used interchangeably and taken as synonymous terms. Both relate to the measurement of changes occurring in an individual after conception in the womb of the mother. Change is the law of nature. An individual, from being a fertilised egg turns into a full-fledged human adult. In this turnover process, he undergoes a cycle of changes brought about by the process of growth and development in various dimensions — physical, mental, social, emotional, and so on. Therefore, in the wider sense, both the terms growth and development can be used for any change brought about by maturation and learning (formal as well as informal education), and essentially is the product of both heredity and environment.

However, in the strict sense of terminology, these two terms have different meanings that can be understood with the following presentation and discussion:

Table 3.1: Distinction between the Terms Growth and Development

S. No.	Growth	Development
1.	The term 'growth' is used in a purely physical sense. It generally refers to an increase in size, length, height and weight. Changes in the quantitative aspects come into the domain of growth.	Development implies overall changes in shape, form or structure resulting in improved working or functioning. It indicates changes in quality or character rather than in quantitative aspects.

2.	Growth is one of the parts of developmental process. In a strict sense, development in its quantitative aspect is termed as growth.	Development is a wider and comprehensive term. It refers to the overall changes in an individual. Growth is one of its parts.
3.	Growth may be referred to describe the changes, which take place in particular aspects of the body and behaviour of an organism.	Development describes the changes in the organism as a whole and does not list the changes in parts.
4.	Growth does not continue throughout life. It stops once maturity is attained.	Development is a continuous process. It goes from womb to tomb. It does not end with the attainment of maturity. The changes, however small they may be, continue throughout the life span of an individual.
5.	The changes produced by growth are the subject of measurement. They may be quantified and are observable in nature.	Development, as mentioned earlier, implies improvement in functioning and behaviour and hence brings qualitative changes, which are difficult to be measured directly. They are assessed through keen observation in behavioural situations.
6.	Growth may or may not bring development. A child may grow (in terms of weight) by becoming fat but this growth may not bring any functional improvement (qualitative change) or development.	Development is also possible without growth as we see in the cases of some children who do not gain in terms of height, weight or size but they do experience functional improvement or development in physical, social, emotional or intellectual aspects.

Hence, observed in minute details, both growth and development show differentiation. But in a wider and practical sense, both terms are used to denote the changes in an organism's physical as well as functional behaviour. These changes which cover physical, emotional, intellectual and social aspects of human life have been roughly divided into four major classes by Mrs. Hurlock (1956, pp. 2-3):

   (i)   Changes in size

  (ii)   Changes in proportion

 (iii)   Disappearance of old features

 (iv)   Acquisition of new features

All these types of changes have qualitative as well as quantitative aspects and hence generally, growth and development go hand in hand. And it is in this sense that the two terms are to be used collectively. Both, when taken together, explain the total changes — functional as well as constitutional within the body and behaviour of an individual with the lapse of time after the conception. In the following pages, these terms will be used in a synonymous sense for the purpose of convenience.

The Field of Operation or Scope of Child Development

The field of operation or scope of the study of child development can cover or be discussed under the following two broader aspects or heads:

a. The discussion about the development pattern of the growing children during the different stages, i.e., age spans or developmental periods.

b. The discussion of the developmental pattern of the growing children in consideration of the different areas or dimensions of child development.

Let us try to understand what is meant by the terms stages and dimensions of the growth and development of children.

Stages of Growth and Development

For all children, the journey of their life starts from a fertilised ovum in the womb of the mother. Not only before birth, but also many years after that, child is a helpless organism unless he is helped by the continuous process of growth and development and attains maturity. When one attains maturity, one ceases to be called an adolescent and becomes an adult member of the society. He is supposed to play a responsible role in the society. Before being called an adolescent, he is called a child or an infant. All these names — infant, child, adolescent, adult etc., are linked with various stages of growth and development through which the child passes during his life span.

There are certain common developmental or practical characteristics belonging to each stage. A human being shows peculiar quantitative and qualitative changes in his body and behaviour with the help of which we can say at what particular age an individual belongs to which definite stages of his life.

If we also include the pre-birth period, the lifespan of a human being can be divided conveniently into the following stages:

Name of the stage	Period and approximate age
1. Pre-natal (pre-birth) stage	From conception to birth.
2. Stage of infancy	From birth to 2 years.
3. Childhood stage	From 3 to 12 years or in strict sense, till the onset of puberty.
4. Adolescent stage	From the onset of puberty to the age of maturity (generally from 13 to 19 years)
5. Adulthood	From 20 years and beyond or in a strict sense from the age of attaining maturity till death.

We do not claim absolute rigidity in the above classification in terms of either the division of lifespan into the above-mentioned stages or the duration of the period mentioned against them. There are certainly vast individual differences and so we should not imagine that every child will necessarily have each stage according to the period indicated above.

Regarding the discussion to be carried out in this text of *Child Psychology and Development* we would be certainly focusing over the pattern of development carried out among children during different stages of their developmental period, i.e., from conception till the end of adolescence. This task will be carried out later on in the relevant chapters of the text.

Various Areas or Dimensions of Growth and Development

If we use the term growth and development synonymously, the major dimensions or areas, in which a human child goes ahead for his complete development, can be named as follows:

- Physical development
- Motor development
- Sensory development
- Cognitive or mental development
- Social development
- Language development
- Emotional development
- Moral or character development

Let us see what we understand by these different aspects or dimensions of development:

a. *Physical development.* The physical development of children includes the development of their internal as well as external organs.

b. *Motor Development.* It includes the development of motor abilities and capacities of children in terms of the use and applications of gross and fine motor skills.

c. *Sensory development.* It includes the development of perceptual and sensory abilities or capacities of children for utilising their senses such as sight, hearing, smell, touch, taste and balance in a proper way.

d. *Cognitive or mental development.* It includes the development of cognitive abilities or intellectual powers like the powers of reasoning and thinking, imagination, concentration, creativity, sensation, perception, memory, association, discrimination and generalisation, etc.

e. *Social development.* Initially the child is selfish and antisocial. Gradually he is developed into a social being by learning to behave according to the rules and norms of his society and makes adjustment to it.

f. *Language development*: It is the most important aspect of social development of a child. Initially when a child is born, she makes her own sounds and babbles but later on as she grows, she mimics sounds and words which subsequently transform into a language for communication with family and friends.

g. *Emotional development.* Under this aspect, starting with the basic instinct, the evolution of various emotions takes place and also the emotional behaviour is developed to the point of emotional maturity.

h. *Moral or character development.* Moral or character development includes the evolution of moral sense and development of character. The children here try to imbibe moral sense and follow learned ethical and moral codes.

It is just a short introduction of the various areas or dimensions of child development. However, we would be carrying a detailed description about the development of the growing children in all these various dimensions later on in the relevant chapters of this text.

General Principles of Growth and Development

The changes brought about in children by the process of growth and development follow some well-defined principles. These are known as principles of growth and development. These principles are as follows:

1. **Principle of continuity:** Development follows continuity. It goes from womb to tomb and never ceases. A child starts his life from a tiny cell and then develops his body, mind and other aspects of his personality through a continuous stream of development in these various dimensions.

2. **Rate of growth and development is not uniform:** Although development follows continuity, yet the rate of growth and development is not steady and uniform at all times. It proceeds more rapidly in the early years of life but slows down in the later years of childhood. Again at the dawn of puberty, there is a sudden rise in the speed of growth and development but it is not maintained for long. Therefore, at no stage does the rate of growth and development show steadiness. It rather takes place by fits and starts.

3. **Principle of individual differences:** According to this principle there exist wide individual differences among children with respect to their growth and development in various dimensions. Each child grows at his own unique pace.

4. **Uniformity of pattern:** Although development does not proceed at a uniform rate and shows marked individual differences, yet it follows a definite sequence or pattern and is somewhat uniform in the offspring of a species. For example, the motor development and language development in all children seems to follow a definite sequence.

5. **Development proceeds from general to specific responses:** In all phases of a child's development, general activity precedes specific activity. His responses are of a general sort before they become specific. For example, the child waves his arms in general, random movements before he is capable of a specific response as reaching. Similarly, when a newborn infant cries, his whole body is involved in the process. But with growth, the crying is limited to the vocal cords, eyes, etc. In language development, the child learns general words before the use of specific ones. He uses the word daddy in greeting many men and it is only afterwards that he uses it for his father alone.

6. **Principle of integration:** While it is true that development proceeds from general to specific or from whole to parts, it is also seen that specific responses or part movements are combined in the later process of learning or development "Development," as Kuppuswamy (1971) observes, *"thus involves a movement from the whole to the parts and from the parts to the whole"*. It is the integration of the whole and its part as well as of the specific and general responses that make a child develop satisfactorily in the various dimensions of his growth and development.

7. **Principle of interrelation:** The growth and development in various dimensions like physical, mental, social, etc., are interrelated and interdependent. Growth and development in any one dimension affects the growth and development of the child in other dimensions as well. For example, children with above average intelligence are generally found to possess above average physical and social development. The lack of growth in one dimension diminishes the bright possibility in other dimensions. That is why, a child having poor physical development also tends to regress in emotional, social and intellectual development.

8. **Development is predictable:** With the help of the rate of growth and development of a child it is possible for us to predict the range within which his mature development is going to fall. For example, X-rays of the bones of the wrist of a child will tell approximately what his ultimate size will be. Similarly, the knowledge of the present mental ability of a child will help in predicting his ultimate mental development.

9. **Principle of developmental direction:** Kuppuswamy (1971), throwing light on this principle points out two specific facts concerning the direction of development. He says that development is "cephalocaudal as well as proximodistal".

   By cephalocaudal development he means that development proceeds in the direction of the longitudinal axis (head to foot). First, the child gains control over his head and arms and then on his legs so that he can stand.

   According to the proximodistal tendency of the development, it proceeds from the centre to the periphery. In the beginning a child exhibits its control over the large fundamental muscles but afterwards due to growth and development of smaller muscles he can also exhibit movements that are refined. For example, control over fingers comes after the control over the arm and the hand.

10. **Development is spiral and not linear:** A child does not proceed straight on the path of development with a constant or steady pace. Actually he makes advancement during a particular period but takes rest in the following period to consolidate his development. In advancing further, therefore, he turns back and then moves forward again like a spiral (Fig. 3.1).

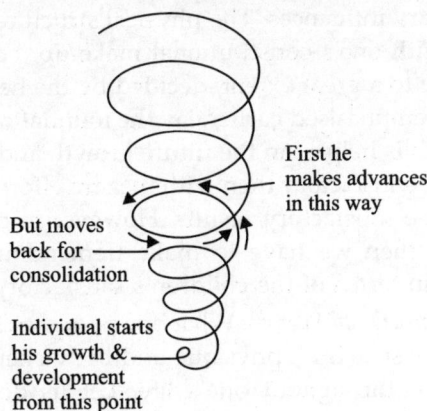

First he makes advances in this way

But moves back for consolidation

Individual starts his growth & development from this point

Fig. 3.1: Development is spiral

11. **Growth and development is a joint product of both heredity and environment:** A child at any stage of his growth and development is a joint product of both heredity and environment. The forces of heredity and environment directly or indirectly influence his growth and development in any dimension at all times.

Factors Influencing Growth and Development of Children

Right from conception, the beginning of life in the womb of the mother, the growth and development of children is influenced by a variety of factors categorised broadly as internal and external. Let us try to throw light on these factors designated as internal and external.

Internal Factors

All those factors which lie within the individual child are designated as internal factors. They may include the following.

1. Heredity Factors
2. Biological or Constitutional Factors
3. Intelligence
4. Emotional Factors
5. Social Nature

Let us discuss the influence of these internal factors on the growth and development of children.

1. *Heredity Factors:* Heredity factors play their part at the time of conception of a child in the womb of the mother. What is transferred to the offspring from the immediate parents in the form of genes and chromosomes at this time constitutes the hereditary contribution. This contribution is the real starting point and base of all the growth and development that take place later in the life of a child. It is like a starting capital for one's later earning from the environmental opportunities or a base for the structure of one's total personality. The height, weight, colour of the eyes, colour of the skin, the characteristics of the hair, etc., are decided by these hereditary influences. The physical structure, nervous system and other things related with one's constitutional make-up, body chemistry and physical development are to a great extent, decided by the hereditary factors. Hereditary factors in fact as emphasised earlier, lay the foundation and it is the quality of this foundation which is helpful in the future growth and development. If hereditary contributions are satisfactory then with meagre efforts of the environment forces, we can expect the satisfactory results. However in case hereditary contribution is quite meagre then we have to make tremendous efforts for achieving the desired success in terms of the children's satisfactory growth and development.

2. *Biological or Constitutional Factors:* What one possesses in terms of his constitutional make up, somatic structure, physique and body chemistry influence his growth and development throughout one's life. Let us describe the impact of these factors in brief.

(i) Children who are physically weak or have internal disturbances within their physical organs can't be expected to achieve satisfactory results in terms of their normal physical growth and development. They usually suffer with illness and diseases which do not only hamper their progress in physical dimensions but also affect their growth and development in other dimensions — mental, social, emotional, etc.

(ii) The Nervous system which he inherits or gets along with him at any stage of his growth and development, affects his further growth and development in the cognitive dimension.

(iii) The endocrine or ductless glands are the potent factors for affecting the growth and development of an individual from a very early age. The chemistry of the body is governed by these glands. Each of these glands secrete their own chemicals known as hormones. These hormones, directly pour into the blood stream and are circulated throughout the body. They influence all those tissues on the function of which the body system, emotional actions and even thoughts depend and therefore, the functioning of the ductless glands exercise a great influence on various aspects — physical, social, mental, emotional and moral — of one's growth and development. For a balanced growth and development, the normal functioning of these glands is quite essential. In case, there is over activity or under activity on the parts of these glands, then it may yield to serious abnormality in one's growth and development. For example, pituitary gland imbalances may lead to quite abnormal increase in height.

(iv) Biological weakness or defective constitutional make up like unattractive face, short stature, deformities of the body, etc., may give birth to feelings of inferiority in the child. Moreover, he may face adjustment problems in the social environment and consequently may lag behind in the race of growth and development pertaining to various aspects of his personality makeup.

3. *Intelligence:* Intelligence, as the ability to learn, adjust and take the right decision at the right time has a significant correlation with the overall growth and development of children. It affects their social behaviour, moral judgement and emotional makeup. An intelligent person is said to exercise reasonable control over his emotions, and is found to carry on well with his personal and social adjustment. In this way, physical, social, emotional, moral and language development of the child is greatly influenced and controlled by the level of his intelligence. Besides this, the course of higher cognitive development is also formed with the type of intelligence one possesses initially with him for this purpose. We can't expect a problem-solving behaviour, creative, imaginative and inventive venture from a child having sub-normal intelligence.

4. *Emotional Factors:* Emotional factors like emotional adjustability and maturity play a big role in influencing one's overall growth and development. Children who are found to be overwhelmed with negative emotions like fear, anger, jealousy, etc., are adversely affected in terms of their normal physical, mental, social, moral and language development. If one can't exercise a reasonable control over his

emotions, he is sure to suffer in terms of his growth and development. He will have to face difficulty in his social adjustment. He may find himself fail in doing some serious mental activity. He may spoil his physical and mental health on account of his bad temperament and abnormal emotional outbursts.

5. *Social Nature.* One's socialisation helps him in achieving adjustment and advancement in other aspects of his growth and development. He may learn from his environment more on account of his social nature and it may prove a boon to him for his proper growth and development.

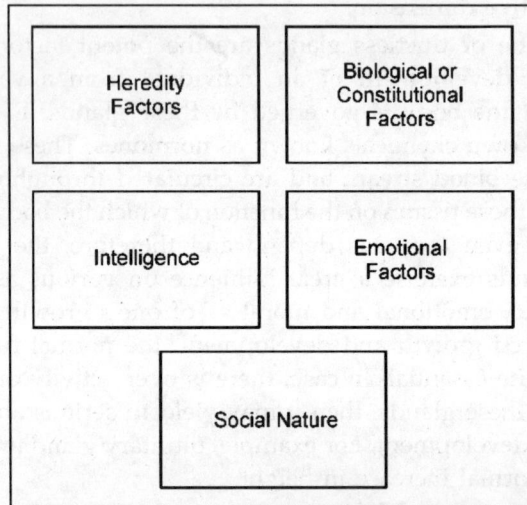

Fig. 3.2: Internal Factors Influencing Development

External Factors

The factors lying outside the individual in his environment are said to be the external factors for influencing his growth and development. They begin their role of influencing one's growth and development just after one's conception in the womb of his mother. They may include the following:

A. *Environment available in the womb of the mother*: What is available to the child for his care and nourishment in the womb of the mother from the time of the conception till birth is quite important from the angle of one's growth and development. A few mentionable things or factors associated with this period may be cited as below:

- The physical and mental health of the mother during pregnancy
- Single child or multiple children getting nourishment in the womb
- The quality and quantity of nutrition received by the embryo within the womb of the mother
- Whether or not the embryo has been subjected to harmful radiation or rays, etc
- Normal or abnormal delivery
- Any damage or accident to the child in the womb

B. *Environment available after birth:* What one gets from the different conditions and forces of one's environment after his birth influence his growth and development in so many ways. These conditions and environmental forces may be described as below:

1. *Accidents and incidents of life:* The growth and development of an individual is greatly influenced by the good and bad incidents and accidents which one happens to meet in his life time. Sometimes a small injury or incident may change the entire development course of the individual. For example,

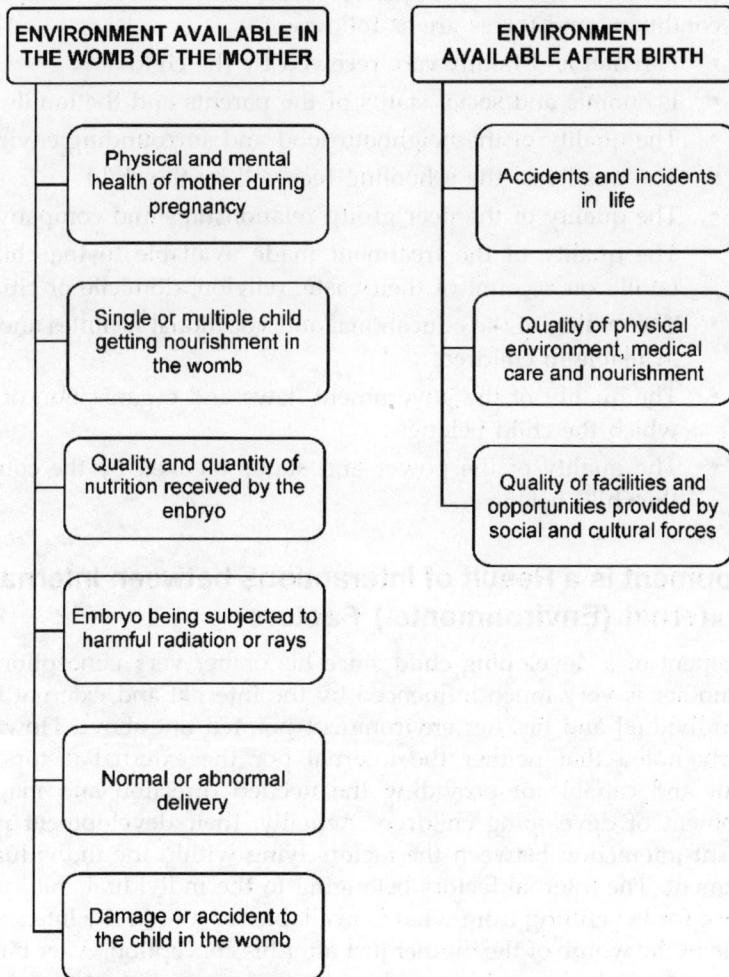

ENVIRONMENT AVAILABLE IN THE WOMB OF THE MOTHER	ENVIRONMENT AVAILABLE AFTER BIRTH
Physical and mental health of mother during pregnancy	Accidents and incidents in life
Single or multiple child getting nourishment in the womb	Quality of physical environment, medical care and nourishment
Quality and quantity of nutrition received by the enbryo	Quality of facilities and opportunities provided by social and cultural forces
Embryo being subjected to harmful radiation or rays	
Normal or abnormal delivery	
Damage or accident to the child in the womb	

Fig. 3.3: External Factors Influencing Development

if the nervous system gets a setback it will affect the mental development of the child and in turn it will affect his development in other dimensions — social, emotional, moral and physical.

2. *The Quality of physical environment, medical care and nourishment.* One's growth and development is greatly influenced by the quality of physical environment,

medical care and nourishment available to him for his living and working. It may demand open space, balanced diet, good living and working conditions, proper timely medical care, etc. One will achieve the heights of his growth and development to the tune of the proper availability of these things.

3. *The Quality of the facilities and opportunities provided by the social and cultural forces:* What one gets from his social and cultural environment and forces for the growth and development of his potentials influences the entire course of his development. In the true sense, one develops and becomes what is permitted and desired by these social and cultural forces. A few of such conditions and forces are as follows:

- Parental and family care received by the child
- Economic and social status of the parents and the family
- The quality of the neighbourhood and surrounding environment
- The quality of the schooling received by the child
- The quality of the peer group relationships and company of the child
- The quality of the treatment made available to the child and child's family on account of their caste, religion, domicile or citizenship
- The quality of the educational and vocational facilities and opportunities available to children.
- The quality of the government, laws and organisation of the society to which the child belongs.
- The quality of the power and status enjoyed by the country to which the child belongs.

Development is a Result of Interactions between Internal (Personal) and External (Environmental) Factors

Development of a developing child since his or her very conception in the womb of the mother is very much influenced by the internal and external factors present in the individual and his/her environment pointed out above. However, it should be clearly noted that neither the internal nor the external factors can alone be sufficient and capable of providing the needed direction and magnitude to the development of developing children. Actually, their development is the result of a constant interaction between the factors lying within the individual and his/her environment. The internal factors belonging to the individual child provides him a solid base for benefitting from what is available for him in the internal environment available in the womb of the mother just after his conception. After birth the external environment available for him in the care and nourishment, physical, social and cultural environment, provides the child opportunities, direction and magnitude for taking his or her development — physical, mental, social, emotional, moral and language — to the maximum height. One progresses and develops to the extent of the results or outcomes reached through the constant interaction of factors lying in him and his environment.

Significance and Importance of the Knowledge about Child Development to the Stakeholders

We the stakeholders in the capacity of parents and family members; instructors and teachers; professionals working as child psychologists, social workers, counsellors, nurses and care takers, and child development specialists; and people who create and carry out policies and programs that affect children and their families all benefit by the knowledge available in the text books and publications, web pages and internet as well as through the continued research work carried out by sincere researchers in the field of child development. The information and the knowledge so gained about child development may help all of us as the stakeholders of children's well being in a variety of ways mentioned as follows:

- To play our roles and performing our jobs with children as properly as possible
- To pay individual attention over the development and welfare of children in view of the diversities and differences found in their rate and progress of development
- To respond empathetically as well as provide the appropriate type of stimulation to support and encourage children to reach their full potential in tune with their developmental capacities and needs
- To help in understanding children better and provide support for children needing intervention for modifying their behaviour and resolving their behavioural problems including stress-generating issues such as child abuse, drug addiction, delinquent behaviour and likewise
- To help in setting a proper level of expectations from children in tune with the rate and nature of their development in one or the other dimensions of their personality for avoiding stress and disappointment on the part of self and children
- To work for the harmonious growth and development of the personality of a child in place of developing a particular aspect at the cost of others
- To work for the settlement of the abnormalities or problems found in the development of children in view of the serious deviation observed in their process and product of development
- To plan ahead and get prepared for helping children in their proper development in the light of the needs and changes to be taking place at the next stage of their growth and development
- To pay needed attention over exercising desirable control on the environmental factors and facilities in view of a key role played by them in the development of children along with the uncontrolled genetic factors.

In this way the knowledge of the process and product of the mechanism of growth and development helps all the stakeholders in the well being of the youngsters.

Summary

Life of an individual starts with his conception in the womb of his mother. Starting from a fertilised egg (like a germinating seed) he develops into a full-fledged being (like a mature plant or tree) with the help of a process named as growth and development. The terms growth and development responsible for making such changes are often used interchangeably and regarded as synonymous terms. However, they differ in some aspects and are capable of conveying different meanings.

The term 'development' carries a wider and more comprehensive meaning than the term 'growth' as it stands for the overall changes occurring in both the quantitative as well as qualitative aspects of one's personality. The term growth on the other hand, carries quite a limited and narrower meaning as it confines itself only with the changes in the quantitative aspect like increase in size, length, height and weight, expansion of vocabulary, etc. In addition, it does not continue throughout one's life. It stops when maturity has been attained while development is a continuous process and a complex one also as the changes brought about development are quite complex in terms of their actual assessment and measurement.

The journey of one's life from conception till death as a result of both the processes of growth and development is divided into certain specific stages referred to as the stages of growth and development namely, infancy, childhood, adolescence, adulthood and old age. Each of these stages chronologically extends over a rather definite period in years exhibiting somewhat definite and typical behavioural characteristic in all dimensions of behavioural and personality makeup.

The major aspects or areas which witness the quantitative as well as qualitative changes in an individual as a result of the processes of growth and development can be seen in the dimensions of one's personality like physical, motor, mental, sensory abilities, social, emotional, moral and language.

The changes brought out in the individual by the process of growth and development tend to follow some well-defined principles like principle of continuity, uniformity of the rate of growth and development, the principle of individual differences, uniformity of pattern, proceeding from general to specific responses, principle of integration, principle of interrelation, predictability of development, principle of developmental direction, spiral nature of development and its evolution as a joint product of both heredity and environment.

Factors influencing growth and development may be broadly classified as internal and external. In the category of internal factors, we may include the factors which lie within the individual. We may designate them as hereditary factors, biological or constitutional factors, intelligence, emotional factors and one's social nature, etc. External factors are those factors contributing towards one's growth and development which lie outside in one's environment. In this category, we may include: (i) Environment available in the womb of the mother, (ii) Environment available after birth in the shape of accidents and incidents of one's life, the quality of physical environment, medical care and nourishment, and the quality of facilities and opportunities provided by social and cultural forces. However it should be clearly noted that neither the internal nor the external factors are alone sufficient and capable of providing the needed direction and magnitude to the development of the developing children. Actually, their development is the result of a constant interaction between the factors lying within the individual and his/her environment.

The knowledge of the things related to the growth and development of children can prove quite useful and valuable for all of us in a variety of ways in helping and assisting children in the harmonious growth and development of their personalities. For example, the correct knowledge of the growth trend of the child may help them in not under or overestimating the expectancy from their child. Similarly, the role of environmental factors may caution them to remain vigilant for providing the best suitable environment for the development of children, and the knowledge of the principle of individual differences may remind them well to plan the education and care for their children in view of their wide individual differences.

References and Suggested Readings

Carmichael, L. (Ed.), (1946), *Manual of Child Psychology*, New York: John Wiley.

Crow, L.D. and Crow, Alice, (1973), *Educational Psychology*, New Delhi: Eurasia Publishing House.

Feldman, Robert S. (2016), *Child Development* (7th edition), Boston: Sage

Hurlock, E.B., (1956), *Child Development, Asian Students,* 3rd ed., Tokyo: McGraw-Hill.

Kuppuswamy, B. (1971), *An Introduction to Social Psychology*, Bombay: Asia Publishing House.

Levin, H.J., (1978), *Psychology: A Biographical Approach*, New York: McGraw-Hill.

Mangal, S. K. (2002), *Advanced Educational Psychology*, New Delhi: Prentice-Hall of India.

4

Methods and Designs of Studying Children

Introduction

We need to know about our children well in order to deal with them effectively for the development of their potential and well-being in all aspects. Certainly in making study or knowing about child our focus is mainly centred over two important aspects, namely, the nature of the journey of their development and pattern of behaviour demonstrated by them in relation to one or the other dimensions of their personality at one or the other stages or age spans of their developmental period. In this connection, we are in constant search for the answers of the questions like: How the children are going on in their developmental journey at a particular age or developmental period of their life? Does their development and behaviour pattern fit well into their expected development or behaviour of their age or stage or not? What types of deviations or abnormalities are visible in their growth and development or demonstrated behaviour and to what extent? Are the steps taken by us for the development of their potential or modification of behaviour going well or not, etc. To seek answers of such questions related to the development, progress and well-being of the children all the stake holders in the capacity of parents, teachers, caretakers, child psychologists, developmental psychologists and researchers in the field of education and welfare of the children try to get engaged in the study of the children individually or collectively. For carrying out their mission they may be found to take help of a number of approaches, methods and techniques by adopting suitable research designs for the study of a number of things and attributes related to the development of the children. Let us try to understand the nature of these means and modes for their effective use on the part of their users.

The Type of Methods and Techniques Used for Studying Children

In a true sense and applied aspect, we need to collect a variety of necessary information for getting acquainted and deriving conclusions about the development and behaviour of a child or children under study. This information can be properly obtained through the observation of the children made either under controlled conditions or in the natural setup. We can also engage in the task of surveying with the use of survey tools such as questionnaire, inventory etc., for the collection of data regarding the children's development and behaviour. Besides this, the study of child behaviour and development on a clear cut individual and comprehensive basis may also be made with the use of the technique of case study.

In view of the earlier means and modes used for studying a child, it is quite customary to divide them under the umbrellas of main methods and modes, namely as follows:

(A) Experimental method, (b) naturalistic observation method, (c) normative survey or field survey method and (d) case study method.

In addition to the utilisation of the earlier-mentioned methods, the stakeholders such as teachers, parents, counsellors, child specialists and psychologists may also seek help from the evaluation of the information gathered from the available means and modes like Reflective Journals, Anecdotal Records, Narratives, etc.

Let us try to know about all these earlier-mentioned methods, means and modes used for studying the children in one or the other situations.

Experimental Method

What is Experimental Method?

In experimental method, due emphasis is laid on the experiments and their subsequent observed results. The word experiment comes from a Latin word meaning "to try" or "put to the test". Therefore, in experimentation we try or put to the test the material or phenomenon, the characteristics or consequences of which we wish to ascertain. In sciences, while doing such experiments in an indoor or outdoor laboratory in natural environment, we may be interested to learn the effect of friction on motion, the effect of sunlight on the growth of the plants, etc. In psychology also, we perform such experiments in our psychological laboratory or outside laboratory in the physical or social settings to study the cause and effect relationship regarding the nature of human behaviour, i.e., the effect of anxiety, drugs or stresses on human behaviour, effect of intelligence or the participation in co-curricular activities on the academic performance of the students. In performing all such experiments, we try to establish certain cause and effect relationship through the objective observations of the actions performed and the subsequent changes produced under pre-arranged or rigidly controlled conditions. From these observations, certain conclusions are drawn and theories or principles formulated.

Features and Characteristics of Experimental Method

Main features and characteristics of the experimental methods may be summarised as below:

— Psychological experiments performed under this method essentially require two persons, the experimenter and the subject or the person whose behaviour is to be observed.

— Psychological experiments are always conducted on living organisms in contrast to experiments in physical sciences which are generally conducted on inorganic or dead subjects.

    — The key factor in this method is the controlling of the conditions or variables. By this control we can eliminate irrelevant conditions or variables and isolate relevant ones. Thus, we are able to observe the casual relationship between the two phenomena keeping all other conditions almost constant.

Let us illustrate this feature of experimental method with the help of an example.

Suppose under an experimental study of behaviour, we want to study the effect of intelligence on academic achievement. For such a study we will definitely need to discover the causative relation between the two phenomena (variables) — intelligence and academic achievement. One of these variables, the effect of which we want to study, will be called independent variable and the other as dependent variable. Thus an independent variable stands for a cause and a dependent variable is characterised as the effect of that cause. The other conditions like study habits, sex, socio-economic conditions, parental education, home environment, health, past learning, memory, etc., which exercise desirable impact upon one's achievement besides intelligence, are termed as intervening variables. In experimentation all such intervening variables are to be controlled, i.e., made constant or equalised and the effect of only one independent variable, is studied on the dependent variable. Here in the present case intelligence is the independent variable whose effect on academic achievement, the dependent variable we want to study. For experimental study we will now try to change and vary the independent variable (intelligence) for observing the concomitant changes in the dependent variable (academic achievement).

The further task is concerned with the objective observation and measurement of these changes and then drawing the relevant conclusions about the relationship of intelligence with academic achievement.

Experimental Designs or Techniques

For exercising control over the intervening variables and studying the exclusive effect of the independent variable on dependent variable, the following experimental designs or techniques can be adopted by an investigator.

The Control Test Method

In this method or technique, we try to differentiate by observing the performance under different conditions. First, we observe under normal conditions and then again with one condition changed. In this experimental design, there is no need of two different groups of subjects for the experiment. Only measures can be taken several times under different conditions.

Example. Suppose we want to know whether students can do better on an intelligence test under the influence of a specific drug (like Benzedrine sulphate, Caffeine or Brahmi).

For its finding, we will take only one group of some students preferably of the same age, sex, health conditions, etc. The process of experimentation will then run in the following steps:

    (i)   These students can be given sugar capsules. After giving these capsules, they can be tested on some intelligence test. This will make the initial testing under normal conditions.

(ii) Some time later, they can be given drug capsules and tested on the same intelligence test. This will make a test under changed conditions.

(iii) The I.Q. scores under these two situations will be noted down and difference calculated. If any significant difference is found, it will be attributed to the influence of the drug.

Control-group Method

Control test method possesses a serious drawback known as positive practice effect. In the control-group method we can minimise the practice effect. In this method, two separate groups, known as experimental group and control group, are taken. They are equated or matched on various traits like age, sex, intelligence and other personality characteristics. There is one to one correspondence in the two equated groups. Now the one group — control group — is given sugar capsules and tested on some intelligence test. At the same time, the experimental group is given drug capsules and tested on the same intelligence test. Then the differences in the intelligence scores of the groups are calculated. In case we find some significant differences, they are attributed to the effect of the drug.

Rotation Method

This method consists of presenting two or more simulating situations to the experimental subjects in as many sequences as necessary to control the serial effects of fatigue or practice.

For example, if we want to determine the relative influence of two specified conditions A and B (say praise and blame) on a group of subjects, we will not measure all the subjects under conditions A and then under condition B. Condition A might so fatigue or train the subjects that the measures under conditions B would not be independent of the fatigue or training effects. Here two alternatives can be adopted:

(i) We may obtain half the measures for condition A, all the measures for condition B and then the other half of measures for condition A. This technique is sometimes called the ABBA order.

(ii) Another alternative is to separate the subjects into two equated groups, one of which first receives treatment A and then B, whereas the other group first receives treatment B and then A. Both sets of A results and both sets of B results may then be combined and the difference between these calculated.

Limitations of Experimental Method

1. The Experimental method advocates the study of behaviour under completely controlled rigid conditions. These conditions demand the creation of an artificial situation or environment and the behaviour studied under these conditions may be or is usually different from spontaneous or natural behaviour. Therefore, experimental method fails to study the behaviour in naturalistic conditions as may be otherwise studied through naturalistic observation.

2. The second limitation or difficulty lies in exercising actual control or handling of the independent variable and the intervening variables. It is quite difficult to know and control all the intervening variables. Similarly, we cannot always control the independent variable. Therefore, it is not always possible to create conditions in the laboratory as we would like to and consequently in the absence of the desired controlled conditions, the success of this method becomes quite unpredictable.

3. In the experimental method, we often make use of animals or birds as subjects for the experimentation. It is also debatable whether experimental results obtained from such sources are applicable to human beings or not.

4. The experimental method has a limited scope. All problems of psychology cannot be studied by this method as we cannot perform experiments for all the problems that may be raised in the heterogeneous subject matter of psychology.

5. The dynamic nature of human behaviour does not always allow an independent variable leading to a change in the dependent variable. Human behaviour is not like that of a machine. The anger or fear-producing stimuli or variables may or may not yield the required responses as desired under experiment and hence it is not possible to get the uniform responses or changes in the dependent variables on account of the concomitant changes in the independent variable.

6. The experimental method is both costly and time-consuming. Moreover, handling of this method demands specialised knowledge and skill. In the absence of such an exercise, this method is not functional.

Naturalistic Observation Method

Naturalistic Observation method may be regarded as one of the most convenient and appropriate methods for the study of human behaviour. We can get valuable information about the behaviour and personality traits of an individual by a systematic and careful observation of his behavioural activities related to his day to day life in his natural setting.

In some cases, we may create the situations or conditions for the occurrence of a particular type of behaviour so that necessary inferences may be drawn by its observation. For example to draw inferences about the trait of honesty, we can leave or drop some cash or valuable for observing the reactions or responses of an individual to such an artificially created situation. In this way the situation, whether natural or artificially created, may be utilised for observation of one's behaviour and the data collected from the observation may be utilised for drawing interferences about one's behaviour or personality characteristics.

What is the Naturalistic Observation Method?

Observation, as we know it in sciences, means knowing the environment through sense organs. In the field of psychology it is concerned with the perception of an individual's behaviour by the other individuals and the interpretation and analysis of this perceived behaviour by them. By this method we can infer the mental processes of other persons through the observation of their external behaviour. In fact it is an indirect approach for the study of the mental processes. If someone frowns, howls, grinds his teeth, closes his fists, by observing external signs of his behaviour we can say that he is angry. In this way as a result of observation-purposive perception of human conduct we can know a lot about his mental processes and personality. This observation stands as one of the important methods of studying the human behaviour.

The Styles and Ways of Observation

Observations may be carried out in many ways, forms and styles. Here we are describing a few such forms and styles:

1. **Formal observation:** In such a type or style of observation, it is carried out in quite a formal way by observing necessary formalities like (i) providing the information to the individual or individuals about the nature and purpose of the observation; (ii) the date, timings and place of observation; (iii) the names and introduction of the observers; (iv) the necessary pre-preparation needed on part of the subjects for such an observation just as showing of any maintained record or preparing them or their environment for such inspection, etc. However, such a type of observation cannot prove more fruitful in terms of drawing some reliable and valid conclusions about one's behaviour or personality. For example, if we announce to the inmates of a hostel that we are going to have an inspection of their rooms regarding their habit of cleanliness on a particular date and time, such type of a formally announced observation will surely fail in its objective of knowing about the habit of cleanliness among the hostel dwellers. The prior information, will automatically make them quite alert. Thus the cleanliness behaviour shown at the time of such formal observation will not be a true representation of their real behaviour. It will have an artificial mask with the aim of turning the results of the observation in their favour. The similar thing may happen at the time of the school's formal inspection or inspection of the house of a bride or groom for matrimonial purpose. This is simply because an account of prior information or behaviour under observation is covered with an artificial mask. Hence no real picture or conclusion about one's behaviour can ever be drawn using the method of formal observation.

2. **Informal observation:** Contrary to formal observation, informal observation is carried out in a quite informal, spontaneous and natural way. Here no prior information about the nature, purpose, timings and place of the observation is given to the individual or individuals. They are thus caught unawares, engaging in their behavioural activities in a quite usual and natural way. In such naturalistic observational situations we may have a relatively true picture of the things and events, traits and characteristics of one's behaviour.

3. **Participant observation:** In this type of observation, the observer tries to observe the behaviour of an individual or individuals by joining them as an associate or participant in any of their individual or group activities. For example, he may join them in their play activities or accompany them on tour and excursion activities for having a close observation of them. Such a type of observation may provide good opportunity for the observation of the behaviour of the individuals.

However, it suffers from a serious limitation as the presence of an observer may obstruct the natural and spontaneous flow of the behavioural activities of those individuals.

4. **Non-participant observation:** This type of observation tries to do away with the earlier cited defects or limitations of the participant observation. Here the observer observes the behaviour of the individuals in such a way that they may not have any idea about the observation of their behaviour in any way by one or the other observer. For this purpose as an observer he may take his position at such a place and in such a way that while the individuals under observation may not be able to see him but he can clearly watch and hear if possible all about their behaviour in action. There may be a screen or a curtain of such a nature so as to help the observer in real observation while hiding his presence.

The use of some modern equipment like secret cameras, video recording, audio recording, etc., may also serve such a purpose. While sitting at quite a far distance, the observer may also take the help of a telescope for a clear secret observation. No matter what the means and methods employed by the observer, his motive during such an observation always is to try and come into contact with the natural and spontaneous behaviour of the subject without making him aware of his presence.

How to Make Use of the Observation Method?

The use of the observation method for the investigation of behaviour generally requires the following four systematic steps:

1. **Planning and preparation for observation:** The success of an observation depends much on its proper planning and preparation. This initial task requires proper attention on the following aspects:

    • What type of behavioural activities or personality traits are to be assessed through observation?

    • How the observation work is to be carried out, and what type of methods or resources will be used for such observation?

    • What type of situation or environment is to be maintained for carrying out effective observation?

    • How can the observation results be made more reliable, informative, objective and valid?

2. **Observation of the behaviour:** This second step is related with the actual observation work done by the observer as per planning and pre-preparation made in the first step. Here as far as possible the best methods and techniques should be used for the observation of the behaviour depending upon the purpose of observation and availability of the resources and environmental situations at the time of observation. In this concern for obtaining better results, the following things should always be kept in mind:

    • The subject should not have any idea that his behaviour is under observation. As far as possible his behaviour is to be observed in a quite naturalistic condition for deriving the sample of his most natural and spontaneous behaviour.

- The observation work must be carried out properly in quite an effective way. The eyes have to play a key role in such an observation. If possible, one should also try to hear about the behavioural activities in action.
- It is always better to make use of a telescope for viewing the activities of individuals specially while sitting at a far off place.
- There must be an adequate arrangement for using modern observation equipment like cameras, video and audio recording. The use of these appliances not only helps in proper observation of the behavioural activities but proves an automatic recording device for the proper analysis and interpretation of the behaviour.
- It is not proper to rely on the results of a single observation of the subject's behaviour for taking decision about his one or the other behavioural or personality trait. For a desirable objectivity, reliability and validity, such observation work must be repeated by the same observer for a desirable number of times or it should be carried out by a number of different observers at one or a number of times.
- The recording about the nature of a behavioural or personality trait should always be done side by side by the observer while making observation of his behaviour. The failure to do so, proves quite costly as the observer may forget or miss out on some or the other important things or links regarding the observed behaviour. It is always better to prepare a check list for tallying or marking things to be observed in one's behaviour during the observation.

3. **Analysis and interpretation of the observed facts:** In this third step. What is observed and recorded in terms of the behavioural or personality traits during the observations of one's behaviour is subjected to a close analysis for deriving the necessary interpretation about his behaviour and personality.

4. **Generalisation of the results:** The interpretation made and results arrived at are then used for establishing a generalised opinion, facts or principles about the occurrence of behaviour and existence of similar personality characteristics among the similar individuals under similar situations. It can help us to have prediction of the behaviour in similar circumstances, search for the roots of a particular type of behaviour and study the effects of some remedial or treatment measure in the correction of a maladaptive behaviour.

Merits of Observation Method

For the investigation of behaviour the observation method is said to possess the following points on its credit side:

1. Observation method makes it possible to study the behaviour in its quite natural and original form, the way it occurs or the way it is performed spontaneously by the subject concerned.

2. Observation and experimentation are said to be the only reliable and valid measures and methods for carrying out any systematic and scientific study. However, it is neither practicable nor feasible to have valid experimentation

(observations in the laboratory like controlled situations) for the study of human behaviour. We may have such experiments for the study of the behaviour of animals like cats, rats, pigeons, chimpanzees, etc., but in the case of human behaviour, observation is the only reliable and valid measure that can be properly adopted for the investigation of behaviour.

3. The observation method needs to study the behaviour of an individual in its present form or state. It makes it possible to draw inferences about one's behaviour on the basis of the observation of his present behaviour. One does not need to care about the individual's past behaviour or previous history for the investigation of his behaviour, as happens with methods like psychoanalysis that face the challenge of digging out the past. This is almost saved through the use of observation method.

4. There is a greater scope for the proper verification of the derived results and conclusion reached through the observation method. We can have repeated observation of the behaviour for taking decisions regarding a particular behavioural characteristic, and this observation work can be done by a single observer at different times or a team of observers at a single or number of times.

5. It is quite an economical method in terms of time, money and labour. We can collect huge amount of information about the behaviour of a single subject or a number of subjects at a time within the limited time and resources. Neither are any special types of laboratory facilities or controlled environment required nor are the services of any professionally trained or special psychologists or researchers needed for the investigation of behaviour by the observation method.

6. It is possible to study the behaviour of any living organisms like plants, animals, insects, birds besides human beings through the application of the observation method. In this way observation method has provided a wide scope and application to the study of psychology in our day to day life.

7. Observation method also proves helpful in carrying out the investigation of the various behavioural characteristics of so many individuals at a particular time and occasion.

8. It can be quite helpful in collecting not only the qualitative data but also the quantitative data. The quantification of the observed behavioural traits thus may help in the maintenance of the required objectivity, reliability and validity in the assessment and measurement of one's behaviour and personality.

Limitations and Defects of Observation Method

Despite all the advantages, the observation method also suffers from a number of limitations and shortcomings as follows:

1. **Difficulty in getting properly trained observers:** Observation method rests on the quality of a good observation. Such good observation requires the services of some relatively competent and skilled persons as observers. In the absence of such competent observers, observation work is bound to suffer and that may ultimately lead to the failure of the observation method in its objective.

2. **Disadvantage due to the factor of subjectivity:** Subjectivity factors on the part of the investigator as well as the process of observation also affect the results of observation. There may be distortion of observable facts depending on the degree of care in observation. An individual's interest, values, biases and prejudices may also distort the contents and results of observation. One may lay over emphasis on some particular part of one's behaviour and may altogether neglect some very important aspect. The interpretations of the recorded events may also be sufficiently coloured. One may read one's own thoughts, feelings and tendencies into the observation.

3. **Partial and revengeful attitude of the observer:** Not only the subjectivity but also the partial and revengeful attitude maintained by the observer towards the subject of observation may colour and distort the results of observation. As a result the favourable and dear ones may get assessed and estimated on quite a higher footing whereas the unfavourable and difficult ones maybe looked down upon and judged with a bias.

4. **Lack of reliability and validity:** The observation method suffers from a lack of reliability and validity on account of its complete dependability on the observation of the external observable behaviour of the subject. Here it is impossible for the observer to know what is going on in the mind of the subject. He is supposed to observe it through external signs of behaviour. It is quite a difficult task. There are chances that the subject under observation may play hide and seek and use his all expertise to hide his feelings, emotions and inner personality. A crooked person thus may be able to disguise his evil nature in the garb of artificial sobriety. Similarly, we may be mistaken in considering a person after observing his disciplined attitude, cool temperament and indifferent behaviour. In this way, over dependence upon the external signs of behaviour may make this method a failure in the investigation of the true nature of the individual concerned.

5. **Difficulty in the occurrence and reoccurrence of events:** Another serious limitation of the observation method lies in the fact that the behaviour observed is dependent on that particular time and place and on the particular individual or groups of individuals involved. It lacks repeatability as each natural situation can occur only once.

6. **Can't help in the establishment of cause and effect relationship:** Another important limitation of the observation method lies in its inability to establish a proper cause and effect relationship. For example, if we observe the two phenomena — poverty and delinquency behaviour, they invariably occur together. We cannot infer from this that poverty is the sufficient and necessary cause of delinquent behaviour or vice-versa.

7. **Not helpful in the study of one's total behaviour:** Observation method takes into account only the observation of the external or observable behaviour of the subject. The external behaviour is a quite incomplete portrait of one's personality. The internal aspects on one's behaviour on inner mechanism of one's personality remain totally unexplorable through the use of observation method. We can't

reach the unconscious or even sub-conscious layers of one's mind through the observation of his observable behaviour. In this way, observation method fails in the objective of the investigation of one's total behaviour and aspects of personality.

8. **Difficulty in recording the observation data:** The other limitation of the observation method lies with the proper timely recording of the observed events or data regarding the occurrence of behaviour. As an observer one has to observe one or the many things occurring at the same time in the behaviour of the subject. All his attention, concentration and energy is then directed to gather information about the ongoing behavioural activities. The task of simultaneous recording at this time becomes an extra burden. Both the tasks are serious and at best can be done properly by tackling them one by one. Now if one does not record the observed phenomena side by side, one is bound to miss a few things or important links afterwards. In case he records them side by side, it may affect the process of proper observation. The subject may become over conscious that his behaviour is being noted. Even in the case when the observer takes the help of recording devices like camera, video recording, etc., the behaviour of the subject cannot remain spontaneous or natural. As a subject one is quite intelligent to guess the arrangement of such a nature and then one may also like to cover up one's true nature and behaviour under artificial showdown and sobriety.

Conclusion

In this way, we can observe that the observation method suffers from a few serious limitations and drawbacks, casting serious doubts about its objectivity, reliability and validity. However, these deficiencies in the application of the observation method cannot be termed as non-repairable. Much depends upon the sincerity, seriousness, abilities and skills of the observer. If he is determined he can find ways and means to conduct a proper investigation of the behaviour of a subject with the limited resources at his disposal.

Normative Survey or Field Survey Method

Field survey method as the name suggests demands from the investigator to go to the field or actual life situations for investigating about the development and behaviour pattern of the developing children. Here in addition to the on the spot observation made by them they may obtain information about the children from the children themselves as well as from those who are well acquainted with the development and behaviour of these children with the help of survey tools like questionnaire, interview, rating scale, etc.

In making use of the survey mode for the study of the child or a group of children, there are two main tools that may be employed by researchers. These are:

1. Use of Questionnaire technique.
2. Use of Interview technique.

Let us discuss their applications one by one.

Use of Questionnaires in Survey

Questionnaire, in general is referred to a device or instrument consisting of some systematically planned questions in the shape of a form which the respondents fill in to provide answers to the questions asked. In this way questionnaires are usually paper and pencil instruments (forms) that are filled up by the respondents of a given population or its representative sample for providing desired information.

Types of Surveys Using Questionnaires

Mail survey. When most people think of questionnaires, they think of the mail survey. All of us have, at one time or another received a questionnaire in the mail. There are many advantages of mail surveys. They are relatively inexpensive to administer. You can send the exactly similar instrument to a wide number of people. They allow the respondents to fill it at their own convenience. But there are some disadvantages as well. Response rates from mail surveys are often very low and mail questionnaires are not the best vehicles to ask for detailed written responses.

Group administered survey. A second type is the group administered survey. Here a sample of respondents is brought together and asked to respond to a structural sequence of questions. Traditionally, questionnaires were administered in group settings for convenience. The researcher could give the questionnaire to those who were present and be fairly sure that there would be a high response rate. If the respondents were unclear about the meaning of a question they could ask for clarification. Hence, there were often organisational settings where it was relatively easy to assemble the group (in a school or club or temple, etc).

Door-to-door survey. A less familiar type of survey made with the help of questionnaires is the door to door survey. In this approach, a researcher goes to the respondent's house or workplace and hands over the instrument to the respondent. In some cases, the respondent is asked to mail it back or the researcher returns to pick it up. This approach attempts to blend the advantages of the mail survey and the group or ask follow-up questions by taking the respondent in confidence.

Use of Interview Technique

Technique of interview may prove an effective device for collecting information from the concerned persons very effectively through face-to-face contacts. The use of interview as a technique may involve the features as discussed in the following text.:

Formats of the Interview

Interview in view of its structural organisation may be shaped in the following two forms:
   (i)   Structured and standardised.
   (ii) Unstructured and non-standardised.

Structured and Standardised Interview

In such a format the interview is structured as well as standardised well in advance before it is put to use for obtaining information from individuals as per the need of the survey study. This is done by taking care of the following:

— Selection of appropriate questions to be put to the individuals.

— Deciding about the order and sequence of the asked questions.

— To decide on the type of answer or responses for an asked question that will be able to provide the required information in the light of the objectives of the study.

Hence, by taking proper definite decisions about the mode, procedure and outcomes of the interview, the desired control can be effectively exercised over the total operation of the interview.

Such control and effective organisation of the interview then automatically makes it more objective, reliable and valid. The path of the interviewer becomes totally clear as he has all the material with him (pre-planned, structured and standardised) for the achievement of the interview objectives.

Unstructured and Non-standardised Interview

In this type of an interview, the interviewer neither possesses the pre-prepared set numbers of questions with him for getting the individual's response nor does he have a set of prior decisions about the evaluation of their responses in terms of the objectives of the study. The interviewer is totally free to ask any type of questions to the subject to obtain the desired information. He may go to any depth to seek such information. This unstructured, unplanned and non-standardised format of the interview may result in losing control over the systematic schedule of the interview. The interviewer may put up unnecessary questions after questions for going deep into a single direction, digging out a single aspect of one's knowledge or personality attribute. The subject may also go on elaborating his response and focussing on an irrelevant theme. Thus, this type of interview is regarded as less objective, reliable and valid in comparison to the structured interview. However, it scores a merit point over the structured interview in its characteristic of providing complete freedom to the interviewer and the subject for setting the direction of the interview as per their perceptions and needs of the situations. The subject gets enough opportunity for self-expression through the spontaneously formed questions of the interviewer and hence there lies greater opportunity for the expression and assessment of the spontaneous behaviour in such kind of an unstructured interview.

Interview as an Instrument in Survey

Application of the interview as an instrument of survey research is usually carried out through the following systematic steps namely (i) preparation for the interview; (ii) taking the interview; and (iii) closure of the interview.

Let us try to discuss the various activities carried out in these earlier mentioned steps.

Preparation for the Interview

The following pre-preparation on the part of interviewer may prove quite helpful in the proper application of the interview instrument in carrying out a survey.

— Be definite about the objectives of the survey study and then plan accordingly what is to be asked and observed.

— Locate the population or sample of the individuals to be interviewed and try to enlist their cooperation in conducting the interview.

— Motivate respondents by convincing them about the importance of the study well in advance.

— Acquire enough knowledge and training about using the interview technique for conducting the survey.

— Ensure that the physical and psychological conditions in which the interview is to be held is properly checked so that the respondent and interviewer do not feel uncomfortable.

— Ensure that the respondent feels as natural and spontaneous as possible for providing desired information.

— Have proper arrangement for recording the responses of the respondents.

Taking an Interview

The following essential points should be kept in mind while taking an interview:

— Introduce yourself with necessary legitimate identification as an interviewer to the respondent.

— Explain the purpose of your study by being as definite and short as possible.

— Give proper time to the respondent to get ready to be interviewed for your survey questions.

— Ask the questions very carefully but in a spontaneous and informal way, surely in the manner and order as planned in your study.

— Do not dominate or monopolise the conversation during the interview. Refrain from putting words unnecessarily into the mouth of the respondent. Be a patient listener and never feel disappointed, irritated or surprised by what the respondent says.

— Use the silent probe technique for getting adequate responses. Just pause and wait. It really works by suggesting to the respondent that you are waiting for his response.

— Encourage the respondent by providing direct encouragement. However, this does not imply that the interviewer approves or disapproves of the responses. It may be as simple as saying okay or nodding your head.

— Try to get more desired information by asking for elaboration, for example, is there anything else you would like to say?

— Ask for the desired clarification, if needed, by putting questions in some other ways or repeating your question.

— Demonstrate warmth and respect towards the respondent. Try to have a rapport by winning his confidence and assuring him of the secrecy of his thoughts and feelings.

— Try to accept the responses and reactions of the respondent in their original form and have its record as adequately as possible.

Closure of the Interview

The following things may be kept in mind at this final stage:

— Ensure optimum realisation of the objectives of the survey, as decided, before holding the interview.

— The information collected should be as complete as possible.

— Thank the respondent for allowing you to take his interview.

— Assure the respondent to send the result of your study.

— Make the respondent feel natural and satisfied with the conversation held at the time of the interview. Allow a few minutes for winding up the interview and never make him feel as though you just rushed after realising your motives.

— Try to draw necessary conclusion from the recorded information and responses of the interview for realising the objective of your study.

Merits and Demerits of Interview

Merits and Advantages

The interview as instrument for carrying out survey studies is said to enjoy the following advantages and merits:

(i) It provides face-to-face contact or relationship between the interviewer and the interviewee in comparison to the questionnaire.

(ii) Accurate answers of the questions put to the individual are obtained through an interview.

(iii) By establishing proper rapport, there is very little danger of not getting answers to the questions and, moreover, one can get most confidential information from the individual, which otherwise the subject may have hesitated to reveal.

(iv) The Interview technique is relatively a more flexible tool. It contains explanation, adjustment and variations according to the situation and thus proves to be one of the essential and important tools for the investigation of behaviour.

Limitation and Drawbacks

Interview suffers from the following limitations and drawbacks:

(i) An interview is often held in an artificial situation. Therefore, the behaviour as investigated may not be typical or representative of his usual behaviour.

(ii)   It suffers from the subjective bias of the interviewer.

(iii) There is no safeguard to stop the individual to hide his feelings or to respond in terms of selective answers.

(iv) It needs a well-trained and competent interviewer.

(v)   It is costly in terms of labour, time and money.

Case Study Method

The term 'case' is used in a number of ways conveying different meanings in our day-to-day life. A lawyer helps his client by arguing his *case* in a court of law. A doctor while attending to a *case* gives the diagnosis of the disease of his patient and prescribes appropriate medicines. A judge decrees after hearing and studying the *case* file of an offender. An officer disposes a number of *cases* put up by his subordinate clerks.

In all such situations, the term 'case' is used for a person or matter put to examination, observation or investigation for the purpose of helping the concerned individual in deciding or solving the problem related to him. In the subject psychology, the term case is used almost in the similar sense. Here the individual who is confronted with an educational, vocational, socio psychological or personal problem is termed as a 'case' and is subjected to proper study, investigation, diagnosis and remedial or treatment measures on similar lines as happen with the cases of the doctors or lawyers. Such investigation and study of one's behaviour related with the task of finding a solution of his problem is termed as 'Case Study' in the subject of psychology. This investigation or study is quite comprehensive as it covers an individual's past history related to the problem, the present status of the problem and the future possibilities of dealing with the problem.

Thinking on these lines, a workable definition of the term 'Case Study Method' for the investigation of human behaviour can be adopted as follows.

The case study method is that method of behaviour investigation in which we try to study the behaviour of an individual in all the essential aspects by analysing the past record, present position and future possibilities regarding his felt problem or otherwise guidance functions.

Purposes or Objectives of the Case Study Method

Case study is carried out mainly to serve the following two purposes:

- **Diagnosis and treatment of behavioural problems.** Some individuals may suffer from one or the other behavioural problems on account of their lack of adjustment to their self or the environment. For example, children may have emotional or social maladjustment or may be lagging behind in their studies or normal mental functioning. Such type of problem children, backward, slow learners, delinquents or antisocial personalities, need careful attention and it is done here by studying them as individual and unique cases. The case study method thus aims at going into the depth of the nature of a problem, and search for the probable cause of eruption of a particular behaviour and then suggest the possible remedial or treatment measures for helping the sufferer get rid of the problem.

- **To provide better guidance and counselling.** The case study methods and techniques are quite helpful in the guidance of personnel and counsellors to help exercise their responsibilities in an effective way. Whether it is the field of educational guidance or vocational and personal guidance, the assistance to the guidance seeker is given by treating him as a case, studying him in relation to his environment and his problem and then providing appropriate guidance. In this way whatever guidance or counselling is given to a guidance seeker or counselee depends to a great extent on the results of his case study, much in the same way as a doctor has to carry out the proper diagnosis of his patient's problem before subscribing any medicines for the treatment.

Subjects of the Case Study

So whosoever is going through any kind of difficulty and problem in adjustment, development or progress, or if we as investigators are interested in the investigation or study of an individual's behaviour, then such an individual may be treated as a case for carrying out the study in a professional and technical way. Thus all individuals, whether normal or abnormal, average, above average or below average in the possession of the abilities or capacities related to their growth and development, personality traits or adjustment, may be treated as a subject for case study. However, in general, a case study is more particularly applied to those in search of any assistance or help for solving their felt problems or for those whose behaviour we want to study in bringing desirable modification for their necessary adjustment, development and progress. This is why case studies of the following types of children or individuals are more commonly carried out in the field of education and psychology: (i) Creative person; (ii) Gifted or Genius; (iii) Backward or Slow learners; (iv) Delinquents or Criminals; (v) Persons suffering from emotional, social psychological and educational problems or maladjustment; (vi) Addicted individuals; (vii) Antisocial personality, etc.

How to Make Use of the Case Study Method

In the case study method, any individual who is under study, is treated as a unique or individual case in himself. Thus the study of his behaviour begins by giving due recognition and respect to his individuality. The next task is concerned with the establishment of a good rapport with him. He must be taken in confidence by winning over his trust and faith in the investigation. Henceforth all attempts are made to know him in relation to his personal identity, past history particularly regarding his felt problem of development and adjustment, all relevant information about the present status, circumstances and situations concerning his behaviour, development and adjustment, and so on. Truly speaking, a case study aims to study the past and present of the subject thoroughly in all its aspects of behavioural or personality dimensions vis-a-vis his environment. In this way, it deeply studies the investigation of all the essential things related to the subject's case in a very comprehensive way. Technically it is quite proper to use a pre-prepared format for such a study. It may provide more objectivity, reliability and validity to the case study work. The use of such a format may be illustrated through the case study of a problem adolescent.

Case Study of a Problem Adolescent

1. Identifying Data

(i)	Name	*Narender Chawla*
(ii)	Sex	*Male*
(iii)	Father's Name	*Sh. R.K. Chawla*
(iv)	Address	*House No. 150, Model Town, Delhi*
(v)	Date of Birth	*10.1.1989*
(vi)	Name of the School	*Govt. Sr. Sec. School, Delhi*
(vii)	Class	*X*
(viii)	Problems	

  — Emotional: *Extremely aggressive*

  — Social: *Excessive sexual interests, teases girls*

  — Education: *Little interest in studies.*

Source of identification: The parents and teachers have identified these problems and mentioned about these in their own way to the investigator.

2. Birth Information

(i)	Place of birth:	*Delhi*
(ii)	The health of the mother at the time of his birth:	*Normal*
(iii)	The health of the subject at the time of birth:	*Normal*
(iv)	Any mishappening at the time of the birth:	*No mishap*

3. Health Record

(i)	General Health	Good/Average/Poor	*Good*
(ii)	Height		*5'4"*
(iii)	Weight		*50 kg*
(iv)	Eyesight	Normal/Defective	*Normal*
(v)	Power of Hearing	Normal/Defective	*Normal*
(vi)	Power of Conversation	Normal/Defective	*Normal*
(vii)	Condition of Teeth	Normal/Defective	*Normal*
(viii)	Condition of Throat	Normal/Defective	*Normal*
(ix)	Does the subject perform daily exercise for health?	Yes/No	*No*

4. *Family Data*

(i) Mention, if

(a) Father is alive or dead
Alive

(b) Mother is alive or dead
Alive

(ii) If both alive, do they live together/
live separately/are divorced
Live together

(iii) Education of the Father
M.B.B.S., M.D.

(iv) Occupation of the Father
Doctor

(v) Education of the Mother
M.B.B.S., M.S.

(vi) Number of real brothers with their age
No Brother

(vii) Number of real sisters with their age
Two (18 & 13 years)

(viii) Total Members in the Family
Five

(ix) Joint Family   Yes/No   *No*

(x) The birth order of the Subject
First/Second/Third/Fourth etc.
Second

(xi) Has the subject been brought
up in the family   Yes/No   *No*

(xii) Does the subject get proper love and
No; there is lack of love
affection from his parents?   Yes/No
and affection

(xiii) Does the subject get proper recreational
facilities at home?   Yes/No   *No*

(xiv) Does the subject get proper education?
     Yes/No   *No*

(xv) Do the parents meet all the basic
His psychological needs
needs of the subject?   Yes/No
are not satisfied

(xvi) Do the parents provide due encouragement to the subject?   Yes/No   *No*

(xvii)	Is the relationship between father and mother quite satisfactory?	Yes/No	*No*
(xviii)	Is the relationship between the subject and parents quite satisfactory?	Yes/No	*No*
(xix)	How does the subject spend his leisure time?		
	(a) Mostly with members of the family	Yes/No	*No*
	(b) Mostly with friends	Yes/No	*No*
	(c) Anywhere outside family	Yes/No	*Yes*
(xx)	His attitude towards siblings	Positive/Negative	*Negative*
(xxi)	The attitude of siblings towards the subject Positive/Negative		*Negative*
(xxii)	The discipline in the home	Strict/Loose	*Loose*

5. Socio-Economic Status

(i) The total monthly income of the family   *More than Rs. 20000*

(ii) The source of the income   *Salary and some private practice*

(iii) Does the family own a house?   Yes/No   *No*

(iv) The source of entertainment within the family environment — Radio/ Television/Magazines/Indoor games etc.   *Radio/Television Magazines*

(v) The surroundings where family is residing lonely/crowded   *Not so crowded*

(vi) The type of society in which the family resides: High/Middle/Low   *High, middle class*

(vii) The status of the family in the society High/Middle/Low   *Middle*

6. (i) Level of Intelligence

(a) The opinion of the teachers   *Above average intelligence*

(b) The opinion of the parents   *Average Intelligence*

(ii) Level of Creativity

(a) The opinion of the teachers   *Demonstrates creativity in his work and adjustment*

(b) The opinion of the parents   *Nothing creative can be expected from him*

7. Educational Record

(i) Academic Achievements (Last three years)

Subjects	Class VII Year 1998	Class VIII Year 1999	Class IX Year 2000
Hindi	55/100	40/100	34/100
English	60/100	50/100	35/100
Mathematics	80/100	40/100	30/100
General Science	70/100	35/100	33/100
Social Sciences	65/100	35/100	33/100
Art	75/100	38/100	34/100
Total	405/600	238/600	199/600
The position in the class	II position	30th out of 50	Passed with grace marks; 46th out of 50

(ii) The subjects he likes most   *English and Art*

(iii) The subjects he does not like   *Maths and Science*

(iv) The relationship with the teachers
Good/Satisfactory/Not satisfactory   *Not satisfactory*

(v) The relationship with the colleagues
Good/Satisfactory/Not satisfactory   *Not satisfactory*

(vi) The opinion of the teachers about the subject
Careless

(vii) The status of his attendance in school
Satisfactory/Unsatisfactory   *Unsatisfactory*

(viii) Has he ever failed in the school examination?   *He has passed class IX with grace marks*

(ix) If yes, the name of the subject in   *Mathematics*
which failed

8. Areas of Interests

(i) Co-curricular activities

The name of	Participated or the activity	The distinction not participated if achieved
(a) Drama/Play	Participated	—
(b) Music	Not participated	—
(c) On the spot painting	Participated	—
(d) N.C.C.	Not participated	—
(e) Social Sciences	Not participated	—
(f) Declamation/Debate	Not participated	—

(g) Games and Sports	Participated	Won some prizes
(h) Literary	Not participated	—
(i) Any other	Participated in excursion	—

(ii) What type of books does he want to read?   *Film magazines, romantic novels and detective novels*

(iii) His specific interests:
  (a) Reading novels and film magazines
  (b) Watching films
  (c) Having friendship with girls and teasing them

9. Adjustment

(i) *Home Adjustment*
  (a) Does the subject feel that his parents are disappointed with him?   Yes/No   *Yes*
  (b) Does the subject enjoy the family environment?   Yes/No   *No*

(ii) *Emotional Adjustment*
  (a) Does the subject feel difficulty in talking to strangers?   Yes/No   *No*
  (b) Does the subject usually remain anxious?   Yes/No   *No*

(iii) *Social Adjustment*
  (a) Does the subject make friendship easily with others?   Yes/No   *Yes*
  (b) Does he take interest in social work?   Yes/No   *Yes*

10. Behaviour in the Classroom

(i) Does the subject behave properly with his teachers?   Yes/No   *No*

(ii) Does the subject take interest in classroom activities?   Yes/No   *No*

11. Behavior in the Playground

(i) Does the subject demonstrate a socially responsive behaviour on the playground?   Yes/No   *No*

(ii) Does the subject remain aggressive and assertive on the playground?   Yes/No   *Yes*

12. Personality Traits

Traits	High level	Middle level	Low level
Self-confidence	H	M	L
Emotional stability	H	M	L
Stability	H	M	L
Leadership	H	M	L
Persistence	H	M	L

Note: The encircled M and L here are indicating the middle and low levels respectively of the possession of the related personality traits. The subject has not reached a high level in respect of the demonstration of any of the mentioned traits in his behaviour.

13. Educational and Vocational Plan or Ambitions

(i) What subjects would the subject prefer for his further studies after class X?

    First choice   *Dramatics*

    Second choice   *Fine Arts*

    Third choice   *Tourism*

(ii) What profession or occupation would the subject prefer to enter after his studies?

    First choice   *Hotel Management*

    Second choice   *Tourism*

    Third choice   *Commerce*

14. Follow-up Work

After collecting relevant information in the earlier form by using a pre-structured pro forma through various sources, attempts were again made to seek interview with his parents, colleagues, family members and friends for bringing more objectivity, reliability and validity to the collected data. The observation of their behaviour was also subjected to repetition for arriving at more appropriate conclusions. All these earlier-mentioned efforts related to the case study of our subject Narendra Chawla finally led us to conclude about him as follows:

Subject and His Problem: Narendra is enjoying a good physical health. He is above average in intelligence. He is ill tempered, emotional and aggressive in his behaviour. He fared well in his studies till class VII. His downfall began from class VIII. It was at this time when his mother took up a job and both his parents were quite occupied in their respective professions. The higher social status made them quite busy at the cost of looking after their home and children. Now there is free-for-all in the home environment. The impact of western culture is clearly reflected in the lifestyle of all the family members. The elder sister has developed heterosexual relationships. Following her steps, Narendra has developed an unusual excessive interest in girls to the extent of teasing and molesting them. He is maladjusted in class and school and it has led to his truant behaviour. He has no attraction for the school life except taking part in dramatic or excursion activities for the sake of fun and enjoyment.

Probable Causes of His Present Behaviour. The more probable causes leading him to this present status may be listed as below:

(a) He is not receiving the desired emotional support from his parents.

(b) His sexually deviant behaviour may be the result of the impact of the behaviour of his family. The subject goes to an all-boys school and this could be one reason that has led him to not pay proper respect to the opposite sex, which has lead him to tease and harass girls.

(c) There is no proper provision and opportunity for co-curricular and social activities in the school curriculum. Teachers are also indifferent to the children's need and there is no proper arrangement for guidance and counselling services in school.

Remedial Work and Suggestions

1. The parents should wake up to the reality of their child. They must try to bring desirable changes in their attitude especially in dealing with their children. They must not neglect their children for their own enjoyment, professionalism and social life. Narendra should get the essential moral, emotional and educational support from his parents.

2. There is need of proper change in the attitudes, behaviour and inter-personal relationships on the part of every member of the family. The parents should set better examples before their young children.

3. The school environment also needs to be restructured in terms of suitable modifications in the methods of teaching, individual attention and care, proper organisation of appropriate co-curricular activities and social work, group activities, tours and excursions, the maintenance of proper discipline in classrooms and school, etc. Narendra, for his behaviour modification, needs some extra care and attention from the teachers and school authorities. He should be properly attended to and given due recognition and appreciation for the goodness shown in any ongoing curricular or extra-curricular activity.

Merits and Demerits of Case Study Method

Merits: Case study method may be credited with some of the following merit points:

1. It provides quite a deep, intensive and overall investigation of the behaviour of an individual with respect to his past and the present. Here he is studied as a complete case in relation to his environmental surroundings, developmental characteristics and adjustment difficulties. Such a thorough study and investigation of his behaviour is only possible through this method. As a result, the method has a unique advantage of the subject under study.

2. The method can play an effective role in the proper identification, diagnosis and subsequent remedial work, adjustment and rehabilitation of problem children, maladjusted or maladaptive personalities, emotionally or socially disturbed individuals, delinquents, criminals or antisocial persons by studying them thoroughly as individual cases.

3. In this method of behaviour study, the scope and range of study is quite wide and comprehensive. The information and data are collected from various persons and information sources. The behavioural data is subject to repeated observation. All such efforts make the results of the investigation or study more objective, reliable and valid.

4. This method provides an opportunity for collecting data on a personal basis, by seeking personal interview, going close to the original source of information, etc. The rapport established and the closeness received may help the investigator reach and search for the most secret and unconscious seated behaviour of the subject. In this way, the information received through the case study method may prove more effective in the solution of the felt problems or rendering proper educational, vocational and personal guidance.

Demerits: The case study method suffers from some of the following limitations and defects:

1. The case study work is quite a technical and professional work. It can't be entrusted to the classroom subject teachers. There is a need for specially trained teachers or professionals for carrying out such studies.

2. There is a need for the collecting of a huge amount of information regarding a case from a number of persons or sources. The work is quite extensive and comprehensive. There are a lot of difficulties and utilisation of individual resources in terms of time, labour and money causes a serious handicap to the collection of the required information for such a study.

3. There is no guarantee of objectivity, reliability and validity of the information or data collected from the variety of sources for the analysis and investigation of the behaviour of the subject.

4. The field of application of this method is quite narrow and limited. It can only be used properly for the investigation of the behaviour of the problem children or antisocial or deviant personalities.

5. There is no provision of studying the behaviour in a properly controlled laboratory like situation. Therefore we can't expect the required objectivity, reliability and validity in the results of the study carried out through the case study method like in the experimental or other scientific observations.

6. The task of proper analysis and interpretation of the collected information, drawing conclusions and then having its proper generalisation is quite difficult and technical. There are plenty of chances of drawing erroneous conclusion about the causes and possible remedial work related to the problems and needed assistance to the subject.

Conclusion

Hence, the case study method may be seen to be affected with a few drawbacks and limitations. However, keeping in view the advantages of this method we must give it a due place in the task of investigating human behaviour. After all, it is the only method that strives hard for the thorough investigation of one's behaviour in all its sorts, forms and dimensions by using one's past and present record for the future possibilities of one's better adjustment, development and progress in the interest of self and the society.

In addition to making use of the earlier-cited methods and techniques a few special techniques and means like mentioned in the following text can also be well utilised for this purpose by teachers in knowing facts about their children.

Reflective Journals about Children

What are Reflective Journals?

Reflective journal is a term used for recording in one's notebook, diary or pieces of paper one's own reflections and insights concerning ideas, personal thoughts, experiences and learning process of a course. Children while maintaining such reflective journals are found to record their own analysis and reflections about what has happened, learned or experienced by them in their encounter with so many formal and informal experiences at their homes, neighbourhoods, communities, schools and playgrounds.

Regarding its content material, thus a reflective journal belonging to a child student may include:

- What he has done; what he has experienced or learnt; and how he has spent his day or week.
- It can include the product of his reflection in the form of thoughts of the experiences that he is having at present with him, the things that he has enjoyed, liked or disliked, wished or felt otherwise for not happening so, the things that he has done well, the things that he could have done better, etc.
- It can include his reflections on his individual work as well as his cooperative and collaborative work with others.
- It can bring into focus his own understanding and application of a learned concept, principle or idea.
- It can mention about his experiences regarding interaction with his classmates, school mates, teachers, parents and other members of the family, neighbours and men of the community; the impact such interactions have made on him and the good or bad impressions he is carrying about such interactions.

In this way, a reflective journal in a form of recorded document presents a valuable platform for a child student to express his reflections and insights related to his school experiences as well his exposure to the external world (home, neighbourhood and community as a whole). The recording on the part of the students in such journals is also quite flexible. They can record their reflections and insights about their encounters and experiences at any time suitable to them. The mode of recording may be adopted according to their convenience. They may write with their own handwriting; type on computers, laptop, tablets or other handy devices; make an audio and video recording, or have it online. The presentation format of reflective journals is also flexible. One can pick a format for writing his journal entries, choose point-wise presentation or narratives as he likes.

Structure of Reflective Journal

Basically, there are two standard forms of reflective journals

1. **Structured Journals:** In the writing of such journals, students are given a specific question: what did you learn today, how do you want to be evaluated, target (students may be asked to study a particular story, do a particular project. Then the children are asked to reflect upon their own analyses, experiences and accomplishments, or on a set of guidelines to base their writings.

2. **Unstructured journals/free-form journals:** Here students are required to record their reflections and insights, thoughts and feelings, interests and attitudes freely with minimal direction on the part or teachers or parents.

How to Proceed for Reflective Writing

Reflective writing requires on the part of students to think deeply and reflect up on their own experiences well and then sit calmly for writing their reflections on a piece of a paper, diary or note book. Generally, for an unstructured journal one has to pick up a free-style of expression involving the writing about:

1. What happened (positive and negative)
2. Why it happened, what it means, how successful it was
3. What one has (individually or collectively) learned from the experience

The overall reflective outcomes, then, can be arranged or sequenced properly for writing in the journals by taking into consideration the following three aspects:

*   Describe what you have experienced
*   Analyze the experienced encounter
*   Evaluate and reflect upon your experience

Reflected journals as a means of gathering information about children

A reflection journal maintained by an individual child may provide access to some valuable information related to the child and his environment in the following ways:

*   It can tell us about the status and affairs related to his adjustment at home, neighbourhood, community and school as well as his adjustment with himself.
*   It acquaints us with the type of interactions and relationships he is having with his parents, elder members of the family, siblings, peers, neighbours and other members of the community such as, teachers, classmates and school mates and school staff.
*   It helps him to know about his specific interests, aptitudes, attitudes, desires and wishes, hopes and expectations, rise and successes, frustrations and failures.
*   It helps us to have access about his physical, mental emotions, social and spiritual health.

- We can know many of the things concerning the individual student that may otherwise directly not be accessible through other methods of collecting information. In fact the reflective journals or diaries maintained by the students provide us a valuable gateway or window for peeping through their inner feelings and mind.

- It helps us to have better knowledge about his intellectual level, higher cognitive abilities, creativity and inventiveness.

- It can help us to know about the difficulties and problems, obstacles and handicaps, stress and anxieties, pulls and pressures felt by the individual student in his day-to-day life and functioning.

- It can help us to know what an individual student already knows, what he wants and needs to know and how he will proceed to increase his understanding and capacity of applying the learned things.

- It helps us to know about the knowing, understanding and reflective capacity of an individual student. The aspects like how does one think and challenge old ideas with new incoming information; synthesise what is learnt and experiences with personal thoughts and philosophy and integrate in with his daily experience and future actions are better known through the contents of his reflective journal.

In this way many of the things and information about the behaviour and personality, learning and grasping new ideas, problems and difficulties, hopes and expectations, dreams and wishes, adjustment and maladjustment, the status of his past, present and future etc., can be better known through the analysis of the contents available in the reflective journals or diary maintained by the individual students and in this sense a reflective journal/diary may prove its worth as a valuable technique or method of gathering needed information about the children.

Maintaining Anecdotal Records

What are Anecdotal Records?

In its word meaning, the term anecdotal record stands for a type of record maintained in an anecdotal form. The adjective 'anecdotal', however, has its root in 'anecdote', a noun meaning a short story or brief narrative. In reference to a particular child an anecdote refers to an account of an event narrated in a form of short story in a child's day. In this sense, an anecdotal record of a student maintained by a teacher represents a factual written record of a student's conduct during a specified period and place of observation in the form of a short story or brief narrative. An anecdotal record, thus, is like a short story containing descriptions of behaviour and direct quotes concerning a significant incident about the student being observed and reported by the teacher. However, in reporting the incident in a story form, the teacher has to maintain objectivity and spontaneity and it contains his own views in a positive tone about the student as opposed to specific assessment or value judgment made about the behaviour of the student. By expressing its views on the meaning and nature of an anecdotal record, American Association of School Administrators (1992:21) writes: *"An anecdotal record is a written record kept in a positive tone of a child's progress based* on milestones particular to that child's social, emotional, physical, aesthetic, and cognitive development". In maintaining the positive tone of his anecdotal record, the teacher should try to report "what a child can do and his or her achievements, as opposed to what he or she cannot do".

For maintaining an anecdotal record, thus, a teacher is required to observe and then record a child's actions and work in the shape of word for word and action for action throughout the day while the activities are occurring. The recording is informal and typically is based on notes or a checklist with space for writing comments. It is done only when appropriate and is not forced; in fact, there may be days between entries.

The following are a few examples of anecdotal records:

Example-1

Name of the Student: Amit   Class & Section: IV A

Date: 10.05.15   Occasion and Place: Project activities

Description of the event/ specific situation

Amit ran over to the table where other students were completing puzzles shouting, "Here I come!" He then approached a student named Rani and asked, "Can 1 have that puzzle?" Rani: No, I'm not finished.

Amit: But I need that one to build my rocket ship.

Rani: Madam says you have to wait your turn.

Amit: Madam, can I have that puzzle now from Rani?

Madam: No, when Rani finishes you may have your turn.

Amit: Sets the timer and says to Rani, "You have 1 minute, right Madam?"

Amit then sat at the table with his face supported by his hands and repeated 5 times: time is almost up.

When the timer rang, Amit took the puzzle and dumped it and began assembling it himself.

Anyone reviewing this record can "see" exactly what occurred at the table. Remember that, an anecdotal record should be written in a positive tone. It needs to emphasise what a child is doing and his or her achievements as opposed to what the child is not doing.

Example-2

Child's Name: Sheela   Class & Section: IA

Date 11/07/15   Place: Play centre

Observed Event and Behaviors:

In the play centre, Jaya and Sheela began to argue over who would drive the dump truck. Jaya said, "Nobody can be my friend if I'm not the driver." Sheela suggested that there were two other trucks and an airplane — she could be the pilot and everyone else could drive a truck.

Example-3

Child's Name: Sonia

Date: 08/07/15

Class & Section: II B

Occasion: Project Group

Observed Event and Behaviours

During project group, the children were painting a mural. Sonia asked Preeti to help. Preeti said she was not ready. Sonia replied, "Don't worry, we'll wait."

The Characteristics and Uniqueness of Anecdotal Records

- The record provides quite simple reports of behaviour without passing any value judgment
- It provides objective, specific and accurate statement of the observed behaviour in a short story or brief narrative.
- It is the result of direct observation.
- It gives context of a child's behaviour
- It provides the record of typical or unusual behaviours
- It is written in a positive tone emphasising what a child is doing and his or her achievements as opposed to what the child is not doing

Benefits and Purposes of Anecdotal Records

Maintenance of anecdotal records, if done in a proper way, represents a true and unbiased account of precisely what is occurring to the child in relation to his progress. On account of their uniqueness and valuable contributions they may be found beneficial in a variety of ways as outlined:

1. Anecdotal records are easy to use and quick to write, so they are the most popular form of record that educators may use for knowing about the progress of the students.

2. These records of child behaviour and learning accumulated over time may help well in enhancing the teacher's understanding of the individual child.

3. They are helpful in assessing development and progress of the children in all areas — physical, social, cognitive and emotional.

4. In keeping anecdotal record, changes in behaviour can be properly tracked, documented, and placed in the child's portfolio in a proper manner. It helps in getting suggestions for future observations, curriculum planning and student or parent conferences.

5. Because they can be written after the fact, when an educator is on his break, for example, or at the end of the day, using anecdotal records allows the educator to continue to work (this is often referred to as the "participant-observer role") without having to stop to write down his observations.

6. Anecdotal records allow educators to record qualitative information, like details about a child's specific behaviour or the conversation between two children. These details can help educators plan activities, experiences and learn more about the children as an individual as well as social being.

7. Maintenance of such records helps in remembering all the essential information about a number of children under the charge of a teacher for planning and implementing policies and programs of their future welfare and progress.

8. The information or data derived from anecdotal records may be shared for taking a number of decisions in the interests of the students and schools.

How to Write an Anecdotal Record

Writing an anecdotal record is quite a methodological and planned activity. In general the following considerations may help a teacher well in this task.

1. Follow a format for writing an anecdotal record much like this:

    Name of the student.................... Class & Section...........

    Date................. Occasion and Place...........

Factual account of incident/situation observed by teacher:...

....

Teacher's Name & Signature

2. Now begin with writing the introductory part involving name of the student, class & section, date, and occasion and place of the observation of behaviour.

3. Now write down exactly all that is being observed in the actions and behaviour of the children by keeping in mind the following things:

    • Since anecdotal records are written after the fact, so always use past tense in writing the description of the behaviour.

    • Try to become as accurate, objective and specific in your observation of the behaviour of the student.

    • Do not make ASSUMPTIONS or use SUBJECTIVE or AMBIGUOUS words in your description of the behaviour and action of the student.

    • Describe the student's behaviour and NOT what you think of the behaviors.

    • Use details of the student's actions and comments, including the responses and actions of other students.

    • Write down the exact words used in the conversation.

    • Be positive in providing description of the events and behavioural actions. However, describe all what is seen and witnessed in the student's behaviour. Try to avoid only writing anecdotes about the "cute things children say."

    • Remember that anecdotal records are like short stories; so be sure to have a beginning, a middle and an end for each anecdote

    • Remember to ask the following question when observing and writing: "Am I writing things in such a way that anyone viewing the same scene would write it in the exact same way," and "when they close their eyes would they see the same scene in their mind's eye?"

    • Since, you have to do your writing later at the end of the day it is useful to keep brief notes of the observed behaviour on index cards or sticky notes carried in your pocket. Jotting one-word reminders or short phrases on the cards about the event can provide you a set of reminders when the anecdote is written.

Taking Help from the Narratives

Narratives are the detailed narrative account of an incident, episode or things observed on the part of an observer in one or the other situations. It can be used as a useful data-gathering device on the part of an investigator while making use of naturalistic observation as a method of investigation. A teacher may also make use of narratives for recording and writing about the information he gathers about the children while observing them and their behaviour in a variety of situations.

Narratives are the running record of a child's behaviour (under investigation or observation) occurring in a particular situation and duration of time. While using narratives as a data-gathering device or technique, an observer or investigator is required to record or write down exactly in great detail all what he sees, hears and finds in the behaviour of a child at the time of his observation. In other words, in using narratives as a data-gathering tool, all that a child does, says, gestures, seems to feel and appears to think about becomes a subject of close observation and recording at the hands of an attentive and alert observer.

How to Carry out the Task in a Proper Way

The following points may prove necessarily helpful for the observers in making use of narratives as a data-gathering device:

1. They should make use of note book or diary to write down or record things observed by them.
2. The observers need to be necessarily alert and attentive in observing and recording things observed in the behaviour of children. They have not to miss anything concerning the behaviour of the child since any missed observation or recording might prove costly in the true observation and analysis of the child's behaviour.
3. Ideally one should note down or record the things regarding the child's behaviour at the time of their occurrence. If in case it is inconvenient or may prove a hurdle in the natural occurrence of the behaviour, then one should be quite careful for its noting down while what has been seen is still fresh in the memory.
4. Since things have to be noted down in detail, it is advisable on the part of observers to make use of abbreviations to speed up the process. However, whatever notes the teacher/observer use need to be both clear and accurate.
5. Observers are needed to make use of present tense in their writing as it helps in presenting the lively status of the child's behaviour truly in the period of its occurrence.
6. Observers should try to record or note down a true account concerning the observed behaviour leaving its analysis to a later stage.
7. Observers should try to be as objective as possible in observing and recording/ writing narrative accounts of the things seen and heard about a child's behaviour.
8. The challenge in writing narratives on the part of observers lies in their capability to write enough detail so that the readers will be able to picture whole situations later.

9. In providing a narrative account of the behaviour observed, the teacher/observer must keep in mind that whereas on one hand it is quite worthwhile to provide a running record of the excitement and tension of the interaction, it is also equally essential for him to provide an accurate and objective account of the events and behaviour observed.

Distinction Between Narratives and Anecdotal Records

The distinction between narratives and Anecdotal records may be revealed through the following description.

Table 4.1: Distinction between the terms Narratives and Anecdotal Records

Narratives as data-gathering device	Anecdotal records as data-gathering device
1. It provides a detailed narrative description of the behaviour observed	1. It provides a brief narrative description of the behaviour observed.
2. It provides description of all the aspects of child's behaviour including the context in which behaviour occurs. It is not limited to a particular incident or aspect of behaviour like anecdotal records.	2. It provides description of an incident of a child's behaviour that is of interest to the observer, instead of providing a detailed account of all what is seen and heard about the child's behaviour then and there.
3. It is a time-consuming and lengthy process	3. They are less time-consuming than narratives.
4. Narratives are recorded and written for the study of child behaviour in a particular context.	4. They are in the form of permanent records, accumulated and collected over the years.
5. Narratives are required to be written and recorded simultaneously with the occurrence of behaviour or just after when a memory is fresh.	5. Anecdotal records are often written and recorded after the incident as they are specifically meant for providing description of an incident (already occurred) related to child's behaviour.
6. Its use is frequently made in the qualitative researches in behavioural sciences. It has been in practice in the developmental and anthropological researches from quite a long time.	6. Since it is a little difficult and cumbersome to make, its use as a data-gathering device is not so common in researches.

Advantages of Narratives

1. No special or specific training is required for the teachers in making use of narratives as a data-gathering device.
2. This technique of gathering data has a special advantage and significance of recording things concerning children behaviour truly at the time of their occurrence.

3.   It helps in obtaining a detailed narrative account of the things observed in the behaviour of the child in an appropriate sequential way. It may prove quite beneficial in drawing valid and reliable inference about the child's behaviour at a later stage.

4.   It helps in gathering information or data about the child's behaviour occurring at the time of observation in a comprehensive way. Here, all aspects of a child's behaviour are subjected to observation and recording. It is not merely limited to a particular incident or aspect of behaviour like anecdotal record.

5.   The data obtained through the use of narratives as a data-gathering device are quite rich and extensive enough to draw essential inferences about the behaviour of a child.

6.   It helps in understanding not only what behaviors occurred but also the context in which the behaviour occurred.

Disadvantages of Narratives

1.   In making use of narratives as a data-gathering device, a teacher has to take decisions about exactly what to record. It becomes quite tedious and challenging for the teacher since a lot of things may be going on for observing and recording and something might get missed.

2.   Since, the use of narratives as a data-gathering device is time-consuming and needs to be done without interruption, the task of its employment and management may prove quite challenging to the teachers.

3.   While it may work well for observing and studying the behaviour of a single child at a time, it is difficult to use it for observing and studying the behaviour of a group.

4.   Here the observer is required to observe and record the behaviour of a child as it happens in a natural way. For such observation, observers are needed to keep themselves apart from the children and this could be difficult for a teacher to do.

5.   The data or information gathered through the use of narratives is most of the time unstructured and requires careful analysis. To draw such analysis in a quite objective way becomes quite a challenging task for the teacher.

Research Designs Used in Developmental Studies

Developmental studies are carried out to know about how children grow and develop in relation to their growth and development in one or the other aspects or dimensions of their personality. They show how and in which manner the variety of changes occur in children's behaviour and their developmental characteristics as they advance in their ages and pass through the developmental stages — infancy, childhood and adolescence. The studies also reveal what type of variations and individual differences are visible in the development of the children across developmental ages and periods in relation to their gender, socio-economic status, schooling, parental care and similar other factors and things associated with their upbringing and education. In short, in all such studies, age of the children is an important variable. We want to assess the type of changes occurring among children on the basis of their increasing age. The task of knowing and assessing all about this is carried out with the help of the methods and techniques discussed in this chapter so far. But the thing which remains unanswered at this stage is that how is the task of conducting such study initiated and what are the subjects that get selected by the researchers for carrying out such developmental studies. Let us think about this in the light of a particular developmental research problem or issue say: *"the development of the trait of independence/ sociability/ moral sense etc, in the developing children as they advance in their age"*.

The researchers for this purpose may adopt two different ways. One may try to select a group of children belonging to the age of a particular year and plan to study them in relation to the trait in question such as independence/ sociability/ morality or development of cognitive abilities etc., as they grow in their age, and pass through the different stages of their developmental periods. He may decide to study them at the gradual interval of one year till they gain maturity at the age of sixteen years such as at the age of two, three, four and so on. The famous cognitive and developmental psychologist Jean Piaget is known for using this type of research mode for carrying out his research work related to the development of cognitive abilities among growing children. He chose his own children for this developmental study as subjects and studied them across their developmental ages from infancy to adolescence for concluding about his famous theory known as Piaget's theory of cognitive development. The other researcher may decide not to depend upon the same group of children of equal age for his study, but try to select different groups of children from the population of the children belonging to different age groups such as two years, three years, four years, etc., (up to the age of 16 years) for studying them simultaneously at the same time and similar situations and not to wait for them to grow and develop in ages for their study much like the former researcher.

In the earlier cited two modes of conducting researches, it is the former which is designated as longitudinal design while the later one is known with the term cross-sectional design.

Let us try to know a little more about the concept, nature and applications of these two research designs.

The Longitudinal Design

It may be defined as a research design which allows the study of the same individuals repeatedly over time. Here the behaviours of interest are first measured at some early point in development and then measured again at various intervals as the child grows. In the study involving longitudinal design, the subject is assessed repeatedly in order to determine the stability of the pattern of behaviour of a particular individual over time.

In longitudinal study, the same and not different individuals would be evaluated at each time point. In this way, for the longitudinal approach, patience is a key since one has to wait until the infants mature in order to understand adolescence. Here by tracking children over time, the psychologist can determine the impact of events on later behaviour.

Advantages

- The main advantage of this method is that it allows the researcher to directly study how behaviour changes as the child grows older.
- The impact of earlier events on later behaviour can be determined.
- Difference in behaviour at different points in development can also be determined, just as in the case of cross-sectional approach.
- The clear advantage over the cross-sectional approach, however, is that the same children are observed at each age point and so the stability of a behaviour for an individual can be noted in a proper way.

Disadvantages

- It is expensive in terms of labour, money and time.
- There is a problem of attrition (the loss of individuals under study). It can occur for a variety of reasons such as moving of the individuals or their families, took ill, or simply lose interest in being tested. The result is a shrinking sample, which not only reduces the reliability of the results but may bias the results.
- Other problems may develop because of the repeated testing. For example, a study concerned with the stability of a child's intelligence requires that IQ tests be administered at regular intervals. But repeated experience with tests itself may make a child aware to the types of responses that are expected and may thus artificially improve the child's performance. (Vasta , Miller and Ellis,2004:56)
- Another problem affecting the study involving longitudinal design is concerned with the cross-generational change. Is the 4-year-old today similar to a 4-year-old of fifty years ago? Decidedly, the experiences of the 4-year-old of fifty years ago and the typical experiences of a modern 4-year-old will be quite different. Therefore, it is difficult to conclude that the long-term effects of the experiences of the 4-year-old of fifty years ago can apply to our present 4-year-old (Hetherington and Parke, 1986:37).Also, there is a very real possibility that the issues involved or the instruments used at the beginning of the study (likely to be continued for long on account of the adoption of a longitudinal design) may become outdated. For example, the experimental questions posed at the outset of the project may become less important as the years pass and other research findings are published. Similarly, the tests and instruments used may become obsolete (Vasta, Miller and Ellis, 2004:56).

The Cross-sectional Design

A cross-sectional design may be defined as a design of the study which allows the researcher to select different groups of children belonging to different age levels and study them simultaneously to examine the effects of age on some aspect of behaviour or developmental change such as degree and quality of independence, sociability, moral sense, etc., shown by them in their behaviour.

Advantages:

1. One unique feature of the adoption of this design is that one can collect his data across a wide age range in a very short time say couple of days or months. Here one has not to wait until the one year old infants of his study become toddlers of four years or adolescents of fifteen years. It is thus much less time-consuming in comparison to the long-struggled and much-awaited results of longitudinal researches.

2. On account of the less time required for study, this design employed for studying developmental outcomes of the children is not plagued by the problems of attrition (loss of the subjects of the study), repeated testing, cross-generational changes, outdated issues and instruments and involved high costs as faced in the studies involving longitudinal designs.

Disadvantages:

- This approach yields no information about the possible historical or past determinants of the age-related changes that are observed because it is impossible to know what these children were like at earlier ages. Nor is there any information about the ways in which individual children develop. (Hetherington and Parke, 1986:37).

- The second problem is concerned with the stability feature of the behaviour or developmental phenomenon in study. This design cannot be used to investigate questions concerning the stability of behaviour or the developmental features of the growing children as it is impossible to determine persistence of an early trait or development feature by examining that behaviour or feature in different older children. (Vasta, Miller and Ellis, 2004:57)

- Moreover, it has a major disadvantage in the fact that in taking children of varying age groups for studying one or the other aspect of developing behaviour one cannot be wholly certain that the groups differ in age alone. For however hard one tries to keep other possible influences such as social class, intelligence and health the same, there may still be various uncontrolled factors of personality and background that could be responsible for the results obtained. (Schaffer, 2004:8). In such a situation, the use of this design may itself put a serious doubt in the reliability and validity of the research study.

Summary

A variety of methods like experimental method, naturalistic observation method, normative survey or field survey, case study method, and maintaining of reflective journals, anecdotal records and reporting through narratives may be utilised for studying the behaviour of growing children.

Experimental method is considered to be the most scientific and objective method for studying behaviour. It allows the study of the cause and effect relationship concerned with a particular type of behaviour by performing experiments in the psychology laboratory or outside laboratory in the physical or social settings, i.e., effect of intelligence or the participation in co-curricular activities on the academic performance of the students. The key factor in the method is the controlling conditions or variables for studying the cause and effect relationships. Independent variable stands for the cause and dependent on the effect of that cause. The other conditions or factors influencing the cause-effect relationship are called intervening variables. These variables need to be controlled by making use of various experimental designs like control test or single group design, control group design, matching group design and design involving relation depending upon the resources in hand and demands of the study.

In observation method the situations, whether natural or artificially created may be utilised for the observation of one's behaviour and the data collected from the observation may then be utilised for drawing inferences about one's behaviour or personality characteristics. The observation for the required purposes may be carried out in many ways and styles like formal observation (e.g., pre-informed formal inspection), informal observation (carried out in most informal, spontaneous and natural way without informing the subjects), participant observation (participation of observer in the events of observation), and non-participant observation (observing without letting the subjects know) etc. The success of the observation method lies in the proper planning and preparation of the observation task and then carefully observing and recording the events of the observed behaviour. However, as a matter of studying behaviour the objective method suffers from a number of limitations and drawbacks casting serious doubts about its objectivity, reliability and validity.

In the use of Normative survey or field survey method the investigator has to go to the field or actual life situations for investigating the development and behaviour pattern of the developing children. Here in addition to the on the spot observation made by them, they may obtain information about the children from the children themselves as well as from those who are well acquainted with the development and behaviour of these children with the help of survey tools like questionnaire, and interview.

A questionnaire, in general is referred to a device or instrument consisting of some systematically planned questions in the shape of a form which the respondents fill to provide answers to the questions asked. In making use of the questionnaire format in survey research, the investigator tries to approach the children or their parents, teachers and elders well acquainted with the things related to the behaviour and development of growing children (the phenomenon under investigation) for providing responses to the well-framed questions appearing in the questionnaire. The work can be done in a number of ways such as (i) mail survey i.e., administration of the questionnaire through the postal service, e-mail etc., (here the tasks of sending questionnaire to the respondents, requesting them for responding to it and getting the filled questionnaire back is done through mail services); (ii) group administered survey i.e., administration of questionnaire in a group setting (here the subjects of the study are approached together in a group such as school class, club or temple gathering for responding to the items of a questionnaire); and (iii) door-to-door survey, i.e., approaching the subjects personally at their houses or work places for responding to the items of the questionnaire. The information provided by the subjects through their responses, may then be subjected to proper analysis and interpretation for deriving conclusions about the things related to the behaviour and development of the children.

Use of Interview tool in survey research is made mainly to collect information about one or the other aspects of individual or group behaviour in a face-to-face situation. In fact, as a method or technique, interviews provide a more personal touch and face-to-face contacts in comparison to other methods for collecting useful information from the subjects. In general we may have three types of interviews for the required information collecting task namely personal interview, group interview and telephonic or electronic interview. While taking interview of the subjects, the interviewer may plan to adopt two types of formats: (i) Structured and standardised and (ii) Non-structured and un-standardised. In the former he has to take definite decisions about the mode, procedure and outcomes of the interview enabling him to exercise effective control over the total operation of the interview. The adoption of the latter format, however, provides complete freedom to both the interviewer and the subject for setting the direction of the interview according to their perceptions and needs of the situation.

Case study method allows studying the behaviour of an individual in its totality by analysing the past record, present position and future possibilities regarding his felt problem or otherwise guidance functions. It can be utilised for the diagnosis and treatment of behavioural problems as well as for the purpose of planning better guidance and counselling to the normal and exceptional ones. In this method, the individual under study is treated as a unique or individual case in himself and then attempts are made to know him in relation to his personal identity, past history, particularly regarding his felt problem/exceptionality, all relevant information about the present status, circumstances and situations concerning his behaviour, development, adjustment, etc. After collecting relevant information (preferably using a pre-structured pro-forma) through various sources, attempts are then made to derive useful conclusions about the probable causes, needs and requirements, possible remedial tasks, etc., for the betterment of the individual.

Reflective journals of children can also be utilised for taking stock of a variety of the things belonging to the behaviour, personality, learning and adjustment process of children. The term reflective journals is used for documents (in the form of diary, notebook, audio, video recording, picture stories etc.), maintained by the children themselves stating their own reflections and insights about the things and events happening in their day-to-day encounters in school and outside school at home, in their neighbourhood, society, etc. What is available in the form of their saying or reporting in these reflective journals can then be subjected to a careful analysis for passing observations about them.

Anecdotal records as a method of studying children's behaviour may provide quite valuable information about behaviour, personality traits, learning and adjustment of the children. Contrary to reflective journals, these documents are maintained and developed by teachers. In maintaining an anecdotal record of a student, a teacher is required to observe and then record a child's actions and work in the shape of word for word and action for action throughout the day at the time the activities are occurring. An anecdotal record, thus, is like a short story or a brief narrative of behaviour and direct quotes concerning a significant incident about the student being observed and reported by the teacher. However, in reporting the incident in a story form, the teacher has to maintain objectivity and spontaneity, and ensure it contains his own views in a positive tone about the student as opposed to specific assessment or value judgment made about the behaviour of the student.

Narratives as a method of studying children's behaviour may also be utilised for deriving conclusions about the things related to their behaviour, personality, learning and adjustment. As a term, narratives represent quite a detailed description and running record of a child's behaviour (under investigation or observation) occurring in a particular situation and duration of time. While using narratives as a data-gathering device or technique, an observer or investigator is required to record or write down exactly in great detail all what he sees, hears and finds in the behaviour of a child at the time of his observation. The narratives differ from the anecdotal records in the sense: (i) these are recorded and stated by the investigators at the time of observation of the child's behaviour and not limited to be carried out only by the teachers themselves, and also (ii) these are quite long and detailed descriptions in comparison to the point-wise brief descriptions (with no comments or reflections) required in the maintenance of anecdotal records.

There are two main research designs that are used by the researchers in carrying out the development studies. These are named as longitudinal and cross-sectional designs.

The longitudinal research design refers to a design in which the same individuals (subjects of the study) are studied repeatedly over time. How a particular aspect of behaviour changes in the developing children from infancy to adolescence, the study of this phenomenon in the adoption of longitudinal design, thus, requires needed patience on the part of the researcher for selecting a group of infants for his study and studying them all along their varying ages and stages till adolescence. The main problem underlying the use of this design is to follow the subjects of the study for a long time and this can prove quite expensive in terms of time, money and labour, as well as the loss of subjects under study for one or the other reasons, etc.

These problems can be solved to a great extent by adopting the Cross-sectional design which allows the researcher to select different groups of children belonging to different age levels or stages of development and study them simultaneously at the present juncture (instead of following them during a long duration of coming years and stages of their development) for examining the effects of age on some aspect of behaviour or developmental change as they grow and develop from infancy to adolescence. However, this design has serious limitations in the sense that (i) this design cannot be used to investigate questions concerning the stability of behaviour or the developmental features of the growing children on account of choosing subjects of the different age groups, and (ii) here one cannot be wholly certain that the groups chosen for the study differ in age alone, for however hard one tries to keep other possible influences such as social class, intelligence and health on the same level, there may still be various uncontrolled factors that may affect the reliability and validity of the study.

References and Suggested Readings

American Association of School Administrators (1992), *Anecdotal Records:* Learning Point Associates. North Central Regional Educational Laboratory (online) available from: infolncrel. org.

Andrews, T.G. (Ed.), *Methods of Psychology*, John Wiley, New York, 1958.

Boring, E.G., *A History of Experimental Psychology*, 2nd ed., Appleton Century, Crofts, New York, 1950.

Hetherington, E Mavis, and Parke, Ross D, (1986), *Child Psychology: A Contemporary Viewpoint*, New York: McGraw-Hill

Horney, K., *New ways in Psycho analysis*, W.W. Norton, New York, 1939.

Schaffer, H.R. (2004), *Introducing Child Psychology*, U.K.: Blackwell

Vasta, Ross, Miller, Scott A. and Ellis, Shari, (2014), *Child Psychology* (4th edition), New York: John Willey & Sons, Inc.

Wilson, E.B. Jr., *An Introduction to Scientific Research*, McGraw-Hill, New York, 1952.

Woodworth, R.S., *Experimental Psychology*, Rev. ed., Holt, New York, 1954.

5

Theories and Perspectives in Child Development

What is Meant by the Term Theory of Child Development?

A theory by its definition may be found to be consisting of the statement of some facts, principles or formulations that may help us in our understanding of a phenomenon associated with the conception of that theory. We have heard as a student of one or the other subjects about one or the other theories describing, explaining and predicting a particular phenomenon related to the study of a subject. In the early years of our schooling, theories of evolution helped us in understanding evolution of our earth and mankind along with the other species inhabiting Earth. Theory of gravitation similarly helped us in our school classes to understand why the stones or anything thrown by us in the air comes back to Earth. In this sense, a theory of child development may be found to provide us a particular type of explanation and description for helping us to know, understand, describe, explain and predict about one or the other aspect of a child's development at a particular developmental age, stage and circumstances.

Nowadays there are a number of developmental theories available for helping us in the task of our understanding and providing prediction regarding one or the other aspect or phenomenon of human development including children. No doubt each of these theories has been formulated on its own philosophical and theoretical foundation, and accordingly provides an altogether unique explanation and description for the phenomenon under consideration. As a result, we may be forced or influenced to accept one or the other explanations given for our understanding of the facts related to a developmental feature or behaviour of the developing child at a particular stage. For example, as illustrated by Levine & Munsch (2014:27) a parent might react to an infant's excessive crying very differently depending on his understanding of what this crying means. If he subscribes to the theory of behaviourism, he might believe that picking up the crying baby will reward that behaviour and make the baby cry more. However, if he subscribes to the theory of ethology, he might believe the crying is a behaviour that signals that the baby needs comfort. If that need is met, it will help the baby develop a secure attachment that will eventually help the baby cry less.

What has contributed in the evolution of a number of developmental theories and perspectives?

The reasons for the accumulation of so many theories and perspectives of development may be summarised as follows:

1. Theorists working for the formulation of a developmental theory are found to have a particular bent of mind under the influence of philosophy and thoughts driven by behaviourism, cognitivism, analytical psychology, ethology or ecology. This has resulted in their drawing different conclusions about the explanation of a developmental phenomena that suits their line of thoughts.

2. Development as seen otherwise is quite a complex and enlarged phenomenon. On one hand it has to do with both stability and change over time and on the other hand it has to leave scope for the occurrence of the ongoing changes in two different modes and ways such as quantitative and qualitative. As a result theorists have the compulsion of developing different and separate theories and perspectives for providing explanation to the issues such as:

   • Why and how changes occur among children during their developmental period and why some aspects of behaviour remain the same.

   • How do changes termed as quantitative, such as increase in height occurring little by little over time and qualitative changes such as change in the voice tone and quality occurring suddenly and substantially at the onset of puberty, be explained in an appropriate way?

3. What is that which is held utmost responsible for bringing visible changes in one or the other areas or dimensions of growth and development? This question can again be answered in different ways. Some may term it as an absolute role of hereditary composition or biological processes, and the others may term it as the sole contribution of one's environment, while the rest may attribute it as the net result of the intersection of the two. It has thus also been a solid reason to bring out different developmental theories and view points for explaining the processes and outcomes of development in children.

It is thus no surprise to witness the presence of a number of approaches or viewpoints developed by theorists and psychologists from time to time in the name of specific child development theories or perspectives. We can broadly divide them in the following two categories:

(A) **The theories or perspectives helpful in explaining the development of the children in general, irrespective of the specificity of the areas or dimensions of development:** We may include developmental theories like Biological theories, Behaviourist theories, Psychoanalytic theories, Ethological theories and Ecological theories, in this category.

(B) **The theories or perspectives specifically helpful in understanding the development of children in one or the other specific area or dimension of their personality** such as cognitive, social, sociocultural, moral, linguistic, etc. The theories like Piaget's and Bruner's theories of Cognitive Development, Erickson's Theory of Psycho-Social development, Piaget's and Kohlberg's Theories of Moral Development, Vygotsky's Socio-Cultural Theory of Development and theories related to the children's language development fall in this category.

Let us have some useful discussion of the theories and perspectives related to child development falling in the earlier mentioned categories. For this purpose let us start from the theories or perspectives falling in the first general category.

Biological or Hereditary Theories

Biological theories or hereditary theories of child development are known to explain the development of the children by adopting a clear cut biological and genetic perspective. Accordingly they may be found to assert that the trend of a child's development is well initiated and the foundations of the future growth and development is well laid down from the blue prints of the genes (comprising genetic code and data) and biological structure (comprising body structure, nervous system, brain and activities of hormones) he or she inherits from his or her ancestors through the immediate parents. A good beginning is always attributed for the successful accomplishment of a task. Accordingly, blessed with a fine heredity contribution and equipped with a strong biological structure helpful in shaping the adaptive ability of their bodies to struggle well in the journey of their life, children may be found to excel well in terms of their development in all the dimensions of their personality and domains of behaviour. The reverse is also true. The children who are sufferers in terms of genetic inheritance and biological structure may also be found to suffer adversely in terms of their adaptation, development and progress in life.

In a nutshell thus, the perspective or view point held by biological or hereditary theories may be known to emphasise and advocate that:

(i)   The genetic code and data as well as biological structure inherited on the part of children from their parents and ancestors exercise a great influence over the development of the children in one or the other dimensions of their personality in the positive as well as adverse way depending upon the nature and quality of such inheritance.

(ii) The inherited biological structure (including genetic inheritance) is responsible for the type of adaptations made on the part of growing children for their survival, as well as struggling for their development and progress in life. The degree of appropriateness of such adaptation thus is further responsible for their success and failure in achieving the mile stones of their developmental journey in their life.

(iii) Initiated and helped by one's hereditary endowments, the mechanism of adaptation, maturation and biological processes may be found to play a quite substantial role in deciding the magnitude and direction of the growth and development of children.

As far as the task of propagating and forwarding the biological and hereditary perspective in relation to the development of children is concerned, the credit for the same is usually given to the famous scholars and psychologists of their times, Charles Darwin (1809-1882) and Arnold Gesell (1880-1961). Each of them through their significant research work tried to bring into limelight the unique role played by the inherited biological makeup on the development of children. In this concern while Darwin through his theory of evolution provided credit to the adaptive value of inherited biological structures for the consequential development of human beings including children, Gesell through his maturation theory tried to link the development of children with the process of maturation attained by them in the course of their natural growth and development.

In case we try to view the pros and cons of the earlier mentioned biological cum hereditary perspective of child development we can come to the some of the following conclusions in this regard:

The Merits and Good Points

1. It revealed to us the role of inherited genetic composition and biological structure in the process and outcomes of the children's development in quite a substantial way, particularly in the matter of strengths supplied or limits imposed by the inheritance of good and poor biological capacities on the part of children for their adaptation, learning, development and progress in life.

2. It helped us in learning about the mechanism of maturation (the natural biological process) and accordingly set the path and principles of children's development.

3. It helped us to get through the basic reasons of the individual differences visible in the growth and development of children reared in similar environmental conditions at one or the other age or periods of life.

4. In view of McDevitt and Ormrod (2013:13), it has helped us draw valuable lessons in the care and development of children by providing the following two key principles:
   (i) Children's maturation levels impose limits on their interests and
   (ii) Children's physical abilities serve valuable functions for them, such as permitting age-appropriate exploration

The Limitations and Fallacy

1. It heavily overemphasised the importance and role of hereditary contributions and biological structure at the cost of paying no consideration for the role of environmental influences on the development of children. It was a major fallacy on the part of the propagators and followers of this theory, as however good the inherited biological make up may be, it can't develop to its expected potential without the assistance of environmental push up.

2. It lead to the discouragement of proper efforts made in the tasks of helping the developing children in their proper learning, adjustment and progress in life simply on the plea that development and progress is the function of one's hereditary and biological composition and environmental influences have no substantial role in this direction.

As a consequence of its underlying weaknesses and fallacy, the biological perspective had to face severe criticism resulting into its required amendment and replacement with the other perspectives and theories of child development.

Behaviourist or Environmentalist Theories

These theories have been brought into existence by a group of psychologists belonging to the school of behaviourism. Behaviourism as a philosophy and doctrine gave the sole credit to the environmental influences for the growth and development of the children right from the time of their conception in the womb of the mother. For the behaviourists, environment was everything for shaping and developing the behaviour and personality of children in all its aspects as opposed to the significance provided to the hereditary contributions by the earlier propagators and followers of biology and hereditary driven theories of child development.

Famous psychologists like J. B. Watson (1878-1958), Ivan Pavlov (1849-1936), B. F. Skinner (1904-1990) and Albert Bandura (1925-) may be named as the main propagators of the ideas and viewpoints associated with the behaviourist or environmental theory of child development. In this connection where Watson and Pavlov through their classical conditioning perspectives tried to conclude that activities related to the development of the children especially associated with the behaviour changes in the affective domain (such as habits, temperament, interests and attitudes, etc.,) are designed and controlled via the learning carried out through the classical conditioning mechanism, Skinner on the other hand explained the development of a number of attributes of one's personality especially belonging to the learning of skilled behaviour and changes in the motor or conative behaviour of children through the mechanism of operant conditioning. Besides this, the famous social and environmental psychologist Albert Bandura propagated the cause of behaviourist cum environmental theory of child development though his theory of observational or social learning by stating that the type of influences and behaviour models available to children for their observation, imitation and practicing in their environment are very much responsible for shaping the behaviour and development of the children in almost all the periods and age span of developing children.

In this way, things emphasised about the development of the children by the above mentioned behaviourist cum environmental theory may be well summarised in the following manner:

- All types of development or behavioural changes occurring in the personality of the developing children may be found to rest on the mercy of the available environmental resources and facilities to children at one or the other times of their developing period.
- Whatever, may be the contributions of one's heredity in terms of available biological make up for initiating the developmental journey on the part of a growing child, it may be well supplemented, enriched and designed through the available or suitably arranged environmental resources and facilities for the desired development of the child.
- The processes as well as the outcomes of the developmental acts and attempts can be well predicted on the basis of nature and quality of the environmental influences arranged for the developing children. A glimpse of such confidence in the ability of environmental influences in the development of individuals can be very well availed in the assertion of the father of behaviourism, J.B. Watson (1926) in the following words:

Give me a dozen healthy infants, well informed and my own specified world to bring them up in and I will guarantee to take any one at random and train him to become any type of specialist I might select — doctor, lawyer, artist, merchant chief and yes, even beggar-man and thief, regardless of his talents, penchants, tendencies, abilities, vocations and race of his ancestors.

- It is useless and unfair on the part of teachers, parents, caretakers and all other well wishers of children to blame the heredity or biological makeup of the children for the lapses and deficiencies in the development of a child in one or the other dimensions of their personality. It is clear escapism on their part for saving face against their own lapses in fulfilling responsibilities towards the developing children in a desirable way.

However, with all appreciation for advocating the role of environmental facilities and well-intended efforts for the development and learning of children, the behaviourist cum environmental theories can also be blamed and criticised much like the biological cum hereditary theories for taking an extreme stand in making environment the sole deciding factor for shaping and moulding the development and behaviour of growing children with neglect and utter disregard shown towards (i) what is provided by the biological and hereditary factors for the development of children, and (ii) what is conveyed by the phenomenon of maturation for the level and nature of development at one or the other stages of children's development.

Psychoanalytic Theories or Perspective

With the emergence and development of the analytical school of thought, attempts were made by psychoanalysts such as Sigmund Freud (1856-1939), his disciple Alfred Adler, and his daughter, Anna Freud, to adopt a psychoanalytic approach for explaining the developmental processes of children. In this approach, they neither provided unnecessary importance to the inherited dispositions or biological makeup like the biologists and hereditarians, nor did they agree with the behaviourists' views of declaring environmental influences as a sole factor in controlling and shaping the development of children. In this regard while displaying its opposition to the previously held views, theories and perspectives about the development of children, the psychoanalytical theories and perspective as claimed by Berk (2009:16) demonstrated quite uniqueness in emphasising that:

- The development of children is the result of an ongoing interaction between what lies in them in terms of the children's genetic makeup and internal conflicts and what is provided to them through their environmental experiences.
- Early experiences play a crucial role in the development of characteristics and behaviour of children in their maturity years.
- The unconscious mind and unconscious behaviour cast a deep influence in directing the development of the children in all the dimensions of their personality
- Children move through a series of stages in which they confront conflicts between biological drives and social expectations. How these conflicts are resolved determines the person's ability to learn, to get along with others and cope with anxiety.

Each of the great figures in the realm of analytical psychology brought out their own perspective and theory of child development. The beginning in this direction was made by the initiator and founder of the school of analytical psychology, Sigmund Freud (1856-1939) by providing us a theory of children's development popularly named as the theory of Psycho-Sexual Development.

Freud's Psycho-Sexual Theory of Child development

According to Freud, sex is the life urge or fundamental motive in life. All physical pleasures arising from any of the organs or any of the functions are ultimately sexual in nature. Sexuality is not the characteristic only of adults. Children from the very beginning have sexual desires also. This, he termed as 'infantile sexuality'. With regard to the development of children, Freud outlined five stages in the development of children and adolescents, which he called psycho-sexual stages. At each of these stages, sexuality (in the form of sexual pleasure and gratification) is attached or associated with a particular part and place of the body, and gratification of the sexual urges associated with those areas of the body is essential for the adjustment and well being of the developing child. In this connection, Freud opined that the way in which gratification of urges is handled during each of these stages determines the nature and status of the things related to his adjustment and development of personality and character. Lack of gratification at any of these psycho-sexual stages may lead the child in to maladjustment and disturbance in his normal functioning and development.

As proposed in the psycho-sexual stage theory, children may be found to pass through the following different stages with respect to their psycho-sexual development:

1. *The oral stage.* This initial stage of child development lasts from birth to about 18 months of age. According to Freud, the zone of pleasure for the child at this stage is his mouth, the first sex organ for providing pleasure to the child. The beginning in this direction is made with the pleasure received from the mother's nipple or the feeding bottle. Thereafter, the child derives pleasure by putting anything, candy, a stick, his own thumb, etc., into his mouth. The need of deriving pleasure from such oral means needs to be satisfied for the child in a satisfactory way. Its denial may bring unhappiness and disturbance to his normal development. Freud in this connection stated that a child can get fixated if her needs are not adequately met or over saturated at this stage. As a result, the developing child may then exhibit characteristics of that stage later in life. For example, the developing individual who is fixated in the oral stage may want to continue to try his oral urges by over-eating, or smoking or be infatuated to see and sucking female nipples (Freud, 1953).

2. *The anal stage.* The anal stage lasts from 18 months to 3 years. At this stage, the interest of the child shifts from the mouth as the erogenous zone to the organs of elimination, i.e., the anus or the urethra. He derives pleasure by holding back or letting go of the body's waste material through the anus or the urethra. The task of the child at this stage is to learn to control his bodily urges to conform to society's expectations. The developing child who is fixated at this stage may become over controlled (referred to as anal compulsive) as

an adult (Freud, 1959). He may be found to see everything in its proper place to an extreme degree. Conversely, another child fixated at the oral stage might become anal explosive, creating "messes" wherever he goes.

3. *The phallic stage.* This phase starts from the age of 4 years and lasts up to 6 years. It is characterised with the shifting of the child's interest from the eliminating organs to the genitals. At this stage children come to note the biological differences between the sexes and derive pleasure by playing with and manipulating their genital organs. This stage, according to Freud, may give rise to a number of complexes like deprivation and Electra complexes in girls and castration and Oedipus complexes in boys. The deprivation complex is the result of the feeling generated in the minds of little girls that they have been deprived of the male organ by their mothers. Castration complex is generated in boys through their fear of being deprived of the male organs certainly as a result of the threat received from elders that the organ would be cut off if they did not give up the habit of playing with it. About the Oedipus and Electra phases, Freud says that they are the result of the sexual attraction or pleasure that children experience in the company of the parent of the opposite sex. In case the parent of the same sex frustrates the desire, expresses his or her resentment and is not friendly to the boy or girl, the child may develop Oedipus or Electra complex by loving the opposite sex parent more and rather hating the like sex parent.

4. *The latency stage.* This period starts from 6 years in the case of girls and between 7 and 8 years in the case of boys and can extend up to the onset of puberty. Latent means inactive, and Freud believed that during his time the sex drive goes underground (Freud, 1953). At this stage, boys and girls prefer to be in the company of their own sex and even neglect or hate members of the opposite sex.

5. *The genital stage.* Puberty is the starting point of the genital stage. At this point, sexual energy becomes focused on the genital area. As a result the adolescent boy and girl now feel a strange feeling of strong sensation in the genitals and attraction towards the members of the opposite sex. At this stage they may feel pleasure by self-stimulation of the genitals, may fall in love with their own self by taking interest in beautifying and adorning their bodies and may be drawn quite close to members of the opposite sex even to the extent of indulging in sexual intercourse.

In this way, Freud tried to adopt a somewhat different and unique approach for knowing and understanding the development of children in terms of their psycho-sexual behaviour. The views expressed by Freud in his psycho-sexual development theory have been quite controversial and often criticised much on account of his over-emphasis and undue importance to sex. However, many of his views, especially related to infantile sexuality and colouring everything related to children's development with the expression of sex desire or motive were quite indigestible to the contemporary psychologists including his own disciples like Alfred Adler and Carl Jung.

However, irrespective of all these things, due credit is also given to Freud for highlighting the role of sex in one's life in terms of shaping his psyche and behaviour and outline the developmental path of children determined through his or her basic instincts and drives. Thus, his theory of psycho-sexual development may be well credited, in fact for opening a new chapter in the history of sex education by:

- Discussing the stage of psycho-sexual development
- Emphasizing the need for spontaneous expression of sex instinct, and
- Changing the general attitude towards sex by treating it as a natural, essential biological function instead of regarding it as shameful, dirty or bad.

Alfred Adler's Perspective About the Development of Children

Alfred Adler (1870-1937), a disciple of Freud disagreed with his mentor regarding his views about the development of children as explained in Freud's theory of psycho-sexual development. He was against Freud's idea of explaining and colouring the development of children unnecessarily with the sexual desires and impulses. Adler broke away from Freud's group in 1911. Along with eight colleagues he formed his own school of individual psychology. This school of psychology established by Adler then brought out new perspectives and thoughts related to the development visible among children across different age spans and rearing situations. As a whole, as emphasised by Meggitt and Ormrod, (2013:161-62),

Adler's theory helped in providing the following key ideas and line of thoughts for explaining the "what and why of children's development".

- The importance of birth order in the formation of personality
- The impact of neglect or pampering on child development
- The idea that the most basic human drive is to strive from an initial state of inadequacy, or what he termed 'inferiority', towards 'superiority', or self-perfection.
- The idea that one must study and treat the individual as a whole person.

For explaining his views related to the feelings of inadequacy or inferiority giving birth to a basic drive striving for superiority, Adler maintained that in younger age right from the period of infancy, as children we face a number of inabilities or incapacities in comparison to the grown up. It instils a deep rooted feeling of inferiority among developing children. In making efforts for dealing with their inadequacy and getting rid of the feelings of inferiority they may be seen to get engaged in the task of striving for superiority. The way in which they strive for superiority in order to overcome feelings of inferiority is called their style of life, or lifestyle. It is the nature or quality of this lifestyle that decides the nature and quality of their development and functioning in the rest of their life. In this connection, Adler further emphasised that those who strive for superiority by beating down others had an unhealthy lifestyle or mistaken lifestyle. On the other hand, if they try to be the best version of themselves by working together with others towards common goals, they are said to be exhibiting a healthy lifestyle. The more healthy lifestyle one picks up for his/her growth and development or functioning, the more appropriate mile stones in the proper growth and development of his/her personality one achieves during the developmental period.

Ethological Perspective or Theories

Ethology, as a subject of study, may be well defined as the scientific study of the behaviour and development of animals (including humans) from an evolutionary angle. For this purpose it may be seen to focus on the study of (i) the development and behaviour of animals that leads to their survival and adaptation to natural environment and (ii) similarities and resemblance between the evolution of human behaviour and that of other species especially the immediate ancestors of humans such as chimpanzees, monkeys, etc.

As its historical evolution, the roots of its development may be traced in the work of the famous evolutionist Charles Darwin who for the first time in the history of mankind introduced concepts like survival, adaptation, evolution of species, etc., for describing the behaviour and development of animals including humans. However, it was the efforts of two European zoologists, Konrad Lorenz (1952) and Niko Tinbergen (1973), that helped the subject ethology to gain proper scientific recognition in the 1930s.

Lorenz's Theory of Imprinting

In reference to describing the evolution of developmental behaviour, Lorenz, the father of modern ethology, took the lead in studying animal behaviour in Munich, Germany through his experiments with ducks and geese. In his observation on the behaviour of ducks and geese in their natural as well as controlled setup, Lorenze noticed that when these animals are born, they immediately follow their mothers or any large objects perceived by them nearby since the time of their birth. To test this phenomenon further, he removed the mother goose as her eggs were hatching. Then, walking by the newborn goslings himself, he found that the babies would follow him just as they would have followed their mother. (Refer Figure 5.1)

Fig. 5.1: Lorenz's experiment on the Phenomenon of Imprinting (Adaptive Attachment Behaviour of the Baby Geese)

Lorenz named this behaviour of these animals as *imprinting* and termed it an adaptive behaviour ensuring closeness with the mother or any first perceived nearby object (such as large ball or the experimenter himself) for providing needed food, shelter and protection for their survival and growing. It is quite imperative here that the newborn animals that follow their mothers or care takers are more likely to grow up and pass their genes on to their babies. But on the other hand, the Babies who do not do so are more likely to starve or be eaten by predators. Lorenz declared that this behaviour results from genetically determined tendencies to respond to very specific stimuli in the environment.

Observation of the phenomenon of imprinting and likewise other researches in the field of ethology have helped in drawing a number of significant conclusions regarding the learning and development in animals including humans in the following manner:

1. The imprinting type of innate behaviors may be found to play a significant role in the adaptation, adjustment, learning and development of animals (including humans) right from their birth. As examples of such innate or inborn behaviour we may cite behaviors like nest-building behaviours of birds, pecking responses of chickens, herding behaviours of antelope, and sucking, grasping, pushing and reaching behaviours of infants. To shed more light on the nature and characteristics of such inborn behaviours, ethologists have identified four qualities that characterise virtually all innate or inborn, behaviors of the animals and humans. (Elbl-Eibesfeldt, 1989).

    • They are *universal* to all members of the species.

    • Because they are usually biologically programmed responses to very specific stimuli, they *require no learning or experience.*

    • They are normally *stereotyped*, meaning that they occur in precisely the same way every time they are displayed.

    • They are only *minimally affected by environmental influences* (in the short run, that is; natural selection pressures affect them across generations).

2. Observation of the phenomenon of imprinting on the part of ethologists and child psychologists has led to a major concept in child development known by the term critical or sensitive period. Lorenz in his experiments with animals referred this term to a limited time during which the newborn animal is biologically prepared or programmed for engaging in adaptive behaviours in a natural way. Actually, during his experiments Lorenz discovered that one of the most important influences on imprinting was the age of the chicks. If the act of following of the mother or any other object on the part of baby animals occurred during a period that began several hours after birth and lasted until sometime the next day, the phenomenon of imprinting (development of attachment bond) was found to occur in a reliable way, But however when the acts of such following occurred only before or after this period, little or no imprinting (development of attachment bond) resulted. Nowadays, modern ethologists, developmental psychologists and educationists use the term critical or sensitive periods to describe points in development when learning is much easier than it is at earlier or later points. Researches and experimental findings have now clearly shown

that the impact of critical or sensitive periods are not restricted to imprinting or even to the area of mother-infant attachment. It can be equally applicable to diverse areas, aspects and dimensions of child learning and development in a quite useful way such as learning of skills, motor and social development, development of cognitive abilities and imbibing of moral and ethical sense, etc. Parents and teachers are therefore advised to be vigilant and cautious about the appearance of the critical or sensitive periods in the developmental life of their children and should put in their efforts accordingly for the teaching and training of children that is in tune with the appropriateness of age and time for such teaching and training.

3. The concept of imprinting has significantly led to researches and further work in the field of ethology in the form of one or the other type of learning and development in the area of social and emotional behaviour of human beings such as understanding the human infant-caregiver relationship; formation of social and emotional bonds between peers, family members and people of the community, the emergence of the theories explain attachment behaviour of the infants and children, as well as the indifferent, aggressive and unattached behaviour of difficult children.

Bronfenbrenner's Bio-Ecological Theory of Child Development

The Russian born American psychologist, Urie Bronfenbrenner (1917-2005), in the 1970s tried to explain the developmental process of children by making use of the fundamental principles of science of ecology. In ecology, the environment in which living organisms (i.e., plants and animals) interact with each other and with the available physical environment is considered quite crucial for their survival, adaptation, growth and development. By taking inspiration and clues from this phenomenon, Bronfenbrenner tried to explain the adjustment and development of children in the context of the environment they live and grow in. However, in tune with the socio-cultural theory of development brought out by Lev Vygotsky, by the term environment, here he purely meant the socio-cultural environment available to children in its various forms and contexts for shaping and moulding their behaviour and development in the developmental period.

But later when he realised that the role of a child's biologically influenced disposition can't be ignored in shaping his development, he re-named his theory as the bio-ecological theory of child development (Bronfenbrenner, 2005). In forwarding such an altogether new perspective for explaining the development of children, Urie Bronfenbrenner may be seen to possess certain strong convictions that are as follows:

• Neither the biological make up (inherited genetic composition and biological structure) nor the environment exposure in their own separate functioning may be found sufficient enough for explaining the development of children in its proper way. It can only be explained by studying the interaction between these two and the resulted outcomes.

• Children's development does not generally take place in laboratory or in the forests along with animals. It is carried out in the socio-cultural environment of home, school, community settings and through wider socio-cultural exposure.

- The things mattering much in the development of children primarily are (i) the social context in which children live and (ii) the people who influence their development.
- The development is always context specific, i.e., the type of opportunities available in the social environment for the development of the child often influences the course of that development.
- It is the nature and type of interaction of the child with his environment that matters much in setting the course of his development. In such interaction, the child does not remain a passive recipient but plays a quite active role depending upon his own unique characteristics.
- To understand development completely we must consider how the unique characteristics of a child (known as personal characteristics) interact with that child's surroundings. These characteristics may be categorised as (i) developmentally generative (capable of influencing other people in ways that are important to the child) and (ii) developmentally disruptive (capable of causing problems in the environment with corresponding negative effects on the child).
- In the course of interaction between the child and his environment, both of them may be seen to continually influence one another in a bidirectional, or transactional, manner. For example, suppose a child has the developmentally generative characteristics of being bright sincere and promising, it may cast a quite positive effect on the child's environment by resulting in the parents' sending him to a better school and caring more for his study at home, which in turn may influence the child by paying more attention resulting in appreciable performance, which again may affect her environment by attracting friends who have high career aspirations, and so forth, in an ongoing cycle of interaction and development.
- It is not proper to lay undue emphasis or complete dependence on the role of the immediate environment, especially the mother-child relationship for explaining the development of children as is done in the ethological theories of child development. Here we must keep in mind that although we cannot undermine the importance of the immediate environment yet much more than this is involved in children's development in the shape of the many socio-cultural forces lying in their immediate surroundings and broader socio-cultural environment.

Bronfenbrenner's Ecological Systems and their Role in Child Development

While proposing his bio-ecological theory of child development, Bronfenbrenner contended that child development is the function of his constant interaction with the type of socio-cultural environment available to him for his living and development. He named these available environmental influences as the prevailing ecological system in which a child is seen to live and seek interaction with for his development. Going further, he hypothesised this eco-system as a blend or synthesis of a number of sub-systems or layers of environmental surroundings named as: (i) The Microsystem, (ii) The Mesosystem, (iii) The Exosystem, (iv) The Macrosystem and (v) The Chronosystem. Each of these subsystems of child's ecological system or environmental surroundings tries to influence the development of the children in its own powerful way.

The Microsystem

In his ecological model of child development, Bronfenbrenner used the term microsystem for describing the immediate environment available to the child for performing his day-to-day activities. The microsystem, thus available for a developing child may be seen to be consisting of interactions and relationship of the child with his parents, family members including siblings and relatives, teachers, peers, friends, neighbours, community people, etc. Development of the child in this system takes place in the manner as the behaviour and interaction with the members of this system have a desirable or undesirable impact on him. However, this impact goes both ways. Accordingly, how the parents or teachers interact with the child affects his development, but side by side the child's behaviour towards them also affects the teachers' and parents' further interaction with him for his care and development.

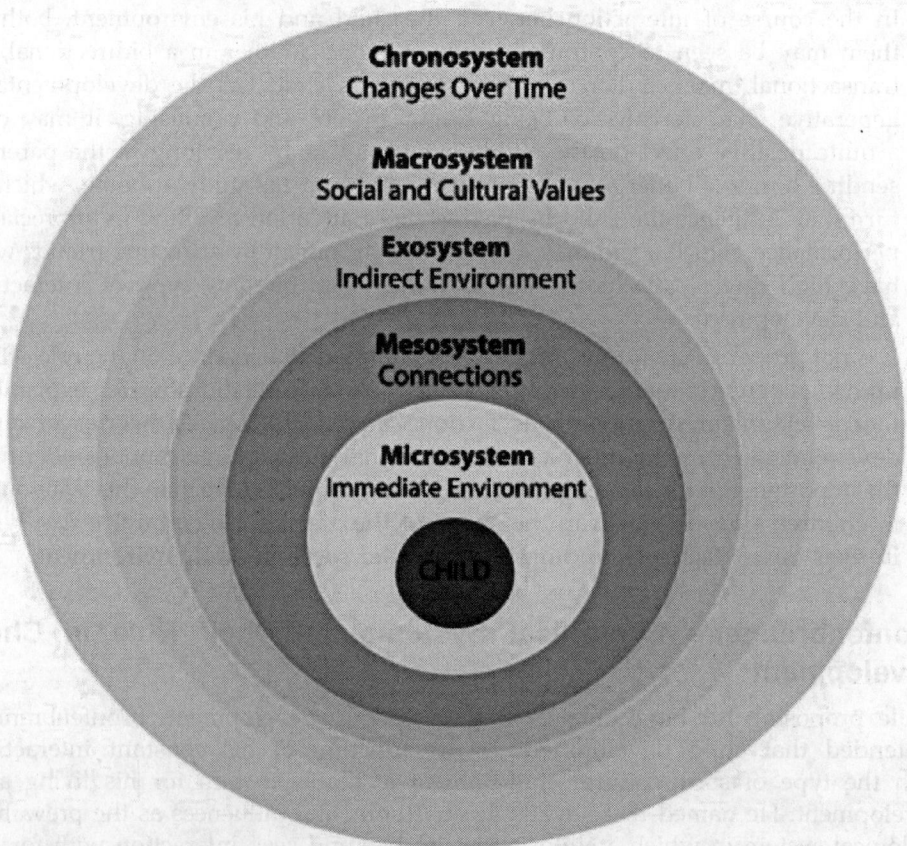

Chronosystem
Changes Over Time

Macrosystem
Social and Cultural Values

Exosystem
Indirect Environment

Mesosystem
Connections

Microsystem
Immediate Environment

CHILD

Figure 5.2: Bronfenbrenner's Ecological Model of the Environment

The Mesosystem

The term mesosystem stands for the interconnections and relationships existing among the different Microsystems of a developing child such as relationship of the child's parents or family with the school or teachers; relationship of family with the parents of the child's peers, neighbours, community, etc. In general, the more interconnection or more positive and healthy relationships prevail among these Microsystems, the more the child's development is likely to be supported in a clear and consistent way. The reverse is also true. For example if the parents of the children take an active part in parent-teacher association meetings, try to cooperate with the teachers in implementing their recommendations as well as of the school authorities about their children, then the development of their children is affected in a positive way, but in case the parents show apathy and negligence towards the functioning of parent-teacher association and the instruction and advice of the teachers and school, then it may prove costly to the proper development of their children.

The Exosystem

The exosystem refers to social settings comprising people and places in which children do not participate in a direct way, but that may still be found to have an important influence over their development. Such places and people may include people in the parents' workplaces, distant relatives and family acquaintances, religious institutions and such places, charitable institutions, media, the social and promotional policies of the government towards education and welfare of the children, etc.

For example, favourable work settings for the parents such as flexible work schedules, paid maternity and paternity leave, sick leave for parents whose children are ill may contribute in a positive way towards the development of children while on the other hand, poor working conditions and maladjustment at the work places of one or the other parent may bring negativity in children's development.

The Macrosystem

The macrosystem, an eco-system, true to its name that represents a broad based and much enlarged sphere of socio-cultural elements or forces helpful in the development of children from an outside external angle. In its practical sense, it represents the cultures and sub-cultures in which the child lives and affects the child's development through its beliefs, attitudes, traditions and values in a substantial way. Things like the type of government ruling the country, the economy and freedom available to citizens, the peaceful or conflicting war-like situations prevailing in the country, etc., also make a part of the macrosystem and we may clearly witness the effects of all such prevailing factors on the growth and development of children in a visible way. The living conditions and the state of development of the children in war torn countries like Syria and Afghanistan, nowadays may present a living example of this phenomenon.

The Chronosystem

The chronosystem represents that eco-system that is responsible for the development of children which governs through the principle of "changes occurring in developmental circumstances with the passage of time both with respect to individual development and to historical changes". For example, with respect to individual development, the separation or divorce of parents will be a more inconvenient, painful and detrimental incident for the development of children in the younger age than occurring at later ages. Similarly with respect to historical changes, we may notice that nowadays in the era of developed means of web information and internet technology, children at quite a tender age have access to information and knowledge that was not available till a few years ago even to the much older children from quite rich backgrounds, but had only direct instructions available to them from teachers or texts.

Evaluation of the Role of Bronfenbrenner's Theory or Model of Child Development

As a part of analyzing the role and working of Bronfenbrenner's theory and model of child development, the following observations have been made:

- In his bio-ecological model, Bronfenbrenner has tried to describe the part played by the different layers (sub-systems) of the child's bio-ecological environment in the development of growing children. In this concern, while starting from the closest and nearest socio-cultural influences available to children from the people and places of immediate touch and closeness in their day to day living, Bronfenbrenner has highlighted the importance of people, places, resources and influences available to children for their development as remote and indirect as the influences and impact of the cultural environment in which they live, and events and happenings through which they pass with the passage of time.

- He has also not forgotten the role played by the individuality and specificity of children in the form of their inherited biological make up and individually acquired characteristics in bringing sizable similarities and differences in their development.

- Not only has he clearly emphasised the active role played by children in determining the course of their development, but also shown that how does there exist a dynamic relationship between the child and the environment and among all systems in which the child develops. The different sub-systems of the child's ecological environment, according to his opinion do not exist and function in isolation, but influence the development of the child in a global way by interacting and interfering in each others' contributions in a quite significant way. For example, the lesson learnt in the bad company of peers or through the demonstrated behaviour of a favourable character on the TV screen, may wash out all what is available in this concern in a positive way at home and lectured by the teachers in the school.

- It is the duty of parents and teachers to remain vigilant to the possibility of any adverse impact on the development of children arising through the influence of one or the other sub-systems of the child's environment and try to seek its remedy by doing extra work in the areas and dimensions related to other eco-systems. For example, the deficiency arising in the development of children on account of the strained relationship between the parents may be overcome to a great extent by the needed handling on the part of a helpful teacher or with the sympathetic attitude of other family members. It has thus tried to advise the parents, teachers and all others interested in the welfare of the children to cooperate, understand and promote each others' efforts in the development of children by taking into consideration the mutually inclusive role constantly played by all the sub-systems of children's ecological environment in one or the other situation.

In the light of the nature, working and significance of Bronfenbrenner's theory and model of child development as described earlier, it can be well concluded that in comparison to the theories and models available so far for describing the development of children, Bronfenbrenner's model possesses all capabilities for being termed as a complete and comprehensive theory or model in itself for fulfilling its responsibility. Its real power in this concern may be seen lying in its capability of capturing all what is there in nature and in the child's own characteristics and activities for setting the direction of child's development.

As already discussed earlier, there is a distinctive category of developmental theories that are helpful in the proper understanding and knowing about the nature and functioning of the developmental process of children going on in the distinctive or specific areas or dimensions of their development such as cognitive, social or socio-cultural, moral and linguistic, etc. We will be dealing with all such theories in their respective chapters ahead in this text.

Summary

There exist a number of theories referred to as 'theories of child development' that help us in our understanding and providing predictions regarding one or the other aspects or phenomenon of children's development. Some of the mentionable ones in this direction are known by the names Biological theories, Behaviourist theories, Psychoanalytic theories, Ethological theories and Ecological theories.

Biological theories or hereditary theories of child development explain the development of children by adopting a clear cut biological and genetic perspective. According to them, it is inheritance of genes and biological structure on the part of a child that is responsible for laying down the foundation as well as the future course of his or her future growth and development. The credit for taking initiative in propagating these theories or perspectives goes to Darwin and Gesell who through their theories of evolution and maturation respectively held the adaptive value of inherited biological structures and process of maturation responsible for the consequential development of living beings including humans.

Behaviourist or environmental theories, propagated by behaviourists like Watson, Pavlov, Skinner and Bandura, provide the sole credit to the environmental influences for the growth and development of children right from the time of their conception in the womb of their mothers. The classical conditioning theories put forward by Watson and Pavlov, operant conditioning principles brought out by Skinner and social learning theory advocated by Bandura, all provide importance to environmental exposure for learning and imbibing one or the other behavioural traits or developmental characteristics on the part of children in the course of his or their growing from one stage to another stage of development.

However, the behaviourist cum environmental theories can also be blamed and criticised much like the biological cum hereditary theories for taking extreme stand in making environment as the sole deciding factor for shaping and moulding the development and behaviour of growing children with the neglect and utter disregard shown towards hereditary and biological contributions.

Psychoanalytical theories propagated by psychoanalysts such as Sigmund Freud and Alfred Adler adopted a psychoanalytic approach for explaining the developmental processes of children. In this connection, Freud tried to put his theory of psycho-sexual development centred round his strong belief in the role of one's sex drive in shaping and moulding one's behaviour. He outlined five stages in development of children and adolescents, which he called psychosexual stages. At each of these stages, a sexual urge is invested in a different part of the body, and gratification of the urges associated with those areas of the body is particularly pleasurable. He believed that the way in which gratification of urges is handled during each of these stages is what determines the nature of the development occurring in an adult's personality and character. Disturbance in any of these stages can result in psychological disturbance in adulthood.

Adler, while disagreeing with Freud's views of colouring the development of children unnecessarily with sexual desires and impulses, put his own views for explaining the development of children visible among children across different age spans and rearing situations by emphasizing on the role of birth order, the style adopted for their rearing and their striving towards superiority or self-perfection in the course of their growth and formation of personality.

Ethological theories or perspectives try to explain the behaviour and development of children from an ethological angle, i.e., the scientific study of their behaviour and development from an evolutionary angle involving their survival and adaptation to the natural environment. Lorenz's theory of imprinting and Bronfenbrenner's Bio-Ecological Theory of Child Development may be cited as two of the important theories representing this perspective.

In reference to describing the evolution of developmental behaviour in children, Lorenz, tried to take help from the phenomenon of imprinting — the following or adaptive attachment behaviour that he noticed during the course of his experiments with ducks and geese, in particular baby geese.

Lorenz declared that this behaviour results from genetically determined tendencies to respond to very specific stimuli in the environment and is able to explain the innate or inborn behaviors of animals and human babies visible in the form of pecking responses of the chickens, herding behaviors of antelope, and sucking, grasping, pushing and reaching behaviors of infants. This behaviour takes its own shape and form as the children pick up new ways of behaving in the course of their adaption to their environment and future needs.

While proposing his bio-ecological theory of child development, Bronfenbrenner contended that child development is the function of the child's constant interaction with the type of socio-cultural environment available to him for his living and development. He named these available environmental influences as the prevailing ecological system in which a child is seen to live and seek interaction with for his development. Going further, he hypothesised this eco-system as a blend or synthesis of a number of sub-systems or layers of environmental surroundings namely, (i) The Microsystem(the immediate environment available to a child for performing his day-to-day activities), (ii) The Mesosystem (the interconnections and relationships existing among the different microsystems of a developing child such as relationship of the child's parents or family with the school or teachers, (iii) The Exosystem (the social settings comprising people and places, in which the children do not participate in a direct way, but still these may be found to cast a potentially important influence over their development), (iv) The Macrosystem (the cultures and sub-cultures in which a child lives and that affects the child's development through its beliefs, attitudes, traditions and values in a substantial way) and (v) The Chronosystem (the eco-system responsible for the development of children which governs through the principle of "changes occurring in developmental circumstances with the passage of time"). Each of these subsystems of a child's ecological system or environmental surroundings tries to influence the development of the children in its own powerful way.

References and Suggesting Readings

Adler, A. (1927), *Practice and Theory of Individual Psychology*, New York: Harcourt Brace and World

Bandura, A., *Social Learning Theory*, Englewood Cliffs, N.J.: Prentice-Hall, 1977.

Bandura, A. and Walters, R.H., *Social Learning and Personality Development*, New York: Holt, 1963

Berk, Laura E. (2009), *Child Development* (Eighth edition), Boston: Pearson Education

Brooks, Robert and Goldstein, S., *Raising Resilient Children*, New York: McGraw Hill

Bronfenbrenner, U. (1979), *The Ecology of Human Development: Experiments by nature and design*, Cambridge, M.A.: Harvard University Press

Bronfenbrenner, U. (2000), *Ecological theory*, In A. Kazdin (Ed.) Encyclopedia of Psychology, Washington, DC, & New York: American Psychological Association and Oxford University Press

Bronfenbrenner, U. (Ed), (2005), *Making human being human*, Thousand Oaks, CA: Sage

Bronfenbrenner, U., and Morris, P.A. (2006), *The Bioecological model of human development*, In R.M. Lerner (Ed), *Handbook of child psychology*: Vol.1, *Theoretical models of human development*, (6th ed.)

Chomsky, N. *Reflection on language*, London: Temple Smith, 1976

Chomsky, N. *Language and mind*, New York, NY: Harcourt, Bruce & World, 1968

Eibl-Eibesfeldt, I. (1989), *Human ethology*, Hawthorne, NY: Aldine de Gruyter

Erickson, E., *Childhood and Society*, New York: Norton, 1950

Erickson, E., *Childhood and Society*, (2nd ed.), New York: Norton, 1963

Erickson, E., *Identity: Youth and Crises*, New York: Norton, 1968

Freud, S.(1910), *The origin and development of psychoanalysis*, New York: Henry Regnery (Gateway Editions), 1965

Freud, S., *An Outline of Psychoanalysis*, London: Hogarth Press, 1953

Kohlberg, L., *Essays on Moral Development*, San Francisco: Harper & Row, 1984

Kohlberg, L., *The Development of Modes of Thinking and Choices in years 10 to 16*, Ph.D. dissertation, University of Chicago, 1958

Kohlberg, L., "The development of children's orientation toward moral order: Sequence in the development of moral thought", *Vita Humana*, 6, 11-33, 1963

Kohlberg, L., 'The Development of Moral Character and Moral Ideology', in M. Hoffman and L. Hoffman (Eds.), *Review of Child Development Research*, Vol. I, New York: Russel Sage Foundations, 1964

Kohlberg, L., "The Child as a Moral Philosopher", *Psychology Today*, Vol 2, pp, 25-30, 1968

Kohlberg, L., "The development of moral character and moral ideology", in M. Hoffman and L. Hoffman (Eds.), *Review of Child Development Research*, Vol. I, New York: Russell Sage Foundation, 1964

Kohlberg, L., "Moral Stages and Moralization: The Cognitive Development Approach" in T. Lickona (Ed.) *Moral Development and Behaviour*, New York: Holt, Rinehart and Winston, 1976.

Meggitt, Carolyn, *Chid Development: An illustrated Guide*, Boston: Pearson, 2012

Meggitt, Carolyn, and Ormrod, J.E., *Understanding Child Development*, (Fifth edition), Boston: Pearson, 2013

Levine, Laura E. and Munsch, Joyce, *Child Development: An Active Learning Approach* (2nd ed.), Los Angeles: Sage, 2014

Lorenz, K.Z. (1952), *King Solomon's Ring*, New York: Crowell.

Lorenz, K.Z. (1965), *Evolution and the modification of behavior*, Chicago: University of Chicago Press

Lorenz, K.Z. (1980), "Here am I-Where are you? The behaviour of the graylag goose", New York, NY: Harcourt Brace Jovanovich

Ormrod, J.E., *Educational Psychology: Developing Learners* (4th ed.), Upper Saddle River, N.J.: Prentice-Hall, 2003

Shaffer, R., *Social Development*, Oxford: Black Well, 1996

Skinner, B.F. (1991), *Verbal behavior*, Action, MA: Copley (original work published in 1957)

Smetana, J. "Pre-School Children's Conceptions of Moral and Social Rules" *Child Development*, 52, 1333-1336, 1981

Tinbergen, N. (1973), *The animal in its world: Exploration of an ethologist*, 1932-1972, Cambridge, M.A.: Harvard University Press

Watson, J.B. (1926), *What is Behaviorism?*, Harper's Monthly Magazine, 152, 723-729

Watson, J.B. (1924), *Behaviorism*, New York: People's Institute (Rev. Ed., 1930)

6

Genetics (Heredity) and Environment

What is Genetics?

The term genetics has its etymological derivation in the Greek word 'Gene'. Gene is a basic unit of heredity that gets transferred from generation to generation from the immediate parents to their offspring. Genetics is the science that helps understand the mechanism of the transfer of hereditary characteristics in the form of genes, chromosomes and DNA through the immediate parents to offspring. In this way, Genetics is particularly concerned with one's heredity and the mechanism of the transfer of hereditary characteristics from the parents to offspring at the time of sexual intercourse. Let us get acquainted with the meaning and nature of the term heredity and the mechanism of the transfer of hereditary characteristics.

What is Heredity?

A cat gives birth to a kitten, a cow to a calf and a human being to a child. The members of one species resemble each other and possess characteristics that are common to their respective species. Now the question arises: what is responsible for a particular type of body, shape and other likewise characteristics in the members of one species. Furthermore we find that there are individual differences even in the members of the same species. A child resembles his sisters, brothers, parents, grandparents and other members of the family more than the people unrelated to him. What is it that causes such similarities and dissimilarities? The answer to this is heredity which means that an offspring inherits most of the personality traits of his parents and forefathers that make him resemble them. It is in this sense that Douglas and Holland have defined heredity as follows:

"One's heredity consists of all the structures, physical characteristics, functions or capacities derived from parents, other ancestry or species." (1947, p. 51)

When does a child inherit such personality characteristics from his parents or forefathers and how is this process of inheritance performed? What helps in such inheritance? These are some of the basic questions that need some clarification at this stage. For the answers, let us try to understand how life begins.

How life begins: Life in human beings actually begins with conception, approximately nine months before birth. The mechanism of conception is explained below:

The male and female reproductive organs produce germ cells. In the males, their testes produce the male germ cells, the spermatozoa, while in the females ovaries produce the female germ cells, the ova.

Normally, one ovum or egg is produced in each menstrual cycle (about 28 days) by the ovaries of a normal woman. The production of the sperm by the testes in the male is not so confined and limited. Normally, they produce 10 million sperms per day per gram of testicular tissue from the onset of puberty till death.

Conception is the result of the union of these male and female cells. In the natural way, this union occurs at the time of copulating between a man and a woman. Here as a result of coitus, the male germ cells (millions in number) usually come in contact with the female germ cells. The male germ cells are deposited at the mouth of the uterus and try to make contact with the single ovum. Out of so many spermatozoa, in a normal case, only one sperm (single male cell) is able to establish contact with the ovum (single female cell) situated in the ovarian duct of the mother and makes it fertile. The fertilised ovum is technically known as *zygote*, the starting single cell structure of a new life.

Human life thus starts from a single cell produced by the union of two germ cells, one from each parent, and gradually develops into a complicated composition of trillions of body cells and all containing the same genetic material as was inherited at the time of conception.

The zygote, i.e., fertilised ovum consists of a semi-fluid mass called *cytoplasm* and within the cytoplasm there is a nucleus which contains the *chromosomes*. Chromosomes always exist in pairs. In a human zygote, there are 23 pairs of chromosomes (46 individual chromosomes), 23 of which are contributed by the mother and 23 by the father and this is why for the transmission of hereditary characteristics in the offspring both mother and father are said to be equal partners. (See fig.6.1)

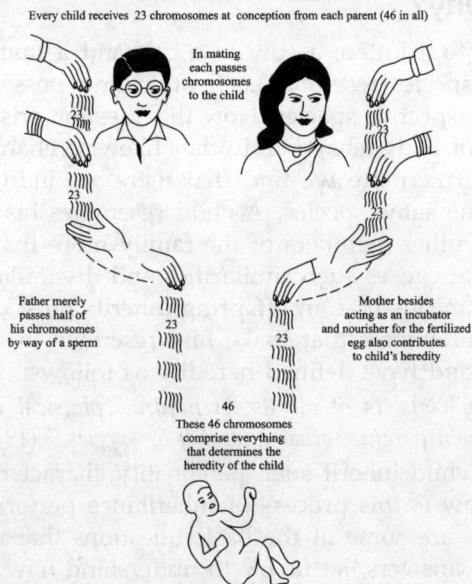

Every child receives 23 chromosomes at conception from each parent (46 in all)

In mating each passes chromosomes to the child

Father merely passes half of his chromosomes by way of a sperm

Mother besides acting as an incubator and nourisher for the fertilized egg also contributes to child's heredity

These 46 chromosomes comprise everything that determines the heredity of the child

Fig. 6.1 Transmission of chromosomes at the time of conception

Chromosomes possess a thread-like structure and are made of very small units called *genes*. It is estimated that there are about 1000 genes in each human chromosome cell. Consequently, the possibility regarding the combination of 23,000 characteristics each from mother and father may help us understand well the uniqueness of each individual.

Regardless of this very minute size, the composition of genes has been determined in terms of "DNA" and "RNA". DNA stands for deoxyribonucleic acid, and is said to be a basic chemical substance primarily responsible for genetic inheritance. RNA stands for Ribonucleic acid, and it acts as an active assistant to DNA for carrying out the genetic code message from parents to offspring, Thus all what we get from our ancestral stock through our parents at the time of fertilisation of the ovum of the mother by the sperm of the father exists in the form of chromosomes, genes and their respective classical constituents.

This inheritance at the time of conception makes up the native capital and endowment of an individual that is present with him in the form of the sum total of the traits potentially present in the fertilised ovum. It is this that is known as the heredity of an individual.

Determination of Gender — Boy Or Girl

The first twenty-two pairs of chromosomes are called autosomes. These chromosomes determine the development of most of our body structures and characteristics. The remaining twenty-third pair consists of the sex chromosomes. These sex chromosomes decide the individual's sex and other sex-linked characteristics.

There are two different types of sex chromosomes, X chromosome (usually big in size) and Y chromosome (comparatively smaller than X). In the male child, one member of the sex chromosome is X chromosome (contributed by the mother). In the female child both of these sex chromosomes, one from each parent, are X chromosomes.

All eggs have X chromosomes, but sperm cells may contain either type. Therefore, the mother's role in the determination of sex is quite neutral. At the time of conception, she can contribute only one type of sex chromosome, i.e., X chromosome. Much depends upon the possibility of the type of sex chromosomes X or Y that may be transmitted by the sperm cell of the father. If X chromosome is transmitted, the child will be female, and if Y chromosome is transmitted it will result in a male child. In this way, it is not the mother but the father who is biologically responsible for determination of the sex of the child.

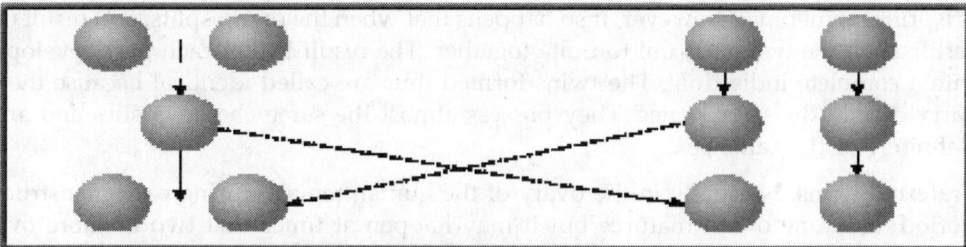

Fig.6.2: Determination of Gender — Boy or girl

(Note: The figure needs a lot of correction, it is incomplete, I will send you the figure for sketching the Right figure)

Heredity and Variations

With the discussion so far, we now know the cause of similarities between child and his immediate parents. However, it is still not clear as to why we sometimes find children possessing altogether different characteristics and traits from their parents. For example:

(i) Both the parents are of black complexion while the baby is white.

(ii) The parents are extra ordinarily genius while the child is not.

(iii) The child does not inherit the blindness, lameness or mental disorder of his parents.

(iv) The child does not resemble any of his sisters and brothers.

Let us try to seek clarification for these doubts. In fact, variations as observed above are the result of chance factors that work as under:

- It is purely by chance that a particular sperm fuses with a particular ovum to form a zygote. Moreover, in zygote there are 23 pairs of chromosomes, 23 of which are contributed by the sperm of the father and 23 by the ovum of the mother. Which chromosomes from ovum will pair with which chromosomes from sperm depend upon chance. A million permutations and combinations are possible for the union of chromosomes which contain genes. This explains why no two individuals are perfectly identical.

- What does an individual get from heredity is determined by the genes which he received through his parents. The traits of the forefathers, besides those of immediate parents, are also transmitted to the offspring through these genes. Therefore, it is possible that a child may possess certain traits that are traceable to one or more of the ancestors, even though they may not be visible in either of the parents.

Twins and Heredity

Normally at the time of fertilisation, a single ovum is fertilised by a sperm of the male. It results in the birth of a single offspring at one time. But sometimes this normal function is disturbed and there are cases of multiple births — the birth of two or more offspring at a time. The birth of twins is one of such cases where two individuals are born at the same time. There are two types of twins namely Identical twins and Fraternal twins.

Identical twins. Usually the fertilisation of one ovum by one sperm produces the offspring. Sometimes, however, it so happens that when the ovum splits, as a result of fertilisation the two parts fail to unite together. The result is that each part develops into a complete individual. The twins formed thus are called identical because they carry exactly the same genes. They possess almost the same characteristics and are definitely of the same sex.

Fraternal twins. Normally in the ovary of the human female during each menstrual period, only one ovum matures but it may happen at times that two or more ova mature simultaneously and may get fertilised at the same time by two different sperms. The result is that two different zygotes are produced. The individuals thus produced are known as fraternal twins or non-identical twins. They have a different combination of chromosomes and genes as both ova are fertilised by different sperms. Fraternal twins, therefore, are sure to differ in many traits. Unlike the identical twins, they may not necessarily belong to the same sex.

Laws of Heredity Governing Transfer of Heredity Characteristics

There exist certain well-known principles and laws for explaining the process and outcome of the mechanism of heredity transmission. These laws are as follows:

Law of Similarity (like begets like)

According to this law of inheritance, children tend to be similar to their parents. Thus following the notion of like begets like, the children of fair-coloured parents are likely to be fair, while those of the dark coloured are likely to be dark in complexion. Likewise, in inheritance of intellectual potentialities, bright parents are likely to have bright children, average parents, average children and dull parents, dull children. While the child of a German or Afghan national has all the possibilities of inheriting a tall height and broad structure from his parents, a Japanese or Nepalese child is likely to inherit a short structure and appearance resembling his parents.

This law of similarity and resemblance may thus work well in explaining the transfer of so many traits and characteristics from parents to their offspring. However, it does not appear to be universal. There are many exceptions. Fair-coloured parents may have dark complexioned children and dark-eyed parents may have blue-eyed children. Similarly bright parents may have dull children or dull parents may produce bright kids. The disparity or variation in the mechanism of inheritance thus needs some other laws or principles for its explanation.

Law of Variation

According to this law of inheritance, children may vary or differ from their parents with respect to one or the other traits or characteristics. As Sorenson (1948) puts it: *"The reason for such variations lies in the characteristics of the germ cells of the parents. Germ cells contain many determiners (in the name of chromosomes and genes) which are in fact responsible for the transmission of hereditary characteristics to the offspring."* (p. 256).

The type of combination of genes and chromosomes (the determiners of traits and characteristics) a child gets from his immediate parents solely depends on mere chance. This explains the differences and variations among the children of the same parents, even the children of same sex and twins. Moreover, as pointed out by the already referred inheritance theory of continuity of germplasm, the parents are said to be the trustee of the age-old hereditary characteristics that they transfer in the form of germplasm to their offspring. In such a transfer, it may be possible that the child inherits many of the characteristics or traits of his ancestors that lie dormant in his immediate parents. This explains why parents with darker complexion may also have fair children. Children of the same parents may also differ widely in terms of the inheritance of one or the other traits.

The reason for such variations may also be explained on the basis of the findings of some other theories of inheritance (already discussed in the text) propagated by well-known personalities like Mendel, Darwin and Lamark. While Mendel has explained the possibilities of variations in the successive generations through his findings in the characteristics of hybrids of peas and rats, etc., Darwin and Lamark have supported the principle of variation through their own explanations of the process of evolution needed to bring bodily and behavioural changes in the species on account of the demands of their environment for survival and progress.

Law of Regression

This law of inheritance is governed by the phenomenon of regression which means that there is an inherent tendency in the human beings to move towards the mean or average for the transmission of traits and characteristics from one generation to another.

As a result, *"Children of tall parents tend to be taller than the average but not as tall as their parents. The offspring of especially talented parent can be expected to be less gifted from their parents and similarly the children of less able parents probably will exceed parental ability."* (Crow and Crow, 1973, p. 38).

Thus, for any trait under transmission through hereditary mechanism, there is a tendency to move towards the average rather than farther below or above it. This is why son of a great artist or scientist seldom becomes as great as his father or the son of a dull parent always show better performance than his parent.

The Mechanism and Role of Dominant and Recessive Genes

Besides the above-mentioned three laws of heredity, the inheritance of traits and characteristics with human beings also needs to be explained in terms of the role played by the dominant and recessive genes. Let us try and understand this.

In search of hereditary functions of genes, through his experiments on garden peas and fruit-flies, Gregor Mendel hypothesised that some genes are dominant while others recessive. Like chromosomes, the genes also occur in pairs. Each of the pairs is donated by one of the parents. An offspring thus may be found to derive a gene pair in one of the following forms:

- A dominant gene from one of the parents and a recessive gene from the other

- Dominant genes from both the parents

- Recessive genes from both the parents

In simple meaning, a dominant gene must exhibit his dominance over the recessive ones. For example, if one parent furnishes a gene for brown eyes (known to be dominant) and the other provides a gene for blue (a recessive gene), the offspring will have brown eyes (characteristic of the dominant gene).

However, the fact that a particular trait is recessive in one generation in no way rules out its appearance in the future. For example, in the above example of the mutation between brown and blue genes resulting in brown eyes, a recessive blue gene lies in wait. If that offspring is copulated with someone with another gene for blue eyes (even if he or she may not possess blue eyes), their offspring, the third generation, might have blue eyes.

The role of genes, as mentioned earlier, may thus provide a solid support (besides the chance pairing of 23 chromosomes and 23,000 genes from the egg and sperm cells) for explaining the variations and dissimilarities in height, weight, intelligence, blood type, eye colour, and the colour and texture of the skin and hair and other similar important characteristics found in the parents and their off-spring as well as within the offspring of the same parents.

Many of the inherited genetic characteristics which cause the most concern (e.g., inheritance of feeble mindedness, certain forms of insanity and a susceptibility to certain diseases such as diabetes) have their potential answer in the mechanism and role played by the strange inheritance caused through a combination of recessive genes. It may give us a surprise that while immediate parents have no such symptom of mental deficiency or disease, the children are said to carry them on account of inheriting them through their immediate parents. It is here that the role of recessive genes suddenly comes into limelight. Let us see how.

The extensive experiments carried out by Mendel and other genetic authorities have resulted in conveying that "a recessive trait cannot be passed on if it is present in the genes of only one parent. It must be carried by both parents. Moreover, the genes carrying the trait must be paired." (Cunningham, 1951: 56)

In Fig. 6.3., the light circle represents the presence of feeble mindedness. The dark circle represents its absence. Each chromosome is represented by a string of genes. A and B are the grandparents (parents of father F) and grandparents C and D are the parents of mother M. There are four children W, X, Y and Z who have received various combinations, of genes. A and C did not have the feeble mindedness genes, B and D did. Child W does not have feeble mindedness and cannot pass it on to his offspring. Children X and Y carry it, but may or may not pass it on to their children. Child Z does have it, and he is feeble-minded. He must pass it on if he has children.

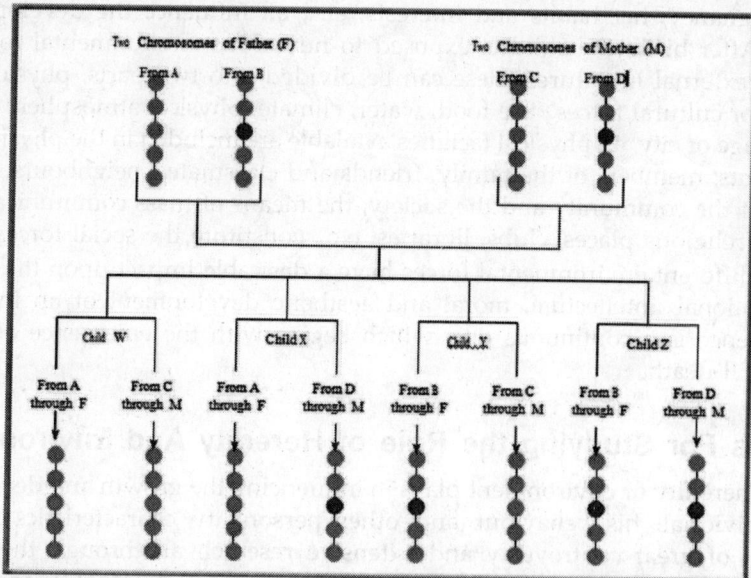

Fig. 6.3: Illustrating how a recessive trait such as feeble mindedness may be inherited. (Adapted from Cruze, W.W, *Educational Psychology*, Ronald Press Co., New York, 1942)

What is Environment

From the above discussion, it is clear that a child inherits the traits and characteristics of his parents and forefathers through genes at the time of conception. Therefore, what he possesses at the time of conception is all due to heredity. It is the native capital given to him for starting his life. After conception, how he develops is the outcome of the interaction between his hereditary characteristics and environment. The forces of environment begin to play their part and influence the growth and development of an individual right from the time of the fertilisation of the ovum by sperm. Therefore, from the environmental point of view, not only what happens after birth is important, but also what goes on inside the womb of the mother after conception has equal significance.

The above point of view has given birth to many meanings and definitions of environment and have been mentioned as follows:

Boring, Langfield and Weld

"The environment is everything that affects the individual except his genes." (1961, p. 422)

Wordsworth and Marquis

"Environment covers all the outside factors that have acted on the individual since he began life."(1948, p. 156)

The views expressed by the above writers lead to the conclusion that environment consists of external forces, which influence the growth and development of an individual right from his conception. Before birth, the mother's womb is the place where these forces play their part. Nutrition is received by the embryo through the blood stream of the mother. The physiological and psychological state of the mother during pregnancy, her habits and interests, etc., all influence the development of the baby. After birth, the child is exposed to numerous environmental forces that are purely external in nature. These can be divided into two parts, physical forces and social or cultural forces. The food, water, climate, physical atmosphere at home, school, village or city, all physical facilities available are included in the physical forces while parents, members of the family, friends and classmates, neighbours, teachers, members of the community and the society, the means of mass communication and recreation, religious places, clubs, libraries, etc., constitute the social forces.

These different environmental forces have a desirable impact upon the physical, social, emotional, intellectual, moral and aesthetic development of an individual. Their influence is a continuous one, which begins with the emergence of life and continues till death.

Measures For Studying the Role of Heredity And Environment

What part heredity or environment plays in influencing the growth and development of the individual, his behaviour and other personality characteristics has been the subject of great controversy and extensive research all through the ages for psychologists. For tendering explanations regarding the individuality and existing variations among the individuals, they quite often resort to the studies as follows.

Selective Breeding: In this method of studying inheritance, members of some specific species high or low in a particular trait copulate with the other members of the species in the same position and then the genetic character of the so-produced offspring is made the subject of study.

Gregor Mendel (1822-1884) was the first to use the method of selective breeding in the investigation of the inherited traits by crossing different types of peas, a fast growing, sexually reproducing plant.

The method of selective breeding has been very useful to agriculturists, tree planters and commercial breeders of live-stock for improving the varieties and yields. In performing such experiments, they usually arrange selective breeding through the copulating of the members of the species that excel in the desired trait such as size. The difference between the average sizes of the males and females in the parental generation and the average sizes of the males and females of offspring (the selection gain) are noted and then the largest offspring are bred and so on. In these experiments, care is taken for maintaining the environmental factors as constant as possible. Therefore, any insignificant difference between the traits of the parental generation and their subsequent offspring can be safely attributed to heredity.

The method of selective breeding for studying inheritance, although found quite useful in case of lower plants and animals, has not been found practicable in case of human beings. This is because human copulating cannot be used for experimental purposes and one human generation lasts for so many years. However, the naturally available results of (the selective breeding in the form of inbred population, the tribes or isolated places where marriage and copulating is permitted within the same blood) provide many important clues for the hereditary transmission of so many traits. With development in Genetic Science regarding artificial insemination, test tube babies, the possibility of producing a body directly from the body of a human being without sex or fertilisation, etc., we may place high hopes for experimental results of selective breeding in humans.

Twins and Family Studies

For studying the impact of heredity or environment on the development and personality characteristics of individuals, psychologists have also tried to take the help of twin and family studies.

Twins, especially identical twins, are supposed to be identical in hereditary potential. Fraternal twins, siblings, cousins, members of family and other blood relations are also supposed to form a group of individuals who show a gradual diminishing resemblance for heredity characteristics but are certainly nearer to the people not related at all. Generally, these studies of twins and other types of family relations often use concordance or coefficient of correlation, to ascertain whether a certain characteristic is the result of heredity or environment.

In carrying out the studies of twins and family, psychologists have adopted the following approach:

(1) A pair of identical twins has been separated and reared apart in different environmental surroundings. The results of such experiments have sprung in favour of both heredity and environment as significant or non-significant differences have been found to exist in one or the other case.

(2) Identical twins have been compared to fraternal twins, siblings, cousins other relatives and individuals not having any blood relationship to ascertain whether or not the affinity in terms of blood relationship causes affinity in terms of physical and other characteristics.

(3) Families have been studied for generations past from the point of the unique presence or absence of some personality attributes. It has been found that members of family and their descendants show a remarkable resemblance. For example, a family known to be rich and of repute may consistently display healthy signs of wealth and intelligence while a family of ill-repute may exhibit a record of the characterless, poor and defamed persons. Similarly, many of the abnormalities and diseases have been found to perpetuate from generation to generation. Consequently, heredity has been made responsible for the subsequent development and behaviour of an individual.

However, from all types of experiments going on to support the role of heredity or environment it may be easily concluded that the findings of these experiments can be interpreted either way. In the real sense, it is too difficult to have proper experimentation for studying hereditary or environmental influences on the development of children.

To study the impact of environment we have to take individuals with the same heredity and then study their differences by keeping them in different environments. Similarly for studying the impact of heredity, environmental factors need to be made constant.

In actual experimentation, it is impossible to get individuals having the same heredity (possessing exactly the same genes). However, if we take the case of identical twins (by assuming they are of similar hereditary stock), we cannot study the impact of environmental influences right from the time of their conception. Hence it is difficult to make the heredity factor a constant.

On the other hand, it is also impossible to get the environmental factors as constant because it is very difficult to provide exactly the same environment for different individuals. Even a mother cannot show equal amount of love and affection to her own children.

What Is Then Contributed By Heredity And What By Environment

It is difficult to find an appropriate answer to this question due to the following reasons:

(1) After the conception of a child, we are unable to pin-point with accuracy whether a particular behaviour or trait emanates from our heredity or from our environment.

(2) With all the available resources at hand and experiments conducted, we still cannot say with certainty what type of behaviour or trait is influenced most by heredity and what by environment.

However, in human beings, hereditary factors are predominantly accountable for the behaviour and characteristics as under:

• Reflex and instinctive behaviour, characteristics like blood type, finger-prints, eye colour, the colour and texture of the skin and hair, defective genes and chromosomal abnormalities, schizophrenia, tuberculosis, cancer, haemophilia, etc.

• Similarly, we can say that environmental factors are predominantly accountable for the interests, attitudes, aptitudes, habits, temperaments, etiquettes and manners, social and culture norms, etc.

However, for most of the characteristics and traits including our somatic structure, and physical, mental, social and emotional makeup, it is the interaction between the individual's genetically determined characteristics and its environment which is said to be responsible for making the individual what he is at a particular time. Speaking in a true sense, both heredity and environment are said to be jointly responsible for the acquisition of any type of behaviour and development of any personality characteristics in human beings.

The respective roles of heredity and environment become clear when we compare the individual's growth and development with that of a tree. Whereas the maximum and minimum growth of a healthy tree is determined by its genes but exactly how tall it will grow within this range can only be determined by the environment — soil, water, manure and the sunlight it gets. In a similar way our heredity endowments provide us with the native capital to start the journey of life. How successful we will be in life depends both on the potential value of our native capital and the opportunities and circumstances favourable or unfavourable that we get from our environment for reaching the maximum out of our starting capital. The future outcome as a result of interaction with one's environment is thus perfectly hidden in one's inherited genetic character. Genetic factors (although influenced, directed and even surpassed in some cases by the environmental forces) play quite a substantial role in providing an approximate range for the minimum and maximum height reached in terms of the personality traits but how much height one will achieve along this range again depends upon the cooperation one receives from one's environment.

Therefore, it is always advisable to take into account the sources like one's heredity, his environment and the inseparable interaction between one's heredity and environmental factors for determining the aetiology of one's behaviour or development of some specific personality traits.

Genetics and Child Development

Many times, a straight question is asked — what may be the most possible effect or influence of genetics on human development and behaviour? What type of abnormalities, disorders and malfunctioning of the health and personality characteristics are most likely to be transferred from generation to generation? Let us try to answer the same in the light of the studies and evidences gathered so far on this account.

1. **Cognitive malfunctioning and mental deficiency:** Genetic factors have been found responsible for causing cognitive malfunctioning and mental deficiencies among children. It can happen in two ways, either through transmission of some defective genes in the chromosome of one or both parents or on account of chromosomal aberrations. The most common types of disorders and deficiencies caused on these accounts may be listed as follows:

   • A disorder and mental deficiency popularly known as PKU (phenylketonuria) results through the pairing of defective recessive genes carrying metabolic disturbances. Signs of neurological and mental retardation and manifestations relating to severe brain damage are common with this disorder.

- In some cases like *Tay Sachs disease*, also known as infantile amaurotic idiocy, mental deficiency or defective cognitive functioning may result from the pairing of single recessive genes.
- *Down's syndrome or Mongolism* (the mentally deficient whose facial characteristics bear superficial resemblance to members of the Mongolian race) is said to be caused by chromosomal aberrations. The majority of the Mongoloid children are found to have 47 chromosomes instead of the usual 46.
- *Klinefelter's syndrome*, also known as Fragile X syndrome, (resulting into abnormality in behaviour and severe mental retardation) is caused on account of a chromosomal abnormality related with the presence of the extra X-chromosome (which appears as if it is fragile and a part of it is breaking off). This disorder occurs in males and symptoms are usually noticed at puberty when the testes remain small and the body develops feminine secondary sexual characteristics such as enlarged breasts and round hips.

2. **Muscular malfunctioning and disorders:** Genetic factors have also been found responsible for causing muscular malfunctioning and disorders such as follows:
   - *Muscular Dystrophy:* Available in the various forms and types, this type of muscular impairment or disorder is a well-known group of inherited diseases (running usually in families) in which the muscles of the body are subjected to the condition of progressive atrophy (weakening and wasting away of muscular tissue).
   - *Osteogenesis imperfecta:* It is a hereditary disorder that goes on in families because of transmission to children by affected parents. It is characterised by improper formations of bones and their easy breaking.
   - *Marfan Syndrome:* It is a genetic disorder in which the muscles of the affected children are found to be poorly developed and their spine is curved. It is why they are advised to avoid heavy exercise and lifting of heavy loads.
   - *Achondroplasia:* It is a genetic disorder in which the affected children have straight upper backs and curved lower backs (sway back), and are therefore subjected to the risk of sudden death during sleep from compression of the spinal cord interfering with their breathing.

3. **Sensory malfunctioning and disorders:** In many cases the defects and disorders related to the sensation of hearing, visual and smell heredity factors including transfer of defective genes may be found a causal factor to affect the power of sensation of the collected children. For example, in case of hearing impairment the blood type incompatibility between a mother and her offspring sometimes may be found a quite pertinent cause.

4. **Learning disabilities and behavioural disorders:** Genetic or heredity factors have been found responsible for causing learning disabilities and behavioural disorders among the children on the pattern of "like begets like" and "transmission of hereditary characteristics" in the following manner:

- Nearly 20 to 25 per cent of hyperactive or impulsive children have been found to have at least one parent of this nature.

- Emotional imbalances, disorders of memory and thinking, speech and learning have been found to run in families.

- Recent research in genetics have shown that genes connected to chromosome 6 and chromosome 15 are said to play a role in the hereditary transmission of reading disabilities.

- The behavioural problems related to stuttering is found to run in families.

- The most severe and profound cases of emotional disturbance like schizophrenia has been found to be linked to genetic factors.

5. **Physiological malfunctioning and diseases:** Genetic factors have been found responsible for affecting adversely the metabolic and health functioning including the inheritance of chronic diseases among children. Among the most distinguishable diseases supposed to be caused through genetic factors some may be named as tuberculosis, muscular dystrophy, Marfan Syndrome, Down Syndrome, phenylketonuria (PKU), cancer, haemophilia, diabetes and heart ailments.

The above-cited multidimensional malfunctioning and disorders caused by heredity or genetic factors give birth to one or the other problems related to one's adjustment to self and his environment which ultimately lead to affect one's way of thinking, feeling and acting in a quite adverse and detrimental way.

Implications of the knowledge related to the mechanism of heredity and environment

Let us see in which manner, all of us are helped by the knowledge and understanding reached through the study about genetic and environmental factors in exercising our role towards the proper development and welfare of children.

(i)   We may learn that by following the principle "like begets like" a child will definitely inherit all those traits and characteristics which are generally attributed to human beings. Going further, he or she is likely to inherit (with some slight variations) all those traits and characteristics which are common and peculiar to the family lines (paternal and maternal) of which he/she is a product.

(ii) Although a child has a tendency to resemble his parents, ancestors or members of the race in many of the traits or characteristics yet there always exists wide possibilities to differ and vary on account of the possibility of a number of permutations and combinations of genes and chromosomes affecting the native endowment of an offspring at the time of conception.

Therefore, we should not be surprised to observe the significant differences or variations among parents and their children or children of the same parents.

(iii) The knowledge of the phenomenon of continuity of germplasm may reveal to us that germ cells (not the somatic or body cells) are the true bases for the transmission of hereditary characteristics. Therefore, the deficiencies or disorders regarding the somatic or bodily structure of the parents are not handed over in their true form as such by the immediate parents to their offspring. As a result, the son or daughter of a physically handicapped or sensory deprived person is not necessarily born handicapped like his mother or father.

On the similar lines, it becomes quite useful for us to know that these are only the potentialities of development, not the acquired skills, knowledge, interests, attitudes and behavioural traits of parents that are known to be inherited by children. Therefore, all the behavioural and adjustment problems of the children and ailing persons may be said to be a product of the uncongenial environmental influences, rearing practices, training and education. Thus in no way, heredity should ever be blamed on this account. The knowledge regarding the role of genetic factors in transferring and germinating the various types of physiological, mental, psychological malfunctioning disorders and diseases among the individuals may help us to look for the aetiology, prevention and cure of various types of health and behavioural problems of the suffering children.

(v) The role of the environment forces getting active right from the conception of the child in the womb of the mother may help the pregnant mothers and the members of family to take every possible care for the proper growth and development of the developing embryo. The pregnant mothers thus may be helped to adopt proper dietary measures and do away with smoking, drinking, drug abuse, or any physical or emotional shocks that can prove detrimental to the health and well being of the child.

(vi) The knowledge that at any stage of its development the child's net growth and development is the outcome of the joint product of its hereditary endowment and environmental influences, may help in assuring the parents and care takers of the children that they should not get panicky for the poor state of the new-born child. If hereditary or internal environment available so far has not been favourable, then there is still much left to be done for the needed growth and development of the child by taking care of the environmental forces. The child may be properly nourished and brought up in such a way as to yield the maximum positive result in terms of his wholesome growth and development.

In this way, the knowledge regarding the mechanism of heredity and environment and their role in the development of human being may help all of us in so many ways for deriving useful lessons for helping children in their development and well being in the desired proper way.

Summary

Genetics is the science that helps in understanding the mechanism of the transfer of hereditary characteristics in the form of genes, chromosomes and DNA through the immediate parents to their offspring. In this way, Genetics is particularly concerned with one's heredity and the mechanism of the transfer of hereditary characteristics from the parents to offspring at the time of sexual intercourse.

Heredity refers to a biological mechanism as a result of which a child receives the traits and characteristics of his ancestors and race through the transmission of particular genes to him by his immediate parents at the time of his conception in the womb of his mother.

The mother's eggs have a pair of X chromosomes, but father's sperm cells may contain both X and Y. Therefore, the mother's role in the determination of sex is quite neutral. She can only contribute X chromosome for her child. Much depends upon the possibility of the type of sex chromosomes X or Y that may be transmitted by the sperm cell of the father. If X chromosome is transmitted, the child will be female, and if Y chromosome is transmitted it will result in a male child. In this way, it is not the mother but the father who is biologically responsible for the birth of a male or female child.

Dissimilarities between the child and his immediate parents may arise on account of the fact that the child may inherit some or the other characteristics of his ancestors (not necessarily present in the parents) through the inherited genes.

Twins are born when two children are conceived by the mother at the same time. Identical twins have exactly the same set of genes and therefore possess the same characteristics and are definitely of the same sex. Fraternal twins have a different combination of chromosomes and genes and are therefore sure to differ in many traits. In addition they may belong to the same or opposite sex.

The theories of heredity have given birth to certain specific principles and laws known as Laws of heredity like the Law of similarity (like begets like), Law of variation (one may vary or differ from their parents), and Law of regression emphasizing an inherent tendency of moving towards the mean or average for the transmission of traits from one generation to another.

The inheritance of traits and characteristics also needs to be explained in terms of the role played by the dominant and recessive genes. In simple meaning, a dominant gene must exhibit his dominance over the recessive ones. For example, if one parent furnishes a gene for brown eyes (known to be dominant) and the other provides a gene for blue (a recessive gene), the offspring will have brown eyes (characteristic of the dominant gene).

The developments in the field of genetics have been helpful in establishing a mentionable link between the hereditary transmission, and occurrence of certain type of abnormalities and disorders in the children classified as, (A) Cognitive malfunctioning and Mental deficiency, resulting in one or the other type of mental disorder such as PKU, Tay Sachs disease, Down's syndrome or Mongolism and Fragile X syndrome; (B) Muscular malfunctioning and disorders such as Muscular Dystrophy, Marfan Syndrome and Achondroplasia; (C) Sensory malfunctioning and disorders related to the sensation of hearing, visual and smell etc.; (D) Learning disabilities and behavioural disorders such as hyperactivity and impulsivity, Emotional imbalances, disorders of memory and thinking, speech and learning etc.; and (E) Physiological malfunctioning and diseases such as tuberculosis, cancer, haemophilia, diabetes and heart ailments.

The forces of environment begin to play their role in the growth and development of an individual right from the time of conception of the child in the womb of the mother. The child is exposed to the influence of such internal environmental forces first in the womb of the mother and later on by so many external environmental factors categorised as physical and socio-cultural factors.

Whether heredity or environment plays a decisive role in the growth and development of the individual has been a subject of wide controversy. Both hereditarians and environmentalists (supported by their observations and experiments) have forwarded their claim of supremacy in this direction. However, nothing is truer than the clear assertion that both are essential for the growth and development of the personality of a child.

As parents, elders and teachers we can be helped by the knowledge related to the mechanism of heredity and environment for serving the interest and welfare of the developing children particularly concerning the principles of heredity transmission, role of dominant and recessive genes, and the acceptance of the role of environment in shaping the future of the children.

References and Suggested Readings

Bhatia, H.R., *Elements of Educational Psychology*, Orient Longman, 1968, Calcutta.

Boring, E.C., Langfield, H.S. and Weld, H.P. (Eds.), *Foundations of Psychology*, (Ind. ed.), John Wiley, New York, 1961.

Crow, L.D. and Crow, Alice, *Child Psychology*, Reprint, Barney Noble, New York, 1969.

– – –, *Child Psychology*, 3rd Indian Reprint, Eurasia Publishing House, New York, 1973.

Cruze, W.W, *Educational Psychology*, Ronald Press Co., New York, 1942

Cunningham, B.V., *Psychology for Nurses*, (2nd edition), New York: Appleton, Century Crofts, Inc., 1951

Douglas, O.B. and Holland, B.F., *Fundamentals of Educational Psychology*, Macmillan, New York, 1947.

Garrett, H.E., *General Psychology*, Indian Reprint, Eurasia Publishing House, New Delhi, 1968.

McDougall, William, *An Outline of Psychology*, Methuen & Co., London, 1949.

McIver, R.M. and Page, C.H., *Society: An Introductory Analysis*, Macmillan, London, 1949.

Pasricha, Prem, *Educational Psychology*, University Publishers, Delhi, 1963.

Sorenson, Herbert, *Psychology in Education*, McGraw-Hill, New York, 1948.

Stern, C., *Principles of Human Genetics*, W.H. Freeman, San Francisco, 1973.

Woodworth, R.S. and Marquis, D.G., *Psychology*, Henry Holt, New York, 1948

7

Pre-natal Development, Birth and Care of Newborns

Introduction

The journey of a child's life begins with the conception in the womb of the mother. The period of development beginning from conception till birth is referred to as the period of prenatal development of the child. How does the conception of the child in the womb of the mother take place, how the conceived child travels the journey of getting developed in the shape of zygote, embryo, foetus and finally in the form of a newborn baby for arriving on this earth? How the mothers conceive or get pregnant and how the babies are delivered by the mothers? What are the possible birth complications and their negative outcomes for the mother and child? How the health and well being of the new born baby is checked and what should be done for the health and safe delivery of the child? Let us try to seek answers of such questions in this chapter.

Conception of the Child and Beginning of Life

Life begins in the womb of the mother with the conception of the child. Conception is the net result of the fertilisation of the ovum belonging to the mother by the sperm of the father. In this regard a few things have already been referred to in Chapter five of the book. Let us elaborate a little bit more in this concern.

Menstruation is a natural process in women during which an ovum bursts from one of her ovaries in the middle of the menstrual cycle. The ovum after its emergence from the ovary travels to the adjacent fallopian tube, a narrow and curved pipe that connects the ovary to the uterus. While the ovum is travelling, a spot on the ovary, from which it was released, secretes hormones responsible for preparing the lining of the uterus to receive a fertilised ovum.

During sexual intercourse between a man and woman, when the man ejaculates, millions of sperms they begin making their way through the woman's reproductive organs — first into the vagina, then to the cervix, through the uterus and up the fallopian tubes toward the ovaries. However, out of these millions of sperms only a few numbering 200 or so are fortunate to make their way first into the uterus and then move toward the fallopian tube where an ovum produced by the woman is waiting for the union. The life span of the sperm is six days and the ovum can survive only for one day after its release into the fallopian tube. Out of the sperms entering the fallopian tube, only one is capable of piercing the ovum for getting it fertilised. It is this fertilisation of the ovum by a single sperm that results in the conception of a child.

The question here may arise why only one sperm is capable of uniting with the ovum. It happens on account of two main reasons. First, it happens on account of the inability of these millions of sperms to cover the distance travelled by them up to the fallopian tube. However large the number may be, the sperms composed of a single cell (although carrying a heavy weight of the 23 chromosomes and a tail) are not exactly skilled at navigation. The distance from the vagina to the ovaries is vast for such a small object as a sperm. Secondly, the woman's body responds to sperm as a foreign substance. As soon as a single sperm makes contact with the ovum waiting in the fallopian tube, the ovum cooperates by rearranging its exterior layers so hard that no other sperm can enter the contact area.

Although this is how conception usually takes place, there are occasional variations resulting in phenomenon such as birth of twins. In one these variations, two ova are released by the woman instead of one, and both are fertilised by sperm, resulting in di-zygotic twins. Through another variation, twins can also result when a zygote that has just begun the process of cell division splits into two separate clusters of cells, named specifically as monozygotic twins.

The Developmental Journey After Conception

After conception (becoming pregnant on the part of a woman), the developmental journey of the child in the womb of the mother begins to take its shape. Duration of this journey is approximately 9 months or 38 weeks. There are two main stages or phases involved in the prenatal development of children namely: (A) Germinal phase (covering the conception and developmental journey of zygote during the first two weeks from the time of conception) and (B) Gestation phase (covering the developmental journeys of embryo and foetus from the third week of pregnancy to the birth of the child). In this way, the developmental journey of the children after conception may be claimed to involve the periods named as (i) the period of Zygote, (ii) the period of the Embryo, (iii) the period of the foetus. Let us try and understand what happens during these periods.

The Period of Zygote

Fertilisation of the ovum by a single sperm results in the formation of zygote. The duration of the period falling between the fertilisation of the ovum (formation of the zygote) and formation of embryo is termed as the period of zygote. It lasts about two weeks is and characterised with the developments of the following nature:

• **Development of blastocyst:** In such a development, the zygote is found to create new cells as it travels through the fallopian tube and toward the uterus. The cell formation here is carried out through a process named *mitosis* (cell duplication). As a result the first cell gets divided into two, two cells into four, four into eight and so on. By the fourth day of the child's conception about 60 to 70 cells are formed and these are found to exist in the shape of a hollow, fluid-filled ball called a blastocyst.

- **Occurrence of implantation:** Implantation refers to the process of attaching firmly of the growing group of cells to the inner lining of the mother's uterus. Regarding the survival of the developing organism, implantation is quite challenging. Many of the conceptions fail to achieve successful implantation resulting in the termination of pregnancy even before the mothers may get aware of their pregnancy.

The developmental activities regarding the implantation going on in the second week of conception may be briefed as follows:

(i)   At first the protective outer layer of the blastocyst (called trophoblast) gets multiplied at a fastest rate for forming a membrane, called amnion. It helps in enclosing the developing zygote in amniotic fluid which in turn helps keep the temperature inside the womb of the mother constant and provides the developing zygote a cushion against any jolts caused by the mother's movement. After that there is development in the form of a structure named yolk sac that takes the responsibility of producing blood cells.

(ii) By the end of the second week, cells of the outer layer of the blastocyst form another protective membrane named chorion surrounding the amnion. From the chorion, there is the emergence of some tiny hair like villi or blood vessels. The burrowing of these vessels into the uterine wall gives birth to a special organ named placenta. It helps in allowing food and oxygen to reach the developing zygote and for the waste products to be carried away. For this purpose there is a development of another organ named umbilical cord that is well connected to the placenta. It contains one large vein that helps in delivering blood loaded with nutrients and two arteries that remove waste products from the zygote.

> The biggest challenge during the germinal phase is implantation. The growing group of cells need to attach to the inner lining of the women's uterus. Surprisingly, an estimated 60 percent of all conceptions never result in successful attachment of the zygote to the uterine wall, thus ending the pregnancy often before the woman is even aware that she was pregnant.

By the end of the period of the zygote (that lasts from conception to two weeks) the developing organism in the form of zygote thus becomes able to avail food and shelter in the mother's uterus. It is now ready to travel its prenatal developmental journey of the gestation phase through its development as embryo and foetus.

The Period of Embryo

Starting from the third week of conception, the period of embryo development goes up to the eighth week. The development going on during this 6-week period may be briefed as follows:

(i)   The placenta along with the umbilical cord becomes larger, stronger and more elaborate to share its responsibility of supplying food, liquid and oxygen; removing wastes; and secreting hormones helpful in the sustaining of pregnancy.

(ii) The mass of cells, now called an embryo, gets differentiated into three distinctive layers, each of which is credited to build the essential structures helpful in providing support to the independent existence of the baby. These following are the distinctive:

- **Ectoderm (the outermost layer):** It is developed into the organs helpful in making contact with the outside world such as skin, hair, parts of the eyes, the ears and the nervous system.
- **Endoderm (the innermost layer):** It is developed into the life supporting mechanism that makes the respiratory system, digestive system and glandular system.
- **Mesoderm (the middle layer):** It is developed into a few other life supporting organs like muscles, bones, heart, kidneys and gonads.

(iii) The embryo itself undergoes rapid structural changes and increases in size. During the period of embryo of 6 weeks duration, the development of life-supporting organs takes a necessary lead. The development is so rapid that by the end of this period, all of the major organs and structures of the body get laid down and are found in place. However, their development here is at a quite initial stage and the later work regarding the strengthening of the support system waits for being carried out at the later stage — the period of the foetus.

The Period of Foetus

The period or duration beginning from the 9th week (or third month) after conception till the birth of the child is referred to as the period of foetus. The one particular significant event in the development of the child during this period is the transformation of the genitalia of the foetus into male and female genitalia. Up to the beginning of the period of foetus, the sex organs of the developing baby are undifferentiated. With the beginning of this period, the foetus of male and female child begins to produce the male and female hormones giving birth to distinctive male and female reproductive organs as well as functions. Moreover this stage or period of development is also characterised by the continued growth and remarkable increase in the size and weight along with the appearance of the distinctive features and functioning of the support organs. How the different types of growth and development take place during the different months of the embryonic period has been briefed by McDevitt and Ormrod (2013:126) as follows:

1. **Development in the third month:** The head is large in comparison to the rest of the body but now slows down in rate of growth. The eyes move to their proper places, and the foetus becomes increasingly human looking. The external genitalia grow. The foetus begins to show reflexes and muscular movement, but the mother does not yet feel these movements.

2. **Development in the fourth month:** The foetus grows rapidly in length. Weight increases slowly. Hair grows on the head and eyebrows. Eye movements occur.

3. **Development in the fifth month:** The foetus continues to grow rapidly in length. Fine hair covers the body and a greasy substance protects the foetus's delicate skin. The mother can usually feel the foetus's movements by now.

4. **Development in the sixth month:** The foetus has red, wrinkled skin and a body that is lean but gaining weight. Fingernails are present. The respiratory system and central nervous system are still developing and coordinating their operations.

5. **Development in the seventh month:** Eyes open and eyelashes are present. Toenails grow. The body begins to fill out. The brain has developed sufficiently to support breathing.

6. **Development in the eighth month:** Skin is pink and smooth. Fat grows under the skin. The testes (in males) descend.

7. **Development in the final ninth month:** The foetus is refining its basic body structures and also gaining weight, slowly at first and more steadily as birth approaches. The brain also expands and matures during the final week of the month.

> The embryo becomes a foetus nine weeks after conception, and the mother's body begins to show signs of pregnancy. By the end of the third month, the sexual organs of the foetus emerge. The mother detects movements of the foetus by the fourth or fifth month. At the same time, the foetus begins to demonstrate sensitivity to lights and sounds from the external environment. During the last couple of months, the foetus prepares to live apart from the mother's body.

Regarding the development of sensory abilities, it is said that the foetus is quite capable of interacting with a complex intrauterine environment available in the womb of the mother, and by the time the baby is born, all of the senses are functional to some extent (Hopkins & Johnson, 2005). The sequence of the development of various senses in the foetus has been pointed out by Levine & Munsch (2014:141) in the following way:

•   The cutaneous senses (or "skin senses" such as touch and pain) and the proprioceptive senses (the one that detects motion or the position of the body) are the first to develop.

•   The cutaneous senses are followed by the chemical senses such as smell and taste and the vestibular senses (the sense of equilibrium and balance).

•   The last to develop are the auditory and visual senses.

In this way, the gradual development going on in the subsequent months of the foetus period coupled with the important last minutes touch given to such development sets the stage for the new born babies to play their role on Earth. However, in between what goes with them during their coming out on Earth from the womb of their mother also carries a great significance. Let us see how babies are delivered and what complications may arise during their deliveries. But before that let us see what we mean by three trimesters of a mother's pregnancy.

Three Trimesters of a Mother's Pregnancy

The nine months time period of pregnancy of mothers is often divided into three sections known as the three trimesters of 3 months period each for describing the kind of experiences encountered on their part with regard to the stage of their pregnancy. Let us learn about them briefly:

1. **First trimester (from conception to 3 months):** During this period of pregnancy, the pregnancy of the mother goes usually unrecognised and unidentified on the part of the others. However, the mothers begin to feel the sensation and movement of their babies to some extent. There are significant changes in their level of hormones resulting in a kind of fatigue, sensation and tenderness in the breasts as well as feelings related to nausea.

2. **Second trimester (from 4th to 6th month):** During this period the pregnancy begins to become apparent to others as the foetus grows larger in size. The mothers now feel the movements of their babies well by their kicking, bending and changing of their positions.

3. **Third trimester (from 7th to 9th month):** During this period of pregnancy the size of the foetus becomes quite larger as not only to get visible to others in a significant way but also begins to cause inconvenience and tiredness to the mother herself. The movements and activities of the babies are also now frequently experienced by the mothers.

Labour and Delivery of Babies

From the time of conception onward, mothers have to pass through an unforgettable experience termed as labour pain for the delivery of their child that results in the birth of their babies. Justifying its name, the term labour stands for an intensive or tiresome job or strenuous physical work that is performed by pregnant mothers to give birth to their children who they have been rearing in their wombs since conception; the baby is delivered through an opening of the uterus called the cervix.

The Stages of Labour

As the mothers get closer to the date of delivery, their body makes them ready for doing the job concerning the delivery of the newborn by going through a chained sequence of the following three stages:

1. **The First Stage:** For first time mothers, in a normal delivery, the first stage of labour usually lasts between 10 to 20 hours. It results in the proper dilation and effacement of their cervix helpful in the delivery of the child and involves the following three phases for its execution.

    *   *The phase of early labour:* Although the mothers experience painless uterine contractions much before the beginning of labour pains as early as the 6th week of pregnancy, yet the true contractions (lasting about 30 to 60 seconds) here now begin to appear in this phase of early labour. The contractions, usually not very painful, are responsible for starting the process of thinning out and opening up (dilating) the cervix to the extent of 4 centimetres.

- *The phase of active labour:* In this phase, the contractions become longer, stronger and painful, and also arise more frequently helping in dilating the cervix with a more rapid pace to the size of 7 centimetres. In general, this phase of active labour lasts between 3 and 8 hours and is forceful enough for the mothers to feel the need of some pain medications or using breathing and relaxation techniques for the relief in labour pains
- *The phase of transition:* Usually, lasting in between 15 minutes and 3 hours, this short phase is known to be the most difficult phase of labour. Contractions now become more rapid and forceful to help in dilating the cervix up to 10 centimetres.

2. **The Second Stage:** At this stage of the mother's labour, when the cervix is fully dilated, the uterine contractions begin to push the baby down through the birth canal. This stage may take about half an hour but for the first time mothers it may last up to 2 hours. With each contraction mothers feel a strong urge to push the baby down and in a natural process of the delivery are often successful in doing so. In other cases medical help is sought for helping the delivery of the child. In the process of delivery (coming out of the child from the uterus) the baby's head emerges first from the birth canal and then in succession the shoulders and rest of the baby's body quickly follows. The second stage ends when the baby has completely exited the mother's body. After the baby emerges from the mother, the umbilical cord is cut, and any mucus present in the baby's throat is removed.

3. **The Third Stage:** In this third and last stage of labour, the uterus again begins to contract to expel the placenta. This stage is the quickest and easiest, usually taking only a few minutes.

The Screening of the Baby in the Mother

Ultrasound is the most common and relatively safe test used in the case of pregnant women for checking growth, gender (not legal in India), amount of amino fluid and the condition of the placenta, as well as to diagnose multiple pregnancies. A few other screenings that may be done during pregnancy include:

Blood chemistry tests: These tests measure changes in the mother's blood chemistry and the foetus's blood. They are helpful in detecting infection, monitoring diabetes and sometimes detecting genetic disorders.

Amniocentesis: Another test, called amniocentesis, involves withdrawing a small amount of amniotic fluid. This test (usually performed sometime between 14 and 18 weeks after conception) may help detect genetic, biochemical and nervous-system disorders. However, as it involves a slight risk of foetal injury, infection or spontaneous abortion, therefore, it is not carried out routinely for healthy mothers.

Chorionic villus sampling (CVS): This test analyses cells from the placenta to check for genetic problems. This test can be done earlier than amniocentesis (between 10 and 12 weeks after conception) and carries similar risks. It can help in detecting a number of abnormalities including chromosomal abnormalities such as Tay-Sachs disease and some diseases of the blood such as sickle cell disease.

Birthing Options and Techniques

There are a number of issues before the mothers and the family members regarding the setting of the delivery place and the method or technique used for the delivery. Let us think in this direction.

The Decision About the Place of Delivery

There are a number of options available to pregnant mothers and their family members for choosing the setting and place for the delivery of the baby. These may be named as (i) delivery at home under the supervision of a professional, (ii) delivery at a private nursing home, (iii) delivery at a child care centre or maternity facility centre provided by the Government and (iv) maternity ward of a hospital. In our country for a long time the first option — delivery at home — was the most selected option. But it has now been almost replaced by one of the other three alternatives for providing better health care and safety to mothers and their babies. The last alternative, however, is opted in the case when there appears some danger to the safe delivery and well being of the mother and baby.

The Decision About the Procedure or Technique Used For Delivery

Regarding the procedures or techniques used for delivery of the child the following techniques are in use:

1. **Natural or prepared delivery:** Most of the deliveries, in general, are first tried to be set up in a natural way unless some complications develop along the way. Here the mothers are found to deliver babies in a natural course in a natural way through the opening of their vagina with no aid from medication or medical intervention. However, due care is taken for getting the mother prepared for going through the labour pains and dealing with the uterine contractions and pushing of the baby for the birth. The mothers for this purpose may be provided opportunities for the learning of appropriate relaxation and breathing techniques and asked to take care of their physical and mental health during pregnancy in a proper way. Besides this here a proper support system is also maintained with the objective of assisting mothers in their looking after and safe delivery with the involvement of their family members, relatives, friends and professionals (midwife and physician).

2. **Medication-supported delivery:** Here, although child birth occurs naturally via the birth canal by the aid of uterine contractions and pushing, yet it is supported by medications in dealing with the labour pains and pushing the baby out from the uterus by the mother. In this connection the type of medications provided may be as follows:

   (i) The appropriate doses of pain reliever drugs like analgesics and anaesthetics may be given to the mothers for dealing with the severe labour pains.

(ii) To help the women in having a painless delivery of the baby a procedure named as epidural analgesia is common nowadays. It results in making the mothers numb from the waist down for helping them to push the baby out during delivery. An epidural block, performed by a physician or nurse anaesthetist, reduces or eliminates all sensation from the mother's breasts down to her feet. The mother can't get out of bed but is awake, alert and able to participate in the birthing process.

Many mothers, whether they have taken classes for learning the relaxation and breathing technique may choose to take medications during their labour or delivery. This choice should not be viewed as weakness. Medications are generally considered to be safe and are not thought to have long-term effects on the baby. Mothers and their medical team may choose to use pain relievers or pain blockers.

3. **Caesarean delivery:** While adopting this procedure for delivery, the baby is surgically removed from the uterus, rather than travelling through the birth canal, by performing an incision in the mother's abdomen and uterus. Most of the deliveries now happening in nursing homes and maternity centres of private hospitals are caesarean deliveries. The reasons may be many. Besides having the compulsion of adopting this alternative, in many cases it may be opted on account of some unprofessional medical practitioners and greedy owners of nursing homes. The compulsion for having a caesarean child may however, happen in the cases where there is greater risk involved for the life and well being of a child or mother such as the following:

- The mother has an infection that could be passed on to the baby.
- The foetus appears to be in danger, as indicated by a sudden rise or drop in its heart rate or if blood is seen coming from the mother's vagina during labour.
- The umbilical cord is wrapped around the baby's neck causing deprivation of oxygen to the baby.
- The baby lies in a breech position, turned in such a way that the buttocks or feet would be delivered first or the baby's head is so large that it creates trouble in the movement through the birth canal.
- The placenta has detached from the uterine wall and the mother is bleeding.
- The mother's cervix has not opened sufficiently.
- The mother is aged or has become incapable on account of her poor health for bearing the labour pains and delivering the baby in a normal way.

Birth Complications

There are situations where we may find that the babies during their prenatal period are subjected to some serious problems giving birth to one or the other complications named as birth complications. We may name them as: (i) oxygen deprivation, (ii) pre-term birth and low-weight, and (iii) post-term birth.

Let us learn about their nature and consequences.

Oxygen deprivation: This is a big complication involved in the birth and well-being of a newborn on account of deprivation of oxygen (the state of anoxia). Newborns may experience it in any one or more stages of their birth: (i) at the time of conception as inheritance, (ii) during labour or (iii) during the birth process.

(i) As a matter of inheritance, the Rh factor incompatibility between the mother's and baby's blood types may give birth to the state of anoxia in the baby. In cases where the father is Rh-positive (rich in Rh protein) and the mother is Rh-negative (poor in Rh protein), the baby may inherit the father's Rh-positive blood type. If even a little of a foetus's Rh-positive crosses the placenta into the Rh-negative mother's blood stream, she begins to form antibodies to the foreign protein. If these enter the foetus's system, they destroy red blood cells reducing the supply of oxygen and causing a number of complications to the developing foetus at times even resulting in infantile death. (Berk, 2009:112).

(ii) During labour there may arise a number of situations which can cause a state of anoxia or oxygen deprivation for the developing foetus such as: (i) premature separation of the placenta causing emergency to prompt immediate delivery, (ii) wrapping of the umbilical cord around the neck of the foetus or pinching of the cord during a prolonged contraction, resulting in cut off in the supply of oxygen. These situations may cause serious complications and a state of emergency calling for the immediate delivery though a caesarean process.

(iii) The state of anoxia or oxygen deprivation may be faced by newborn babies during the birth process. It is quite usual for the newborn babies to automatically make the transition from taking in oxygen via the placenta to using their lungs to breathe air. Consequently, after immediately emerging from their mother's body, a cry spontaneously helps newborns clear their lungs and breathe on their own. However, for some reason if there arises complications in doing so and babies fail to start breathing within a few minutes of their birth due to lack of oxygen it can cause brain damage or other developmental problems to them in future.

Pre-term and low-birth: The normal period for the birth of a child is 9 months or 38 weeks. However, for one reason or the other babies may be born three weeks or more before the scheduled period. These babies are referred to as pre-mature babies and are usually found to be quite weak in their body composition and strength characterised with low-birth weight, reduced height and fragile muscles and bones. Many babies born prematurely and with birth weights significantly below average, face a tough challenge for their survival and development. They are quite vulnerable to infection, and because their lungs have not had sufficient time to develop completely, they face an acute problem of oxygen deprivation resulting in serious respiratory and breathing problems in future.

Post-term birth: It is not the preterm but the post-term birth that may also invite a number of complications, health and well-being problems for newborn babies. By the term post-term or post mature birth we here mean the babies still unborn 2 weeks after the mother's due date. The usual complications involved and the health problems encountered in their cases may be the following: (i) inadequacy or insufficiency of the supply of blood from the placenta for the nourishment of the developing foetus obstructing the supply of blood to the brain and becoming a potential cause of brain damage, (ii) mother having problem for the birth of the child from the birth canal on account of the bigger size of the foetus. Since there is a much danger in such cases for a normal delivery, the efforts are made for inducing artificial labour and performing caesarean deliveries.

The Occurrence of Events Immediately After Birth

What happens to a newborn baby (neonate) immediately after birth is a matter of immense importance to children as well to the mothers and other well wishers. The happenings in this concern on the part of the neonates in normal delivery cases may be briefed as follows:

1. The spontaneous cry of the child immediately after the birth.
2. Automatically making transition to inhale oxygen by using their lungs.
3. After the baby emerges, the umbilical cord is clamped and cut after it stops pulsing.
4. The newborns are covered with a thick, greasy substance called vernix for smoothing their passage through the birth canal; it is no longer needed once they are born. Their eyelids may be puffy due to an accumulation of fluids during labour and they may have blood or other fluids on parts of their body. In order to get rid of all these things, the newborns are cleaned before being handed to the mother, father or any responsible member of the family.
5. A few drops of an antibiotic such as tetracycline or erythromycin are added to the baby's eyes to prevent infection that could be caused by any organisms that were present in the birth canal.

The overall condition and health of the baby gets assessed usually one minute after the birth by using the Apgar scale.

The Apgar Scale and Its Use for The Assessment of a Newborn

The Apgar scale developed by physician Virginia Apgar represents a standard measurement system that helps in providing a variety of indicators of good health in newborns. In its use it seeks to provide scores ranging from 0 to 2 on each of the five basic qualities of the new born, namely: (i) appearance (colour), (ii) pulse (heart rate), (iii) grimace (reflex irritability), (iv) activity (muscle tone) and (v) respiration (respiration effort) in the manner as provided in Table 7.1:

Table 7.1: Apgar Scale

A score is given for each sign at 1 minute and 5 minutes after birth. If there are problems with the baby, an additional score is given at 10 minutes.

Total score: 7-10 = Good to excellent condition; 4-6 = Requires assistance to breathe; 3 or below = Life-threatening danger

Sign	0 Point	1 Point	2 Points
Appearance (skin colour)	Blue-gray, pale all over	Normal, except for extremities	Normal over entire body
Pulse (heart rate)	Absent	Slow: less than 100 beats per minute	Fast:100-140 beats per minute
Grimace (reflex irritability)	No response	Grimace	Sneezes, coughs, pulls away
Activity (muscle tone)	Absent	Arms and legs fixed	Active movements
Respiration (Breathing)	Absent	Slow, irregular	Good breathing with normal crying

Source: Adapted from Apgar (1953)

Weighing and Screening of the Baby

The newborn is weighed for the assessment of its normal good health and then may be subjected to screening for getting assured about the normal health and well being of the child as well as detecting the possible abnormality or birth defects and developmental deficits in the newborns. The newborn screening may help in permitting early treatment of a number of disorders and problems that might go undetected for years. In conducting such screening, either the help of imaging techniques is taken or a tiny sample of the blood (such as a very small amount of blood drawn from an infant's heel) is used for the detection of a variety of disorders and birth defects or malfunctioning.

Factors Affecting the Prenatal Development of a Child

The prenatal period carries a unique significance from the point of view of giving start to a new life, erecting a solid base for the future development of neonates and keeping the child and mothers in good physical and mental health during the entire duration from conception to birth. The mothers, fathers and the other people responsible for caring of the mothers should take due precautions in terms of what to do and not to do in the interest of pregnant mothers and the newborns. For this purpose, they should be properly aware about the many factors affecting the health and well being of pregnant mothers and their new born. Let us focus on this aspect in the light of the factors affecting the prenatal development of the children from conception till their birth.

A. Genetics and age of parents

The genetics and age of the prospective mothers and fathers may exercise a considerable impact on the well being and developmental journey of the expected newborns. In the cases of early marriage and early pregnancy, much before the proper maturity of the child bearing/reproductive organs of the mothers, a number of complications and developmental problems may arise for the child and well being of the mothers. On the other hand, an advanced age in mothers and fathers especially after 35 in women and 40 in men is associated with several types of risks to the well being of the neonates and pregnant mothers. Genetic background and structure of the father and mother have also been associated with miscarriages, genetic defects and abnormalities among newborns. This is why proper advice is a must for prospective couples and parents and they should seek genetic counselling when they have the desire of bearing a child.

B. The quality of prenatal caring

The caring and look after of pregnant mothers in a proper way is very essential for the health and well being of the neonates and their mothers. We can expect good or poor results for the health and well being of the neonates and mothers based on the quality of attention given to them or deficiencies suffered in providing care and support to pregnant mothers. The following essentially matter in this direction:

(i) **Quality of the maternal diet:** The health and well being of the child and the mother rests very much on the quality of diet received by the mother during the period of her pregnancy. The diet schedule and its quality in the form of a well-balanced diet must be maintained in a way so as to prove sufficiently appropriate for the mothers along with their developing foetus. It has been found and confirmed that the mothers who take a varied diet high in nutrients suffer from fewer complications during pregnancy, go through an easy labour and give birth to healthier babies in comparison to mothers who do not receive healthier diets or are denied so on account of one or the other unfavourable conditions.

(ii) **Quality of maternal health:** The mothers need to be in proper physical and mental health for being fit for bearing the labour pains, adapting to changes in their daily routine and keeping and supporting the child in their wombs for the needed duration and later giving birth to healthier and happier babies. They should try and remain healthy so that no physical illnesses and diseases trouble them. They should also attempt to be in a happy mental state and avoid unnecessary agonies, maintain an appropriate and healthy weight, and remain appropriately active for carrying out their necessary day-to-day activities. On the opposite side their poor health and illness (physical or mental), their inappropriate weight and inactivity may lead to a variety of problems and complications to their pregnancy and to the well being of the neonates in the following manner:

- Suffering from diseases like chicken pox and mumps on the part of the pregnant mothers may give birth to birth defects and developmental deficits in the newborns and increase the possibilities of miscarriage.

- Some sexually transmitted diseases such as syphilis are said to be transferable directly to the developing foetus and diseases such as gonorrhoea are communicable to newborns as they pass through the birth canal.

- Mothers infected with AIDS or even carrying its virus may pass it on to their foetuses through the blood that reaches the placenta and as a consequence the newborn child may forcibly suffer from AIDS much before its birth.

- The onset of rubella (German measles) in the mother prior to 11th week of pregnancy is found to cause serious health problems in the baby, including blindness, deafness, heart defects or brain damage.

- Mothers infected with the herpes simplex virus are found to have a miscarriage or giving birth prematurely to babies with physical problems.

Besides this the mental state of pregnant mothers is also found to exercise a strong influence on the overall health and well being of mothers and the developing foetus. The mothers who remain tense, suffer from mental agonies on one account or the other or pass through a trauma or devastating experience during their pregnancies are usually found to go through a number of birth complications and ill consequences including miscarriage. Besides this they are also found to give birth to infants with low birth weight and short tempered dispositions and, later in life, with difficulties in focusing attention and dealing with negative emotions. It is why, it is always advised to caregivers and family members to keep mothers in their pregnancy safe and sound in terms of their physical and mental health.

(iii) **Regular check-up and medical care:** The health and well being of pregnant mothers and their newborns also depends much on the quality of medical care and check-up facilities available to pregnant mothers on time and with ease. The facilities available in this connection at the nearby maternity centres and hospitals established especially for the care of the mothers and children may serve the purpose well in case the needed quality is maintained in terms of the service provided by them to the public. Moreover, the mothers should also be properly motivated and urged to maintain due regularity for their medical check-up and screening as and when needed for their care and well being along with their developing foetus. It becomes more essential on the part of pregnant mothers to visit the centres and consult the concerned medical personnel for helping them in their chronic diseases and ailments like diabetes, asthma or allergies for their own well being as well safety of the developing foetus. The carelessness observed on their part or unavailability of such medical facilities for them may prove quite detrimental for the safety and well being of their own as well as to the child rearing in them.

One thing that should also be kept in mind while taking any medicine or prescribed/ unprescribed drugs for getting rid of problems associated with the mother's illness or diseases is that there may be some serious side effects of taking such medicines/drugs resulting in issues for both them and their neonates. As examples of some harmful medications/drugs we may name Soriatane (prescribed for treating skin disorder), and Thalidomide (used for treating multiple myeloma, complications of AIDS and leprosy) that are found to result in missing or malformed arms and legs in the child. It is therefore quite essential on the part of pregnant mothers to avoid taking any such medicine or drug without the proper recommendation and advice of their gynaecologist/physician.

C. The Consequences of Harmful Substances or Teratogens

The exposure to or consumption of a number of harmful substances present in the external environment of pregnant mothers is found to be a great potential factor for causing heavy damage to the health and well being of mothers and the developing embryo or foetus. These harmful substances causing a birth defect or malformation in the developing embryo or foetus are technically known as teratogens. As examples of such teratogens we may categorise them as follows:

(i) Substances that the mother ingests or consumes such as alcohol, nicotine, medications or illegal drugs like cocaine, marijuana, heroin, etc.

(ii) Diseases that the mother has or picks up during pregnancy such as rubella, herpes simplex, syphilis, or HIV and AIDS).

(iii) The toxins in the environment and food products such as mercury in the food consumed by the mother and her exposure to radiation or environmental pollution

The teratogens specified above cast a quite damaging effect on the developing embryo or foetus in their own ways. It may be a structural abnormality such as missing or malformed limbs, or a functional deficit, such as hearing loss or mental retardation. However, the nature and magnitude of the effects ranging from mild to severe depends up on the duration or phase of the prenatal development and the amount of doses taken or exposure experienced by the mother during her pregnancy. We have already thrown light on the damaging effects of the mother's diseases such as rubella, herpes simplex, HIV infection and AIDs on their children. The effect of some other important teratogens on the well being of the children is further briefed in Table 7.2:

Table 7.2: A few important Teratogens and their harmful effects

Name of the harmful substance (Teratogen)	Description of the structural malformation, developmental deficit and functional limitations imposed on the offspring
Alcohol consumption	The consumption of alcohol on the part of mothers can give birth to infants with foetal alcohol syndrome (FAS), which includes: (i) physical characteristics such as abnormal facial features, small stature, and a small head, (ii) functional problems such as problems with learning, memory and attention span as well as trouble controlling behaviour and regulating emotions, (iii) developmental difficulty such as mental retardation and learning disabilities.
Organic Mercury consumption through diet	The ingestion or consumption of high levels of mercury from their regular diets on the part of mothers may result in giving birth to children with abnormalities in brain, intellectual disabilities and motor problems.
Nicotine consumption through smoking	The consumption of nicotine through smoking (cigarettes, *bidis*, *hukkas*) may result in miscarriages, premature birth, sudden infant death and later developmental problems for the child.
Consumption of illegal drugs like cocaine, marijuana, heroin etc.	The mothers consuming illegal drugs like cocaine, marijuana, heroin, etc. during their pregnancy have a risk of miscarriages and premature birth of their children. The babies born may also have small head size and may also suffer from respiratory problems. Besides this they are also found somewhat lethargic as well as irritable in their motor and social behaviour and their intellectual potential and functioning is also adversely affected.
Exposure to radiation	Pregnant women are at risk of exposure to non-ionizing radiation (resulting from medical intervention such as ultrasonography and using appliances such as microwave), ionizing radiation (resulting from the exposure to Gamma and X-rays, atomic radiation). Where the exposure to the non-ionizing radiation is not associated with significant risks, the exposure to the ionizing radiation may cause damaging effects to the human embryo and foetus resulting in growth retardation, prenatal or neonatal death, congenital malformations and mental retardation.

Summary

The life journey of a child begins right from the time of its conception (fertilisation of the mother's ovum by the sperm of the father) in the womb of the mother. The period of development approximately covering 9 months, spent by the children in the womb is known as pre-natal development. The development carried out at this stage involves the periods named as: (i) the period of Zygote, (ii) the period of the Embryo and (iii) the period of the foetus.

The period of zygote, falling between fertilisation of the ovum (formation of the zygote) and formation of embryo, is about two weeks in duration. The developmental activities of this period involve: (i) creation of new cells through a process named mitosis (cell duplication), (ii) the attachment of the growing group of cells firmly to the inner lining of the mother's uterus in the name of implantation, (iii) acquiring the capability of availing food and shelter in the mother's uterus and (iv) becoming ready to travel its prenatal developmental journey through its development as embryo.

The period of embryo (from the third week of conception to eighth week) is covered with developmental activities such as: (i) enhancement in the capacity of placenta along with umbilical cord to share its responsibility of supplying food, liquid and oxygen; removing wastes; and secreting hormones helpful in the sustaining of pregnancy, (ii) differentiation of the mass of cells into three distinctive layers,(the outermost layer 'Ectoderm', the innermost layer 'Endoderm' and the middle layer 'Mesoderm'), each of which is credited to build the essential structures helpful in providing support to the independent living of the developing baby.

The period of foetus (from the 9th week after conception till the birth of the child) is covered with developmental activities characterised as: (i) the transformation of the genitalia of the foetus into male and female genitalia, (ii) the growth and remarkable increase in the size and weight along with the appearance of the distinctive features and functioning of support organs and (iii) finally, in the last couple of months, preparing itself to live apart from the mother's body.

The mothers have to pass through an unforgettable experience termed as labour pain for the delivery of their child. Justifying its name, the term labour stands for an intensive or tiresome job or strenuous physical work that is performed by pregnant mothers to give birth to their children who they have been rearing in their wombs since conception; the baby is delivered through an opening of the uterus called the cervix. Usually it involves three stages. At the first stage (lasting between 10 to 20 hours), the mothers have to pass through the painful experience of uterine contractions resulting in the proper dilation and effacement of their cervix that helps them in the delivery of the child.

At the second stage of labour (lasting for 2 hours or so), when the cervix is fully dilated, the contractions of the uterus begin to push the baby down through the birth canal. After the baby emerges from the mother, the umbilical cord is cut, and any mucus in the baby's throat is removed. In the third and last stage of labour, the uterus again begins to contract for expelling the placenta. This stage is the quickest and easiest, usually taking about a few minutes.

For the **screening of the baby during pregnancy**, ultrasound is the most common and relatively safe test generally used for checking growth, gender, health, multiple pregnancies and detecting possible genetic disorders. A few other screenings that may be done during pregnancy are blood chemistry, amniocentesis, and chorionic villus sampling (CVS) tests.

For **choosing a place for the delivery** of the baby several options are available. In our country for a long time the option of delivery a child at home was the most preferred option. But now it has been almost replaced by having pregnancies done under proper medical supervision at maternity wards of the government-run hospitals, maternity centres or private nursing homes. Regarding the procedures or techniques used for the delivery of the child they are the following: (i) natural delivery (ii) medicated supported delivery and (iii) caesarean delivery.

During the prenatal period in the womb of the mother and at the time of their birth, babies may be subjected to some serious problems resulting in complications known as birth complications. We may name them as: (i) oxygen deprivation (the state of anoxia), (ii) pre-term birth (babies born 3 weeks or more before the scheduled period) and low-weight, and (iii) post-term birth (the babies who remain unborn 2 weeks after the mother's due date).

After birth, attempts should be made to take every attention and precaution for the care of the baby. For assessing the overall condition and health of the newborn baby it is advisable to make use of: (i) a standard measurement scale such as Apgar scale usually one minute after the birth and (ii) completing the task of screening and weighing the baby for getting assured about his or her normal health and well being as well as detecting the possible abnormality or birth defects and developmental deficiencies.

Some of the factors affecting prenatal development of children from conception till their birth may be the following: (i) genetics and age of parents, (ii) the caring and look after of pregnant mothers in terms of the quality of their diet, their physical and mental health, provision for regular checkups and medical care, and (iv) the ill consequences of harmful substance consumption or Teratogens (such as alcohol, nicotine, medications or illegal drugs like cocaine, marijuana, heroin etc., on the health and well being of mothers and their babies.

References and Suggested Readings

American Academy of Pediatrics, (1999), Media Education, *Pediatrics*, 104, 341-343

Apgar, V. (1953), A proposal for a new method of evaluation in the newborn infant, *Current Research in Anesthesia and Analgesia*, 32, 260.

Arnett, Jeffrey Jensen & Maynard, Ashley E. (2017), *Child Development: A Cultural Approach* (2nd edition), Boston: Pearson.

Berk, Laura E. (2009), *Child Development* (Eighth edition), Boston: Pearson Education

Brazelton Berry and Nugent J.K., (1995), Neonatal Behavioral Assessment Scale (3rd ed.), London: Mac Keith Press.

Harwood, Robin, Miller, Scott A., and Vasta, Ross (2012), *Child Psychology-Development in a Changing Society*, (Fifth Ed.) New York: John Wiley & Sons, Inc.

Hopkins, Brian and Johnson, Scott P. (2005), *Prenatal Development of Postnatal Functions (Advances in Infancy Research)*, New York: Praeger.

Johnson, M.D. (2008), *Human biology: concepts and current issues*, Upper Saddle River, NJ: Prentice –Hall

Jones, R.E. (2006), *Human reproductive biology*, New York, NY: Academic Press.

Jorde, L.B., Carey, J.C., Bam shad, M.J., & White, R.L. (2006), *Medical genetics* (3rd ed.), St. Louis, MO: Mosby.

Levine, Laura E. and Munsch Joyce (2014), *Child Development - An Active Learning Approach*, (2nd edition), Los Angeles: Sage

Lipsit, L.P. (2003), Crib death: A bio-behavioral phenomenon? *Psychological Science*, 12, 164-170.

McDevitt, T. M., & Ormrod, J. E. (2013), *Child Development and Education* (5th ed.), Upper Saddle River, NJ: Pearson.

Meggitt, Carolyn and Ormrod, J.E. (2013), *Understanding Child Development*, (fifth edition), Boston: Pearson.

National Human Gerome Research institute (2011), *Chromosome abnormalities*, Retrieved from http://www.genome.gov/11508982#6

National Human Genome Research Institute (2010), *An overview of the human genome project*, Retrieved from http//www.genome.gov/12011239

Nugent, K.J. & Brazelton, T. B. (2000), Preventive infant mental health: Uses of the Brazelton scale, In J.D. Osofsky & H.E. Fitzgerald (eds), *WAIMH Handbook of infant mental health* (Vol 2), New York, NY: Wiley.

Rutter, M. (1991), *Maternal Deprivation Reassessed* (2nd ed.), London: Penguin.

Shepard, T.H. (2001), *Catalogue of teratogenic agents* (10th ed.), Baltimore: Johns Hopkins University Press.

Shaffer, David R. (2007), Developmental Psychology-Childhood and Adolescence, (7th ed.), Canada: Thomson/Wadsworth.

8

Physical Development and Physiological Habits Formation

Meaning of the Term Physical Growth and Development

The term 'Physical growth and development' refers to a process which brings bodily and physiological changes — internal as well as external — in an organism from conception till his death. Generally, these changes take place in the following dimensions:

(i) **In his gross physical structure or physique:** It involves changes in terms of height, weight, body proportions and general physical appearance.

(ii) **In his internal organs:** It involves changes in the functioning of glands, nervous system and other body systems — circulatory, respiratory, digestive, muscular, lymphatic and reproductive.

The process of physical growth and development plays a significant role in the proper adjustment and progress of an organism. In the beginning, an infant is quite helpless. It depends upon its parents and other members of the family for the satisfaction of his bodily needs. As a result of the changes brought by physical growth and development, the baby's body organs become adaptable to his increasing body needs and gradually he develops into a mature adult.

General Pattern of the Children's Physical Growth and Development

Although there are wide individual differences among human beings and it is not possible to describe a perfect general pattern of the growth and development, yet physical growth and development seems to follow, to some extent, a general pattern which can help us to think about some definite structural changes in the case of normal children at each stage of their growth and development.

We have tried to summarise this general pattern of growth and development along with definite structural changes as follows.

Increase in Height and Weight

On an average, at birth a baby measures about 45-47 cm in height and between 3 and 4 kg in weight, boys being slightly taller and heavier. During the first two years, there is rapid increase in both the height and the weight. There is a steady and slower growth from the third year till the onset of puberty. By the age of five, the height of the child becomes almost double and he weighs almost five times of his birth weight. During the period of adolescence, we again find a sudden increase in both height and weight. Girls reach puberty about a year or two earlier than boys. Therefore, during the age 12 to 14 they are found slightly taller and heavier than boys. But they are again surpassed by the boys. By the end of adolescence, young men are generally higher and heavier than the young women. Generally, both men and women attain their maximum height and weight up to the end of adolescence. However, there are a lot of variations in weight as it is more susceptible to environmental influences. Therefore, it is no surprise to note the sudden increase or decrease in weight in later years even after attaining maturity.

Weight of the brain gets increased rapidly in the early years of life. By the time the child attains the age of four, his brain would have gained almost 80 per cent of its final weight, another 10 per cent being added by the time he completes his eight years. By the 20th year, the brain gains almost all its weight.

Table 8.1: Increase in height and weight with age

Age	Height (in cm)		Average Weight (in kg)	
	Girls	Boys	Girls	Boys
Below 3 months	55.0	56.2	4.2	4.5
3 months	60.9	62.7	5.6	6.7
6 months	64.4	64.9	6.2	6.9
9 months	66.7	69.5	6.6	7.4
1 year	72.5	73.9	7.8	8.4
2 years	80.1	81.6	9.6	10.1
3 years	87.2	88.8	11.2	11.8
4 years	94.5	96.0	12.9	13.5
5 years	101.4	102.1	14.5	14.8
6 years	107.4	108.5	16.0	16.3
7 years	112.8	113.9	17.6	18.0
8 years	118.2	119.8	19.4	19.7
9 years	122.9	123.7	21.3	21.5
10 years	128.4	124.4	23.6	23.5
11 years	133.6	133.4	26.4	25.9
12 years	139.6	138.3	29.8	28.5
13 years	143.9	144.6	33.3	32.1
14 years	147.5	150.1	36.8	35.7
15 years	149.6	155.5	38.8	39.6
16 years	151.0	159.5	41.4	43.2
17 years	151.5	161.4	42.4	45.7
18 years	151.7	163.1	42.4	47.4
19 years	151.7	163.4	42.4	48.1

Source: Growth and Development of Indian infants and children, Technical Report Series No. 18, Indian Council of Medical Research, 1972.

Changes in Body Proportions

A child not only grows in size but also shows a marked change in the proportion of the different parts of the body. For example, the head constitutes about one-fourth the height of the body at birth, its size being relatively much larger than the arms and legs. As the child grows older, the proportion of the head decreases and by the end of adolescence it becomes one-eighth of the body. In addition to head, the other body parts, legs, arms, torso, etc., also show change in proportions as the child requires them more and more in his adaptation to coming life.

Anatomical Growth and Development

The bones of a child are not only smaller in size than the bones of an adult, but they also differ in the composition. A child's bones contain, relatively, a larger amount of water and smaller quantity of mineral matter than those of an adult. They are softer and more blood flows through them than through the bones of an adult. This accounts for their greater reliability. But it also increases the chances of bones deformities and infection.

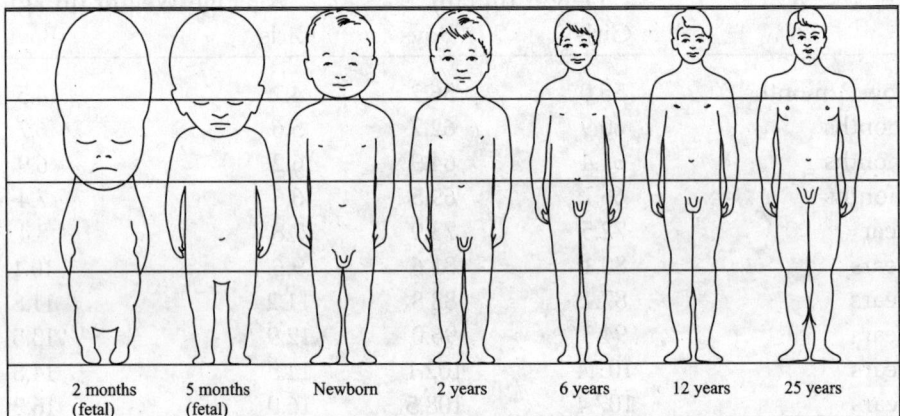

| 2 months (fetal) | 5 months (fetal) | Newborn | 2 years | 6 years | 12 years | 25 years |

Fig. 8.1: Changes in body proportion from birth to 25 years.

As regards the development of teeth, it has been found that most of the children acquire their milk teeth by the time they are two years of age. Near the end of the fifth year, permanent teeth begin to appear, the growth of which takes a long time. The last four of the permanent teeth, the wisdom teeth, develop between the ages of 17 and 25, if they appear at all. Girls usually show more advanced teeth growth than the boys except in the case of wisdom teeth, where boys are usually ahead of the girls.

Growth and Development of Internal Organs

Once a child is born, the internal organs of his body undergo constant development. As a result, the child's body systems show desirable change in order to satisfy the growing needs. Let's consider the growth and development of these internal organs as follows.

Nervous System

It shows rapid growth during the prenatal period and the first four years after birth. Before birth the development consists primarily of an increase in the number and size of nerve cells. Because no new cells are formed after birth, therefore the development in the first four years consists of the development of immature cells present at birth. After the age of 4, the growth of the nervous system proceeds at a relatively slow rate.

Muscular System

The muscular system also shows a remarkable development, although no new muscle fibres develop after birth. The muscles of a child are more delicate and less firmly attached to the bones than the adult muscles. However, gradually the muscles change in shape, size and composition and become firmer and stronger.

Circulatory and Respiratory Systems

Lungs as well as heart are very small in early childhood but they gradually grow in volume as well as in weight and reach their maximum by the end of adolescence. They also show desirable improvement in their functioning. The veins and arteries do not follow the same growth pattern as that of the heart and lungs. Prior to adolescence, they grow rapidly, whereas they show little growth during adolescence.

Digestive System

Young children have a small tubular shaped stomach in comparison with the bag-like shape stomach of the adults which not only holds a large amount of food but also empties more slowly. Therefore children require more feeding in the earlier years of their life than they will need later. In addition to the greater quantity of food, they need food with essential energy value for their rapid growth and development.

Lymphatic System

It is involved in the elimination of waste and the destruction of bacteria in the body. From birth onwards, this system shows signs of rapid development until it reaches its maximum between the ages of 11 and 12 years, when the death rate is about the lowest. After 12 years it decreases rapidly.

Reproductive System

The development of sex organs shows a peculiar trend in contrast with the overall growth and developmental pattern. Their rate of development is very slow during early childhood but picks up its speed as the child advances towards adolescence and becomes almost developed by the end of adolescence.

A close observation of the earlier-mentioned pattern can reveal the following important facts regarding the general trend of physical growth and development:

1. It is very rapid from birth to the age of two or three years.

2. Then, it continues at a diminished rate till the beginning of adolescence.

3. The first three years of adolescence are marked as the years of rapid growth and development.

4. This is followed by a period of slow growth and development to the time of maturity.

Factors Affecting Physical Growth and Development

The physical growth and development of an individual is conditioned by both heredity and environment. Some of the important heredity and environmental factors which influence the process of physical growth and development are:

1. The traits and characteristics inherited at the time of conception.
2. Single birth or multiple births.
3. The physical as well as mental health of the mother during pregnancy.
4. Nutrition received by the embryo within the womb of the mother.
5. Normal or abnormal delivery.
6. Conditions and care at the time of delivery.
7. Care of the baby and its mother.
8. Nutrition received by the child after birth.
9. Presence or absence of physical defects.
10. The living conditions — physical, social and cultural.
11. The opportunities of recreation, self-expression, play and exercise.
12. Presence or absence of illness and diseases.
13. Emotional and social adjustment of the child.
14. Adequate or inadequate rest and sleep.
15. Proper or improper medical care.

Physiological Habits Formation

Habits are the habitual acts that are performed by all of us with a great ease and convenience with or without some intentional efforts on our part. There are a number of habits categorised as physical and physiological habits, social and cultural habits, reasoning and moral habits, etc., that help or harm the developing children in proceeding well on the path of their proper development and well being. Physiological habits in this concern may be found to affect the physical development of the children in their own way depending upon the nature of their development in the children. Some of the more pronounced physiological habits observable among the children from their very birth may be identified as sleeping behaviour, eating behaviour, bladder and bowel control, handedness, etc.

Let us try to know about the nature, development and functioning of these physiological habits among developing children.

Sleeping Behaviour: Nature and Development

Sleeping is quite an essential and useful habit for all of us to safeguard our health and well-being. The children need it as well for their development and well-being right from their existence in the womb of their mother. The things related to the nature of changes occurring in the sleeping behaviour of the children from the time of their birth onwards in this concern may be discussed well under the following heads.

The Sleeping Behaviour of Newborns

- Most newborns spend more time in their sleep than awake. On an average the newborns are found to sleep 16 to 17 hours a day.
- In addition to spending so much time in sleeping, the pattern and quality of newborns' sleep is also found to differ a lot from infants and older children. Rather than sleeping 16 to17 hours straight, they sleep for a few hours, wake up for a while, sleep a few more hours and wake up again. Their sleep-wake patterns are governed by when they get hungry, not whether it is light or dark outside. This unique pattern of sleep-awake of the neonates, however do not fit very well with how most adults prefer to sleep, so parents are often sleep-deprived in the early weeks of their children's lives. (Arnett &Maynard, 2017:104)
- Another important distinction in the sleeping pattern of the newborns lies in their spending quite a high proportion of their sleeping time in rapid eye movement (REM) sleep. The REM sleep may be known as a sleep in which (i) the eyes move back and forth rapidly, and (ii) one also experiences other physiological changes as well, such as irregular heart rate and breathing. The newborns are found to spend 50 percent of their total sleeping time in REM sleep in comparison to adults' 20 percent for the same.

  Furthermore, adults do not enter REM until about an hour after falling asleep, but neonates enter it almost immediately.

Sleeping Behaviour in The Period of Infancy and Beyond

The sleeping behaviour of the neonates shows a remarkable change as they enter the stage of infancy in the manner briefed as follows:

- Instead of sleeping 16 to 17 hours, now they are found to sleep for longer duration about 14 hours a day. The time of continued sleep is also increased and they may be found to enjoy 6 to 7 hours sleep in a row at night.
- There is also a sharp decline in their REM sleep. By about 3 months of age, time spent in their REM sleep falls to 40 percent. There comes rapid change in their sleep cycle and the older infants are no longer found to begin their sleep cycle with the REM sleep.
- As the children advance in their age, we may find a quick sharp decline in the duration of their natural sleep as well as REM. Both of these decrease more and more with the increase in age. The duration of the continued sleep at stretch is also increased as they grow in age and they may be found to reach soon the

levels of the sleep and REM duration visible in the mature adults well before entering adolescence.

Development of Eating Behaviour

Life needs food and nutrition for support and survival. It is true for all living beings including plants and animals. Human beings right from their very conception in the womb of the mother need a proper amount of nutrition for their growth and survival. It gets available to them in their prenatal period with the courtesy of their mothers. What the mothers take in their regular diet, not only stands as a complete single source to fulfil the nutritional needs of the developing foetuses but also lays down the solid base for influencing and affecting the future dietary behaviour of the children after their birth in terms of types, smell and taste. At this stage therefore, it is absolutely essential to take care to consume a well-balanced nutritional diet by pregnant mothers in the interest of both the mothers as well as the developing foetus.

From the birth onwards, the children in their period of infancy need quality food full of nutritional energy for their rapid growth and development. In this concern the eating behaviour of the children may be found to make use of means like breast feeding, bottle feeding and eating solid food. The child may use either one form of diet or a combination. Let us try and understand these means and modes that are reflected in the eating behaviour of developing children after their birth.

Breast Feeding

The beginning of the eating behaviour in children is reflected through their habit of remaining fully dependent on the milk for their nutrition. The best way to obtain quality nutrition during infancy is through breast milk. At this stage also therefore, the mothers have to take great care of their diets. The breast feeding may go on up to 2 to 3 years and it may fulfil the needed nutritional needs of the developing children in a quite satisfactory way.

The practice of breast feeding, however best it may be for the child, cannot be continued for long. At one or the other stage it has to be supplemented or substituted by bottle feeding and or solid food introduction for any one of the reasons such as (i) the mother's milk alone is not able to fulfil the nutritional needs of the growing infant, (ii) the mothers are not in a position to breastfeed their infants due to one or the other reasons, (iii) mothers worry about becoming unfashionable if they breastfeed their children, or if (iv) the child has reached the stage of eating solid food and has almost given up breast feeding.

Bottle Feeding

The infants from their birth onwards may also be found to be fed through the help of bottled milk. It can be used as a supplement or substitute to breast feeding. The milk from cows, buffalos, goats or even other women can be filled up in the bottles and infants are habituated to get it from the nipples fixed in the bottle just as to have the feelings of their mother's nipple. Although, breast feeding is the best for the health and well-being of the mothers and children both, yet it needs to be stopped or replaced with bottle feeding at one or the other stage as the infants grow in their age. The earlier it is done, the better it is. But it always faces resistance of one or the other nature. Throwing light on this fact (Arnett &Maynard, 2017:107) writes:

> If breast feeding takes place for only a few weeks or months during infancy, the transition from breast to bottle usually takes place fairly smoothly, especially if the bottle is introduced gradually. However, the longer breast feeding continues into toddlerhood, the more challenging weaning becomes when the mother decides the time has come for the child to stop drinking breast milk. The toddler is much more socially aware then the infant, and much more capable of exercising intentional behaviour. The toddler can also speak up, in a way the infant cannot, to make demands and protest prohibitions. Consequently, most traditional cultures have customary practices for weaning toddlers from the breast. Often, the approach is gentle and gradual at first, but becomes harsher if the toddler resists, for instance, in the form of coating the breast with bitter tasting herbs.

Introduction of Solid Food

It is good for the health and well-being of the infants to make them habituated to the eating of solid foods as early as possible. The starting in this direction can be made as the infants enter into the age of 4 or 5 months by giving them mashed or semi-liquid food such as rice cereal mixed with breast milk, the soup of cooked pulses, mashed banana or mashed boiled potato, etc. At this stage it is not unusual to witness the small babies spit out any solid food put into their mouth. It happens on account of a gag reflex that causes such spitting and resulting in a scene where more foods end up on them than inside them. However, gradually they become habituated, at first with a variety of the semi liquid and quite soft food items and then with other types of solid foods that need chewing and pressing on their part after acquiring teeth for doing the same. In this way, the diet of children in their younger ages universally in all parts of the world usually consists of the breast and bottle feeding milk accompanied with some solid food suiting their age, preferences and adaptability.

In the years to follow, the developing children must be put into a habit for making use of healthy and nutrient supplying items in their diet along with picking up the healthy habits of taking meals on time and in a proper way. This helps them attain proper physical and mental health, and all round growth and development by getting rid of the problems arising on account of malnutrition and unhealthy eating.

Toilet Training

The process of urination and defecation in its own forms is quite natural as well as essential for the heath and well-being of all the living species at all times of their living. For the foetuses it starts in the wombs of their mother and from their birth onwards the young infants are found to urinate and defecate anytime and anywhere around them with or without their will. It happens on account of their inability to exercise needed control over their bowel and bladder movements.

To make developing children urinate and defecate in a regular and proper way at the proper places needs proper training designated as toilet training.

However, it has been seen that children, in general, have no bladder or bowel control until the age of 12 months and only slight control for 6 months after that (American Academy of Paediatrics, 1999). It is thus very much clear that children up to this stage cannot be expected to be left on their own for urinating and defecating or providing any instructions or training for the purpose. Therefore, it is quite customary at this stage to make use of diapers for allowing children to urinate and defecate at their will.

Later on, in the toddler years after the age of 18 months or so a need is felt to getting the children learn to control their urination and defecation and become "toilet trained". There is a lot of controversy regarding the age and stage of commencing toilet training for younger children. However, there has been a general consensus on the decision that their training should be started only after ensuring their readiness for such training. Generally most children show signs of readiness for toilet training between 18 and 30 months of age with the following visible signs: (Arnett & Maynard, 2017, Feldman, Robert, 2016)

*   Staying "dry" at least 2 hours at a time during the day or waking up dry after naps;
*   Regular and predictable bowel movements, occurring at about the same time each day;
*   Increased anticipation or indication about the occurrence of urination or a bowel movement through facial expression or words;
*   The ability to follow simple directions;
*   The ability to get to the toilet and undress alone;
*   Feeling discomfort with soiled diapers;
*   Directly asking to use the toilet or to wear underwear instead of diaper.

In providing toilet training to the young children, parents and older members of the family should try to show the needed patience in doing so. It does not happen overnight but needs a lot of effort and wilful intention on the part of trainers and children continuing some time for several months or even years. The help of peers and older siblings may work well in this direction in terms of providing guidance or becoming a role model for the toilet trainees.

The task of exercising needed control over urination and defecation cannot be said to be fully finished by achieving initial satisfactory results in toilet training. It remains under trial for some more time. For this reason, it is better to wear "training pants" in between diapers and underwear for a period after learning toilet training.

After getting better toilet trained, it is quite probable for the developing children to experience occasional "accident" especially when they are tired, excited or stressed. Even getting full success during the day, it may often take a quite long duration before they are able to exercise control at night. This is why many of the younger children may be found to wet their beds at the night. It is quite natural for the younger ones to wet their beds occasionally. Gradually as they grow in age they may begin to demonstrate the quite leak proof results in this direction. As an estimate around three quarters of boys and most girls are able to stay dry after the age of 5 years.

The lack of proper bowel and bladder control, especially wetting the beds at night on the part of elder children however, may put them in trouble. It may upset the child besides making the child a target of ridicule from siblings and peers. The problem then becomes a subject of great concern for the parents and they are advised to seek guidance from a counsellor and child specialist for helping the children get out of this troubling issue.

Handedness and Left-handed

The habitual act of handedness in its technical sense may be defined as one of the physiological habit found in individuals including children showing a clear preference for the use of one hand over the other.

This habit of preferring one hand over the other may well come into the notice of others when the children get engaged in a variety of motor and conative acts such as using a table spoon for putting food into their mouth, throwing and hitting a ball, and using pen and pencil for writing and drawing. The research studies in this concern have concluded that by the age of 5, most children display a clear tendency to use one hand over the other, with 90 percent being right-handed and 10 percent left-handed (Feldman Robert, 2016).

In fact even prenatally, foetuses show a definite preference for sucking the thumb of their right or left hand, with 90 percent preferring the right thumb. The same 90 percent proportion of right hands continues into childhood and throughout adulthood in most cultures. (Arnett & Maynard, 2017).

The question here may arise that what contributes towards one's handedness — heredity or environment? The evidences gathered and research conclusions arrived on this issue are mixed, some advocating the role of environment and others blaming heredity for the left or right handedness of the children. Actually, the physiological habit of handedness is an acquired phenomenon and a learned habit that gets equally influenced with one's hereditary endowments and environment available to him from the time of conception.

The children right from the time of coming into action may be found to prefer the use of left or right hand for their day to day use and functioning. In the formal sense, a child is deemed a left-hander when he gets better results with the left hand, in addition to when he prefers the left hand in activities that need good co-ordination, strength and accuracy (Meyer, 1998).

Dominance of the right hemisphere of the brain predicates left-handedness. When one is left-handed there are sensory and motor differences in behaviour, perception and thinking. This is a powerful reason that makes left-handers especially unique in terms of a number of learning and adjustment demands.

As a habit, left-handedness, in general on the practical side, is found to create a number of obstacles in the learning and performance of the children in a variety of ways. Usually what is available everywhere in terms of the everyday objects for use as well as equipments and facilities for reading, writing, doing experiments, and performing in visual arts and workshops to the developing children at their homes, schools and other environmental situations favours the right-handed while creating many hurdles in the path of the left-handed. The difficulties faced by the left-handed on this account may be of the nature stated as follows:

- Different difficulties are mostly connected with perception of direction and handedness that requires accuracy and co-ordination skills.
- Difficulties occur in script techniques, handicraft and art. In these subjects, a child needs individual, methodological and adequate guidance, no matter where it is received.
- Left-handed children are also more likely to be diagnosed with conditions such as dyslexia as schools misinterpreted common writing difficulties.
- Pupils are often unable to use the mouse in computing lessons, and find scientific instruments such as microscopes, with controls on the right, harder to reach.
- In cookery classes, kitchen scissors, peelers, can openers and serrated knives are often right-handed, while in woodwork and metalwork, safety overrides on heavy machinery and power tools are harder to access for left-handed people.

In the light of the difficulties and inconvenience suffered on account of being left-handed, it has been perhaps a strong reason to view left-handedness as dangerous and evil on the part of so many cultures and societies of the world in the past.

However, there stands no valid reason or scientific evidence for the myths and negative feelings towards left-handedness. Actually as experience reveals, handedness, weather right or left, cannot be blamed or praised for the success of the individuals in one or the other lines of pursuit. Although, most children and adults in our population are right-handers and therefore their percentages of the success may be more vocal than the left-handed. However, we should not forget that many of the great men, artists, architectures and men of inventions such as Michelangelo, Benjamin Franklin, Leonardo da Vinci, Pablo Picasso, Sir Isaac Newton, Beethoven, Mahatma Gandhi, Henry Ford were all left-handed, and nowadays also many of our left-handed cricket players are known to be the most successful bowlers or batsmen in the international arena. It is therefore our duty to see that no undesirable complex or negative feelings should be allowed to develop among growing children with respect to their handedness, especially for their being left-handed. In addition we ourselves should not be any fussy over the handedness of the children and should not insist upon them to pick up a particular style of handedness.

Regarding, helping and dealing with left-handed children, it is not the case that they are incapable. But it is the case that things take longer, and may be handled more clumsily, because left-handed children's requirements are not being met adequately at home, school and in other environments. Thus, as a matter of proper consideration, a left-handed child should receive special attention, and left-handedness should be considered a child's inborn right to be different, not as a disability or a sign that the child will have certain difficulties in acquiring the skills of learning.

However, most failings were due to lack of awareness, rather than poor equipment. Children could be taught to write without smudging ink or straining their wrist by angling the paper properly, relaxing their arm and positioning themselves on the correct side of the desk. In the similar way, attempts should be made to get the left-handed feel at ease in performing one or the other tasks at home, school, and in other socio-cultural situations.

Significance and Implications of the Knowledge Related to Physical Development and Physiological Habits Formation

All the aspects of growth and development — physical, intellectual, emotional, social, moral etc., — are closely interlinked. The growth and development of any one of these aspects affects the growth and development of the other. Physical growth and development is not an exception. Certainly, it influences the development in other directions. For example, growth and development of the nervous system influences the growth and development of intellectual powers. Emotional and social adjustment is also linked with physical growth and development. While the children having normal physical growth and development are accepted by their age group, the physical deviates — who are very small, very large, too fat, too thin, etc., — remain isolated. They are often nicknamed, ridiculed and denied participation in play and recreational activities enjoyed by their age associates. This leads to serious maladjustments and personality problems. A young child is intelligent enough to become aware of the fact that he differs in appearance and physical abilities from other children. His attitude towards self is injured and self-confidence is shaken. In this case, he either becomes shy and timid or becomes aggressive in order to compensate for his inferiority feelings.

Moreover, on the balanced growth and development of the internal as well as external organs depends the balanced functioning of the body systems. The functioning of the body systems decides the interest, attitude and the total behaviour of all individuals. For example, glands and their functioning affect his emotional behaviour to a great extent. Similarly, his anatomical development, the development of circulatory, respiratory systems, etc., give the person the required abilities for participating in various motor activities. Hence, physical development influences the total make-up of an individual and thus needs careful attention. Similar is the story with the knowledge of the development of a number of physiological habits related to the children's sleeping and eating behaviour, bowels and bladder control, handedness, etc. All these physiological habits also influence and affect the behaviour and development of the growing children in a variety of ways.

The knowledge and understanding of the process of physical development as well as development of the one or the other physiological habits among growing children thus can help the parents and teachers well to achieve their most important purpose — helping children in bettering their overall well-being and to bring an all-round development of their personality. Specifically this can serve them in the following ways:

1. They can become aware of the physical deviates, their psychology and problem of adjustment. Consequently, parents and teachers can help them with their social and emotional adjustments as well as in their school and social learning.

2. Children are the backbone of a nation. The development of appropriate physiological habits and the acquisition of good health and proper physical development is an asset to the progress of a country. Our schools, families and communities have to play a decisive role in the task of physical welfare of the children. Parents, teachers and community people with the knowledge of physical development and physiological habit formation process can render valuable help in this direction.

3. Needs, desires, interests, attitudes, and in its own way the overall behaviour of an individual is controlled, to a great extent, by his physical development and physiological habits. Therefore at a particular age level, what would be the expected behaviour of the child of that age group can be estimated through the physical development and physiological habit pattern. For example, with the study of the trend of the physical development in adolescence, one can be aware of their growing physical, emotional and social needs. Accordingly, adolescents can be helped by us in the adjustment to their rapid development and changes.

4. Study of the pattern of physical development and physiological habits helps us in knowing what can be expected normally from the children of a particular age level. In turn it can help us (i) to provide for the needed help and facilities to the developing children in relation to their level of physical development, physiological habits formation and (ii) suitably arrange school programmes like curricular and co-curricular experiences, methods and techniques of teaching, time-table, text-books, aid material, seating arrangement, learning environment, etc., for the wholesome development of the children.

In this way we can see that the knowledge of process of physical development and physiological habits formation helps all of us in fulfilling our responsibilities towards our children. Its knowledge equips one to set an agenda according to the needs of the developing children for helping them improve their health and attain proper physical strength and abilities in a wholesome and desired manner.

Summary

Physical growth and development refers to the process responsible for bringing bodily and physiological changes — internal as well as external — in an organism from the time of conception till his death.

In spite of the wide individual differences, the process of human physical growth and development may be seen to exhibit a somewhat general pattern characterised as (i) uniformity in the increase of height and weight with the growing age (till the end of adolescence), (ii) change in body proportions, (iii) uniformity in anatomical growth and development, (iv) uniformity in growth and development of internal organs like nervous, muscular, circulatory digestive, lymphatic and reproductive systems.

In a general way, the process of physical growth and development is quite rapid from birth to the age of two or three years. After that it continues at a diminished rate till the beginning of adolescence. As soon as the child enters the adolescence era, his first three years are marked as the years of rapid growth and development. It is then followed by a period of slow growth and development till the time of maturity.

Factors affecting the physical growth and development of an individual begin to play their role right from their conception till death. The traits and characteristics transmitted through genes, the internal environmental forces affecting the growth and development after birth, etc., may be named as some of such factors.

Physiological habits may be found to affect the physical development of the children in their own way depending upon the nature of their development in children. Some of the more pronounced physiological habits observable among the children from their very birth may be identified as sleeping behaviour, eating behaviour, bladder and bowel control, handedness, etc.

In the **development of sleeping behaviour** among the children we may find that initially the newborns spend more time in their sleep than when awake. Moreover, rather than sleeping 16 to17 hours straight, they sleep for a few hours, wake up for a while, sleep a few more hours, and wake up again. At this stage their sleep-wake patterns are governed by hunger, not whether it is light or dark outside. Besides this, they are found to spend 50 percent of their total sleeping time in REM (rapid eye movement) sleep in comparison to adults' 20 percent for the same. However, as they enter the stage of infancy and grow further, there is a sharp decline in the durations of their sleeping hours and REM sleep along with a considerable increase in the time of their continued sleep.

Regarding the **development of the eating behaviour** of children it may be well noted that during the prenatal stage, the children get supply of their nutritional needs from the regular diet of their mothers. After birth, their eating or feeding behaviour may be found to pass through the stages of breast feeding, bottle feeding and solid meal taking.

Regarding the **development of the habit of exercising needed bowel and bladder control** for going through the natural process of urination and defecation, it may be seen that the young infants urinate and defecate anytime and anywhere around them with or without their will. During the early infancy years, therefore, it is quite customary to make use of diapers for allowing children to urinate and defecate at their will. But later on, they essentially need proper training for helping them in this concern known as toilet training. After getting better toilet trained, however, it is quite natural for the younger ones to wet their beds occasionally. Gradually, it improves and in general most children up to the age of five or six are able to demonstrate the quite leak proof results in this direction.

The habitual act of handedness in its technical sense may be defined as one of the physiological habits found in the individuals including children showing a clear preference for the use of one hand over the other. The children pick up the habit of handedness as an acquired phenomenon that gets equally influenced with one's hereditary endowments and environment available to them from the time of conception. In some cases, the dominance of the left or right hemisphere of the brain may be found to be a great predictor for the right and left-handedness among children. In some of the cultures and societies the left-handedness is regarded as dangerous and evil. However, there stands no valid reason or scientific evidence for the myths and negative feelings towards left-handedness. Many of the great persons all over the world have been left-handed.

As a whole, the knowledge of the process of the physical development and physiological habits formation may help all of us well in the task of helping children develop their overall well-being and shape their all-round personality. By caring for their physical development and physiological habits formation, we may help them to grow and develop not only in physical aspects but also in the other aspects of their personality make up like intellectual, emotional, social, moral, etc., (as all these aspects of one's personality are closely inter-linked). Moreover, a study of the pattern of physical development and physiological habits formation may help us in understanding what can be expected normally from the children at a particular age level. It may help further, in the planning and organisation of the facilities, programs and curricular and co-curricular experiences for the education and welfare of the children in school and home.

References and Suggested Readings

American Academy of Pediatrics, (1999), Media Education, *Pediatrics*, 104, 341-343

Arnett, Jeffrey Jensen & Maynard, Ashley E., (2017), *Child Development: A Cultural Approach* (2nd edition), Boston: Pearson.

Carmichael, L. (Ed.), *Manual of Child Psychology*, John Wiley, New York, 1946

Feldman, Robert S., (2016), *Child Development* (7th edition), Boston: Sage

Hurlock, E.B., *Child Psychology*, McGraw-Hill, Tokyo, 1959.

Indian Council of Medical Research, *Growth and Development of Infants and Children, Technical Report*, revision 19, 1972.

Marry, F.K. and Marry, R.V., *From Infancy to Adolescence*, Harper & Brothers, New York, 1940.

Meyer, R.W.(1999), Quoted In Pilvi Kula, *Left-handedness, Journal of Teacher Education for Sustainability*, Vol.9, 2008, pp. 58-67.

9

Motor Development

Meaning of Motor Development

Motor development in general, means the development of motor capacities and abilities of an individual. Motor capacities and abilities as Crow & Crow (1953) define stand for *"the various kinds of bodily movements that are made possible through the co-ordination of nerve and muscle activity."* (p. 34)

As examples, of these bodily movements we may cite a number of activities concerning conative aspects of the human behaviour like walking, running, jumping, swimming, grasping, throwing, catching, writing, using tools and equipment, etc. We may easily observe that a newborn child or an infant is quite helpless with regard to the performance of these activities. His helplessness can be very well identified. He see but cannot stare or focus at a particular object. He may remain lying down but cannot crawl, stand or walk. He is unable to grasp and hold things and engage himself in the individual or collective play activities. He is so helpless in his motor capacities that he cannot even manage his urgent affairs like passing stool and urine, protection himself from harmful situations and satisfying the need of food and water. However, with the passage of time, he is able to gain control over his neuromuscular apparatus as a result of the maturation and the art of learning various motor movements and develop his motor abilities and capacities so much so that he is able to perform many complex motor activities demanded by his environment. Now he does not remain helpless but gains confidence. This change in the motor abilities and capacities of the child is brought by a developmental process known as motor development.

Therefore, as a term motor development, in general, may be referred to the development of motor activities, i.e., development of control over bodily movements. Since this control is a natural outcome of the gross as well as finer co-ordination of the nervous and muscular system, the term motor development according to E.B. Hurlock (1987) may be properly defined as *"the development of control over bodily movements through the co-ordinated activity of the nerve centers, the nerves and the muscles."* (p. 138)

The control over bodily movements requiring gross or finer co-ordination of the nervous system and muscular system, thus constitutes the subject of the process of motor development that starts from the very early stage of one's life and goes on till one has a will and strength for acquiring such control for the acquisition of motor abilities and skills.

How this development process goes on at the different stages of life, what are its general characteristics and principles, etc., and how this development is useful for the individual child are some of the basic questions that need to be answered for understanding the mechanism of motor development going on in our children. Let us try to seek answers for these queries in the subsequent discussion carried out in this chapter.

How Does Motor Development Take Place in Growing Children?

Watching a small baby take their first step to your outstretched arms is something that you will probably always remember and talk about proudly by utterances like "look, Anita took her first step last week." Why not? It is a significant milestone in the motor development of your child. Like this, there happen a variety of milestones related to gross and fine motor development of the youngsters that are not only fascinating but are in fact very much essential for the survival, adjustment, welfare and progress of the child in the existing and coming days of his life. Motor development is an essential as well as universal phenomenon in the sense that each newborn baby passes through it as a result of the close interaction between his hereditary endowments and environmental influences. Yet even though each child is different, generally children attain the major milestones with regard to their gross and fine motor developments at a fairly predictable order in the subsequent ages of their development. For the clarity of the discussion here we would be discussing development of gross motor and fine motor skills side by side in the period of infancy, childhood and adolescence.

Motor Development in Infancy (from birth to 2 years)

In infancy the newborn demonstrates quite significant changes, as he grows in age in terms of his gross and fine motor ability and skills, in various areas and aspects. The motor development and activities performed by the infants may be seen to follow the usual law of developmental direction emphasising that motor development happens from head to foot, i.e., the development of strength, co-ordination and reflexes start with the head and gradually work their way down to the trunk, arms and legs. Consequently, we would like to discuss the motor development and activities of the infants in relation to such downward development.

A. Motor Development and Activities in the Region of Head

1. Eye co-ordination:

During a few hours after birth the newborn has quite poor eye coordination but in a few months the baby becomes quite capable in demonstrating various motor abilities related to eye co-ordination such as focusing his eyes on stationary objects and following his eyes on moving objects.

2. Control and movements of head:

- During the first month of life, the baby has little control of his head. It lags when you lift him to a sitting position. It is for this reason you should keep one hand behind the baby's head when you pick him up.

- Between one and two months of age, the baby is able to raise his head up above a flat surface. As he continues to grow, he can hold his head up longer.
- At three months, the baby's head still bobs when he sits, but he is beginning to hold his head erect. When laying on his stomach, a baby, three to four months old can raise his head and chest well above the mattress, supporting his weight on his forearms.

B. Development and Activities of Trunk

- When the baby is about four or five months old, he will probably roll over the first time, usually from the belly to the back, it is therefore advisable not to leave the baby alone at this time on a table or bed. Before long, if you put the baby on his back, he may roll over on his stomach and get on his hand and knees, as though ready to crawl. While lying on his back, he may lift his head and shoulders as though he is trying to sit up.
- During the age of 5 to 8 months the baby is able to pull himself to a sitting position when someone lifts his hands and he can sit alone for about half an hour if he is well propped. Some placid infants, particularly if they are plump, will lie on their back a little longer and not sit alone with support until seven months or so.
- By nine or ten months, an infant can crawl on his stomach or hands and knees. And he can support his weight by holding on to the sides of his cot or playpen.
- During ages 9 to 12 months the baby reaches out into his environment, not only with his hands but with the whole body. He can sit, lie on his back and then sit again. Most babies of this age can pull themselves to a standing position without help. In the beginning, he may not know how to sit down again.

C. Development and Activities of the Arms and Hands

- A three-month old baby plays with his hands as with a toy. At around four months of age, the baby can bring his hands together in front of him and before long actively suck his thumb.
- Although at about three months the baby does have an ever-increasing amount of arm and hand movements, he still cannot reach out and grasp an object as he has still not acquired the much-needed eye-hand co-ordination.
- At the early stage of the acquisition of eye and hand co-ordination in the fourth month, the baby can only look at the objects but is not able to reach and grasp it. Later on, as his eye co-ordination improves, he begins to reach the object for its grasping. As a result, by completion of four months, he can hold and shake a rattle.
- By the age of six months and so, the baby is able to reach for an object, grasp and then carry the object to his mouth.
- At six or seven months of age, the baby develops the ability to pass objects from one hand to another. The infant can grasp an object, move it over to the opposite hand and hold it.

- Initially infants grasp with the whole hand, (called a *palmar* grasp), latter, by about eight or nine months, the baby usually starts to develop the ability to use his thumb and index finger (called pincer grasp) to grasp small objects. And he uses both hands simultaneously-feeding himself a biscuit with one hand while he bangs his cup or plate with a toy held in the other hand.

- By about 9 to 12 months the baby learns to do many things with hands and fingers like poking, pointing, touching, lifting, twisting, squeezing, picking up and dropping, etc.

- The child of 12 to 15 months of age gets joy from dumping items out of a bottle or box and may practice this skill by emptying waste-baskets and pouring liquids out of bottles. As well as being very active, the baby will sit for long periods of time, turning the pages of a magazine or picture book or playing with blocks and toys. He now also tries to assist in dressing and undressing himself, although his 'help' may lengthen the process.

- An average 18-month toddler generally can eat without help, drink from a cup, use a spoon, stack a few blocks and pretend to do housework.

- By the end of two years, the toddlers can perform some or the other delicate acts associated with co-ordination of fine movements like turning of pages and may enter well into the practice of toilet training.

D. Development and Activities of Legs

When a baby is just able to stand with or without support, he may be seen trying to begin his journey on foot by learning the skill of walking. The milestone earned by him in the field of locomotion with the use of his legs and foot may be summarised as follows:

- In the beginning, during the age of 9 to 11 months the child tries to walk while holding on to something for support with one hand. In the beginning they demonstrate a poor balance in terms of their walking movements. Throwing light on this aspect Hurlock (1956: 147) writes:

  At first balance is poor. As an aid to maintaining equilibrium, the baby's arms are held outright, much like those of a tightrope walker or are pulled up to the body. The feet are turned outward and the legs are stiff. A rhythmic alteration of the two legs occurs. The head is held slightly forward and the baby looks straight ahead of him, instead of at the floor. This is necessary if balance is to be maintained, though it usually results in many falls.

- However, by their first birthday, usually most of the babies are able to walk properly with or without support and then later on in one or two months they may be seen to walk alone, with a new degree of confidence and independence.

- By the age 14 to 18 months the children's motor activities using their legs are reaching such a fine level of control that:

  (i) They start to run instead of walk. In fact, it may appear as though they are on the run constantly, going from room to room with frustrating speed.

(ii) Besides, running in this style, they climb on to and off furniture and also may walk up and down stairs while holding your hand. It may also be seen that the children first walk up the stairs independently but are unable to get down without support.

(iii) It may also be seen that the children have acquired ability to balance on their feet in a squat position while playing with objects on the floor, walk backward and walk on tiptoe without losing their balance, stand and kick a ball without falling, stand and throw a ball and jump in place.

- Later on, by the second birthday, they begin to demonstrate their capability of getting up and down the stairs properly in a quite independent way besides climbing, getting down and sliding from some high slopes or slides.

- At two, toddlers can run well, throw a ball, catch it, etc.

- By the end of infancy children are often torn between dependence and independence. They set out on their own to explore — climbing, walking, opening doors, trying to dress themselves and helping to foot them independently. But they still must be helped down from the steps they have climbed, protected from accidents and cuddled and cooed over when they scrape a knee.

Table 9.1: Motor Milestones — Gross and Fine Motor Development in Infancy

Motor skill	Average age achieved	Age range in which 90 percent of infants achieve the skill
When held upright, holds head erect and steady	6 weeks	3 weeks-4 months
When prone, lifts self by arms	2 months	3 weeks-4 months
Rolls from side to back	2 months	3 weeks-5months
Grasps cube	3 months, 3 weeks	2-7 months
Rolls from back to side	4½ months	2-7 months
Sits alone	7 months	5-9 months
Crawls	7 months	5-11 months
Pulls to stand	8 months	5-12 months
Plays pat-a-cake	9 months, 3 weeks	7-15 months
Stands alone	11 months	9-16 months
Walks alone	11 months, 3 weeks	9-17 months
Builds tower of two cubes	13 months, 3 weeks	10-19 months
Scribbles vigorously	14 months	10-21 months
Walks upstairs with help	16 months	12-23 months
Jumps in place	23 months, 2 weeks	17-30 months
Walks on tiptoe	25 months	16-30 months

Source: Adapted from Bayley, 1993.

Note: These milestone figures indicate the general trend. However, there exist individual differences with relation to age-specific development.

Motor Development in Childhood (from 3 to 12 years)

As understood from the developmental milestones acquired during infancy, children entering age three are equipped with necessary locomotion control and movement for carrying out the process of motor development with reasonable speed and efficiency as they have not to worry about staying upright, to move around in the environment, use their arms and hands in grasping, holding, pulling and performing their many age-related activities. As a result of such development, the children at their pre-and later childhood years may be found to acquire various milestones regarding their gross and fine motor development detailed as follows:

1. *During 2-3 years,* children are generally found to demonstrate the following types of gross and fine motor abilities.

    (i) They walk more confidently and rhythmically.

    (ii) Engage in simple movements such as hopping, jumping, throwing and catching (often with rigid upper body) and take pride and delight in performing these activities.

    (iii) Push their tricycle or a riding toy with feet. At this stage they are in the habit of using little steering or pedalling for their tricycle.

    (iv) Have the ability to pick up the tiniest objects between their thumb and index fingers for some time, but they are somewhat clumsy at it.

    (v) Can build surprisingly high towers but not in a completely straight line.

    (vi) While playing with a foam board or a simple puzzle they are rather rough in placing the pieces.

2. *During 3-4 years,* the children are still enjoying the same types of motor activities as they used to earlier but at this age now they become more adventurous and thus are found to exhibit the following types of gross and fine motor development:

    (i) Although they have been able to climb stairs previously with one foot on each step for some time, now at this age they begin trying to come down the same way.

    (ii) They begin to jump on the spot, hop with flexing upper body and copying a circle, etc.

    (iii) They now begin to throw the objects with slight involvement of their upper body, however, they are still found to catch the ball by trapping it against their chests.

    (iv) They demonstrate their ability to ride a tricycle by steering and pedalling it properly.

    (v) They begin to demonstrate much more precision in their fine motor co-ordination. However, they may still have trouble in building high towers with blocks due to the hurry and impatience on their part.

3. *During 4-5 years* children are found to be more adventurous than they were at 3-4 years. At this age they are found to demonstrate the following types of gross and fine motor development:

    (i) They can walk downstairs with one foot each step (alternating feet) and run smoothly.

(ii)   They are able to gallop and skip with one foot.

(iii) They can throw ball with increased body rotation and transfer of weight on feet and are also able to catch it with one hand.

(iv)   They ride on their tricycle by steering it smoothly and rapidly. The way a child uses a tricycle says a lot about his motor skill development during this age span. He is no longer a silent sitter or experimenting with pedals as he used to be at the age of three. Now he sees how fast he can make the tricycle go without caring for the turn and obstacles in his path.

(v)   Their fine motor co-ordination gets further improved resulting in their hands, arms and fingers all moving together under better command of the eye. As an example, the difference may be observed in relation to their dressing themselves. When a child is four he may begin to dress himself with little assistance from others.

4. *During 5-6 years* children become more active and stronger in terms of the development of their gross and fine motor abilities in the manner as follows:

(i)   They can run faster and enjoy races with each other and their parents.

(ii)   They are able to jump more smoothly now and are found to be engaged in skipping and sideways stepping activities.

(iii) They show improvement in their throwing and catching skills by displaying mature whole body throwing and catching pattern. Their speed of throwing the ball also increases.

(iv)   They now begin to ride on a bicycle (small sized or with training wheel.)

(v)   As a matter of further improvement in their fine motor co-ordination children now are able to use their hands more adroitly as tools. A child of six years can hammer, paste, tie shoes and fasten clothes. However, a child of 5-6 years of 4 to 5 years age is not ready for writing. The small muscles that control his fingers and hands are not developed well enough. He also does not acquire enough hand eye co-ordination at this age. For this purpose he has to wait a little more.

5.   *During 7-12 years* when children are studying in elementary school, they are found to demonstrate a quite reasonable development of their gross and fine motor abilities summarised as follows:

(i)   They gain greater control over their bodies and can sit and pay attention to the activities for longer periods of time. However they become more fatigued by long periods of sitting as they are not adequately matured in physical terms.

(ii)   Their running speed is quite enhanced and they pay more attention and take more interest in the activities related to running, continuous skipping, sideways stepping, jumping or bicycling without getting fatigued. Their skill regarding balancing on beam, throwing, catching, batting, kicking and dribbling improves in terms of body movements, technique, accuracy, distance and speed.

(iii) There comes a lot of improvement quite speedily in the fine motor abilities of the children during this age span. For example, where at the age of four months, a baby could hold a block for a short time using his whole palm, gradually, in the age span of seven the block moves over toward the thumb side of the hand and by eight or nine months, the baby uses just the thumb and first finger (also known as the forefinger) a more efficient and accurate way to handle objects.

(iv) Moreover, by seven years of age, children's hand become steadier and they begin to prefer a pencil to a crayon. A, seven year old child may concentrate hard when writing. He grips his pencil tightly and holds it close to the point. By the time he is eight years old, his hand-eye co-ordination and the small muscles in his hands and fingers are much better developed. As a result, he may write more evenly and easily.

(v) At 10 to 12 years of age, they begin to show manipulative skills for the execution of the tasks and activities similar to the abilities of mature adults like such as using hands independently with more ease and precision, writing words with smaller spelling and smaller letter size, playing a difficult piece on a musical instrument and producing fine quality crafts.

Table 9.2: Motor Milestones — Gross and Fine Motor Development in Childhood

Age	Gross Motor Skills	Fine Motor Skills
2-3 years	1. Walks more confidently and rhythmically, hurriedly walking or slow running.	1. Picking up the tiniest objects between thumb and index finger.
	2. Shows simple movements as hopping, jumping, throwing, catching (often with rigid upper body) and feeling delight in performing these activities.	2. Building high towers with blocks but not in a completely straight line.
	3. Pushing tricycle or any riding toy with feet using little steering or pedalling.	3. Roughly placing pieces while playing board games or simple puzzles.
3-4 years	1. Climbing stairs with one foot on each step and trying to come down the stairs in the same way.	1. Feel trouble in building high towers with blocks due to hurry and impatience on their part.
	2. Begin to jump and hop with flexing upper body.	2. Begin to demonstrate much more precision in their fine motor co-ordination.
	3. Begin to throw the object with slight involvement of their upper body and catching the object by trapping it against their chest.	
	4. Ride a tricycle by steering and pedalling it.	

Age	Gross Motor Skills	Fine Motor Skills
4-5 years	1. Walk down the stairs with one foot ahead of each step (alternating feet) and run smoothly.	1. Their hand, arm and fingers, all move together under better command of the eye.
	2. Able to gallop and skip with one foot.	2. Begins to dress himself with little assistance from others.
	3. Can throw the ball with increased body rotation and catch ball with hand. 4. Can ride on tricycle by steering it smoothly and rapidly without caring for the turn and obstacles in his path.	3. Begin to read and write letters, colouring with crayons, sketching, dancing, acting (copying others), playing instruments and swimming according to their interests.
5-6 years	1. Can now run much harder and enjoy races with each other and parents.	1. Able to use their hand more adroitly as tools.
	2. Able to gallop more smoothly, true skipping and sideways skipping.	2. Can hammer, paste, tie shoes and fasten clothes.
	3. Shows improvement in throwing and catching skills. 4. Begins to ride on bicycle (small sized or with training wheels)	3. Show increase in the ability to read, write, colour, sketch, dance, play instrument, swim, act, etc.
7-12 years	1. Gain greater control over their bodies. Can sit and pay attention to the activities for a little longer duration.	1. Show advancement to handle objects in a more efficient and accurate way by using just their thumb and forefingers.
	2. Running speed is enhanced. They pay more attention and take more interest in the activities related to running, skipping, sideways stepping, jumping, swimming or bicycling without getting fatigued.	2. Show a great improvement in their hand eye coordination. 3. Show considerable fine movements with the use of the small muscles of their hands and fingers. 4. They become quite adept at the execution of tasks and activities involving fine motor skills similar to the abilities of a mature adult.
	3. Improvement in throwing, catching, batting, kicking, dribbling, balancing on beam skill, etc.	

Motor Development in Adolescence and Adulthood

Adolescence is said to be a period of intensive growth and development in all the aspects and spheres of human growth and development including motor development. The development and functioning of our gross as well as fine motor skills, thus, reach their peak at the end of adolescence and just a few years after that (mostly between the ages of 19 to 25). It is true for the average young adult and for outstanding athletes or sports personnel. It has been also commonly observed that there starts a decline in the efficiency and output of the gross and fine motor abilities of human beings as they step into their late adulthood. They begin to demonstrate decline in their moving / running, balancing, jumping and the co-ordination activities of the smaller muscles in terms of their speed, duration and precision.

Delayed Motor Development

Motor development, as already pointed out, follows a generalised pattern of growth and development in relation to the gross and fine motor abilities and skills of the children during the different ages of their development period. However, exceptions are there as some children demonstrate forwardness or backwardness in terms of the development of their gross and fine motor abilities and skills. To some extent such exceptions, within reasonable limits of differentiation do not cause much trouble, however, deviation to a greater extent (especially on the side of retardation or delayed development) becomes a thing of concern to parents, teachers and other persons interested in the welfare of the children. The children, said to be the victim of their delayed motor development, may be found to be quite delayed in reaching the normal or generalised pattern of age-specific milestones of their gross and fine motor development. It can prove harmful to the developing child in a variety of ways, mainly, as follows:

- The delayed development is responsible to keep the child from reaching the stage of independent action when normally he is expected to do so.
- It affects their normal process of physical growth and development.
- It affects their social interaction with their peers and thus hampers their normal social development.
- The delayed motor development − gross and fine − put obstacles in their normal mental development and functioning.

It affects adversely their socio-emotional behaviour. Because as a result of this early backwardness in the development of motor control, many young children develop feelings of inferiority which cause them to withdraw from the social group and this lays the foundation for unsocial attitudes and behaviour (Hurlock, 1956, p. 167).

Causes of Delayed Motor Development

The causes of delayed motor development in the children may be briefly outlined as follows:

1. The improper growth conditions or inadequate nutrition received by the child in the womb of his mother.
2. Poor physical health of the child due to illness, malnutrition, glandular or chemical deficiencies and similar other reasons.
3. Inappropriate or abnormal size and body proportions of the child.
4. Low grade intelligence.

5. Improper or inadequate development of muscle control due to (i) lack of adequate space for carrying out motor activities, (ii) lack of proper facilities for play, exercise and other motor acts, (iii) lack of incentive, (iv) lack of proper environment experiences, proper model for observation and imitation and timely training.

6. Improper effects of hampering or tight clothes and shoes.

7. Lack of proper tuning between learning or practising a motor skill and maturation.

8. Forcing a child for a skilled movement to the extent of making him fearful or rebellion.

Importance and Implications of the Knowledge of Motor Development

The knowledge of the nature and mechanism of the process of gross and fine motor development among the children may prove quite helpful to parents, teachers, counsellors and other care takers of the children in a variety of ways summarised as follows:

1. They may be aware of the fact that motor development is essential for the all-round balanced development of their personality as it works as a foundation and base for carrying out proper growth and development in physical, mental, social, emotional, moral and aesthetic development of the child.

2. There must be perfect co-ordination between the age specific maturation and acquisition of motor skills, the knowledge of this specific fact helps them to arrange for the proper learning or training experiences to the children at an appropriate time.

3. The knowledge of the various laws and trends governing the gross and fine motor development of the children makes them quite knowledgeable about their expectations from their children about their general and specific acquisition or motor skills. It can then prove quite useful to them for the organisation of suitable environment and learning facilities to their children for their proper motor development.

4. The knowledge of the factors responsible for the delayed motor development, may help them to take necessary preventive and curative measures.

5. There are some generalised milestones for the development of gross and fine motor skills among the children of various ages related to different developmental periods like infancy, earlier and later childhood years, adolescence, etc. These milestones in general may tell us in advance about the nature, characteristics and features of the children's motor development. Thus, what can be expected from growing child in general about his motor abilities is better known through the study of these age- or stage-specific milestones. Such knowledge may prove quite advantageous in the ways given as follows:

   (i) We can be better prepared for providing our children the needed care, security and preventive safeguard for their adequate adjustment well being and progress. For example, if we know that during the first month of life the baby has almost no control of his head, then it would help us to take the needed precaution of keeping our one hand behind the baby's head while picking him up. Similarly, if we know that by the age of six months or so the baby is able to reach for an object, grasp it and carry it to his mouth, we would be quite cautious that baby should not put any harmful object in his mouth. Similarly, we can take a number of precautions for saving the children with their immature adventures for which they are not fully capable at a particular development period.

(ii)   Besides taking precautions for protecting them from their untimely adventures, the knowledge of these milestones can also prove helpful in our planning and providing needed facilities, congenial adequate environment, incentives, etc., for the expression of their motor potential and practice as well as exercise of their motor skills. We can plan for the needed learning experiences and training schedules, etc., for the children in a proper way in the light of these milestones.

(iii)   A wise study and observation regarding the attainment of these milestones may also help us in educating ourselves that we should never feel too much anxious, over jealous and enthusiastic for the development of motor abilities and skills on the part of our children during specific ages of their developmental periods. These milestones are only the guidelines telling us about the average gross and fine motor development of most of the children in a normal set up. The children may experience delayed development due to so many personal and environmental reasons. The variations in their developments to a moderate range is thus to be accepted by us without any anxiety. Every child possesses his own individuality and we should not thrust our own expectations on them with regard to their excelling in the motor skills related tasks. We should also avoid putting unnecessary pressure on the children for the fear that they are not reaching their milestones.

(iv)   While the attainment of the laid down milestones should not be made a subject of utter concern and anxiety, but their values as providing red signal for getting cautious about the nature of motor development of our children cannot also be minimised. Milestones are helpful in the unlikely event that there really is something missing in a child. In this way the knowledge of the milestones can help us in timely diagnosis of the motor incapacities and disabilities of children leading to the planning and implementing of suitable special education programmes for them. For such diagnosis, you do not need to take into consideration the average age that children do certain things, but rather take into account the red-flag age (the age by which 90 percent or more of healthy normal children are expected to attain that milestone). Such comparison, then, may essentially help you to experience some doubt or concern about the normal motor development of your child and it is the time when you can approach the counsellor or doctor for the necessary help to your developing children.

(v)   Knowledge of motor development along with the milestones related to cross and fine motor skills may help teachers, curriculum planners and trainers to plan for suitable learning experiences, method and training techniques for helping children in their proper education, development and efficiency gained in games and sports, craft and vocational activities.

Summary

Motor development, in general, means the development of motor capacities and abilities (bodily movement possible through the coordination of nerves and muscular activities) of an individual. The control over bodily movements requiring gross or finer coordination of the nervous and muscular systems begins from the early stage of one's life and goes on till one has a will and strength for acquiring such control.

All though each child is different, yet, generally children attain their major milestones with regard to their gross and fine motor development at a fairly predictable order in the subsequent ages of their development.

In infancy a newborn baby demonstrates quite significant changes, as he grows in age, in terms of his gross and fine motor ability and skills in the various areas and aspects. Here, the motor development and activities performed by the infants may be seen to follow a set pattern of proceeding from head to foot, i.e., the development of strength, co-ordination and reflexes starts with the head and gradually works down to the trunk, arms and legs. As a result of the necessary developmental milestones acquired during the infancy, children entering age three are equipped with necessary locomotion control and movement for carrying out the process of motor development at the later stages of their motor development with reasonable speed and efficiency. On reaching the age of 10 to 12 years of age, they begin to show manipulative skills for the execution of tasks and activities similar to the abilities of mature adults, such as using hands independently with more ease and precision, writing words with smaller letter size, playing a difficult piece on a musical instrument and producing fine quality crafts. Going further, the development and functioning of one's gross as well as fine motor skills, then may be found, to reach their peak at the end of adolescence.

Although, in its course of development from infancy to adolescence the phenomenon of motor development follows a generalised pattern of growth and development in relation to the gross and motor abilities and skills of children during the different ages of their developmental period. However, some children may be found to suffer from the phenomenon of delayed motor development. A lot of delay in reaching the normal and generalised pattern of age-specific milestones of their gross and fine motor development can prove harmful to their overall growth, development and general welfare.

The knowledge of the nature and mechanism of the process of gross and fine motor development among the children may prove quite helpful to parents, teachers, counsellors and other care takers of the children in the following ways: (i) to become better prepared for providing the children the needed care, security and preventive safeguard for their adequate adjustment well being and progress, (ii) to prove helpful in planning and providing needed facilities, congenial adequate environment, incentives, etc., for the expression of their motor potential and practice as well as exercise of their motor skills, (iii) to make us learn that there are individual differences on the part of developing children in reaching milestones and we should avoid showing undue stress for their delayed motor development at one or the other stages of their development.

References and Suggested Readings

Bayley, Nancy (1993), Bayley Scales of Infant Development (2nd ed.), *Psychology Corporation*, USA.

Carmichael, L. (Ed.), *Manual of Child Psychology*, John Wiley, New York, 1946

Crow, L.D. and Crow, Alice, *Psychology*, Barney & Noble, New York, 1953.

Crow, L.D. and Crow, Alice, *Child Psychology*, (Reprint), Barney & Noble, New York, 1969.

Garrett, H.E., *General Psychology*, 2nd ed., Eurasia Publishing House, New Delhi, 1968.

Halverson, H.M., The acquisition of Skills in Infancy, *Journal of General Psychology*, 1933, 43, 3-48.

Hurlock, E.B., *Child Psychology*, (Asian Student edition), Tokyo: Kogakusha, 1956.

Hurlock, E.B., *Child Development* (International edition, 8th printing), New York: McGraw Hill, 1987

Indian Council of Medical Research, *Growth and Development of Infants and Children, Technical Report*, revision 19, 1972.

Marry, F.K. and Marry, R.V., *From Infancy to Adolescence*, Harper & Brothers, New York, 1940.

Ormrod, J.E., Educational Psychology: Developing Learners (4th ed.), Upper Saddle River, N.J.: Prentice-Hall.

Skinner C.E. and Harriman, P.L. (Eds.), *Child Psychology*, 6th print, Macmillan, New York, 1937.

Thomson, G.G., *Child Psychology* (First Indian Reprint), New Delhi: Surjeet Publications, 1979.

10

Sensory Development

Introduction

In the previous two chapters we learned how newborn children are helped in their physical and motor development by acquiring necessary abilities and capacities for this purpose. As they advance in age by passing through different stages of growth and development such as infancy, early and later childhood they become quite capable of exercising their physical and motor abilities and skills in a proper and desired way that aids them in their needed adjustment, learning and progress in life. Besides these two types of growth and development linked with the physical and biological needs of their body as well as developmental abilities and capacities of their physical organs, there is still another dimension or aspect of their physical growth and development that needs to be properly developed side by side along with the process of their physical and motor development. This is known as sensory development. Let us understand what it means and how it works out in their developmental period.

What is Sensory Development

In its simple meaning sensory development stands for the development of sensory abilities and capacities of children in the shape of the development of their capability to see, hear, feel, smell and taste in a way much like adults in their culture and society. These sensory abilities may also be referred to as perceptual abilities of children. Perception as we know is known as the sensation attached to its meaning. The child's sense organs say eyes for example helps him to catch hold of a visual image or impression of the perceived object and this impression is provided some meaning by his brain. When this happens, we may say that the child has some perception of the visual object and the ability demonstrated by him in this connection is called his sensory or perceptual ability to see and identify or recognise the objects.

In this way, the process of sensory or perceptual development is well connected with the discussion of the process of growth and development of the abilities and capacities being demonstrated through the use and application of the human senses such as senses of sight or vision, hearing, touch, taste and smell.

Regarding the development of these sensory abilities, it was believed in earlier days that nothing like development of sensory abilities exists among the children before their birth and as a result the newborns cannot be expected to make sense of their world. However, the studies carried out in the area of child psychology and development have now clearly revealed that the developmental process of the sensory abilities goes out well in its own way even in the womb of the mother. Let us therefore try to see how the growth and development in all the sensory abilities proceeds gradually in developing children right from the conception in the womb of their mothers. However, what goes inside the womb of the mother in the name of development of sensory abilities can be identified properly by looking through the behavioural activities of the newborns. Therefore for the discussion of the outcomes of the development of sensory abilities in the prenatal period we will be using the yardstick of the type of sensory abilities visible in newborns.

Development of Vision or Sight

The sensory abilities concerning sight or vision is found to be least developed among developing children in their prenatal period. A number of key features of the eyes such as muscles of the lens, the cells of the retina and the optic nerve etc., are still immature at birth. They can make out objects or images that are close to their eyes, and on this account also they may be found to exhibit a quite blurry vision. That is why children are regarded as legally blind at the time of their birth. However, we may witness a quite positive sign of quick development of the visual sensory abilities among the newborns during infancy and afterwards in the manner described as follows:

- At birth, the newborn's **visual acuity** (the ability to see things in sharp detail) is estimated as ranging from 20/200 to 20/800 which means that he can see at 20 feet what an adult with normal vision could see at 400 or 800 feet. Regarding the use the visual acuity of newborns it is best at a distance of 8 to 14 inches. This poor state of the children's visual acuity, however, improves steadily as their eyes mature. It becomes 20/200 to 20/400 at the age of one month, and reaches 20/20 sometime in the second half of the first year.

- The visual ability of the children with regard to their **binocular vision** (the ability to combine information from both eyes for perceiving depth and motion), is also limited at birth but it also improves quickly as they cross the age of 3 to 4 months. Acquisition of this sensory ability carries a special importance to them once they become mobile and get engaged in activities such as crawling, walking, climbing, running, etc.

- The visual ability regarding the **perception of colour** is also limited among the newborns. They can distinguish between black, red, and white but not between white and other light colours. However, their colour perception ability improves with a lot of pace and as a result by the end of 3 months of age, infants can discriminate all the basis colours, and by the age of 4 months they become capable of grouping colours of slightly different shades in to distinct basic categories such as red, green, blue, yellow, orange purple and violet much like adults.

- One special feature regarding the development of the sense of sight or vision clearly visible among the children right from their birth is concerned with the demonstration of the **ability of visual preferences**. As emphasised by Arnett and Maynard (2017: 109), even shortly after birth they prefer patterns to random designs, curved over straight lines, three dimensional rather than two dimensional objects, and coloured over gray patterns. Above all they prefer human faces in comparison to any other patterns. This indicates that they are born with cells that are specialised to detect and prefer certain kinds of visual patterns. Moreover, neonates show a clear preference for images of human faces, and especially for the face of their mother and other caretakers. This ability concerning visual preferences also rapidly develops in the period of infancy.

- Although children from their very birth are found to be looking at the faces of people and having direct eye contact with the people around them, yet the **ability to extract the most relevant information from a face** is something that develops over infancy. In this connection where a one-month-old infant may be found to look at the periphery of faces, 2-month-old infants may be found to focus on the eyes for getting signals from others for getting or not getting close to them. This ability of this then gets further developed as they advance in their age and get feedback from their experiences on this account.

Development of Visual Ability After Infancy

Although the task of development of visual ability of the children gets completed by the beginning of their childhood in reference to the development of various capacities and activities of their sense of vision, yet it can't be termed as completely over. Maturation of brain as well as expanding experiences for visual encounter now play a key role in the development and fine functioning of the visual ability of developing children. It helps them in the better controlling of their eye movements, as well as getting focused on perceived objects, events and processing. What we term as the high order tasks requiring fine distinctive visual capacities on the part of individuals may then be carried out by a developing child in the later years of his development.

Development of Hearing Ability

The development of hearing ability among the children begins well for them in the womb of the mother before their birth in the shape of the development of hearing organs and availability of hearing experiences. The availability of the hearing experiences in the prenatal period to the developing foetus may exist in the form of voice of mother, father, family members and others, external sounds, talks and noises as well as internal sounds related to the mother's heart beat and sound of digestion, etc. The studies conducted and observations carried out of the movements of the developing foetuses provide a number of significant evidences of responding well to all such hearing experiences on the part of developing foetuses in the womb of the mother.

Besides this, studies conducted on newborns may be found to reveal that hearing becomes functional well in the prenatal period. They are in the capacity of recognising the sounds and voices heard by them in the womb especially related to their mother's voice or frequently repeated sounds or voices of their surroundings. It is therefore no surprise to see that most of the newborn babies show a preference for their mother's voice within the first 3 days of life. They even remember specifically what is told and repeated to them regularly by the mothers or someone else. We in India are quite familiar with the incidence quoted in our great Epic *Mahabharat* in which Abhimanyu (the son of the Great warrior Arjun) remembered well all what was told by his father to his pregnant mother regarding the art of "Chakra Vyooh Bhedan" in the capacity of a developing foetus in the womb of his mother. We also have quite a large number of scientific evidences nowadays for the confirmation of the learning made through the hearing ability of foetuses. In this connection, the authors Levine and Munsch (2004:197) have quoted in their text a study/experiment in the manner given below:

> In a well-known experiment mothers were assigned a story to read aloud twice a day to their unborn foetus during the last 6 weeks of their pregnancy. Within hours of their birth, the newborns were given a special pacifier. If the infants sucked on the pacifier in a certain way, they heard a recording of either their mother or another woman reading the assigned story, but if they sucked in a different way they could hear a recording of a different story. The researchers concluded that babies showed memory for what they had heard prenatally because they were more likely to suck the pacifier in the way that would produce the recording of the story they had heard prenatally.

The other things regarding the evidences of the development of hearing abilities among the children at their prenatal stage may also be revealed through the following types of behaviour demonstrated by neonates in the earlier days of their functioning.

- They are found to identify and recognise well the distinctive sounds and voices they heard in the womb.
- They are also found to have an innate sensitivity to human speech. Moreover here also they prefer their mother's voice to other women's voices and their mother's language to foreign language.
- Furthermore, neonates are born with preferences for particular sound combinations. Because they have had some practice of its hearing before birth.
- In addition to their language sensitivity, neonates show a very early sensitivity to music. It is why we may find newborns preferring musical sound in the form of lullabies in order to sleep.
- In the first few days of their life, newborns are found to turn their heads toward the source of a sound.

Development of Hearing Ability After Birth

The process of the development of hearing ability among the newborn children picks up a very good speed in their period of infancy just within 2 years of their birth after the necessary maturing of their hearing system in the manner as witnessed below.

- At the time of birth newborns are found to experience difficulty in terms of some confusion over the sounds localisation (telling where a sound is coming from). However, in the course of their first year development they may be found to reach adult levels of success in the attainment of the ability of sound localisation.

- At the time of their birth and also afterwards in their early infancy, children are not able to hear some soft sounds, and they are also unable to discriminate between the sounds having fine tuning, pitch, shrillness, etc. However, their ability in this regard gets momentum as they advance in their age in infancy and by the time they enter the age of childhood, they become capable of seeking a proper degree of satisfaction in the discrimination of different sounds in terms of their patterns and other acoustical characteristics.

- In the age of their infancy, children are also found to acquire the ability of making fine discriminations that their future understanding of language will require. Moreover, during this period they are also able to acquire the ability to discriminate one language from another. In this concern, it is found that by the age of four and half months, infants are able to discriminate their own names from other similar-sounding words, distinguish different people on the basis of voice and demonstrate a clear preference for some voices over others (Feldman, 2016: 137).

Although, hearing is more fully developed up to the end of infancy, yet there remains a quite significant scope for its further refinement in the coming years as a result of the further maturing of their brain and the varying hearing experiences encountered as they grow and develop in their age. It helps them in getting focused on the objects and events of hearing, and making use of their power of memorisation and information processing speed in a quite appropriate way for interpreting and encoding the information and all other auditory aspects available in a hearing encountered situation.

Development of the Sensory Ability of Touch

Developmental process of the sensory ability related to touch of the developing children also begins its journey right in the womb of their mothers. The ongoing researches and observations made of the children in the womb reveal that touch is the first and foremost sensory ability developed in children. As early as the second month following conception, the foetus responds to stroking at the side of the mouth (tested in naturally aborted foetuses). As the foetus grows this ability gets more developed to the extent that by 7 months after conception (i.e., 2 months before a full time birth) all the body parts of a developing foetus are found responding to touch. The truth of this fact can be further revealed to us through the behavioural activities exhibited on the part of neonates in the manner discussed as follows:

- Babies right from their birth have a quite reasonable sense of touch as a soothing means to them in the time of distress or otherwise. We may find they stop crying or feeling comfortable and happy while having skin to skin contact with the mother right from their birth.

- The infants, right from the time of their birth, are found to respond well with the touching of their mothers and other caretakers in the form of getting a massage for helping them in their proper physical and motor development.

- The neonates, right from their birth, are found to make use of their sensory ability of touch for exploring their environment. A newborn child knows much to sense a touch near the mouth in order to seek automatically his mother's or a feeding bottle's nipple to suck. At this stage he is also capable of making use of the sensibility of touch to identify and recognise familiar objects in his environment. He may reject the use of a feeding bottle's nipple and cry for breast feeding simply on the basis of getting habituated to the touch of the mother's breast and nipples.

- The neonates are also capable of making use of their sensory ability of touch in reaching, grasping or catching hold of things for their exploration and use. Within the first year of their birth, babies begin to use their sense of touch to explore objects — first with their lips and mouth, and later with their hands. So touch is a primary means by which infants acquire knowledge about their environment, which contributes so crucially to their earlier cognitive development (Piaget, 1960).

- Touching is important for relations between children and adults. A hand placed on the newborn's chest can quiet a crying episode, and gentle stroking can soothe even premature babies. Moreover, neonates are also found to make use of their sensory ability of touch for their needed socio-cultural development in future. Body touch is said to stimulate the production of certain chemicals or triggers like responses in the brain of the developing children for helping them to getting closer and acquiring intimacy with their near and dear, caretakers, and acquaintances and also for remaining away from strangers for their safety and survival.

Development of the Sensory Ability of Taste

Like touch, taste is also found to be well developed during the prenatal period in the womb of the mother. The related evidences in this regard are very much available in the taste preferences shown by newborns and babies for drinks and foods taken by them for their nourishment and survival. They show preferences for their mother's milk and local food taken by their mother and family members. It happens for the reason, that as foetuses they have been conditioned to the taste of such food well in the womb of the mother. Amniotic fluid that foetuses float in has the flavour of whatever the mother has recently eaten, and the nourishment they get for their survival and development in the womb is only available for them with the type of foods taken by the mothers during their pregnancy. It is therefore no surprise that as infants they have a total preference for the taste and flavour in the food and drinks they experienced at the prenatal stage particularly at the later months of their prenatal stage. This fact has been well investigated and established through well-established researches. In one of the studies quoted by Feldman (2016:138) in his text, it was found that the women who drank carrot juice while pregnant had children who had the preference for taking foods and drinks having the taste of carrots.

In addition to showing an early preference for whatever is familiar to them from the time of their existence in the womb, neonates have a variety of innate responses to taste in the manner given as follows:

- Infants are born with some very definite taste preferences. For example, they apparently prefer sweets tastes over bitter or sour ones. It becomes quite apparent with the observations such as: (i) Both full-term and premature babies are found to show pleasure and suck faster and longer for sweet liquids than for bitter, sour, salty or neutral (water) solutions and (ii) If they taste something biter or sour, they at once leave it and are also found to display facial expression of disgust and displeasure.

- As neonates and infants children are fully capable of distinguishing and differentiating between different tastes and also elicit different facial expressions for responding to these tastes. Emphasising well on this fact Shaffer and Kipp, (2007:171) write:

Sweets reduce crying and produce smiles and smacking of the lips, whereas sour substances cause infants to wrinkle their noses and purse their lips. Bitter solutions often elicit expression of disgust — a down turning of the corners of the mouth, tongue protrusions, and even spitting. These facial expressions become more pronounced as solutions become sweeter, much sour, or more bitter, suggesting that newborns can discriminate different concentrations of a particular taste.

- It is true that in the beginning newborns show their absolute preference for sweet taste over salty and other mixed tastes. It is perhaps for this reason that the milk they suck from the nipples of the mother or bottles is sweet in taste and moreover in the beginning they are also provided food that is sweetened. However, as they grow in age and get exposed to a variety of foods and drinks, they may be found to develop tastes for salty, sour, bitter and mixed ones. For example, where as a baby in early infancy a child is found to totally reject any food or drink that is not sweet in taste, after growing a little more in age the same infant may be seen to show liking for salty, sour or mixed taste foods and drinks.
- The ability and capacity of a child with regard to the sensory ability of taste is further strengthened and enhanced as they mature in terms of development of their brain and are exposed to a wide variety of tastes in their foods and drinks in their social and cultural surroundings.

Development of the Sensory Ability of Smell

Much like taste, the sensory ability of smell is found to be reasonably developed among children during the prenatal period. After spending a long period in the womb of the mother in their prenatal development, the children get conditioned to the smell or odour of amniotic fluid in which they have been living at that time. This odour or smell has a direct association with: (i) the milk produced by the glands of their mothers, (ii) the chemical reactions and odour of the foods and drinks that mothers usually or heavily take in their day-to-day diet and (iii) the body smell or odour of the mother. Due to such conditioning, the ability as well preferences for the smell or odour of the newborns is found to be automatically guided by what is familiar to them during their prenatal period in the womb. Therefore, it is no surprise to find neonates showing preference for the milk and specially the milk from the breast of their mothers containing the smell or odour experienced by them in the womb.

In addition to showing an early preference for whatever is familiar from the womb, neonates have a variety of innate responses to smell such as their strong likings and preferences for the pleasant and fair smells over the unpleasant and foul ones. If they smell something unpleasant or foul, their noses crinkle up, their forehead wrinkle, and they are seen showing a displeased expression.

In addition to the use of familiar experiences and innate preferences, we may find that neonates quickly engage in the task of the development of their sensory ability of smell as visible in their day-to-day behaviour as follows:

- After birth and from the earlier days of their life, neonates begin to discriminate between the various smells surrounding them. Where, at two days after birth, breast feeding neonates show no difference in response between their mother's breast smell and the breast smell of another lactating mother, they may be found to get oriented more toward their mother's smell only at the age of 4 days.

- Rapidly, in the coming days the newly growing babies of 12 to 18 days old become able to distinguish their mothers on the basis of smell alone. In this concern in the beginning, (i) they recognise and discriminate their mothers from other women by the smell of their breast and underarms. It becomes possible for the babies on account of the possession of a unique characteristic known as "olfactory signature" a characteristic odour that babies can use as an early means of identifying their closest companions (Shaffer and Kipp, 2007:172), and (ii) then afterwards become able to distinguish their mothers on the basis of the scent of clothes they are wearing.

- In the coming days the developing infants are found to become able of distinguishing and discriminating between the varieties of odours, and reacting vigorously in positive and negative ways to any pleasant and unpleasant smell or odour.

The task of developing sensory ability of smell, like other sensory abilities, is almost complete for children in their period of infancy. However, like other developmental characteristics it continues for its further refinement and enhancement with the development of the brain and the exposure available to the developing children for using their sense of smell.

Summary

The process of sensory or perceptual development is well concerned with the discussion of the process of growth and development of the abilities and capacities being demonstrated on the part of children right from the time of their conception through the use and application of the human senses such as senses of sight or vision, hearing, touch, taste and smell.

The sensory abilities concerning sight or vision are found to be least developed among developing children in their prenatal period. At birth, a newborn's visual acuity is best at a distance of 8 to 14 inches. This poor state of the children's visual acuity, however, improves steadily as their eyes mature. The visual ability of children with regard to their **binocular vision** (the ability to combine information from both eyes for perceiving depth and motion), as well as perception of colour is also limited at birth but it improves quickly as they cross the age of 3 to 4 months. One special feature regarding the development of the sense of sight or vision clearly visible among children right from their birth is concerned with the demonstration of the ability of visual preferences such as a clear preference for images of human faces, and especially for the face of their mother and other caretakers. All such abilities concerning the visual perception among children may be seen to be almost developed to the required strengths among children up to the beginning of childhood. However, at a later stage, with the maturation of their brain and exposure to the expanded experiences, they gain better control and focus of their eye movements that enable them to perform high order tasks requiring fine distinctive visual capacities with accuracy.

The development of hearing ability among children begins well for them in the womb of the mother before their birth in the shape of the development of hearing organs and availability of hearing experiences. The newborns are found to recognise the sounds and voices heard by them in the womb especially related to their mother's voice or frequently repeated sounds or voices of their surroundings. In the first few days of their life, newborns are found to turn their heads toward the source of a sound providing proof for their capability of hearing. The development of hearing ability among the newborns picks up at a very good speed in their period of infancy just within 2 years of their birth after the necessary maturing of their hearing system to the adult level almost. After infancy, it also goes on improving as a result of the further maturing of their brain and encountering varying hearing experiences as they grow and develop in age.

Touch is the first and foremost sensory ability developed in children. As early as the second month following conception, the foetus has been found responding to stroking at the side of the mouth. After their birth, newborns are found to be quite comfortable and happy while having skin to skin contact with the mother or feeling the touch of breast feeding/ bottle feeding. After then, within a few days of their birth, they may be found to make use of the sensibility of their touch in identifying, reaching, grasping or catching hold of things for their exploration and use (in the sequence of first using their lips and mouths and later on their hands). With their advance in age, children become more sensible and capable of using their sensory ability of touch in identifying, recognising and exploring things lying in their environment, developing a relationship and intimacy with their near and dear, caretakers, and acquaintances, and also for staying away from strangers for their safety, and survival.

Like touch, **taste** is found to be well developed during the prenatal period in the womb of the mother. It is therefore no surprise that as infants they have a total preference for the taste and flavour in the food and drinks they experienced at the prenatal stage particularly at the later months of their mother's pregnancy. Besides this, as neonates and infants the children are fully capable of distinguishing and differentiating between different tastes and also elicit different facial expressions for responding to these tastes. It is true that in the beginning newborns infants show their absolute preference for sweet taste over salty and other mixed tastes, but as they grow in age and get exposed to a variety of foods and drinks, they may be found to develop tastes for salty, sour, bitter and mixed ones. The ability and capacity of the children with regard to the sensory ability of taste is further strengthened and enhanced as they mature in terms of the development of their brain and are exposed to a wide variety of tastes in their foods and drinks.

Much like the taste, the **sensory ability of smell** is found to be reasonably developed among children during the prenatal period. Therefore, it is no surprise to find neonates showing preference for milk and especially milk from the breast of their mothers that contains the smell or odour experienced by them in their mother's womb. In addition to showing an early preference for whatever is familiar from the womb, neonates have a variety of innate responses to smell such as their strong likings and preferences for the pleasant and fair smells over the unpleasant and foul ones. As a matter of further development, small babies begin to use their sensory ability of smell for discriminating between the various objects, and people surrounding them. Afterwards, they begin to make its use in distinguishing and discrimination between the varieties of odours, and reacting vigorously in positive and negative ways to pleasant and unpleasant smells or odours. The task of developing sensory ability of smell, like other sensory abilities, gets almost complete as children complete their period of infancy. However, like other developmental characteristics it also gets continued for its further refinement and enhancement with the development of the brain and the exposure available to them for using this sense of smell.

References and Suggested Readings

Arnett, Jeffrey Jensen & Maynard, Ashley E. (2017), *Child Development: A Cultural Approach* (2nd edition), Boston: Pearson.

Berk, Laura E. (2009), *Child Development* (Eighth edition), Boston: Pearson Education

Berk, L.E., (2012), *Young Children: Pre-natal through Middle Adulthood*, New York: Allyn & Bacon.

Feldman, Robert S. (2016), *Child Development* (7th edition), Boston: Sage

Levine, Laura E. and Munsch Joyce (2014**)**, *Child Development- An Active Learning Approach*, (2nd edition), Los Angeles: Sage

Piaget, J. (1960), *Psychology of Intelligence*, Patterson, NJ: Littlefield, Adams.

Shaffer, David R. and Kipp, K. (2007), *Developmental Psychology-Childhood and Adolescence*, (7th ed.), Canada: Thomson/Wadsworth.

11

Mental or Cognitive Development

Meaning of The Term Mental Or Cognitive Development

In chapter seven, we saw how the mechanism of physical growth and development brings desirable changes in the internal as well as external body organs of an individual in order to increase his physical skills and strength. This development enables him to do physical work and play games he could not when younger. Similarly, a child at the time of his birth or in early childhood cannot be expected to perform such tasks that require high mental abilities. As he advances in his age, his mental abilities and capacities gradually develop and he is able to solve the problems he could not when younger. *The growth and development of the mental abilities and capacities which helps an individual to adjust his behaviour to the ever-changing environmental conditions or to enable him to accomplish a task that needs complex cognitive abilities is referred to as mental or cognitive development.*

Actually, the process of mental growth and development is responsible for the development of an Individual's - all cognitive, mental or intellectual abilities like sensation, perception, imagination, memory, reasoning, understanding, intelligence, generalisation, interpretation, language ability, conceptual ability, problem-solving ability and decision-making ability. These abilities are interrelated and never develop in isolation. Therefore, mental development of an individual at any stage of his development includes the overall development of these abilities.

Various Areas or Aspects Of Mental Development

As mentioned earlier, mental or intellectual development takes into consideration the development of various mental abilities and capacities. How these abilities grow and develop from birth onwards is an interesting as well as a useful thing to know. Though the development in the areas of various abilities proceeds simultaneously and is continuous, yet the studies have revealed possibility of the differences in the rate of overall mental development at various ages. Similarly, it has also been noted that there is a personality of greater growth and development in one aspect or area of mental activity than in other at one or the other stage of life.

As far as the general characteristics or trends of mental growth and development at various stages are concerned, we will discuss it in Chapter 18 of this text. However, in the following pages we will try to discuss the changes and development in some of the important mental abilities or aspects of mental power of a small child as he grows older and older.

Sensation and Perception

Both sensation and perception are considered important aspects of one's mental development. Sensations are elementary impressions gathered by sense organs. When these impressions are interpreted and some definite meanings are attached to them, they take the form of perception.

In the beginning, a child lacks in sensation as well as in perception. His sense organs are not developed. As a result, he cannot discriminate between things and understand their meanings. Focusing the eye towards the lamp, bright coloured objects, etc., can be said to be the beginning of an infant's perceptual growth. Later on, he distinguishes people from objects and then familiar people from strangers and in this way his environment gradually becomes differentiated into perceived objects. These perceived objects later on become associated with a verbal sound that he is able to recognise when heard.

When he becomes able to use his sense organs, he becomes increasingly conscious of the things around him and begins to ask a series of questions such as why, what and who. At this point he has a poor perception of space, time, form, movement and distance. For example, due to lack of perception of the size of distant objects, the train, when viewed from a distance, may appear to him as a toy train.

But gradually, his ability of perception gets developed. As the individual passes through the years of his adolescence, the sensory acuity reaches almost its peak and perceptual patterns become most organised and refined. His perceptions now become more definite, rich and detailed which are now beginning to be influenced by his beliefs, opinions, ideas, etc., besides his needs, interests and mental sets. They now need not necessarily be associated with concrete objects.

Concept Formation

Acquiring conception is another important aspect of the child's mental development. A concept is the generalised meaning that is attached to an object or idea. It is the result of one's perceptual experiences and involves both discrimination and generalisation.

Discrimination begins early in life. Sometimes, the child tries to generalise his perceptual experiences and thus begins to acquire concepts. Experience is a great factor in concept formation. In early childhood, the concrete experiences in the form of actual objects help the child in the formation of concepts. He tries to develop various concepts from direct experiences.

In the later period, vicarious experiences offered by reading, watching movies, attending lectures, etc., also provide the base for concept formation. In the later years, not only new concepts are formed, the old concepts may also get a new shape. They may be broadened, developed or the wrong concepts can be altogether abandoned. Normally during development concepts go from abstract to concrete to vague to clear and from inexact to definite, depending on the type of experiences one receives as one grows older.

In this way, the concepts of the child in the beginning are characterised by vagueness, indefiniteness and inadequacy. For example, the child has very poor time concepts. As Crow and Crow put it, *"Time as such means little to the young child. He cannot distinguish among 'today', 'tomorrow' and 'next week' except as they represent words rather than actual duration of time."* (1969, p. 73)

Development of Language

Development of language adds to the mental growth and development of an individual. The growth and development in speech, vocabulary, length of response are some of the important aspects of language development.

At birth, the child can only utter some crying sounds. By the age of one and a little later, he may learn to speak a few words. After that spoken vocabulary increases rapidly. Much of the speech pattern that the child learns is the result of imitation of others in the environment. During the course of learning to speak, it is possible that certain speech disorders like omissions, stuttering, stammering, etc., may develop. Therefore, the parents as well as the teachers of small children must remain very cautious about this.

The vocabulary of children in the beginning is too limited. There is continuous increase in the size of one's vocabulary during childhood. Later on as the result of environmental needs and opportunities in learning, the vocabulary develops. Maintenance of the past and addition of new words in one's vocabulary may continue even till the period of old age depending upon one's reading habit and interests.

In addition to the change in vocabulary and speech, the pattern of giving responses also changes with age. In early childhood the child's responses are characterised by the one-word response. Also, generally, he uses more nouns than other forms of language. Later, he gradually begins to use descriptive words like adjectives and adverbs and his responses include a large variety of words and almost every form of sentence structure.

Development of Memory

Memory is also an important aspect of mental development. At birth, there is little memory; but, gradually with maturation and experiences memory increases. The developmental schedule, as discussed by Hurlock and Schwartz, indicates that *"Memory of an impressionistic kind appears in the first half of the year and instances of true remembrance appear by the end of the first year. During the first year, memory is only aroused by sensory stimuli. With the learning of speech, the child is able to remember ideally by the end of the second year. During the first and second years, the memory is stronger for persons and objects than for situation. During early childhood, from 3 to 6 years, situations become significant factors in the child's memory. Also, the emotional quality of the impressions influences memory. By 2 years the child can recount the story heard a few days ago and he can also give information about past experiences."* (Kuppuswamy, 1964, p. 98).

Therefore, a child shows signs of memory from early childhood. The memory which the child possesses in his young age, is generally a rote memory. He enjoys repetition and seldom uses logic and insight in memorising a thing. During later childhood and adolescence, the memory tends to function more logically and a selection process of remembering and forgetting begins to operate. In the later years of childhood, memory tends to decrease. But the age from which the downfall begins, is difficult to say with certainty. It varies from individual to individual and generally besides the age and health, the situation and stimuli which are associated with a particular kind of memory significantly affects its remembrance or forgetting.

Development of Problem-Solving Ability

Problem-solving ability is an important constituent of mental development. An individual needs this type of ability in discovering the solution of the problems. Therefore, problem-solving ability depends upon the development of thinking and reasoning. Thinking and reasoning powers begin to grow as early as two and a half or three years. However, reasoning at this stage is confined to concrete and personal things from the child's immediate environment. A younger child deals more easily with the concrete than with the abstract. We cannot expect him to solve complicated problems which require abstract thinking and more developed reasoning. But gradually, he shows an increase in the ability to deal with abstract as he grows older. He begins to compare and evaluate ideas and solve problems through the utilisation of verbal symbols and imaginary concepts.

It can be drawn from this discussion that in the beginning, children should be provided with simple realistic problems depending on concrete situations and related to their own experiences and environment so that they can solve them with insight and understanding. As they grow older, more complicated problems requiring abstract thinking and widened experiences may be given to them. In this way children should gradually be made to increase their problem-solving ability.

In addition to these aspects, the other aspects of mental growth and development include attention, imagination, decision making and ability of interpretation, etc. Like other aspects they also change, grow and mature with the increase in age due to maturation and learning.

Factors Affecting Mental Growth and Development

Mental growth and development is controlled by both hereditary and environmental factors. An individual's mental abilities, at any age of his life, are the products of his heredity and environment. For a child what he gets from his ancestral stock through his immediate parents at the time of conception in terms of mental traits or characteristics and mental apparatus is in fact a valuable asset to his future mental growth and development. But the environment which he gets afterwards for the development of these innate mental abilities is no less significant. The social and cultural experiences, learning opportunities and education which he avails for the developmental process as he advances in age, contribute significantly towards his mental growth and development.

In fact, maturation and learning are responsible for controlling the process of mental growth and development. Maturation helps in achieving physical growth and development which in turn affects the process of mental growth and development. Brain and the nervous system play a significant role in this direction. At birth, the brain and the nerves that lead to it are not fully developed. They grow and develop rapidly after birth and mature in due course. As the nervous system advances toward maturity, the mental powers of the child also go on developing. Therefore, organic growth of the nervous system is the basic factor in mental development.

Learning in the form of experiences and education helps the developmental process and in fact intensifies it to reach its optimum level. It is said to play the same part as exercises play in developing physical skills and power as Sorenson puts it — *"A child's legs, arms and body are made stronger by healthful play. We can deduce that the mind with its organic counter-part, the nervous system, improves and becomes better equipped because of use and exercise in the form of reading, calculating, memorizing, speaking, imagining and other mental activities."* (1948, p. 32).

Cessation of Mental Growth

At what age does the increase in mental growth cease is a controversial question. Mental growth is a complex process. There is no universal pattern of mental growth for all individuals. Neither is the pattern same for all mental functions or abilities. Therefore, it is difficult to tell the age at which mental growth, with all its aspects, will cease to grow. Actually, the age of cessation of mental growth varies with different individuals and with different mental functions or abilities.

Psychologists have tried to give various ages ranging from 13 to the early 20s or even a much later age after which there is no further mental growth. The variation in the results is due to the fact they have worked on different groups and used different tests of mental ability. Despite such differences in opinion, Sorenson has tried to arrive at some conclusion regarding the age of cessation of mental growth. He writes:

"It is probably safe to conclude that a person reaches his maximum mental level at about the age of twenty or perhaps a little before or a little after twenty. It is true that on the average there is only a little mental growth during the late teens — nevertheless this small amount may be very important." (1948, p.44)

Therefore, the age of cessation of mental growth can be estimated as 20 or little before or a little after 20. But now the question again arises: Does the development of mental capacity or power also cease with the cessation of mental growth at the age of about 20?

In this connection, latest researches have shown that development in mental power and capacity does not necessarily stop with the cessation of mental growth. In most of the cases, the mental power or capacity reaches its maximum in the mid 30s. But whatever changes after the natural mental growth occur in the mental abilities of capacities, are definitely the result of learning, experience and education. After attaining their maximum height, mental capacity declines gradually but can be maintained effectively even in the old age by those who keep their minds alert and active.

Significance and Implications of The Knowledge About Mental Development

The knowledge of the trend of mental growth and the subsequent changes in the various mental abilities is of great use for all of us who are associated with the task of helping the children in their cognitive or mental development in one or the other ways. Briefly, we can summarise this utility as follows:

1. It can help them in the selection of curricular and co-curricular experiences at various age levels.

2. It can also help them to arrange learning situations, and decide methods and techniques of teaching, training and providing suitable learning experiences to the children suitable for their desired development.

3. It can also help them bring appropriate reading and audio-visual material as per the intellectual growth and development of children at different age levels.

4. It makes them conscious that a particular type of work or activity which needs some or the other developed mental abilities, needs to be introduced when the age of acquiring that approaches. We must not be too hasty to give him a particular piece of knowledge to train him in a particular act if the mental abilities required for that knowledge or act have not been acquired by the child. Definitely, in such cases, we should wait for the ripe stage.

5. Proper understanding of the pattern of mental growth, can lead elders to help the children in acquiring their maximum mental capacity and power. In light of such knowledge children can be given training in problem solving and creative expression. Also, they can be helped in the development of their logical understanding for taking them to intelligent learning in place of mechanical fumbling and parrot-like cramming. Their ability of using language, perception and ability to interpret and generalisation can also be developed through the natural course of their mental growth and development pattern.

In this way, knowledge related to the process of growth and development of the children can be utilised for leading the children to acquire their maximum mental capacities and powers and help them to use these intelligently and judiciously for their own welfare as well as that of the society.

Piaget's and Bruner's Theory of Cognitive Development

How do the children become capable of exercising their cognitive skills as they grow and develop? How does cognitive development, related to the process of change in the ways of thinking, reasoning and problem solving, etc., among children, take place among the different ages and stages of their developmental period? Such questions have been answered by the psychologists through their view points, named as theories of cognitive development. For this purpose, here we would like to focus on two important theories, namely, Piaget's Theory of Cognitive Development and Bruner's Theory of Cognitive Development.

Piaget's Theory of Cognitive Development

Jean Piaget, a Swiss biologist who later turned into a cognitive and child psychologist is known well for providing a stage theory of cognitive development for explaining the development of thinking in human beings from infancy to adulthood.

So keen was his interest in the study of cognitive and child psychology that he along with his wife (a former student of his at the Rousseau Institute) devoted almost all the precious years of their early married life to studying the cognitive development of their own three children by making them the subjects of their laboratory studies. As a result, today his theory of cognitive development has no parallel in the history of research in the field of developmental, cognitive and child psychology. For understanding this theory concerning the stages of cognitive development, let us first try to understand the major theoretical premise on which the theory stands.

Piaget's Theoretical Notions

Piaget designed a proper framework to understand the structure, functioning and development of the cognitive network of the human mind. He postulated that, like physical organs of the human body, there are two aspects of the human mind: one is referred to as cognitive structure and the other as cognitive functioning.

Jean Piaget (1896-1980)

Cognitive Structure

Unlike other creatures, a human baby is born with a few practical instincts and reflexes such as sucking, looking, reaching and grasping. Therefore, the initial cognitive structure of infants is supposed to incorporate only those cognitive abilities or potentials which help them to do such acts such as look, reach out or grasp. Piaget named these abilities or potentials as *schemas* and termed them as the basic building blocks of our thinking. He defined them as the organised systems of actions or thought that allow us to mentally represent or 'think about' the objects and events in our world (Woolfolk, 2004, p.30). Let us try to understand the meaning conveyed by the term 'schema' more clearly by referring to a particular schema like the 'sucking schema'. It refers to one's general cognitive ability or potential to suck objects. This schema is more than a single manifestation of the sucking reflex. It can be thought of as a cognitive structure that makes all acts of sucking possible. However, the description of this act of sucking differs in relation to contents, i.e., specific responses to specific stimuli such as the mother's nipple, a spoon, a toy, etc. We thus conclude that a schema represents a unit of one's cognitive structure in the shape of a general potential to perform a particular class of behaviours (like sucking, grasping, calculating, etc.), the content of which is related to the conditions that prevail during any particular manifestation of that general potential.

The various schemas with their contents thus form the basic structure of the human mind. The earlier schemas represent those reflexes and instincts that are biologically inherited. However, as a child grows, with the interaction of physical and social environment, he is able to form different schemas, resulting in changes and modifications in his cognitive structure.

Cognitive Functioning

The structure of an organism is said to play a decisive role in its functioning. Therefore, what is available to an individual in terms of his schemas decides how he is going to respond to the stimuli present in his physical or social environment. On the other hand, an individual has to adapt to his environment for survival as well as proper growth and development. The key to his cognitive development thus lies in his constant interaction with an adaptation to his physical and social environment. The task of such adaptation is carried out through the processes of assimilation and accommodation.

Assimilation refers to a kind of matching between the already existing cognitive structures and the environmental needs as they arise. In a situation where a six-month-old infant is given a new toy it is likely to respond by putting the toy in his mouth. This is assimilation, as what the child did was to assimilate, incorporate or fit ideas about the new toy into already existing cognitive structures about old toys. His cognitive structure about old toys revolved around the sucking schema, therefore, he at once responded by performing the act of sucking.

Now, in case the new toy is too big to be picked up and placed in the mouth, it will certainly need a change or modification in the already existing cognitive structure. The child will have to change his old ways of thinking and behaving in order to adapt or adjust to the new situation. Consequently, now instead of sucking, the child may respond by pushing or grasping the toy. This is called accommodation as one tries to accommodate or adjust to new ways of thinking and behaving in place of assimilating or behaving in the same old fashion. Thus, whereas in the process of assimilation, one's responses are supposed to bank upon one's past experiences and already compiled stock of information, in the process of accommodation one has to learn new ways of thinking and behaving by making changes or modifications in one's existing cognitive structure. For instance, when a child is offered milk in a tumbler instead of the feeding bottle, first he tries his old way of behaving, i.e., sucking. Afterwards, as a result of accommodation he picks up the new ways and consequently makes the necessary modification in his old cognitive structure.it will certainly need a change or modification in the already existing cognitive structure. The child will have to change his old ways of thinking and behaving in order to adapt or adjust to the new situation. Consequently, now instead of sucking, the child may respond by pushing or grasping the toy. This is called accommodation as one tries to accommodate or adjust to new ways of thinking and behaving in place of assimilating or behaving in the same old fashion. Thus, whereas in the process of assimilation, one's responses are supposed to bank upon one's past experiences and already compiled stock of information, in the process of accommodation one has to learn new ways of thinking and behaving by making changes or modifications in one's existing cognitive structure. For instance, when the child is offered milk in a tumbler instead of the feeling bottle, first he tries his old way of behaving, i.e., sucking. Afterwards, as a result of accommodation he picks up the new ways and consequently makes the necessary modification in his old cognitive structure."

Parallel to the concept of the processes of assimilation and accommodation linked with the process of the child's cognitive development, Piaget postulated the concept of equilibration. He asserted that the process of assimilation or accommodation helps an organism to adjust or maintain a harmonious relationship between himself and his environment. This adjustment mechanism was called equilibration by Piaget. It can be defined as an innate tendency or continuous drive on the part of an organism to organise its experiences (through assimilation or accommodation) for obtaining optimal adaptation to the changing demands of its environment by maintaining a proper balance between its cognitive structure and the changing demands of its environment. In fact, it is the need of seeking optimal adaptation or maintaining a balance between himself and his environment that makes an individual feel uncomfortable and start reorganising his cognitive structure for equipping himself with new ways of thinking and behaving.Piaget postulated the concept of equilibration. He asserted that the process of assimilation or accommodation helps the organism to adjust or maintain a harmonious relationship between himself and his environment. This adjustment mechanism was called equilibration by Piaget. It can be defined as an innate tendency or continuous drive on the part of an organism to organise its experiences (through assimilation or accommodation

In this way Piaget highlighted the role of the following factors in one's cognitive make-up and its functioning:

1. The biologically inherited reflexes and mental dispositions as the fundamental cognitive structure.
2. The changes and development brought about in the cognitive structure through maturation (i.e., the process of natural growth).
3. The changes and development in the cognitive structure brought about through experiences (interaction with the physical and social environment) involving the processes of assimilation, accommodation and equilibration.

Stages of Intellectual Development

As already pointed out, Piaget, on account of his biological background, traced the initiation of human cognitive development in terms of biologically inherited ways of interacting with the environment. He further postulated that the changes and developments in one's cognitive structure are brought about by interaction with one's physical and social environment. This task is carried out through the mechanism of equilibration, resulting in constant organisation of one's cognitive structure by the interplay of accommodation and assimilation. This task of constant organisation of the mental structure is an individual phenomenon; we may, therefore, find wide differences between children in terms of possession of cognitive abilities. However, as Piaget concluded, this organisation of the mental structure in all children always takes place in a particular order involving definite stages of intellectual development. Thus, although children of the same age may differ in terms of possession of mental abilities, the order, in which the abilities evolve, and the pattern of development are quite constant and universal. Let us discuss this pattern of intellectual development in terms of the following four developmental stages suggested by Piaget:

Sensori-motor Stage (From birth to about 2 years)

Piaget called the first stage of intellectual development the sensori-motor stage because (a) it is characterised by the absence of language, and (b) it is limited to direct sensory and motor interactions with the environment. The cognitive development at this stage occurs along the following pattern:

1. At birth the infant exhibits a limited number of uncoordinated reflexes such as sucking, looking, reaching and grasping.
2. During the next four months the uncoordinated reflexes are coordinated into simple schemas providing the child with a general potential to perform certain

classes of behaviour. For example, the infant now tries to suck anything which is put into his mouth, stares at whatever he sees, reaches for everything and grasps all that is put into his hands.

3. By the age of 8 months the infant is able to react to objects outside the self. He begins to realise that the objects around him are separated from himself and they have their independent and permanent existence. Prior to such development, his view of the environmental objects is quite transitory, i.e., what is out of sight is purely out of mind. For example, if the infant is playing with a toy and you pick it up, hide it somewhere while allowing the child to watch your act of hiding the toy, he will at once forget about it. For him the toy placed under a blanket or hidden somewhere has disappeared and is no more. With the passage of time, gradually the concept of object permanence evolves in the cognitive structure of the infant. He begins to realise that the objects continue to exist even though he cannot see or experience them. Thus he begins to search for the objects that are hidden. For example, if you hide a toy in the blanket the infant will try to lift the blanket and search for the toy. In case you have shifted it somewhere, he will proceed to investigate its whereabouts under the assumption that the object has its permanent identity. When he does so we may infer that the child has been able to see or experience the object in his mind by making its mental image. Now he can proceed to the next stage of intellectual development involving the symbolic world of language by leaving behind the pure sensory or motor exploration.

4. Another significant achievement for the child of sensory motor stage according to Piaget is that by the end of the period of infancy he may step into logical goal-directed actions. Throwing light on this aspect Woolfolk (2004) writes *"Think of the familiar container toy for babies. It is usually plastic, has a lid, and contains several colourful items that can be dumped out and replaced. A six month old baby is likely to become frustrated trying to get to the toys inside. An older child who has mastered the basics of the sensori-motor stage will probably be able to deal with the toy in an orderly fashion by building a 'container toy' scheme, (1) get the lid off (2) turn the container upside down, (3) shake if the items jam, (4) watch the items fall. Later on the child is also soon able to reverse this action by refilling the container"* (p. 32-33).

Pre-operational stage (about 2 to 7 years)

While stepping into this stage, the child begins to replace direct action in the form of sensory or motor exploration with symbols. The learning of the language provides him with a good tool for thinking. He begins to utter words to ask for something rather than just reaching out to get it. In addition to words, his thinking is also characterised by other symbolic representations or images of the things in the environment. This stage can be further sub-divided into: (1) the pre-conceptual phase (approximately two to four years) and (2) the intuitive phase (approximately four to seven years).

1. **Pre-conceptual phase:** This is the period of the rudimentary concept formation and is characterised by the following features:

(a) In the early part of this stage, the children seem to identify objects by their names and put them into certain classes. However, they usually make mistakes in this process of identification and concept formation. For example, they think all men are 'daddy', all women are 'mummy' and all dogs are 'montu'.

(b) Their mode of thinking and reasoning is quite illogical at this stage. It is neither inductive nor deductive but rather transductive in nature. For example, the child at this stage would reason like: as "cows are big animals with four legs and a long tail, this animal is also big and has four legs and a long tail, therefore it is a cow".

(c) Their thinking is sometimes too imaginative and far removed from reality. It may be seen in their play activities when a block of wood is turned into a riding horse or motor cycle and a doll into a baby. Moreover, at this stage they are unable to distinguish between living and non-living objects. For them the doll in their hands is a live baby who can cry, smile and sleep. Similarly the dreams they have are, for them, real and concrete events.

(d) The other major characteristic of the cognitive structure of the child at this stage is concerned with his egocentric nature. By egocentric Piaget means that the child can see the world only from his own standpoint. He considers that the sun and moon are following him, the rain falls to delight him, and obviously what exists in the external environment is specifically meant for him. He cannot think that people may have different opinions and differ in their modes of thinking and conclusions. He considers himself as the centre of a world of people who are supposed to perceive the things the way he does.

2. **Intuitive phase (approximately 4 to 7 years):** At this stage the child progresses towards the formation of various concepts at a more advanced level. For example, now he will agree that apples, oranges and bananas are all fruits despite the difference in their shape, colour or taste. But what he thinks or solves at this stage is carried out intuitively, rather than in accordance with any logical rule. Consequently, as Piaget concludes, the child's thinking at this stage is not logical and is full of contradictions. It is clearly reflected in the absence in him of the two main cognitive characteristics namely, reversibility (ability to reverse) and conservation (ability to see an object as permanent even though its arrangement or appearance is changed as long as nothing is added or taken away).

For example when a child realises that not only has he a brother but his brother also has a brother in him, it can be said that the child has developed the reversible quality in his cognitive operations. However, at the pre-operational stage children are seen not to possess the reversible characteristic in their mental functioning. For them moving from point A to B may not carry the same meaning as moving from point B to A.

Similarly, the thinking of pre-operational children at the intuitive stage is marked by an inability to conserve in terms of quantity as well as number as may be understood through the following experiments:

Experiment No. 1. A child belonging to the pre-operational age say five years old is shown two identical containers filled with the same quantity of coloured water. The child will agree that both have the same amount. Now the experimenter pours the water from one of the containers into a taller but narrower container and asks the child to compare the amount of water in this taller container with the amount in one of the old containers.

The inability to conserve in terms of quantity makes the child think that there is more water in the taller container even when the child has observed that the same amount of water has been poured into it (see Figure 11.1). The child in this experiment is likely to say that the taller container has more water because the level of the water is higher in this container. According to Piaget this happens because the child at this stage fails to realise that the amount or quantity of a material does not change with the change in the shape or appearance of its container. In other words, the child belonging to the pre-operational stage shows a marked inability to conserve continuous quantity.

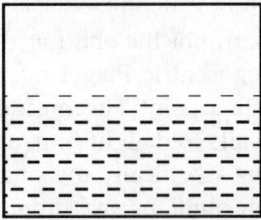

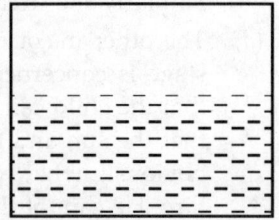

Experimental stage-1 (Two containers of the same shape and size)

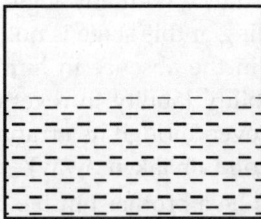

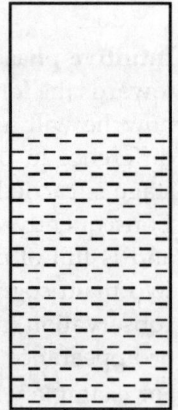

Experimental stage-2 (Containers differing in size and shape)

Fig.11.1.Experiment demonstrating inability for conservation in terms of quantity

Experiment No. 2. A child is shown two sets of beads arranged in one-to-one correspondence. The child is asked if the beads in the two rows are equal in number. The child would say that they are. The beads in one row are then spaced further apart (or spaced closer together) and the child is then asked to tell which row has more beads.ÿÿÿÿÿÿÿÿÿÿDÿ

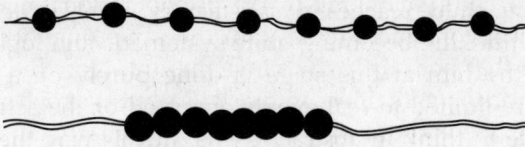

Fig. 11.2.Experiment demonstrating inability for conservation in terms of number

Here with reference to Figure 11.2 the child belonging to the pre-operational stage is likely to say that the bottom row has more beads. What leads the child to think in such an illogical manner? The answer according to Piaget lies in the fact that the concept of the conservation of numbers is not yet developed in the child. He is therefore, unable to realise the simple fact that a mere change in appearance or arrangement of some objects cannot increase or decrease their number. As a conclusion it may be said in connection with intellectual development of the child belonging to the pre-operational stage that although the child's cognitive structure or thinking is seen to be operated through symbols instead of motor and sensory actions, yet his thinking at this stage is characterised as illogical and full of contradictions.

Concrete Operational Stage (about 7 to 11 years)

This stage shows marked developments in the cognitive functioning of the child.

1. The child now learns to deal with concepts and ideas that exist only in mental terms. He can now think about things and figure out discrepancies and relationships.

2. He begins to think in terms of a set of interrelated principles rather than single bits of knowledge. As a result he can think in terms of systems.

3. His thinking becomes more logical and systematic. He can now make use of inductive and deductive approaches in terms of reasoning and arriving at conclusions.

4. The child now develops the ability to conserve both in terms of quantity and number of objects. He can now very well think that the change in appearance of an object does not alter either its quantity or its number.

5. The thinking of the child is no longer 'rigid' and 'irreversible'; a female child who has a sister clearly realises that her sister also has a sister.

6. The child now is no longer ego-centric in his thinking. He does not think of himself as the centre of the external world and does not perceive the world only from his own standpoint. He does not find it difficult to appreciate that other people have experiences, views and ideas that differ from his own.

7. The child now develops the abilities to deal adequately with classes. He can classify objects. He develops the ability of serialisation like arranging things from largest to smallest and vice versa. The number concept is also developed, but it all happens in a very simple concrete form.

8. The child now learns to carry out rather complex operations or tackle problems as long as they are concrete and not abstract. For example, the child now realises the importance of cardinal numbers and ordinal numbers. He can operate symbolically by combining, reversing and forming associations among different objects.

In this way, the child reaches a satisfactory level in terms of intellectual development by his thinking becoming quite systematic and logical. However, what is done or thought by him at this stage is done purely on a concrete level. His thought processes are limited to real events observed or the actual objects operated by him. He is unable to think in abstract terms. In this way the concrete operation stage can actually be a pre-preparation for the final stage of formal operations mainly concerned with abstractions.

Formal Operation Stage (about 12 to 15 years)

The intellectual development and functioning takes a very sophisticated shape at this stage as the child learns to deal with abstraction by logical thinking. Actually he learns to utilise the tool of symbolism as effectively as possible in the process of thought and problem solving. The child now gets interested in forms. He begins to construct relationships between concrete operations and between symbols. Generalisations and framing of rules by operating in abstract terms become quite possible at this stage. The child now begins to appreciate that some hypothetical problems can be solved mentally by applying the same rules as would be applied to concrete problems. He begins to look at problems in many ways and explore various solutions but in a very systematic and logical way. For example, if a child of this stage is shown five colourless, and odourless liquids in test tubes and is asked to find out what combination of the five will produce a brown liquid, he is likely to discover the possible combination by adopting a systematic approach, e.g., combining the first and second, then first and third, then first and fourth and so on. Thus it is quite distinctive in comparison to the children belonging to earlier stages of cognitive development who will simply resort to trial and error for finding the solution.

Moreover, the child's thinking at this stage does not remain only concrete but becomes hypothetical, with considerations given to the most unusual ideas. Hence the creative aspects in the child are very visible during this age not only in terms of concrete operations but also in terms of abstraction and pure imagination. For example, previous to this stage, if we were to ask a child to imagine he has three fathers, he might reply that it is no use imaging such a thing as one can only have one father. However, in the formal operational stage such thoughts involving unusual ideas are possible. Here one can imagine figures and shapes and can fly in the air without wings as is often done by children when studying poetry, algebra and geometry.

The other noticeable characteristic of this stage, as Piaget found, was the child's interest in dealing with things that do not exist in reality instead of the things concerning the present which are actually perceived by him.

In fact, Piaget was of the opinion that the thought processes and the intellectual functioning of a child at the formal operational period reflect the beginning of the most advanced stage in the functioning of his cognitive system. It provides a ladder to reach the limits of a person's intellectual development and actualise his potentiality to the maximum in the available circumstances. The high order of intellectual functioning developed through this stage, according to Piaget, is usually characterised by the presence of the most sophisticated cognitive abilities like the ability to (a) build up multiple hypotheses and a number of alternate solutions; (b) verify all possible solutions in a systematic and logical way; (c) generalise and arrive at abstract rules that cover many specific situations.

In this way, according to Piaget, after the expiry of the formal operation stage the child may reach full intellectual potential. He may discover the solutions of problems through mental manipulation of symbols by adopting a logical and systematic procedure known as scientific thinking and problem solving rather than a reflexive, motor or sensory manipulation as is done at the sensory motor stage; or by exposing his thinking operationally in more concrete terms as done at the concrete operation stage. It thus represents a stage which helps the child to attain mental maturity with respect to the development of his cognitive abilities.

Critical Evaluation of Piaget's Theory

Piaget's theory on intellectual development has been questioned and challenged on the following grounds:

1. Piaget's views on the pattern of intellectual development are not as uniform and universal as claimed by him. He based his theory on detailed observations of European children as they grew up in 1920s, 1930s and 1940s. The subsequent researches in Europe and outside have demonstrated significant deviations from the chronological ages linked with different stages of intellectual development by Piaget.
2. The Piagetian view that thinking proceeds in distinct stages has also been seriously challenged. It has been found that cognitive performance at particular ages is usually very inconsistent.
3. Piaget's claim that children below the age of concrete operations are incapable of logical thinking and are egocentric has been refuted by a number of research studies. It has been established that children are able to both think logically and show sensitivity and concern for the feelings and viewpoints of others at very early ages.
4. The claim that a child is unable to perform an intellectual task like conservation at ages below those specified by Piaget has also been questioned. A number of studies have shown that it is possible to train children to carry out not only tasks like conservation but also very typical complex formal operations at ages below those specified by Piaget.
5. Piaget has linked biological maturation with the development of cognitive abilities and thus made a certain stage of maturation necessary for learning the cognitive task related to that maturation age. He is thus often blamed for being a pure nativist who gives singular importance to biological maturation for the intellectual development of the child. However, this criticism is one-sided, as Piaget believes that maturation works only as the framework for intellectual development and the necessary material and means are supplied by one's physical and social environment. His stand on this issue may become quite clear through the following assertion of Inhelder and Piaget (1958):

The maturation of the nervous system can do no more than determine the totality of possibilities and impossibilities at a given stage. A particular social environment remains indispensable for the realization of these possibilities. It follows that their realization can be accelerated or retarded as a function of cultural and educational conditions.

If we examine the nature of the criticism levelled against Piaget's theory we find that most of it is one-sided. For example, as is clear from the mentioned quotation, it is not true that Piaget's theory does not take the environmental experiences into account. Similarly, we can visualise that, while laying down different stages of cognitive development, Piaget does not mean that all children belonging to all cultures essentially pass through these stages in the chronological periods specified by him. As he gives due recognition to the forces of biological inheritance, maturation and environmental experiences in the formation and functioning of one's cognitive structure, the possibility in terms of variation in ages for reaching a particular stage of intellectual development cannot be ruled out. Consequently, the actual age at which certain types of mental abilities appear varies from child to child or from culture to culture. Irrespective of this acknowledgement linked with the individual differences with regard to intellectual development, the contribution of Piaget's theory can never be underrated. Whatever points we may raise against the universality and validity of his theory, it would always be remembered that intellectual development involves stages as specified by Piaget and occurs in the same order irrespective of the individual and environmental differences or geographical and cultural barriers.we can visualize that, while laying down different stages of cognitive development, Piaget does not mean that all children belonging to all cultures essentially pass through these stages in the chronological periods specified by him. As he gives due recognition to the forces of biological inheritance, maturation and environmental experiences in the formation and functioning of one's cognitive structure, the possibility in terms of variation in ages for reaching a particular stage of intellectual development cannot be ruled out. Consequently, the actual age at which certain types of mental abilities appear varies from child to child or from culture to culture. Irrespective of this acknowledgement linked with the individual differences with regard to intellectual development, the contribution of Piaget's theory can never be underrated. Whatever points we may raise against the universality and validity of his theory, it would always be remembered that intellectual development involves stages as specified by Piaget and occurs in the same order irrespective of the individual and environmental differences or geographical and cultural barriers."

Appreciation and Contribution to Education

Piaget, an acknowledged international authority in the field of child psychology and cognitive development, has contributed a great deal to the theory and practice of education. His contributions may be briefly summarised as follows:

1. Piaget interpreted and defined intelligence in a practical way. From birth onwards, the individual has to struggle for survival and seek adjustment with his environment. Intelligence in terms of his cognitive structure and its functioning helps him in this task. Therefore, the intelligence of an individual

can only be assessed in terms of the nature of adjustment (balance between him and his environment) he is making at a particular time under the prevailing circumstances. This means that one's intelligence is a dynamic function. It really has some purposes or functions and it is these functions that help us to measure the intelligence of a person. Interpreting intelligence in this way has led to intelligence tests being devised with emphasis on the mechanism of adaptation on the one hand, and maintenance of the balance between abilities and environmental demands for the development and welfare of the child on the other.

2. Piaget's theory has highlighted the importance of drives and motivation in the field of learning and development. It has utilised the concept of equilibration for this purpose by defining it as the continuous drive towards equilibrium or balance between the organism and its environment. Piaget's equilibration can be equated with Freud's sex gratification and Jung's self-actualisation for activating one's behaviour.

3. Piaget's theory provides valuable information and advice on curriculum planning and structuring the schemes of studies. Since children of a particular region tend to reach a particular stage in their intellectual development at a particular age, what is to be planned in terms of their curriculum or scheme of studies must always be in tune with the expected level of their maturation and mental abilities. In other words, an ideal curriculum should provide the appropriate experiences at the proper time. For example, it is no use teaching world geography to students studying in first or second standard because at that age they have not yet acquired the necessary concepts like country, stage or even city. Therefore, it is more appropriate to teach them local geography such as their neighbourhood, school, classroom, and so on. Similarly, teaching algebra to students of fourth or fifth standard is pointless, as children of this age may not have acquired the ability to deal with abstractions. Piaget's theory may help in this direction by providing a suitable framework of the learning experiences in view of the cognitive development of children and the needs of society.

4. The knowledge of Piaget's theory may prove quite valuable to teachers and parents for making them aware of the nature of the thought processes of the children at a particular level of maturation or chronological age. They may also get some idea of the changes that take place in the cognitive structure and functioning of their children. This type of knowledge may prove quite beneficial to them in dealing with children and planning their training and education.

5. The major contribution of Piaget's theory is its analysis and suggestion of the optimal conditions for an individual's learning and development by introducing the concept of assimilation, accommodation and equilibration. According to Piaget, learning and development are the net result of interaction between a person's cognitive structure and his environmental experiences. For optimal learning to take place, the experiences or information presented must be of such a form and nature that it can be assimilated into the present cognitive structures, but

at the same time different enough to necessitate a change in those structures calling for accommodation and resulting in new learning. Consequently, if the new information or learning is completely unrelated to previous learning, it will certainly not fit in with the present cognitive structure and so would not be understood. On the other hand, if it is too simple or unchallenging, it will be completely assimilated and hardly any need for further learning will arise. Therefore, according to Piaget's theory, for acquiring learning it is essential that experiences or material presented to the learner are somewhat new and moderately challenging to initiate the phenomenon of accommodation, but at the same time these experiences should be sufficiently linked and related with one's old learning so that they may be reasonably easy for being assimilated and understood by the learner.

6. Since the Piagetian theory considers both physical and social experiences as quite indispensable for one's intellectual development, it has placed a major responsibility on parents, teachers and others directly or indirectly connected with the education and welfare of children to arrange for the most appropriate and stimulating environment for their children.

7. Piaget's theory may be said to have the following implications vis-a-vis the children of nursery and elementary school:

   (a) Since the children of this age are able to think only in concrete terms, it is advisable to allow them to experiment with materials in order to accommodate new understanding and to acquire new learning by themselves. For instance, to give the idea of the fraction 1/4, it would be best to cut an apple into four equal parts and then show one piece physically to show that the meaning of the fraction 1/4 is 'one out of four parts'.

   (b) The teacher must try to emphasise discovery learning rather than teaching or telling each and every part of information to the students. They should try to set up environments in which the students can have a wide variety of experiences for self or discovery-learning.

8. Piagetian theory conveys that symbolic thinking adopted by children in their thought process after the sensory motor stage is not limited to the use of language only. There may be children who prefer to use images, relationships and other symbols instead of language as a tool for their thinking and may make better progress in terms of further learning and cognitive advancement. Therefore, the teaching-learning process should not be limited to the use of verbal communication, but should involve other symbolic expression and means for the communication of ideas suited to the circumstances and nature of the learner.

9. The last but not the least contribution of Piagetian theory is its emphasis on the individualisation of education. It has advocated the need of child-centred education by saying that the educational experiences must be built around the learner's cognitive structure. What is suitable, appropriate and challenging to his cognitive structure must be given for him to acquire new experiences and develop his cognitive abilities. Since cognitive structures are sure to vary from child to child, in providing education, we have to think in terms of tailoring

the educational material according to each child's cognitive structure. For this purpose the teacher has to know the level of functioning of each student's cognitive structure and then plan his further learning and cognitive development accordingly.

Bruner's Theory of Cognitive Development

Jerome S. Bruner, born in 1915 in New York and later educated at Duke University and Harvard (USA) is credited to be a quite known and influential cognitive and educational psychologist. His works like: (i) A Study of Thinking (1956), (ii) The Process of Education (1960), (iii) Towards a Theory of Instruction (1966), (iv) Processes of Cognitive Growth (1968), (v) The Relevance of Education (1971), and (vi) The Culture of Education (1996) are recognised for their worth and contribution towards the development of psychological principles and educational applications.

His concern with cognitive psychology, particularly, his interest in the cognitive development of children (and their modes of thought representation) gave birth to a theory of cognitive development known as Bruner's Theory of Cognitive Development. Let us discuss his views and his theory in brief.

1. Bruner at the earlier stages of his cognitive views on the development of children was very influenced with Piaget's stages of cognitive development. Therefore, on the lines of Piaget's stages, he proposed that human intellectual ability develops in stages from infancy to adulthood through step by step progress in how the mind is used. However, Bruner's theory of cognitive development cannot be treated as stage theory as such (like Piaget's stage theory of cognitive development) but may be credited to suggest that children gradually acquire cognitive skills (referred by him as modes of thinking or modes of representing or symbolizing human thought). He named three modes of thinking for this purpose as Enactive mode, Iconic mode and Symbolic mode.

    (i) **Enactive mode:** According to Bruner, enactive mode of representing thought is the beginning or initial stage of a child's cognitive development. It may be recognised as a characteristic of an infant's cognitive development in the early years. In this mode, one thinks in terms of physical manipulation of the things and events of his environment. Here physical presence of a thing or event is essential for having its thought in the mind. This mode of thinking, makes one learn by repeatedly manipulating a thing or action in its physical terms. Infants are, therefore, may be seen to rely extensively upon enactive modes to learn. As they learn to roll over, sit up and walk, they are learning to do so through their own action, i.e., repeatedly physical manipulation of a particular activity. Due to the presence of enactive mode, thus, most of the activities of small children are motor activities. Bruner, however, further clarified that this mode of thinking (as an initial stage of thinking, or way acquiring skills through the use of one's cognitive ability) is although present in people of all ages, yet it is more dominant when a person is young. Our learning of tying shoelaces or driving a car, thus is easier for us when we are young than later in our old age. However, enactive mode of thinking overall helps us in the development of motor capacities and includes activities such as using tools. This is the first type of cognitive skill that Bruner suggests babies are able to use and is thus fits well with Piaget's sensory-motor stage where children may be seen learning by manipulating things and repeating movements by learning the things in their environment.

(ii) **Iconic mode:** An icon is something that is visual and in this way, iconic mode of thinking according to Bruner, involves building on our part a picture or visual image of a thing being experienced in our mind. This mode of thinking follows the enactive mode of thinking and thereby iconic representation normally begins to initiate during childhood, just after infancy. As a result, children may be able to shut their eyes and imagine the room they are in. They can also imagine a triangular, circular or rectangular plot through the figure drawn by the teacher on a blackboard or demonstrated through a chart. In contrary to involvement of motor capacities in the enactive mode, iconic mode is characterised by the involvement of the sensory capacities for the acquisition of knowledge and doing things. It is why most of the activities of the children in the age group 2-7 years are guided by their mental visualisation and imagery. They are able to form their own mental images and express themselves on that basis. While drawing analogy with Piaget's developmental stages, iconic mode of thinking relates much to Piaget's pre-operational stage.

(iii) **Symbolic mode**: Symbolic mode of thought representation follows the iconic and enactive modes. Now the child may begin to use symbols particularly of language instead of visual and physical representation of things and events. He now develops ability to understand and work with concepts that are abstract in nature. He can now have a mental sense of time and distance and make use of his reasoning and symbolic representation (particularly language) as a means not only for representing experiences but also for transforming it. In symbolic mode, thus thinking can take place without its direct experience on our part. For example, we may listen to the news on the radio and retain the information even though we have not directly witnessed the events mentioned. While drawing analogy with Piaget's developmental stages, symbolic mode of thinking may be equated with Piaget's operational stage and may be roughly linked with the cognitive development of children belonging to the pre-adolescence and adolescence age.

2. Bruner with the help of his cognitive development theory tried to demonstrate how our thought processes could be sub-divided into three distinct modes of thinking and reasoning. Unlike Piaget who tried to link the development of cognitive abilities or modes of thinking to some specific stage or periods of child development (emphasising that a child can enter the next stage of his cognitive development only when he successfully attains mastery over the previous one). Bruner, on the other hand, did not believe in stages. He merely defined different representations and saw each mode as dominant during each

developmental phase, but present and accessible throughout. Bruner's model of cognitive development thus presents before us a synthesised picture of enactive skills (manipulating objects: spatial awareness), iconic skills (visual recognition: the ability to compare and contrast) and symbolic skills (abstract reasoning) for being used by an individual for performing or learning an intellectual task. Bruner, in this connection, put a heavy emphasis on strengthening all the three modes of thinking in their proper combination for seeking maturity in terms of one's cognitive development.

3. In addition to Piaget, Bruner's theory of cognitive development drew much inspiration from the works of and views of the famous Russian psychologist Lev Vygotsky who strongly advocated the need of social interaction and language for the cognitive development of children. Bruner was critical of Piaget's underestimation of the importance of culture, social interaction and language in the cognitive development of children. As a result, he tried to pay due attention on the environmental and experiential factors influencing each individual's specific cognitive development pattern. In this connection, while differing form Piaget and agreeing to Vygotsky, he tried to emphasise that:

(i) Interpersonal communication is quite essential for the desired cognitive development of the children.

(ii) Cognitive development of children is much helped through active intervention of experts, parents, teachers and peers who are at higher level of the cognitive development.

(iii) Cognitive development is much helped in case adults try to develop reciprocal behaviour/communication/dialogue with the child.

(iv) Development of language plays a quite substantial role in the cognitive development of children. It is a quite important tool and vehicle for carrying out the thought processes. Limitations in language cause limitation in thoughts. Therefore, due care should be provided from the very beginning for the proper development of linguistic and communication abilities among the children. How social interaction coupled with language acquisition is helpful in the gradual development of cognitive abilities, may be understood through the following sequence proposed by Bruner.

• Games and rituals form the basis of the birth of pre-linguistic thoughts among the children.

• These act as thought-provoking agencies that are gradually replaced by adult interaction that adds new information in the cognitive structure of children.

• With the learning of language, the communication and interaction with adults and peers receives a needful boost for carrying out the task of cognitive development on desired lines.

4. According to Bruner, the process of cognitive development is much helped if children are allowed to construct the knowledge or acquire information through

their own efforts. He argued that children for this purpose should be got engaged in the knowledge-getting process rather than pouring knowledge directly in their minds. For utilising the mode of knowledge-getting process as an instrument for the proper cognitive development of children, he tried his best to advocate its very adoption in the teaching-learning process by commenting in the way as below:

"To instruct someone — is not a matter of getting him to commit results to mind rather it is to teach him to participate in the process that makes possible the establishment of knowledge. We teach a subject not to produce little libraries on that subject, but rather to get a student to think mathematically for himself, to consider matters as an historian does, to take part in the process of knowledge getting. Knowing is a process not a product" — Bruner (1966:72)

5. Bruner gave due recognition to the child by providing him a key role in his knowledge construction and cognitive development process. He asserted that in any process of learning or development, the child needs to be quite active rather than being a passive recipient. He has to make use of thinking skills inherent in the enactive, iconic and symbolic mode acquired by him in their best combination for the discovery of new knowledge and information in order to seek or reach the required level of his cognitive development.

6. According to Bruner, the task of proper cognitive development is more facilitated if the learning task and methods are utilised in the manner as to facilitate the knowledge construction by the child himself. For this purpose, Bruner tried to provide a theory of instruction and learning known as Bruner's cognitive development of children, in which he clearly emphasised that a teacher or instructor should essentially play the role of a facilitator for the construction of knowledge by the student himself rather than putting the already constructed knowledge before him. The instructor's task as Bruner (1966) emphasised is to *"translate information to be learned into a format appropriate to the learner's current state of understanding (enactive, iconic or symbolic) and organise it in a spiral manner so that the students continually build upon what they have already learned"*. In this way, Bruner brought into picture the idea of "Spiral Curriculum" in any instructional scheme of the child's schooling and termed it as the basic requirements for the proper cognitive development and constructivist learning on the part of an individual learner.

Similarities and Differences with Piaget's Theory

The question here may arise that in what aspects the theories of cognitive development propagated by Bruner and Piaget are similar or dissimilar. Let us think on these lines.

1. Both the theories may be described and put in the category of socio-cognitive stage theory as essentially both of them emphasise that one's cognitive development is the coefficient of friction between his/her cognitive structure and environment. What one learns is the product of his interaction with the environment (particularly the social and cultural environment). However, in this connection, where Bruner

(influenced by Vygotsky) provided a quite high place and dominant role to the culture, social influence, interaction with the adults and language development in the cognitive development of children, Piaget made the cognitive development as a subject of individual phenomena and intrapersonal focus by paying least attention to the role of social interaction and language in the development of one's cognitive abilities.

2. Bruner and Piaget both provided a sequence for the development of children. Piaget for this purpose put before us stages like sensory-motor, pre-operational, concrete operational and formal operation. Bruner while drawing inspiration from Piaget, provided quite parallel stages in the name of enactive mode, iconic mode and symbolic mode. He also like Piaget, argued that abstract thinking develops out of concrete thinking. Apart from such similarities, Bruner's cognitive development theory differs from Piaget's theory in the sense that while it tries to provide sequential steps by dividing the thought process into three distinct modes of thinking or reasoning, it like Piaget does not relate each mode or make it strictly confined to a specific period of childhood development. Rather it says that although each of these three modes may be dominant during specific developmental phase, yet they remain present and accessible throughout. As a result, these three modes of thinking are always present in a lesser or greater degree in the execution of a task involving cognitive abilities in one's life.

3. Bruner's theory strongly emphasised that the organised experiences and interaction with adults in the form of active dialogue, direction and guidance may help children in their cognitive development. Piaget, on the other hand, did not advocate the interpersonal communication, guidance, direction, role modelling, etc., on the part of adults for the cognitive development of children. He simply put the idea that cognitive development of children does take place gradually during their specific ages of developmental period as a result of changes in their inherited cognitive structure through the processes of assimilation, accommodation and equilibration.

4. Piaget and Bruner both are considered constructivists as each of them propagated that knowledge should be gained by its construction or discovery on the part of an individual learner. With the adoption of such a constructive approach, both of them argued that if we want to help children in their proper cognitive development, we have to engage them in knowledge-getting or discovery task. However, where Piaget made the knowledge-getting task a properly an independent persona phenomenon (with no interaction, instruction, guidance or help from the teacher, elders or knowledgeable peers), Bruner as a propagator of social constructivism, had no hesitation of the adult's role and social and cultural influences in shaping the cognitive development of children.

5. As far as designing instructions for students with an eye to seek their desired cognitive development is concerned, both Piaget and Bruner emphasised that teachers should have a clear-cut understanding about the level or stage of cognitive development of their students before they proceed with any designs for instruction. Piaget in this concern, however, emphasised that the learning

experiences and methods organised for the learners should match their cognitive development at the specific developmental age periods. Therefore, in the eyes of Piaget, the curriculum should be organised on the pattern simple to complex and concrete to abstract principles. Bruner had a reservation on such thinking for the organisation of curriculum. He put forward the idea of spiral curriculum by hypothesising that *"any subject can be taught effectively in some intellectually honest form to any child at any stage of development"* (Bruner, 1960:33). Based on this hypothesis he, unlike Piaget, advocated the development of spiral curriculum —*"a curriculum as it develops should revisit the basic ideas repeatedly, building up on them until the student has grasped the full formal apparatus that goes with them"* (Bruner, 1966:13).

6. Unlike Piaget, who did not believe in providing any importance to interpersonal communication, and interaction for the cognitive development of children, Bruner took a stand that adults had a very important role in developing children's cognitive skills by working alongside them and by asking questions and helping children vocalise their thoughts. In this way, Bruner may be found to be much influenced by Russian psychologist Vygotsky's idea of scaffolding. Similarly, Bruner demonstrated more proximity to Vygotsky's theory of cognitive development than Piaget's theory for assigning the status and responsibility to the language development in children by declaring that the development of language was the key to children being able to move from iconic mode into symbolic mode of higher thinking.

Implications of Bruner's Theory

On the basis of what has been discusses earlier, the implications of Bruner's theory of cognitive development may be summarised as follows:

1. Educationists, teachers and parents should recognise and know about the nature and importance of all the three modes of thought representation. They must capitalise on these modes accordingly for the development of capacities and abilities of their students. For example, a proper emphasis and utilisation of enactive mode thinking may be helpful in the development of motor capacities and mechanical skills (e.g., using tools) among the students. Similarly, emphasis on the utilisation of iconic mode may prove helpful in the development of sensory and imagery capacities, and symbolic mode may help in developing the ability of abstraction and higher order thinking skills.

2. As per Bruner's advice, we should not think that enactive, iconic or symbolic mode is the monopoly of a particular developmental period or specific age. A mental task or activity requiring the use of cognitive skills may demand the use of one or the other types of thinking mode. In such a situation, it is advisable to teachers to make use of a single mode or a combination of modes for making their students understand a concept or undertake a task in a proper way. This viewpoint emphasised by Bruner has thus been responsible for the use of the multimedia approach in the field of education.

3. Enactive, iconic or symbolic modes of thinking and reasoning according to Bruner, although present to some extent at all ages and periods of development are found to be dominated at some specific developmental periods, i.e., enactive mode of thinking is dominated in infancy and early childhood. Similarly, iconic and symbolic modes of thinking are more dominant in the childhood and adolescence respectively. It is therefore, imperative that educational experiences and methods must be planned and organised in view of the thinking mode of enactive, iconic and symbolic nature for the learners belonging to infancy, childhood and adolescence. Moreover, we can expect much in terms of motor development and motor skills from the child belonging to infancy, development of sensory and imagery abilities from the child belonging to childhood, and development of abstract reasoning on the part of adolescents. Therefore, where education of the children belonging to infancy and childhood should involve concrete objects and use of audio-visual material, the students belonging to the age of adolescence may be adjudged capable of taking advantages from the abstraction, and use of reasoning and other higher order cognitive abilities.

4. Bruner has emphasised that development of children (including cognitive) is best possible if the learners are made to construct and discover their knowledge by themselves. Accordingly, the teacher should act as a facilitator for providing opportunities and needed help to the students for seeking knowledge. Teachers must treat education as a knowledge-getting process and should avoid pouring knowledge directly into the minds of their students.

5. As emphasised by Bruner, one can be successful in going higher and higher in the course of his cognitive development in case he is ready (interested) as well as busy in utilising his cognitive structure (already developed cognitive skill and acquired experiences) for gaining new information, knowledge and skills. A teacher, therefore, should try to seek active participation and involvement of his students in the teaching-learning process. He should also try to make use of his prior experiences and existing cognitive structure for planning and organising appropriate learning experiences and methodology of teaching suiting his/her nature and level of cognitive development.

6. Suitability of curricular/co-curricular experiences counts much for seeking proper cognitive development of students and vice-versa. Bruner has suggested use of spiral curriculum for gaining maximum benefit on this account. Accordingly, the curriculum developer should initiate some concepts and things suitable to early ages in the lower classes and gradually build up the knowledge concerning these topics in the subsequent higher classes by allowing the students for the repetition of material learned in the previous classes so that all what is learned at present or previous classes may be available from them

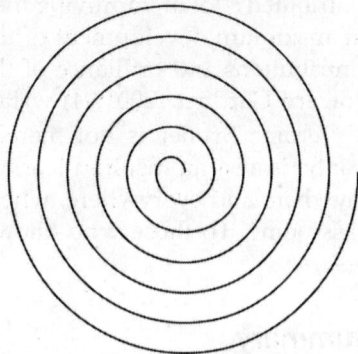

Fig.11.3: Spiral Curriculum

to have continuous increase in their cognitive potential. The spiral curriculum may take the following imagery presentation.

7. Bruner's theory of cognitive development has tried to provide quite a big importance to the cognitive processes and cognitive theories of learning for the purpose of needed development and attainment of educational objectives at any age of the developmental period. It is therefore, imperative for teachers to make use of the methods and processes suggested by Bruner for seeking better outcomes of their teaching endeavours. Accordingly, we as teachers, should try to learn to make use of Bruner's cognitive methods and means like discovery method, enquiry approach, concept attainment model, dialogue and discussion method, constructive learning methods (like cooperative and constructivist learning), etc.

8. Bruner has given due stress on the role of language and social interaction in the development of children. We as teachers should, therefore, pay due emphasis on the development of linguistic abilities and communication skills so that students may harvest rich dividends with the utilisation of these abilities in the acquisition of knowledge and developing their cognitive potential.

9. Bruner has also emphasised the importance of culture, social interaction and guidance of the elders in the development of children. It is, therefore, needed on our part to organise the content material, methodology of teaching, teaching-learning environment in such a way to have the needed facilities and help on the part of elders including teachers for the maximum development of learners.

10. The last but not the least, a teacher must learn the art of making use of the existing cognitive structure or potential of the students in terms of a proper synthesis of their enactive, iconic and symbolic modes of reasoning. For example, a teacher aiming to help children learn about dinosaurs could use all these three modes in a synthesised form. For this purpose, he can ask his students to construct models of dinosaurs (conative), he may make his students watch a film about or involving dinosaurs (enactive), and persuade them to consult reference texts and then discuss their findings (symbolic).

In fact, in this way, Bruner through his progressive ideas and theories has contributed a lot in improving the processes and products of education, aimed towards the maximum development of the students' cognitive potential. Commenting on the contributions and brilliance of this famous cognitive psychologist cum educationist, Howard Gardner (2001:94) writes:

Jerome Bruner is not merely one of the foremost educational thinkers of the era: he is also an inspired learner and teacher. In his words, "Intellectual activity is anywhere and everywhere, whether at the frontier of knowledge or in a third-grade classroom". To those who know him Bruner remains the complete educator in the flesh.

Summary

Mental growth and development refers to a process responsible for the development of an individual in all cognitive, mental or intellectual abilities (interrelated to each other) like sensation, perception, imagination, memory, reasoning, understanding, generalisation, interpretation, language ability, conceptional ability, problem-solving ability, decision-making ability, etc. All these aspects of mental growth and development change, grow and mature with increase in the age of the child due to maturation and learning.

In fact maturation and learning are responsible for controlling the process of mental growth and development. Maturation helps in achieving physical growth and development specifically in terms of the organic growth of the nervous system which in turn helps in one's mental development. Learning in the form of experiences and education helps the mental developmental process to reach to its optimum level.

There is neither a universal pattern of mental growth for all individuals nor is the pattern same for all mental abilities. However, it can be seen that there is a cessation of mental growth in all individuals with respect to one or the other mental abilities. Latest researchers have concluded that the age of cessation of mental growth can be estimated as 20 or little before or little after 20. However, with such cessation of mental growth, development in mental power and capacity is not necessarily stopped.

The knowledge of the trend of mental growth and development and the resulting changes in the various types of mental abilities may prove quite useful for the teacher to plan and organise his teaching-learning material, teaching-learning situations and environment as to ensure for the maximum growth and development of the mental abilities of his students for their own as well as social welfare. Piaget's theory of cognitive development discusses the intellectual development of children in its two broader aspects — cognitive structure and cognitive functioning. The initial cognitive structure of the child consists of a few inborn instincts and reflexes like sucking, looking, reaching, grasping, etc. called schemas by Piaget. Helped by the process of assimilation, accommodation and equilibration, significant changes are brought into initial cognitive structure involving definite sequential stages of intellectual development, named as sensori-motor stage, pre-operation stage, concrete operational stage and formal operational stage. The sensory motor stage (birth-2years) is characterised by the absence of language and limited to the child's direct sensory and motor interaction with the environment. As a main development, the child acquires the concept of object permanence. At the pre-operation stage (3-7 years), the child reacts through words or other symbolic representations or images to the things in the environment. His thought process at this stage is highly ego-centric showing inability to consider other's point of view.

During *the concrete operational stage* (7 to 11 years), children begin to think logically but are unable to think in abstract terms. Their thought processes are limited to concrete objects and events. However, they are able to understand the cognitive concept such as number, classification and conservation.

During *the formal operation stage* (12 years to 15 years or later), individuals are able to think abstractly, test hypotheses and deal with problems that are not physically present in their environment. Actually, this stage reflects the most advanced period in the functioning of the cognitive system. The individual here may reach the intellectual potential to discover solutions to problems through mental manipulation of symbols by adopting a logical and systematic way known as scientific thinking and problem solving.

Bruner's theory of cognitive development much like Piaget's theory proposes that there are three stages or sequential steps for the development of intellectual abilities among children. He named them as enactive, iconic, and symbolic modes of thinking or symbolising human thought.

Enactive mode of representing thought is the beginning or initial stage of a child's cognitive development. Infants therefore, may be seen to rely extensively upon enactive mode to learn which allows them to think in terms of physical manipulation of the things and events of their environment. This stage, thus, fits well to the Piaget's sensori-motor stage.

Iconic mode of thinking involves building on one's part a picture or visual image of a thing being experienced in one's mind. Since this mode of thinking follows the enactive mode, normally it begins to develop among the children in the age group 2-7 years are guided by their mental visualisation and imagery. In this way, Bruner iconic mode of thinking relates much to Piaget's pre-operational stage. Symbolic mode of thought representation follows the iconic and enactive modes. Now the child may begin to use symbols particularly the language in place of visual and physical representation of things and events. He can now develop the ability to understand and use the concepts that are abstract in nature. This mode of thinking thus may be equated with Piaget's operational stage linked with pre-adolescence and adolescence.

Bruner, however, while providing sequential steps by dividing thought process into three distinct modes of thinking does not relate each mode or make it strictly confined to a specific period of childhood development much like his predecessor, Jean Piaget. Rather he says that although each of these three modes may be dominant during specific developmental phase, yet they remain present and accessible throughout. As a result, these three modes of thinking are always present in a lesser or greater degree in the execution of a task involving cognitive abilities in one's life.

References and Suggested Readings

Brunner, J.S., *Toward a Theory of Instruction*, Cambridge Man: Bel Kapp Press, 1966.

Brunner, J.S., *Actual Minds Possible Worlds*, Cambridge MA: Harvard University Press, 1986.

Brunner, J.S., *Culture of Education*, Cambridge MA: Harvard University Press, 1996.

Carmichael, L. (Ed.), *Manual of Child Psychology*, John Wiley, New York, 1946.

Crow., L.D. and Crow, Alice, *Child Psychology*, (Reprint), Barney & Noble, New York, 1969.

Gardner, H. "Jerome, S. Bruner" In J.A. Palmer (Ed.), *Fifty Modern Thinkers on Education*, London: Routledge, 2001.

Gilligan, Carol, *In a different voice: Psychological theory and women development*, Cambridge MA: Harvard University Press, 1987.

Inhelder, B. and Piaget, J., *The Growth of Logical Thinking from Childhood to Adolescence* (Trans. by Anne Parson and Stanley Milgram), New York: Basic Books, 1958.

Harlock and Schewartz, quoted by Kuppuswamy, B., *Advanced Educational Psychology*, Delhi, University Publication, 1964.

Kuppuswamy, B., *An Introduction and Social Psychology*, Asia Publishing House, Bombay, 1971.

Kuppuswamy, B. (1964), *Advanced Educational Psychology*, Delhi, University Publication.

Marry, F.K. and Marry, R.V., *From Infancy to Adolescence*, Harper & Brothers, New York, 1940.

Sorenson, Herbert, *Psychology in Education*, McGraw-Hill, New York, 1948.

Piaget, J., *Judgement and Reasoning in the Child*, New York: Harcourt & Brace, 1926.

Piaget, J., *The Construction of Reality in the Child*, New York: Basic Books, 1954.

Piaget, J., *Psychology of Intelligence*, Totowa, N.J.: Littlefield Adams, 1966.

Piaget J., *Equilibration of Cognitive Structures*, New York: Viking Press, 1977.

Piaget, J., *The Moral Judgement of the Child*, New York: Harcourt and Brace, 1932 (and New York: Free Press, 1965).

Piaget, J., *The Origins of Intelligence in Children*, New York: International University Press, 1952 (and New York: Norton, 1963).

Woolfolk, Anita, *Educational Psychology* (Ninth edition), First Indian Reprint, New York: Pearson, 2004.

12

Social Development

What is Social Development?

Human beings possess unique characteristic which differentiates them from animals. Their behaviour is social. Society to them is as essential as food. They believe in the maintenance of social relationships and try to adjust with others. But this does not mean that the child is born with such social behaviour and social qualities. Like other aspects of growth and development, he develops the necessary social characteristics in him as he grows. The process of the development of such qualities which brings desirable changes in his social behaviour is referred to as social development or socialisation of the child. Social development occupies very important place in the overall process of growth and development. We cannot even describe an individual a person if he has not passed through the process of social development or socialisation.

Let us try - to analyse this further. What does this term social development (also described as socialisation) mean? Various thinkers have tried to define it. The following are some of the definitions:

- **Sorenson:** By social growth and development we mean increasing ability to get along well with oneself and others. (1948, p. 50)

  Thus Sorenson explains that during the process of social development there is a progress in the social abilities or skills of an individual. With these increasing abilities he tries to bring improvement in the maintenance of social relationships. He tries to mould his behaviour and seek adjustment and harmony with others.

- **Freeman and Showel:** Social development is the process of learning to conform to group standards, mores and traditions and becoming imbued with a sense of oneness, inter-communication and co-operation. (Hurlock, E.B., 1959, p. 257)

  The definition lays stress on the following:

  (i) Social development refers to the process by which a person acquires the necessary knowledge, skills and disposition that makes him an acceptable member in his own group.

  (ii) It develops group loyalty and encourages mutual dependence, co-operation and cohesiveness.

(iii) It is the process which helps an individual behave in accordance with social traditions and mores and thus makes him able to adjust in his social environment.

- **Hurlock:** Social development means the attaining of maturity in social relationships. (1959, p. 257)

This brief definition carries a wide meaning. It asserts that as in the case of emotional development, the goal is to attain emotional maturity; similarly in the case of social development, the goal should be the attainment of social maturity. An individual should have all the opportunities to modify or improve his social behaviour so that he may be able to maintain proper social relationships and can adjust himself to his social environment.

- **Garrett:** Socialisation or social development is the process whereby the biological individual is converted into a human person. (1968, p. 555).

This definition is based upon the distinction between the term 'individual' and 'person'. We cannot name each and everybody as person. The person always possesses some personality. The personality is the product of social interaction between him and his social environment. Socialisation and social development — the process of social interaction — helps individuals attain essential personality characteristics.

In the light of all these views, we can come to the conclusion that social development or socialisation is a process which:

(i) Begins with the infant's first contact with other people and continues throughout his life,

(ii) Is the net result of the constant interaction with his social environment,

(iii) Helps in learning and acquiring various social qualities and characteristics, and

(iv) With the result of learning helps the individual become adjusted to his social environment and maintain proper social relationships.

Development of Social Behaviour At Different Stages Of Development

Social Development in Infancy

The behaviour of a human infant is not social at birth. He is extremely self-centred and is only concerned with the satisfaction of his physical need. He does not even distinguish between people and inanimate objects.

Social behaviour is said to be taking its birth when the infant first communicates with the adults for the satisfaction of his needs. Therefore, normally the baby's first social contacts are with an adult. Mrs. Hurlock in her book 'Child Psychology' has beautifully explained the process of social development during the first two years of a child as a result of the contact with adults. The following is the summary of her findings:

Table12.1: Social development of infants as a result of contact with other adults

Duration of age	Pattern of social behaviour
During the first month	Cannot differentiate between human voices and other noises.
Second month	Recognises the sounds of human beings and smiles.
Third month	Recognises the mother and feels unhappy on separation.
Fourth month	Shows selective attention to the human face and feels happy in company.
Fifth month	Reacts differently to smiling and scolding and distinguishes between friendly and angry voices.
Sixth month	Recognises familiar persons with a smile and shows definite expressions of fear of strangers.
Eighth and ninth month	Attempts to imitate the speech, simple acts and gestures observed in others.
Between the tenth and twelfth month	Plays with his image and even kisses it as if it were another persons.
At twelfth month	Can refrain from doing things in response to 'no-no' or some other form of request.
At second year	Can cooperate with adults in a number of routine activities and becomes an active member of the family.

With regard to an infant's social reactions to another infant or child, it has been observed that his early behaviour is egocentric and selfish. He cannot share his toys with others. He wants to have all things for himself and does not tolerate any external interference. From the 13th to the 18th month, the young child's interest shifts from play materials to playmates. There is a decrease in fighting for toys and increase in cooperative use of them. Up to 3 years, he learns to divide and share his possession with others and to cooperate with them. Children of this age are now in a position to engage themselves in cooperative and organised play activities. Up to 7 years or so, children seek companionship regardless of gender of the other children. Usually the boys and girls play together at this stage.

Like emotions, the early stage of social behaviour during infancy is characterised by negative social characteristics. Imitation, timidity, shyness, rivalry and desire for possession dominate the first two years of development. Between 2 to 6 years, both negative and positive aspects of social behaviour are seen. Negativism, rivalry, quarrelling, teasing and bullying, cooperation, sympathy and social approval are some of the new social behaviours which are learned at this stage.

Social Development During Childhood

As we have seen that during the period 2 to 6 years, a child progresses from being relatively unsocial to becoming a distinctly socialised individual. He learns to share, cooperate and do things with others. But the circle of his social contacts is limited at this stage. Therefore, we cannot expect much from him regarding his social development.

With the entrance in childhood, most of the children begin to go to school. The area of their social contacts is now widened. We note the following changes in the social behaviour of a child:

1. This period is marked by greater degree of social awareness. There is a great expansion in the child's social world. Most of the important types of social behaviour, necessary to adjustment with others, begin to develop at this stage.

2. He tries to seek independence from his parents and other elders and spends less time with them. In actual sense, he now derives no enjoyment from them. Thus interest in playmates of his own age gets increased.

3. He becomes an active member of a 'peer group' and this group gradually replaces the family group in its influence over his behaviour and attitudes. The members of such a group are almost of the same age. They believe in group loyalty and thus try to conform to the rules and values maintained by their group.

4. We find a sort of segregation among boys and girls of this age. They form their groups among members of their own gender because of a definite and clear differentiation between their habits, interests, attitudes, etc.

5. The interests and values of the peer group often clash with the interests and values of the teachers and parents. The child at this age is caught between the two. On one hand, he aspires for the social values of his own group; on the other hand, he is equally anxious to win the love and affection of his parents as well as teachers. Therefore, a proper balance between these two influencing forces — peer group, parents and teachers — is essential. If neglected by either side, he may develop a maladjusted and antisocial personality.

6. Till the end of the stage of childhood, i.e., 11th or 12th year, the child enters the peak of "gang age" with increasing loyalties towards his own gang and conflicts with other gangs, parents and teachers. The gang life develops many good and bad social qualities in a child.

Social Development During Adolescence

Adolescence is the period of rapid change and adjustments, and holds a greater significance in the social sphere. The social development of this age is marked by the following characteristics:

1. Adolescence is marked with too much sex consciousness, sexual development and the accompanying attraction for opposite sex. Boys and girls of this age try to attract and hold the attraction of each other through their style of dress, manner of talking and other forms of social behaviour. They also try to seek friendship and even sexual relationships. Therefore, the social behaviour pattern during adolescence is almost dominated by sexual needs and desires.

2. During this stage, group loyalty becomes very pronounced. Like childhood, it does not confine itself to the gang only but extends to the school, community, province and the nation. Martyrs and patriots are the product of this age. Cooperation reaches its peak during this period and the individuals are in a mood to sacrifice their own interests for the greater cause of the group, society and the nation.

3. Adolescence is also marked with an increase in friendly relationships. The nature of friendship maintained at this stage differs much from that of the childhood. While the childhood friends are generally chosen from the neighbourhood or class, in adolescence there is no such bar of distance. Adolescents tend to choose friends of their own age, mental level and from the same socio-economic group to which their own family belongs. Their friendships are based on their common interests, hobbies and skills or the satisfaction of their mutual needs and subsequently tend to last longer than the friendships made in early childhood. It sometimes cements life-long relationships.

4. Adolescence is a period of intense emotions. Emotional behaviour dominates the social characteristics and qualities of adolescents. An adolescent is highly sensitive, an idealist and a social reformer by nature. He feels strongly for the weak. He is always ready to do some sort of social and community service. From time to time, he exhibits his desire for bringing reforms in the social setup and is highly critical of social evils and injustice.

5. Their areas of specific interests and social contacts get widened during adolescence. Besides individual characteristics, culture, socio-economic status of the family, sex education — all affect their social interest and contacts. We find too much diversity in the adolescents regarding their interests and sociability. While some are highly extrovert and sociable, others like to remain aloof and shirk from social contacts and participations.

In the end, we can say that adolescence is a period of maximum social awareness, increasing social relationships and intimate friendships. During this age the individual is provided with wide area of interests and opportunities for making social adjustment as well as learning so many social qualities. During this period, an individual prepares himself to play the role of an adult in his social life. By the end of this stage, the social behaviour of the child becomes almost matured.

Social Maturity

As we have seen earlier, the aim of social development is to gain social maturity. A child while passing through various stages from his very birth strives to attain it. Let us see what does the term social maturity indicate or what characteristics are supposed to be present in a socially mature individual?

1. A socially mature individual likes to mix and interact with people. He is capable of making and keeping friendships.

2. He is not self-centred. He is always ready to sacrifice his interests for the greater cause of groups, society and the nation. While demanding and asserting for his rights, he always cares for the social obligations.

3. He possesses the ability of sharing and shouldering the social responsibilities. He is prepared to play the role of a leader or of a staunch follower as the situation demands from him.

4. He is able to make proper decisions and take suitable action at the time of any social crisis, problem or situation in which his help is needed.

5. He is very cooperative. He believes in maintaining relationships and working with others. He does not do anything that hurts the feeling of others. He possesses social virtues like the feeling of sympathy, kindness, courtesy and cheerfulness. He believes in justice, equality and fraternity and never does anything to disrupt the cohesiveness and unity of the social structure.

   Actually, he is imbued with all important social qualities like patience, respect for others' opinions, kindness and sympathy, cooperation, courtesy and politeness, cheerfulness, self-confidence, self-control, sentiment of self-regard, respect for the opposite gender, religions, culture, etc.

6. The area of his social interests and participation is very wide. He possesses refined tastes and adequate social etiquettes.

7. His social behaviour conforms to the norms, mores, social codes and ethics. He never engages himself in any sort of activities or behaviour which is anti-social and looked down upon by society.

8. He possesses a strong desire to serve the cause of the society. He is critical of the evils and malpractices in the society and tries to bring desirable reforms.

9. He possesses a greater degree of adaptability and adjustability. He can easily adjust himself to the varying needs of the society and social circumstances.

Factors Affecting Social Development

How does one help a child in the task of his social development is a relevant question at this stage. In this task, the individual in addition to his own physical, mental and emotional development is helped by various social agencies. All these factors — personal and environmental — work together in influencing the social development of a child. What are these factors and how they influence the pattern of social development have been discussed as follows:

Personal Factors

1. **Bodily structure and health:** Development of social behaviour is influenced by the physique and health which one possesses. A healthy child with a normal physique develops self-confidence and a sense of self-respect. He has the strength and ability to adjust in the challenging social situations. He is always cheerful and cooperative. He is able to mix with people and maintain proper social relationships. A child suffering from an illness or having poor health or any physical deformities and defects develops a feeling of inferiority and feels difficulty in social adjustment. Therefore, proper care should be taken for the balanced physical development of children.

2. **Intelligence:** Intelligence is defined as the ability to make and take the right decision at the right time and the ability to adapt or adjust to new situations. These qualities are very essential for effective social behaviour. The more intelligent a person, the more adjustable and social he will prove to be.

3. **Emotional development:** Emotional development of a child bears a positive correlation with social development. Emotional adjustability and maturity is one of the very important elements of social maturity. Those who can express their emotions in a proper degree at a proper time are found to possess a healthy social personality. Emotionally maladjusted personalities possess poor social qualities. Therefore, due care should be taken for the training of the emotions of a child so that he may not feel any obstacles in the path of his social development.

Environmental Factors

1. **Family environment:** Family is named as the most important primary agency for the socialisation of a child. The home atmosphere and family relationships exercise much influence upon his social development. A child learns the first lesson of social qualities from his parents. Consciously or unconsciously, he imitates the behaviour of his parents and other members of the family and thus picks up many good or bad social characteristics which stay with him till the end of his life. The size of the family, relationships within the family, attitude of the parents and family members, socio-economic status and position of the family in the society, traditions, culture, values and the ideals of the family — all influence the social development of the child.

   A family, which provides healthy social atmosphere and where basic needs of children are satisfied, produces socially balanced personalities whereas those houses where the family relationships are under strain and the elders possess negative social characteristics, the child is not brought up properly and consequently he produces socially undesirable and negative behaviour. Therefore it is essential to seek active cooperation of parents in providing suitable atmosphere at home for the proper social development of children.

2. **School environment:** Social development in children is greatly influenced by the social environment and functioning of schools. Human relationships maintained by the school; the kinds of programmes and activities performed; its traditions, values and principles; the social qualities; and behaviour of teachers and schoolmates — all influence the social development of a child. A school, having a healthy social and democratic atmosphere, inculcates many social virtues among its students while poor and unhealthy atmosphere at the school and negative social behavioural characteristics of the teachers and schoolmates cast a bad influence on the social behaviour of a child. Therefore, teachers as well as authorities should try their level best to make the school environment as healthy as possible for the proper social development of children. They must produce good examples of social virtues and democratic living before children and through curricular and co-curricular activities, proper methods of instruction and personal contact, should help children in their proper social development.

3. **Peer-group relationship and gang influence:** The playmates, school or classmates also influence the social development of a child. He picks up the habits and social qualities of his companions. Good company helps him to learn good qualities while bad company provides all opportunities to spoil him and turn him into an anti-social person. On the positive side, through peer group relationships and gang influence he learns to cooperate, lead and follow, think for a common cause and adjust in the challenging social situations. It inculcates the sense of loyalty, sympathetic attitude and the willingness to obey social rules and regulations in him.

    Parents, teachers and other responsible members of the society should remain very careful to see that a child gets healthy company. Negative influence of the peer group and the gang in the form of an unsocial behaviour should be checked. A child should be accepted by his peer group. He should get proper environment and opportunities to mix with his peers.

4. **Community and neighbourhood:** As a child grows older, he comes in contact with the social circle of his neighbourhood and the community to which he belongs. The social interests, habits and characteristics of neighbours, unconsciously and consciously, influence the social behaviour of the child. Every community and society is characterised by its unique cultural pattern, social mores, traditions and social characteristics. The child, as a member of the community and society, picks up these things which go in shaping his social behaviour and influence his social development.

5. **Religious institutions and clubs:** Social agencies like temples, churches, social clubs, etc., also influence the social development of a child. These places serve as a meeting ground for members of the society and help in developing social contacts and relationships. The social behaviour of an individual is greatly influenced by traditions, values, ideals and social characteristics maintained by these institutions.

6. **Information and entertainment agencies:** Agencies like newspapers, magazines, radio, cinema, television, etc., also exercise their influence on the social development of children. Such sources constantly inform the readers, listeners and others about the changes in the social structure, customs, traditions and values and thus bring desirable changes in the social behaviour of the individuals. The mass entertainment agencies like radio, cinema, television etc., play a vital role in moulding and shaping the behaviour of the members of the society. The impact of these agencies in social life can very well be recognised. What a hero or heroine does on the screen is at once imitated. The values of life, style of living, traditions and cultural pattern of the society — all undergo a drastic change by the impact of these modern mass agencies.

    These agencies should not be allowed to function unchecked. Society or the government should exercise a desirable control and check upon the functioning of these agencies so that no undesirable and anti-social influence is left over for the masses. Directly or indirectly, these agencies should be made an important means for the assimilation of the social and democratic virtues among citizens.

Erickson's Theory of Psycho-Social Development

Erik Erikson was a native of Germany. He spent his early adult years studying art and travelling around Europe. A meeting with the famous psychoanalyst Sigmund Freud in Vienna led to an invitation from Freud to study psychoanalysis. It was a turning point of his career. He immigrated to America for this purpose and it was perhaps also to escape from the threat of Hitler. In America, he studied Native American traditions of human development and continued his work as a psychoanalyst. In 1950, he brought out his psychosocial theory — a developmental theory of the Eight stages of Man covering the entire life span rather than childhood and adolescent development like all other theories of development.

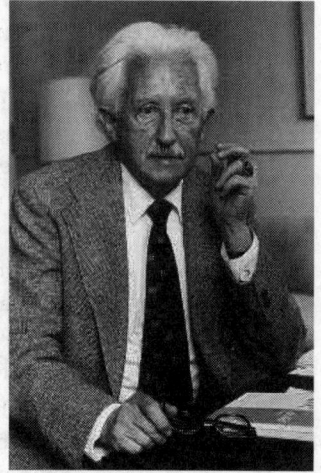

Erik H. Erikson (1902-1994)

Introducing his theory, Erickson postulated that the development of an individual is the result of his interaction with his social environment. Right from his birth, his social development puts him under specific pressures or conflicts (called crises) by making specific demands at different ages or developmental stages of his life. The individual tries to meet these specific demands or resolve the crises by reacting psychologically in his own way, depending upon his circumstances. The complexity of the demands from society or social environment go on increasing as the child advances on the ladder of growth and development. So, at each stage of his development, the child faces a new crisis, i.e., an issue that needs to be resolved at that particular stage of development. The way in which the 'crisis' of each stage is resolved has a major bearing on the development of one's personality which in turn is reflected as the positive and negative aspect of one's behaviour. Erickson discovered eight such issues or crises of life arising at different ages or periods of one's development and linked them with the eight stages of one's psycho-social development covering one's entire life span as outlined in Table 12.2.

Table 12.2. Age Span for the Stages of Psycho-social Development

Stage of psycho-social development	Specific age or period
Trust vs. Mistrust	Birth to 1½ years
Autonomy vs. Shame and Doubt	1½ years to 3 years
Initiative vs. Guilt	3 to 6 years
Industry vs. Inferiority	6 to 12 years
Entity vs. Role Confusion	Adolescence (12 to 20 years)
Intimacy vs. Isolation	Early adulthood (20 to 45 years)
Generativity vs. Stagnation	Middle adulthood (45 to 65 years)
Ego integrity vs. Despair	Later adulthood (65 years onwards)

The above division outlines the types of crises that need to be resolved at particular stages or periods of one's life. It also identifies the different stages of psycho-social development, i.e., the personality traits that are likely to develop at a particular stage. For example, one may go on acquiring positive traits like trust, independence, initiative, industry, identity, etc., to develop into a meaningful personality. On the other hand, one can develop into a troublesome, confused and doomed personality by failing to successfully resolve the crisis of one's age and developing negative traits like mistrust, shame, doubt, guilt feeling, inferiority and the like. Since these behaviour traits, modes of adjustment or psychological build-up are acquired through one's active interaction with the social environment, the stages of development are referred to as psycho-social development. These different stages of psycho-social development should not be considered as begin sudden or end abruptly. In fact, one stage evolves into another through the whole life cycle and the crisis of issues not resolved during one stage is supposed to carry over into the stages that follow in some way or the other as revealed through the following discussion:

Stage I: The period of trust vs. mistrust (birth to 1½ years): In the first one and a half years of life, the infant is confronted with the crisis termed trust vs. mistrust. During this period the baby is completely dependent upon its mother or caretaker for the satisfaction of its needs. The way it is nourished, handled, protected and kept safe and comfortable at this stage may provide the baby with a sense of security or insecurity, a feeling of trust or mistrust in the mother or caretaker and ultimately in its surroundings. The sense of trust or mistrust with regard to the environment gained in this way at this stage of development may then be carried over to the stages of development to follow and consequently reflected in the developing personality.

Stage II: The period of autonomy vs. shame and doubt (1½ to 3 years): Having gained a primary sense of trust and security with regard to his environment, in the second and third years of his life, the child now passes through the second stage of psycho-social development. With the newly developed motor or physical skills and language ability, the child now engages in exploring his environment and experimenting with his strengths and limitations for achieving a sense of autonomy and independence. The child now needs proper safety measures against the risks involved in activities like walking, running, pulling and handling the objects of his environment or in terms of learning undesirable language but this does not mean that he should be denied a reasonable degree of freedom to acquire a sense of independence. Within the bounds of safety, he must be provided adequate opportunities for the acquisition of a sense of autonomy and knowledge about his limitations.

Children who are denied the opportunity to develop a sense of independence by over-protective, harsh or restrictive parents begin to doubt their ability and ultimately begin to feel embarrassed or ashamed in the presence of others. However, the development of the sense of doubt and shame within reasonable limits is not harmful. A healthy sense of doubt helps the child to set his own limits and the development of shame helps him to develop a sense of right and wrong. Therefore, at this stage of psycho-social development, the child needs to be helped in striking a balance between the conflicting needs of his social environment to acquire a sense of autonomy and develop a sense of doubt and shame for the adequate development of his personality.

Stage III: The period of initiative vs. guilt (3 to 6 years): The third stage of psycho-social development between three to six years of age is characterised by the crisis of initiative versus guilt. Equipped with the sense of trust and autonomy the child now begins to take initiative in interacting with his environment. He asks questions about each and everything, explores his environment ceaselessly, and engages in planning and carrying out activities of various kinds. The extent to which the initiative for carrying out physical and mental exploration is encouraged or discouraged by parents and the available social environment, goes a long way in developing ability in the child to initiate plan and carry out these activities in later life.

In case the child is discouraged from taking the initiative by his parents and guardians not having faith in him, or is pulled down by unhealthy criticism, punishment or rebuke for minor failures, the child is sure to develop a sense of guilt leading to hesitation, indecision and lack of initiative in planning and carrying out his life activities. Although in case of failure he feels a reasonable amount of guilt for having failed to take the initiative at the right time or made mistakes in planning and carrying out his activities, this enables him to learn from his failures. However, to allow this to develop into a guilty conscience is harmful to the development of the child's personality. Therefore, there is a need to resolve the crisis of initiative vs. guilt at this stage of psycho-social development and it can be properly done if we allow the child to experiment with his initiative by properly supervising and guiding his activities and encouraging him to develop a habit of self-evaluation of the results of his initiative.

Stage IV: Period of industry vs. inferiority (6 to 12 years): Generally, by this age children begin to attend school where they are made to learn various skills and the teachers as well as the school environment generate pressures on them to work hard in order to perform well. Parents also now begin to make demands upon the children to lend their hand in household duties or in some cases saddle them with occupational responsibilities. They have also to compete with their peers in terms of competence and productivity in school and other social situations. Now, in case the child performs well in school, home or in other social environments or is admired for his intellectual or motor pursuits, he will likely develop a sense of industry filled with a sense of achievement. Such a child will consequently be motivated to work harder and achieve more in terms of competency and productivity. On the other hand, if his performance remains inferior to that of his peers or he does not satisfy his teachers and parents with his performance, he may begin to look down upon himself and develop a sense of inferiority.

The teachers and the school environment thus play a very significant role in helping the child out of the industry versus inferiority crisis. For the child, the school becomes a place where success and failure are defined. Therefore, it is the duty of the teachers and school authorities to structure their classroom and school environment in such a way so as to help the students maintain a positive attitude and view themselves as capable and valuable individuals.

Stage V: The period of identity vs. role confusion (12 to 19 years): This stage, beginning with the advent of puberty, is marked with the crisis of identity vs. role confusion. Equipped with the sense of trust, autonomy, initiative and industry, adolescents begin to search for their own personal identity. The sudden changes in their bodies and mental functioning and the altered demands of society compel them to ask questions of their own self like, who am I? What have I become? Am

I the same person I used to be? What am I supposed to do and in which manner am I to behave?

Erickson asserts that at this stage, the adolescent's search by questioning and redefining his own socio-psychological identity established during earlier stages is definitely linked with (a) his sudden and rapid bodily changes and (b) anxiety and pressures related to this need to make decisions about his future education and career. Consequently, the adolescent tries to search for his new role and identity. He experiments with various sexual, occupational and educational roles to understand who he is and what he can be.

The extent to which an individual is able to develop a sense of identity will depend upon the degree of success he achieves in resolving the crisis related to all the previous stages. Failure in resolving the crises of those periods would be likely, at this stage, to result in role confusion and consequently the individual will not be able to find himself. He may then feel completely bewildered, not knowing what to do and how to behave on his own. He may be unable to make the decision about his educational or professional career or about making friends. The lack of self-identification and role confusion may also lead to over identification with villains and clowns, showing a type of childish and impulsive behaviour or developing conformity in taste and style and intolerance of others. On the other hand, if the psycho-social development of the adolescent results in his achieving a sense of identity, it will result in the individual developing the required confidence in his ability to do things, make him properly balanced in terms of emotional reactions and will place him in harmony with his environment.

Teachers and parents can play a very constructive role in helping adolescents through this identity versus confusion crisis. The adolescents, craving for identity must be fully recognised and it should be clearly understood that adolescents want to be identified as adults and must, therefore, be treated as such and not as children as many teachers and parents tend to do. They should never be belittled or humiliated in front of their peers or anyone else for that matter. They must be assigned responsibilities independently or collectively and be trusted for their promises and conduct.

Stage VI: The period of intimacy vs. isolation (20 to 45 years): This is the sixth stage of psycho-social development, and spans the years of early adulthood. During this stage the individual tends to develop a sense of intimacy or commitment to a close relationship with another person.

Throwing light on this aspect Erickson (1950), writes:

Thus the young adult, emerging from the search for and the insistence on identity, is eager and willing to fuse his identity with that of others. He is ready for intimacy, that is, the capacity to commit himself to concrete affiliations and partnerships and to develop the ethical strength to abide by such commitments even though they may call for significant sacrifices and compromises.

Thus, during this stage, the individual seeks to form close personal attachments by merging his identity with that of another person. The relationships develop into such a close involvement that he tends to risk even the loss of his ego or image as is evidenced in the harmonious relationships between husband and wife and intimate friends, and in the ideal relationship between a teacher and his pupil. The ultimate sense of closeness is clearly visible in terms of the mutual identity experienced at the time of sexual intimacy with one's beloved. Another form of such intimacy is seen in sacrifices made for one's close friends or for members of one's family.

The opposite of intimacy is isolation. When one fails to develop an adequate sense of intimacy by merging one's identity with that of another person or when relations deteriorate for one reason or another, one tends to develop a sense of isolation — a pulling away from relationships and breaking off of ties. Alternatives have to be developed for intimate relationships. It is essential to maintain equilibrium in such cases as the deviation from or denial of intimate relationships is costly in terms of a normal and happy life. This does not mean, however, that isolation is altogether undesirable or harmful. A certain degree of isolation is crucial to the maintenance of one's individuality and the development of one's personality in the desired direction, but if it exceeds certain limits, it may become a serious handicap to the establishment and maintenance of close ties and may lead to loneliness and self-absorption. The crisis of *intimacy* vs. *isolation* needs to be resolved by striking a balance between the two contradictory needs — the need for intimacy and the need to maintain one's individuality. The degree to which one succeeds in resolving this crisis is said to secure one's adjustment with one's self and the world one lives in.

Stage VII: The period of creativity vs. stagnation (middle adulthood — 45 to 65 years): An individual's life up to this stage is taken up with trying to establish himself in a professional career. Now, he needs to satisfy his need for generativity, a concern to establish and guide the next generation. This is realised through nurturing his own children, guiding and directing other young people and by engaging in some kind of creative, productive or fruitful activity that may prove beneficial to society. Instead of caring only for himself or for those in his family or friends who are close to him, he participates in the welfare of the future generation as represented by his own children, pupils, subordinates and young people in general. This is, in fact, an effort at extension of one's self and its merger with self or others in society.

As opposed to the sense of generativity, there is a tendency on the part of the individual to become egoistic and selfish. This leads to stagnation and personal impoverishment. Although it would be quite natural to pause in one's life's work to reflect upon, evaluate and consolidate one's achievements and to regroup one's energies for future productivity, an excess of this habit may result in self-indulgence and psychological invalidism. A balanced adjustment between the extremes of the need for generativity and the need for inactivity is thus required so that in the time of inactivity one may become more energetic and be able to put renewed efforts into rendering service to society and future generations.

Stage VIII: The period of ego-integrity vs. despair (old age, about 65 years onwards): This stage of psycho-social development is associated with later adulthood or old age. Although the precise commencement of old age cannot be determined because some people remain physically and mentally active well into their eighties and nineties, others feel, look and act old even in their fifties, yet biologically speaking, old age may be said to begin when people cease to reproduce.

During this last stage of psycho-social development one is confronted with the final crisis of one's life span, termed ego-integrity vs. despair. Ego-integrity refers to the integration or culmination of the successful resolution of all the seven previous crises in the course of one's life. The successful resolution of the previous crises provides a sense of fulfilment and satisfaction to one's ego. When one reflects on one's past and feels satisfied over what has been done, one is sure to develop a positive outlook about oneself and the world around. A person with a developed sense of ego-integrity is at peace with the life he has lived and has no major regrets over what could have been or for what should have been done differently. On the other hand, persons who have not been able to successfully resolve the previous crises of the developmental stages are sure to feel differently. They look back on their lives with despair and feel dissatisfied with the way they have lived their lives. The thought that they now have no time left for changing the course of their lives and doing what should have been done, makes them feel miserable and, consequently, they are doomed to develop a deep sense of despair. These people can become desperately afraid of death. On the other hand, people who have no regrets for the way their lives have been lived and who have an admiration or love for their ego are easily able to accept the inevitability of their death and live life as fully as they can till their last breath.

At the same time, despair is not the absolute negative aspect of one's personality. To feel satisfied or dissatisfied about one or the other issue is common and natural. One may regret many mistakes and deficiencies of one's life, but this should not be stretched to the point where one develops a sense of disaffection with one's ego and begins to hate oneself and then sinks into a state of utter depression. It is, therefore, essential to strike a balance between the conflicting needs of ego-integrity and despair and to successfully resolve the final crisis of one's life resulting in a well-balanced optimistic outlook for oneself and the outside world in order to live the remaining days of one's life as gracefully and productively as possible.

In a summarised form, Erickson's stages of psycho-social development covering the entire life span of an individual may be represented in the following manner:

Table 12.3. Erickson's Stage of Psycho-Social Development

Stages of Psycho-Social Development	The person and Specific age	Description of the nature of development
1. Trust vs. Mistrust	Infant (Birth to 1½ years)	Development of trust between Caregiver and child
2. Autonomy vs. Shame and Doubt	Toddler (1½ years to 3 years)	Development of control over bodily functions and activities
3. Initiative vs. Guilt	Pre-Schooler (3 years to 6 years)	Testing limits of self-assertion and purposefulness
4. Industry vs. Inferiority	School age child (6 years to 12 years)	Development of sense of mastery and competence

5. Identity vs.   Adolescent   Development of identity and
                           Role confusion   (12 to 20 years)
                                                acknowledge of identity by others

6. Intimacy vs. Isolation Young Adult   Formation of intimate relationships
                           (20 years to 45 years) and commitments

7. Generativity vs.   Middle Age Adult   Development of creative or productive
   Stagnation   (45 to 65 years)   activities that contribute to future
                                                generations

8. Integrity vs.   Older Adult   Acceptance of personal life history and
   Despair   (65 years onwards)   forgiveness of self and others

Vygotsky's socio-cultural theory of development

Lev Vygotsky (1896-1934), a Soviet psychologist, who began his work following the Russian Revolution of 1917, is most closely identified with socio-cultural theory. Vygotsky has developed a socio-cultural approach to children's development (cognitive as well as socio-cultural). He developed his theories at around the same time when Jean Piaget was starting to develop his ideas (1920s and 30s).

According to Vygotsky's socio cultural theory, no single principle (such as Piaget's equilibration) can account for development of the growing children. Actually, individual development cannot be understood without reference to the social and cultural context within which it is embedded. The development of a child in the various dimensions or aspects of his personality including development of higher mental processes has its origin in socio-cultural processes. How does the socio-cultural process related to a developing child affect and influence his development may be broadly discussed as follows:

1. Development as a function of learning carried out in socio-cultural environment

According to Vygotsky individual development in all its dimensions is in fact an acquired phenomenon realised through one's learning efforts. Unlike Piaget's notion that children's development must necessarily precede their learning. Vygotsky (1978: 90) argued *"learning is a necessary and universal aspect of the process of developing culturally organised, specifically human psychological function"*. In other words, social learning tends to precede (come before) development. It is this social leaning made possible through one's social interaction that enables him to get the desired development in all dimensions or aspects of his personality. Regarding the role of learning in development, Vygotsky believed everything is learned on two levels. First, through interaction with others, and then integrated into the individual's mental structure. Emphasizing on this aspect Vygotsky (1978: 57) writes:

Every function in the child's cultural development appears twice: first, on the social level, and later, on the individual level; first, between people (inter-psychological) and then inside the child (intra-psychological). This applies equally to voluntary attention, to logical memory, and to the formation of concepts. All the higher functions originate as actual relationships between individuals.

2. *Vygotsky's views about children's cognitive and socio-cultural development*

According to him children's cognitive development and social development are closely related. In fact one's cognitive development is influenced by the level of one's social development, as well as the impact of his social interaction and culture to which he belongs. Let us see how he tries to explain the cognitive development of children in a close relation of social and cultural influences through some specific concepts and views expressed by him.

- **Children make use of culturally determined tools for intellectual adaptation**

  Regarding the process of cognitive development in children, Piaget was of the view that every child is born with certain motor reflexes and sensory abilities for going ahead in the journey of cognitive development. Unlike him, Vygotsky claimed that infants are born with certain basic materials/abilities for intellectual development referred to as (i) attention, (ii) sensation, (iii) perception and (iv) memory.

  Vygotsky refers to these four as tools of intellectual or cognitive adaptation. His intellectual or cognitive capacity is developed in the way these four tools are found to help him in this task. However, the development and refinement of these tools are quite social and culturally specific. These are picked up and developed in the child through social interaction and social learning. Vygotsky, (1978) believed strongly that community plays a central role in the process of "making meaning." A child's intellectual development cannot be understood without reference to the social and cultural context within which it is embedded. In fact it is very much socially and culturally determined and not directed by biological or innate ones as claimed by Piaget in his theory of cognitive development. As a result, the capacity of the children to attend, sense, perceive and memorise varies from culture to culture. These help children to use their basic mental functions more effectively/adaptively for interacting well in their social circle and culture. Eventually, through interaction within the socio-cultural environment, these are developed into more sophisticated and effective mental processes/strategies which he refers to as Higher Mental Functions.

- **Effects of social influences on child's cognitive and socio-cultural development**

  Like Piaget, Vygotsky believes that young children are curious and actively involved in their own learning and in the discovery and development of new understandings/schemas. However, Vygotsky placed more emphasis on social contributions to the process of development, whereas Piaget emphasised self-initiated discovery. According to Vygotsky (1978), much important learning by the child occurs through social interaction with a skilful or More Knowledgeable One (MKO) who may be a tutor, parent or the more knowledgeable peer. The MKO have the capacity to model behaviors and/or provide verbal instructions for the child. Vygotsky refers to this as cooperative or collaborative dialogue. The child first tries to understand the actions or instructions given to him by his parent or teacher, and then internalises the information using it to guide or regulate his own performance, resulting in his proper cognitive and social development. In this way much of the cognitive and social development of children takes place on account of his interaction with his social environment and particularly the persons he thinks know more than him. He can learn so many simple things by just observing and imitating the behaviour of others but for the higher order cognition he has to take active help and guidance from the more knowledgeable ones.

Highlighting such learning on the part of the small children, Shaffer (1996) has provided an illustration of a young girl who is given her first jigsaw. Alone, she performs poorly in attempting to solve the puzzle. The father then sits with her and describes or demonstrates some basic strategies, such as finding all the corner/edge pieces and provides a couple of pieces for the child to put together herself and offers encouragement when she does so. As the child becomes more competent, the father allows the child to work more independently. This is called social learning; learning through cooperative or collaborate dialogue between a child and the more knowledgeable one that accounts for most of the cognitive and social development of children.

3. The concepts of MKO and ZPD (used for explaining the role of socio-psychological factors in a child's development)

In order to explain how the process of social interaction helps a child in his learning and the subsequent intellectual development, Vygotsky put forward two new concepts coined as More Knowledgeable Other (MKO) and the Zone of Proximal Development (ZPD). Let us see what did these terms mean and how he used them for putting up his theory of socio cultural development.

More Knowledgeable Other (MKO): The more knowledgeable other is somewhat self-explanatory; it refers to someone who has a better understanding or a higher ability level than the learner, with respect to a particular task, process or concept. Although the implication is that the MKO is a teacher or an older adult, this is not necessarily the case. Many times, a child's peers or the elder children may be the individuals with more knowledge or experience; for example, a child who knows more about the diversified application of a mobile phone, tablet or recently loaded video game.

Zone of Proximal Development

A second aspect of Vygotsky's theory is the idea that the potential for cognitive development depends upon the "zone of proximal development" (ZPD). This is an important concept that relates to the difference between what a child can achieve independently and what a child can achieve with guidance and encouragement from a skilled or more knowledgeable partner. (See Figure 12.1). In this way, ZPD actually represents that zone or area where a child can solve a problem with the assistance (scaffolding) of a more knowledgeable one (an adult or more able peer). Proximal simply means "next". It carries two meanings. The first one is that for the child in his task of problem solving or behaviour modification, the person lying next to him in knowledge and experience (superior) may help a lot. He can learn and develop himself intellectually and socially, more so in supervision or collaboration with the adults or peers. In its second meaning, the term proximal or next conveys that

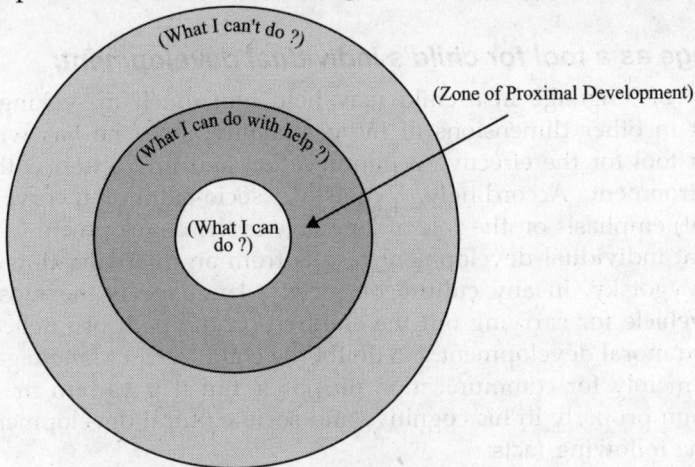

(What I can't do ?)

(Zone of Proximal Development)

(What I can do with help ?)

(What I can do ?)

Fig. 12.1: Zone of Proximal Development

"the key to stretching the learner for taking him on the path of cognitive and social development rests on the part of we adults to know well in advance what lies in that person's ZPD, to what extent he can be helped to go ahead on the path of his cognitive and social development in view of his existing potential". The ZPD of children according to Vygotsky depends on a number of factors, like age, their individuality, the differing nature of the impact of home and family, society and culture in which they are brought up, etc. The circumference of the children widens as the child advances in their age, gets opportunities for learning and are exposed to wider social and cultural experiences.

Taken together, the MKO and the ZPD form the basis of the scaffolding component of the cognitive apprenticeship model of instruction. In this regard, Vygotsky explained that when a student is at the ZPD level for a particular task, providing appropriate assistance (scaffolding) will give the student enough of a "boost" to achieve the task. Once the student, with the benefit of scaffolding, masters the task, the scaffolding can then be removed and the student will then be able to complete the task again on his own. For example, the child could not solve the jigsaw puzzle (in the earlier example) by herself and would have taken a long time to do so (if at all), but was able to solve it following the interaction with the father, and has developed competence at this skill that will be applied to future jigsaws.

4. Role of socio-cultural factors in language development:

Vygotsky's socio-cultural theory clearly emphasises that the language a child uses for his communication is all learned through his interaction and communication with the members of the society and culture he belongs. The initial lessons of his language development are thus learned by a child in the company of his mother, caretaker and other members of the family. The neighbourhood, peers, school and community influences then add to his language development further as he grows and his interaction circle widens. The development of language among the children, thus maybe seen as a clear handy work of the forces and factors present in the socio cultural environment of the child.

5. Language as a tool for child's individual development:

Development of language in a child may help him much in seeking a desirable development in other dimensions of his personality, since he has with him now an important tool for the effective communication and interaction within his socio cultural environment. Accordingly, Vygotsky's socio-cultural theory places more (and different) emphasis on the role of language in the development of the child by signalling that individual development results from an internalisation of language. In view of Vygotsky, in any culture or society, language is the most significant and potent vehicle for carrying out the children on the path of intellectual, social, emotional and moral development. No doubt the child learns a language from social interactions, mainly for communication purposes. But it pays him much in return for helping him properly in his cognitive and socio cultural development chiefly on account of the following facts:

(i) The more proficient he becomes in the learning and use of a language, the more help he gets for having better communication and interaction with others in his social circle and culture resulting in his proper socio-cultural development.

(ii) The development of language helps him in getting ahead of his intellectual development by (i) communicating and getting assistance from the MKO for the needed learning and development of his cognitive abilities and (ii) using language as a tool for thinking and carrying out mental tasks and helping in the development of higher cognitive functioning. Let us understand how Vygotsky talked about the role of language as a tool for the cognitive and intellectual development of children.

- Vygotsky (1987) differentiates between three forms of language:

  (i) social speech which is external communication used to talk to others (typical from the age of two); (ii) private speech (typical from the age of three) which is directed to the self and serves an intellectual function; and (iii) finally private speech goes underground, diminishing in audibility as it takes on a self-regulating function and is transformed into silent inner speech (typical from the age of seven).

- With regard to the initiation of the development of language in the children, Vygotsky differs from Piaget's assertion that language depends on thought for its development, (i.e., thought comes before language). In his opinion, language development does not need thought or thinking of any kind for its development. In the beginning period of life approximately up to two years, thoughts and language are two separate systems and the child learns a form of language termed by him as social speech from his social environment as a means of communicating with other.

- After two years, the development of language in the children takes a new form when there is some coordination between their thoughts and language. At this point speech and thought become interdependent: thought becomes verbal and speech becomes a means of expressing one's thoughts in an open way. This newly developed form of the children's language has been named as "private speech" by Vygotsky. Private speech can be typically defined in contrast to social speech, as an external speech addressed to the self (not to others) and is specifically used by the children for the purpose of self-regulation (rather than communication). What they think needs to be done for doing a task (solving a problem) is uttered and talked by them to their self (in a shape of self-talk). Vygotsky sees "private speech" as a means for self-regulation, i.e., to plan activities and strategies on the part of children and therefore aid their development. Vygotsky believed that children who engaged in large amounts of private speech are more socially and intellectually competent than children who do not use it extensively. Vygotsky (1987) notes that private speech does not merely accompany a child's activity but acts as a tool used by the developing child to facilitate cognitive processes, such as overcoming task obstacles, enhancing imagination, thinking and conscious awareness.

- After, the development of private speech, then begins the era for the development of inner speech, the most useful form of the language that works as a potent tool for the cognitive development of children. Unlike private speech which is overt, inner speech is covert (hidden). Commenting on the very nature of inner speech Vygotsky (1962: 149) writes:

  Inner speech is not the interior aspect of external speech - it is a function in itself. It still remains speech, *i.e.*, thought connected with words. But while in external speech thought is embodied in words, in inner speech words die as they bring forth thought. Inner speech is, to a large extent, thinking in pure meanings.

The internalisation of language is important as it drives the child to his needed gradual cognitive development. He makes use of inner speech as a an important tool for the necessary thinking about the processes and activities necessary for his task of problem solving and thus allowing himself to be developed intellectually as well as socially.

Classroom Implications

Vygotsky's socio-cultural theory may be found to carry with it a number of useful instructional and classroom implications summarised as follows:

1. According to Vygotsky, children from their early childhood have to make use of a set of four abilities named (i) attention, (ii) sensation, (iii) perception and (iv) memory as tools for their needed intellectual or cognitive adaptation. In classroom learning and instruction also, the proper equipping of the children

with these four abilities pays quite a rich dividend. Hence, due care from the very beginning should be observed for the development as well as the utilisation of these abilities for the proper learning, grasping and application of the facts learned and experiences gained in and outside the school environment. The children should be trained to pay attention, utilise fully their abilities of sensation and perception while observing the things and phenomenon, and remember the learned and practiced things for their needed application in further learning and utilisation in life.

2. According to Vygotsky, the development of children is very culture specific and thus when a child comes to school he brings with him the level of cognitive, social, emotional, and language development and potential background for the school learning determined by the social and cultural environment of his home, family, community and society. The teacher and trainer should always keep in mind such individual differences among students before venturing to help and guide them on their path of learning.

3. The views expressed by Vygotsky concerning, MKO, and ZPD carry wide educational implications. Children have the natural curiosity to know, explore and construct knowledge. They can learn and practice many things with their own as a result of their social and cultural exposure and self-experiences. However, there is a limit of such learning on their part. They can't learn, do and behave beyond a certain limit of their own. For their further learning, cognitive and social development thus they are essentially needed to provide appropriate assistance by parents, teachers. instructors or their more knowledgeable peers. However, in doing so as Vygotsky warns we should be careful that (i) the child should not be made dependent on such assistance for his further learning and development and (ii) he should not be too stretched for his learning and development as he can't go on this path beyond the limits of his ZPD.

4. Vygotsky's view concerning ZPD also provides us quite useful hints about the abilities, experiences and skills of teachers, instructors, guides and counsellors who are entrusted with the task of providing needed assistance to children in their learning and development. Decidedly these people should be sufficiently more knowledgeable, experienced, trained and competent than students they are guiding, training or teaching.

5. Vygotsky's views concerning ZPD also provide direction and guidelines for setting the curriculum and planning teaching-learning experiences for individual learners in view of their generalised and specific ZPD levels. What learning experiences should be provided in a particular grade or age level to developing children? How and to what extent these should be enriched as students step in the higher grades? The concept of ZPD here helps us much in enlightening the path.

6. Language plays quite a significant role in the overall development of children from their earlier childhood. The language in speech form (verbal, non-verbal, oral or written) helps much in proper communication of ideas, views, feelings, interests and attitudes between and among the people and thus proves a strong

media of social interaction, cooperation and collaboration between human beings. As a result, Vygotsky's views regarding the development of language in the speech form, guide and inspire teachers and parents to focus properly on the development of language in its appropriate way in the children as a means of effective communication and social and cultural development. The other second form of language called private speech (self-talk) is also essential as it prepares the individual to get self-motivation, readiness and step wise preparation for the execution of a task or behaviour in its desired form. However, it should be converted into a silent inner speech (not to be heard by others) as a child steps into a growing responsible age. What is to be done in its external form through active behaviour is actually rehearsed and executed internally in the mind by an individual through his inner speech. It thus stands as a powerful tool for carrying out higher order thought processes and behavioural functioning in a desired way. Gradually with the increase in age, thus, children should be helped by their teachers and parents in making use of the self-talk desirably in the form of their inner speech for getting them well on the path of their cognitive, social, emotional, and moral development.

Summary

Social development refers to a process as a result of which a child acquires various social qualities and characteristics through his constant interaction with his social environment. It helps him to adjust in the social environment by maintaining proper social relationships.

The process of social development begins with an infant's first contact with other people and continues throughout his life. The early stage of social behaviour during infancy is characterised by negative social characteristics like shyness, rivalry, desire for possession, imitation, etc. Later on, in early childhood positive aspects of social behaviour like co-operation, sympathy and social approval, etc., begin to take roots. During later childhood, a child begins to acquire distinctive social qualities with the widening of his area of social contact. In his further journey towards social development, adolescence provides him valuable opportunities for the acquisition of maximum social awareness, increasing social relationships and intimate friendships. By the end of this stage, the social behaviour of a child almost matures.

Social development aims at helping a child attain social maturity. A socially mature individual proves a valuable asset to himself (by being properly adjusted in his social world through the maintenance of proper social relationships) and to the society (by becoming conscious of his social obligations).

Both personal as well as environmental factors work side by side in the process of social development of a child. Among the personal factors we can include bodily structure and health, intelligence and emotional development. Environmental factors include factors like family environment, school environment, peer group relationships and gang influence, community and neighbourhood, religious institutions, clubs, information and entertainment agencies as a potent means for shaping and moulding the social behaviour of a child.

Erickson's theory of psycho-social development brings into light the distinctive eight stages of psycho-social development spanning from one's birth through adulthood named as Trust v/s Mistrust (birth-1.5 years), Autonomy v/s Shame and Doubt (1.5-3 years), Initiative v/s Guilt (3-6 years), Industry v/s Inferiority (6-12 years), Identity v/s Role Confusion (12-20 years), Intimacy v/s Isolation (20-45 years), Generativity v/s Stagnation (45-65 years), and Ego Integrity v/s Despair (65 years onwards). According to Erickson, at each stage of his development, the child faces a new crisis, i.e., an issue that needs to be resolved at that particular stage of development, the way in which the crisis of each stage is resolved has a major bearing on the development of one's personality. It is well reflected in the shape of positive and negative aspect of one's behaviour leading to his adjustment or maladjustment to his self and the environment resulting in his success or failure in life.

According to Vygotsky's socio-cultural theory of development, individual development cannot be understood without reference to the social and cultural context within which it is embedded. The development of a child in the various dimensions or aspects of his personality including development of higher mental processes has its origin in socio-cultural processes.

According to Vygotsky much important learning by the child for his needed development occurs through social interaction with a skilful or more knowledgeable one (MKO) who may be of a more knowledgeable (termed scaffolding by Vygotsky) the developing child progresses on the path of knowledge construction and skill acquisition for his needed progress and development in various aspects or dimensions of his personality. The development of language also helps the children in their proper social interaction which in turn helps them in seeking development in one or the other aspects of their personality.

References and Suggested Readings

Carmichael, L. (Ed.), *Manual of Child Psychology*, John Wiley, New York, 1946.

Crow, L.D., and Crow, Alice, *Child Psychology*, reprint, Barney & Noble, New York, 1969.

Erickson, E., *Childhood and Society*, (2nd ed.), New York: Norton, 1963.

Erickson, E., (1950) *Childhood and Society*, New York: Norton.

Erickson, E., *Identity: Youth and Crises*, New York: Norton, 1968.

Freeman and Showel, quoted by Hurlock, E.B., *Child Psychology*, Asian student 3rd ed., McGraw-Hill, Tokyo, 1959.

Garrett, H.E., *General Psychology*, 2nd ed., Eurasia Publishing House, New Delhi, 1968.

Hurlock, E.B., *Child Psychology*, Asian student 3rd ed., McGraw-Hill, Tokyo, 1959.

Marry, F.K. and Marry, R.V., *From Infancy to Adolescence*, Harper & Brothers, New York, 1940.

Sorenson, Herbert, *Psychology in Education*, McGraw-Hill, New York, 1948.

Vygotsky, L.S., *Thought and Language* (E. Haufmann & G. Vakar, Eds. And Trans.), Cambridge, MA: MIT Press, 1962.

Vygotsky, L.S., *Mind and Society: The Development of Higher Mental Process*, Cambridge, M.A.: Harvard University Press, 1978.

Vygotsky, L.S., 'The Kind of Speech', in R.W. Rieberd and A.S. Carton (Eds.), *The Collected Works of L.S. Vygotsky*, Volume I: 'Problems of General Psychology' (pp 39, 285), New York: Plenum Press, 1987 (Original Work Published, 1934).

13

Language Development

Meaning of Language

Language is such a powerful means of communication that can be employed effectively for exchanging ideas, feelings and expressions between and among people. It has quite a comprehensive meaning, as it also - includes all types of non-verbal expressions like facial expressions, gestures, use of symbols and signals, and artistic creations. In this way, conveying our thoughts and feelings through symbolic expressions and gestures like speaking through eyes, and movements of hands, foot, head, nose and eyebrows may be termed as the various forms and shapes of the use language on our part. However, in case we try to pick up a real and accurate meaning of the term language, then we can come to the conclusion that it is not so extensive and broad as indicated above, but stands to be quite simple, brief and straight forward. In its simple and technically sound meaning, it stands for a well meaningful composition or aggregate of words and sounds capable of providing maximum assistance for the expression and communication of our thoughts and feelings.

Forms of Language

In the light of defining the term language, we can very well distinguish two main forms/kinds of language identified as oral and written language. We can further classify these two forms/ kinds of language in the manner shown in figure 13.1

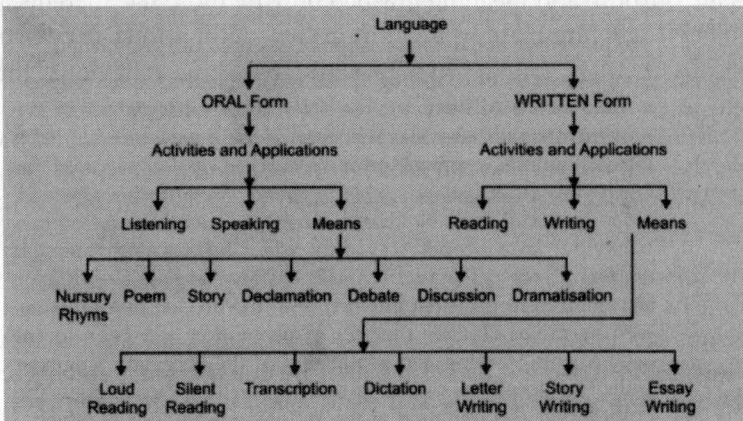

Fig. 13.1 Forms of Language and their prevalent uses or applications

The Process of Language Development

Language is learned and acquired like other skills. The process of such learning or acquisition starts with the birth of a child. Things and factors like observation and imitation, interaction with the environment and the demands placed for realisation of the physiological and socio-psychological needs play a significant role in the proper development of language among children. The developmental process of learning goes on in quite a steady and slower place as explained here in detail.

The Stage Prior to Actual Language Development

In this initial or starting stage of language development the child seems to get ready or prepare himself for comprehending and utilising the form of language expressed through symbols or signs. Such readiness on his part may be visible through the following actions and activities:

(i) In the initial step just after birth, the child may be seen to get engaged in activities like weeping and crying.

(ii) Along with weeping and crying, actions and sounds, the child gradually may be able to produce other sounds well accompanied with the actions or activities like yawning and fast breathing. These actions or activities are absolutely natural automatic and innate and no wilful attempts are made for their learning and execution.

(iii) Subsequently, children may be seen to get engaged in the actions and activities involving babbling as a sign of the initial emergence of language development among children. The children are able to demonstrate such early language behaviour at the earlier age of two to three months. Such babbling on the part of infants provides them opportunities for the drill and practice of the vowels and consonant sounds. They may be found to repeat the utterance of others as heard and grasped by them in their own ways. In doing so, they may be seen to produce the sound of vowels earlier than the consonants. They try to utter vowels and consonants in a repeated way and it is this utterance that is termed as babbling on the part of children. Their babbling although has no parallel in encyclopaedia yet it carries a specific purpose and meaning grasped only by those (i.e., parents and family members) who are close to them in understanding their needs and actions.

(iv) Along with their sound producing and babbling behaviour, the children begin to express or communicate their thoughts and feelings with the help of gestures, symbols and signals. In this connection, every child has his own sign or signal system that can only be grasped and understood by his parents and intimate ones. Accordingly, they may be seen to make use of different signs, symbols or signals for conveying that they are hungry, their stomach is now full, they want you to be with them, etc. In this way, during this period or stage of language development a child is not able to use words or sentences in his utterance. He can only communicate his thoughts and feelings either with the use of his own invented signs, symbols and signals or by uttering a few vowels and consonants graspable only by his parents or intimates.

The Stage Related to Actual Language Development

After the initial stage of readiness or preparation, the actual stage of language development among the children usually begins to emerge at the age of 10 and 11 months. In the course of language development here the task starts with the acquisition of the skill or ability related to oral expression. A child, thus, first learns to speak and grasp the meaning of certain specific words, sentences and the language composed of these words and sentences. His oral vocabulary increases and the abilities and skills related to oral expression improve. In subsequent years after getting access to school education and receiving training in using writing skills, he begins to demonstrate efficiency in using language in its writing form. In this way, now he may be seen to progress gradually on the path of acquiring and using both the forms of language — oral and written for his communication, development and progress. He can develop his language abilities and skills to the extent of utilising them not only for the purpose of communication but also for the learning of other curricular subjects and seeking his wholesome all round development in different aspects or dimensions of his personality. How does a child's language development proceed during the different ages or stages of his developmental period? Let us try to seek the answer by classifying/categorising a child's language development under the following aspects or dimensions:

A. Development of oral vocabulary
B. Development of oral expression or speech power
C. Development of reading ability or expression
D. Development of writing ability or written expression

A. Development of oral vocabulary

Words related to a language and their vocabularies possess a wide significance in the language development of children. In oral vocabulary, children first try to pick up words. These words later on take the form of sentences and the formation of sentences give birth to a capable form of applied language that can be successfully used for the exchange or communication of their thoughts and feelings. The development of the oral vocabulary takes place in the child gradually at a slow pace. After birth as soon as he begins to utter sounds along with their inherent meanings, he becomes capable of grasping the words along with their pronunciation. Every new word grasped or pronounced by him becomes a solid means or instrument of fulfilling one of his needs or purpose and in turn it becomes an appropriate source of reinforcing his language learning behaviour. As a result, he may be seen trying for the grasping, understanding and pronouncing of many new words helpful in the appropriate development of his oral vocabulary.

How the oral vocabulary of children gradually develops has been studied by a number of psychologists and language scholars. Table 13.1 shows the consensus reached on the part of scholars in terms of the development of oral vocabulary on the part of growing children.

Table 13.1: Development of Oral Vocabulary across ages among children

Age of children	Vocabulary of children
From birth to 8 months	0
From 9 months to 12 months	3 or 4 words
One and half years	10-12 words
Two years	272 words
Two a half years	450 words
Three years	1000 words
Three a half years	1250 words
Four years	1600 words
Five years	2100 words
Eleven years	50000 words
Fourteen years	80000 words
Sixteen years	More than one lakh

In this we may see that as soon as the child enters the school-going age after getting five years old, his oral vocabulary increases with a good speed. In fact the developed vocabulary is very much dependant on the subsequent growth and development in the intellectual abilities and social skills as well as the appropriate environment and opportunities available for learning and progress. The oral vocabulary of the children thus gets increased in the proportion of the facilities and opportunities available to him for its adequate development.

The development of oral vocabulary may exhibit many other characteristics and uniqueness besides a mere increase in the acquisition of new words in the following manner:

1. Generally there are two types of words available in the oral vocabulary of children one of which are those that are actively used by them for serving their purposes. They understand and grasp their meaning well. The others belongs to the category that are not made into use by children themselves but they can understand their meaning well if spoken or uttered by someone else.

2. In taking into consideration the value or significance of the utilised words the children's oral vocabulary may be classified into two main categories — General vocabulary and Specific vocabulary. In the first category, we may include the words that are used by children generally in all situations. In the second category, we may include or put those words that are used by children in particular situations for serving specific purposes. In the development of general vocabulary among children, the words signifying nouns appear in the vocabulary of children first, followed by the words signifying adjectives, pronouns, verbs, adverbs, etc. The development in the area of specific vocabulary goes on with the increase in age. In addition, the development in specific vocabulary is also guided and directed through the type of interactions children make with their environment, and the nature and quality of education and upbringing they receive at the hands of teachers and parents. In general, the specific vocabulary of children may be found to provide space for the following words:

(i)   The words related to colour sense.

(ii)   The words related to time sense such as yesterday, today, tomorrow, morning, evening, day, night, winter, rainy, summer, etc.

(iii) The names of animals, birds, vegetables and fruits.

(iv)   The body parts such as eyes, ears, nose, hand, feet, legs, stomach, etc.

(v)   The words related to currency and money counting.

(vi)   The words used in measurement.

(vii) The improper, uncultured and abusive words.

(viii) The words used for showing courtesy and respect such as thanks, sir, your honour, excuse me, etc.

(ix)   The words related to the use of transport and entertainment means like television, cinema, mobile and computer appliances.

(x)   The secrete coded language used by children for interacting with their peers.

3. In the children's oral vocabulary, first we may witness the presence of the words related to the satisfaction of their physical or physiological needs and then the words associated with the satisfaction of their socio-psychological needs. In relation to the development of the vocabulary concerning the satisfaction of their socio-psychological needs, the scope is initially limited to the parents, siblings and other family members. However, as the child grows and develops, the area and scope of his social contacts and interaction widens and accordingly he matures in terms of his increased vocabulary concerning social behaviour and environmental surroundings.

B. Development of Oral Expression or Speech Power

In the task of developing oral expression or speech power among children, things like pronunciation and understanding of sounds, words and sentences carry an immense importance. The attempts in this direction get initiated just after birth. The task of oral expression and speech power development actually begins with the attempts made on the part of children with their babbling (meaningless and vague pronunciation of sounds). At this stage, they may also try to grasp the meaning conveyed through the sounds and words pronounced by others. Such ability acquired on the part of the children is named as their comprehension ability. Development of this ability actually helps a lot in the oral expression or speech power of children. Its development takes place in the children before they pick up the ability to speak. When they hear the words like take water, bring milk to the Baby, where is the toy, etc., it makes them quite alert and attentive signifying that they comprehend the meaning of these words and sentences uttered by others. In this way, development of comprehension ability of the spoken words may be termed as a first solid step in the direction of developing oral expression or speech power among children.

The second major step in this direction is concerned with the development of appropriate vocabulary along with its desirable pronunciation. However, a child in the beginning is not able to pronounce the sounds and words used in his language expression. At this stage, generally children may be seen to have incorrect pronunciation of the words and sentences.

In the initial stage, children feel pleasure in pronouncing speedily all the words that are present in their vocabulary. However, gradually they learn to speak a particular word that is relevant at a time in a particular situation. Moreover, the speaking of the words precedes the speaking of a full sentence. For example, instead of saying that "I am thirty and want to take water," the child utters the word 'water' or 'mum', gradually instead of using a single word for conveying his purpose he may begin to use two or more words in combination and thus gradually by the end of two years he learns to speak word sentences like: 'Give me milk', 'I want toy', 'come near me', etc. Later on as he grows in age he begins to make use of simple sentences with a developed vocabulary with him according to his age. Initially the sentences spoken by him are quite small and incomplete. However, up to the age of five years there is sufficient improvement and as a result before entering school he may be capable of using compound sentences in his language expression.

After entering school, there is a significant development in his oral and speech power. It happens because he gets wide opportunities of enough exposure, interaction and communication with his peers and teachers. Language is specifically taught as the subject of school, curriculum and he makes its use as a medium of learning and understanding other subjects of the school curriculum. As a result, there happens a great increase in the expressive and speech power of children.

C. Development of Reading Ability

By the term reading ability we here mean the language ability of a child helping him to identify or recognise the written and printed language symbols, words and sentences in a proper way along with their needed comprehension and understanding on his part. It helps him well in receiving the message, idea or feelings inherent in a written piece of statement. The stages of the development of reading ability among the children may be summarised as follows:

(i)   The task of the development of reading ability among children starts just after they become capable of utilising their sense organs for getting information or knowledge. Their ability to identity and classify objects may help them in identifying or recognising letters of the alphabets. The acquisition of the ability to identify and name the letters may be regarded as the first step taken towards developing reading ability among children. Usually a child of three years may exhibit such ability. When a child is shown an apple in the chart he may first identify it as a picture of an apple and then can associate it with the letter 'A'. This visual experience can lead the child to know and learn that the letter 'A' stands for apple.

(ii) Acquaintance and understanding of the letters of alphabet is followed by the knowledge and comprehension of words. Children who get early mastery over the letters may be able to pick up word comprehension also at quite a earlier stage. The starting in this process is made with the learning to read the words composed of quite a few letters.

(iii) It is followed by learning to read a full sentence. Initially they try to read simple and short sentences and then the more difficult and complex ones. Here, the silent as well loud reading can play an important role in helping children to develop appropriate ability of reading the paragraphs of texts.

D. Development of Writing Ability or Written Expression

By the term writing ability or expression we mean a language ability of a child helpful for him in expressing his thoughts and feelings in a written form. With the acquisition of such ability the child can now acquire the power of expressing his ideas and feelings through the visual form of the symbolic language, alphabets, words and sentences instead of merely expressing them in an oral form.

It must be clearly noted that the task of developing writing ability is carried out well only after the acquisition of proper reading comprehension and ability on the part of children. A required level of physical and mental maturity is also needed for initiating the acquisition of writing skill on the part of children. It is essential because writing on their part requires proper development of the coordinated muscles of the fingers as well as the development of proper cognitive focusing and attention for copying the alphabets in their appropriate form. It is why, we can't think of developing the writing ability among children during the period of infancy. The following usually may help much in developing appropriate writing ability or skill among children:

(i) Attempts should be made to create the state of readiness and motivation among children for the acquisition of writing skills by paying attention over the proper identification of the structure and formation of letters, words and sentences.

(ii) We should wait for the necessary acquisition of the level of physical and mental maturity on the part of a developing child in order to becoming a necessary fit and capable of doing writing work.

(iii) The initial attempts for the development of writing skill among children may be made to assist the child manually (by holding their hand desirably at the time of their writing) till the time they become capable of holding the writing material in an independent way.

(iv) The teachers or parents may draw the letter figures on sand with their fingers or on papers with a pencil or writing pen. They may then ask the child to go over it with their fingers or pencils. With sufficient practice they can thus learn gradually the writing of all the letters of the alphabets.

(v) After learning to write single letters children should be made to learn writing of simple words and sentences.

(vi) The help of transcription and dictation may be properly taken for the development of proper writing ability among children. For this purpose, children may be given the home task or drill work of copying passages of a text and they may also be told to write in their notebooks whatever is dictated by the teacher in the class.

(vii) Next step in the development of the writing ability among children is concerned with providing them desired freedom and opportunity for expressing their thoughts and feelings in the written form. The writing of essays, letters, short stories, episodes, poems, dramas, critical analysis, etc., falls under the domain of such creative writing. At this stage, they should also be given appropriate knowledge and understanding of grammar of a specific language and also should be encouraged to demonstrate the required creativity and constructiveness in their written expression.

Factors Influencing Language Development

As discussed earlier, the development of language among children takes place only after their birth. As a result, heredity may be said not to play any mentionable role in the development of language. In practice also it actually happens. Language is not inherited, it is acquired, no genes and chromosomes are responsible for getting the linguistic abilities transferred from one generation to another. However, it is not also appropriate to deny any role for children's heredity in the development of their language. The children inherit a number of things in the form of their physical and mental capacities that may actually work as a potent deciding factor for the learning, acquisition and functioning of language skills among children. For example, in a case where a child is born with deformity and defects in his vocal apparatus — lungs, lips, tongue, teeth, throat or he suffers from acute physical or mental disability then decidedly it may cast quite a damaging and negative effect on the development of proper linguistic ability in him. However, no control can be exercised over such happenings. It is a natural process and accordingly we should not expect from the sufferers to have a normal level of language development. In this direction, what can be done is limited only to taking appropriate steps for their adequate adjustment and needed emotional development helpful in their living and developing.

By leaving aside the factors associated with inheritance, if we try to think over the other things responsible for the development of language among children then, we can talk about them in the following manner:

1. **Physical Health:** Language development of a child is greatly influenced by the nature and quality of his physical health. A physically strong and healthy child may be found to put up necessary energy in the task of acquiring language, but a child having health and suffering from ailments may remain deprived of the opportunities to learn language. A physically healthy and fit child enjoys the privilege of having his physical organs or components in a quite healthy and workable fashion. He knows that the fitness and adequate health of the physical organs such as, vocal apparatus, lips, tongue, teeth, lungs, brain and nervous system play quite a significant role in the proper development of language among children and this can be only possible through the acquisition of good physical health and normal development on the part of children.

2. **Mental Health:** An adequate mental health is quite essential for the proper language development of a child. Children who enjoy good mental health may be found to proceed on their language learning path in a satisfactory way. On the contrary, children passing through the states of anxiety, stress and conflicts may face a lot of difficulty in the task of acquiring desirable language skills. Mentally unhealthy and disturbed children may be found to fall victims of speech and writing disorders.

3. **Maturation:** The children's language development is affected and influenced with the natural growth in their age and maturity level. For the development and functioning of language skills like speaking, reading, comprehending and writing Children require a desired level of physical and mental maturity. Attainment of a desired level of such maturity on their part can help them

well in the task of the development of language. That is why it is quite useless to try the development of speech power among children unless they acquire necessary maturity for this purpose. Similarly, it is not fruitful to try for the acquisition of writing skills on the part of children unless they acquire necessary physical (proper coordination capability and holding power of their fingers) and mental maturity.

4. **Intelligence and Mental Development:** There is quite an intimate relationship between the acquisition of language and development of the intellectual and mental capacities. The inadequacy and deficiency arising in the development of mental and intellectual capacities may create a great hurdle in the proper development of language among children. Contrarily, the adequate development of mental and intellectual capacities among children may help them well in their efforts of gaining useful language skills. It is why the gifted and genius may be found to be imbibed with necessary developed language skills.

5. **Social Development:** Language is learned properly by children through their social interaction and contacts with elders and peers. Such interactions and contacts can be made by children after gaining desired sociability and social traits and it can be possible only through their adequate social development. Consequently, when children having adequate social development are found to get ahead on the path of language development, the child suffering from the inadequacy of their social development may be affected quite adversely in terms of their language development.

6. **Emotional Development:** One's emotions are intimately related with the expression of their thoughts and feelings. Language also serves the function of helping children in the adequate expression of their thoughts and feelings. Accordingly language and emotional developments both may be found to have quite an intimate relationship. The children who are found to be adequately developed and adjusted in respect to the expression of their feelings and emotions may also be seen quite developed in terms of the acquisition of language skills. Contrarily children facing emotional maladjustment may be found to fall victim to a number of language disorders and deficiencies.

7. **Role of Family:** Language is learned through the observation and imitation of the language behaviour of elders and peers. In this connection, mother is his first teacher. The other members of the family also prove as models for his language acquisition task. He picks up the language spoken in his family. The goodness and limitations shown on the part of family members in terms of the use of language are automatically transferred to the developing children and it affects their language development in either a positive or negative way. Besides this the congenial or uncongenial environment prevailing at home, the economic and socio-cultural status and conditions available in the family may be found to influence the physical, mental, social, emotional and educational development and adjustment of children which in turn may be found to influence the children's language development in a favourable or adverse way.

8. **Peer group and friend circle:** In the task of acquiring language through the observation and imitation of the behaviour of others, the peer group and friend circle of the child also play quite a decisive role. The child spends most of the time outside his family in the company of his peers and friends. Accordingly, the child acquires the language spoken and used by them. Sometimes, the parents and his family members may be astonished to see that the small child is speaking a language other than the language spoken by the family members. However, it is very natural for a child of a Punjabi family to speak in Haryanavi tone or make use of Haryanavi words, on account of having so many Haryanavi friends and peers. The elders in spite of living in Haryana for so many years may not be able to make use of Haryanavi, but the child in spite of having Hindi as the medium of instruction is capable of speaking and using Haryanavi dialect merely on account of the effect and influence of his peers and friends.

9. **Society and community:** In the acquisition of language, society and community may also play quite an important role. A child is motivated and gets interested in the learning of the language that is spoken and used by the members of his community and society. As a result, a child belonging to an Anglo-Indian Society may naturally develop a tendency to use many English words and accents in his speech and writing of the language. Similarly we can usually visualise the effect of local dialect and regional languages such as Bihari, Rajasthani, Haryanavi, Punjabi on the dialects used and language spoken and written by the children belonging to the communities who make use of these local or regional languages.

10. **School education and environment:** The school environment and education available to children for their language development may also affect the language development of the children in quite a substantial way. The quality of teachers available in schools, the methods and techniques used for language teaching, the media of instruction employed in schools, the types of experiences provided to the students for the development of language and its use through the organisation of curricular activities, the interaction and communication carried out among students and teachers etc., may be cited as a sizable factor contributing towards the proper development of language among children.

11. **Learning potential and factors associated with learning:** The language is the subject of learning. It is learned and acquired like so many skills and traits of one's personality. Its acquisition therefore depends on the quality and level of the learner's learning potential. The children who have potential to learn better in a short time may also pick up better speed and learn language skills in a better way in comparison to those who have little interest or enthusiasm and are relatively slow in learning. Moreover, as we know one's learning is also influenced and affected through a number of other related factors like level of aspiration, achievement motivation, interest and attitude, opportunities for healthy competition and cooperation, rewards and incentives, learning environment, methods and techniques used for learning,

time devoted and energy spent for learning, as well as the environmental situation prevailing at the time of learning. The suitability and unsuitability of these factors may positively or adversely affect language development in children. In addition, the availability of appropriate direction, guidance, timely assistance, provision of appropriate evaluation and feedback also may prove a potent contributing factor for the proper development of language ability and skills among children.

Theories of Language Development

The task of language development taking place among growing children has been investigated and explained by a number of scholars and researchers in the field of language in their own ways. As a result, they have arrived at various viewpoints or theoretical perspectives termed as theories of language development. Out of all these, we will discuss a few important ones. Let us begin first with the most common and practical theory named as Imitation and Reinforcement theory of language development.

Imitation and Reinforcement Theory of Language Development

According to this theory children acquire language through a simple learning process known as imitation of the model language behaviour of their adults and its subsequent reinforcement. How it happens can be best explained through the ideas put up in Bandura's social learning theory and Skinner's operant conditioning theory.

Albert Bandura's social learning theory conveys that while engaging in the learning of a language, a child first observes (looks and listens) what is conveyed by the utterances of some specific sounds and gestures by adults and then imitates and practices what is being observed and imitated. Thus, the sequence suggested by Albert Bandura for language learning is quite systematic, logical and practicable, i.e., the child observes, imitates, practices and then learns what is observed, imitated and practiced (Levine & Munsch, 2014:290).

The other proper explanation for language learning springs from Skinner's theory of operant conditioning. According to this theory, the beginning in this direction is made by responding on the part of the parents and elders to the babbling sounds (resembling useful words) of toddlers with smiles, hugs and speech. Commenting on such early language learning behaviour of the toddlers, Meggitt Carolyn (2012:185) writes:

Adults particularly parents react to random, babbling sounds made by babies and toddlers. They conclude that the baby is asking for something, e.g. "bi-bi or bis-bis" means biscuit. They respond by providing the biscuit and by giving the correct name for it. As the toddler is eating the biscuit, they repeat the sound bi-bi, and the association between the sound and the child's experience of eating the biscuit is reinforced by the adult saying: "yes, that's right, you've got a biscuit"

In fact, the principle of operant conditioning emphasised by Skinner in his theory provides quite a reasonable explanation for the learning of all types of learning including language skills on the part of children. According to Skinner (1957, 1991) language is also shaped through operant conditioning and the use of reinforcement.

When we respond to a baby's babbling with a smile or vocalisation of our own, babies babble more. If we respond to a request for "cookie" with desired cookie, it becomes more likely that the child will use that word again the next time she wants a cookie. Consistent with these ideas, research has shown that the more mothers respond to their babies' vocalisations, the sooner their babies develop language.

In this way, according to the imitation and reinforcement theory of language development the task of language development begins with the process of modelling (observation and imitation of the behaviour of elders) as well as reinforcement of the early attempts of the child for the utterances of the sounds and word resembling the native language. In Skinner's view, when infants make a variety of speech sounds in a seemingly random fashion, adults respond favourably and so encourage children to repeat only those sounds used in the local language. As children grow older, Skinner proposed, adults begin to reinforce the use of actual words, then the use of multiword combinations, and eventually only word combinations that are, from an adult's perspective grammatically correct (McDevitt and Ormrod, 2013:326-27). In this connection, it is also important to add that sounds and words that are not part of the language that the child will eventually speak are not reinforced and therefore are extinguished.

The behavioural perspective involving imitation and reinforcement has been found quite capable for explaining many of the things concerning the development of language among children. However, it also suffers from a number of shortcomings and limitations for fulfilling its responsibilities on this account such as follows:

- Children often may be found to utter a number of novel words and sentences and committing errors (e.g., boaties, shoppies) that are not reinforced by or copied from elders and peers. From where have these crept in their language behaviour? The imitation and reinforcement theory does not provide any valid explanation for this.

- To teach language through the adoption of operant conditioning much like the learning complex skills is not an easy task. Adults would have to engage in intensive tutoring, continuously modelling and reinforcing to yield the extensive vocabulary and complex sentences of a typical 6 year old — a physically impossible task. (Berk, 2009:359)

Nativist Theory of Language Development

In pointing out the limitations of the theory of imitation and reinforcement, we have just said that it has been incapable of explaining the language behaviour of developing children in which they are found uttering a number of such words and sentences they have never said or heard before from their parents, elders and other members of their social surroundings. It clearly implies then there must be something inherited among the children for this purpose and certainly it is as advocated by the nativist perspective of language development. In this connection, the credit for bringing and popularising this perspective goes to an American psycholinguist named Noam Chomsky. He through his writings in the 1960s argued that although children are not born with knowing any particular language, yet they inherit some predispositions that help them in the acquisition of the knowledge and skills related to a language. Noam Chomsky, in this connection clearly asserted that developing children have a biological built-in mechanism — a language acquisition device (popularly called as LAD) that enables them to learn many complex aspects of one or the other languages in a very short period of time. Throwing light on this aspect Chomsky (1976) has opined as follows:

There lie necessary aspects of a universal grammar within the instrument LAD. It may be thought as a built-in storehouse of rules applicable to all human languages. Young children use this knowledge to decipher grammatical categories and relationships in any language to which they are exposed. Because the LAD is specifically suited for language processing, children master the structure of language spontaneously, with only limited language exposure.

In this way, according to Chomsky children are born with a basic instrument LCD in the shape of basic language principles or rules of grammar hardwired in their brain. We can equate them with the basic principles that underline the operation of the hard drive of our computer. Just as our computer's hard drive can run many different types of software, the language structures in our brain can process the specific characteristics of many different languages (Levine & Munsch, 2014:291).

In addition to bringing the concept of LCD for highlighting the role of inborn biological characteristics of children, the nativist perspective of language development may also be given credit for evolving the concept of sensitive or critical periods associated with the development of language among children. According to nativist, thus, there lie certain periods or timings in the life of developing children known as sensitive or critical periods in which they are best helped by their LCD to acquire one or the other aspects of language learning.

In this way, the nativist perspective is found to do a good job in highlighting the role of inheritance and biological maturity in the development of language among children. However, it has also been subjected to criticism on the following grounds:

1. The claim that human beings inherit a specific neurological mechanism (known as LCD helpful in the acquisition of language) has no research-based evidence. In case if children are born with an innate capacity for language learning, then why it is so that they need a number of years and strenuous efforts to learn one or the other language.

2. The claim that there lies a system of universal grammar or a set of rules for all world language is not properly digestible.

3. The sensitive or critical period hypothesis is also not properly justified as we may find the cases of learning one or the other languages at any period of the life time.

4. The Nativist perspective that grammatically knowledge is innately determined, does not fit in with the general observations of language development. Once children begin to use an innate grammatical structure, we would expect them to apply all relevant instances in their language. But later we find evidences that children refine and generalise many grammatical forms gradually, engaging in much piecemeal learning and making errors along the way. Complete mastery of some forms (such as the passive voice) is not achieved until well into middle childhood. It confirms that language is not inherited but it is a function of deliberate attempts through modelling, reinforcing and practicing a lot in a variety of ways. (Berk, L.E.,2009:360)

Interactionist Theory of Language Development

The theory of language development known as interactionist theory lies midway between the native and imitation theory of language development providing equal weightage to heredity disposition and environmental exposure for the development of language among developing children. Accordingly, neither heredity dispositions in the form of innate grammatical structure or biological maturity, nor the environmental experiences alone are enough to help in the development of language among children. Both of them should join hands and work together and thus there is an urgent need of close interaction between them for the learning and development of language among the developing children. How such an interaction may be carried out, has been explained by the interactionists in the following manner:

- While trying to communicate and develop language among children, parents and elders generally take notice of the biological and cognitive maturity of the child. Accordingly, they try to simplify their speech or conversation with them in the manner understandable to the infant and later on as the child grows older, they interact with him/her to provide higher structure to the development of language.

- Children learn the language of the land with a useful social interaction with their parents, elders and peers as they have a natural urge to get them socialised and adjusted in their socio-cultural environment. In this task, they are adequately helped by their parents, elders, teachers and peers through direct instruction as well as self-efforts.

- Children construct language much like the way they construct knowledge regarding their environment and curricular subjects or co-curricular areas. Social constructivist Lev Vygotsky has emphasised the role of social interaction with elders and knowledgeable peers for acquiring language skills on the part of children. Social interaction helps them to discover the functions and regularities of language spoken and used in their social environment. In addition to such self-help, the parents, elders and peers also assist them to acquire the necessary concepts and skills related to the learning of a language.

- Furthermore, social interactions provide a means through which children internalise language. Consistent with Vygotsky's theory of cognitive development, children use words first in their interactions with others, and then, through the process of internalisation, gradually incorporate these words into their everyday thought processes. (Berk, 2009:329-30)

- The organised formal interaction with teachers and language experts may help children in acquiring the essentials of one or the other language including the associated grammatical rules and structure.

Cognitive Processing Theory of Language Development

The cognitive perspective explaining learning of a language on the part of children emphasises well the role played by their cognitive abilities and capacities in this regard. The views expressed by them in this connection may be summarised as follows:

- Children are born not with a specific capacity for language learning but rather with essential perceptual abilities and thinking skills for understanding and inferring the underlying patterns of the language of the land.

- Learning language on the part of children right from the early years of their development is a process of "data crunching or information processing", in which children take in and process the language they hear from their parents, elders and peers for using it in their own ways. Thus, the cognitivists view the task of language learning as a function of the computational ability of human brain. The children receive the language learning data from their social environment as input, carry out its processing and bring out its output for their use.

- The information or data related to language used in the socio-cultural environment of the developing children after its processing with the help of their cognitive abilities helps them to discover the way their native language works. Later on, such data crunching or information processing work done on their part may help them in understanding the complex rules of grammar.

- Cognitive processing theorists argue that language learning takes place independent of a mother's responsiveness to her children's speech and to her children's social abilities. They point to the fact that even socially limited children with autism can develop language as evidence that language development is not solely dependent on social interaction (Levine & Munsch, 2014:291).

- From a cognitive process perspective, one essential ingredient to many aspects of language is attention. Infants pay attention to human speech from a very early age. In addition to careful listening and watching the actions of elders in conversation, the reasoning acquired by the children at one or the other stage of their cognitive development also plays quite a crucial role in their language development (Berk, 2009:328).

In this way, we can observe that the various theories or perspectives put up to explain the development of language among the developing children try to say it in their own ways. All of them are right in their field of operation but none of them can solely explain the process of language development among children of all ages and environmental surroundings. However, an eclectic approach synthesising the viewpoints of these theories providing due importance to the hereditary and environmental contributions, and utilising the perspectives of behaviourists, cognitivists and constructivists may work well for understanding the mechanism of language development among developing children.

Summary

Language as a term may be defined as a composition or constitution of meaningful words and sounds capable of providing maximum assistance for the expression and communication of our thoughts and feelings.

Language development in the form of learning and acquiring language skills just starts with the birth of the child and goes on till death.

At the initial stage of language development, a child tries to get ready or prepare him or herself for comprehending and utilising the form of language expressed through symbols or signs.

After that the task of language development the children during the different ages or stages of their developmental period follows a sequence in the form of (i) development of oral vocabulary, (ii) development of oral expression or speech power, (iii) development of reading ability or expression and (iv) development of writing ability or written expression.

In this development factors like physical and mental health, maturation, mental, social and emotional development as well as socio-cultural determinants such as family, peer group, society and community, school education and their own level of learning potential and efforts made for the acquisition of language play quite a substantial role.

A number of theories of language development exist for explaining the development of language among the children. We can group them as (i) Imitation and Reinforcement theory of language development, (ii) Nativist theory of language development, (iii) Interactionist theory of language development and (iv) Cognitive processing theory of language development.

Imitation and Reinforcement theory has been well emphasised by Albert Bandura through his social learning approach and B.F. Skinner through the principle of operant conditioning. According to Bandura, in the learning of a language, a child observes, imitates, practices and then repeats what has been observed, imitated and practiced in a given situation. According to Skinner, language is learned through the shaping of one or the other language behaviour, i.e., a baby's babbling or uttering a sound or word for a particular thing through operant conditioning and the use of reinforcement.

Nativist theory provides credit to the role of inheritance and biological maturity in the development of language among children. According to the notable nativist Noam Chomsky, children are born with a biological built-in mechanism or instrument known as LAD (Language Acquisition Device) in the shape of basic language principles or rules of grammar hardwired in their brain that help them in the acquisition of knowledge and skills related to a language. In addition, there lie certain periods in which they are best helped by their LAD to acquire one or the other aspects of language learning.

Interactionist theory of language development urges to have close interaction and cooperation between the forces or potential provided by hereditary disposition and environmental exposure for the development of language among developing children. According to them, biological maturity coupled with environmental exposure, particularly the interaction with elders and peers help children acquire the necessary concepts and skills of a language.

Cognitive processing theory of language development views the task of language learning as a function of the information processing carried out through the computer-like working ability of the human brain. Here the children receive the language learning data from their social environment as input, carry out its processing and bring out its output for their use.

References and Suggested Readings

Bandura, A., *Social Learning Theory*, Englewood Cliffs, N.J.: Prentice-Hall, 1977.

Bandura, A. and Walters, R.H., *Social Learning and Personality Development*, New York: Holt, 1963

Berk, Laura E. (2009), *Child Development* (Eighth edition), Boston: Pearson Education

Chomsky, N, *Reflection on language*, London: Temple Smith, 1976

Chomsky, N., *Language and mind*, New York, NY: Harcourt, Bruce & World, 1968

Levine, Laura E. and Munsch, Joyce, *Child Development: An Active Learning Approach* (2nd ed.), Los Angeles: Sage, 2014.

Ormrod, J.E., *Educational Psychology: Developing Learners* (4th ed.), Upper Saddle River, N.J.: Prentice-Hall, 2003.

Meggitt, Carolyn, *Chid Development: An Illustrated Guide*, Boston: Pearson. 2012

Meggitt, Carolyn, and Ormrod, J.E., *Understanding Child Development*, (Fifth edition), Boston: Pearson. 2013

Ross, J.S., *Ground Work of Educational Psychology*, George G. Harrap, London, 1951.

Shaffer, R., *Social Development*, Oxford: Black Well, 1996.

Skinner, B.F. (1991), *Verbal Behavior*, Action, MA: Copley (original work published in1957).

Vygotsky, L.S., *Thought and Language* (E. Haufmann & G. Vakar, Eds. And Trans.), Cambridge, MA: MIT Press,1962.

Vygotsky, L.S., *Mind and Society: The Development of Higher Mental Process*, Cambridge, M.A.: Harvard University Press, 1978.

Vygotsky, L.S., 'The Kind of Speech', in R.W. Rieberd and A.S. Carton (Eds.), *The Collected Works of L.S. Vygotsky*, Volume I: 'Problems of General Psychology' (pp 39, 285), New York: Plenum Press, 1987 (Original Work Published, 1934).

14

Emotional Development

Introduction

Our emotions play quite a significant role in guiding and directing our behaviour. Many a time they are seen to dominate our behaviour in such a way that we have no solution other than behaving as per their wish. On the other hand, if a person has no emotional current in him then he becomes crippled in terms of living his life in a normal way. Hence, emotions play a key role in providing a particular direction to our behaviour and thus shaping our personality according to their development. In this chapter, we would like to throw light on the emotional aspect of our behaviour.

What are Emotions?

Etymologically, the word emotion is derived from the Latin word 'emovere' which means 'to stir up' or 'to excite'. Therefore, emotion may be understood as an agitated or excited state of our mind and body. Taking clue from such derivation, various psychologists have tried to provide the definition of the term 'emotion' in their own ways. Let us reproduce a few such definitions.

- **Woodworth**: Emotion is a 'moved' or 'stirred-up' state of an organism. It is a stirred-up state of feeling that is the way it appears to the individual himself. It is a disturbed muscular and glandular activity that is the way it appears to an external observer. (1945, p. 410).

- **Crow and Crow**: Emotion is an affective experience that accompanies generalised inner adjustment and mental and physiological stirred-up states in the individual and that shows itself in his overt behaviour. (1973, p. 83).

- **Charles G. Morris**: Emotion is a complex affective experience that involves diffuse physiological changes and can be expressed overtly in characteristic behaviour patterns. (1979, p. 386).

- **McDougall** (1949): Considering instinct as an innate tendency, he maintains that emotion is an affective experience that one undergoes during an instinctive excitement. For example, when a child perceives a bull coming towards him (cognition) he experiences an affective experience in the form of the arousal of accompanied emotion of fear and consequently tries to run away (conative aspect of one's behaviour). McDougall discovered 14 basic instincts and concluded that each and every emotion, whatever it may be, is the product of some instinctive behaviour.

These instincts with their associated emotions can be listed as:

Table 14.1: Instincts and Emotions Accompanying Them

S. No.	Instinct	Emotion accompanying it
1.	Flight or escape	Fear
2.	Pugnacity or combat	Anger
3.	Repulsion	Disgust
4.	Curiosity	Wonder
5.	Parental	Tender emotion, love
6.	Appeal	Distress
7.	Construction	Feeling of creativeness
8.	Acquisition	Feeling of ownership
9.	Gregariousness	Feeling of loveliness
10.	Sex, Mating	Lust
11.	Self-assertion	Positive self-feeling or elation
12.	Submission	Negative self-feeling
13.	Food-seeking	Appetite
14.	Laughter	Amusement

Thus, whatever may be the terminology used by all these different writers and psychologists, their definitions tend to describe emotions as some sort of feelings or affective experiences which are characterised by some physiological changes that generally lead them to perform some or the other type of behavioural acts.

Nature and Characteristics Of Emotions

From the definitions and discussion above, we may be able to conclude following things about the nature and characteristics of emotions.

1. **Emotional experiences are associated with instincts or biological drives.** When the basic need is satisfied or challenged (the satisfaction is in danger), emotions play their part.

2. **Emotions are the product of perception.** The perception of a proper stimulus (object or situation) is needed to start an emotional experience. Organic changes within the body (favourable or unfavourable) may then intensify the emotional experiences.

3. **The core of an emotion is feeling.** Actually every emotional experience, whatever it may be, involves feelings — matter of the heart. Feelings and emotions both are affective experiences. There is only the difference of degrees. After perceiving a thing or a situation, feelings like pleasure or displeasure can be aroused. There may be some intensity or degree of strength in these feelings. When the feelings are so strong that they are able to disturb the mind and excite an individual to act immediately — they are turned into emotions. Therefore, the urge to do or act (conative aspect) is the most important emotional experience.

4. **Emotions bring physiological changes.** Every emotional experience involves many physical and physiological changes in an organism. Some of the changes which express themselves in overt behaviour are easily observable. Examples of such changes are — bulge of the eyes, flush of the face, flow of tears, pulse rate, beating of the heart, choke in the voice, fleeing from the situation or attack on the emotion arousing stimulus. In addition to these easily observable changes, there are internal physiological changes as well. Examples of such changes are changes in the circulation of blood, impact on digestive system and changes in the functioning of some glands like adrenal glands, etc.

These changes become so specific and distinguishable in human beings that a simple glimpse can enable us to detect a particular emotional experience in an individual and we can see whether he is in anger or scared.

In addition to the above characteristics, emotions have some more specific features that need to be mentioned here. These are:

(i)   Emotions exist in every living organism.

(ii) They are present at all stages of development and can be aroused in young as well as in old.

(iii) Emotions are extremely individualistic and they differ from person to person.

(iv) Same emotions can be aroused by a number of different stimuli — objects or situations.

(v)   Emotions rise abruptly but die down slowly. An emotion once aroused tends to persist and leaves behind emotional mood.

(vi) Emotions have the quality of displacement. The anger aroused on account of one stimulus gets transferred to other situation. The anger on account of the rebuking by boss is transferred in beating the children at home.

(vii) One emotion can give birth to a number of likewise emotions.

(viii) There is a negative correlation between the upsurge of emotions and intelligence. While reasoning and sharp intellect provides a careful check on the sudden upsurge of emotions, under emotional experiences, the reasoning and thinking powers are decreased.

Kinds of Emotions

If we try to analyse the impact of various emotional experiences upon the well-being of an individual, we can come to the conclusion that emotions have both positive as well as negative effects. Whether an emotion will prove to be helpful or harmful to an individual depends upon the following factors:

(i)   Frequency and intensity of emotional experience.

(ii) Situation, occasion and nature of the stimulus which arouses the emotion.

(iii) Kind of emotional experience or emotions.

The last factor — the kind of emotional experience — counts much in this direction. Emotions, in general, can be categorised in two kinds — positive and negative emotions.

Unpleasant emotions like fear, anger, jealously which are harmful to an individual's development are termed as negative emotions while pleasant emotions like affection (love), amusement, curiosity, joy and happiness which are very helpful and essential in the normal development of an individual are termed as positive emotions.

By their nature of positiveness and negativity, it should not be assumed that all the positive emotions are always good and negative emotions are bad. While weighing their impact, other factors like the frequency and intensity, situations and the nature of stimuli should also be considered. Excess of everything is bad. Emotions with too much intensity and frequency, whether positive or negative, bring harmful effects. On the other hand, the so-called negative emotions are also very essential for human welfare. The emotion of fear prepares an individual to face danger ahead. A child who has no emotion of fear is sure to get injured because he has not learnt to save himself against a possible danger.

Physiological or Bodily Changes Accompanying Emotions

When we are in the waves of positive or negative emotions, our behaviour is totally controlled and directed by that emotion. During this period, various types of internal or external changes occur in our body which may be briefly summarised as follows:

Internal Bodily Changes

The internal structure and functioning of our body is influenced and affected by the ongoing emotional experience. Some of these bodily and physiological changes may be judged through outward observation or simple instruments but for others we often have to make use of sophisticated special instruments like galvanic skin reflex instrument, electro encephalograph (EEG), sphygmomanometer (blood pressure checking instrument), polygraph (lie detector), etc. Some of these internal bodily changes can be mentioned as follows:

1. Functioning of our heart is affected by emotional experience. Generally the heart beat increases under the states of agitation and excitement provided by emotion.

2. Blood circulation system is very much affected by emotional experiences. Generally it increases but in some cases of fear, anxiety and shock it may also go down deeply.

3 Rate of respiration and breathing is deeply affected by an emotional experience. Generally it increases but in some cases of excessive fear, happiness, shocks and excitements it may go down to the extent of becoming absent.

4. Digestive system is adversely affected by emotions. Experimental studies have concluded that under the current of emotions, our stomach and intestines work quite slowly and sometimes become inactive. The secretion of the digestive glands including saliva is also sufficiently decreased resulting in the malfunctioning and inactivity on the part of our digestive system. This is why extremely emotionally charged individuals are mostly found to suffer from the malfunctioning of their digestive system.

5. Emotions bring changes in the chemical composition of our blood like (i) increase in the amount of adrenaline; (ii) increase in the amount of sugar level; (iii) changes in the number and proportion of the red corpuscles.

6. There is a change in the temperature of the body. At the time of intense excitement, it generally goes up.

7. There are significant changes in the secretion of the duct and ductless glands. The flow of these secretions in the form of saliva, tears, sweat, etc., may also be easily identified through external observation.

8. There are significant changes in the electrical or galvanic skin responses. There is a decrease in the case of emotions like distress, disgust and anger which results into sweating or perspiration. On the other hand, there is increase in the case of emotions like fear, love, wonder, etc., which results in the goose bumps, a condition in which hair or the skin rises.

9. Muscles of our body harden and get tense during an emotional moment. It may bring destabilisation and disequilibrium to our body functioning. The twisting and hardening of the muscles of the stomach, arms, legs, neck, etc., may be easily detected from external observation.

10. The functioning of the brain is also adversely affected during intense emotional currents. The sensory and perceptual processes are also influenced through these emotional experiences. Quite often, the emotions play a dominant role by almost making our brains inactive and ineffective making us behave in an improper and delinquent way.

External or Observable Bodily Changes

Apart from the covert changes mentioned above, there are many such overt changes in our body during the current of the emotions that can be detected through simple observation without the need of any special instrument. These may be of the following nature.

Changes in Facial Expression

Face, to some extent, is said to be the index of human behaviour. It equally applies to our emotional behaviour. Under the influence of an emotional current, there are significant changes in our facial expression that can be identified through simple external observation. By looking at one's facial expression, we can judge one's intended emotion and term it as anger, laughter, fear, disgust, contempt, love, happiness or surprise. The basis for the correlation between facial expressions and emotions may be discovered both in one's innate dispositions and socio-cultural environment. While the way of expressing emotions may vary from culture to culture, it may also represent innate responses to particular situations like jumping at the time of hearing a sudden noise and baring teeth at the time of anger.

Behavioural expressions in the form of facial expressions and non-verbal communications, however, cannot be understood as sufficiently objective, reliable and valid instrument for the identification and measurement of one's emotions. One can hide one's feelings in the garb of an apparent mask of false facial expressions and other non-verbal communications, and thus may make the task of identification difficult and most unreliable.

Changes in Body Postures

Besides the changes in facial expression, there are significant changes in one's body postures during emotional experiences. For example when one is angry, besides the redness of his face, his bodily postures and movements may also tell the same story. He may begin to walk fast, push and pull his hands and feet, take a fighting posture, utter non-sensible words, etc. In this way, his whole body and its movements through their various forms and postures may provide identification of a particular type of emotional behaviour. That is why when one is trembling or trying to hide or run away in a bid to save one's life, we say that one is in the grip of some fear. Similar identification may also be made in the case of other emotions like love, delight, disgust, wonder, distress, etc.

However, there lies less objectivity and reliability in the identification of the emotions through one's body postures. One may be able to hide one's emotional feelings by exhibiting different types of body postures other than those expected for the display of one's actual feelings. Apart from this, there lies another difficulty in the identification of emotional behaviour on the basis of the observed body postures and movements simply on account of the fact that many of the emotions have similarities in terms of the observable body postures and movements.

Changes in Voice or Vocal Expression

There are significant changes in one's voice or vocal expression during an emotional current. Laughing, weeping, speaking in loud voice with an unusually high pitch, crying, talking slowly with some hesitation, feeling difficulty in speaking, uttering abusive language, speaking in a very sweet and affectionate manner, whistling, murmuring, humming, etc., demonstrate our various emotions. That is why when we listen to the dialogues of the various actors in a play or programmes on the radio and television broadcasting we can very well say that at this particular time one is displaying the emotion of anger, fear, disgust, love, lust, etc. However, it is also not a reliable method for the identification of one's emotional experience simply on the ground that many of the emotional expressions may demonstrate similarities in terms of the voice or vocal expressions. Besides this, there may be individual differences with regard to the vocal expression of a particular emotional behaviour. In such cases, therefore, no general conception for the vocal expression of an emotion, may come to our help and hence we may remain undecided or take a wrong decision about one's emotional behaviour.

Emotional Development During Different Stages of Development

Development, in general, applies to the changes brought about with the passage of time. Emotional development in this respect reflects the following changes:

- There is a gradual birth of different emotions in an individual since his birth.
- There are changes in the conditions or nature of the stimuli that arouse child's emotions.

•   There are changes in the manner in which a child expresses his emotions.

In the light of these changes, we will try to discuss the process of emotional development during different developmental stages.

Emotional Development During Infancy

1. Right from the time of his birth, an infant cries and his bodily movements seem to give evidence of the presence of emotional element in him. What are the specific emotions, if any, that he experiences at this stage is a difficult question to be answered.

2. Truly speaking, as Mrs. Hurlock puts it, "At birth and shortly afterwards the first sign of emotional behaviour is general excitement to strong stimulation. There are no indications of clear-cut, definite emotional patterns that can be recognised and identified as specific emotional states." (1959, p. 216).

   Thus, it is the stage of an undifferentiated excitement to any stimulus.

3. The stage of undifferentiated excitement is over in a very short time, when the general excitement becomes differentiated into simple responses that suggest pleasure and displeasure. Stimuli like sudden loud noise, wet, cold or hot objects applied to the baby's skin, feeling hungry, uncomfortable, etc., bring unpleasant responses. The stimuli like sucking, patting, warmth, etc., bring pleasant responses.

4. The differentiation of general excitement into pleasant and unpleasant responses takes the following pattern according to Spitz:

   "During the first two months, pleasure and displeasure come in response to 'physical' stimulation. By the third month, pleasure is aroused by 'psychological' stimulation as shown in the baby's smile in response to human face. Slightly later displeasure can be aroused by psychological as well as physical stimuli as may be seen in the baby's reaction to being left alone." (Hurlock, E.B., 1959, p. 217)

5. As mentioned earlier, before the age of 6 months, emotional behaviour is expressed through pleasant and unpleasant responses, that is, there are only two emotions (distress and delight) up to this stage. When the infant completes his six months, the negative emotions take the lead and gradually in the coming months, fear, disgust, anger, jealousy all are distinguishable. Between the 10th and 12th months positive emotions like elation, love, sympathy, enjoyment all enter the field. Up to 2 years, as the study of Bridges conducted in 1931 shows almost all the emotions, positive as well as negative, take their shape and become quite distinguishable.

6. There is continuous variation in the manifestation of emotions during infancy. In the earlier months it is very difficult to distinguish on the basis of facial expression and bodily positions. Only mothers can determine the reasons behind her child's crying and yelling. Later on they gradually become distinguishable. Moreover in the earlier months of infancy, the child reacts more violently to emotionally disturbing situations; but as an infant approaches childhood, his crying, yelling and the vigorous movements of the body parts become less and less violent. Gradually with increasing age there is an increase in linguistic responses and a decrease in motor responses.

Emotional Development During Childhood

As said above, almost all the emotions make themselves distinguishable by the beginning of childhood. Therefore, emotional development after the stage of infancy, concerns itself only to the changes in the nature of situations or stimuli arousing emotions and the changes in the expression of emotional experiences. The following changes are found in a child during childhood:

1. In infancy, the child is only concerned with his own well-being. Therefore, the emotions are generally aroused by the conditions which are related with his immediate well-being. But as he grows, his world grows larger and he has to respond to a variety of stimuli. During childhood, peer group relationship and school atmosphere and other environmental factors influence his emotional behaviour. His emotions get linked with new experiences and interests, and his emotional behaviour gets linked with new stimuli. At the same time, he does not react to various old stimuli. For example, he does not show anger at being dressed or bathed, nor does he show any fear of strangers.

2. There is a remarkable change in the expression of emotional behaviour. In infancy his behaviour is usually dominated by too much intensity and is usually expressed through motor responses like crying, yelling, etc. But in childhood and especially in later childhood, the child tries to express his behaviour through reasonable means and is the result of many factors. In childhood, the child is in a position to express his feelings through language. Secondly, he becomes social and realises that it may not be desirable or proper for him to show his emotions at all times. Thirdly, his intellect begins to play a proper role in exercising check over emotional outbursts.

Thus, the child advances towards emotional stability and control and during the later period of his childhood, demonstrates an appreciable degree of control over his emotions.

Emotional Development During Adolescence

The emotional balance is once again disturbed in adolescence. An individual once again experiences the violent and intensive current of emotional experiences. With regard to emotional experiences, this is the period of intensive storm and stress. At no stage this emotional energy is as strong and dangerous as in adolescence. It is very difficult for an adolescent to exercise control over his emotions. The sudden functioning of sexual glands and tremendous increase in physical energy makes him restless. Moreover, adolescents are not consistent in their emotions. Emotions during this stage fluctuate very frequently and quickly. It makes them moody. In a very short span of time they could switch between being happy and extremely sad. So there is too much uncertainty in the nature of their emotional state.

At this stage, there is a strong need for training of emotions and proper channelization of emotional energy. The Hadow report has emphasised this need in the following words:

"There is a tide which begins to rise in the veins of youth at the age of eleven or twelve. It is called by the name of adolescence. If that tide can be taken at the flood, and a new voyage begun in the strength and along the flow of its current, we think that it will move on to fortune." (Ross J.S., 1951, p.153).

Emotional Development in Adulthood

Emotional development reaches its maximum in adulthood. During this stage, generally, all individuals attain emotional maturity. Let us try to understand what is meant by emotional maturity.

Meaning of Emotional Maturity

In brief, a person can be called emotionally mature if he is able to display his emotions in an appropriate degree with reasonable control. An emotionally mature person will possess the following characteristics:

(1) Almost all the emotions can be distinctly seen in him and their pattern of expression can be easily recognised.

(2) Manifestation of emotions is very refined. Usually he expresses his emotions in a socially desirable way.

(3) He is able to exercise control over his emotions. Sudden inappropriate emotional outbursts are rarely found in him. He is able to hide his feelings and check his emotional tide.

(4) The person no more hangs in mere idealism, but he actually perceives the things in their real perspective. He is not a daydreamer and does not possess the desire to run away from realities.

(5) The intellectual powers like thinking, reasoning, etc., are properly exercised by him in making any decision. He is more guided by his intellect than his emotions.

(6) He does not possess the habit of rationalisation i.e., he never gives arguments in defence of his undesirable or improper conduct. Also he never puts the responsibility of his own mistakes on others. He is always honest in his behaviour.

(7) He possesses an adequate self-concept and self-respect. He never likes to do the things or to show such behaviour as can injure his self respect and is adverse to his self-concept.

(8) He is not confined to himself. He thinks for others and is keen to maintain social relationships. He never engages himself in such a behaviour which is antisocial and can result in the social conflicts and blockage of social relationships.

(9) He has the courage to exercise his emotions at a proper time in a proper place. If there is a danger to his self-respect or if an innocent person is attacked, he can rise to the occasion by exercising his emotion of anger. But if he commits a mistake and is rebuked by his boss, he is equally able to check his emotion of anger. Mature emotional behaviour is characterised by greater stability. A person having such maturity shows no sudden shift from one emotion to another.

As a conclusion regarding the meaning of emotional maturity, I would like to quote Arthur T. Jersild. He is of the opinion that emotional maturity should not involve only simple restriction and control. According to him, it is a very narrow view of emotional maturity. He writes:

"An adequate description of emotional maturity must take account of the full scope of the individual's capacity and powers, and of his ability to use and enjoy them. In its broadest sense emotional maturity means the degree to which the person has realised his potential for richness of living and has developed his capacity to enjoy things, to relate himself to others, to love and to laugh: his capacity for whole-hearted sorrow when an occasion for grief arises... and his capacity to show fear when there is occasion to be frightened, without feeling a need to use a false mask of courage." (Skinner, C.E., 1968, p. 281).

Emotionality of Childhood Vs Adulthood

The emotional experiences during childhood differ markedly from those of adulthood. This difference can be easily seen through some of the following distinguished characteristics:

Intensity

Children's emotions are characterised by too much intensity. There are sudden outbursts of emotions among children. If a child weeps, he weeps bitterly. In anger, he loses control over himself. But an adult's emotional experiences are not so intense. Volcano-like sudden emotional outbursts are seldom observed in adults.

Briefness

Children's emotional experiences are very brief. Their emotions last for a short time and these end all of a sudden. However, in adults the emotions play their part for a long time and in the end, make their existence drawn over a period of time in the form of 'mood'.

Transitory

Children's emotions are transitory in character which means there is a rapid shift from one emotion to another. We find that for a weeping child, a piece of chocolate is enough to shift his emotion from distress to delight. Similarly, we find a quick shift in his emotion from delight to distress. We also find a rapid shift from anger to smile, from laughter to tears or from jealously to affection. Contrary to this, emotions of adults do not shift so rapidly. They are marked by a greater degree of stability.

Frequency

On an average, the number of emotional experiences experienced by a child during a day is significantly greater than those experienced by a normal adult. A child undergoes different currents of emotional streams during a period of time, sometimes a specific emotion being repeated a number of times. But as the child grows older, he learns to make adjustments and tries to handle situations by reactions other than the emotional ones, hence resulting in a gradual decrease in the frequency of emotional responses.

Detection of Emotionality

The emotional state of a child is easily detectable. He is very innocent and does not know the art of hiding his feelings and emotions. The behaviour symptoms like speech difficulties, frequent crying, restlessness, nail-biting, thumb sucking, etc., give indications of his emotionality. Adults, on the other hand, are generally able to hide their feelings and emotions. Therefore, in their case, it is difficult for others to know how they feel and detect their emotionality.

Differences in Emotional Expression

An infant is quite unable to exercise control over his violent emotional outbursts. Emotions at this stage are expressed through motor responses. As the child grows, the way of emotional expression gets modified. This modification goes on till the attainment of maturity in adulthood. A mature adult seldom engages himself in motor activity during emotional stress. He learns to exercise control over his emotions and expresses them in a refined and socially approved way. The emotional expression either in the form of motor responses or in a socially unacceptable way is labelled as 'childish'. The emotional response of an adult is always guided by his intellect while in the child, the intensity of feelings rules over the reasoning and thinking power. The adults are able to keep their emotions reserved for a future expression but in childhood it is a difficult task.

Factors Influencing Emotional Development

The emotional development of a child rests on many factors. Six of the important ones are as follows:

Health and Physical Development

Physical development and health has a positive correlation with emotional development. Any deficiency on physical front — internal or external — creates emotional problems. Children, weak in somatic structure or suffering from illness, are more emotionally upset and unstable than those with better health. The normal functioning of the glands is very important for the balanced emotional development. Any abnormal increase or decrease in their power of secretion creates obstacles in the proper emotional development.

Intelligence

Intelligence, as the ability to make adaptation, has a significant correlation with emotional adjustment and suitability of a child. Meltzer (1937) concluded that:

"There is less emotional control, on the average, among those of the lower intellectual levels than among children of the same age who are bright." (Hurlock, E.B., 1959, p. 254).

An intelligent person, with his reasoning and thinking powers, exercises control according to the situation and makes proper use of his emotions. At every stage, the child's intellectual power guides and controls his emotional development.

Family Atmosphere and Relationships

Emotional development is significantly influenced by the family atmosphere and relationships. The emotional behaviour of parents and elder members and the cordial atmosphere prevalent at home develops positive emotions among the children, while conflicts, fights and tensions in family relationships give birth to negative emotions. Also the treatment given to a child by parents and the members of the family influences his emotional development. The order of birth (whether the first or the youngest child), the size of the family, the socio-economic status of the family, the parental attitude (neglected, pampered or over-protected child) — all are decisive factors in the emotional upbringing of the child.

School Atmosphere and Teachers

School life plays an important role in the emotional development of children. The healthy conducive atmosphere of the school always results in the balanced emotional development of children. All such things like the physical facilities provided in school, the methods of teaching, the organisation of co curricular activities and social life in the school, the relationship among the staff members and the head of the institution, attitude of teachers towards the students and the self-example of the teacher's emotional behaviour influence the emotional development of children.

Social Development and Peer-Group Relationship

Social development of children is closely linked to their emotional development. The more social the child is, the more emotionally adjustable he will prove. Socially rejected or maladjusted children always face difficult emotional problems. The maintenance of proper social relationships and acquisition of social virtues are the effective means for bringing essential modification in the emotional behaviour of the child. The proper social development can only bring desirable and socially approved emotional development in children.

Neighbourhood, the Community and the Society

The other social agencies like neighbourhood, the community and society, of which an individual is the member, also exert significant influence upon his emotional setup. He picks up so many traits of his emotional behaviour from these surroundings. A brave community is sure to produce fearless and courageous children. A society where the elder members unnecessarily exhibit emotional outbursts of anger leads the youngsters to such negative development. Similarly, so many good or bad things related to emotional behaviour of an individual can be acquired due to the impact of neighbourhood and the society.

In this way, the factors influencing the emotional development of an individual can be labelled into two categories. In the first category there are personal factors like his physical, physiological, mental and social development. In the second category there are social factors like parents, family, school, neighbourhood, community and the society. Both these factors exert a significant influence upon the emotional development of the child. While taking care of the proper emotional development of a child, parents as well as the teachers should keep in view all the factors belonging to both the categories.

Methods for Training of Emotions

Emotions in their crude form are harmful to the individual and the society. One of the major objectives of any good scheme of education is to train and modify the emotions for the welfare of the individual and that of the society. The various methods employed for this purpose are:
1. Repression or inhibition.
2. Industriousness or mental occupation.
3. Redirection and sublimation.
4. Catharsis.

Repression or inhibition

Here the undesirable emotional behaviour of the child is checked by imposing restrictions and giving punishment. No outlet or opportunity is provided to the child for the emotional expression. Rules and regulations are very strictly observed and the child is always required to express his emotions in socially desirable ways. Actually it is a negative method of exercising control over the emotions and is in no way helpful for the healthy emotional development.

Industriousness or Mental Occupation

Another method for exercising desirable control over emotions is to keep oneself busy in some constructive activities. Empty mind is said to be a devil's workshop. Therefore, it is essential to have provision for co-curricular and leisure activities for the balanced emotional development of the children.

Redirection and Sublimation

The direction of flow of emotional energy is changed through the process of redirection and sublimation from an undesirable goal to a socially desirable one. In both these processes, there is only a difference of degrees. While, in redirection there is no change in the nature of the emotion and only the direction of the flow is changed, in sublimation, there is modification of original instincts or emotions. Sublimation changes the very form of the emotion.

As far as the method of controlling the emotions is concerned, redirection serves the best purpose. Unlike repression or inhibition, it does not have negative effect on the personality development of the children. It does not destroy the emotion, but only brings desirable changes in the mode of its expression. If a child is very aggressive and displays emotion of anger frequently, his emotion of anger can be diverted towards the enemies of the country and the devils of the society. In this way, his energy can be utilised in the defence of the country and for the weaker members of the society. Similarly, the sublimation of love in the cases of Tulsidas and Kalidas presents clear example of the role of sublimation in changing the emotional setup of an individual.

Catharsis

In this method, desirable channels are provided for the release of emotional energy. In some way or the other, the individual is provided with the opportunity of self-expression so that the pent-up emotions get appropriate outlet. Under the clouds of emotions, tensions are created in the minds of the individuals. By providing a proper outlet for emotional expression, the tensions can be removed and one is made to feel better and lighter. Listening patiently to the verbal expression of an individual under emotion is the simplest catharsis process. The opportunity for self-expression in the form of co-curricular activities, participation in festivals and fairs and rituals of the society — all provide means for the catharsis of emotional energy.

Role of Parents and Teachers in Proper Emotional Development of Children

Role of home and specially that of teachers in bringing balanced emotional development in children deserves special mention. The emotional development of children are influenced and controlled by many factors. These factors have been mentioned earlier. Let us analyse the part played by parents and teachers in bringing balanced emotional development of children in the light of these factors.

(1) Emotional development, as mentioned earlier, depends upon physical and physiological development. Therefore, every care is to be taken for the proper physical development of children. Children should be made to learn the ways of healthy living. With due collaboration among family and school and the state authorities, children need to be cared for proper nourishment. The parents and teachers should try to be fully aware of the physical weaknesses, deformities and illnesses of the children and necessary provision for the treatment should be made at homes, schools or state hospitals.

(2) Home atmosphere exercises a good amount of influence over the emotional character of children. Parents and elder members of the family should exhibit better examples of emotional expression before their children. They should try to develop a healthy attitude towards their children and in no way spoil them by their own modes of behaviour. The teachers in the school should also try to know the causes of emotional maladjustment of children and find out how far home atmosphere and parents are responsible for this. Accordingly, they

should take suitable steps for the proper emotional development of the children in active collaboration with the children's family.

(3) The teachers in school, with the active cooperation of authorities, should take care of the following things:

(i) There should be an adequate provision for various co-curricular activities for the full expression and outlet of emotional energies of the children.

(ii) Instructional methodology and curriculum should be dynamic, progressive and child-centred.

(iii) Children should get desired love and sympathy from the teachers. Their individuality should be respected and individual differences recognised. The teacher should see to it that the basic emotional needs of children are satisfied in the classroom or school.

(iv) With the help of positive methods of controlling and training the emotions, the emotional tension present in the minds of the children should be removed and the creation of undesirable complexes avoided.

(v) Moral and religious training should form a part of the school programme. High ideas of life and moral principles should be made the guiding factors of the children's lives.

(vi) Emotions are caught, they are not taught. Therefore, teachers should refrain from any act or behaviour which can bring undesirable influence on the emotional development of children. They must put their own example before children for the refined emotional expressions and behaviour.

(vii) Proper care should be taken for the balanced social development of children. Each child should get due recognition in his group and in no case he should feel isolated or rejected by his peer group and classmates.

(viii) Teachers need to understand when behaviour is normal and when it is a symptom of something wrong. The causes for emotional deviation should be sought and in case the behaviour is expressively immature, services of a skilled guidance personnel should be obtained.

(ix) Teachers should recognise the place of emotion in the learning process. Balanced emotional feelings can serve as a tonic to the body and can make the learning an active and exciting experience. Therefore, teachers should make the child emotionally involved in his work.

Summary

Emotions are some sort of feelings or affective experiences which are characterised by some physiological changes that generally lead them to perform some or the other types of behavioural acts.

A particular type of emotion has distinguished characteristics like (i) its association with some basic instincts or drives, (ii) aroused as a result of perception (iii) intensity of feelings (iv) accompanied with the specific physiological changes (v) its sudden rise but slow death, (vi) displaying the quality of displacement i.e., transferred to other situation, target, etc.

Emotions in general can be categorised into two kinds — positive or pleasant emotions like love, amusement, curiosity, etc., and negative and unpleasant emotions like fear, anger, jealously, etc.

Emotions are always accompanied with some distinctive physiological or bodily internal and external changes. Examples of such internal changes — increase in heart beat, decrease in blood pressure, increase and decrease in the rate of respiration and breathing, malfunctioning of the digestive system, change in the body temperature, chemical composition of the blood, and secretion of the duct and ductless glands, hardening and tensing of muscles of the body and changes in the electrical or galvanic skin responses. Among the external changes (detected only through simple observation) are changes in facial expression, body postures and voice or vocal expressions.

The process of emotional development in an individual during different developmental stages is mainly characterised by changes like (i) gradual birth of different emotions since birth, (ii) changes in the conditions or nature of stimuli that arouse the emotions and (iii) changes in the manner in which emotions are expressed.

Emotional experiences during childhood differ markedly from those of adulthood mainly in terms of (i) intensity, (ii) briefness, (iii) transitory, (iv) frequencies, (v) detection and (vi) differences in the emotional expression.

Emotions development of the children may be influenced by so many factors like his health and physical development, intelligence, family atmosphere and relationships, school atmosphere and teachers, social development and peer group relationships, neighbourhood, the community and the society, etc.

The welfare of the individual and society lies in the proper emotional functioning. For this purpose, there is a need of proper training and modification of the emotions. The various methods employed for this purpose may be named as (i) repression or inhibition, (ii) industriousness or mental occupation, (iii) redirection and sublimation and (iv) catharsis.

Teachers and parents can play a big role in bringing balanced emotional development of children by taking due notice of (i) getting imbibed with the knowledge and understanding of the methods and ways of regulating the emotions, (ii) taking care of the children's physical, social and mental development, (iii) providing guidance and education to children for knowing and regulating their emotions, (iv) arranging experiences related to exemplary behaviour of emotions display and control, and (v) providing outlet for the emotional energies of the children through proper curricular and co-curricular experiences and so on.

References and Suggested Readings

Arnold, M.B., *Emotion and Personality* (2 Vols.), Columbia University Press, New York, 1960.

Cannon, W.B., *Bodily Changes in Pain, Hunger, Fear and Rage,* 2nd ed., Appleton-Century-Crofts, New York, 1929.

Crow, L.D. and Crow, A., *Educational Psychology,* 3rd Indian reprint, Eurasia Publishing House, New Delhi, 1973.

Darwin, C., *The Expression of the Emotions in Man and Animals,* reprint, Chicago University Press, Chicago, 1965.

Delgado, J.M.R., *Physical Control of the Mind: Towards a Psycho-civilized Society*, Harper & Row, New York, 1969.

Drever, J., *Instinct in Man*, Cambridge University Press, Cambridge, 1917.

Hurlock, E.B., *Child Psychology* (Asian student edition), Tokyo: Kogakusha Co. Ltd., 1956.

Hurlock, E.B., *Child Psychology*, McGraw-Hill, Tokyo, 1959.

James, William, *Psychology: Brief Course*, Collier Macmillan, London, 1969.

Jersild, A.T., *In Essentials of Educational Psychology*, Skinner, C.E. (Ed.), Prentice-Hall Inc., 1968.

Jersild et.al., *Child Psychology*, New York: Macmillan, 1975.

Lindsley, D.B., *Emotion* in S.S. Stevans (Ed.), *Hand Book of Experimental Psychology*, John Wiley, New York, 1951.

McDougall, William, *An Introduction to Social Psychology*, 28th ed., Methuen, London, 1946.

– – –, *An Outline of Psychology*, 13th ed., Methuen, London, 1949.

Morris, Charles G., *Psychology*, 3rd ed., Englewood Cliffs, Prentice-Hall, New Jersey, 1979.

Schachter, S. and Singer, J.E., "Cognitive, Social and Physiological Determinants of Emotional State," *Psychological Review*, 69, 369–399, 1962.

Schachter, S., *Emotion, Obesity and Crime*, Academic Press, New York, 1971.

Selye, H., *The Stress of Life*, McGraw-Hill, New York, 1956.

Skinner C.E. and Harriman, P.L. (Eds.), *Child Psychology*, 6th print, Macmillan, New York, 1937.

Skinner C.E. (Ed.), *Essential of Educational Psychology*, Prentice-Hall, New York, 1968

Young, P.T., *Emotion in Man and Animal*, 2nd ed., Krieger, Huntington, New York, 1973.

Wood, J., *How Do You Feel?* Prentice-Hall, Englewood Cliffs, New Jersey, 1974.

Woodworth, R.S., *Psychology*, Methuen, London, 1945.

15

Development of Attachment and Temperament

Attachment: Meaning and Concept

There exists a close loving relationship between mothers and their babies giving birth to a particular type of emotional behaviour termed as attachment among all the living species including the human beings. It can be experienced as well as witnessed by all of us in its varieties of forms and shapes signified as follows:

- For instance, we see a mother monkey on her journey with the baby monkey riding on her back or clinging to her chest. She stops at a place and the baby monkey gets engaged in exploring the nearby environment by jumping here and there in a quite joyful mood. However, in such exploration, he gets out of sight and approach to her mother. Suddenly he sees a dog approaching him; he gets frightened and baffled at that moment, and then runs in the direction of his mother's resting place and keeps calling out to her. After getting a glimpse of his mother, the baby monkey rushes and jumps into her laps, expresses his agony and gets normal after getting consolation from the mother and clinging to his mother's chest.

- In the other situation, look at the behaviour of your pet puppy or kitten. He or she follows you, welcomes you when you enter the home with one or the other acts of showing affection towards you such as moving his/her tail vigorously, touching you here and there, etc. See that his or her, so performed behaviour is reserved to you and a few family members; this gets quite different and annoying to strangers and unfamiliar visitors to your house.

- What is seen in the behaviours of the baby monkey and pet puppy may also be witnessed in the behaviour of young infants and children. For this purpose you may recall your own experiences of witnessing the scene of separation and reunion of the small babies with her mothers or other caregivers.

Summing up, in all such examples and instances witnessed by you in the interaction of children with their mothers, caregivers and other close family members, there lies a common factor or link in the form of a unique emotional behaviour in the form of a close relationship and a bond between the child and mother/caregiver.

It is commonly referred to as attachment in the language of the subject psychology. Let us try and understand the meaning and concept of this term in a more clear manner through the views expressed and definitions provided by the various scholars and authors on this account.

John Bowlby (1969): The term attachment refers to the presence of the strong affectionate ties that we have with the special people in our lives. People who are securely attached take pleasure in their interactions and feel comforted by their partner's presence in times of stress or uncertainty.

Harwood, Miller and Vasta (2012): The term attachment can be defined as the enduring emotional bond that exists between a child and those people significant in his or her life.

Shaffer and Kipp (2007): Attachment refers to a close emotional relationship between two persons, characterised by mutual affection and a desire to maintain proximity.

Meggitt, Carolyn, (2012): We can define the term bonding for denoting the feelings of love and responsibility that parents have for their children. Attachment is, however, a two-way process which develops over time. It can be defined as an enduring emotional bond that an infant forms with a specific person.

Levine and Munsch (2014): Attachment a key concept related to the emotional behaviour of human beings can be defined as a strong enduring emotional tie uniting one person to another in the prevailing socio-cultural environment.

Feldman, Robert (2016): Attachment is the positive emotional bond that develops between a child and a particular special individual. When children experience attachment to a given person, they feel pleasure when they are with them and feel comforted by their presence at times of distress.

The things revealed and views expressed in the cited definitions may help us in drawing the necessary conclusions about the meaning, nature and characteristics of the term attachment in the following way:

- A child in his or her interaction with the mother/caregiver is said to be well attached or demonstrating an attachment behaviour when we witness the presence of a strong affectionate tie or emotional bond between them.
- The nature of these emotional ties or bonds is relatively quite enduring and stable.
- The child is able to establish and maintain strong emotional ties or relationship not only with his mother/caregiver but also with all other people who care for him and are significant in his life.
- The nature of the emotional tie or bond existing between the child and mother/caregiver is generally somewhat pleasurable and satisfying to both of them. It is also capable of providing soothing touch, consolation and comfort to the distressed partner in the time of need.
- There lies an essential presence of mutual affection, love and desire to maintain proximity with each other in the relationship involving attachment.
- There lies a considerable difference between the terms bonding and attachment. Where in bonding the relationship between the child and mother/other people is totally one sided (on the pattern of one-sided affair or love), the relationships

or emotional ties existing in the behaviour characterised as attachment behaviour are two-sided bringing mutual satisfaction and pleasure to both the parties.

Theories of Attachment

A number of theories and viewpoints have been put forward by thinkers and scholars to explain why and how infants become emotionally involved or attached with the people around them. The theories and viewpoints available on this account may be classified as Psychoanalytic theories, Behavioural theories, Cognitive developmental theories and Ethological theories. Let us discuss them one by one.

Psychoanalytic Perspective or Theories

Psychologists belonging to the school of psychoanalysis such as Freud, Erik Erickson have tried to explain the mechanism of attachment found in the infants on the basis of satisfaction of their biological needs in a satisfactory way. In this concern while Freud tried to explain the attachment behaviour of infants on the lines of the development of infants expected at the oral stage of their psycho-sexual development, Erickson linked it with the state of trust v/s mistrust visible among infants in relation to their psycho-social development.

According to Freud, at the oral stage of his development from the very birth an infant's most important immediate need is related to his feeding and the only means available to him for the purpose is oral. At this stage he derives great pleasure in sucking and mouthing objects and thus is automatically bound to feel attracted and attached with the individual who is special to him in satisfying his feeding need as well as providing him the sucking pleasure. In this concern breast feeding is the most pleasurable choice to infants and then comes bottle feeding. It is why infants are seen to make strong emotional ties or attachments with their breast feeding mothers at a greater priority and then comes the turn of those who provide bottle feeding.

Erickson while agreeing with the role of the satisfaction of feeding needed in the development of attachment behaviour stressed that it is not only the mother's feeding practices but her overall responsiveness to her child's needs (in the form of providing warmth, tender touches, soft reassuring vocalisation, changing of diaper, etc.,) that is responsible for establishing trust or mistrust in the developing infants for the development of a particular type of attachment or non-attachment behaviour. The emergence of such attachment-related behaviour evolved through trust and mistrust on the caretakers is not limited to the period of its arousal but is found to be carried over the entire life span of an individual as evident from the instances where people are found to avoid establishing close mutual trust relationship throughout life on account of such aversive tendency generated in their mind though the careless behaviour of their caregivers in infancy.

Behavioural Perspective or Theories

The behaviourists while agreeing with the role of the satisfaction of feeding and other needs in the formation of attachment relationship emphasise on explaining how this relationship is developed among developing children and care takers in infancy and later periods of their life. According to them all behaviour is learned, including the attachment behaviour shown by infants and toddlers towards their mother and other care givers by following the principles and process of classical and operant conditioning explained as follows:

• In the attempts of feeding and caring for the newborns and small babies the initiative in this direction is taken by mothers and other caretakers. Here the milk, other food material and caring of children in many other ways such as providing tender touches, hugging, holding them in the arms and comforting them in their lap, works as a primary or natural stimuli for generating positive responses on the part of the receiving children. After some time as a result of the repeated association of these natural stimuli with the secondary stimuli (mothers and caretakers) in the task of generated responses of the babies (such as feeling happy and satisfied, smiling and looking towards the caregivers with affection etc.), the secondary stimuli begin to play the part of primary stimuli (feeding and care) for generating the similar positive responses on the part of the babies for imbibing a conditioned behaviour known as attachment behaviour. Commenting on the outcomes and processing of such conditioning, Shaffer and Kipp (2007:438) write:

Overtime, then, an infant would come to associate his mother with pleasant or pleasurable sensations, so that the mother herself becomes a valuable commodity. Once the mother (or any other care giver) has attained the status as a secondary reinforce, the infant is attached, and he or she will now do whatever is necessary (smile, cry, coo, babble or follow) in order to attract the care giver's attention or to remain near this valuable and rewarding individual.

• The mechanism of operant conditioning may also be found to play a quite significant role in the formation and shaping of attachment behaviour and development of affectionate relationship between infants and caregivers. As initiation, some caring and feeding may be done on the part of mothers and caregivers for one or the other account. (Such as the mothers and family members must be feeling a burning desire to have a new member in the family and thus waiting a long time for his or her arrival; the mothers have a need to feed the newborn with her breast milk, feeding and caring is taken as a must for the survival and well being of the newborn and small children, etc). Such feeding and caring of the infants, after eliciting positive responses on the part of infants may work as a good reinforcing agent for providing more attention and affection on the part of mothers and caregivers which in turn may be properly accounted for reinforcing the ongoing behaviour cycle and shaping a particular type of attachment behaviour between the child and caregivers. By following the key word of operant conditioning that a behaviour is shaped and maintained through its consequences, the attachment once shown for a caregiver or object gets continued, modified or replaced depending upon the life circumstances.

Cognitive-Developmental Perspective or Theories

The cognitive-developmental perspective, in its simple meaning talks about a close link between the cognitive developmental level of children and the developing attachment behaviour. It is thus found to convey that the ability to form attachment depends a lot on the infant's level of cognitive development. We should therefore not expect the emergence and perpetuation of one or the other type of attachment behaviour among developing children until or unless they happen to acquire a certain stage or excellence level in their cognitive maturity. Commenting on this aspect, Shaffer and Kipp (2007:439) write:

> Before an attachment can occur, the infant must be able to discriminate familiar companions from strangers. He must also recognise that familiar companions have a *permanence* about them (object permanence), for it would be difficult to form a stable relationship with a person who ceases to exist whenever she passes from view (Shaffer,1971). So perhaps it is no accident that attachment first emerges at age 7 to 9 months — precisely the time when infants are entering Piaget's fourth sensori-motor sub-stage, the point at which they first begin to search for and find objects that they've seen sometimes hidden from them.

In the later period and stages of cognitive development, the pattern of attachment towards, people, places, objects and events get developed, modified or replaced depending on the development, functioning and use of the cognitive abilities on the part of individuals in one or the other life situations. In the later stages of their development, the developed cognitive competency is capable enough to provide individuals the needed insight for the identification and recognition of the fairness and truth in the love and affection showered on them by others in a relationship. Its positivity and fairness then work as a strong motivating force for forming and maintaining a close relationship and developing intact attachment bonds with them. It goes on multiplying on the footprints of the saying "love begets love" but may also pick up the adverse direction depending on the nature of the circumstances and the behavioural responses received in return from others in a relationship.

Ethological Perspective or Theories

Ethological perspective and related theories are based on the learning and thinking of the discipline Ethology. As a discipline or subject of study Ethology refers to a branch of biology concerned with the adaptive behaviour of different animal species including human beings. While adopting an ethological approach for the study of attachment behaviour, researchers tried to peep through the adaptive behaviour of children.

A beginning in this direction, was initiated by the famous ethologist Konrad Lorenz with the study of adaptive behaviour of the children of animals. For this purpose, he made young goslings (the baby birds of a duck) the subject of his study. He found that the young goslings followed their mother immediately after their birth demonstrating a typical attachment behaviour towards the mother by turning and moving in the direction of their mother's mobility. In the next phase of his experiment, with the goslings, he placed himself as a parental bird by rearing them all alone from the moment of their hatching. He found that the young goslings followed him in the same manner the mother duck was followed by her goslings in the first phase of his experiment. (See Figure 5.1 provided in Chapter 5)

He named the 'follow behaviour' of the goslings as adaptive attachment behaviour and the mechanism lying behind the demonstration of such behaviour as imprinting. The adoption of such attachment behaviour helps the young goslings from the time of their birth for adapting to the environmental situations for their needed assured security and survival. The term imprinting as explained by Lorenz stands for an innate or instinctive form of permanent learning that occurs for a limited time (called a critical period) early in life, particularly in pre-social species (such as ducks, geese, sheep, horses, etc.,) in which they are found to show attachment behaviour for their mothers or first nearby objects seen by them helping in their adaptation and survival.

The work done and conclusions derived by Lorenz through his experiments helped in reaching an understanding that the bonding and attachment in humans is similar to imprinting as it is important to survival and usually happens within a particular period – popularly known as 'sensitive period'.

Bowlby's Theory of Attachment

Inspired by Lorenz's study and the derived conclusions, the British psychiatrist cum ethologist John Bowlby (1907-1990), brought out a theory of attachment known as Bowlby's theory of attachment in the year 1951. In the development of his theory, Bowlby tried to apply the phenomenon of imprinting and findings of Lorenz's study to explain the affectionate and attachment behaviour of infants towards their caregivers especially the mothers. Bowlby, in this connection, theorised that the human infants, like the young of other animal species, are endowed with a set of built-in behaviors that help them to remain in close proximity of their mothers and other caretakers for their needed protection, care and survival. Moreover, as happens in the case of rearing of babies in other species, the mother, father or other care takers of human infants also remain always nearby for providing them needed security and satisfying their needs as immediately and properly as possible. In this way, in Bowlby's theory, attachment is based primarily on infants' needs for safety and security – their genetically determined motivation to avoid predators. As they develop, infants come to learn that their safety is best provided by a particular individual. This realisation ultimately leads to the development of a special relationship with that individual, who is typically the mother (Feldman, 2016:179).

In general, as claimed in Bowlby's theory, babies who develop attachment to their mothers or caregivers are found to show the following behavioural characteristics towards their attachment figure:

- They wish to remain always near to their attachment figure.
- They are found to return or approach always the attachment figure for comfort and safety in the face of a fear or threat.
- They choose the attachment figure as a security base for exploring the surrounding environment.
- They can't bear separation and demonstrate a lot of anxiety and fear-related symptoms in the absence of the attachment figure.

In fact, Bowlby's theory has discussed a lot concerning the nature, aetiology, emergence, types, outcomes, effects, etc., related to the development of attachment among children. However, the important lessons learnt and things emerging from this discussion, according to Meggitt, Carolyn, (2012), may be stated as follows:

1. The first five years of life are the most important in a person's development.
2. A child's relationship with their parents (in particular with the mother) has an enormous effect on the child's overall development.
3. Separation from a parent, particularly from the mother, is a major cause of psychological trauma in childhood.
4. Such separation and consequent psychological trauma has long-lasting effects on the overall development of a child.
5. The attachment is 'monotropic'. This means that it is established between the infant and one other person.
6. There is a critical period for attachment formation. Bowlby thought that the period between 6 months and 3 years was critical for attachment formation. The child must form an attachment by about 6 months, after which, until around 3 years, they have a strong need to be continuously with or close by their mother. Any obstacle to the forming of an attachment, or any subsequent disruption of the relationship, constitutes maternal deprivation.
7. The secure attachment and continuous relationship a child needs is far more likely to be provided within their natural family than anywhere else.

The Development of Attachment behaviour among children

How do infants acquire a typical behavioural characteristic named attachment in the course of their development or how does such an attachment develop between the infant and caregiver, mother or another affectionate person? By paying consideration on this issue, much like Piaget's stage theory of cognitive development, Bowlby (1969) in his theory of attachment mentioned the following four distinctive stages or phases in the attachment development among developing children.

1. Pre-attachment phase *(from birth to 6-8 weeks):*

During this phase or stage of attachment development, arriving at the earliest days of their development, infants are seen to be characterised in the following manner with regard to the development of attachment behaviour:

- They demonstrate no signs of attachment towards the people or objects surrounding them.
- They are quite neutral in showing their preference to the familiar or unfamiliar social and non-social stimuli present in their environment simply for the reason of not possessing the needed ability to discriminate between them.
- At this stage they are not able to recognise their mothers or caregivers on the basis of their voice, smell, touch, face, looks and the other likewise characteristics.
- They are found to act in ways that attract others to care for them (such as smiling, crying, grasping and seeking eye contact) to seek attention and care of the caregivers, mothers and other persons available in their social environment.

2. Attachment in the making phase (*from 6-8 weeks to 6-8 months*):

During this phase or stage of their readiness as well as the initiation of well-intended steps towards the attachment development, the infants are in general found to demonstrate the following signs and symptoms:

- They begin to show their capability of identifying and recognising the familiar ones by getting them separated from the unfamiliar ones
- They now begin to provide their preference for a few selected ones (e.g., caregiver, mother, a close family member) in the matter of providing security, comfort and company to them.
- Although, at first instance, they may be found to react positively with the unfamiliar and strangers such as passing them a smile or going into their arms (especially while in the mother's arm), but soon it gets transferred into displeasing and anxiety signs such as crying and getting away from the arms.
- They begin to demonstrate stranger anxiety (fearfulness towards strangers) in their social encounters.
- They respond differently to a familiar caregiver than to a less familiar one. Hence, especially now they feel more comfortable and secure in the company and care of a regular caregiver especially the mother.
- The developed ability of recognising and reacting accordingly to the familiar and unfamiliar ones, begin to lay foundation of the formation of a close emotional tie between infants and caregivers.
- However, since it is a beginning stage of attachment formation between the caregiver/mother and the infants, they are not found to show much resentment and protest when separated from their mothers as more often visible at the later stage of attachment development.

3. Clear-cut attachment phase (*from 6-8 months to 18 months-2 years*):

At this stage infants begin to show a full-fledged attachment to one or the other closer persons responsible for providing security, comfort, company and care to them by exhibiting the following behavioural signs:

- As toddler, now the infants become able to actively maintain contact with their caregivers and discriminating quite clearly between their attachment figures and unfamiliar/strangers.
- Infants now strongly desire the assured full time company of their mother, caregivers and adults on whom they have come to rely. They can't bear separation from them and exhibit their separation anxiety in a quite expressive way such as crying loudly, running after them, lying on the ground, etc.
- Besides the expression of such separation anxiety, the stranger anxiety is also quite vocal and expressive now among them. They strongly express their liking and disliking, shyness and fear towards the strangers in quite clear terms.

  With the signs and symptoms indicated above thus now at this stage the developing infants can be well described to imbibe with their first genuine attachments.

4. Reciprocal relationship phase (*from 18 months-2 years afterwards*):

This phase of attachment development among developing infants occurs generally by the end of two years when they are found to attain a somewhat reasonable stage of their cognitive understanding for developing quite satisfactory emotional ties with the people on a give and take reciprocal relationship. This stage has also been referred to as Goal-Corrected Partnership stage or phase of attachment development on account of a necessary mutually satisfying goal-directed relationship developed between developing children and caregivers or others in their socio-cultural environment. The development of such goal-corrected partnership in the opinion of Bowlby (1969) happens in the following way:

> As the baby becomes a toddler, she becomes increasingly aware that her mother has goals and motives that are different from her own. At this point she realises that she must create a partnership with her mother through their interaction. This partnership is based on the idea of two separate individuals interacting, each with an equal role in keeping the interaction going (Levine and Munsch, 2018: 388).

Children belonging to the goal-corrected partnership or reciprocal relationship attachment phase may be found to exhibit the following characteristics in their day-to-day behaviour:

- They are no more seen to be grappled with unnecessary and undesirable feelings related to the separation and stranger anxieties as exhibited by them in the earlier days or stage of their development.
- The knot of their emotional ties and strength of the emotional bonds established with their parents, caregivers and family members get much tightened and strengthened during this phase.
- The basis of getting attached with others for the children now does not remain confined to the satisfaction of their own needs or goals (such as feeding, safety, security, company or other socio emotional needs) as a one-sided affair but gets extended to the process of establishing mutually satisfying relationships on an equal partnership ground.
- As a result of the development of their cognitive understanding now children begin to understand the expectation of others in relation to them. As a result, they may now begin to act and behave in the manner liked and needed by others for establishing mutually satisfying relationships and a reciprocal bond of mutual liking, love and affection with their caregivers, siblings, friends and other familiar adult members interacting and assisting them in their day-to-day living.
- At the end of this phase or stage of attachment development, the developing children in general are found to get engaged in multiple attachments at a time with a number of people at a time in the given socio-cultural environment instead of getting attached with one such as their mother/caretaker or some more familiar and intimate individuals.

Types or Styles of Attachment

It is certain that children in the first few years of their life say up to three or four years are found to imbibe a sense of attachment towards their caregivers, parents, siblings, members of the family and other adults of their social circle. As a matter of individual differences however, the quality of the sense of attachment imbibed by them shows a wide variation. Researchers in this connection through their findings have identified a secure attachment style and three other styles up surging on account of their feeling insecure.

1. **Secure attachment**: The infants showing this type of attachment are found to use the mother (or caregiver) as a secure base. In her presence they may be found to be engaged in all types of pleasure and exploring activities but feel somewhat distressed when she is out of sight or absent. After her return they actively seek contact and their crying stops. They are not responsive to strangers and feel scared and distressed when approached by them, no matter in whatever comfortable or motivational ways.

2. **Insecure-avoidant attachment**: As a reactionary measure for feeling insecure, here the infants may be seen to adopt an avoidance or apathetic attitude towards their mother or caregivers. They are somewhat unresponsive to her presence and do not feel distressed after her leaving. When the mother (or caregiver) returns, they do not rush to greet or cling to her. Instead, they go about their business independently, and many times show themselves busy for avoiding contact and approaches of the mother.

   With respect to their behaviour with unfamiliar people and strangers, they are often rather sociable with them but may sometimes avoid or ignore also much in the same way that they avoid or ignore their mothers.

3. **Insecure-resistance attachment**: As a reactionary measure for feeling insecure, the infants here try to pick up a rebellion and resistive attitude towards their mother or care giver. Their insecurity forces them to remain close to the mother and they resist her separation, but even in her closeness they can't engage in carefree activities. The fear of separation haunts them and they feel quite distressed when she leaves. After her return they combine clinginess with an angry resistive behaviour demonstrable through their struggle to be released after being picked up and not to be comforted easily by the attempts of the mother.

4. **Insecure-disorganised and disoriented attachment**: This attachment style is the outcome of the utmost insecurity felt by infants in their upbringing. The infants exhibiting this style are characterised by confusion, a clueless behaviour lying between attachment and non-attachment such as (i) crying out unexpectedly after having calmed down, (ii) crawling towards caregiver and then suddenly freezing with apprehension, (iii) looking away with flat, depressed emotion while the mother is holding or approaching her, (iv) displaying fear of familiar caregivers instead of getting comfortable in their company, etc.

This last category is often linked with parental abuse or neglect and is connected with unmanageable fear. Throwing light on its etiology and disorganised nature, Levine and Munsch, (2018:390) write:

> Think about how this pattern would develop. The very person to whom the baby would normally turn when afraid is the same who is causing the fear. The babies don't know what to do or where to turn. They cannot organize their behaviour because they do not have a predictable environment. They never know what to expect or what is expected of them.

The impact of the Type of Early Attachment on Later Development

The type of attachment developed by infants toward their mother and caregivers is said to carry quite an influential impact over their later developments in all the dimensions of their personality. While the children who have been securely attached as infants to their mother and caregivers tend to follow a properly appropriate developmental path and feel adjusted to their self and environment, those imbibed with insecure attachment styles of one or the other nature are found to be somewhat a failure in achieving satisfactory progress in their development in one or the other personality dimension. They also have been found to be developed in an insecure maladjusted personality causing hurdles in the welfare of their self and others.

In general, researchers engaged in this field have pointed out a number of instances and examples glorifying the impact of the type and nature of early attachment of children on their later development and behaviors in the following manner:

1. The children who got imbibed with a secure attachment style in their early infancy were more often found in their later life to display behaviors such as:

   • As toddlers at the age of 2-3 years they are recognised as better problem solvers and more complex and creative in their symbolic play, display more positive and fewer negative emotions, and are more attractive to their peers as play mates than those who were insecurely attached.

   • As preschoolers they are able to demonstrate reasonable independence, empathy, social competency in their day-to-day functioning.

   • In their school years they are judged as children possessing a lot of self-confidence, capability to adjust in the school environment, establishing satisfactory relationships with teachers and peers, and performing well in their studies and other co-curricular activities.

   • In their adulthood they are found to demonstrate a reasonable level of adaptability to their day-to-day functioning and professional responsibilities contributing positively towards their own progress and welfare of the society.

   • In their married life they are found to be quite adjustable, happy and fulfil their responsibility towards their family and children in a satisfactory way.

2. Quite opposite and contrarily to the securely attached children, the children imbibing insecurity-ridden attachment types in their infancy and early childhood are found to exhibit the behavioural characteristics true to their type at the later stage of their developmental and adult years. Accordingly, where the insecurity-avoidant show a lot of apathy, avoidance, withdrawal, social aloofness, inconsistency of behaviour, lack of decisive ability, suspicion, anxiety and nervousness in their functioning and behaving, the insecurity-resistant are known for their aggressive, hostile, resentment and revengeful attitude and behaviour in their life. They are unable to maintain satisfactory relationships with the peers and other people in their social and professional interaction and may thus not live a satisfactory married life. The insecurity-disorganised on the other hand have a quite disturbed and disorganised life characterised with a lot of signs and symptoms of a disturbed and disorganised personality, antisocial and abnormal behaviour.

Assessing or Measuring Attachment

The methods and measures employed for assessing or measuring the type, nature and quality of the attachment developed among children may be outlined and discussed as follows:

Strange Situation Method

This method has its origin in the study and work of Mary Ainsworth, a developmental psychologist who used it in her one of the longitudinal study of the attachment process of the small babies in 1960s (Ainsworth &Wittig, 1969).

In its working, this method involves a laboratory procedure of observing and evaluating the child responses and reactions to a series of the *Strange Situation Episodes,* eight in number. In these sequential episodes a child is exposed to a varying degree of stressful situations involving the mother, child and an adult stranger in an unfamiliar setting for a limited specified time (30 seconds for first episode and 3 minutes or so for the other ones).

The sequence of events occurring in these eight episodes of the Ainsworth study has been summarised by Vasta, Miller and Ellis (2014:460) through Table 15.1:

Table 15.1: Strange Situation Procedure for Assessing Attachment

Episode	Persons present	Duration	Brief Description of Action Number
1	Mother, baby and observer	30 second	Observer introduces mother and baby to experimental room, then leaves.
2	Mother and baby	3 minutes	Mother is non-participant while baby explores.
3	Stranger, mother and baby	3 minutes	If necessary, play is stimulated after 2 minutes Stranger enters. Minute 1: Stranger silent,
4	Stranger and baby	3 minutes or less	Minute 2: Stranger converses with mother,
5	Mother and baby	3 minutes or more	Minute 3: Stranger approaches baby, After 3 minutes mother leaves unobtrusively.
6	Baby alone	3 minutes or less	*First separation episode*: Stranger's behaviour is geared to that of baby
7	Stranger and baby	3 minutes or less	*First reunion episode*: Mother greets and comforts.
8	Mother and baby	3 minutes	Baby, then tries to settle baby again in play; mother then leaves, saying bye-bye. Second separation episode *Continuation of second separation*: Stranger enters and gears behaviour to that of baby *Second reunion episode*: Mother enters, greets baby, then picks baby up; meanwhile stranger leaves unobtrusively.

Note: A particular episode is curtailed if the baby gets unduly distressed or prolonged and if more time is required for the baby to become re-involved in play.

The Steps for Using Strange Situation technique

The method or procedure named as "Strange Situation Procedure" can be put to use to measure and classify the attachment behaviour of a particular child into one or the other types of attachment behaviour described earlier in the name of Secure, Insecure-avoidant, Insecure-resistance, and Insecure-disruptive attachment. One can go ahead for this by making use of the following steps:

- The experimenter should try to become quite proficient in making use of the Strange Situation prescribed by Ainsworth for assessing the attachment behaviour of children

- He should call the mother/caregiver of the child along with a stranger (nominated for this purpose) for knowing well the task performed and role played by them in the experiment with the small baby whose attachment behaviour needs to be assessed.

  (The video recording of the episodes involving the child, mother and stranger may be properly shown and repeated for this purpose to them along with proper instructions issued to them in this concern).

- Now selection of a proper place (quite unfamiliar to the child) should be made and the child, his mother/caregiver and stranger should be made to act out their own from passing through the experiences exactly on the lines as shown to the mother and stranger in the video before the commencement of the experiment.

- The task of video recording of what happens during the experiment is properly performed by the experimenter or his assistant side by side as the experiment goes on with no interference in the natural process of role playing on the part of child, mother and stranger.

- The experimenter is then required to draw necessary conclusion from the experimental observation data (lying in the recorded video). His task here is now mainly concerned to classify the attachment behaviour of the child in one or the other well-specified four attachment types. Table 15.2 and Table 15.3 may facilitate his task well in this concern for reaching a somewhat reliable and valid conclusion. While Table 15.2 describes in brief the type of behaviour shown by children classified in different attachment types during the different episodes of Strange Situation experiment, Table15.3 provides a criteria for putting children into different attachment types on the basis of the intensity of behavioural characteristics associated with attachment behaviour.

Table 15.2: Ainsworth's four types of attachment with their associated behaviours

Types or Styles of Attachment	Associated Behaviors
Secure	Children feel secure enough to explore freely during the pre-separation episodes, but they display distress when the mother leaves, seek her out, respond enthusiastically when she returns and gets easily soothed by her.

Insecure-Avoidant	Children may explore with or without mother's presence, show little distress at separation, and when the mother returns, they tend to avoid her.
Insecure-Resistance	Children need to stay close to the mother and don't leave her at all for exploration. They give evidence of distress throughout the procedure, particularly during separation. On reunion with the mother they may simultaneously seek close contact but also hit and kick her.
Insecure-Disorganised	An infant with this attachment pattern displays quite unpredictable, disorganised and distressed responses in the whole duration of the experiment. There is great confusion among them whether to approach or avoid the mother and hence they may be seen to show a lot of inconsistency and contradiction in their behaviour such as approaching her mother when she returns but not looking at her.

Source: Adapted from Ainsworth, (1983)

Table 15.3: Criterion for the Classification of Infant Attachment

------------------------------------- Classification Criteria -------------------------------------

Types and Styles of Attachment	Seeking Proximity with Caregiver	Maintaining Contact with Caregiver	Avoiding Proximity with Caregiver	Resisting Contact with Caregiver
Secure	High	High (if dismissed)	Low	Low
Insecure-Avoidant	Low	Low	High	Low
Insecure-Resistance	High	Often (pre-separation)	Low	High
Insecure-Disorganised	Inconsistent	Inconsistent	Inconsistent	Inconsistent

Adapted from Feldman, Robert (2016:180)

The use of Strange Situation method or technique for the assessment of attachment behaviour of children suffers from a number of weaknesses and limitations such as:

- Its use is strictly limited to laboratory-like conditions. The study of attachment behaviour in natural conditions in the home and day-to-day life situations is not possible through this technique.
- Here the study of child behaviour is not properly possible unless we have a quite trained and professional experimenter (i) to experiment well with the use of Strange Situation episodes and (ii) derive needed conclusions from the observed behaviors.

- The study of the behaviour here involves strange situations characterised with the acts and influences that may make the infants extremely fearful, anxious, withdrawn or resentful in their future behaviour.
- It does not suit for assessing the attachment behaviour of children much older than 2 who are becoming quite accustomed to (and less stressed by) brief separations and encounters with strangers (Shaffer and Kipp, 2007).

The Method of Employing Attachment Q-Set

This method can be usefully employed in studying the attachment behaviour of the 1-5 year olds. Here instead of getting confined to assess the attachment behaviour of children in the laboratory setup, it can be studied in the most natural setups even in the children's own residences over a much longer period of time.

The use of this method for the evaluation of the attachment behaviour of a child requires the presence and involvement of the following.

(i)   A trained observer/evaluator (a family member or friend may also perform this act after due preparation)

(ii) The mother or caregiver of the child

(iii) The child whose attachment behaviour is to be assessed or evaluated.

As an assessment tool, Attachment Q-set (AQS) consists of a set of 90 items each of which is printed on a card and thus making a total of 90 cards used by the experimenter /observer for the study or assessment of a child's behaviour. The printed material of these items is meant for describing one or the other type of situations involving an interaction between the mother/caregiver and the child. For illustrating the nature of the item used in an AQS we are hereby producing a few sample items.

- Child looks to mother/caregiver for reassurance when wary.
- Child greets mother/caregiver with big smile/running hug.
- Child enjoys climbing all over the mother when they are sitting nearby or playing.
- When child returns to mother after playing, he is sometimes fussy for no clear reason.

The Procedure or Steps Involved in the Use of AQS method:

1. The process begins with the arrival of a trained observer (or family member or friend taking the responsibility) at the scene of the behavioural observation task carried out in familiar settings such as home or residence of the child under study.
2. His task here is to make an objective and proper observation of the behavioural activities involving interaction of the child with the mother in a variety of situations highlighting one or the other thing related to the attachment behaviour of the child with his mother/caregiver.
3. He can visit the home or other place several times as needed for observing and confirming the things related to the attachment behaviour of the child with his mother/caregiver.

4. Now he may sit at his own place for arriving at the conclusions about the attachment behaviour of the child on the basis of what has been observed by him during these days in this concern. For this purpose he makes use of Q-sort method — a rating technique used in social science research in which prepared statements are sorted into categories.

5. Accordingly he is now engaged in the task of sorting the 90 cards into 9 piles ranging from "least like the child's observed behaviour " (piles 1-3) to "most like the child observed behaviour" (piles 7-9).

6. After sorting the cards the observer/evaluator (i) develops a profile of the child's attachment behaviour, (ii) compares it with the profiles of children (categorised and placed in one or the other types/styles of their attachment behaviour) developed by experts in the field.

7. On the basis of such comparison now he tries to say that (i) the child is secure and insecure, (ii) what are the nature and types of his security or insecurity and (iii) in what category of the well known four attachment types his or her behaviour falls.

What is Temperament?

You must have often heard that a particular individual is temperamentally fit or unfit for a job or facing a particular type of life situation. Similarly in their day-to-day life we may find some people designated as timid, fearful and anxious; some as fearless and outgoing; and others as aggressive and angry. It does not happen exclusively with mature elders but is also common with children of any age and the foetuses rearing in the womb of the mother. The infants may differ in exhibiting quite a unique type of emotional response in the day-to-day behaviour. While some are known for getting easily disturbed and cry easily, others are relatively easy going and peaceful in their reactions and responses to the encountered situations. For the typical responses of the foetuses developing in the womb, while some mothers may be found complaining about their quite restless movement kicking and pushing most of the time, the others may feel relatively comfortable and at ease with the developing foetus. All of such differing behaviour styles adopted by the individuals, right from the prenatal period onwards, in the course of their life journey in dealing with faced situations and circumstances are attributed to a particular characteristic or trait of their personality known by the term temperament. Let us know more about the meaning, nature and concept of the term temperament from the writings and views expressed by different authors and scholars.

1. **Levine and Munsch, (2014):** Temperament may be defined as the general emotional style of an individual displayed by him or her in responding to events going on in one's environment.

2. **Kagan and Fox, (2006):** Temperament refers to a child's typical ways of responding to events and novel stimulation and of regulating impulses.

3. **Arnett & Maynard, (2017)**: Temperament may be defined as innate responses to the physical and social environment, including qualities of activity level, irritability, soothability, emotional reactivity and sociability

4. **Berk, (2009):** When we describe one person as cheerful and upbeat, another as active and energetic, and still others as calm, cautious, persistent or prone to angry outbursts, we are referring to temperament — early appearing, stable individual differences in reactivity and self-regulation.

5. **Feldman, Robert S, (2016):** Temperament encompasses patterns of arousal and emotionality that are consistent and enduring characteristics of an individual. It refers to how children behave, as opposed to what they do or why they do it.

6. **Rothbart & Bates, (1998):** For infants, personality does not yet include many components that are evident later on, such as beliefs, attitudes and values. For this reason, the study of infant personality is generally restricted to *emotional expressiveness and responsiveness to environmental stimulation.* These components of personality are called temperament.

7. **Bates & Wachs, (1994):** Temperament is meant to describe the baby's behavioural style, reflecting not so much what babies do as how they do it. For example, two babies may both enjoy riding in a mechanical swing, but one may react exuberantly, shrieking with delight, whereas the other may remain calm and even fall asleep. Most researchers view temperament as simply one of the many individual differences, or traits, that make each child unique.

The analysis of all what has been said above in general and emphasised in various definitions may help us in deriving the following conclusions about the nature and characteristics of the term temperament:

- Temperament as an important trait of human personality is well visible among developing children from the time of their birth onwards in the infancy — the time when many of the personality traits such as attitudes, beliefs and values have no appearance among them.

- Temperament in its usually visible form may be taken as a generalised tendency of reacting and responding emotionally to the events and stimuli in their environment.

- Temperament represents a somewhat generalised way of one's behaving in terms of responding and reacting emotionally to the environmental stimuli on one hand and showing capability of regulating and managing the emotional expression on the other.

- Temperament is meant to describe the style of one's behaviour in a generalised way paying more attention to how it is expressed rather than what and why of this behaviour.

- The quite early appearance of the temperamental characteristics among the individuals right from their very birth and even earlier in the womb may make us conclude that emergence of temperament is genetically guided and biologically derived.

- The differences in the temperament are responsible for bringing a lot of things concerning variability and individual differences among children in their present and future behaviour and ways of life.

- The emergence and functioning of the temperament in human beings is relatively quite stable travelling from one age span to other in one's life. One's temperament thus may be helpful in saying and predicting about the present and future outcomes of his or her functioning.

In the end, as a matter of defining the term temperament, we may say that the term temperament, as one of the important personality traits, stands for a general behavioural style adopted by individuals in their life since the beginning of their life for reacting and responding emotionally in certain ways to a variety of stimuli and events in their environment.

The discussion about the concept and nature of the term temperament can't be termed over until some of the following basic questions remain unanswered.

1. Is temperament inherited or environmentally decided?
2. Is temperament stable and beyond the task of modification and change?
3. Can something be done for helping children in their temperament development?

Let us try to seek answers to these questions.

Role of Heredity and Environment in Temperament Development

The things and findings favouring a strong genetic and biological base to the development of temperament among human beings can be summarised as follows:

(i) The children as developing foetuses rearing in the womb of their mothers are found to exhibit particular types of behaviour patterns quite specific and distinguishable from others in terms of their movements, sleeping behaviour, arousal, etc., quite similar as visible in their temperaments after birth and age of infancy.

(ii) The variability and differences in terms of reacting and responding to the environmental stimuli and event is clearly visible and gets more vocal and expressive in the behaviour of newborns and babies of a few days. In real situations in our day-to-day life we may find that while some newborns are found to be crying a lot and need immediate caring and feeding, the others remain calm and do not need such immediate caring and feeding. In the similar way, when we have an opportunity to look at the few hours old babies in the nursing homes or maternity hospital lying in the same ward, we may notice them exhibiting varying temperamental tendencies; while some may be seen sleeping contently, others can be seen moving around grimacing, some staring quietly, others thrashing, a few red-faced and crying, etc.

(iii) It has been observed that children differing in their temperamental characteristics in a quite significant manner are also found to differ in a great way in the possession of distinct capacities of their neurological development and functioning. It seems that there is a direct correlation between one's neurological functioning and temperament display and it is therefore right to provide a biological base (and consequence the genetic disposition) to the differences found in the temperaments of babies and developing children.

The observational findings noticed as such in the behavioural reactions and responses of the developing foetuses, newborns and few hours old in the manner given above have a substantial ground in forcing us to believe that we all are born with a certain temperament based to some degree on our genetic inheritance. (Rothbart, 2007)

However, it is one side of the story. The evidences cited and things said in providing sole credit to the genetic and biological factors for the temperamental differences among children are neither sufficient nor valid in their assertion. Actually, what we call the genetic and biological influence on the development or emergence of a particular type of temperament at any stage of a child's development in the womb of the mother, at birth and early period of infancy can never be excluded or separated from the influences and effects of the powerful and dominating forces of the environment available to the developing children right from their conception in the womb of the mother in the form of internal environment and after birth as physical and social environment. Therefore it is not fair to provide sole credit to the heredity for the temperamental differences among developing children.

Moreover, the role of environmental forces in influencing and affecting the temperamental characteristics of developing children becomes quite evident when the employed suitable environmental measures like good practices of child rearing, re-structuring and modification of the environment available to children for their living, education and development etc., begin to show positive results in bringing needed change and alterations in the child's so called innate temperaments.

As a result, it is almost agreed on the part of the thinkers, scholars and researchers in the field of child and developmental psychology that temperament development as well as differences among children on this account are neither absolutely genetically or biologically determined nor environmentally controlled but are quite inter-actionist in nature, implying that an ongoing interaction between forces of heredity and available environment is responsible for what happens to them in relation to their temperaments.

The Stability and Modification in Temperament

As a rare distinction, temperament represents a characteristic of one's personality that is present in developing children right from their rearing in the womb of the mother. Apart from this, it is also a characteristic and trait that remains fairly stable after its first appearance in developing children. The longitudinal studies done on this account have sufficiently revealed that what goes with the children in relation to their inherent temperamental characteristics in the womb of the mothers travels to them well up to a quite long distance in the subsequent developmental stages. The work done by Thomas and Chess in the 1950s by following 3 months old to their adult years in their 30 years' duration longitudinal study may be cited as a quite glaring example for this purpose. In the form of maintaining stability in his temperamental characteristics, thus, a child showing a lot of restlessness, hyperactivity and demanding nature as a foetus maintains these characteristics in his or her behaviour at the time of birth, infancy and also at the later stages of future life. For example, children showing characteristics such as impulsivity, restlessness, demanding nature and boldness in their childhood behaviour may be found to be quite adventurous and accident prone in their later life. They move into less safe situations more readily than a child with a more cautious temperament. (Meggitt, Carolyn, 2012).

Now the question arises that whether such stability claimed in the temperaments of children is absolutely rigid or there are possibilities for modification, alteration and change in its structure and functioning in the coming future?

In this concern it has been seen that although most of the children in general show a great amount of fairness in maintaining stability in their temperamental characteristics from conception onwards in their developing years, still then, there lies necessary scope for modification and change in the so stabilised temperament as a consequence of the coming life events and wilful attempts doing in this direction. Apart from this, it has also been found that all children and adults are not at all so temperamentally stable and may show significant variations in this regard. Among them the earlier temperamental characteristics sometimes do and sometimes do not carry over into later life. Confirming such possibility Feldman, Robert (2016:187) has commented in the following way:

> Infants show temperamental differences in general disposition from the time of birth, and temperament tends to be fairly stable well into adolescence. On the other hand, temperament is not fixed and unchangeable: child-rearing practices can modify temperament significantly. In fact some children show little consistency in temperament from one age to another.

The Concept of 'Goodness of fit' and Child Rearing

Chess and Thomas on the basis of their longitudinal study in the 1950s also introduced the concept of "goodness of fit" with the objectives (i) to describe the interactional relationship between the child and the environment and (ii) to suggest better patterns of child rearing used by parents. Let us discuss this.

The term 'Goodness of fit' in relation to the proper development and functioning of temperament in the developing children refers to a proper degree of fitness or suitability observed between the child's temperamental characteristics and the environmental conditions including the rearing practices utilised for dealing and behaving with the developing children. In other words the term Goodness-of-fit refers to a theoretical principle propagating that children develop best if there is a good fit between the temperament of the child and environmental demands. (Arnett & Maynard, 2017:165).

For applying the principle of goodness of fit in dealing with the children, parents thus need first to recognise and identify well the unique temperament of their children through the observation of the displayed behaviour of the children and then try to adjust their responses and rearing styles much in tune with the demands of the identified temperament.

How such goodness of fit is observed and how it results in positive outcome with the difficult children has been illustrated by Shaffer and Kipp (2007:433-34) in the following manner:

Difficult infants and toddlers who fuss a lot and have trouble adapting to new routines often become less cranky and more adaptable over the long run if parents remain calm as they insist their children comply with rules. It also helps if parents exercise restraint and allow them to respond to new routines at a more leisurely pace. Indeed many difficult youngsters who experience such patient, sensitive and yet demanding care giving are no longer classifiable as temperamentally difficult or displaying problem behaviour later in childhood or adolescence. However, true to their form, difficult infants and toddlers are especially likely to remain difficult and to display behaviour problems later in life if their parents are often impatient, angry, demanding and forceful.

In the rearing of easy going, shy and slow to warm up children, the parents have to be quite watchful in pushing them gently and gradually towards the more acceptable social, activity ridden and anxiety free behaviour with the application of the principle of classical and operant conditioning. However, whatever temperamental characteristics the children possess, the first and foremost thing to remember in child rearing is that "the well being of both children and parents is promoted when goodness of fit exists".

In this way, parents and caregivers can learn quite valuable lessons from the theory and application of the principle of goodness of fit in the manner such as it is always good for them (i) to adapt their expectations in the manner of providing good fit to the demands of their children's temperament and (ii) to take help of the well-tested measures as well as the trained counsellors for understanding and managing the behaviour of the temperamentally challenging children.

Theories or Models of Temperament

Psychologists and theorists have put up a number of theories and viewpoints (also referred to as model of temperament) for explaining the nature and mechanism of temperament. Here in this chapter we would be describing three of them one by one.

Thomas and Chess's Theory or Model of Temperament

The oldest as well as most popular theory or model of temperament known as Thomas and Chess's theory or model of temperament owes its propagation in the 1950s at the hands of two USA paediatricians — Alexander Thomas and Stella Chess. It was the result of their persistent efforts through a research project, named the New York Longitudinal Study (NYLS), which continued for a record time of more than 30 years. In this study they followed 141 children from the age of 3 months well into adulthood. With the help of their study they identified initially nine main dimensions of temperament present at birth in the developing children described in Table 15.4:

Table 15.4: Dimensions of Temperament

Dimension	Definition (meaning of the concerned dimension)
Activity level	Proportion of active time periods to inactive time periods
Approach-withdrawal	The response to new person or object, based on whether the child accepts the new situation or withdraws from it
Adaptability	How easily the child is able to adapt to changes in his or her environment
Quality of mood	The contrast of the amount of friendly, joyful and pleasant behaviour with unpleasant, unfriendly behaviour
Attention span and persistence	The amount of time the child devotes to an activity and the effect of distraction on that activity
Distractibility	The degree to which stimuli in the environment alters behaviour
Rhythmicity (regularity)	The regularity of basic functions such as hunger, excretion, sleep and wakefulness
Intensity of reaction	The energy level or reaction of the child's response
Threshold of responsiveness	The intensity of stimulation needed to elicit a response

Source: Thomas, Chess and Birch (1968)

On the basis of these dimensions of temperament, Chess and Thomas found that about 60% of the babies and young children in their study fell into one of the following three groups:

1. **Easy children:** These children are found to be quite at ease and comfortable in their day-to-day actions and behaviour. They adapt to the demands of the environment easily, establish regular routines and are generally cheerful. They are found to show quite positive response in new situations, and could accept frustration with little fuss. Their rearing and handling causes less problems to the parents and teachers.

2. **Difficult children:** Difficult children show a lot of irregularities in their day-to-day routine activities such as sleeping, eating and elimination cycles. They are not able and even offer resistance in getting adjusted to new situations and environmental demands. They get easily disturbed and frustrated with the denial or delay in the satisfaction of their immediate needs and agitate quite intensively on this account with loud crying or throwing tantrums. These children are said to be difficult in their rearing and handling on the part of the parents, elders and teachers.

3. **'Slow-to-warm-up' children:** As the name signifies, these children take time for getting activated and responding properly to the environmental demands and situations. As a result, initially they may be found to show negative responses of mild intensity when exposed to new situations, but slowly come to accept them with repeated exposure. They have a fairly regular biological routine. In spite

of showing some negativity in their mood in the beginning, they get reasonably interactive and adaptable after getting some support from elders.

It was also realised on the part of these researchers that there may arise exceptions when it becomes difficult for placing a child into one of these three specified categories in terms of his temperament development on account of demonstrating the unique mixed blends of temperamental characteristics in his behaviour.

EAS Theory or Model of Temperament

Following a biological approach and viewing temperament as an inherited personality trait, the American psychologist and geneticist Robert Plomin along with his team members brought out another model of temperament in the year 1984 for throwing light on the mechanism of temperament. On the basis of their research findings the propagators of this model concluded that a child's temperament can be predicted or measured along a few basic dimensions of his or her behavior named as (i) emotionality, (ii) activity, (iii) sociability and(iv) shyness. Since in knowing and defining the temperament with the use of this model, first three components or dimensions play a quite key role, the method has become popular in the name of EAS model (letters EAS standing for emotionality, activity and sociability, respectively). Let us have an understanding of all the four basic dimensions of one's temperament referred to in this model.

Emotionality in this model refers to how quickly a child becomes aroused and responds negatively to stimulation from the environment right from his or her earlier days of infancy. It is quite apparent in small babies and developing children through their emotional reactions and responses to environmental stimuli such as:

* Awakened easily by a sudden noise and crying intensely in reaction.
* Showing resentment and resistance by refusing the acceptance of the things offered or done for him or her.
* Exhibiting anger or fear responses such as temper tantrums

Plomin believes that differences on this dimension represent inherited difference in infant's nervous system, with some infants having a quicker 'trigger' and automatically experiencing greater arousal than others. (Vasta, Miller and Ellis, 2004)

Activity in this model refers to the energy level, tempo and vigour demonstrated by the child in reacting emotionally to environmental stimuli or faced situations. The activity level possessed by a child may very well predict how fast and strong he will react in an emotionally aroused situation. In general, the nature of the activity level of the emotionally aroused children is revealed through the following behavioural activities:

* They may be found to be quite restless and full of energy in responding to environmental stimuli with a great force and speed;
* Moving all the time without taking rest and getting easily tired;
* Exploring new places and showing the spirit of adventurism;
* Frequently engaging in various types of activities at a time.

Sociability in the model refers to an infant's preference and attempts for being social, i.e., getting along with other people. Accordingly children demonstrating sociability in their behaviour may be found to get engaged in the following activities:

- Instead of remaining alone, they are found to enjoy the company of others.
- At their own they try to initiate contact and interaction with others.
- He has little or almost no hesitation of initiating contact and being social to the strangers and unfamiliar people.

Shyness, as the fourth component or dimension of temperament, stands quite contrary and opposite to the behaviour shown in the third component sociability of the model. Here the child has no tendency or inclination for initiating contact or being social to other people. He avoids or rather fears the arrival or company of the unfamiliar and strangers at his home and elsewhere. Although what gets measured under this component may get covered much under the sociability component, however, measures of temperament taken under this sub-scale or component can further add to the reliability and validity of the instruments utilising the EAS model.

Regarding, the role of the EAS model describing temperament as a biological or environmental phenomenon, a mid-course stand has been taken by the propagators of the model. Emphasising on this aspect Vasta, Miller and Ellis, (2004:450) write:

> Although the EAS model views temperament as a biological concept, the researchers are interactionist in their conception of social development. In their view, although the baby's levels of key temperamental characteristics may be determined by genes, the baby's overall social development will depend on how these characteristics interact with characteristics of the social and physical environment.

Rothbart's Theory or Model of Temperament

A third approach or model named as Rothbart's model of temperament has been proposed by the American psychologist Mary Rothbart and her colleagues. This model too in the line of previous models has a strong biological flavour. It tries to explain the temperamental differences among developing children through the differences in their neurological development and physiological functioning. Rothbart in this connection clearly emphasised that "particular temperaments emerge as children's brains develop distinctive capacities for responding to impulses and regulating attention, emotions and activity" (Rothbart, 2007). These two capacities have been named as reactivity and self-regulation in Rothbart's model.

Accordingly, in Rothbart's model the temperamental characteristics of developing children first have been bifurcated in two broad categories or dimensions named as (i) reactivity (the nature and capacity of responding to the internal and external environment and (ii) self-regulation (the nature and capacity of exercising an effective control over their reactions and responses) and then attempts have been made to list out the sub-dimensions along with the typical behaviour characterising the sub-dimension in the manner as illustrated in Table 15.5:

Table 15.5: Rothbart's Model of Temperament

Dimension of Temperament	Description
Reactivity Activity level	Level of gross motor activity
Attention Span/Persistence	Duration of orienting or interest
Fearful distress	Wariness and distress in response to intense or novel stimuli, including time to adjust to new situations
Irritable distress	Extent of fussing, crying and distress when desires are frustrated
Positive affect	
Self-Regulation Effortful control	Frequency of expression of happiness and pleasure
	Capacity to voluntarily suppress a dominant, reactive response in order to plan and execute a more adaptive response.

Source: Berk, 2009:418

In this way, in the initial attempt of developing a temperament model, Rothbart and her colleagues tried to place before us a total number of six dimensions (five belonging to the reaction tendency and one to the regulating). They further worked on this pursuit aiming to arrive at some basic dimensions (reduced categories of temperamental dimensions) for explaining or measuring the temperament of an individual. For this purpose they took the help of a sophisticated statistical technique named factor analysis and got success in establishing

three fundamental dimensions of temperament, namely, (i) Extraversion/Surgency, (ii) Negative affectivity and (iii) Effortful control for the measurement of temperament of the children.

In relation to the role played by Rothbart's model in describing temperament as hereditary or environmental phenomenon, it can be well emphasised that it is interactionist in nature and thus may be found paying equal importance to both the biological and environmental contribution. The major characteristics or determinants of temperament — reactivity and self regulation described in this model although seem to be genetically or biologically determined on the basis of clear cut perceived differences in the temperament of the children right from the prenatal period, yet the role of environment available to them in the womb of the mothers and after birth in the form of physical surroundings and caring, cannot be underestimated.

Measuring Temperament

The task of assessing or measuring temperament can also be performed much in the similar way as performed in assessing or measuring other personality traits such as intelligence, attitudes, aptitudes, interests, etc., with the use a questionnaire or tool developed for the assessment of temperament. There are specific tools available for use in this concern. These have been developed by making use of the theoretical considerations put up by the propagators of the models of temperament described earlier in this chapter.

Besides this a researcher and user can also develop and use his own questionnaire (based on the theoretical notions of a temperament theory or model) for knowing the quality of a child's temperament on various dimensions of temperament as indicated in the model. For the purpose of illustration here we are giving a set of probable questions appearing in a questionnaire developed by making use of 'The Thomas and Chess' Model for the measurement of children's temperament.

Critical Questions Indicating a Particular Type of Temperamental Dimension:

Is the child always 'on the move' and doing something or has a more relaxed style?
Are the child's eating, sleeping and bowel movements, etc., regular or somewhat haphazard?
Does the child get adjusted to changes in routines or plans easily or resist transitions?
Does the child never meet a stranger or tend to shy away from new people or activities or does not have such problems?
Is the child bothered by external stimuli such as loud noises, bright lights, or food textures or does he tend to ignore them?
Does the child react strongly to situations, either positive or negative, or does he react calmly and quietly?
Does the child's mood shift frequently or does he remain usually even-tempered?
Is the child easily distracted from what he is doing or can he shut out extended distraction and stay with the current activity?
Can the child stick with an activity for a long time or does his mind tend to wander?
Does the child give up as soon as a problem arises with a task or does he keep on trying?

In a measure of temperament developed with the use of Thomas and Chess model, any individual child can score high, low or average on each of the nine dimensions of temperament specified in the mode. With the help of all such information, one can arrive at having three temperament profiles: an easy temperament, a difficult temperament and a slow-to-warm temperament. Table 15.6 shows where children with each of these temperament profiles fall on each of these dimensions.

Table 15.6: Temperament profiles

This table shows where children classified by Thomas and Chess into three categories fall on each of the nine dimensions of temperament.

Dimensions of Temperament	Easy Temperament	Slow-to-warm Temperament	Difficult Temperament
Activity Level	Varies	Low to moderate	Varies
Adaptability	Very adaptable	Slowly adaptable	Slowly adaptable
Approach/Withdrawal	Positive approach	Initial withdrawal	Withdrawal

Attention Span and Persistence	High or low	High or low	High or low
Distractibility	Varies	Varies	Varies
Intensity of Reaction	Low or mild	Mild	Intense
Quality of Mood	Positive	Slightly negative	Negative
Rhythmicity	Very regular	Varies	Irregular
Threshold of Responsiveness	High or low	High or Low	High or Low

Source: Adapted from Chess, Thomas & Birch (1965)

In making an attempt to measure temperament in accordance with the theoretical ideas put up in the EAS model, one can conveniently use a well-known tool, *EAS Temperament Survey*. It consists of a well-developed questionnaire (set of appropriate questions). The administration of this questionnaire demands from the parents' caretakers of the developing children (whose temperaments we intend to measure) to supply the answers of the asked questions related to child's behaviour patterns.

In the case of measuring temperament with the use of an instrument developed on the ideas provided in Rothbart's model, the scores earned by the subjects on the three basic dimensions — extraversion/surgency, negative affectivity and effortful control — are first computed and then efforts are made for drawing a conclusion about the quality of temperament with the interpretation of the earned scores. In this connection, for drawing conclusions about the quality of temperament of the children Rothbart and her colleagues have provided appropriate interpretation for the scores earned on these dimensions in the following manner as shown in Table 15.7 (Berk, 2009).

Table 15.7: Interpretation of Scores on Rothbart's Dimensions of Temperament

Dimension of temperament	The quality of the temperament
High score on Extraversion/ surgency	High levels of optimistic anticipation, impulsivity, activity and sensation seeking; smiling and laughing often
High score on negative affectivity	Shy and often fearful, frustrated, sad, uncomfortable and not easily soothed.
High score on effortful control	Proficient in strategically focusing and shifting their attention: effective planner for the future, able to suppress inappropriate responses, and take pleasure in complex and novel stimuli.

Summary

The term **attachment** refers to a particular type of emotional behaviour in the form of a close relationship, affectionate tie or bond existing between two individuals who may be seen to shower love and affection and express desire to maintain proximity with each other. The most glaring example of such attachment behaviour may be witnessed in the emotional tie or bond existing between an infant and his mother or caregiver.

A number of theories such as Psychoanalytic theories, Behavioural theories, Cognitive-developmental theories and Ethological theories are available to explain how infants become emotionally involved or attached with the people around them.

Psychoanalytic view point put forward by the psychologists like Freud and Erikson have tried to explain the mechanism of attachment found in the infants on the basis of the satisfaction of their biological needs in a satisfactory way. In this concern, Freud said that infants at the oral stage of their psycho-sexual stage of development get attached with the individuals who are special to them in satisfying their feeding need as well as providing them the sucking pleasure. Erikson on the other hand linked it with the state of trust v/s mistrust visible among infants in relation to their psycho-social development by saying that the behaviour of the people capable of establishing a trust worthy relationship with the infants by fulfilling not only their feeding need but also assuring them warmth, tender touches, soft reassuring vocalisation, changing of diaper etc., is responsible for the development of attachment ties.

The behaviourists like Watson, Pavlov and Skinner emphasise that attachment behaviour is a learned and acquired phenomenon and it can be well explained through the principles and process of classical and operant conditioning. The positive responses generated and the satisfaction felt by the babies as a result of feeding and caring is responsible for generating attraction and attachment towards mother or other caretakers. Similarly by following the operant conditioning principle that a behaviour is shaped and maintained through its consequences, the attachment once shown for the mother, a caregiver or object gets continued, modified or replaced depending upon life circumstances.

According to the **cognitive-developmental perspective**, the ability to form attachment depends a lot on the infant's level of cognitive development. That is why the sign of emergence of attachment behaviour among the babies does not appear before the age of 7 to 9 months — precisely the time when infants are entering Piaget's sensori-motor stage of cognitive development. In the later period and stages of cognitive development, the pattern of attachment towards people, places, objects and events get developed, modified, or replaced depending on the development, functioning and use of the cognitive abilities on the part of individuals in one or the other life situations.

A somewhat more useful explanation of the children's attachment behaviour comes from the ethological perspective put forward by the Ethologists like Lorenz and Bowlby. Lorenz tried to mention a phenomenon of imprinting (the instinctively generated adaptive behaviour of young goslings for their survival and protection) to provide explanation of the development of attachment behaviour among babies of all species include humans. John Bowlby through his theory of attachment theorised that human babies (like the babies of other animal species) are endowed with a set of built-in behaviors that keep them in close proximity of their mothers and other caretakers for their needed protection, care and survival. In the course of their further development, infants come to learn that their safety is best provided by a particular individual. This realisation ultimately leads to the development of a special relationship with that individual, who is typically the mother.

Regarding the development of attachment behaviour among the children, Bowlby says that it goes on through a sequence of the four distinctive stages or phases, namely, (i) Pre-attachment phase (from birth to 6-8 weeks), (ii) Attachment-in-the-making phase (from 6-8 weeks to 6-8 months), (iii) Clear-cut Attachment Phase (from 6-8 months to 18 months-2 years), and (iv) Reciprocal relationship phase (from 18 months-2 years afterwards).

The Attachment behaviour developed among children according to its very nature, functioning and consequences can be mainly divided into two broad types — secure and insecure. Going little further, the insecure attachment behaviour visible in the children may be further categorised as (i) insecure-avoidant, (ii) insecure-resistance and (iii) insecure-disorganised and disoriented.

The type of attachment developed by the infants toward their mother and caregivers is said to carry out quite influential impact over their later developments in all the dimensions of their personality. While children who have been securely attached as infants to their mother and caregivers tend to follow a properly appropriate developmental path and feel adjusted to their self and environment, those imbibed with insecure-attachment styles of one or the other nature are found to be somewhat of a failure in achieving satisfactory progress in their development in one or the other personality dimension. They also have been found to be developed in an insecure maladjusted personality causing hurdles in the welfare of their self and others.

There are two methods that can be usefully employed for assessing or measuring the type, nature and quality of the attachment developed among children, named as Strange Situation method and Attachment Q-Set (AQS) method. In the strange situation method, a child (the subject of the study) is exposed to a varying degree of stressful situations (under a series of the eight Strange Situation episodes) involving the mother, child and an adult stranger in an unfamiliar setting for a limited specified time. The responses and reactions shown by the child then makes way for taking decision about the nature and quality of the child's attachment behaviour. The use of AQS method, involves an assessment tool (used by the evaluator) called attachment Q-set consisting of a set of 90 cards. On each of these cards there lie an item/statement describing one or the other type of situations involving an interaction between the mother/caregiver and the child. The evaluator first tries to collect information about the attachment behaviour of the child (well in the light of the statements of the Q-set) by observing his behaviour in the familiar settings such as home, nearby park, etc., and then makes use of Q-sort method (a rating technique used in social science research) for arriving at the needed conclusion about the child's attachment behaviour.

The term temperament as one of the important personality traits stands for a general behavioural style adopted by individuals in their life since the beginning of their life for reacting and responding emotionally in certain ways to a variety of stimuli and events in their environment.

About the relative role of heredity and environment in the temperamental development of the growing children it has been commonly agreed that an ongoing interaction between the forces of heredity and available environment is responsible for what happens to them in relation to their temperaments.

Regarding the stability and modification in temperament it can be well inferred that although most of the children in general show a great amount of fairness in maintaining stability in their temperamental characteristics from the conception onwards in their developing years, still then, there lies necessary scope for the modification and change in the so stabilised temperament as a consequence of the coming life events, and wilful attempts doing in this direction.

The term Goodness of fit refers to a theoretical principle propagating that children develop best if there is a good fit between the temperament of the child and environmental demands.

For applying the principle of goodness of fit in dealing with the children the parents thus need first to recognise and identify well the unique temperament of their children through the observation of the displayed behaviour of the children and then try to adjust their responses and rearing styles much in tune with the demands of the identified temperament.

There exist a number of theories and models helpful to us in understanding the nature and mechanism of temperament. In this connection, the work done under the propagation of the famous Thomas and Chess's theory or model of temperament has a distinction of first placing before us nine main dimensions of temperament (such as activity level, approach-withdrawal, adaptability, quality of mood, attention span and persistence, distractibility, regularity, intensity of reaction and threshold of responsiveness) present at birth in developing children, and then using these dimensions for classifying babies and young children into one of three groups named as (i) Easy children, (ii) Difficult children, (iii) "Slow-to-warm-up" children.

EAS Theory or Model of Temperament has a distinction of following a biological approach and viewing temperament as inherited personality trait. It says that a child's temperament can be predicted or measured along a few basic dimensions of his or her behaviour named as (i) emotionality (the quickness demonstrated on the part of child in arousing and responding negatively to environmental stimuli), (ii) activity (the energy level, tempo and vigour demonstrated by the child in reacting emotionally to the environmental stimuli, (iii) sociability (ability to get along with other people), and (iv) shyness (avoiding or rather fearing the arrival or company of the unfamiliar and strangers).

Rothbart's Theory or Model of Temperament tries to explain the temperament differences among the developing children through the differences in their neurological development and physiological functioning. Accordingly, it has been clearly emphasised in this theory that particular temperaments emerge as children's brains develop distinctive capacities for responding to impulses and regulating attention, emotions, and activity. These two capacities have been named as reactivity and self-regulation in this model of temperament. These capacities or broader components of temperament have been further sub divided into sub categories, giving birth to six basic capacities or characteristics helpful in describing one's temperament. For providing their model as a base or means of measuring one's temperament in an objective way, the propagators of model have also mentioned about three fundamental dimensions of temperament, namely, (i) Extraversion/Surgency, (ii) Negative affectivity and (iii) Effortful control.

The task of assessing or measuring temperament can also be performed much in the similar way as performed in assessing or measuring other personality traits such as intelligence, aptitudes, interests etc., with the use of a questionnaire or tool developed for the assessment of temperament. There are specific tools available for use in this concern. These have been developed by making use of the theoretical considerations put up by the propagators of the various theories or models of temperament such as Thomas and Chess's model, EAS model and Rothbart's model of temperament.

References and Suggested Readings

Ainsworth, M.D.S.(1983), 'Patterns of infant-mother attachment as related to maternal care: Their early history and their contribution to continuity', In D. Magnusson & V. Allen (Eds), *Human development: An interactional perspective*, New York: Academic Press.

Ainsworth, M.D.S. & Wittig, B.A. (1969), Attachment and exploratory behavior of one year old in a strange situation, In B.M. Foss (Ed.) *Determinants of Infant behavior* (Vol.4), London: Methuen.

Arnett, Jeffrey Jensen & Maynard, Ashley E. (2017), *Child Development: A Cultural Approach* (2nd edition), Boston: Pearson.

Bates, J.E. & Wachs, T.D.(Eds) (1994), Temperament: Individual differences at the interface of biology and behavior, Washington , D.C., American Psychological Association

Berk, Laura E. (2009), *Child Development* (Eighth edition), Boston: Pearson Education

Bowlby, J.(1969), *Attachment and loss:Vol.1. Attachment*, New York, N.Y: Basic Books

Bowlby, J.(1973), *Attachment and loss: Vol. II Separation*, New York: Basic Books, Bowlby, J.(1980), *Attachment and loss: Vol. III Loss*, New York: Basic Books.

Bowlby, J.(1988), *A secure base: Parent-child attachment and healthy human development*, New York: Basic Books.

Bowlby, J., Maternal care and mental health, *Bulletin of the World Health Organization*, 3, 355-534.

Chess, S., Thomas, A. & Birch, H,G.(1965), *Your child is a person: A psychological approach to childhood without guilt*, New York, NY: Viking Press.

Feldman, Robert S. (2016), *Child Development* (7th edition), Boston: Sage.

Freud, S.(1910), *The origin and development of psychoanalysis*, New York: Henry Regnery (Gateway Editions), 1965.

Harwood, Robin, Miller, Scott A., and Vasta, Ross (2012), *Child Psychology-Development in a Changing Society*, (Fifth Ed.) New York: John Wiley & Sons, Inc., Hoboken, NJ, Wiley,

Chess, S., and Thomas, A. (1999), *Goodness of fit: Clinical applications from infancy through adult life*, Philadelphia, PA: Brunner/Mazel.

Kagan, J. and Fox, N. (2006), Biology, culture, and temperamental biases. In: Eisenberg, N., Damon, W. and Lerner, R.M. Eds., *Social, Emotional, and Personality Development, Handbook of Child Psychology*, Wiley, New York, 167-225.

Levine, Laura E. and Munsch Joyce (2014), *Child Development-An Active Learning Approach*, (2nd edition), Los Angeles: Sage.

Levine, Laura E. and Munsch Joyce (2018), *Child Development- An Active Learning Approach*, (3rd edition), Los Angeles: Sage.

Lorenz, K.Z. (1952), *King Solomon's Ring*, New York: Crowell.

Lorenz, K.Z. (1965), *Evolution and the modification of behavior*, Chicago: University of Chicago Press.

Lorenz, K.Z. (1980), Here am I-Where are you? The behavior of the graylag goose, New York, NY: Harcourt Brace Jovanovich.

Meggitt, Carolyn, and Ormrod, J.E. (2013), *Understanding Child Development*, (Fifth edition), Boston: Pearson.

Rothbart, M.K. & Bates, J.E.(1998), Temperament in W. Damon (Series Ed.) & N. Eisenberg (Vol.Ed.), Handbook of child psychology, Vol.3., Social, emotional, and personality development, (5th ed.), NewYork: Wiley.

Rothbart, M.K. (2007),Temperament, development and personality, Current Dimensions in Psychological Science, 16 (4), 207-212.

Shaffer, David R. and Kipp, K. (2007), Developmental Psychology-Childhood and Adolescence,(7th ed.), Canada: Thomson/Wadsworth.

Thomas, A. & Chess, S. (1977), *Temperament and development.* New York, NY: Brunner/Mazel

Thomas, A. & Chess, S.(1980), *The dynamics of psychological development.* New York, NY: Brunner/Mazel

Thomas, A., Chess, S. & Birch, H.G. (1968), *Temperament and behavior disorders in children,* New York: New York University Press.

Vasta, Ross, Miller, Scott A. and Ellis, Shari, (2014), *Child Psychology* (4th edition), New York: John Willey & Sons, Inc.

16

Moral or Character Development

Introduction

Development of morality or character formation is regarded as one of the important and essential aims for a system of education and the pattern of bringing up children in almost all societies and communities of the world. The fundamental principles and practices of all the different religions and sects also propagate and emphasise on the development of morality and character formation among their followers. Universally, thus it is almost believed by societies and communities of the world that the welfare of human beings as individuals and the group as a whole depends upon the proper development of morality and character formation among all the members of the group or community and for this purpose efforts should be made right from early upbringing and education of children. The questions that arise are: What is this morality? Is it inherited or learned? What is the nature or pattern of its development among human beings? Can it be explained on the basis of stage-specific developmental theories discussed in the preceding chapters? How can we help our youngsters have proper development in their morality or character? Let us think over these issues in the present chapter.

What is Morality?

Etymologically, the term morality, has been derived from the Latin word 'mores', meaning manners, customs or traditions. Societies and communities from their very birth throughout the world have tried to establish essential ways, manners and norms for helping them co-exist and progress properly in the form of certain moral or ethical codes for being followed by every member of their group. Such observance of the moral codes on the part of the members of the group has been referred to as conduct or morality. In this way, morality is nothing but a pure conformity to the moral or ethical code of a society on the part of its members. Emphasising further on such meaning of the term morality Hurlock (1956: 404) writes:

> "To act in a moral way means, thus to act in conformity or group standards of conduct. Immorality is failure to conform or behaviour directed against the interest and welfare of the group."

Therefore what is moral or immoral, totally rests on the decision of right or wrong of a conduct as prescribed in the moral or ethical code of a society. It is natural that such moral codes or standards may be found to vary from group to group or society to society and it is therefore an accepted fact that there cannot be any uniform and generalised criteria of judging morality or immorality. However, as a concept, one's morality may be taken or regarded as an equivalence to his character that has been defined as "sum of all the tendencies which an individual possesses". (Dumville, 1938, p. 311).

The definition provided by Dumville is somewhat capable of providing a comprehensive view as it tries to suggest that character or morality possessed by an individual is the sum total of all his tendencies — innate as well as acquired. As a whole it takes into consideration the following:

(i) In the first place there are instincts which are inborn and innate. They provide the native mental capital for a person at the time of birth in order to start his life.

(ii) With increasing age and experience, instinctive behaviour is replaced by habit formation. At this stage habits mechanise the behaviour of an individual. But as they are mechanical in nature they have no power to control or manipulate the behaviour pattern.

(iii) Instincts give birth to emotions and these emotions play an important part in personality or character development. The various emotions centred round an object or idea often combine themselves to form a composite group or organisation. When this organism or structure takes a permanent structure in the mind of an individual he develops a sentiment regarding that particular object or idea.

(iv) In the last stage the various sentiments are combined so as to form a system or organisation. The equilibrium of this system is maintained by the intellect and the master sentiment.

This system of properly organised sentiments, which is known as morality or character of an individual, is completely an acquired disposition. In actual sense the moral development or character formation of an individual can be compared with a building which possesses the foundation in the form of (refined) instincts. The emotions can be considered the bricks for building the walls and roofs of the sentiments. The sentiment of self-regard is the cement or the adhesive material. In this way, morality or character like a building consists of the foundation material and the other constructive material and thus is defined as the sum total of what an individual possesses.

In this way, in a general sense, as it may appear most of the time, "the domains of morality or character" in the words of Ormond (2003): "May include such traits (acquired-tendencies) as honesty, fairness, dependability, concern for the rights and welfare of others, and other pro-social behaviour helping, sharing and comforting, and so on. The term immoral behaviour typically refers to actions that are unfair, cause physical or emotional harm or violate the rights of others". (p. 86).

In conclusion we can repeat the saying of Ross that "morality or character is just the organised self", (1951, p. 129). Instincts, emotions, habits, temperament, will and sentiments — all are the constituents of one's morality or character. The organisation of these constituents into one whole in the form of a permanent mental structure is taken as a morality or character of an individual. Therefore the study of one's morality or character needs complete understanding of one's habits, motivation, will, sentiments, intellect, self-image and many other factors affecting this total personality. The person's behaviour in the social situation is governed by his moral sense. Therefore, morality or character in its essence can be defined as an organised and stable mental structure of an individual existing in the form of one's moral sense or reasoning which determines his social behaviour.

Morality is an Acquired or Learned Phenomenon

The traits of good or bad conduct, conformity or non-conformity to the moral code of the social group or capability of behaving by judging an act as right or wrong is not an inherited phenomenon. Its blue prints do not lie in the chromosomes or genes of an individual. Although, the inherited physiological and cognitive structure, to some extent, may be considered to provide some basic foundation to the inclination and preferences for psycho-social behaviour but as far as the studies of concept development and patterns of behaviour have revealed, the existence of moral sense and demonstration of moral behaviour on the part of individuals are purely the subject of their environmental influences rather than hereditary contributions. Calling morality an acquired or learned phenomenon, Hurlock (1956: 405) writes:

> At birth, the child has no conscience and no scale of values. Thus, he is neither moral nor immoral. Instead, he is 'non-moral in the sense that his behaviour is not guided by moral standards. Before he can behave in a moral way, he must learn what the group to which he belongs believes to be right or wrong. This he will learn gradually through the childhood years.

Morality, in this way, should be taken as an acquired and learned phenomenon both in terms of acquiring moral sense or reasoning and demonstrating moral or ethical behaviour in conformity to the moral or ethical code set by society. The ability to judge one's own conduct and that of others (moral reasoning) in terms of evaluating what is right or wrong comes through actual personal experiences and training received by the child as he passes through the various ages and stages of his developmental period.

Levels of character or morality

According to Cronbach, there are five levels of character or morality which are shown in Fig. 5.3.

1. **Amoral stage:** This stage lasts from birth to two years. At this stage, the performer does not know or realise whether his choice has a good or bad effect on others or affects the welfare of others, e.g., plucking flowers from a neighbour's garden. Wants are the sole motivation for a newly born infant who has no concept of good or bad. At this stage he has no control over emotions, cries at the time of every need without bothering whether or not the cry disturbs others.

2. **Self-centred stage:** It lasts from 2 to 6 years. At this stage the person gratifies his own needs and wishes without caring for the effects of his own act on others. His action interferes with the happiness of others though he may not desire to violate the rules. The choice in this case is selfish and if fixation takes place, the person may develop miserly and selfish habits, source of trouble to himself and others. The selfish choices are gradually reduced by socialisation. Selfish choices may also sometimes be seen in case of a man of character.

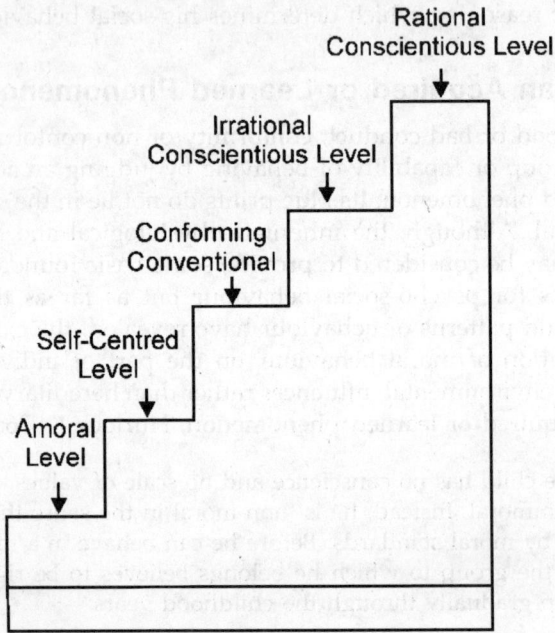

Fig. 16.1: Levels of Character or Morality

3. **Conforming-conventional stage:** The child in his early life is at this stage. The person may do as the Romans do even when his behaviour harms others. A person may not copy because of resulting punishment. Many good citizens follow a conventional pattern of behaviour to avoid bad consequences by breaking the norms.

4. **Irrational-conscientious stage:** The internal self-criticism which is responsible for making a person dissatisfied with some conduct even though that conduct will satisfy his external goals is called conscience. It can be compared with the concept of super-ego as given by Sigmund Freud.

When a person acts in the light of the values held emotionally rather than rationally, e.g., speaks the truth irrationally, he is said to exhibit irrational conscientious behaviour. He will always speak the truth even if he were to be hanged for it.

Some people opine that since we attach topmost importance to value, we should consider it the best form of morality whereas others believe that people not able to tell gracious social lies will find it most difficult — rather impossible to get along with the world. No doubt many irrational conformers have good adjustment with the community in spite of the fact that rigid truthfulness proves an obstacle or hindrance in certain social situations.

5. **Rational conscientious stage:** It is the highest stage of one's morality or character development and it characterised by rationally (not emotionally) sticking to the values, e.g., war is undesirable because of the undesirable destruction of life which accompanies it. But destruction of life may not matter much to a person because war is a means to prevent oppression which again is undesirable. We commonly observe that if two values are important for a person, he may reconcile both of them or subordinate one value to the other.

Helping Children in their Moral Development or Character Formation

In general, the following techniques and provisions can prove as valuable guide-lines in the task of moral development or character formation among developing children.

1. **Proper training of instincts and emotions:** Instincts form the rock-bottom of character. Therefore, the first step in the formation of character is the sublimation and modification of instincts. The emotions, which control the behaviour of an individual, take their energy from different instincts. In fact instincts and emotions give birth to so many elements of one's character. Nature of instinctive and emotional behaviour contributes much to the character development. Therefore, proper care should be taken to modify and sublimate the instinctive impulses and emotions along socially desirable channels. For instance, the crude instinct of combat and emotion of anger after sublimation can be channelized into patriotic and philanthropic deeds, and thus they may help in character formation.

2. **Training of will power:** Proper care should be taken for the development of a strong will power among children. Firm determination and power of taking the right decision at the right time are products of will power and these two qualities are very essential for the development of a strong character. There is a perfect correlation between will and character. There are so many undesirable and negative things which we do and know they are bad but due to weakness of our will cannot do away with them. A man of strong will can free himself from these harmful factors and can remove obstacles from his path of character development.

3. **Organisation of good habits:** Habits also form a path of character. Therefore, due care should be taken to develop healthy habits among children through proper conditioning. The wrong habits need to be done away with - de-conditioning and proper understanding.

4. **Development of worthy ideals:** What a person does and how he will behave in a particular situation depends much on his aims of life and the ideals for which he strives. In other words the character of a person can be judged through his values and ideals. The higher the ideals and goals of life, the stronger is the character of a person. Therefore, children should be made to develop worthy ideals, higher values and noble aims of life so that they can imbibe good virtues in them.

5. **Organisation and development of proper sentiments:** Character is referred to as the system or organisation of sentiments, therefore, every care should be taken to develop a well-organised stable system of healthy sentiments among children. First of all due consideration should be given for developing the right type of sentiments such as patriotism, moral sentiment, social sentiment, intellectual sentiment, aesthetic sentiment and self-regarding sentiment. Then on all these positive sentiments should be well organised with the help of the master sentiment, i.e., the self-regarding sentiment. The strength of one's character always depends upon the sentiment of self-regard. Therefore, children must be helped to develop a strong sense of self-respect and a sentiment of self-regard. In developing this very important sentiment the following points should be kept in mind:

   (i) Due respect must be shown for the individuality of the child.

   (ii) The child should be given reasonable freedom in day-to-day work.

   (iii) He must be encouraged to do his work independently and every care should be taken to build his self-confidence.

   (iv) He must get proper love and affection coupled with an adequate sense of security.

   (v) He must be helped to share and play a role of responsible individual in his school and social life.

6. **The role of suggestion:** Suggestion occupies an important place in the formation and development of character. Children are very sensitive to suggestions. Therefore, help of suggestions should be taken in character formation. But as far as possible, positive suggestions should be given to the children for bringing desirable improvement in their behaviour. This can be achieved through ideal stories and reading about great men and women. Teachers and parents may become living examples. After stepping in for character development, the children should be told that they are making satisfactory progress. Auto-suggestion can also bring very good results at this stage. The feeling, that he is improving day by day and acquiring good habits and characteristics, can immediately help the child to become a man of character.

7. **The role of imitation:** A child is imitative by nature. He imitates what he sees and hears. To him his parents, elders and the teachers are ideals. He imitates them consciously and unconsciously. Hence, it is essential that teachers, parents and other elder members of society should place the ideal examples of their own conduct and character. Every care should be taken by the parents and teachers that nothing undesirable be imitated by their children. They must be provided with a healthy and inspiring atmosphere inside their schools and at their homes. They should not be made to fall prey to bad company and unhealthy society.

8. **Role of reward and punishment:** Punishment and reward both occupy an important place in the development of a character. In the modern age of democratic values and applied Psychology, the role of punishment in character formation is decried. It is said that it creates complexes in the mind of the students and does more harm than good. The main function of punishment is negative as it can

only check wrong things, but it certainly cannot develop the desired attitude. No doubt there is some truth in these observations, but we cannot give up punishment completely in our educational system. Sometimes punishment appears to be the only tool that can curb down undesirable activities. But as far as possible punishment should be resorted to only when other measures fail. Most of the time, positive measures like rewards, praise, appreciation and other methods for due incentive and encouragement should be applied.

9. **Role of moral instructions and religious education:** No one can question the utility of moral and religious education as an instrument for character formation. In one form or the other, provision should be made for its inclusion in a sound system of education. Religious education in a secular state like India creates some doubts in the mind. Such a type of education need not be based upon some narrow rigid sectarian feelings. In fact it should emphasise the lofty moral and human values and keep itself away from the rituals of various religions. It should teach the children to pay respect to all religions and men of character irrespective of caste, colour and creed.

    Moral values may be inculcated in children by making them read stories from the *Panchtantra* and *Hitopdesh*, the *Ramayana* and the *Mahabharata*. Biographies and autobiographies of great personalities may also serve the purpose. Prayer assemblies, talks on morality and other programmes of co-curricular activities can also be made use of for moral and religious instruction.

10. **Proper socialisation of the child:** Social development and character development bear a positive correlation. A socially developed child always behaves according to the norms and values of the society and therefore is more conscious of his character. Therefore every care should be taken for the proper social development of the child. He must be helped in the inculcation of desirable social virtues and maintenance of essential social relations with his peers and other members of the society.

11. **Proper mental development of the child:** Character formation is also linked with the proper mental development of the child. Intellect plays a vital role in the organisation of the elements of character. How a person will behave in a particular situation and face the realities of life depends much upon his intellectual powers. Therefore proper care should be taken to develop intellectual powers like reasoning, thinking, imagination, memory, concentration, etc.

12. **The role of the school, family and society:** Environment plays a vital role in the development of character. From the very birth or right from the time of conception, the environmental forces begin to influence the behaviour of the child. The parents and the family are the first social institution where the foundation stone regarding the character of the child is laid down. Outside the family, the neighbourhood, community and social forces influence the conduct of the child. When he goes to school, the school atmosphere along with the teachers and schoolmates cast their influence upon the character of the child. Therefore, it is essential that all these social forces join hands in the task of the children's

character formation. The social environment as a whole must be so suggestive and inspiring that the children can pick up the habits and characteristics essential for proper character development.

In fact moral development or character formation is a gigantic task. Without the active cooperation of all the involved individuals — children, parents, teachers and all the important social agencies — it is difficult to achieve fruitful results in this direction. We have to exploit all the resources at our command and should strive hard by all the methods and techniques in our possession. The observation made by Skinner and Harriman (1937:261) reminds us of the same. In their words:

"There is no curriculum or method that will produce character (or develop morality) by magic. On the contrary, every experience in the home, at church, on the playground or at school presents an opportunity for character development."

Character formation, in its true sense, is an all-round development and needs an all-round effort. Paying attention to all the aspects it is needed that a programme of character formation be chalked out and it should be implemented with the hearty cooperation of all the involved partners.

Theories of Moral Development

Morality as emphasised earlier, is an acquired and learned phenomenon. However, the acquisition of moral sense or learning to behave in a socially approved way does not come overnight. Instead, it moves slowly but steadily right from birth through infancy and childhood years and into adolescence. How it happens across these developmental stages, has been explained by a number of psychologists and sociologists through their observational studies that consequently have given birth to some theories of moral development. In this chapter, here we would be discussing two of these important theories named as Piaget's Theory of Moral Development and Kohlberg's Theory of Moral Development.

Piaget's Theory of Moral Development

Jean Piaget, famous for his theory of cognitive development is also credited for providing a quite relevant and useful theory of moral development. For studying moral development as a developmental process like cognitive development, Piaget adopted two types of different approaches as follows:

1. The first of these was to observe children of different ages playing marbles, and ask them questions about the rules of the game in order to learn more about children's beliefs about right and wrong. Through such observation and clinical interviews, Piaget (1932:65), concluded as follows:

   • Children younger than 5 essentially had no rules at all.
   • Children falling in the age group 5-10 years were found to observe rules, but they saw them as fixed and non-changeable.
   • Finally, by the age of 10, the children were able to think of their own rules and recognise that these could be adopted by mutual consent.

2. In his other technique, Piaget tried to present to children moral dilemmas, each consisting of a pair of stories. In one, a child (hero of the story) caused a small amount of damage. In the other, the damage done by the hero of the story was accidental but much greater. Piaget asked his clinical interviewed children which of the characters deserved to be punished the most. Piaget then tried to find out not just their answers but the reasoning they used to arrive at them.

The findings of his clinical interview based upon his second approach highlighted that while younger children merely focused on consequences (of the acts like steeling, lying, etc.,) the older children went ahead by taking intent into account.

Stages of Moral Development

On the basis of the results of the observations and clinical interviews involving both the earlier-mentioned approaches, Piaget concluded that the moral development of the children passes through two distinct stages of moral reasoning named (i) heteronomous stage and (ii) autonomous stage.

Let us first see how Piaget tried to conclude that a particular child is demonstrating heteronomous stage of morality or autonomous stage of morality. For this purpose, let us take one of Piaget's pair of story involving moral dilemma :

(i) A little boy named John was in his room. He was called to dinner and went into the dining room. Behind the door there was a chair and on the chair, there was a tray with 15 cups on it. John couldn't have known that the chair was behind the door, and as he entered the dining room, the door knocked against the tray and the tray fell on the floor breaking all the cups.

(ii) One day, a little boy called Henry tried to get some jam out of a cupboard when his mother was out. He climbed onto a chair and stretched out his arm. The jam jar was too high up, and he couldn't reach it. But while he was trying to get it, he knocked over a cup. The cup fell down and broke.

Piaget asked random children of who was naughtier between John and Henry and should be punished more.

Piaget found that even though the younger children were able to distinguish between deliberate and unintentional acts, they still tended to base their judgements on the outcome of the act: the more severe the outcome, the naughtier the act. The younger children were passing through the stage of Heteronomous Morality. Older children (10 years or more) were able to make judgements based on the person's motives: Henry was doing something he shouldn't have been doing, so he is naughtier. The thinking of older children thus represents the stage of autonomous morality. However, it should be noted carefully here that Piaget did not see moral development as consisting of separate stages (as in his cognitive development theory), instead, he saw moral development as progressing through two broad phases that overlap; so sometimes a child's moral reasoning will be in the heteronomous phase and at other times it will be autonomous regardless of his matured age.

Heteronomous Stage of Morality

According to Piaget in a course of their moral development, children first pass through the heteronomous stage of or phase of their morality. It usually occurs in the age group 5-10 years. Development of morality at this stage is usually characterised by the following beliefs and behaviours on the part of younger children:

1. "Heteronomous" means bring subject to rules imposed by others. At the heteronomous stage of morality, thus younger children (age group 5-10 years) consider rules as fixed and absolute. They believe that rules are handed down by authorities, such as God, parents, teachers and other elderly members and therefore, are permanent and unchangeable. One should not challenge or doubt the correctness or appropriateness of the rules and these should be observed in strict obedience.

2. Younger children (5-10 years) base their moral judgement more on consequences (i.e., the largeness of the amount of damage made) rather on intentions. For example, when the younger children were made to comment upon the relative acts of naughtiness, in the previously cited stories, on the part of John (who broke 15 cups while trying to help his mother) and Henry (who broke only one cup trying to steal cookies), the younger children thought that the first boy, John did worse. In this way, their moral judgement is usually based on the amount of damage — the consequences irrespective of the motive — good or bad, for doing the act.

3. They believe in expiratory punishment meaning thereby, that punishment given to the rule breaker or doing wrong or improper things should be proportional to the gravity of consequences (damage done or naughtiness of behaviour). They believe in the theory of immanent justice — if you do something bad and later slip and hurt yourself then that is your punishment.

The question arises why younger children believe and behave in moral realism characterised with a strict adherence to rules and duties and obedience to authority. Piaget in this concern has tried to pinpoint the following two factors:

- The one reason lies in the cognitive development of these children, particularly, egocentrism. That is to say, that, young children are unable to simultaneously take into account their own view of things with the perspective of someone else. They think that everybody has the same views as they have. Their egocentrism thus leads them to project their own thoughts and wishes onto others. Since, they themselves believe in the theory of immanent justice (expectation that punishments automatically follow acts of wrong-doing) and moral realism (valuing the letter of the law above the purpose of the law), they insist on obeying the rules by taking them as fixed eternal features of reality, rather than something that can be negotiated.

- The second major cause lies in their subjugation to their elders — parents, teachers and others. In the natural authority relationship between adults and children, power is handed down from above. The relative powerlessness of young children, thus, may orient them to comply with the rules framed by the adults without question.

Autonomous Stage of Morality

As children grow in age, their thinking gets improved and developed. There is also a change in their cognitive structure from egocentrism to perspective taking. They now stop thinking that everybody thinks in the same way as they think and it makes them realise that people may differ in their moral values and judging the appropriateness or inappropriateness of the rules. Moreover, they now enter into the state of interaction and social relationship by getting rid of their feelings of egocentrism and self-centeredness. The mutual reciprocity and feelings of mutual respect help them to enter the autonomous stage of morality characterised as below:

- Older children (10 years or more) come to understand that people make rules and people can change them. These are not eternal or unchangeable. The rules can be broken in some circumstances.

- As children interact with others, develop perspective-taking emotional abilities and see that different people have different rules, there is a gradual shift from moral realism to morality of cooperation in the moral thinking and reasoning of the older children. As a result, the child of this stage may easily think that people differ in their moral views and morality is not static and universal.

- Piaget said that for the older children belonging to the autonomous phase of morality, intentions are more important than the consequences of action and therefore, their morality should be judged on the basis of their intention-based behaviour. He quoted the example of Henry, a boy who broke only one cup trying to steal cookies in contrast to John, another boy, who broke 15 cups trying to help his mother. The older children like the younger ones did not take into account the gravity of consequences (the heavier loss in terms of breaking 15 cups) for deciding the relative inappropriateness of the behaviour of John and Henry. As a proof of their maturity and entering the stage of autonomous morality, they were found to judge wrongness in terms of the intentions or motives underlying the act (Piaget 1932:137).

- The older children belonging to the autonomous stage of morality no longer believe in immanent justice like the younger children.

- They believe in reciprocal punishment — that punishment should fit the crime.

- Older children believe in coordinating one's own perspective with that of others implying that what is right needs to be based on solutions that meet the requirements of fair reciprocity. Thus according to Piaget, the older children may be said to acquire autonomy in taking judgements over the appropriateness or inappropriateness of an act in comparison to the younger children.

Table 16.1: Piaget's Two-Stage Theory of Moral Development

	Heteronomous Stage of Morality (The Morality of Constraints)	Autonomous Stage of Morality (Morality of Cooperation)
Age span	*5-10 years, typical of 6 years olds*	*10-12 years, typical of 12 years old*
Point of view	Single, absolute moral perspective (behaviour is either right or wrong) and believes that everyone sees in the same way	Awareness of different viewpoints regarding rules. Children put themselves in place of others. They are not absolute in judgement but see that more than one point of view is possible.
Rules	Child believes that rules are fixed and unchangeable or 'carved in stone'.	Child recognises that rules are made by people and can be altered by people. Children consider themselves just as capable of changing rules as everyone else.
Judgement of Act	Children base their moral judgement on consequences, i.e., amount of damage done by an action.	Act by intentions and not by consequences. He considers the intention of the wrong-doers when evaluating an action.
Respect for Authority	Unilateral respect for authority, leading to feelings of obligation to conform to adult standard and obeying adult rules. Believes that wrong doers should be punished by adults.	Mutual respect for authority and peers allows children to value their own opinions and abilities and judge other people realistically. Children obey rules because of mutual concern for the rights.
Punishment	Child favours severe punishment. He believes that punishment itself defines the wrongness of an act. An act is bad if it leads to punishment	Child favours milder punishment that compensates the victim and helps the culprit recognise why the act is wrong, thus leading to reform. In fact, he believes in reciprocal response. A good or bad behaviour on the part of his peers should be paid in same coin.
Concept of Justice	Children should obey laws because they are established by those in authority. Child confuses moral law and believes that any physical accident or misfortune that occurs after a misdeed is a punishment willed by God.	Children believe that laws or rules are established for the welfare of the individuals and society. He does not confuse natural mishappenings with punishment for wrong doing.

Piaget, thus, tried to sketch the process of moral reasoning and development of morality among children. Beginning from the stage of heteronymous morality the children, as they in their age, are seen to demonstrate autonomous morality in their reasoning and behaviour. Such changes in their moral behaviour, according to Piaget results from their social interactions. In this way, Piaget emphasised the role of social interaction, mutual give and take and cooperation as the very basis of bringing changes in the moral behaviour of younger children. It is this cooperation and interaction that makes the individuals work out resolutions or take decisions and judgements which all deem fair. In the light of such observations, Piaget then advised teachers and educational authorities that they should emphasise cooperative decision-making and problem-solving for healthy social interaction and cooperation among children. It will help in nurturing moral development by requiring students to work out common grounds, interaction and mutual cooperation based on fairness.

However, as pointed out by the critics of Piaget's theory of moral development, Piaget was just a beginner in putting up his views about moral development of children. He did not go beyond childhood (the stage of concrete operation of his theory of cognitive development) for the study of the development of moral reasoning and morality among children. However, his initiation to the study of moral development among children and his assertion about of the role of experience and socialisation in the development of morality, certainly influenced the latter psychologists especially Lawrence Kohlberg for bringing a comprehensive stage theory of moral development.

Kohlberg's Theory of Moral Development

Lawrence Kohlberg a psychologist belonging to the University of Harvard, was born in 1927 and grew up in Bronxville, New York. In his years as a student, he stayed on at Chicago for graduate work in psychology, at first thinking he would become a clinical psychologist. However, he soon became interested in Piaget and began interviewing children and adolescents on moral issues as an extension of Piaget's work on children's moral reasoning and development. As a result of his study he got success in putting forward a theory of the development of moral judgement. The sample of his study consisted of hundreds of children belonging to different ages of childhood and adolescence from different family setups, cultures and countries.

Lawrence Kohlberg
(1927-1986)

In his concept of morality and moral judgement it may be seen that he differs from the popular view that children imbibe the sense and methods of moral judgement from their parents and elders by way of learning. According to him, "As soon as we talk with children about morality, we find that they have many ways of making judgements which are not internalised from the outside, and which do not come in any direct and obvious way from parents, teachers or even peers," (Kohlberg, 1968). Going further he clarified that internal or cognitive processes like thinking and reasoning also play a major role in one's moral development,, i.e., the way children make moral judgement depends on their level of intellectual development as well as on their upbringing and learning experiences.

For studying the process of moral development in human beings, Kohlberg first defined moral development as the development of an individual's sense of justice. For estimating one's sense of justice he concentrated on one's views on morality with the help of a test of moral judgement consisting of a set of moral dilemmas. For instance, should a man who cannot afford the medicine his dying wife needs, steal it? Should a doctor mercy-kill a fatally ill person suffering terrible pain? Is it better to save the life of one important person or a lot of unimportant persons? For the purpose of creating interest among the children he interviewed, he tried to put before them these moral dilemmas in the form of story or narrative descriptions like below.

Heinz Steals the Drug

In Europe, a woman was near death from a severe kind of cancer. There was one drug that the doctors thought might save her. It was a form of radium that a druggist in the same town had recently discovered. The drug was expensive to make, and the druggist was charging ten times what the drug cost him to make. He paid $200 for the radium and charged $2,000 for a small dose of the drug. The sick woman's husband, Heinz, went to everyone he knew to borrow the money, but he could only collect about $1,000 which is half of what the drug cost. He told the druggist that his wife was dying and asked him to sell it cheaper or let him pay later. But the druggist said: "No, I discovered the drug and I'm going to make money from it." So Heinz got desperate and broke into the man's store to steal the drug for his wife. Should the husband have done that? (Kohlberg, 1963, p. 19)

After putting such dilemma before the subject, he persuaded him to respond. However, Kohlberg was not really interested in whether the subject said "yes" or "no" to this dilemma, he wanted to know the reasoning behind the answer that could reflect the level of moral reasoning needed to assess the subject's level of moral development. For this purpose, he went ahead and put question like: "Why do you think Heinz should or should not have stolen the drug?" For further probing he planned to ask questions like: "Do you think that Heinz had the right to steal the drug?" "Was he violating the druggist rights? What sentence should the judge give Heinz, once he was caught?" In this way, many such questions were put up by Kohlberg for finding out the reasoning behind his subject's answers.

Finally after analysing the responses Kohlberg got from his subjects, he came to the conclusion that like the Piaget's stages of cognitive development, there also exist universal stages in the development of moral values, and the movement from one stage to another depends on cognitive abilities rather than the simple acquisition of moral values of one's parents, elders and peers. He then identified three levels of moral development, each containing two stages as shown in Table 16.2.

**Table 16.2: Kohlberg's Three Levels and
Six Stages of Moral Development**

Level I	Pre-moral or Pre-conventional Morality (Age 4 to 10 years)
Stage 1:	The stage of obedience for avoiding punishment
Stage 2:	The stage of conforming to obtain rewards and favours in return
Level II	**Conventional Morality (Age 10 to 13 years)**
Stage 3:	Good Interpersonal relationships
	(The stage of maintaining mutual relations and approval of others)
Stage 4:	Maintaining social order
	(The stage of obedience for avoiding censure by higher authority or social systems)
Level III	**Post-Conventional Morality involving self-accepted moral principles (Age 13 or not until middle or later adulthood or never)**
Stage 5:	Social contract
	(Stage of conforming to the democratically accepted laws and mores of community welfare)
Stage 6:	Universe ethical principle
	(Stage of conforming to the universal ethical principles and the call of one's conscience)

Let us now briefly discuss these levels and stages of morality.

Level I. Pre-moral or Pre-conventional Morality (4-10 years)

At this level, the child begins to make judgements about what is right or wrong, good or bad. However, the standards by which he measures the morality are those of others. He is persuaded to take such judgements either to avoid punishment or to earn rewards. Development of morality at this level usually follows the following two stages:

Stage 1. Obedience and Punishment Orientation

In the beginning, the child's morality is controlled by the fear of punishment. He tries to obey his parents and elders purely to avoid reproof and punishment. Actually Kohlberg's Stage 1 resembles Piaget's first stage (Heteronomous Stage of Morality) of moral reasoning. The child assumes that powerful authorities hand down a fixed set of rules which he or she must unquestioningly obey. To the Heinz dilemma, the child typically says that Heinz was wrong to steal the drug because, "It's against the law," or "It's bad to steal," as if this were all there were to it. When asked to elaborate, the child usually responds in terms of the consequences involved, explaining that stealing is bad "because you'll get punished" (Kohlberg, 1958).

Stage 2. Individualism and Exchange

At this stage of moral development children begin to recognise that there is not just one right view that is handed down by authorities. Different individuals have different viewpoints. "Heinz," they might point out, "might think it's right to take the drug, but the druggist would not." Since everything is relative, each person is free to pursue his or her individual interests. One boy said that Heinz might steal the drug if he wanted his wife to live, but that he doesn't have to if he wants to marry someone younger and better-looking (Kohlberg, 1963, p. 24).

In this way, at the second stage of the pre-moral or pre-conventional level, children's moral judgement is based on self-interest and considerations of what others can do for them in exchange or return. Here they value a thing because it has some practical utility for them. They obey the orders of their parents and elders and abide by some rules and regulations, because it serves their interests.

Level II. Conventional Morality (10-13 years)

At this level of moral development also, children's moral judgement is controlled by the likes and dislikes of others — conventions, rules and regulations and the law and order system maintained within the society. Stealing or mercy-killing would thus be judged wrong because it is considered wrong by society at large and by the legal system. In this way, the conventional level of morality may be regarded as the level where the child identifies with authority. It is characterised by the following two stages:

Stage 3. Good Interpersonal Relationships

In the early years of second level of moral development, the child's moral judgement is based on the desire to obtain approval of others and avoid being disliked by being declared a good boy or a good girl. For this purpose he begins to judge the intentions and likes or dislikes of others and acts accordingly. As concluded by Kohlberg, children of this stage of moral development believe that children should live up to the expectations of the family and community and behave in "good" ways like a good boy or good girl. Accordingly as Kohlberg discovered many of his subjects argued that Heinz was right to steal the drug because, "He was a good man for saving the life of his wife simply because no husband would have sat back and watched his wife die." As example, Kohlberg quotes the response given by his subject Don (aged 13 years) as follows:

> It was really the druggist's fault, he was unfair, trying to overcharge and letting someone die. Heinz loved his wife and wanted to save her. I think anyone would. I don't think they would put him in jail. The judge would look at all sides and see that the druggist was charging too much. (Kohlberg, 1963, p. 25)

Kohlberg concluded from such responses of his subjects that by responding in such a way, they were demonstrating the level of their conventional morality because it assumes that the attitude expressed would be shared conventionally by the entire community — "anyone" would be right to do what Heinz did.

In case we try to find similarities and dissimilarities between Piaget's theory of moral development and Kohlberg's theory of moral development, we can fairly analyze that there lie substantial similarities between Kohlberg's first three stages and Piaget's two stages being covered during the entire period of childhood. In both the developmental theories, we may observe a similar sequence characterised with a shift from unquestioning obedience to a relativistic outlook and to a concern for good intention on the part of wrong doers. The difference lies in the fact where in Kohlberg's theory these shifts occur in three stages rather than two as emphasised in Piaget's theory of moral development.

Stage 4. Maintaining the Social Order

According to Kohlberg, stage 3 reasoning works best in two-person relationships with family members or close friends, where one can make a real effort to get to know the other's feelings and needs and try to help. At stage 4, in contrast, the respondent becomes more broadly concerned with society as a whole. Now the emphasis is on obeying laws, respecting authority and performing one's duties so that the social order is maintained. In support of his conclusion Kohlberg again cites the responses of his subjects to the Heinz story. Many of his subjects were found to utter that they understand that Heinz's intention or motive was good, but they cannot condone the theft. What would happen if all of us started breaking the laws whenever we felt we had a good reason? The result would be chaos; society could not function.

In this way children reaching the moral stage 4, begin to take moral decisions from the perspective of the society as a whole. At this stage children's moral behaviour and judgements are governed by conventions as well as the laws and mores of the social system. The standards of others are now so established that it becomes a convention to follow them. Children now follow the rules and regulations of society and take decisions about things being right or wrong with a view to avoiding censure by the elders, authorities or the social system.

Level III. Post-conventional Morality Involving Self-Accepted Moral Principles (13 years and afterwards)

This marks the highest level of attainment of true morality, as the controlling force for making judgements now rests with the individual himself. He does not value a thing or conform to an idea merely because of consideration of the views of others, conventions or the law and order system of the society, but because it fits onto the framework of his self-accepted moral principles. However, to reach this level is not an ordinary thing. One may be able to attain it in the beginning or middle of his adolescence or it may be postponed for him till the middle or later adulthood or he may never attain it in his life time. This highest level of moral development is also characterised by two separate stages as described below.

Stage 5. Social Contracts and Individual Rights

At stage 5 as Kohlberg concludes, individuals begin to ask. "What makes for a good society?" They basically believe that a good society is best conceived as a social contract into which people freely enter to work toward the benefit for all. They recognise that all rational people would agree on two points (i) getting certain basic rights, such as liberty and life, to be protected and (ii) needing some democratic procedures for changing unfair laws and for improving society. In support of his conclusion Kohlberg quotes the responses of his subjects to the Heinz dilemma. Many of his respondents make it clear that they do not generally favour the breaking of laws; laws are social contracts that we agree to uphold until we can change them by democratic means. Nevertheless, his wife's right to live is a moral right that must also be protected.

In this way, at this stage the individual's moral judgements are internalised in such a form that he responds positively to authority only if he agrees with the principles upon which the demands of authority are based. The individual at this stage begins to think in rational terms, valuing the rights of human beings and the welfare of society. For example, at this stage in reference to the rights of the human being, the decision about mercy-killing may be left to the individual who is suffering, and if so needed, the concerned laws may be amended for the welfare of society at large.

Stage 6. Universal Principles

This stage of moral development is the highest stage or perfection achieved in terms of moral reasoning and development of morality. In propagating his theory of moral development, Kohlberg believes that there must be a higher stage of moral development (as just conceived by him through his stage 6) which defines the principles by which we get the type of justice as conceived by the great moral leaders like Mahatma Gandhi and Martin Luther King. The principle of justice is universal and requires us to treat the claims of all parties in an impartial way, respecting the dignity of all people as individuals and humans. According to Kohlberg, we can reach this stage in case we begin to look at a situation purely through one another's eyes. Take the case of Heinz dilemma, reaching this stage would essentially require that all parties — the druggist, Heinz and his wife — try to view the things from other perspectives for seeking justice and fair solution of the problem. As a result, in the end, they would all agree that the life of the wife must be saved by sacrificing the narrow interests related to money or conventional laws.

In this way at Stage 6 of our moral development the controlling forces for making moral judgements are highly internalised. The decisions of the individual are now based upon his conscience and the belief in universal principles of respect, justice and equality. He does what he, as an individual thinks right, regardless of legal restrictions or the opinion of others. Thus, at this stage people act according to the inner voice of their conscience provide evidence of sharing, helping and defending the victims of injustice and lead a life that they can, without self-condemnation or feeling of guilt or shame.

From this discussion of Kohlberg's stages of moral development, it is clear that although children begin to think about morality in terms of justice or right and wrong at a very early age, yet they have to wait until adolescence or adulthood for the dawning of the stage of true morality. Also, it is not essential that all people pass through the third level of moral development. Most adults are not able to cross the second level and few can reach stage 5, and among these there are very few who, being intellectually quite sound, can think rationally and base their moral judgement purely on the dictates of their conscience at the risk of life and property.

Evaluation of Kohlberg's Theory of Moral Development

Appreciation

Kohlberg's theory of Moral Development is appreciated on the following grounds:

1. Kohlberg is the first psychologist who tried to present a comprehensive stage theory of moral development by stating that the development of moral reasoning is characterised by a series of qualitative distinctive stages. He claimed that an individual progresses through them in order, without skipping any. Each of Kohlberg's stages build upon the foundation laid by earlier stages but reflect a more integrated and logical consistent set of moral beliefs than those before it. (Ormrod, 2003, p. 88)

2. Kohlberg's theory of moral development provided a unique description for explaining the progression to higher stages of our moral reasoning by taking into account Piaget's stage of cognitive thinking or logical reasoning. Kohlberg proposed that advanced moral reasoning (post-conventional reasoning) requires formal operational thought for abstract understanding of the purpose of the laws and rules to help society run smoothly (Kohlberg, 1976). Hence the post-conventional level of morality does not appear until adolescence (the concrete operational stage of their cognitive development). In this way, for the development of his theory of moral reasoning, Kohlberg tried to adopt the base provided through Piaget's stages of cognitive thinking. Consequently, it appears that development of moral reasoning and cognitive thinking travel side by side. However, in his theory of moral development, in explaining advanced moral reasoning Kohlberg put up a different view. He asserted that progression to an advanced stage of cognitive development does not guarantee equivalent moral development. One may have quite a developed cognitive structure and functioning, but it is not essential that he must demonstrate the same higher level of his moral reasoning in tune with his higher cognitive development. It was thus a unique feature in the moral development theory of Kohlberg in its assertion that it is quite possible to be logically operational in logical reasoning but pre-conventional in moral reasoning, implying that cognitive development is a necessary but insufficient condition for moral development to occur (Ormrod 2003, p. 90).1976

3. In addition to making use of Piaget's stage of cognitive thinking or logical reasoning for building his sequential stages of moral reasoning, Kohlberg also tried to make use of Piaget's concept of disequilibrium as an instrument or explanation for the development of advanced moral reasoning among children. As we know Piaget proposed that when a child is unable to assimilate new learning, he experiences a state of disequilibrium, which makes him eager to expand his ways of thinking and reasoning to accommodate and learn the new thing. Following the footsteps of Piaget, Kohlberg in his theory of moral development advocated that one progresses to a higher stage of moral development only when he faces disequilibrium by realising that his beliefs about morality are unable to address the events and dilemma he is experiencing at present. In this way,

Kohlberg's theory of moral development produced a unique way of presenting certain problematic situations or dilemmas before the growing children for letting them experience disequilibrium and gradually restructure their thoughts about morality for moving to the subsequent higher stages of moral development. Kohlberg in his theory of moral development advocated that one progresses to a higher stage of moral development only when he faces disequilibrium by realizing that his beliefs about morality are unable to address the events and dilemma he is experiencing at present. In this way, Kohlberg theory of moral development produced a unique way of presenting certain problematic situations or dilemmas before the growing children for letting them experience disequilibrium and gradually restructure their thoughts about morality for moving to the subsequent higher stages of moral development."

4. Kohlberg's theory of moral development provided substantial weightage to the role of experience, modelling and social interaction in the development of morality among children. It emphasised that morality is a learned behaviour and moral reasoning is developed through successive stages with close interaction of child's individuality with his environment — particularly social and cultural.

5. Kohlberg's theory of moral development has been able to suggest and expect from individuals to demonstrate a higher stage of moral reasoning where they no longer accept their own society and existing rules but think reflectively and autonomously for bringing changes to make the society progress and humanity flourish. In this way, his theory may provide enough ground to work its way towards the thinking of great men like Socrates, Martin Luther King and Mahatma Gandhi and thus inspiring us to proceed toward the challenging vision of our highest moral development.

Criticism

Kohlberg's theory of moral development has been the subject of criticism too highlighting its fallacies as follows:

1. An important limitation of Kohlberg's theory of moral development lies in the fact that it deals with moral reasoning rather than with moral behaviour. Many individuals at different stages of moral development may be found to demonstrate a similar type of moral behaviour and individuals at the same stages may behave morally in different ways. In practice, there may be a quite weak link, between moral reasoning and moral behaviour. A child may have reached a higher stage of moral reasoning as established by Kohlberg through the analysis of responses to the presented moral dilemmas, but it is not essential that he should also behave and demonstrate morality suitable to this moral stage. Thus children might learn so many things about moral decisions or moral reasoning at various ages, but what they do may be another matter. Therefore, it can be properly said that Kohlberg's theory is not able to provide a proper answer for the simultaneous development of moral reasoning and moral development across the various ages.

2. Kohlberg through his specific stages of moral development has tried to draw a line among the types of moral development reached by the individual at different ages. In practice, however, the picture regarding such fixed pattern across the varying ages involving different individuals may not be so clear. An individual at one period of his life span may be found to demonstrate more than one type of morality — pre-conventional, conventional or post-conventional depending upon the situation he faces for doing so. In this way, contrary to Kohlberg's assumption, moral behaviour is more context or situation oriented than the age-specific moral development attained by individuals.

3. Kohlberg's theory is also criticised on the ground that young children are probably more advanced in their moral reasoning then established by Kohlberg. Even pre-schoolers have some internal standards of right and wrong, regardless of what authority figures might tell them and regardless of what consequences certain behaviours may or may not bring (Smetana, 1981).

4. It is also said that Kohlberg's stages are culturally biased. It is argued how the stage is model based on a Western philosophical model and cannot be applied to non-Western cultures without considering the extent to which they have different approaches and outlooks towards morality. It is also doubtful to apply this model to the moral developmental pattern found in children belonging to traditional village and tribal cultures.

5. Carol Gilligan (1987), believes that Kohlberg's theory is gender biased as it does not adequately describe female moral development. Gilligan observes that Kohlberg's stages were derived exclusively from interviews with males and therefore reflect a decidedly male orientation. She charges that Kohlberg's stages focus on the issues of rights and rules, fairness and justice but omit other aspects of morality especially compassion and caring for those in need that are more characteristic of the moral reasoning and behaviour of females.

6. Kohlberg's concept of post-conventional morality has also been a subject of severe criticism. Kohlberg has advocated for the morality of consciousness or autonomous thinking on the part of the individuals reaching the post-conventional level. Practically it is nothing but sort of an open war with the established ethical codes and organised functioning of the society. If everybody acts according to the morality of his own, then certainly there will be chaos. It is absolutely dangerous for people to place their own principles and ethics above society and the law. Moreover, everybody cannot be so worthwhile and selfless as the great thinkers and reformists like Martin Luther King or Mahatma Gandhi, therefore, it is unwise to preach and advocate for the development of such unbridled level of consciousness and morality among individuals.

7. Lastly, it can also be said that Kohlberg's theory of moral development is not as comprehensive as claimed to provide answers for all the moral dilemmas and thus is not able to guide our moral reasoning to face all the situations in our life without ambiguity and confusion. It has its weakness and limitations like other theories of development. Although Kohlberg claims that his stage six of moral development is capable of equipping an individual with the decision-making

tools needed for the toughest moral dilemmas, however, in practice there may lie many issues that the principle of justice arrived at this stage frequently fail to resolve. One such issue may be abortion. Justice for whom and in what ways is it an issue that can hardly be resolved properly at the satisfaction of all the parties involved. The decisions have to vary with the situation. In this way, the stages described in Kohlberg's theory are certainly not aimed for providing a ready-made answer to moral dilemmas. These represent a particular mode or pattern of moral reasoning at specific ages and thus can never be thought as universally applicable to provide solution to all types of moral issues raised in varying situations.

However, on the basis of the criticism laid down, it should not be assumed that Kohlberg's theory is to be discarded or it has little significance for understanding the mechanism of moral development among human beings. Despite the criticism, there is no doubt that Kohlberg's accomplishment in bringing his theory of moral development is great. His theory offers valuable insights into the nature and development of moral reasoning among children and adolescents. He has not just expanded on Piaget's stages of moral judgement but has done so in a quite convincing and appropriate way by having a beautiful blend of individualistic and socialised trends of constructive approach for the development of moral reasoning on the part of human beings.

Educational Implications of Moral Development Theory

The moral development theory provided by Kohlberg has enough potential to direct and guide the way of teachers and parents for helping the children develop morally by highlighting some of the following essential facts:

1. The moral development is essentially a learned phenomenon. As Kohlberg (1968) asserts the stages of moral development are not the product of maturation. The sequence related to development of moral reasoning does not simply unfold according to genetic blueprint. It is therefore much needed on the part of ourselves as elders that we should never blame heredity for the child's level of moral reasoning and moral development.

2. The child in his early years of development (infancy and early childhood till the age of 4 or 5 years) is neither moral nor immoral but is essentially non-moral, in the sense that he has no moral thinking regarding good or bad of an act. He may pick up things belonging to others without feeling any need of asking or informing them about it simply due to the reason that he feels nothing bad or wrong in doing so. Since no moral sense or reasoning lies with children of this age, we elders should behave accordingly without blaming them for their act of disobedience, unsocial or antisocial behaviour as these children are quite ignorant about the goodness or wrongness of their behaviour.

3. The children belonging to Kohlberg's first three stages of moral development believe in the eternal nature of the rules and the authority of the elders. They want to obey their orders and rules without questioning their validity. Accordingly we elders must be quite cautious in putting rules and regulations before the

children belonging to this age span. The rules once made should not be altered. The children without any discrimination should be made to follow them. It is essential at this stage because children have not attained enough mental maturity for deciding on their own that what is right or wrong for them. It is in the interest of the children, their peers, parents, teachers and community as a whole that they should be made to observe rules and regulations regarding their appropriate individual and social behaviour,

4. The children prior to their entry into the age of adolescence can only grasp the concrete ideas and form related to morality. At this stage, for them, examples are always better then precept. In childhood, therefore, they should be presented with models of appropriate behaviour by the elders for being observed and imitated. The abstraction regarding moral reasoning or concept is out of reach to the children belonging to the development period of childhood. It is therefore futile to expect from them to talk about soul, the fruits of Karma, rudiments of religion and God

5. With the development of their intellectual abilities, older children belonging to the adolescence stage now no longer believe in the eternity or non-changing pattern of the rules. They can't be expected to obey the elders and observe the set rules silently as happens in childhood. They need reason and satisfactory answers to their question "why". Therefore, we should be quite cautious in emphasising about the rules and moral conduct at this stage. Rather than making them follow the rules and ethical norms blindly, they should be told about the significance of such behaviour from the individual as well as social point of views. They should be allowed to ask questions and remove their doubts about the appropriateness and inappropriateness of their behaviour in practising morality at home, schools and other social situations. Discussion and debates on moral issues should also be encouraged and children need to be given opportunities as well as freedom to reason about the prevalent social and ethical norms for better adoption in their lives.

6. The parents and teachers should also recognise the importance of the principle of reciprocity as believed by individuals in their period of childhood. If you do good to others, others also behave with your nicely. Judging the impact of a bad act or foul saying on one's self may force children to behave in a proper way. If one thing is pinching them, it will do the same to others. Stimulating and encouraging such thinking and feelings on the part of children may help them imbibe and practice good things.

7. Kohlberg strongly emphasises that the goal of moral education is to encourage and help individuals advance to the next stage of moral reasoning and morality. According to him the most common tool for doing this is to present a "moral dilemma" for making the child confronted with a situation involving his moral reasoning and judgement. The child may adopt views, characterizing his developmental age but may not be able to resolve the moral dilemma; he may then be forced to adopt the moral reasoning belonging to the next stage of moral development. Kohlberg's device of inducing conflict resembles equilibration model emphasised by Piaget. When a new thing does not fit into the existing

cognitive structure through assimilation, one has to go for the due enlargement of his cognitive structure for doing away with the state of disequilibrium. In this way, both the moral development theories (given by Piaget and Kohlberg) urge to adopt a cognitive conflict inducing approach for helping the child to move further on the higher stages of his moral development. In this method, teachers are urged to lead discussion groups in which children have a chance to grapple actively with moral issues. For the proper inducement of cognitive conflict, it is well cared to encourage arguments that belong to one stage above those of most of the class. Since students do not find sufficient, the level of moral reasoning which they presently have with them for resolving the confronted moral issue, they will be stimulated and interested in the acquisition of the moral reasoning belonging to the higher stage of their moral development and this will definitely help them in their pursuit of higher and higher moral development.

8.   Kohlberg's theory of moral development inspires and motivates us that it is quite possible to attain the true morality characterised with selfless feelings of doing good to others, adherence to the principles of equity, equality, moral justice and human rights being preached and practised by the great men of history like Mahatma Gandhi and Martin Luther King. Students, for this purpose, should be exposed to the lives and works of great social reformers, freedom fighters, social revolutionaries, philosophers and religious figures. They should also be given reasonable freedom to express their original ideas and views about the prevalent social structure, laws and ethical norms along with their zeal to replace them with some suitable ones. May be that there may be quite a few to attempt to reach this highest stage of moral reasoning, but surely these are the ones who are responsible for leading the society and humanity to a more illuminated path and certainly we should make provisions for them in our system of education.

Summary

The term morality or character stands for an organised self. Instincts, emotions, habits, temperament, will and sentiments — all are the constituents of one's morality or character. The organisation of these constitutes into one in the form of a permanent mental structure (capable of guiding one's social behaviour) is taken as a morality or character of an individual.

Character formation or moral development in children passes through some specific age-linked stages or levels, named as Amoral stage (birth to 2 years), Self-centred stage (from 3 to 6 years)Conforming-conventional stage (7 to early adolescence), Irrational conscientious stage (adolescence) and Rational conscientious stage (adulthood). In this way starting from the negation of maturity and sociability a mature person reaches the highest level of character development when he acts rationally and not merely emotionally sticking to conventions and values.

Children can be properly helped in the task of moral or character building by following a number of techniques and provisions like (i) proper training of their instincts, emotions and will power; (ii) developing healthy and desirable habits, as well as ideals of life; (iii) helping them in the organisation and development of proper sentiments, like sentiment of patriotism, social sentiment, aesthetic sentiment and self-regard sentiment, etc.; (iv) applying behaviour modification techniques like suggestion, imitation, reward and punishment, moral instructions, religious education and socialisation of the child; (v) caring for the proper physical, mental and emotional development of the child; (vi) seeking proper involvement of parents, family members, school and society in character building of the child.

Piaget's theory of moral development lays down two distinct stages of moral reasoning named heteronomous stage (5-10 years) and autonomous stage (10 years or more) for explaining the nature of moral development among developing children. At the heteronomous stage of morality, children are found to believe and behave in the moral realism characterised with a strict adherence to rules and duties and obedience to authority, However, while reaching the autonomous stage the older children are found to acquire autonomy in taking judgement over the appropriateness or inappropriateness of an act in comparison to younger children.

Kohlberg's theory of moral development emphasises that like the Piagetian stages of cognitive development, there also exists universal stages in the development of moral values, and the movement from one stage to another depends on cognitive abilities rather than the simple acquisition of moral values of one's parents, elders and peers.

Kohlberg identified three levels and six stages of moral development incorporating two stages of moral development. He named these levels Pre-moral or Pre-conventional Morality (4-10 years), Conventional Morality (10-13 years) and Post-conventional Morality (13 years onwards). The six stages associated with these levels are named as (i) the stage of obedience for avoiding punishment, (ii) the stage of conforming to obtain rewards and favour, (iii) the stage of maintaining mutual relations and approval of others, (iv) the stage of obedience for avoiding censure by higher authority or social systems, (v) stage of conforming to the democratically accepted laws and mores of community welfare and (vi) stage of conforming to the universal ethical principles and the call of one's conscience. By providing these stages, Kohlberg claimed that an individual progresses through them in order, without skipping away. Each of Kohlberg's stages builds upon the foundation laid by earlier stages but reflects a more integrated and logically consistent set of moral beliefs than those before it.

References and Suggested Readings

Carmichael, L. (Ed.), *Manual of Child Psychology*, John Wiley, New York, 1946

Crow., L.D. and Crow, Alice, *Child Psychology*, (Reprint), Barney & Noble, New York, 1969.

Dumville, Benjamin, *The Fundamental of Psychology*, 3rd ed., University Tutorial Press, London, 1938.

Gilligan, Carol, *In a different voice: Psychological theory and women development*, Cambridge MA: Harvard University Press, 1987.

Hurlock, E.B., *Child Psychology*, McGraw-Hill, Tokyo, 1959.

Hurlock, E.B., *Child Psychology* (Asian student edition), Tokyo: Kogakusha Co. Ltd., 1956.

Kohlberg, L., *Essays on Moral Development*, San Francisco: Harper & Row, 1984.

Kohlberg, L., *The Development of Modes of Thinking and Choices in years 10 to 16*, Ph.D. dissertation, University of Chicago, 1958.

Kohlberg, L., The development of children's orientation toward moral order: Sequence in the development of moral thought, *Vita Humana*, 6, 11-33, 1963.

Kohlberg, L., The Child as a Moral Philosopher, Psychology Today, Vol 2, 25-30, 1968

Kohlberg, L., The development of moral character and moral ideology, in M. Hoffman and L. Hoffman (Eds.), *Review of Child Development Research*, Vol. I, New York: Russell Sage Foundation, 1964.

Kohlberg, L., 'Moral Stages and Moralization: The Cognitive Development Approach' in T. Lickona (Ed.) *Moral Development and Behaviour*, New York: Holt, Rinehart and Winston, 1976.

Marry, F.K. and Marry, R.V., *From Infancy to Adolescence,* Harper & Brothers, New York, 1940.

Ormrod, J.E., Educational Psychology: Developing Learners (4th ed.), Upper Saddle River, N.J.: Prentice-Hall,2003

Piaget, J., *The Moral Judgement of the Child*, New York: Harcourt and Brace, 1932 (and New York: Free Press, 1965).

Piaget, J., *The Origins of Intelligence in Children*, New York: International University Press, 1952 (and New York: Norton, 1963).

Ross, J.S., *Ground Work of Educational Psychology*, George G. Harrap, London, 1951.

Skinner C.E. and Harriman, P.L. (Eds.), *Child Psychology*, 6th print, Macmillan, New York, 1937.

Smetana, J. "Pre-School Children's Conceptions of Moral and Social Rules" *Child Development*, 52, 1333-1336,1981

17

Emergence and Development of the Self

Introduction

The goal and purpose of any scheme or the practice of child rearing, education and welfare is to help children in developing them in their totality and dimensions such as physical, motor, mental, emotional, social, linguistic, and expressive in all their ways and shapes for the overall welfare of their own and the society to which they belong. The journey of walking on this pursuit, definitely needs an active and wilful involvement of the children themselves and it can't be properly possible till the children get acquainted with their self. The knowledge and understanding of the self and its needed proper development is found to involve a number of the associated attributes and aspects such as self-awareness, self-concept, self-esteem, self-efficacy, self-regulation, etc. Let us try understanding them one by one in some essential details.

Self-awareness: Meaning and Development

The term self-awareness in its word meaning stands for the awareness of one's self. Let us see now what is meant by the term 'self' and 'awareness'.

Self in its common sense understanding as well dictionary meaning is known as the distinct identity and individuality of a person. In other words, it is one's essential being that distinguishes him or her from others. Specifically, it is the outcome or product of one's own introspection or reflexive action.

Awareness as a term stands for the capacity and ability of a person for being acquainted identifying, recognising or taking cognition on his part of one or the other things lying all around including his self with the application of one or the other tools helpful in his task of recognition including his own introspection.

The term self-awareness, in this sense may now be defined as (i) the ability to recognise oneself as an independent social entity, i.e., an individual quite separate from the environment and other individuals and (ii) a capacity for introspecting one's self.

In connection with its presence and development among individuals, it can be properly said that it is not innate and inherited. No child at birth is found to be equipped with the ability or capacity of what is known as self-awareness. It develops among the children much like the other traits or characteristics of behaviour after getting needed environmental exposure and acquiring the necessary cognitive capacity for separating his identity from other people or objects lying in his environment.

Commenting on this aspect Feldman, Robert (2016:174) writes:

> We are not born with the knowledge that we exist independently from others and the larger world. Very young infants do not have a sense of themselves as individuals; they do not recognise themselves in photos or mirrors. The roots of self-awareness, knowledge of oneself, begin to grow at around the age of 12 months.

Thus starting in the infants with the recognition of their faces and body in the mirrors, pictures and photos, voices from the audio-video recording, the sense of self-awareness goes on developing in children as they go on advancing in their ages and stages of development. During their developmental years this ability or capacity of recognising and indentifying one's self reaches its top in the period of adolescence. Now they are seen to get engaged in seeking the answers of questions related to the identity of their self such as: Who am I? From where I have come? For what am I here? With the development of higher cognitive abilities to think, reason, analyze and conceptualise, they are now also in the process of seeking and understanding the available philosophical explanation about knowing and understanding one's self. Is it my body or physical appearance which is called my 'self', or should it be my voice, smell, brain or my thoughts and views that are to be identified as my 'self' or is it the composition of all such as body, mind and spirit that makes the sense of 'self' for me? The thinking and searching the answers of such questions now may be helping the developing children in making attempts for getting acquainted with their self.

Apart from this continuous process of evolving and developing self-awareness among developing children, one thing is quite clear that whatever the developmental level may be, the development of self–awareness, i.e., awareness about one's self in a developing infant provides sufficient ground and opens up channels for the proper development of his self in its higher forms such as the emergence and development of his self-concept, instilling him with a sense of self-esteem or self-regard and self-efficacy, and enabling him to demonstrate self-regulation in his behaviour.

Self-concept and its Development

Self-concept in its word meaning stands for the possession of a certain type of concept on one's part about his or her self. We have known and defined the term self and its awareness. It is thus imperative now to define the term concept before knowing and understanding the term self-concept in its proper way.

Meaning of the Term Concept

In our day-to-day life, we are found to possess some generalised ideas or socially accepted notions about objects, persons or events lying in our environment and thought process. These generalised ideas or notions are termed as concepts about these objects, persons or events. A particular concept stands for a general class and not for particular object, person or event. In fact, it represents a common name given on the basis of similarities or commonness found in different objects, persons or events. A large proportion of the words used and other symbolic expressions found in our language communication represent what we term as 'concepts'. The names horse, tree, dog, table, chair, etc., represent our concept of objects; father, mother, teacher, Indian, American etc., represents our concept of persons; honesty, truthfulness, cleanliness, positivity, goodness, etc., represent our concept of qualities and characteristics; and small, big, low, high, equal, similar, etc., represent our concepts of relations. Similarly we can have concepts of life, death, soul, God, etc. In this way, we may have the concepts of objects, persons, qualities, characteristics, relations, events or to say for all what we can perceive or imagine in our thought process.

Our thinking about the objects, persons or events carries two types of mental images or ideas. One in particular and the other in general. When we say "Mohan's horse" the word "horse" refers to its particular meaning (a horse owned by Mohan) but when it is said that "A horse is a useful animal", the word horse clearly stands for a general class, for all the horses in the universe. It is in this latter sense or meaning of the word horse (generalised meaning) that we use the term concept.

Formation or Development of Concepts

Regarding the formation of our concepts about various things or events, it can be said that these are the results of our own experiences (direct or indirect) as well as formal and informal learning. The task of concept formation starts quite earlier in the period of childhood when as an infant we begin to interact with our physical, social and cultural environment; the type of experiences the child begins to accumulate about an object, person, or event, as he grows and develops give birth to the formation of generalised ideas about it known as its concept. It is not necessary for all children or adults to have similarity regarding their concepts about objects, persons and events in their environment. It depends upon the type of their experiences, learning or training associated with these objects, persons or events. Since there remains a lot of variation in the experiences and learning on the part of children, it is not surprising to find wide individual differences among them with regard to their concept formation. A child, who has been pushed by a cow or has seen it eat rotten food material or human waste, must naturally have a negative concept about cows in comparison to those who have not gone through such negative experiences. As a result, children may be found to exhibit a wide variation in terms of the formation of concepts about things, persons or events in their environment.

Meaning of the Term Self-concept

Children are not only found to form specific concepts about objects, persons or events related to their environment, but are also characterised with the possession of specific concepts about the self. The concepts and forms possessed by children about their self are termed as self-concepts. A self-concept formed by an individual child may thus represent a mental image, notion, or generalised idea formed by him through his own experiences, learning or training about his self. The self-concept possessed by the child in fact is the mirror of one's self. It reflects or mirrors all what he thinks in totality about himself. In the words of famous psychologist H.J. Eysenck, the totality of attitudes and qualities may thus be referred to his self-concept.

The concept of the self is thus found to reflect one's own ideas and picture about his total self, revealing to us things such as: (i) what we think about our self, (ii) how we perceive ourselves in our eyes, (iii) what are our strengths and weaknesses, (iv) what are our abilities and incapacities, (v) how are we expected to behave in a particular situation, (vi) how can we stand against odds (vii) and how can we win co-operation, love, confidence, etc., of others. In this way, the self-concept of an individual child is nothing but a generalised idea or image formed by him about his self. It helps him assign the required worth and value for his 'self' in his own eyes (the reflection of his own about himself) irrespective of what is judged and said about others. As a matter of definition thus, the self-concept of a child may be defined as a generalised idea, notion or mental picture drawn by him about himself through his prior experience or learning enabling him to distinguish himself from other children, persons or objects and to have a proper estimate about his strengths and capacities.

Development of Self-concept Among Children

Self-concept or any other concept possessed by an individual child is not a matter of one's heredity. It is acquired like other traits and characteristics of one's personality or behaviour through experience and learning. What a child gets after his birth in the form of direct and indirect experiences from his interaction with the physical, social and cultural environment and how he is reared and receives his education, all cast a powerful impact over the formation of his concept about the self.

The process of self-concept formation starts in baby infants with their attempts to get their voice and face distinguished and recognised as different from their mother and other persons around them. After standing against the mirror they are able to rub off any substance poured, powder spread over their face, nose, etc., and respond well to the questions identifying their body parts. They can recognise themselves in their family photo and turn their head after being called by a certain name. It is the stage of the development of their awareness about their 'self'.

The next phase of the development of self-concept is concerned with the development of his ideas or notions of the benefits he may derive through the type and nature of his weeping, smiling and behaving in one way or the other. He may also have an idea of what is there in him that is liked by others and in what way. The task of formation or development of the concept about self is thus concerned with the task of the formation of an image or drawing of a picture by the individual himself — his totality of behaviour, personality characteristics, strengths and weaknesses, power and limitations, etc., in a composite way. In doing so, he may be seen to form two types of self-images, one termed as physical self-image and the other named as psychological self-image.

Physical self-images are concerned with images formed by an individual child about his body structure, colour, shape, weight and height, strength and stamina, physical and motor abilities, intelligence and cognitive functioning, etc. The formation of such image helps him in taking evaluative judgments about his physical appearance, strengths, and stamina, physical and mental capacities, and making anticipation about the reaction of others in reference to the possession of these physical attributes by him.

The psychological self-images are concerned with the psychological-self, i.e., thinking and feelings. The realm of these are covered thorough the concepts related to thoughts, emotions, attitudes, interests, aspirations and feelings of the individual child and how he sees them in relation to the possession of such concepts. Where the task of developing physical self-image is related with the satisfaction of physiological needs and experiences associated with them, the development of psychological self-images is concerned with the experiences associated with the satisfaction of socio-psychological needs. Since, the satisfaction of physiological needs comes well before the satisfaction of psychological needs, the children may be seen to acquire physical self-image quite earlier than the acquisition of psychological self-image on the part of developing children. However, as children witness the end of the period of adolescence, both physical and psychological images get merged into each other resulting in a unifying and integrated picture of one's self-concept. It has also been seen that while in childhood concrete self-concepts get developed in a substantial form rather than abstract ones, the adolescence witnesses the development of abstract concepts in an increasing way.

There is one more striking feature regarding the development of self-concept among children in the early years of their childhood. The opinions and judgments of their parents, members of the family, peers and teachers play a more dominant role than their own opinions in helping them form concepts about their self. A child identifies and knows himself in the way and manner as identified and told by others. He is naughty, he is a coward, he does not fear anybody, he is too adamant, he does not listen to anybody, that girl is black, unholy or unfortunate — such types of comments addressed to children persuades them to pick up the same feelings and concepts about them. They try to pass value judgment about them and mirror them accordingly as judged and declared by others.

However, as they advance towards maturity, the scope and field of their experiences of learning, cognition and understanding also increases in a substantial manner. Now he becomes capable of engaging in the task of developing self-concept in an independent way. He no longer mirrors himself in the way as viewed and judged by others. The past experiences as well as his present interaction with persons and the environment guides the process of formation of his self- concept. However, with the gains of maturity on his part it does not guarantee the formation of a proper and desirable concept about his self. He may not be able to form the correct concept about his self, meaning that he may evaluate himself in a quite low way or estimate himself too highly in terms of his actual abilities and capacities. Development of such faulty and improper concepts leads him towards mal-adjustment, failures and frustrations. Here it becomes the duty of parents, elders and teachers to save the child from the ill impacts of the developed faulty concepts by helping them understand the reality about themselves.

Understanding Development of Self-concept from Diverse Aspects

As discussed earlier, one's self-concept is the function of one's interaction with his environment and gaining of experiences (direct or indirect). Since there is too much diversity in the environment or experiences available to developing children, the formation of the self-concept among them also shows significant variations and diversities. Accordingly, children may be found to view themselves differently in the way as coloured or designed by the diversities present in their environmental experiences. We may name and know these diversities from a number of angles such as social, cultural, community, religion, caste, gender, location, language, socio-economic status and literacy of parents, each of which has a strong potential for affecting and influencing the nature of self-concept among developing children. Let us try to adjudge their relative or diverse role in this respect.

1. **Socio-cultural impact**: The type of society, social exposure and cultural interaction available to children in their developmental age is responsible for shaping the formation of their self-concept in a particular way. We may witness the differences observed in the development of self-concept among children brought up in one or the other types of socio-cultural environments. For example, the socio-cultural environment available to children studying in famed residential public schools may thus be seen to work for the development of a particular type of self-concept among children characterised with an egoistic attitude, dominating and ruling nature, superiority complex of an high achievement motivation opposed to the less privileged children of government and economy schools who are found to possess a negative self-concept coloured with inferiority feelings and low achievement motivation.

2. **Community or society variation**: The community and the society in which children live and develop, has a strong potential for colouring the development of self-concept among them. Rural and urban community, orthodox and progressive community, civilised and uncivilised community, criminal and non-criminal community, illiterate and educated community thus may be found to nurture a quite diverse type of self-concept among developing children. The image of a community as the habitat or abode of pocket pickers, smugglers or criminals may impress upon its developing children to imbibe a self-concept of such undesirable behaviours or ill character. They may begin to think or accept themselves in such a negative role.

3. **Religion impact**: Religion or faith observed by the family, parents or by the children themselves may also be found to play quite a decisive role in the development of a particular type of self-concept among developing children. The followers of religions who advocate adoption of non-violence in one's thoughts and actions may be found to develop a non-violent, non-aggressive and peace-loving attitude and self-concept among their children in contrast to the reactionary, aggressive and 'violent' natured self-concept that develops among children following religions that advocate killing of animals in the name of offering sacrifice.

4. **Caste factor:** The caste factor, i.e., sense of belongingness to a particular caste may cast quite a strong impact over shaping the self-concept of developing

children in a particular form. Where the sense of being a Brahmin (an upper caste) may develop a particular type of dominating and superiority complex ridden self-concept among children, the children belonging to the lower castes and scheduled tribes may get infected with a type of concept coloured with inferior feelings, low achievement motive and poor self-expectations. Similarly the sense of belongingness to a business community/caste may be found to be helpful in the development of self-concept coloured with adventurism, risk-taking behaviour and laborious attitude for establishing their own businesses among children belonging to *vaish* or other business community castes; and the children belonging to 'warrior' communities like Jats, Gujjars, Yadavs and Rajputs may develop a self-concept characterising brave and heroic behaviour among them.

5. **Gender influence:** Belongingness to a particular gender male, female or neutral may be found to develop a particular type of self-concept characterised with masculine, feminine or transgender type nature, attitude and temperament among developing children. Consequently boys try to imbibe the behavioural traits characterised as masculine and girls begin to accept themselves fit and appropriate for playing the feminine role. Neutral-gender children similarly develop the self-concept involving the acceptance of neutral gender role for their interaction and behaviour in life.

6. **Location factor:** The nature of the habitat and place where the children reside may also be found to play a decisive role in the development of a particular type of self-confidence among developing children. The truth in this regard may be properly visualised by comparing the self-concepts developed among children belonging to localities such as urban and rural, posh and slum, green and industrial, thin and thickly populated areas, etc. Similarly belongingness to a particular region, state or geographical location such as north and south states, hilly and plain areas, being known as Haryanvi, Punjabi, Rajasthani, Gujarati or Madrasi may direct the developing children to imbibe the diverse self-concepts conceptualised for their respective residential location or habitat.

7. **Language factor:** The skill of communicating with others and its use in learning and self-study may exercise a great role in the development of one's self-concept. One may feel handicapped or benefit to the extent of one's proficiency in understanding and using a particular language for his development and progress. The related awareness of this efficiency or deficiency may cater to form a particular image for his self. A migrated child may experience a certain type of social and emotional isolation in the company of his peers using local language in their communication and interaction. The children from a vernacular-medium school may similarly experience a lot of inconvenience in seeking admission to a higher class in an English-medium school. Here the language barrier may be found responsible for instilling a sense of inferiority complex and looking down upon for adjusting to the new environment. It may become a life-long event for some children who experience difficulty in using English for communicating with others especially verbally. The efficiency of communicating in a day-to-day or learning media language, thus may work as an influencing factor in the development of positive as well as negative self-image among children.

8. **Socio-economic status impact:** It is quite usual for developing children to feel elevated or looked down upon on account of their raised or low socio-economic status. The higher, middle or lower socio-economic status of their family and parents become a deciding factor for them to evaluate and place their self before their peers and others in interaction. Privileges enjoyed by the higher socio-economic group children may automatically add to a raised self-confidence, self-esteem, a care-free attitude and other things that shape their self-concepts in quite favourable ways. On the other hand, children belonging to poverty-ridden families or to the lower socio-economic status may remain quite occupied and anxious for the satisfaction of their day-to-day basic needs or fulfilment of the demands of the school and peer group relationships. These things may influence them to form a negative self-image. However, in case where they emerge victorious in terms of excelling while competing with those belonging to higher socio-economic status they may seen to win over their self resulting in quite an appropriate positive concept about their self.

9. **Literacy of parents:** The literacy levels, and the lower or higher educational levels of the parents of children may add a lot in the formation of positive or negative, higher or lower self-concept among the developing children. It works in two ways. In one way, the educational level of the parents either helps or obstruct the learning and development of children on account of the level of know-how or ignorance of their parents, and on the other side they may experience either elevated or a looked-down-upon feeling in front of their peers, teachers and others on account of the higher or discouraging educational level of their parents. The children of illiterate parents may feel discouraged or find them at a disadvantageous position and thus may form a poor self-image in comparison to their peers who are at the advantageous side on account of the raised educational level of their parents. This is more apparent when parents happen to visit the school of their children to participate in the teacher-parent meetings and functions of the school. In this way, what they feel for themselves and the kind of desirable or discouraging image they develop for their self depends a lot on the literacy level of their parents.

Self-esteem and its Development

What is Self-esteem?

Self-concept and self-esteem both these terms are connected with our self. In their meaning and development both of them differ in quite a considerable way. In a most generalised sense where one's self-concept helps him in knowing what he is, the developed self-esteem signifies his liking and paying due regard to his self. Differentiating between these two terms, Feldman, Robert (2016:414) writes:

> Knowing who you are and liking who you are two different things. Although children, particularly reaching adolescence become increasingly accurate in understanding who they are (their self-concept), this knowledge does not guarantee that they like themselves (their self-esteem) any better. In fact, their

increasing accuracy in understanding themselves permits them to see themselves fully — warts and all. It's what they do with these perceptions that, leads them to develop a sense of their self-esteem.

In this way, while the term self-concept as we have known and discussed in this chapter, stands for what we think about the self, self-esteem denotes the liking shown and value, worth, regard or respect we give to our "self" in the light of its positive or negative evaluation. In literature, therefore, the term self-esteem is often used as almost synonymously with the terms self-worth, self-regard, self-respect and self-integrity.

Whatever meaning we attach to the term self-esteem, in its roots basically it stands for the value judgment passed by an individual himself about his worth and capability in terms of facing problems and difficulties, feeling happy and adjusted, and getting successes in his personal, academic, social and professional life. What is his attitude towards his self, how he values and respects his self, what he thinks about his abilities and capabilities, how much he feels satisfied or dissatisfied with his functioning, how much respect, love and affection, regard and respect he receives from others, all such things singly or in combination work towards defining the self-esteem of an individual child.

Much has been explored about the term self-esteem by scholars. The humanistic psychologists like Karl Rogers and Abraham Maslow have termed self-esteem as a higher order and as a basic need for the attainment of which each one of us struggles and gets a feeling of inner satisfaction and happiness only after knowing and valuing one's self. One's self-esteem, besides helping one to pay respect or regard to his self is also properly linked with one's sense of confidence in his worth and capability. Reflecting on such nature and form of the term self-esteem, Branden, Nathaniel (1969) has provided an understanding of the term self-esteem in the following words:

> Self-esteem is the sum of self-confidence (a feeling of personal capacity) and self-respect (a feeling of personal worth). It exists as a consequence of the implicit judgment that every person has of their ability to face life's challenges, to understand and solve problems, and their right to achieve happiness, and be given respect.

Thus, as conveyed in the assertion, self-esteem may be found to represent an ability, disposition or trait of one's personality that helps him first in making an overall evaluative judgment about one's self (incorporating both positive and negative aspects) and then assists him in maintaining a healthy positive attitude towards "self" for valuing and respecting his self.

Looking in this way, self-esteem may be thought as a unique ability possessed by an individual enabling him to respect and appreciate his self by accepting and owning it as a whole with both its positive as well as negative aspects.

Characteristics of Persons Having a High Self-esteem

1. An individual equipped with an appropriate amount of self-esteem may be found to feel good about his self and capabilities despite a number of weaknesses, limitations and negative attributes of his personality and behavioural functioning.

In fact, the person having a high self-esteem may be said to have a blind love for his self. A true lover loves, admires and accepts his beloved with all her positive and negative aspects. The person having a high self-esteem also in the similar way admires and pays regard to his self by accepting it in its existing form — a mixture of positive and negative attributes. He has an overall good "impression" and attitude marked with the feeling of "all is well" towards his self. It results in making him feel better and developing a sense of satisfaction, love and respect for the self.

2. The people with a high self- esteem have no complaint and never blame or curse their self for their inadequacies and failures. Instead of cursing their self and blaming others for their failures and hardships they begin to think of doing away with their limitations and shortcomings by working on them in a desirable way.

3. With a healthy self-esteem, they feel that they have positive characteristics and skills they can offer to other people, and they also feel they are worthy of being loved, admired and accepted by others. Persons with a healthy self-esteem are more likely to be happy, to make and keep positive relationships and friends circle, and to persevere in working through difficult situations that occur in relationships.

4. A high self-esteem serves a motivational function by making it more or less likely that people will take care of themselves and explore their full potential. People with a high self-esteem are therefore found to demonstrate a natural inclination and favourable motivation for taking care of themselves and to persistently strive towards the fulfilment of personal goals and aspirations.

5. Persons with a high esteem are more likely to see challenging situations as opportunities to try something new, even if they're not completely successful. They prove themselves as capable problem solvers. When challenges arise, they work towards finding solutions and voice discontent without belittling themselves or others. For example, rather than saying, "I'm an idiot," a child with a healthy self-esteem says, "I don't understand this."

6. They remain away from the feelings and thinking of frustration and depression by giving themselves positive suggestions and engaging in appropriate self-talk, and thus remain always surrounded with hopes and optimisms even in the time of difficulties and troubles.

7. Since they value and pay regards to the self, they always try to remain away from the acts and activities that can bring them down in the eyes of others and particularly their own "self".

Characteristics of Persons Having a Low Self-esteem

1. Persons having a low self-esteem are persons who have little or no confidence in their abilities and capabilities. They are always worried about their weaknesses and limitations instead of having appreciation for their goodness and capabilities.

2. Instead of believing and having faith on self-evaluation, they are guided by negative observations, comments and criticism of their abilities by others. They, thus, are naturally bent upon developing an unhealthy and negative attitude towards their self.

3. On account of devaluing their own self, development of a negative attitude towards their capabilities and lack of self-confidence, they are accustomed either to feeling ashamed, embarrassed, guilty, sad or angry with their self or they fall in the trap of frustration, depression, anxiety and stress resulting in the impairment of their mental health and failures in terms of adjusting and being successful in life.

4. Persons with a low self-esteem feel hesitant to try new things and may speak negatively about themselves: "I'm stupid," "I'll never learn how to do this," "What's the point of doing this or that? "I am the person who is not liked by anybody."

5. People with a low self-esteem don't tend to regard themselves as worthy of happy outcomes or capable of achieving targets, and as a result are found to possess quite a low level of achievement motivation. They may have the same kinds of goals as people with a higher self-esteem, but on account of their lack of motivation, they tend to let important things slide and to be less persistent in pursuing their goals.

6. They may exhibit a low tolerance for frustration, giving up easily or waiting for somebody else to take over. They tend to be overly self-critical and habitual to condemn and blame their self for anything happening worse or any unfavourable outcomes of the efforts.

7. Persons with a low self-esteem see temporary setbacks as permanent, intolerable conditions and a heap of troubles from all round the corners. They are thus in the habit of getting into the arms of utter despair and pessimism by laying down their arms without fighting.

Development of Self-esteem Among Children

Nobody is born with the concept of the self and traits of self-esteem. Both are invariably the product of environmental exposure and organised experiences called learning. The type of experiences (good or bad, positive or negative, pleasant or unpleasant) one gathers from his environment, work for the formation of positive or negative attitudes towards the self. It is the formation of such positive and negative attitudes that may result in creating a sense of liking and respect or disliking and disrespect towards the self. However, the best period of habit formation and imbibing of proper traits is the developmental period. Here also it is quite beneficial to start quite early so that the child may pick up the right things at the right time. It is therefore essential that earnest attempts be made by parents, members of the family, teachers and elders to provide the child a rich congenial environment right from his early developmental period for the development of self-esteem in an appropriate way. In doing so they may be advised to take care of the following:

1. **Presenting a proper role model:** Parents, elders and teachers helping children in building their self-esteem should try to present them as an ideal figure or model for imbibing a sense of respect to the self and others. They can support the child in developing a healthy self-esteem through their actions as well as their words. In particular, parents and teachers can model the behaviors they want their children and students to learn by acting out those behaviors out in front of children. One important behaviour they can teach in this manner is how to discuss, express and cope with powerful feelings such as embarrassment, sadness, frustration, disappointment, anger, etc.

2. **Be careful what you say or utter to the child:** Words carry much weight. They have the power to cast most desirable or damageable impact on the minds and hearts of the children. Therefore nothing should be uttered by us that can prove a fertile ground for lowering their self-esteem. "Nothing good can be expected from an idiot like you"; "You are not fit for this assignment" — such outbursts on our part can damage the self-confidence of children and may make them feel worthless and incapable of leading their every-day lives. Instead of uttering such improper words, we should always use praiseworthy and encouraging language for appreciating their good work and motivating them to do away with their mistakes and overcoming their limitations.

3. **Try to identify and rectify inaccurate perceptions and beliefs:** Children having a low self-esteem are found to be nurturing one or the other types of inaccurate perceptions and beliefs about one or the other aspects concerning the self (i.e., perfection, attractiveness, ability, intelligence, sociability and capacity of doing one or the other things).For example a child who does very well in school but struggles with mathematics may say, "I can't do math. I'm a bad student." Not only is this a false generalisation, it's also a belief that can set a child up for failure. We the elders should try to identify such misconceptions and beliefs being nurtured in the minds of our children. They should then be helped in getting rid of such false perceptions and beliefs about themselves that are leading them to feel small, inferior and inadequate. They should be told that no one is perfect in this world. All of us are the creations of the Almighty and as such we all are unique in ourselves. There is nothing to feel small or inadequate about. We should accept ourselves with all of our goodness and limitations and try to make the best use of our limitations with our good behaviour, dedication and hard work.

4. **Encourage positive suggestions and appropriate self-talk:** Auto suggestions and self-talk have a lot of power in influencing the thinking and feeling of children in a positive or adverse way. If one is feeding ideas thorough a continuous flow of auto-suggestions and self-talk that the child is good for nothing, he is the unfortunate one then such feeding will drift him towards limitations and failures. But in case we alter the direction of this flow by making the child use his power of auto-suggestions and self-talk in a positive way; then surely he will be filled with the necessary confidence in his abilities and capacities. "I am capable; I can do it; I am improving and going higher and higher; nobody can stop me from realising my dreams." The use of such motivational ideas certainly

will bring the desired result in raising the level of the child's confidence and the status of his self-esteem.

5. **Creating a positive atmosphere at home and school:** Environmental influences have a strong impact on the shaping of one's behaviour. Therefore earnest attempts should be made to create a positive and favourable environment at the home and school for helping children imbibe an adequate self-esteem. Children who don't get the needed love and affection at home or proper treatment at the hands of their teachers, feel unsafe or are abused at home or school are at greatest risk for developing a poor self-esteem. The parents and teachers should always have an open channel for communicating with children and should try to understand and accept them with their all goodness and limitations, and help them in becoming capable of solving their difficulties and leading life of their own on their own terms with a proper level of self-esteem.

6. **Taking care of peer group influence:** Peer group relationships and interactions should be planned and looked after so the developing children do not get any adverse or negative experience resulting in the diminishing of their regard to the self. They should not be made to feel inferior and think of themselves as worthless or incapable in comparison to their classmates or neighbourhood peers.

7. **Taking care of teaching and teacher behaviour:** Defective teaching methods and improper behaviour of teachers may become a big cause for infecting the child with feelings of inadequacy and low self-esteem. Therefore, the teachers should always remain quite cautious in dealing with their students both at the time of formal instructions as well as during the organisation of co-curricular activities. They should never say or do anything that may hurt the phenomenon self of their students and make them feel inferior, worthless or incapable. Teachers should always have proper communication and desirable interaction with their students in a democratic style. The students should feel properly listened to, being spoken to respectfully, receiving appropriate attention and affection, and having their accomplishments recognised and mistakes or failures acknowledged and accepted. Teachers should accept and love their students with both their positive and negative aspects without letting them feel degraded in any way.

8. **Doing away with unnecessary comparison and competition:** Parents, teachers and other elders should always try and lay emphasis on the maintenance of successful relationships between peers and classmates. They should never resort to comparisons as it may give birth to unnecessary rivalries, jealousies, grudges and complexes among children. Such development is not at all desirable for the well-being of the children as it may result in the spoiling of a good living or working environment besides proving a potent cause for the degradation of the self-esteem to many.

9. **Caring for the proper physical, mental, social, emotional and moral development of children:** The parents, teachers and other elders should take proper care for the development of appropriate physical, mental, social, emotional and moral development of their children. Development in terms of physical and mental dimensions help the children in getting adequately satisfied, feel respected in the

eyes of the self and others. The development of physical and mental capabilities, proper moral sense and imbibing of the needed social and moral values on the part of children makes them feel strong, capable, desirable and the people of worth in the eyes of self and others. They are adjudged as the men of character and values which in turn helps them in paying due regards to their self.

10. **Provide the needed social and cultural exposure:** Self-esteem is in a large part the product of a social process. One of the main reasons people feel important and special is because they have friends and belong to social groups which regard them as important and special. Children who feel like they have an important role to play in their family, peer groups, school, community and culture are found to feel good about them. For this reason, parents and teachers should make sure that children have opportunities to the needed proper social and cultural exposure and have time and space available to play with friends.

11. **Encouraging children to take on challenges:** The children feel confident, proud and develop a sense of adequate self-esteem when they are given proper opportunities to take up challenges for solving difficult problems and complicated puzzles, doing hard tasks and sharing heavy responsibilities. Therefore attempts should be made by teachers and parents to provide suitable opportunities to take up challenges with regard to social tasks and curricular assignments.

12. **Encourage children's self-assessment:** It is customary for people to pass value judgment on the ability, appearance, physique, intelligence, sociability, emotionality and host of other behavioural tendencies and personality traits. The children's self-esteem is affected by such evaluation and comments made by others. However, in case they have the habit of knowing about their capacities and abilities through self-assessment, then they can pick up the reality about their strengths and limitations in a most desirable way. The conclusions reached about their self with their own self-assessment helps them in proper self-awareness and acceptance of the self in its true colour adding to a proper increase in the level of their self-esteem. The parents and teachers should therefore earnestly try to encourage and train the child in going through the self-assessment of their abilities and capabilities.

13. **Help children become involved in co-operative and constructive experiences.** Activities and experiences that provide opportunities to children for creative expression and encourage cooperation rather than competition are especially helpful in fostering self-esteem. Where through his creative expression, constructiveness, ingenuity and adventurism a child feels satisfaction and proud about his achievements, cooperation and collaboration gives him relief from the unnecessary and unhealthy comparison and competition responsible for generating the feelings of inferiority and inadequacy of his abilities and capabilities. Therefore, reasonable attempts should be made by parents and teachers to engage the children in cooperative and constructive activities.

14. **Finding professional help:** As a last resort, in case when needed most, teachers and parents should not hesitate to take help from professionals (therapists and counsellors) in identifying the needed coping strategies to help in dealing with the problems of children suffering from low self-esteem

Self-efficacy and its development

What is self-efficacy?

Why are some students eager to learn and willing to tackle new challenges while others seem uninterested or unmotivated in similar situations? Why do some students demonstrate high levels of confidence in their abilities in the learning of one or the other material, while others seem unsure of themselves? Psychologists may reply to such questions by saying that the interested and willing ones are endowed with a unique ability known as self-efficacy while the uninterested and unwilling ones may fall short of such necessary ability. But what is then this unique ability known as self-efficacy?

Self-efficacy in its simple meaning stands for a state or quality of efficacy demonstrated on the part of an individual. In dictionaries (Merriam-Webster, Oxford, etc.) the term efficacy is defined as (i) the power or capacity to produce a desired result or effect or (ii) effectiveness.

Consequently, we can understand by the term self-efficacy of an individual, his effectiveness or the confidence demonstrated by him in his capacity to produce a desired result or effect (i.e., doing and performing a task, achieving a target).

The famous psychologist Albert Bandura has also tried to endorse the similar meaning by defining the term self-efficacy in the following manner:

(i) Self-efficacy refers to an individual's belief in his or her capacity to execute behaviors necessary to produce specific performance attainments (Bandura, 1986)

(ii) Perceived self-efficacy is defined as people's beliefs about their capabilities to produce designated levels of performance that exercise influence over events that affect their lives (Bandura, 1994)

The term self-efficacy in this way stands for the confidence shown by an individual in his ability or capacity to perform a particular activity or attain a desired thing or objective. It conveys the effectiveness of an individual in respect of facing a particular situation as judged by the individual himself.

Nature and Characteristics of Self-Efficacy

The following characteristics may help us more in understanding and grasping the meaning and concept of the term self-efficacy in a better way:

1. Self-efficacy is a person's judgment about being able to perform a particular activity. It is an individual's "I can" or "I cannot" belief.

2. Self-efficacy beliefs determine how people feel, think, motivate themselves and behave.

3. Unlike self-esteem, which reflects how one feels about his worth or value, self-efficacy reflects how confident one is about performing one or the other tasks.

4. High self-efficacy in one area may not coincide with high self-efficacy in another area. Just as high confidence in playing cricket may not be matched with high confidence in playing tennis, high self-efficacy in mathematics may not necessarily accompany high self-efficiency in English.

5. Self-efficacy is specific to the task being attempted. However, having high self-efficacy does not necessarily mean that one believes he will be successful. While self-efficacy indicates how strongly one believes she has the skills to do well, he may believe other factors will keep him from succeeding.

6. A growing body of research however reveals that there is a positive, significant relationship between one's self-efficacy belief and his performance in the related task (i.e., student's performance in an academic task).

7. It has also been found that while individuals with low self-efficacy toward a task are more likely to avoid it, those with high self-efficacy are not only more likely to attempt the task, but they also will work harder and persist longer in the face of difficulties.

8. Self-efficacy is also found to exert considerable influence in the following matters:

   (i) What activities people select, (ii) how much effort they put forth, (iii) how persistent they are in the face of difficulties and (iv) the difficulty of the goals they set.

Role of Self-Efficacy in the Learning and Development of Children

Self-efficacy beliefs determine how children feel, think, motivate themselves and behave, and as a result may be found to play a significant role in their desired learning and holistic development. In fact a strong sense of efficacy enhances human accomplishment and personal well-being in the following many ways:

1. **Helps in appropriate goal setting:** A desired success in terms of attaining desired progress and development in all the personality dimensions and pursuits of life can be successfully achieved if one has the ability of setting appropriate goals for his striving. Personal goal setting is influenced by self-appraisal of capabilities. Self-efficacy helps a child to have a proper appraisal of his capability of doing a task and achieving the target. It helps him to meet the challenges and set the proper goals for his learning and striving in one or the other situations of his life. The stronger the perceived self-efficacy, the higher the goal challenges people set for themselves and the firmer is their commitment to strive for achieving the targeted objectives.

2. **Helps in seeking proper motivation:** The motivation is found to work as wonder in providing desired success for a learner in his goal directed behaviour. Self-beliefs of efficacy play a key role in the self-regulation of motivation. Most human motivation is cognitively generated. People motivate themselves and guide their actions anticipatorily by the exercise of forethought. They form beliefs about what they can do and achieve. It is why the people loaded with a high degree of self-efficacy are found to be imbibed with a high sense of intrinsic motivation. It helps them in absorbing themselves fully in the tasks and activities related to their wholesome development and targets designed to realise valued futures.

3. **Helps in setting proper level of aspiration:** It is essential for an individual in striving towards his desired development and progress to establish a proper level of his aspiration much in tune with his own abilities and capacities. The setting of a higher or lower level of aspiration much above and below his capacities

may result in unnecessary frustration and despair on one's part. However a good sense of self-efficacy helps learners to set a proper level of their aspirations and thus getting desired success in proceeding well on the path of their proper learning and development.

4. **Helps in equipping children with a sense of necessary self-confidence:** One's self-efficacy is known for his confidence shown in his ability or capacity of performing an act or attaining a specific target. Equipped with a proper sense of self-efficacy, thus an individual may be naturally found to demonstrate a necessary level of self-confidence in the ability or capacity of striving towards the attainment of his goal or performing a task of his choice. The demonstration of such self-confidence thus may help an individual in seeking maximum towards his learning and development.

5. **Helps in pursuing goals in an appropriate way:** The children endowed with a high degree of efficacy are found to have a positive outlook about their efforts in achieving the set targets. They are found to approach difficult tasks as challenges to be mastered rather than as threats to be avoided. They heighten and sustain their efforts in the face of failure. They quickly recover their sense of efficacy after failures or setbacks. They attribute failure to insufficient effort or deficient knowledge and skills which are acquirable. They approach threatening situations with assurance that they can exercise control over them. Such an efficacious outlook produces wonderful impact on their wholesome development and personal accomplishments.

6. **Helps in making right choices for proper learning and development:** The power of self-efficacy belief helps individuals to make correct choices in the course of their learning and development. The higher the level of people's perceived self-efficacy, the wiser they prove themselves in pursuing the most suitable course for their learning and development in perfect tune of their inherent talents and capacities.

7. **Helps in seeking proper adjustment with the self and environment:**
An individual remains adjusted with his self and environment until his basic needs (biological and socio-psychological) remain satisfied or are in the way of getting satisfied. The person endowed with a good sense of self-efficacy is fully aware of his ability or capacity of doing a task or attaining a specific target. He is aware of the extent to which his needs may be gratified and thus may not expect or strive for attaining much beyond his perceived capacities and abilities. This habit helps children in remaining adjusted with their self and environment which in turn may prove a big helping hand in their proper learning and development.

8. **Helps in attaining wholesome health and well-being:** Equipping the children with a good sense of self-efficacy helps them in the attainment of wholesome health and well-being in respect to its physical, mental, social, emotional and moral dimensions. In the support of this assertion the following may be especially mentioned:

- Stress and anxiety caused in any way leads to the impairment of physical and mental health of an individual being. People's beliefs in their coping capabilities affects how much stress and depression they experience in threatening or difficult situations. Self-efficacy loaded individuals who believe they can exercise control over threats do not conjure up disturbing thought patterns and thus do not become victims of anxiety, stress, depression and impairment in their level of physical and mental functioning.

- Perceived self-efficacy affects every phase of personal change. The stronger the perceived self-regulatory efficacy the more successful people are in developing healthy habits and imbibing desirable virtues helpful in their proper social, emotional and moral development.

How to Help Children in the Development of Self-Efficacy

The self-efficacy possessed by the individuals is an acquired phenomenon. It is learned as a consequence of one's experiences and interactions occurring in one's socio cultural environment. The measures like below taken on the part of parents and teachers may prove quite beneficial in helping the children get imbibed with the power of self-efficacy.

1. **Orientation about the concept and significance of self-efficacy:** The children should be provided due orientation about the nature and significance of the behaviour loaded with self-efficacy. Help of the well framed-documentaries, audio-video presentations, availability of appropriate literature highlighting incidence of the success achieved in life through the power of self-efficacy may be taken for acquainting children with the concept and significance of the power of self-efficacy.

2. **Producing models of exemplary behaviour:** A behaviour is learned well through its observation and imitation on the part of learners. Therefore attempts should be made to produce models of exemplary self-efficacy behaviour before the children. For this purpose, children may be provided opportunities at home, community places and schools for getting exposure and interaction with persons of repute and who are living examples of self-efficacy. In addition, parents, teachers and elders should themselves work as a model of the self-efficacy behaviour to the children or provide examples of elder children, senior students and peers for motivating and preparing their children to get engaged in the self-efficacy behaviour.

3. **Providing opportunities for demonstrating self-efficacy:** The skill of using self-efficacy power can be acquired well by children only when they avail the opportunities of getting engaged in the self-efficacy behaviour through their own experience. The parents and teachers therefore, should provide reasonable freedom and opportunities to children for taking challenges of doing and performing the acts and attain the learning and developmental objectives well in tune with their inherent capacities and abilities.

4. **Reinforcing the self-efficacy behaviour of children:** A behaviour is learned well when it gets reinforced in an appropriate way. The parents, elders and teachers, therefore, should try to provide due reinforcement to the self-efficacy behaviour demonstrated on the part of a child in one or the other situations by resorting to methods like praise and appreciation, making him feel satisfied and proud with his achievement, grading the students well and providing his example to the other children of the family, class and school.

Self-Regulation and its Development

What is Self-Regulation?

In its word meaning the term self-regulation stands for regulating or controlling one's self by the individual himself in terms of its functioning and performing one or the other types of behavioural acts and thus giving birth to a special type of behaviour named as self-regulated behaviour helpful in his adjustment, development and progress in a proper way. In this way what is known as the self-regulated behaviour of a child is said to be described as a type of behaviour that is regulated or controlled by the child himself. For knowing more about the meaning and concept of self-regulated behaviour let us take the help of a few available definitions of the term "self-regulating behaviour" and "self- regulated children".

1. **Ormrod (2009):** Self-regulated behaviour describes a process of taking control of and evaluating one's own behaviour for the good and welfare of the self and others.

2. **Paris and Paris (2001):** Self-regulated behaviour emphasises autonomy and control by the individual who monitors, directs and regulates actions toward goals of information acquisition, expanding expertise and self-improvement.

3. **Dweck & Leggett, (1988):** In particular, self-regulated children are cognizant of their strengths and weaknesses, and they have a repertoire of strategies they appropriately apply to tackle the challenges of day-to-day functioning at home, school and community. These children hold incremental beliefs about intelligence (as opposed to entity or fixed views of intelligence) and attribute their successes or failures to factors (e.g., effort expended on a task, effective use of strategies) within their control.

4. **Pintrich & Schunk (2002):** We may conclude well that the characteristics exhibited by self-regulated children may help to explain why self-regulated children usually exhibit a high sense of self-efficacy.

5. **Winne & Perry (2000):** Self- regulated children are successful because they control the environment of learning and functioning. They exert this control by directing and regulating their own actions toward their learning, performance and developmental goals.

In light of these definitions of the term self-regulated behaviour and self-regulated children we can conclude about the meaning and nature of the term self-regulation and self-regulated behaviour in the following way.

- Self-regulation stands for the characteristics of one's ability or capacity to regulate and exercise restraint or control over his behaviour (conative, cognitive and affective) through his own initiative and attempts.
- Self-regulation or self-regulated behaviour is not thrust upon the children from outside. It is a wilful act undertaken by the child himself for serving his own ends.
- Self-regulation and self-regulated behaviour as a whole is initiated, undertaken and executed to its desired end with the full intention, motivation, attention and involvement of the child.
- In a self-regulated behaviour, the behaviour gets fully regulated and controlled by the child himself from the beginning till end in terms of the objectives set, strategies planned and methods used for his functioning in one or the other situation.
- In a self-regulated behaviour, children are found (i) to take responsibility of their behaviour for attaining their immediate and far-reaching life goals (ii) to direct and regulate their behavioural acts well by making use of their thought processes, (iii) to enjoy full autonomy and control over the processes and products of their functioning, (iv) to show the necessary potential of self-efficacy (confidence in their ability to perform an act and attain the desired objectives, (v) to take work or interactions opportunities as a challenge for meeting their developmental goals and (vi) to exercise necessary restraint and control over their working and interactive environment in attaining their desired immediate and life goals.

Role of Self-Regulation and Self-Regulated Behaviour in the Functioning and Development of Children

The habit and practice of resorting to self-regulation in performing or engaging in one or the other types of behavioural activities on the part of children pays a rich dividend in terms of their adequate adjustment, effective work performance and overall developmental outcomes. In fact one's functioning in its proper way is responsible for bringing desired changes in all the dimensions of his personality and aspects of behaviour in a quite appropriate way. In case children follow a proper path of their functioning and behaving with a clear cut proper intension and goal, then it will surely lead them to their wholesome proper development in the interest of their own as well as others' well-being. The value and contribution of such functioning and behaving get automatically enhanced in a big way when the behavioural acts performed by the children become self-oriented, self-initiated, self-motivated, self-directed and controlled, as happens usually in the case of self-regulated behaviour. What is done and performed by the child in one or the other environmental situation gets facilitated and desirably productive when it is carried out by the child himself under the spirit of self-regulation. The contributions and significance of self-regulation and self-regulated behaviour in this connection may be briefly summarised as follows:

1. The child develops his own mechanism in exercising control over his functioning and behaving rather than being dictated and controlled through some external agency. He knows what can go well with him in terms of doing and behaving and thus automatically tries to remain on the track of proper functioning and behaving.

2. The working and functioning on the part of children in the course of their self-regulated behaviour almost remains under their ownership and control. They do not have to wait or depend on the direction, warning, managing and disciplining of their behavioural acts on the part of others and it helps them in quite a valuable way to remain goal-oriented and regulated in their functioning and behaving.

3. The child here takes all types of responsibilities and burdens of carrying out the task of behaving and functioning and thus what gets to be done or performed in a particular situation becomes his own task valued by him in all ways. It pays in a big way to help the child in behaving and performing in a given situation in quite a responsible and effective way.

4. Self-regulated behaviour is characterised with the full involvement of the child in its execution. A self-regulated child is found to take genuine interest and demonstrate a lot of intrinsic motivation towards his functioning and behaving in a particular situation. It helps him remain focused on his behaviour despite facing odds and difficulties in his path.

5. A self-regulated child is found to possess a strong sense of self-efficacy. He knows his strengths and limitations in respect of doing or performing one or the other tasks, solving one or the other problems, reacting and responding to a situation, interacting and behaving with others, etc., and thus remains in command of things to be done and behaviour to be demonstrated on his part. It helps him to benefit through his performance and demonstrated behaviour in a fruitful way.

6. A self-regulated child is found to exercise proper control over the process of his functioning. He can take on the task of performing according to his own pace, convenience, time and amount of efforts. He is free to go on functioning independently with his own efforts or may choose to take guidance and help from others in the way and amount as and when needed by him. He manages the behavioural situations and environment in the manner as required by him in getting success in his behaviour performance. Such regulation and control exercised by him in his behaviour and functioning makes him a good child resulting in his desired development and progress.

7. A self-regulated child is found to make use of the process and mechanism of self-assessment or evaluation for getting needed feedback about the appropriateness of his functioning and behaving. On its basis he may be seen to introduce necessary changes in his performance or behavioural goals, work strategies, motivational spirit and environmental surroundings helping him to exercise needed control over the process and product of his functioning and behaving.

8. A self-regulated child is equipped with a number of useful traits and habits that adds to the effectiveness of the following behavioural acts:
   - He is keen to know and investigate into the nature of things.
   - He does not need constant pushing but is found to take initiative for attempting to know things on his own.
   - He asks questions and makes enquiries from the relevant sources for acquiring necessary knowledge and skills.

- He is self-confident, self-reliant and self-dependent in regulating and managing his affairs regarding the use of his abilities and capacities for his effecting functioning and behaving.

- He knows the art of exercising proper control over his motor, cognitive and emotional behaviour. While functioning and behaving in a particular situation he tries to manage his capabilities and resources in an effective way.

- He tries to adopt his own course and regulate the process of his functioning in his own ways by setting his own behavioural goals, seeking his intrinsic motivation, choosing a particular work strategy, getting him focused on his functioning and behaving, and reinforcing or modifying his efforts on the basis of self-assessment for attaining the desired outcomes of his functioning and behaving.

Needless to say that all such useful habits and qualities of a child and the essentials involved in the execution of self-regulated behaviour have enough potentiality to provide a needed direction and magnitude for the endeavour of a conscious child resulting in his holistic development , progress and well-being.

Development of Self-Regulation and Self-Regulated Behaviour Among Children

The ability or capacity to exercise control over one's functioning and behaving is not at all an inherited phenomenon but gets developed and acquired by children much like the acquisition of other characteristics of one's behaviour and personality traits. It is why no child at the time of his or her birth is found to demonstrate needed ability to regulate his or her behavioural functioning on his or her own. It does not happen or to say can't happen unless the developing infants and children acquire a reasonable level of their cognitive capacities for guiding and exercising control over their functioning and behaving in one or the other ways. At this stage of their development, they have no alternative but to remain completely dependent upon their parents and caregivers for their needed functioning and behaving. They receive feeding and caring for their adjustment, living and development at the hands of their parents and caregivers and learn and imbibe many habits and acts such as walking, climbing, speaking, jumping, etc., in the close company and directions of their elders. In their developmental years also the parents, elders and teachers try to dictate their developmental path by regulating, controlling and managing their functioning and behaviour in accordance with their own likings and disliking, wishes and goals set by them for their children. However, as experience reveals, the parents, elders and teachers also wish and attempt for making their children relatively independent and self-reliant in regulating and managing their behavioural acts on their own. Their efforts in this direction may be well witnessed in helping the infants in demonstrating self-regulated behaviour in terms of taking meals, dressing, taking bath, toilet functioning, combing, tying shoe laces, playing games, etc. As infants grow in age, they try to seek independence in exercising their different roles in their various types of functioning and behaving in their day-to-day life and working at their homes, community surroundings and schools. They can be helped in this task by parents, caregivers, elders and teachers in a variety of ways by adopting the habit and practice of self-regulation in their functioning and behaving. The following measures may help parents, caregivers, elders and teachers well in this direction:

1. They should try to switch over from the practices of authority or dictating behaviors of the children (such as issuing directives and instructions, dictating and deciding their learning paths and ways of behaving, helping and assisting them always in their functioning as well as spoon feeding them in their learning attempts) to the role of an effective guide and facilitator for helping them in their demonstration of the ability of self-regulation and self-control in their functioning and behaving.

2. The children should be properly oriented with the practice of self-regulated functioning and behaving along with its inherent usefulness. For this purpose, attempts should be made to provide opportunities in exposing them to good literature got from a library or showing them documentary films and audio-video presentations highlighting the incidence and significance of self-regulation and self-regulated behaviour.

3. The children should be provided opportunities for modelling their functioning and behaving on the pattern of self-regulated behaviour. The parents, family members, elders, capable peers and teachers themselves may work as models before the younger children so that they can learn and imbibe essentials about self-regulated behaviour.

4. Suitable exposure in the form of formal or informal learning or training experiences should be provided to the developing children for catching hold of the idea and practice of regulation and regulated behaviour in their conative, cognitive and affective functioning. Why and how they have to exercise needed restraint and control over their physical and physiological habits, motor acts and physical activities, cognitive functioning and emotional expression should be invariably known to them. They should be trained and taught to use their cognitive abilities for regulating their behaviour and functioning. Especially in relation to the expression of emotions, they should essentially know the way of expressing their emotions in the right way at the right time and in the right proportion and intensity.

5. The children should be provided the needed freedom for regulating their behaviour and its outcomes by setting their own behavioural goals, seeking their own measures of intrinsic or extrinsic motivation, choosing suitable working strategies and applying their own method of self-assessment for exercising desirable control over their functioning and behaving.

6. Children should not be allowed to develop distaste, apathy or frustration with the adoption of self-regulation in their functioning and behaviour by holding help and assistance from elders for the sake of developing independence and self-regulation but be helped at the time of their need in a proper amount in the proper way by keeping alive the spirit of self-regulation and self-regulated behaviour side by side.

7. Well-intended attempts should also be made to reinforce self-regulated behaviour of children by providing them encouraging feedback. We need to appreciate and acknowledge their hard work, initiatives and enthusiasm in one or the acts of their self-regulated functioning and behaving for helping them well in the pursuit of their proper development and progress.

Summary

The term 'self' stands for one's essential being that distinguishes him or her from others. Specifically, it is the outcome or product of one's own introspection or reflexive action.

The knowledge and understanding of one's self and its needed proper development is found to involve a number of the associated attributes and aspects such as self-awareness, self-concept, self-esteem, self-efficacy and self-regulation, etc.

The term self-awareness, as one of the concepts essential for knowing and understanding the self, may be defined as (i) the ability to recognise oneself as an independent social entity, i.e., an individual quite separate from the environment and other individuals and also (ii) a capacity for introspecting one's self. In connection with its presence and development among individuals, it can be properly said that it is not innate and inherited. No child at birth is found to be equipped with the ability or capacity known as self-awareness. It gets developed among children much like the other traits or characteristics of his behaviour after getting needed environmental exposure and acquiring the necessary cognitive capacity for separating his identity from other people or objects lying in his environment.

The generalised ideas or socially approved notions about a thing, object or person is termed as concepts. In this sense, the term self-concept may be known to stand for the concept formed by an individual about his self. It reflects or mirrors all what he thinks in totality about himself. The self-concept or any other concept possessed by an individual child is not a matter of one's heredity. It is acquired like other traits, characteristics of one's personality or behaviour through experience and learning.

The process of self-concept formation starts in baby infants with their attempts to get their voice and face distinguished and recognised as different from their mother and other persons around them. With the exposure to their environment and learning, the children, may be further helped in the development of two types of self-concepts — physical (related to physique and physical or motor functioning) and psychological (thinking and feeling). The task of self-concept formation in the early years of childhood is influenced and coloured by the opinions and judgments of their parents, members of the family, peers and teachers. They begin to form images about their self in complete shadow of the views expressed for them by others. However, as they advance towards maturity, they become capable of engaging in the task of developing self-concept in an independent way with the help of varying experiences available to them in their environment. But, since there is too much diversity in the environment or experiences available to developing children, the formation of self-concept among them also shows significant variations and diversities. Accordingly, children may be found to view themselves differently in the way as coloured or designed by the diversities present in their environmental experiences. We may name and know these diversities from a number of angles such as social, cultural, community, religion, caste, gender, location, language, socio-economic status, literacy of parents, etc., each of which has a strong potential for affecting and influencing the nature of self-concept among developing children.

The term self-esteem stands for a unique ability possessed by an individual enabling him to respect and appreciate his self by accepting and owning it as a whole with both positive as well as negative aspects. Persons having high self-esteem are found: (i) to feel good and developing a sense of utter satisfaction, love and respect for the self, (ii) not to blame or curse their self for their inadequacies and failures, (iii) able to make and keep positive relationships and friends circle, (iv) persistently strive towards the fulfilment of personal goals and aspirations, (v) meeting challenges by remaining away from the feelings and thinking of frustration and depression and (vi) remaining away from the acts and activities causing damage to their self-respect. Contrarily persons having low self-esteem, do, think and feel all what is damaging to their self, lowering them in their own eyes.

Regarding the development of self-esteem, it can be well said that nobody is born with the concept of the self and traits of self-esteem. Both are invariably the product of environmental exposure and organised experiences called learning. For this purpose, growing children may be helped through presenting role model of the self-esteemed behaviour and biographies, and behaving and treating them in an appropriate way suitable for inculcating among them the trait of self-esteem and characteristics of the persons having high self-esteem.

The term self-efficacy stands for the confidence shown by an individual in his ability or capacity to perform a particular activity or attain a desired thing or objective. It conveys to us the effectiveness of an individual in respect of facing a particular situation as judged by the individual himself. Unlike self-esteem, which reflects how one feels about his worth or value, self-efficacy reflects how confident one is about performing one or the other tasks. A strong sense of self-efficacy possessed by an individual may be found to help him in ways like (i) appropriate goals setting, (ii) seeking proper motivation, (iii) setting a proper level of the term self-esteem stands for a unique ability possessed by an individual enabling him to respect and appreciate his self by accepting and owning it as a whole with both its positive as well as negative aspects. The persons having high self-esteem are found: (i) to feel good about themselves and developing a sense of satisfaction, love and respect for the self, (ii) to not blame or curse their self for their inadequacies and failures, (iii) able to make and maintain positive relationships and a good friends circle, (iv) to persistently strive towards the fulfilment of personal goals and aspirations, (v) to meeting the challenges by remaining away from the feelings and thinking of frustration and depression, and (vi) staying away from acts and activities causing damage to their self-respect. On the contrary persons having a low self-esteem, do, think and feel all that is damaging to their self, lowering them in their own eyes.

The development of self-efficacy behaviour among children is a learned and acquired phenomenon that takes place as a consequence of their experiences and interactions occurring in their socio-cultural environment. For helping them in this direction, it can be useful for adopting measures like (i) providing orientation about the concept and significance of self-efficacy, (ii) producing models of exemplary behaviour, (iii) providing opportunities for demonstrating self-efficacy and (iv) reinforcing the self-efficacy behaviour of children.

The term self-regulation stands for regulating or controlling one's self by the individual himself in terms of its functioning and performing one or the other types of behavioural acts and thus giving birth to a special type of behaviour named as self-regulated behaviour helpful in his adjustment, development and progress in a proper way contributing towards the good and welfare of the self and others.

The ability or capacity to exercise control over one's functioning and behaving is not at all an inherited phenomenon but gets developed and acquired by children much like the acquisition of other characteristics of one's behaviour and personality traits. It also needs a reasonable level of mental maturity on the part of children for the self-regulation of their behaviour. In the task of getting equipped with such behaviour, the children may also be helped by their parents, teachers and elders with measures like (i) playing the role of guide and facilitator in place of dictating and controlling everything about them, (ii) providing orientation about self-regulated behaviour, (iii) working as model and producing exemplary behaviour opportunities before them, (iii) providing exposure in the form of formal or informal learning or training experiences for catching hold of the idea and practice of regulation and regulated behaviour, (iv) giving needed freedom to the children for regulating their behaviour and its outcomes and (v) reinforcing the self-regulated behaviour of children by providing them encouraging feedback.

References and Suggested Readings

Bandura, A. (1986), *Social foundations of thought and action: A social cognitive theory*, Englewood Cliffs, NJ: Prentice-Hall.

Bandura, A. (1994), Self-efficacy. In V. S. Ramachandran (Ed.), *Encyclopedia of Human Behavior* (Vol. 4, 71-81), New York: Academic Press.

Boekaerts & M. Seidner (Eds.), *Handbook of self-regulation*, Orlando, FL: Academic Press.

Branden, Nathaniel, Honoring the Self, Personal Integrity and the Heroic Potential of Human Nature, LA: J.P. Tarcher, Inc., 1987

D.H., & Zimmerman, B.J. (2008), *Motivation and Self-Regulated Learning: Theory, Research, and Application*, New York, NY: Routledge.

Dweck, C.S., & Leggett, E.L. (1988), A social-cognitive approach to motivation and personality, *Psychological Review*, 95, 256-273.

Feldman, Robert S. (2016), *Child Development* (7th edition), Boston: Sage

Iran-Nejad, A., Chissom, B. (1992), Contributions of Active and Dynamic Self-Regulation to Learning, *Innovative Higher Education*, 17 (2), 125-136

Ormrod, Jeanne Ellis, (2009), *Essentials of Educational Psychology*, New York: Pearson Education Inc.

Paris, S., Paris, A. (2001), Classroom Applications of Research on Self-Regulated Learning, *Educational Psychologist*, 36 (2), 89-101.

Perry, N.E., Phillips, L., & Hutchinson, L.R. (2006), Preparing student teachers to support for self-regulated learning, *Elementary School Journal*, 106, 237-254.

Pintrich, P.R. & Schunk, D.H. (2002), *Motivation in education: Theory, research, and applications*, Upper Saddle River, NJ: Merrill-Prentice Hall.

Winne P.H., and Perry N.E. (2000), Measuring self-regulated learning. In: Boekaerts M, Pintrich PR, Zeidner M, (editors), *Handbook of Self-regulation*. San Diego: Academic Press, 531–566.

Zimmerman B.J. (2000), 'Attaining self-regulation: A social cognitive perspective', In: Boekaerts M., Pintrich P.R., Zeidner M., (editors), *Handbook of Self-regulation*. San Diego: Academic Press, 13-39.

18

Characteristics of Various Stages of Development — Infancy to Adolescence

Introduction

As we discussed earlier in chapter three of this text, the life span of human beings can be divided into some specific stages for the study of pattern of growth and development as well as the resulted behavioural characteristics of the individuals during theses specific stages. However, every stage of human development is a unique stage with regard to its stage-specific characteristics. It is perfectly true for all the developmental stages — infancy, early childhood, childhood and adolescence. All these stages, called as developmental stages, are quite crucial in terms of attaining the required developmental milestones as well as educational gains in one's life. In the present chapter, here we would like to discuss the special features of the developmental trend and behaviour patterns visible in individuals during these developmental stages of life.

The Stage of Infancy and Early Childhood

The special features of the developmental trend and behaviour pattern at this stage (up to 5 years) are as follows:

1. **Rapid growth and development:** It is the period of rapid growth and development. Inner as well as outer organs develop rapidly at this stage. There is a rapid growth in terms of height, weight and size. There is also rapid development of emotions and almost all the emotions are developed in the child during this stage. This stage is marked by intensive motor activity and restlessness.

2. **Dependence:** At this stage, a child depends upon his mother, father and other family members for the satisfaction of his basic needs. He is a helpless creature and can move and function only with the help of others. Even for emotional satisfaction, he depends upon others. He expects that everybody around him should love him and give him his entire affection and attention. He wants to love and to be loved and in exchange he totally depends on the mercy of others. Hence a child at this stage is dependent but as he moves into the later years of his infantile behaviour, he slowly proceeds towards independence.

3. **Self-assertion:** Although the child is helpless and depends upon others for the satisfaction of his needs, he is quite self-assertive. He tries to dominate his superiors and elders. His wishes must be fulfilled. He thinks he is always right and all people around him should obey him. He is the prince although without a crown and tries to assert himself all the time in all the situations.

4. **Period of make-believe and fantasy:** Here, children live in the world of their own creation. This is a period of rich but baseless imagination. As in this stage the child has limited potentialities and aspires more than what he can actually get in actual life, he compensates this in fantasy and make-believe.

5. **Selfish and unsocial:** At this stage the child is almost completely ego-centric and selfish. He does not want to share his toys or give any of his possessions to anyone else. He wants to have all the things, even love, admiration and affection reserved for him. He does not care for the social and moral codes and principles and places his self-interest at the premium.

6. **Emotionally unstable:** It is the period of violent emotional experiences. Emotions at this stage are marked by intensity, frequency and instability. They are spontaneous and the infant is hardly able to exercise control over them. He is not capable of hiding his feelings and in this way, the emotional expression of the infant is generally in the overt form.

7. **Characteristics of mental development:**

   (i) **Developing curiosity and questioning attitude:** At this stage the child is very curious about the things around him. The world and the environment is new to him. He is full of questions like what is this, why does it happens or not happen, etc. His queries are virtually endless. Answers do not interest him as much as asking questions.

   (ii) **Intellectually not developed:** A child at this initial stage is very immature in intelligence. He lacks in reasoning and abstract understanding. He can think only in concrete terms and is not developed in abstract reasoning and thinking. The powers of observation, perception, concentration, etc., are also not developed.

   (iii) **Rote memory:** The child, though not much developed intellectually, has a very good memory. However, this memorissation is without reasoning and is purely a rote memory. He can cram and reproduce the matter easily.

   (iv) **Creativity:** This period is also characterised by the tendency of creative impulse in the child. He develops a creative attitude and often engages himself in making or collecting many things. He tries to draw satisfaction realising that he can make, construct and perform the activities like his elders.

   (v) **Time concept not developed:** For a child at this stage, the divisions of time such as yesterday, today, tomorrow, month, year, etc., are meaningless as he has not yet developed the concept of time.

8. **Sexual development:** Although the sex organs at this stage are not developed, the sex tendency is in a continuous stage of development. The findings of psycho-analysts like Freud and others have clearly shown that the sexual life of

a child at this stage is as rich as that of an adolescent. He passes through three stages of sexual development — stage of self-love, homosexual and heterosexual. At the initial stage, the child derives pleasure from his own body by sucking his thumb or touching the sex organs. Later on, he seeks satisfaction of his sex impulse outside and develops sentiments of love for the mother or father depending upon his sex. Finally the child develops heterosexual tendency and in this respect a male child gets attached to the mother and the female child to the father.

The Stage of Childhood

Main Characteristics

A child may be said to enter the period of childhood, when he or she completes the age of five and steps into the school-going age. It continues till the onset of puberty. During this period, significant changes in the sphere of physical, intellectual, emotional and social aspects take place. The main characteristics of development during this stage can be named as follows:

1. **Period of slow and steady growth:** While infancy is the period of rapid and intensive growth, the stage of childhood is characterised as the period of slow, steady and uniform growth. Development rate, although continuous and uniform, is very slow at this stage.

2. **Independence:** An infant seeks help in every sort of work even if he is able to do it independently, whereas a child at this stage desires independence. By acquiring experiences and developing physically, intellectually and socially he tries to adjust in his environment. In fact at this stage he feels more at home with the world and takes satisfaction in doing his work with his own efforts. He becomes increasingly independent of his parents whom he considers merely convenient persons to provide food and shelter.

3. **Emotional stability and control:** Childhood in the emotional aspect is the period of stability and control. Intense emotional outbursts which usually find their expression in motor activity and physical form during infancy are rarely repeated at this stage. The child learns to hide his feelings, he can exercise control over his emotions and express them in appropriate and socially approved ways. His emotional behaviour is not guided by instinctive cause but has an appropriate rational behind it.

4. **Developing social tendency:** In contrast to an infant who is egocentric, the child at this stage develops social tendencies and picks up many social virtues. He likes to play in a group and shares his toys with others. Feelings of mutual cooperation, team spirit and group loyalties are developed among children of this stage. This period of childhood is often named as gang-age as the child of this age is always a member of some group and develops a very strong sentiment for the group. He is so loyal to his group that sometimes he does not even mind the displeasure of his parents and teachers.

5. **Realistic attitude:** Child at this stage begins to accept and appreciate the hard realities of life. He no longer remains in his own world of make-believe, fantasy and fairy-tales. He now becomes a perfect realist from being an imaginative idealist. He begins to take a close interest in the world of realities and tries to adapt himself to the real environment.

6. **Formation of sentiments and complexes:** Infancy is the age of innocence. A child at this stage is used to neither hiding his feeling nor checking his emotions. Therefore, no complexes are formed at this stage whereas childhood stage gives birth to many complexes due to inhibition, repression, and so on. At the stage of infancy, emotional behaviour does not turn itself into a permanent structure for giving birth to sentiments. But at this stage of childhood, emotional behaviour gets structured into sentiments. Various sentiments like religious, moral, patriotic and aesthetic sentiments begin to develop at this stage. The formation of each sentiment leads towards character development.

7. **Sexual development:** With regard to sexual development, this stage is called 'latency period.' Sexual energy, generally, at this stage remains dormant but emerges with great force at the end of this stage. The sexual behaviour of the children at this stage is characterised by the development of an attitude of antagonism and indifference towards the opposite sex. While at the infancy stage boys and girls play together, a child likes to play with the members of his own sex. Due to their varied interests, children gradually develop a general attitude of antagonism towards the opposite sex. As a result of this antagonism during family gatherings, boys and girls of this age are barely civil to one another. Sex antagonism is more pronounced in boys than in the case of girls. They do not want anything that resembles a girl. In the case of girls, the attitude of antagonism generally takes the form of indifference. They try to ignore the boys in place of tormenting, teasing and interfering with their games.

8. **Intellectual development:** This stage is the period of intellectual advancement. The rate of intellectual development is quite rapid at this stage which resembles the rate of physical growth at infancy. At this stage, the child acquires new experiences and tries to adapt himself to his environment and prepares himself to solve the problems. His power of reasoning, thinking, observation, concentration, perception, imagination, etc., are developed. He cannot very well go with abstract thinking. He develops the concept of length, time and distance and learns to express himself in various ways.

9. **Development of interest and aptitudes:** In childhood, the child's field of interests widens and he shows special aptitudes, likings and disliking towards various things and work. The children of this age are usually extrovert and very fond of excursions and visits. They develop interest in reading various types of books. Radio, television drama and movies hold a strong appeal for them. They are interested in everything which is mysterious and romantic. Wide differences in the interest pattern can be seen among boys and girls. Boys are interested in the activities requiring fearlessness, courage and adventures while girls are inclined towards the activities requiring tenderness, softness and other feminine characteristics.

The Stage of Adolescence

The developmental stages of infancy and childhood are followed by the stage of adolescence i.e. the stage of pre-preparation for playing the role of an adult (responsible member of the society). Etymologically speaking, the word 'adolescence' comes from the Latin verb 'adolescere' which means 'to grow'. So, the essence of the word adolescence is growth and it is in this sense that adolescence represents a period of intensive growth and change in nearly all aspects of a child's physical, mental, social and emotional life. It is a very crucial period of one's life. The growth achieved, the experiences gained, responsibilities felt and the relationships developed at this stage destine the complete future of an individual. As a result, the adolescents need careful attention from their parents, teachers and other members of the society for their proper development and welfare. Let us know about them in detail.

Who is an Adolescent?

When does this crucial period start and end in one's life? Who should be labelled as an adolescent? These are some pertinent questions which should be answered at this stage.

Technically speaking, a child is described as an adolescent when he achieves puberty, i.e., when he has become sexually mature to the point where he is able to reproduce his kind. He ceases to be an adolescent when he has acquired maturity to play the role of an adult in his society or culture. Maturity, as the term used here, does not mean mere physical maturity it also implies mental, emotional and social maturity.

It is very difficult to point out the exact range of the adolescence period in terms of chronological years. Achieving puberty and becoming mature cannot be bound to a universal span or period. Therefore, the range of adolescence not only differs from country to country but also varies from community to community and from individual to individual. Generally, girls become sexually as well as socially mature at an early age. The standard of living, early or late marriage, health and climate, cultural traditions and environment, attitude towards sex, role expected from the child at different ages are some of the other factors which control the dawn of puberty and attainment of maturity by human beings.

Compared to Western countries, the period of adolescence starts early in our country as Indian children achieve puberty earlier because of favourable climate and cultural factors. Also it ends early due to early attainment of maturity whereas in the West — "the adolescence extends roughly from 13 years of age till 21 for girls and 15 till 21 for boys", (Harriman, 1946, p.3). In India, it usually ranges from 13 to 19 among boys and from 11 to 17 years among girls.

The above classifications of the range of the period of adolescence are not rigid. There are wide individual differences. However, with a view of a rough estimate for universal applicability, adolescents, also referred to as teenagers, are individuals having chronological age between 13 to 19 years.

Pattern of Growth and Development During Adolescence

As mentioned earlier, human growth and development takes a spiral form and not linear. Therefore, within the alternate stages of life, we find a sort of repetition and resemblance of characteristics. The old adults are often found to behave like children. In adolescence also, we find a sort of repetition and recapitulation of what has been done during infancy. The observation of Ross reflects the above idea when he says, "Adolescence is best regarded as a recapitulation of the first period of life, as a second turn of the spiral development (1951, p. 146). Like infancy, adolescence is the also referred to be the period of too much disturbance or as Stanley Hall regard it "a period of great stress and strain, storm and strife."

Let us see how far these observations are true. The adolescence's growth and developmental pattern, along with the peculiar characteristics of this age, can help us in understanding our adolescents. In the following lines, we will make an attempt in this direction:

Physical Growth and Development

During adolescence, the physical growth and development reaches its peak and the human body finds its final shape. The maximum limit with regard to increase in size, weight and height is achieved. Bones and muscles increase to the greatest possible extent leading to a great increase in our activities. The growth and function of all other outer and inner organs also reach its maximum and almost all the glands become extremely active at this stage.

There is a growth of hair in the underarms and around the genital organs. Boys and girls develop the characteristic features of their respective sexes. There is roundness of breasts and hips among the girls and growth of beard and moustaches among the boys. There is a distinct change in voice among the two sexes. While the girls' voice acquires shrillness and becomes sweet, the boys' voice deepens and becomes harsher. The girls begin to menstruate monthly during this period and the boys have nocturnal emissions (discharge of semen during sleep) accompanied by erotic dreams. In this way physiologically boys and girls attain all the male and female characteristics respectively during this age and are ready to be called men and women or gentlemen and ladies. The typical physical changes during this age may be studied through Figure 18.1.

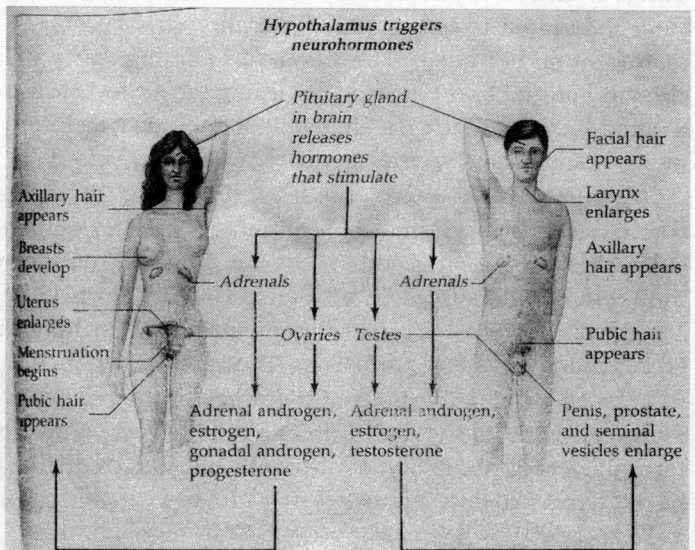

Fig.18.1 Typical physical changes in boys and girls during adolescence

Emotional Development

Emotional development reaches its maximum during adolescence. It is the period of heightening of all emotions like anxiety, fear, love, anger, etc. Once again like an infant, an individual experiences emotional instability and intensity during adolescence. The physical growth and development being maximum, the strength of the boys gives them the opportunity for maximum motor activity. Therefore, in the matters of emotional expression and experiences, adolescence provides the highest peak. At no stage is a child as restless and emotionally perturbed and touchy as in the adolescence stage. He is too sensitive, inflammable and moody. In the words of Ross: "the adolescent lives an intensely emotional life, in which we can see once more the rhythm of positive and negative phases of behaviour in his constant alternation between intense excitement and deep depression". (1951, p. 147). That is why the period is often designated as a period of stresses and strains.

Thus, as Ross clarifies, adolescents are not consistent in their emotional expressions. Their emotions fluctuate very frequently and the current of emotional flow is also very intense. It is very difficult to put a check on the emotions during the peak of adolescence. In fact, during adolescence emotions take their roots into sentiments. Self-consciousness, self-respect and personal pride soars. Group loyalty and sentiments of love, etc., are developed making an adolescent sentimental and passionate. What he feels, he feels very strongly and when he reacts, he reacts vigorously.

Social Development

Adolescence is the period of increased social relationships and contacts. While a child cares very little for the society, an adolescent develops a good amount of social sense. He ceases to be egocentric, selfish and unsocial. Now he wants to mould his behaviour according to the norms of the society.

The social circle of an adolescent is very wide. Contrary to childhood, he becomes interested in the opposite sex. The friendships are no longer nominal. He believes in making intimate friendships and attaches himself closely to a group. Peer group relationship controls the social behaviour of this age. The child develops a strong sense of loyalty towards his group. He wants to be accepted by the group of which he is a member. The rejection is costly as it creates many adjustment problems.

Another significant change in the social aspect of a child during adolescence lies in his relationship with his parents and the family. Now there is a craving for independence. He wants that his personality should be recognised by the parents and elderly members of the family. He must not be treated as a child. He gives more importance to the values and beliefs maintained by his peer group than to the advice of his parents. There may even be hidden or open rebellion if the parents try to impose their opinion and values on their adolescent children.

Intellectual Development

Adolescence is the period of maximum growth and development with regard to mental functioning. Intelligence reaches its climax during this period. Intellectual powers like logical thinking, abstract reasoning and concentration are almost developed by the end of this period. An adolescent learns to reason and seeks answers to 'how' and 'why' of everything scientifically. His power of critical thinking and observation is much developed. He does not try to follow the beaten track. He is critical of almost everything. He develops a fine imagination. Writers, artists, poets, philosophers, and inventors are all born in this period. Improper channelization of imagination and dissatisfied needs may turn an adolescent to daydreaming. Therefore, great care is to be taken for properly cultivating their power of imagination.

Hero worship is most prominent in this period. Adolescents generally love adventures, wandering, fairly tales and develop interest in reading such books. Their area of interest is actually widened. Adolescence is the age of action. According to the difference in tastes and temperaments, nearly all adolescents have some or the other hobbies and strong likes and dislikes for the world of nature, man and things.

Moral and Religious Development

With the development of social and civic sense, children during this period learn to behave according to the norms of their society and culture. Also the 'group' sense makes them follow some moral or ethical code. It prepares a stage of proper moral development. The formation of strong sentiments during this period intensifies the process of moral development. The character by which we know a person in his life to a great extent is the product of the experiences gained, complexes formed and sentiments made during this age.

The impact of religion and religious practices is also felt for the first time at this age in one's life. An adolescent tries to talk about God and religion. He often engages himself in the discourse about philosophical concepts like soul, Brahma, the meaning of life, the question of death, etc.

Sexual Development

Sexual development reaches its peak during adolescence. An adolescent is sexually mature. In fact, the whole personality structure and behaviour of an adolescent is dominated by sex. During adolescence, the sexual development, like infancy, is divided in the following three stages as described:

Stage of Auto-Erotism or Self-Love

At this stage, young boys and girls fall in love with themselves. They try to derive pleasure with their own bodies. Self-decoration and spending time before mirror is their common practice. Self-enjoyment by indulging in masturbation is also prevalent at this stage.

Stage of Homosexuality

At this age boys and girls are attracted towards the members of their own sex and seek gratification from each other's body by grouping in two or three at one time.

Heterosexual Stage

At this age boys and girls are seen attracted towards each other. They are keen to make friendship or even establish sexual relationship with members of the opposite sex.

Special Characteristics of Adolescence (with reference to their needs and problems)

After arming ourselves with a little knowledge about the growth and developmental pattern during adolescence, it is worthwhile to point out some of the special characteristics of this stage. Adolescence, often termed as the age of storm and stress, has many a conflicting situation and problem of adjustment which needs a careful study. Let us think over the origin of such problems and try to analyze the specific needs and demands of adolescents.

Perplexity with Regard to Somatic Variation

Every adolescent has more or less the difficult task of adjusting to 'somatic variation' which may occur during or after puberty. As discussed earlier, during the period of adolescence maximum physiological changes take place. These rapid changes create problems for the adolescents in the following ways:

(a) Menstruation creates worries among girls and gives rise to many fears and anxieties. Similarly, the discharge of semen during nocturnal emission among boys horrifies them. They become quite perturbed about this phenomenon. These particular physiological changes bring many complexes in the minds of the children. These changes make them introvert and secretive.

(b) There are always individual differences among human beings and so one cannot deny the possible differences with regard to bodily development, looks and appearance among the adolescents. An adolescent with his nearly developed body is constantly making comparisons between himself and his contemporaries. Differences are almost certain to cause him some anxiety, particularly regarding height, weight, fatness, thinness, facial blemishes, largeness or smallness of hips and breasts in girls and of genitals in boys.

For both boys and girls, appearance and bodily condition, which is not in keeping with what is considered the norm, will cause some anxiety. Girls want to look feminine and attractive to boys. Boys want to look manly to gain prestige among other boys and particularly from girls. To be reasonably satisfied with one's physical appearance, thus becomes an important task for an adolescent. He needs to become accustomed to new bodily changes. Any deviation from the norms and standards of the peer group can produce complexes in the mind and make him maladjusted.

Intensification of Self-Awareness

Self-consciousness is extremely developed in adolescence. There is a strong desire in an adolescent that his or her bodily changes should be noticed by the elders as well as by the members of his own age group. Adolescence can be described as an age of self-decoration. Boys and girls pay more attention to their dresses, make-up, manner of talking, walking, eating, etc. In fact, there is a craving for recognition in adolescents. Every adolescent desires that he or she should be the centre of attraction for the opposite sex and his abilities, intelligence and capabilities should be recognised by the peer group and elders. Moreover, adolescents are very sensitive, touchy and 'inflammable'. They aim to maintain at any cost their concept of themselves and whenever possible to enhance their status among their peers. An attack on their phenomenal self invites strong reactions and behavioural problems. It makes an adolescent either aggressive or withdrawn depending upon the circumstances.

Intensification of Sex-Consciousness

Sex-consciousness becomes too intense at this stage. Most of the adolescents' problems are concerned with the sudden functioning of their glands, secretion of sex hormones and the awakening of the strong sex instinct.

Firstly, menstruation and ejaculation though natural occurrences at puberty give a shock to most of the adolescents. Afterwards every adolescent feels a sort of strong sensation in the sex organs. This motivates him to seek satisfaction through masturbation and homosexual relations. In the third stage of their sexual development, adolescents are attracted to the opposite sex. Sex sensation combined with curiosity about sex draws the members of the two opposite sex nearer and nearer. This nearness sometimes develops into relationships and creates many problems and complexes for the future.

These activities create many worries and complexes in the minds of the adolescents. They become perturbed and develop a sense of guilt. In most of such cases, they opine that by acquiring these habits they have ruined their lives and they will now remain unfit for future sexual life.

Independence v/s Dependence

An adolescent is on the boundary line of childhood and adulthood. So, he is typically a person who needs security, guidance and protection like a child and independent views, maturity of opinion and self-support like an adult. He is still immature. His abilities and capacities are still in the process of growth and development. He depends for the satisfaction of his so many needs — physical, emotional, etc. — on his parents and elders. The emotional instability of his behaviour and difficulty in coming in terms with the somatic changes makes him quite restless and often insecure.

He needs security and complete freedom from unnecessary worries and anxiety at this stage and in some way he is again in search of his mother's lap and father's affection. Also, his intense love for thrill and adventure, coupled with his uncontrolled emotions, needs to be guided, and his unbridled flow of energy should be checked.

On the other hand, as his social circle is widening, he tries to emancipate himself from the care and look after of his parents and elders. He thinks himself a mature and full-fledged adult. He reacts strongly when the parents and the elders still consider him a child. He tries to assert or show that he is now a mature person and not a child. His opinion should now be given weightage. He has every right to give suggestions and directions in family matters. He can very well manage his own affairs and the elders should not interfere unnecessarily. He begins to feel ashamed and embarrassed about the protection and care shown by the parents.

It is not only the adolescent who suffers from the duality in his behaviour, but even the parents are not clear about the roles of their child at this age. Sometimes, they expect him to behave as an adult and at other times, they treat him like a child. Therefore, the poor adolescent is caught between the role of a child and an adult.

He possesses a strange mix of the needs of dependence and independence which creates conflicting situations and problems for him.

Peer Group Relationship

Peer group relationship plays a substantial role in the life of an adolescent. He drifts away from his parents and elders and spends a lot of his time with the members of his peer group. He values the ideals of the group and develops a sense of loyalty towards it. He is now directed by the standard and norms of his peer group and pays least attention to the desires and advice of his parents and elders. He is more concerned with gaining prestige and recognition in the eyes of his peers. Every child at this stage wants that he should be fully accepted by his peers. Nothing can be more devastating to adolescents than to be rejected by his age mates. There is sure to exist a difference in the opinions, views, liking and disliking of the elders and adolescents. It is here that the difficulty arises. The adolescents find themselves the victims of conflicting demands of social and cultural norms of adults and their peer group and they often become confused and perplexed with regard to any decision making.

Idealism v/s Realism

A typical feature of adolescents lies in their interest in ideals. They desire to help in the creation of an ideal society. They are very critical of the existing circumstances, happenings and think of bringing reform. They often engage themselves in questions like — Where is the world going? What is the meaning of our life? Where is God? What is humanity? Why are there so many sufferings and inequalities? In this way, they try place themselves on a superior level by searching some lofty aims and ideals and want a set of moral principles they can understand as well as some guiding principles by which they can operate.

But in this search of idealism an adolescent moves away from realism. In fact, lack of experience makes him somewhat unrealistic. He tends to accept the impossible. When this is not attainable, he becomes quite disturbed and unreasonable. Many of the adolescents grow up into problem youths. Some of them become pessimistic and believe in destroying whatever comes in the way of realising their dreams. Some become withdrawal and begin daydreaming. They begin to live in their own make-believe world of imagination and fairy-tales, and thus have possibility to turn into maladjusted personalities.

Vocational Choice and Need of Self-Support

An adolescent's strong desire is to achieve self-sufficiency and become independent like an adult member of the society. Also, the life ahead demands from him that he should prepare himself for the future vocation which he wants to adopt. Therefore, the period of adolescence requires from the individuals to take a decision about their vocations. Vocational decision is an important one for an adolescent and he often finds himself not quite up to the mark in making a right choice. Emotional instability, lack of experience and maturity prove as obstacles in making the right choice. Moreover, his interests, aptitudes and abilities are still in the process of making. This uncertainty about the interests and abilities makes him quite puzzled. Therefore, adolescents want proper guidance and advice with regard to their interests, aptitudes and vocational choices.

If we try to make a close analysis, we can find that adolescence is like a crossroad, which provides an equal opportunity to the adolescents to choose and proceed in wrong as well as the right direction. It has every chance of turning adolescents into maladjusted personalities, the chief cause of which is the frustration of needs and conflict of motives. At the adolescent age, there emerges new physical, social and emotional needs. With regard to physical needs the adolescent needs to become accustomed to new bodily changes and desires to have others notice the changes.

In the social aspect, he has a strong need for the belongingness to a peer group. Emotionally, he needs to be loved, accepted and admired. He needs security, freedom from anxiety and recognition of self. He is striving for independence from parental control and is struggling to make the active sexual instincts and urges satisfied or sublimated within the norms of society and culture.

Current Issues Related to Adolescent Stress

So far in this chapter, we have discussed the most common and general problems and stress-inducing situations regarding adolescents. However, with the changed scene many new problems have immerged for making the life and living of the adolescents a little more difficult and stressful. Here, we are taking a few for discussion sake.

A. Increasing Loneliness

Adolescents of modern age are facing a new emerging problem in the name of increasing loneliness. They are finding themselves all alone for coping with their environmental needs and the stress-inducing situations of one or the other kinds.

Reasons Behind Loneliness

In search of the reasons for the rising trend of loneliness among adolescents, the following may be considered as some of the probable causes:

1. The children and adolescents are finding themselves bewildered and all alone on account of the changes visible in the structures of families. The trend is towards setting of nuclear families in place of the traditional system of combined family. In the combined families there were elders (other than the busy parents) who were there to listen and attend to the problems of growing children. On account of their love and affection to their children and life experiences, they were very much there in standing beside them in helping and guiding at the time of their need and difficulties.

2. The cohesiveness and closeness traditionally visible in the social and community fabrics has also almost vanished. The neighbours and community people are now limited to their own affairs. Nobody has the time and concern for listening and caring for the growing up of others families. It has resulted in the loneliness of adolescents. With no contact and help from their neighbours and community people, thus, adolescents of today are forced to lead a life of loneliness.

3. Parents have no time and guts to give company to their growing up children because:
    (i)   Both mother and father have to remain out of the home for a considerable long period of the day on account of the compulsion of serving and earning livelihood.
    (ii) Their life style does not permit them to caring and looking after their children in a needed way.
    (iii) They have no desirable communication with their children and do not take initiative in talking and listening to their problems.
    (iv) Children feel fear to talk and disclose their problems and difficulties,
    (v)   Children feel that there is no use talking to parents as their parents are lacking in guts and capabilities to guide and help them in a proper way.
4. Friendships and peer relationships have also been turned into a self-centred and feeling less affair. It is surrounded with a lack of trust and empathy towards each other. Hence it has become too difficult for the adolescents to rely and take help from their peers and so called friends at the time of their needs and stress.
5. Teacher-pupil relationship has also turned into a mere formality and professionalism. Teachers have no time and attachment with their students for listening to their problems and addressing their stress. Students, also, do not have much trust in their teachers for opening up and talking about their feelings and difficulties.
6. Adolescents in their habitant, neighbourhood, community and school may come across a number of incidents of their harassment, discrimination, marginalisation, sexual abuse and intimidation like bullying, misbehaviour and punishment. It has resulted in the feeling of insecurity and loneliness among adolescents.
7. There lies no proper provision of guidance and counselling services in schools for helping the children at the time of their needs and stressful situations.

Consequences and Impacts of Loneliness

Loneliness suffered by adolescents on one or the other accounts may prove costly to them in terms of their adequate development, progress and well-being. In general, it may be found to cast the following types of negative consequences and impacts in this direction:

1. It may hamper the process of their adequate physical, mental, social, emotional and moral development in an adverse way.
2. With no help from any one for coming out from their problematic and stress inducing situations.
    • They may develop symptoms of mental illness and abnormality in their behaviour.
    • They may develop withdrawal symptoms and get detached from the mainstream of social, educational and cultural fields.

- They may develop into a timid, shy, cowardice and unpleasing personality.
- It may drift them towards educationally failure and defeated personality in their life.
- They may pick up the habit of smoking, liquor consumption, substance abuse or may become drug addicts.
- They may seek asylum in the company of socially undesirable elements and may indulge in delinquent behaviour, truancy and other problematic behaviour.
- They may develop a negative attitude towards their parents, elders and teachers and may even engage in revengeful and rebellion acts.

B. Changing Family Structures

In this modern age of rapid industrial growth, globalisation, urbanisation, modernisation, multiculturalism and technological advancement, there has been a tremendous change in the structures of the family all over the country that may be characterised as follows:

(i) There is a shift from the combined family system (allowing all the family members of old and new generation to live and work under the same roof) to the nuclear family (characterised with the concept of me, you and our children).

(ii) The adoption of two children policy has drawn a limit to the size of nuclear families. The relations like *Bhooa-phopha, Chacha-chachi, Taou-tai, Nanad-bhabhi* are rarely available to the adolescents for support and guidance.

(iii) On account of the nuclear character of the family, the children and adolescents are now almost deprived with the valuable support and guidance of their grand-parents and other elders previously present in the combined family system.

(iv) There also exists a family structure comprising of single parent, mother or father bringing up the children on account of being alone as a result of separation, divorce, unwanted pregnancies or death of one of the spouses, etc.

(v) There has also emerged an altogether new and strange family structure in the name of living relationship in which parents live and have children without getting engaged into formal marital relationships.

Causes

In search for the causes lying behind such rapid changes in the family structures, we may think mainly for the following possible explanations:

1. In many cases, the pace of industrialisation, urbanisation and the subsequent economic compulsion has made a number of families move from their places of native residence to employment-generating places for earning their livelihood. It has caused the shrinkage in the size of the family in the form of a nuclear setup.

2. The influence of modernisation especially the Western culture input and believe in the philosophy of materialism has made people to adhere to the concept of nuclear family system. In the Western culture dominated by the attitude of serving the interest of the self only, the parents or other relations have no place in the family of their sons or daughters. The same is also happening with our country nowadays. The people have started to neglect their elders, cousins and near relatives and believe in the family comprising their spouse and children only.

3. The spread of education and literacy among the masses coupled with the population control drive launched by the Government has been responsible for making the people believe in population control measures and limit their families to up to two children irrespective of their gender.

4. The negative influences of the Western civilisation, globalisation, modernisation and rising permissiveness in the society has resulted in the practices of a live-in relationship and bearing children out of wedlock.

Impact

The changes going on in the structures of family system have been responsible for the outcomes or impacts mentioned as follows:

1. The things like family business and sharing the same work (agriculture, shop or business) is gradually vanishing from the scene. The nuclear families have forced the people to get engaged in independent pursuits for earning their livelihood.

2. The notion of collective responsibility has been transferred into individual responsibility. In a combined family, one or two people were the main earners or say frankly the only earners. Others took the liberty of enjoying at the cost of them.

3. In the absence of assurance, security and safety available in the name of family business, agriculture holdings and income of the elderly people in the family adolescents have now been forced to think about seeking measures for getting capable of earning their livelihood in coming future and it has trapped them into one or the other types of stresses.

4. The presence of one or two children in the family have forced the parents to consider them as the most valuable possession and get over fearful and conscious about their growth and development, career and future. They have started to demand and expect more and more from them in terms of their educational outputs and career building. It is putting a lot of stress and stains on the developing children.

5. In the changed structures of family, there are little opportunities to have interactions and get to gather among the members of the family. All the members of the nuclear families have their own agenda for spending their leisure time, somehow left from their own schedules and adolescents may thus find themselves all alone in fighting with their own needs, problems and stresses.

6. In the changed family structures, the support and guidance available to children from their grand-parents and other elderly members, relatives, elder brothers,

sisters, cousins, etc., is altogether missing. They are not getting any opportunity to speak their mind, open their hearts, and share their problems and stresses, with any one at their home and it is creating great damage to the adjustment and wellbeing of the developing children.

7. In the case of a single parent family and children of the parents having no legal marital relationships, the adolescents have been found to suffer from feelings of insecurity, unsafety and dissatisfaction in relation to the satisfaction of their one or the other basic needs. As a result, they may be found relatively more tense, disturbed and inflicted from one or the other behavioural problems.

C. Rising Permissiveness

Another significant issue arising in the way of proper development and adjustment of children is concerned with the trend of rising permissiveness in the family and social setup. Permissiveness as a term has been defined in the Cambridge Dictionary Online as "a situation in which behaviours that some people might disapprove of is allowed". In view of Dictionary.Com, another dictionary available on line, the term permissiveness stands for "the habit or characteristic accepting or tolerant of something as social behaviour that others might disapprove or forbid."

In reference to behaving with the children thus permissiveness may be viewed as a practice, attitude or habit employed by the parents, teachers or community to be more lenient towards them and permitting them to enjoy more liberty or sometimes unbridled freedom for doing and behaving in their own way. Permissiveness thus stands quite contrary and opposite to the strictness observed in the behaviour of parents, teachers and community for dealing and behaving with the children and adolescents. It is a typical type of leniency, loosy-goosey attitude and tolerance exhibited by elders and members of the community for the otherwise undesirable, unsocial and forbidden behaviour of children and adolescents. This type of tolerance when exhibited by boys and girls towards sexual advances to each other is known by the term sexual permissiveness often visible nowadays in the adolescence friendships and dating.

In the present scenario, we may witness a trend of rising permissiveness everywhere on our globe including our country. Why is it happening, it needs to be earnestly investigated. Let us try to work in this direction.

Underlying Causes

In search for the causes lying behind the rising trend of permissiveness we may think of the probabilities of nature outlined as follows:

1. On account of rapid industrialisation, urbanisation, rising prices and of the struggle for earning livelihood, parents (both mother and father) have been forced to get engaged in the service, business or a means of earning livelihood. They have no time or energy left in interacting and attending their developing children in a needed way. In the absence of the needed attention on the part of their parents, children especially adolescents are finding them free to do and behave in the ways that suits them.

2. In some cases, the parents who are over Westernised, may be seen busy in spending their leisure time in enjoying club life and remaining in holiday mood with their spouses or friends. It has necessitated on their part either to remain quite indifferent towards their children or allowing them to enjoy liberty on their own lines.

3. The parents while giving no proper attention and caring for their developing children may be found to suffer from a sense of guilt on their part and as a compensatory measure may be found to provide a number of concessions and undue privileges to their developing children.

4. The emergence of the nuclear family system and single parent family has also been responsible for the rising permissiveness among adolescents.

5. The neighbourhood, society and community that happened to be quite conscious and vigilant about the behaviour of children and adolescents have adopted a non-interfering, indifferent and even permissive attitude towards the conduct and behaviour of the adolescents for the fear of facing strong undesirable reactions on the part of adolescents and their parents.

6. The teachers who were the best custodian and means for maintaining desirability in the behaviour of their adolescent students have started to keep themselves in the background. They are no more serious about the enforcement of the rules and norms and have adopted a permissive attitude and easy go style of dealing with them. Many times, they may be seen surrendering before the free styles of their adolescent student for the sake of avoiding probable confrontation and humiliation.

7. The peer pressure is forcing the children to feel proud in availing maximum concessions and privileges from the parents for living and behaving in their own ways. The parents many times feel handicap in resisting even the undue and improper demands of their grown up children for the fear of their revolt or unhappiness. The others are also the same, with this feeling the incidence of permissiveness on the part of parents are increasing day by day.

8. The impact of multiculturalism, globalisation and modernisation coupled with the access to mass media, internet and electronic devices has made tremendous change in the attitudes, and ways of behaving and living of the adolescents necessitating to bring a lot of permissiveness on the part of their parents, elders and society as a whole.

Impact

The increasing trend of permissiveness as depicted above for one or the other reasons has been responsible for the type of ill impacts and negative consequences on the development and well-being of the adolescents in the following way:

1. It has given them a boundless freedom to spend their time and energy in useless or somewhat harmful activities such as gossiping and surfing on the internet or smart phones with no real purpose to be served, engaging in picnics, parties and outdoor programs, staying away from the home and returning quite late in night, playing truancy from the classes and school, playing and watching movies in the school time, etc.

2. It has resulted in picking up unhealthy and improper living habits such as late sleeping, late rising, consumption of junk and unhealthy food, spending money in useless buying, expecting from parents to equip them with the items and facilities as enjoyed by their privileged peers, disobeying the elders and teachers, etc.

3. It has increased all possibilities of letting the adolescents fall prey to unsocial, immoral, undesirable, problematic and delinquent behaviour. It is why it is not unusual in any way to see nowadays our adolescents involved in the acts of liquor consumption, drug addiction, unwanted pregnancies, smoking, chain snatching, stealing vehicles, rash driving and road rages, engaging in the bloody fights, bullying, eve teasing, passing remarks on the opposite gender, sexual abuses, rape, and even committing murders.

4. Increasing permissiveness with unlimited freedom to do the things of their choice and likings has created all possibilities for the adolescents to have confrontation and conflicts with their teachers, peers, and other members of the community. It has increased all possibilities for letting our adolescents suffer from the stress and strains arising from such conflicts. On the other side, the pressure for showing themselves superior to others and enjoying life by doing and planning nothing for the same has also made the adolescents quite perplexed and bewildered in their action and behaviour. It has put many of them in a distressing state of stress, frustration, aggression and depression. As a result there has been a striking increase in the cases of committing suicides, running away from the house, and engaging in aggression, fighting and rages among the adolescents.

Increasing permissiveness in this way is not only causing great harm to the adolescents in terms of their wholesome development and well-being but also proving a red signal for the well-being of the parents, families, societies and nation. In fact it is not wise to provide unbridled freedom, unlimited concessions and permission to the adolescents to do and behave as per their likings. It needs to be replaced with the concept of guided freedom and restricted concessions with a sense of feeling more responsibilities on the part of parents, elders, teachers and society as a whole aiming to serve the interests of the adolescents in a better way.

What Can We Do For Our Adolescents?

The needs of the adolescents have to be satisfied and their problems realised in a proper way in order to help them in their proper growth and development. The task is serious and desires all dimensional efforts. Some of these efforts are as follows:

1. **To have the proper knowledge of adolescent's psychology:** Adolescence is the bridge between childhood and adulthood. The behaviour of an adolescent and his personality needs a careful study. It is essential to have the knowledge of the adolescent's psychology in order to understand him. What are his specific needs? What types of changes take place during this period? What are the problems faced by the adolescent? How should they be treated? All this is essential to be known by the parents, teachers and administrators who have to deal with the adolescents.

2. **Providing suitable environment for proper growth:** We already know growth stops at the end of adolescence after attaining maturity. Adolescence is the stage where maximum growth takes place. To attain maximum during this stage, all that one can get with respect to physical and mental growth, suitable environment should be provided by the parents and teachers at home as well as in schools. Adolescents must be provided with a balanced diet. Their eating habits should be properly checked upon. They must be taught about health, personal hygiene, cleanliness, various diseases and their prevention, etc., to keep them fit for growing. Adequate provision for physical exercise and activities should be made in the school curriculum and necessary facilities provided.

3. **Rendering proper sex education:** Sex plays a very dominant role during adolescence. The rapid physiological changes, secretion of sex hormones, sudden awakening of sex instinct and urges — all necessitate the provision of adequate sex information and education for adolescents. The following things may help in this direction:

    *   They should be helped in making adjustments with regard to their new bodily changes and somatic developments. Girls should know that flow of blood during menstruation is not a disease. It is a natural process which prepares them for becoming mothers. Similarly boys should be told that the occasional discharge of semen during sleep is not in any way harmful to them and should not be a cause of worry.

    *   Their curiosity about sex also needs to be satisfied. For this purpose parents and teachers should provide adequate information on sex hygiene and physiology, the process of the birth of a baby, the hazards of immature and pre-marriage intercourse, etc., in a very frank, scientific, judicious and impersonal manner.

    *   The sex instinct and urges also need to be cared properly. There should be proper sublimation of sex instinct and canalisation of sexual energy. Forceful inhibition, taboos, and restrictions imposed in this direction bring disastrous results. With the provision of wide field of interests, a network of co-curricular activities and social situations, boys and girls should be given a chance to know and get along to work with each other. This will remove their many misconceptions about each other and will lead to their healthy adjustments.

4. **Proper dealing with adolescents:** Recent researches in the field of adolescents' psychology have revealed that adults, parents, elders and teachers and their unreasonable ways and points of view are the real problems of adolescence. They are in the habit of criticising the adolescents and always impose their authority and assert their liking and disliking. They forget that there is a generation gap between them and the adolescents. In dealing with them, parents and teachers should realise that the demands of their peer group are more important than their own expectations.

    Secondly, among adolescents, there is a craving for recognition and they also try to maintain their self-prestige and status among their peers. They assert that they are now mature individuals. Their opinions should be valued and they should be given a patient hearing. Therefore, it is badly needed on the part of the teachers as well as parents that they stop treating them as children and give them their due recognition. Their opinions should be invited and they should be given opportunities for free expression. They must refrain from activities damaging the pupil's self-concept. The adolescents must not feel that they are insulted and their phenomenal self has been attacked unnecessarily. The teachers and parents should stop murmuring and blindly criticising the attitudes and actions of the adolescents. Youths are more in need of models than critics. The elders must give a deep consideration to adolescent's needs and problems. It is futile to punish their misbehaviour.

5. **Training of emotions and satisfaction of emotional needs:** The age of adolescence is marked by a lot of intensity, force, instability and immaturity of emotions. The adolescent youths are highly inflammable and restless. Their emotions can be aroused with slight provocation. The political parties and opportunist leaders can easily fool them and use them in destroying national property. Therefore, there is a strong need of providing emotional education to adolescents. Their emotions should be properly trained and emotional energies should be diverted towards constructive ends.

Moreover, adolescents suffer from certain emotional needs. They have a strong desire to love and to be loved. They need to be accepted by their age mates and every adolescent aspires that he should be admired and praised. He wants that he should be given freedom to proceed in his own way and adopt his own style of life but on the other hand, he needs protection, shelter and affection from parents, elders and teachers. He becomes disturbed if he is not provided proper security and freedom from anxiety. The parents and teachers should take care of these needs of the adolescents. They must be given what they need in terms of their emotional requirements.

6. **To take care of the special interests of the adolescents:** Adolescence is the age of wide interests and aptitudes. There are wide individual differences among the adolescents with regard to their special interests and aptitudes. Great care should be taken to locate their special interests and aptitudes. According to their interests and aptitudes, they should be provided with learning experiences and opportunities for participation in co-curricular activities. The curriculum should provide an open choice for various subjects and activities according to the tastes and temperaments of the adolescents.

Their curiosity, wandering and adventurous tendencies should be taken care of by activities like excursions, N.C.C., mountaineering, scientific exploration, etc. The love for humanity and ideals should be utilised in rendering social services and community services in the neighbourhood and distressed areas. In brief, adolescents should be provided with useful activities according to their interests so that they are constantly busy and their mind is preoccupied with healthy and constructive ideas.

7. **Providing religious and moral education:** One of the causes of increasing restlessness, indiscipline, dishonesty and aimlessness among the youth of India is that there is no proper provision of religious and moral education in our system of education. Ours is a secular state and therefore doubts are expressed on erroneous grounds. Actually the roots and the goals of all the religions are one and the same. If we try to do away with the rituals, the essence of all the religions is morality. Therefore, it is education of morality and character formation that should be provided by religious education and every school, home and other social agency can work in this direction. The parents, teachers, social workers and administrators should join hands in creating a suitable atmosphere and offering opportunities of practicing moral qualities.

8. **Provision for vocational education:** There is a strong desire of achieving independence in adolescents. Economic factors obstruct their way. Therefore, they are worried about acquiring self-sufficiency on the economic front. What occupation should they choose, how can they earn their livelihood are some questions, the answers of which they try to seek. Here arises the need of proper vocational guidance and vocational education for them. The youth of today is bewildered and aimless because of the indefiniteness of his vocation. The education imparted to him does not provide jobs and occupations. Therefore, the strong need of today is to provide job-oriented and vocation-based practical education for the adolescents. The government, society, parents and teachers should make their efforts in this direction.

9. **Arranging guidance services:** Lack of guidance creates aimlessness, indefiniteness and restlessness among adolescents. They have their problems which need careful attention and proper solution. They are at the crossroads of life. A slight mistake can lead them on the wrong path. Therefore, it is the utmost duty of the state, society and schools to provide proper guidance services to the students as well as to their parents. Guidance services should be organised in a proper form both inside and the outside the schools. There should be well trained guidance workers and personnel. As far as possible, individual guidance should be provided.

The list of suggestions regarding the solution of the adolescents' problem and the satisfaction of their needs cannot be called complete with the earlier-mentioned few points. The task is gigantic and requires strenuous efforts from all directions. Moreover, it is difficult to prescribe some common rule or formula for the direction and guidance of adolescents with respect to their problems and needs. It is not a mass phenomenon. In actual sense, there are no problem adolescents. Therefore, the focus of guidance is always the individual and not the problem. Every adolescent is to be studied carefully as he requires special guidance and help for the solution of his problems and satisfaction of his needs.

Summary

Every stage of human development is characterised by some unique characteristics named as stage-specific characteristics. For example the stage-specific characteristics of the stage of infancy and early childhood (up to 5 years) may be named as (i) the period of rapid growth and development, (ii) child's dependence on others, (iii) self-assertive nature of child, (iv) children living in the world of make believe and fantasy, (v) child's selfish and unsocial behaviour, (vi) emotional instability, (vii) lacking in terms of intellectual and sexual development. Similarly the childhood (6 years to the beginning of adolescence) stage may be distinctly marked with the stage-specific characteristics like (i) period of slow and steady growth, (ii) independence, (iii) emotional stability and control, (iv) development of social tendency, (v) adoption of realistic attitude, (vi) formation of sentiments and complexes, (vii) developmental progress in terms of intellect, interests and aptitudes, (viii) development of indifference and antagonism towards the opposite sex.

In his journey of growth and development, a child is entitled to be called as an adolescent when he attains puberty (ability to reproduce his kind) and he ceases to be an adolescent when he has acquired maturity (in terms of physical, mental, social and emotional aspects) to play the role of an adult in his society or culture. However, in day-to-day functioning, adolescents can be referred to as teenagers — individuals having chronological age between 13 to 19 years.

In most of the syllabi of the secondary schools teacher preparation courses, we always find one or the other topic in relation to the study of adolescence. It is simply because secondary school teachers have to deal with adolescent students (studying in the secondary or higher secondary classes) ranging in the age group from 11 to 18 years. For their proper growth and development as well as desirable behaviour modification, it is utmost essential to get acquainted with the needed adolescent psychology, the nature needs and problems of their growth and development and so on.

As a consequence of the process of growth and development carried out in the period of adolescence, a child tries to attain his maximum in terms of the physical, mental, social, emotional, moral and sexual development. This is why it is termed as the period of intensive as well as maximum growth and development. However, such sudden growth and development on a large scale may generate specific types of problem and adjustment needs for the developing adolescents so much so as to designate their period of adolescence as "period of great storm and stress".

Adolescents like infants and children possess many age-specific and stage-specific needs, characteristics and problems like (i) perplexity with regard to somatic variation or adjustment with new bodily charges, (ii) intensification of self-awareness and sex consciousness, (iii) conflicting demands of social and cultural norms of adults and their peer group, (iv) caught between the role of a child and an adult in taking decisions about independence v/s dependence, idealism v/s realism, vocational choice and self-support etc.

The stage-specific characteristics of adolescents are also very much reflected clearly in their various personality/behavioural traits like desires and aspirations, attitudes and self-concept. Here the adolescents differ not only in the shape, dimension and magnitude of these traits with respect to the infants and children or adults but also exhibit marked difference in terms of the motivation and anxiety felt for their fulfilment.

Adolescent boys and girls may exhibit significant differences in their respective growth and development. They develop the characteristic features of their respective sizes, physical and stamina, specific attitudes, interests, aesthetic sense, emotional make-up, etc., suiting to their gender needs.

With the so called globalisation, materialisation and modernisation of society, there is now an additional significant development in the life of children and adolescents in the shape of facing a number of new types of stress-generating problems in the name of (i) increasing loneliness (finding themselves all alone for coping with their needs and problems), (ii) changing family structure (nuclear in place of combined family system) and (iii) rising permissiveness (leniency, loosy-goosey attitude and tolerance exhibited by elders towards them for their undesirable and unsocial behaviour).

Our adolescents on account of their age-specific characteristics, needs and problems as well as for facing the new modern age-stress generating issues need help, assistance and guidance for the proper growth and development of their personality. It is the duty of the parents, teachers, school authorities and members of the society to join their hands for providing best means and opportunities not only for realising the felt needs of the adolescents and coming out of the modern stress-related issues but also for the maximum development of their potentialities in the interest of their self and the society.

References and Suggested Readings

Carmichael, L. (Ed.), *Manual of Child Psychology*, John Wiley, New York, 1946

Crow, L.D. and Crow, Alice, *Child Psychology* (Reprint), Barney & Noble, New York, 1969.

Harriman, P.L. (Ed.), *Encyclopaedia of Psychology*, Phil Lib., New York, 1946, Student 3rd ed., McGraw-Hill, Tokyo, 1959.

Hurlock, E.B., *Child Psychology*, McGraw-Hill, Tokyo, 1959.

Kuppuswami, B. (Ed.), *Advanced Educational Psychology*, University Publications, Jalandhar, 1963.

Marry, F.K. and Marry, R.V., *From Infancy to Adolescence*, Harper & Brothers, New York, 1940.

Paplia, D.E. and Olds, S.W., *Psychology*, McGraw-Hill, New York, 1987.

Ross, J.S., *Ground Work of Educational Psychology*, George G. Harrap, London, 1951.

19

Developmental Tasks—Concept and Implications

Meaning and Definition of the Term Developmental Tasks

The term and concept regarding 'developmental tasks', was first introduced historically by the famous American Psychologist Robert Havighurst. For this purpose, he defined the term 'developmental task' in his book "Developmental Tasks and Education" in the words given below:

"Developmental task is one which arises at a certain period in the life of the individual, successful accomplishment of which leads to his happiness and success with later tasks, while failure leads to unhappiness and difficulty with later tasks."-Havighurst, R.J. (1972)

A close analysis of the above definition may lead us to conclude the meaning of the term developmental tasks as under:

(i) Development task is essentially linked with the development and developmental period (from birth till the expiry of the adolescence) of an individual.

(ii) Developmental tasks are age-specific and essentially linked with the developmental stages of one's life.

(iii) An individual at a particular age or stage of his growth and development is expected to perform certain tasks (performing certain types of conative, cognitive and affective behaviour) quite specific to his age and stage of development.

(iv) Adjustment with the self and the environment depends upon the extent to which one in capable of performing these age-specific and stage-related developmental tasks.

(v) In case one is successful in accomplishing the related developmental tasks (specific to his age and developmental period), he feels happy at his present and is expected to perform future tasks successfully in his later life. Failure, on the other hand, makes his present life miserable and puts a question mark on his ability to perform future tasks successfully in his later life.

(vi) Key to happiness and adjustment thus lies in the proper identification of developmental tasks and learning the ways and means of their successful accomplishment during the related developmental periods of one's life.

After having some acquaintance with the meaning and nature of the developmental tasks, the questions can now be raised regarding — (i) The identification and naming of the developmental tasks; (ii) The sources contributing towards the upsurge of the developmental tasks at a particular age and development period; (iii) Critical ages at which the society expects its members to master the developmental tasks of that age; (iv) Purposes and goals of such tasks; (v) Role of the cultural and social pattern regarding expectation of certain developmental tasks from its growing youngsters; and (vi) Specific tasks associated with the stages of developmental period.

Let us think over all such issues. However, in doing so, we would be limiting our discussion to the developmental period ranging from infancy to adolescence.

Identifying and Naming the Development Tasks

Developmental tasks are related with the changes in behaviour belonging to its all three domains namely conative, cognitive and affective. What a developing child is expected to do, think and feel at a particular age or stage of one's developmental period for his adequate adjustment in one's social and cultural environment can then work as a base for the identification and naming of various developmental tasks at a particular age or stage of one's life. Since there lies a number of activities or tasks belonging to these three behavioural domains that can be expected to be executed by the growing children of developmental period, the list for the identification and naming of the developmental task will naturally be too lengthy and exhaustive. However, for illustration purpose let us try to mention the name of the developmental tasks needed to be performed by the growing children as below:

(i) **Conative developmental tasks:** Crawling, sitting, standing, walking, riding, jumping, running, throwing, catching, controlling elimination of bodily wastes, combing, dressing, eating, biting, stretching, stopping, drinking, kneeling, holding, leaning, smashing, balancing, identification by touching, seeing, smelling or hearing, writing, handling the instruments, dancing, dining, driving, knitting, playing a musical organ, teasing, posing, handling of the technologically advanced instruments etc.

(ii) **Cognitive developmental tasks:** Recognizing, recalling, reproducing, selecting, listing, measuring, counting, reading, underlining, classifying, distinguishing, explaining, justifying, interpreting, choosing, modifying, illustrating, comparing, analyzing, synthesizing, concluding, contrasting, arguing, generalizing, associating, criticizing, evaluating, summarizing, verifying, reporting, supporting, predicting, using, solving, relating, etc.

(iii) **Affective developmental tasks:** Accepting, attaining, showing specific interests attitudes and aptitudes for things, ideas, processes and persons, demonstrating particular or generalised habits of thinking, feeling and actions, demonstrating a particular level of social and emotional maturity, sex behaviour, personal and social adjustment and moral sense, etc.

Sources Contributing Towards the Upsurge of Development Tasks

Development tasks specific to an age and stage of development may be necessitated and brought in existence on account of the following factors:

(i) **Maturation:** As the child matures, *i.e.* grows in age, he definitely needs to perform certain tasks so as to adjust himself according to the changing needs of his growing age. Examples of such tasks are learning to crawl, stand, walk, dress, etc.

(ii) **Adjustment to the physical, social and cultural environment:** Many developmental tasks are necessitated on account of seeking proper adjustment to one's physical, social and cultural environment. Sometimes physical environment puts pressure on a growing child to learn proper ways and means of adjusting according to the condition prevailing in one's physical environment. Hilly, desert or coastal areas demand specific activities and ways of living from the growing children and as a result it generates some typical development tasks for them. Similar is the case with the needs and pressures put up by one's social and cultural environment for learning the execution of specific development tasks suiting to one's age and developmental stage. One needs to learn the use of special devices like telephone, mobile, Internet, or read, write and speak a particular language, learn specific social and cultural behaviour, etc. according to the demands of one's social and cultural environment at a particular age or stage of one's life.

(iii) **Adjustment to one's self:** Many developmental tasks are necessitated on account of seeking harmonious relationships or adjustment to one's self. Sometimes one needs to fulfill the demands of his own desires, basic interests, liking and disliking, philosophy of life, values and aspirations, somatic structure and cognitive and emotional characteristics. Aspiring to study a particular course of instruction and choosing a particular course or profession are examples of such demands needed for the adjustment of one's self. Accordingly, an individual is forced to include the related tasks in the list of developmental tasks suiting to his growing age like trying to get entry into a specific academic and professional course or preparing oneself for the entry in the desired profession and vocation.

In this way, developmental tasks are mostly generated naturally on account of maturation or the pressures put on the individual for getting adjusted to one's self and his environment.

Critical Ages and Developmental Tasks

As emphasised earlier, developmental tasks are quite age and developmental stage specific. Hence particular type of developmental task needs to be carried out at a particular age and developmental stage level. The age spans during which the growing children are expected to perform a certain type of developmental task in a particular society and cultural group are termed as *critical ages* and *periods of the life*. These critical ages and periods of life present quite a ripe stage in terms of maturation and learning experiences gained from one's environment for performing the developmental tasks relevant to the critical ages and periods of life. As a result, we can't expect a growing child to perform a certain type of developmental task unless he or she has not reached the required stage of maturation and development, *i.e.* entered in the period of the relevant critical age. Further, we can't also expect from a more mature child or adult to perform certain developmental tasks after the expiry of the critical age period, *i.e.* learning gymnastic skills etc.

Purposes and Goals of Developmental Tasks

It is well in the interest of the growing children, parents and teachers that they are acquainted with the nature of the developmental tasks needed to be performed by the children at a specific age and developmental period of the life. The purposes and objectives realised through such knowledge may prove fruitful in the following way:

- It may provide the norms and expectations of a particular society or cultural group from its growing children in terms of the general behaviour pattern (demonstrable through conative, cognitive and affective tasks) during the various ages and developmental periods of life.

- It may help in setting the minds and attitudes of the children for making desirable attempts to learn the execution of the developmental tasks relevant to different developmental periods of their life.

- It may provide proper guidelines to teachers and parents to help youngsters in their adequate growth and development by providing richer experiences for the execution of the developmental tasks related to the critical ages and stages of their lives.

- It may help the society or a cultural group to develop its own set of developmental tasks needed to be performed at one or the other stage of development by their children in view of the changes of future developmental course of that very society and cultural group.

- The knowledge of developmental tasks specific to critical ages may help the children, teacher and parents to plan their obligation and duties well in advance in view of the targets lying ahead in terms of the required expected stage of maturity and experiences gained for executing the tasks. What is expected at present and what lies ahead in terms of the level of developmental tasks to be performed by the growing children, the knowledge of such aspects may prove a boon to the education and development planner, besides being a source of self motivator to the youngsters themselves.

Role of Cultural and Social Patterns in Developmental Tasks

The developmental tasks, besides being age-specific, are also said to be influenced by the nature of the life patterns prevalent in a social and cultural group. That is why we can't expect our youngsters to perform developmental tasks performed by the English, American, Japanese or African children. For example, in our social and cultural set-up children acquire puberty at quite an early age in comparison to the children of European nations. It will definitely affect the expectation from them in term of the developmental tasks selected to their sex behaviour, emotional and social maturity etc. Similarly, there may be many types of social and cultural behaviour patterns, mental make-up, etc. that may be expected from the children of the developed countries and fast moving societies in a sharp contrast to the children belonging to developing and deprived social segments. Such differences may essentially force to adopt somewhat different approaches in planning the developmental tasks relevant to specific periods of life. In reality it does happen and thereby we may clearly observe that the list of developmental tasks needed to be performed by the growing children at the specific ages and periods of their life varies from culture to culture and society to society.

Developmental Tasks of the Various Stages of Development

The developmental period, as we know in the human beings ranges from birth to the attainment of maturity, *i.e.* expiry of the adolescence period. The significant stages of development during this period may be named as the stages of infancy, childhood and adolescence. Let us try to know something about the nature of development tasks needed to be performed by the youngsters during the above mentioned three development stages of our life.

Development Tasks of Infancy (up to 2 Years)
- Learning to crawl, stand, walk, run, climb, jump, throw, etc.
- Learning to drink and take solid food
- Learning to talk
- Learning to acquire physiological stability
- Learning to control elimination of bodily wastes
- Learning to explore the physical environment surrounding him
- Learning to play with toys
- Learning to accomplish the skill of tri-cycling
- Learning to pay attention towards the things, persons and events
- Learning to recognise and identify things and persons
- Forming simple concepts of social and physical reality
- Learning to recite poems and stories
- Learning to imitate the behaviour and actions of others
- Learning to acquire almost all the positive and negative emotions in his behaviour expression
- Learning to shift his attention from the play material to his playing mates
- Learning to take interest in the company of his age mates and other growing children
- Learning to relate oneself emotionally to parents, sibling and others.

Development Tasks of Early Childhood (from 3 to 5 years)
- Learning to acquire competencies in motor skills like walking, jumping, climbing, sliding, tri-cycling, hopping, galloping, skipping, throwing, bouncing and catching

- Learning to acquire simple basics in language skills like speaking, listening, reading and writing
- Learning sex differences and sex modesty
- Learning to distinguish between right and wrong and developing a conscience
- Learning to develop right concepts related to social and physical reality
- Learning to remain away from the parental fold and enjoy the companionship of other children
- Learning to give up the 'I' feeling and develop the 'we' feeling
- Learning to acquire the ability to sense similarities and dissimilarities and compare and contrast things
- Learning to control overt expression of emotions.
- Development Tasks of Later Childhood (from 6 to 12 years)
- Learning motor and physical skills necessary for playing different indoor and outdoor games
- Learning to get along with age-mates
- Learning to appropriate sex roles
- Building wholesome attitudes towards oneself as a growing organism
- Developing necessary skills in language and communication, computation, sketching and drawing etc.
- Developing interest, attitudes, liking and dislikings towards things, persons and ideas
- Developing concrete and abstract concepts regarding things, persons, ideas and processes
- Development of conscience, morality and scale of values
- Development of the capacity to reason, think and problem solving
- Development of loyalty towards the group.

Development Tasks of Adolescence (from 13 to 18 Years)

- Development of abilities, motor and physical skills for playing difficult, complex and hard indoor and outdoor games
- Development of abilities, motor and physical capacities for performing mental tasks and physical capacities for performing mental tasks and physical labour
- Development of mental and cognitive abilities to perform difficult mental tasks and operations
- Development of all types of concept — requiring concrete or abstract operations
- Learning to accept one's physique and satisfaction with one's appearance
- Learning to play a masculine or feminine role
- Learning to develop new relations with age mates of both the sexes
- Learning to acquire maturity in sex behaviour
- Development of sentiments towards things, persons, places and values

- Learning to acquire civic sense, social responsibilities and ways of democratic living
- Learning to build a sense of belonging to one's social group, culture, community and nation
- Learning to adjust with a sense of self-sacrifice and martyrs like feelings for the cause of society, religion, nation and humanity
- Gaining vocational awareness and getting ready for entering into higher academic or professional courses of study
- Gaining competencies and skills for meeting the needs of specific interests and aptitudes
- Striving to gain desired height on the mental, emotional and social maturity scales
- Preparing for playing the roles of a mature adult in future life.

In this way, every society and cultural group has a list of general and specific developmental task specifically associated with ages and developmental periods of life. It expects the youngsters belonging to the developmental age to successfully execute these tasks for their proper adjustment with themselves and their physical, social and cultural environment. Similar schemes of developmental tasks expected from the adult and older generations may also be planned for serving the individual and social interests and seeking proper harmony with their self and the environment resulting happiness in the personal and social lives.

Implications of Developmental Tasks

Developmental tasks as stated earlier are quite age specific and stage specific. The well- being, development and progress of the developing children very well depends on the successful executions of these developmental tasks very much expected from them at a particular age or stage of their development. The parents and teachers must be quite careful in providing appropriate opportunities and facilities to their developing children for the performance and execution of these age and stage specific developmental tasks in proper way. It is true for them in caring for the children belonging to the entire period of developmental age i.e. infancy to adolescence.

A glimpse on the list of the developmental tasks of adolescence provided earlier in the chapter may make us to conclude that an adolescent is expected

  (i) to attain maximum limit in terms of his physical and cognitive development.
 (ii) to gain proper emotional and social maturity in respect to his emotional and social development.
(iii) to get prepared for playing the role of a mature girl/boy in future life
(iv) to earn the necessary civic sense and morality in tune with the demands of his community/society.
 (v) to prepare him for acquiring self- sufficiency in economic aspect by getting entry into courses or vocation of his choice
(vi   to have an adequate adjustment to the members of opposite sex and his/her sex instincts and urges.

In view of the developmental tasks of the above nature expected from an adolescent, it is expected from the elders, teachers and parents to do all what can be possible for them in carrying over these developmental tasks in a proper way. What can be done on their part in this concern can be summarised in the way given ahead.

- To provide suitable curricular and co-curricular, formal and informal experiences for the proper cognitive development of the adolescents.
- To provide needed opportunities and help to the adolescents to reach at their maximum in terms of their physical development, strength and stamina.
- To arrange for the needed educational, vocational and personal guidance and counselling to the adolescents for their educational, vocational and personal adjustment and progress in their life.
- To arrange for the needed sex education to the adolescents
- To care for meeting the needs, interests, attitudes and aspiration of the adolescents.
- To provide desired curricular and co-curricular experiences and needed formal and informal opportunities for helping the adolescents to attain the needed emotional, moral and social maturity for playing the role of a mature responsible adult.
- To act as a role model or producing role example to the adolescents for helping them in the proper execution of their development tasks.

Summary

Robert J. Havighurst, the American psychologist, is credited to introduce the term and concept related to the developmental tasks. In describing the developmental tasks, he asserted that the entire life span of an individual may be properly divided into six stages and at each stage of development one has to execute developmental tasks quite specific and essential for that developmental stage. In his attempt for clarifying the concept of developmental tasks he also provided a list of some generalised developmental tasks stage wise quite common to all cultures and lands. The things like below may be safely concluded about the nature and development of these tasks.

The developmental tasks are known to be age and stage specific. The adjustment with the self and the environment depends upon one's capacity to properly perform these age and stage related developmental tasks. It is, therefore, the duty of the parents and teachers to get acquainted with the nature of developmental task for helping their children in the proper execution of their tasks at each of their developmental stage.

Developmental tasks belonging to all the three domains of behaviour may be classified into three broad categories namely conative developmental tasks, cognitive developmental tasks and affective developmental tasks (related to doing, thinking and feeling aspects of one's behaviour).

Developmental tasks specific to an age and stage of development are mostly necessitated and brought into existence naturally on account of maturation or the pressures put on the individual for getting adjusted to one's self and his environment.

The age spans during which the growing children are expected to perform a certain type of developmental task in a particular society and cultural group are termed as critical ages and periods of the life. Children for their own and social welfare are necessarily directed to perform the needed development tasks within the boundary of these critical ages/periods.

The developmental tasks, besides being age-specific, are also culture specific as these are known to be greatly influenced by the nature of the life pattern prevailing in a social and cultural group. That is why every society and cultural group has its own list of general and specific developmental tasks specifically associated with ages and developmental periods of life. After such specification, it then expects the youngsters (from infancy to the end of adolescence) to execute these tasks properly for their adequate adjustment.

With respect to the educational implications of the knowledge and skills related to developmental tasks on the part of parents and teachers, it can be properly inferred that first they should try to know that what is expected from the growing children at each stage of their development in relation to the tasks needed to be executed by them at that very specific stage and afterwards should try to help them in the proper execution of these developmental tasks by acquiring needed knowledge and skills for this purpose.

References and Suggested Readings

Berk, L.E., Young Children: Pre-natal through Middle adulthood, New York: Allyn & Bacon, 2012.

Doherty, J. and Hughes, M., Child Development : Theory and Practice, Essex: Pearson, 2009.

Crow, L.D. and Crow, Alice, *Child Psychology*, Reprint, Barney & Noble, New York, 1969.

Havighurst, R.J., *Developmental Task and Education*, 3rd ed., David McKay, New York, 1972.

Hurlock, E.B., *Child Psychology*, Asian student 3rd ed., McGraw-Hill, Tokyo, 1959.

Marry, F.K. and Marry, R.V., *From Infancy to Adolescence*, Harper & Brothers, New York, 1940.

Skinner C.E. and Harriman, P.L. (Eds.), *Child Psychology*, 6th print, Macmillan, New York, 1937.

20

Maturation: Concept and Implications

Concept of Maturation

Maturation is quite a known term in the field of developmental psychology and constitutes a significant factor in the process of growth and development from the very conception of the child in the womb of his mother. What is generally conveyed through the term maturation can be known properly by paying attention to some important issues related with its concept such as: (i) meaning of the term maturation, (ii) effect of maturation on growth and development of children.

Meaning of the Term Maturation

Maturation is known for its uniqueness and specificity as a natural process for the growth that takes place within an individual. It was A. Gesell, who used the term maturation in the field of child development in 1919. The changes brought out by maturation are said to be the result of unfolding and ripening of inherited traits and are relatively independent of activity, practice or experience. We can take the help of some well known definitions of the term maturation for knowing and understanding about its meaning and nature.

McGeoch (1942): Maturation includes any change with age in the conditions of learning which depends primarily upon organic growth factors rather than upon prior practice or experience.

Thompson (1979): "Maturation" is a name for the growth process during which a structure or function is more and more becoming adult, that is "mature".

A. Gesell (1929): Maturation is the maturity and firmness of the nerves and muscles brought out by the internal mechanism of the body quite independent of the impact of the environmental factors external to the organism.

H.J. Eysenck et al. (1972): Maturation is an autonomous process of somatic, psychological and mental differentiation and integration spread over developmental stages and phases which condition and build on one another in the course of time; as a result of this process the individual growth is completed and consolidated somatically, maturely and spiritually as well as socially and he can thus adapt to life.

A.T. Jersildet al. (1975): Maturation is the process by which underlying potential capacities of the organism reach a stage of functional readiness. This process involves both the changes in structure that come with growth and the progressive exercise of structures that provide ground work for later performances.

Biggie and Hunt (1968): "Maturation is a developmental process within which a person, from time to time manifests different traits, the blue prints for which have been carried in his cells from the time of his conception."

The definitions cited earlier may help us in drawing the following conclusions about the meaning and nature of maturation:

- Maturation in its purest sense is the result of the mechanism of heredity. It is the heredity contributions that decide the course of the changes (behavioural and developmental) observed in children since their conception in the womb of their mother.

- The effect of the process of maturation continues throughout the developmental period i.e., upto the end of the period of adolescence.

- Maturation helps the children to get mature in terms of their growth and development in all the various aspects — physical, motor, mental, social, moral and spiritual for playing the role of a mature adult in their lives.

- As a natural phenomenon of growth and development, maturation helps in the development of inner potential of human organisms making them ready and capable of reaching the heights or attaining possible milestones of their personality.

- Maturation is essentially linked with one's organically internal growth processes that are primarily or momentarily, independent of environmental factors external to the organism.

In this way, *maturation as a term and concept stands for a natural and spontaneous process of growth and development guided through the genetically controlled internal mechanism of an organism (quite independent of the impact of training or experience) responsible for bringing changes (behavioural and developmental) with the passage of the time during the developmental age.*

Effect of Maturation on Growth and Development

1. As one grows in age, he or she is naturally bound to be accompanied with some changes in his body, mind and behaviour purely because of the phenomenon of maturation. This is much clearer and revealing in the case of lower species like birds and animals. Let us have a look at examples from our environment around us. A bird conceives and as a result lays eggs in its nest. If we observe, we find that after a few days, there are signs of life in those eggs. A little later, young chicks come out from the eggs, jumping here and there, being fed by the parent birds but still unable to fly. However, one day, we find that they have grown enough and developed the capacity to fly like the other grown-up birds.

2. Similarly, we observe in the case of tadpoles that as a result of maturation, i.e.,
    the natural process of growth and development, there is definitely a major change
    in their behaviour. They are able to swim and after sometime they begin to jump
    like an adult frog. What is observed in terms of their growth and development
    here can be purely attributed to the process of maturation. It is also true in the
    case of the young ones of other animals. No training or experience is received
    by them in the beginning for growing and developing their abilities to walk
    and run alike their adult parents. A baby deer is able to run quite fast just after
    its birth. How does it manage to eat grass and drink water, is just the result of
    the process of maturation as there is no such attempt of providing any formal
    experience or training to it by the parents or the other members of the species
    for the performance of such behaviour.

    In this way, we have enough evidence from the surrounding nature that
    explains the role of maturation in bringing desired growth and development in
    the behaviour and functioning of the small babies of insects, birds and animals.

3. In the case of human beings too, we may observe and notice the impact of
    maturation on the growth and development of youngsters from their very birth
    in almost all the aspects and dimensions of their personality as illustrated below:

    •   With the passage of time, they grow and develop physically in their height,
        weight and body proportions as well as in the functioning of the internal
        and external organs. The process of maturation must help them in acquiring
        physical maturity and thus they turn into fully mature adults physically at
        the end of the period of adolescence,

    •   Same is true with the other dimensions of their personality as well. They
        grow and develop as mentally, socially, emotionally, morally and aesthetically
        mature personalities at the time of acquiring adulthood. The process of
        maturation, i.e., an act of natural growth and development helps them well
        in this task. However, the question here may arise as to whether the growth
        and development acquired in the case of human babies for turning them into
        a fully mature personality in terms of the mental, social, emotional, moral
        and ethical standards is purely a function of the process of maturation or
        environmental influences, including training, or a combination of both.

    •   Definitely here the last one is the appropriate answer and as such it may be
        easily concluded that growth and development in the case of human beings
        for gaining maturity is a combined function of the process of maturation and
        learning. How does it become a combined function, may be well illustrated
        through a number of instances described as below:

        (i) A child is not able to speak or utter words correctly until he reaches a
             certain stage or age in maturation. We can't expect a baby of 6 months
             to speak and utter words correctly even if he belongs to a very high
             hereditary stock (like the parents are too rich and scholars in the linguistic
             capacity, say Ph.D. in language) or is being constantly inspired and
             formally trained in speech. He has to grow and develop his linguistic

capacity in accordance with the maturation level he needs for doing so. In the natural process, he will learn to speak with the maturation of his vocal chords and other similar physical and mental functioning required for learning correct language. At the same time, it is also true that here we can't rule out the impact of favourable or unfavourable environmental influences, including schooling, formal or informal training, for acquiring proper and excellent linguistic ability.

A child at any stage of his schooling or life does not learn the language or develop his language ability just because he attains that stage. Definitely, the language is taught to him. The language which he learns is the one he hears and more specifically the one he gets through specific training. As a result, what a child acquires in terms of his language development at any stage of his life is a joint product of the natural process of growth and development, i.e., maturation and the environment influences including training.

(ii) What is true for language development is also true for the development of other mental functioning. The development of mental facilities like thinking, reasoning, problem solving, decision making, analyzing, synthesising, discriminating, drawing inferences, all need maturation as well as planned experiences and training on the part of the youngsters. Normally, we can't expect a child of tender age to be too logical, consistent, methodological in his approach and systematic in thinking and abstraction. He has to wait before he acquires the ability of abstraction, i.e., a certain stage of maturation, for developing his mental faculties enabling him to perform mental tasks requiring power of abstraction, creative imagination, innovation and novelty.

(iii) In case of emotional development also, we can observe a similar phenomenon. A child develops in terms of emotional maturity on account of the process of maturation helped and influenced by the environmental influences. It is true that a child has to be a child in terms of his emotional behaviour. We can't expect him to behave like a grown-up adult. There is definitely an age characteristic emotional behaviour. That is why we can observe a definite pattern of emotional behaviour at each stage of maturation, i.e., infancy, childhood, pre-adolescence, adolescence, adulthood and old age. However, how one behaves and why one behaves under the influence of a particular emotion depends heavily on the impact of environmental influences or feedback one gets from his formal or informal surroundings. The same is true for social, moral, religious or aesthetic standards and aesthetic sense from individuals belonging to different stages of their maturation.

(iv) Sure, age is a great factor. One learns and picks up so many things related to these aspects as he or she grows in age. Take the case of sexual development, a distinctly visible area showing the impact of maturation. As one grows in age, he or she is sure to pick up many things and practices related to sexual activities even without any prior experiences or formal training. Attraction towards opposite sex, to feel the necessity of the satisfaction of sexual urge are thus some developments that are bound to emerge as and when a child reaches the adolescence stage. However, his attitude and practices towards sex may now be coloured or influenced side by side by the exposures, experiences or formal/ informal training he receives for doing so.

Thus, from this discussion, it may be clear that growth and development in the various aspects and dimensions of personality of an individual are helped and influenced by the process of maturation. As one grows in one's age he is helped by the process of maturation for having grown and developed into a full-fledged matured personality. However, how much maturity in the deeds and kinds is shown by an individual again depends upon the quality of experiences, environmental influences, formal or informal training, education, etc., that is received by an individual.

Significance and Implications of the Phenomenon of Maturation

The knowledge of the nature and process of maturation contributing towards the growth and development of children and its valuable inter-relationship and interaction with the process of learning may prove quite beneficial to parents, teachers and counsellors for planning and providing care, education and guidance to children in the way described as follows:

1. Maturation is a natural process of growth and development. It is guided through hereditary potential and genetic factors. There are many functions, and the phenomenon of growth that are entirely governed through the process of maturation are thus quite automatic and spontaneous among living organisms including human beings. No prior experience, learning or training is needed for such development and behavioural functioning. In this connection McGraw provides the example of psychogenetic functions (functions common to race) such as crawling, sitting, standing, stair climbing, etc. Piaget provides the example of cognitive schemas like reading, grasping, sucking, looking, etc., that are purely the functions of maturation; exercise or training is of little advantage in the development and execution of these functioning. In this way many of the gross motor skills and general intellectual functioning develops naturally in growing children. The parents and the caretakers should wait patiently for the outcome of such natural growth. They should not unnecessarily worry or become over-enthusiastic to bring about early development or changes in the behaviour of their infants or children. However, in the case of ontogenetic functions (those that are specific to an individual) such as swimming, roller-skating, tricycle riding, categorised as fine motor skills or the development of language and other higher cognitive abilities, experiences and training is necessary. Therefore, teachers, parents and counsellors should make themselves quite conscious to recognise what functions are purely guided through maturation (not requiring any training) and what are to be supported through training. It can help them in planning the education and guidance of their wards.

2. Maturation as a close associate of learning or training in fact provides a solid base for any programme or scheme of effective learning or training. Here, it serves its function in two ways:

    (i)   Setting the stage of learning by providing necessary readiness to learn.

    (ii) Acquainting oneself about the limits of development reached through learning or training.

Let us discuss these two aspects of maturation, the knowledge of which carries a lot of valuable educational implications.

    (i)   Maturation helps children to grow and develop physically and mentally for becoming essentially mature and ready for acquiring their age-linked learning experiences and training. The knowledge about the role played by maturity in this respect will surely help us in planning education for the child. We can certainly know that at what age what type of education and training should begin and in what sequence it should occur. We are adequately warned through such knowledge that:

    •   In case the child is not old enough or mature enough to profit by the teaching or training, it has almost no value for him and can be regarded as a mere wastage of time, energy and resources on the part of teachers or trainers. For example, forcing a child to speak, walk or use language before reaching critical age of maturity will prove futile and many times harmful for the well being and proper development of the child.

    •   When a child acquires the necessary developmental readiness through maturation, then no time should be wasted for providing him desirable learning experience and training for the acquisition of his age-linked developmental abilities and skills. To miss the train at this time will be a great cardinal educational error. Pointing towards such error Hurlock (1956, p. 8) writes:

        "Should the child not be permitted to learn, even though ready, his interest is likely to wane? Later, when he is expected to learn, his interest may have reached such a low ebb that he will be unwilling to put forth the efforts needed for successful learning."

In this way, knowledge of the outcome of maturation, critical development periods and acquired developmental readiness through maturity, brings into limelight the *so called valuable teaching moments* in the words of Havighurst (1953). It is these moments when the task of development or behaviour modification should be performed by the teachers and parents for having better results in the welfare of children.

    (ii) Maturation is governed through the forces of heredity mechanism and genetics that are known to put the limits and boundaries on the extent of growth and development of a child during various ages and periods of life span. Commenting on this aspect Hurlock (1956, p. 7) writes:

Maturation, which depends upon the hereditary endowment of the individual, sets limits beyond which development cannot go even when learning is encouraged.

Therefore, we should always keep in mind the limits of one's educability and developmental progress drawn by the genetic structure of the child in the form of his maturation level. We can consider here the cases of severe mentally retarded children whose neural maturation or natural development of the brain has been arrested at quite a low level. For such children, it may be observed that no amount of learning, training or environmental stimulation is sufficient to help them in bringing their behaviour and development into the normal range.

Therefore, it should be clearly recognised by us in planning individual or group education to the children that educational efforts should always be in tune with the limits imposed by the maturation level of the individual child. In this connection, we must always listen to the warning issued by Gesell (1929) in the following words:

> All educability is dependent upon innate capacities for growth. This intrinsic growth (observed in the shape of a maturation level) is a gift of nature. It can be guided, but it cannot be created; nor can it be transcended by an educational agency.

3. Knowledge of the nature and mechanism of maturation can help us know about the mile stones to be attained by children at the various ages of their developmental period. It has been observed and verified through a number of research studies that the majority of children of the same chronological age or at critical periods of their development are more similar than dissimilar in the rates of their physical and mental maturation. This similarity has been responsible for helping educators to create and develop a common programme of training and education to the children of a particular age and maturation level in the classrooms with similar techniques and teaching equipment. It has also helped parents, caretakers and counsellors to make use of generated principles and approaches for the guidance of their children.

4. Maturation stimulated by customary environmental experiences is said to help children reach certain milestones in terms of physical, motor and cognitive development, and acquire specific behavioural patterns quite normal to their age and developmental period. Such criteria may prove quite helpful in the diagnosis of exceptionalities and abnormalities in the development and behaviour of the grown-up children. It can happen in the way given below:

    (i) A child may be observed to remain quite ahead and advanced in comparison to the milestones fixed for his age and developmental period. It can help us plan for his special education by identifying and labelling him as creative or gifted.

(ii) Through comparison with the milestones settled through maturation at a
particular age, a child may be observed to lag behind or we may find that
his behaviour is more infantile and less complex than would otherwise be
possible. It may help us to identify and level him a slow learner, backward
mentally retarded, learning disabled or deprived by diving deep into the
causes of his deficient behaviour. Consequently, when a child is observed to
be slow or inferior in terms of his growth and development and behaviour
patterns that are normal for his age and developmental periods, we must
seriously think about the deficiencies that have remained in his process of
maturation or deprivation of customary environmental experiences including
educational practices employed in his rearing and schooling.

In this way knowledge of the nature, functioning and outcomes of maturation,
and active part played by the joint contribution of maturation and learning may
prove quite helpful to parents, teachers, counsellors and others interested in the
welfare of these youngsters, to plan for the practices of better rearing and education
to them.

Summary

Maturation refers to a developmental process which brings specific changes in a
developing organism mainly associated with his normal growth. These changes
are the results of unfolding and ripening of one's inherited traits and are therefore,
relatively independent of activity, practice or experience.

As a clear-cut example of the effect of maturation (the process of natural growth)
on the growth and development of organisms, we can cite the growing behaviour
of species like birds and animals. The offspring of the birds may come out from the
eggs of their mother, begin to jump and fly like the other grown-up birds without
receiving any experience or training for this purpose. The same is true with a baby
deer who is able to run quite fast just after its birth and also with a tadpole who
can swim and jump like an adult frog without being trained to do so.

In the case of human beings also, maturation brings significant changes leading
to the attainment of maturity in terms of the growth and development of the various
aspects of their personality. However, impact of maturation in their cases is not
as clearly defined as observed in the cases of lower species. It is why growth and
development in human beings for gaining maturity is always considered a combined
function of the process of their maturation and learning or training.

The knowledge of the nature and process of maturation contributing towards the
growth and development of children and its valuable inter-relationship and interaction
with the process of learning may prove quite helpful in providing care, education
and guidance to the children for seeking their needed progress and development.
In doing so, therefore, the principle of providing appropriate learning experiences
or training at the right time of maturation should always be followed in the matter
of seeking the children's desired growth and development in a proper way.

References and Suggested Readings

Biggie, M.L. and Hunt, M.P., *Psychological Foundations of Education*, Harper & Row, New York, 1968.

Crow, L.D. and Crow, Alice, *Educational Psychology*, Eurasia Publishing House, New Delhi, 1973.

Daly, W., "Gessel's Infant Growth Orientation" *A Composite Journal of Instructional Psychology*, 31, 321-324, 2004.

Eysenck, H.J. et.al, *Encyclopedia of Psychology*, New York: Phil. Lib., 1972.

Gessel, A., *Child Development*. New York: Macmillan, 1928.

Gessel, A., *Maturation and Infant Behavior Pattern*, New York: Lancaster Press, 1929.

Havighurst R.J., *Human Development and Education*, New York: Longman, 1953.

Hilgard, E.R. and Bower, G.H., *Theories of Learning*, 4th ed., Prentice-Hall, Englewood Cliffs, New Jersey,1975.

Hurlock, E.B., *Child Psychology* (Asian student edition), Tokyo: Kogakusha Co. Ltd., 1956.

Jersild et.al., *Child Psychology*, New York: Macmillan, 1975.

Kingsly, H.L. and Garry, R., *The Nature and Conditions of Learning*, 2nd ed., Prentice-Hall, Englewood Cliffs, New Jersey, 1957.

Mc Geoch, J.A, *The Psychology of Human Learning*, New York: Longmans, 1942.

Mc Grow, M.B., *Growth: A Study of Johny and Jimmy*, New York: Appleton-Century Crofts, 1935.

Thompson, G.G., *Child Psychology* (First Indian Reprint), New Delhi: Surjeet Publications, 1979.

21

Personality: Concept and Development

The Concept of Personality

The term personality has a unique place and importance in the life and development of children. We as teachers, parents, community personnel and well wishers of our children are always interested and engaged in the tasks and activities aimed towards the integrated development of the personality of our children. It is, therefore, quite imperative to all of us in getting acquainted with the meaning and concept of the term personality. We would therefore like to throw light on the concept by discussing some of the following significant things:

1. Certain wrong notions and misconceptions about personality
    2. Meaning and definitions of the term personality
    3. Facts regarding personality

Let us discuss them one by one.

Certain Wrong Notions and Misconceptions About Personality

Let us first make ourselves acquainted with the wrong notions and misconceptions about the term 'personality'.

Etymologically, the word 'personality' has been derived from the Latin word 'persona'. At first this word was used for the mask worn by the actors to change their appearance, but later on it began to be used for the actors themselves. Since then, the term 'personality' has been used to depict outward appearance or external behaviour, etc. It is in this sense that we have developed a wrong notion about the term 'personality'. We often listen to comments like this man has a fine or magnetic personality or that man has a poor personality. We try to paste such labels as fine, good or poor on individuals on the basis of their physical make-up, their manner of walking, talking, dressing and a host of other similar characteristics.

Sometimes, we use personality as equivalent to one's character. This too is a wrong notion. Character is, by all means, a moral or ethical term which refers to the standards of right and wrong, whereas personality is purely a psychological term and hence it is not proper to use it in reference to the study of ethical values.

Moreover, we cannot take personality as an equivalent word for outward appearance or behaviour. It would be a very superficial approach. We cannot ignore the inner aspect of one's personality. Personality includes the totality of one's behaviour and hence, both inner and outer (covert as well as overt) behaviour should be taken into consideration.

Meaning and Definition of the Term Personality

Psychologically speaking, personality is all that a person is. It is the totality of one's behaviour towards oneself as well as others. It includes everything about the person, his physical, emotional, social, mental and spiritual makeup. It is all that a person has about him.

So definitely, the term personality signifies something deeper than mere appearance or outward behaviour. How should it be given a proper meaning or definition is a difficult problem. Actually subjective nature does not allow us to arrive at a clear-cut, well-agreed definition. That is why it has been defined by many psychologists in so many ways according to their own points of view. Let us first begin with J.B. Watson (1930) the famous behaviourist. He defined personality in the following words:

> *Personality is the sum of activities that can be discovered by actual observations over a long enough period of time to give reliable information. (1930)*

Thus, Watson gives emphasis on the behaviour of an individual and considers personality as nothing but the useful effect one makes upon the person coming in close contact.

Morton Prince, accepting the role of both heredity and environment, defines it as:

> *Personality is the sum total of all the biological innate dispositions, impulses, tendencies, appetites and instincts of the individual and the dispositions and tendencies acquired by experience. (1929, p. 532)*

After evaluating 49 definitions of personality written by many eminent persons, Allport summarises his own concept in the following words:

> *Personality is a dynamic organization within the individual of those psycho-physical systems that determine his unique adjustment to his environment. (1948, p. 28)*

Although Allport has tried to give a comprehensive definition of the term 'personality' by including the words organisation, dynamic, psycho-physical system, unique adjustment and environment, etc., yet he, like his predecessors, only describes it. By emphasizing merely on theoretical aspect and describing it in terms of behavioural or dynamic concepts, the true nature of personality cannot be understood. Contemporary psychologists like R.B. Cattell and Eysenck have so opined. They very strongly feel that if personality cannot be demonstrated, measured and quantified, it should be called philosophy or art and not personality theory in psychology.

Below we give their ideas vis-a-vis the meaning of the term 'personality'.

R.B. Cattell

Personality is that which permits a prediction of what a person will do in a given situation. (1970, p. 386)

Eysenck

Personality is the more or less stable and enduring organisation of a person's character, temperament, intellect, and physique, which determine his unique adjustment to the environment. (1971, p. 2)

Let us have a close view of Eysenck's definition. He has tried to make certain terms clear in the following way:

Character denotes a person's more or less stable or enduring system or organisation of conative behaviour (*will*).

Temperament denotes a person's more or less stable or enduring organization of affective behaviour (*emotions*).

Intellect denotes a person's more or less stable or enduring organisation of cognitive behaviour (*intelligence*).

Physique denotes a person's more or less stable or enduring organisation or bodily configuration and neuro-endocrine endowment (*glands + nervous system + bodily configuration*).

Evaluation of Eysenck's Definition

(i) The definition gives a balanced consideration to heredity and environment in building one's personality.

(ii) Eysenck stresses on the concept of structure and organisation and criticises just naming some of the behavioural characteristics like bricks in describing a home.

(iii) This definition gives personality a physiological base.

(iv) It gives a complete picture of the human behaviour patterns by including cognitive, conative, affective and somatic (constitutional) aspects.

(v) This definition aims at making personality somewhat measurable and assessable and thus gives it a scientific base.

The above-mentioned characteristics do not suggest that Eysenck's definition has explained everything about the term 'personality' nor does it claim that it does not have any weak point. Like other definitions, this definition also suffers from some limitations and drawbacks, which are as follows:

(i) Eysenck advocates that personality must have a physiological base, but such is not the case always. Due to the very complex nature of personality, we cannot always have a physiological base.

(ii) His definition leads us to form an opinion that personality is fixed and cannot be changed.

This is an extreme approach. It is true that personality should be evaluated on the basis of generality of the behaviour (behaviour must be consistent in a number of situations). However, on the other hand, changes cannot be denied. A person, who is an extrovert, may turn into an introvert depending upon so many intervening factors.

Thus for understanding the concept of personality, the evolution of an ideal definition still needs further research. In fact, concepts like personality are difficult to be explained as they have the identity like sound or electricity where the impact can be felt but their real nature is always undisclosed. Something about them can be known by their utility or by describing some of their characteristics and distinguishing features. Let us seek the meaning of the term 'personality' on similar lines.

Some Glaring Facts About Personality

Based on our discussions so far, we can conclude the following points about personality:

1. Firstly, personality is something unique and specific. Each one of us is a unique pattern in ourselves. No two individuals, not even identical twins, behave in precisely the same way over a period of time. Everyone of us has specific characteristics for making adjustments.

2. The second main characteristic of personality is self-consciousness. The man is described as a person or as having a personality when the idea of 'self' enters into his consciousness. In this connection H.R. Bhatia (1968) writes. *"We do not attribute personality to a dog and even a child cannot be described as a personality because it has only a vague sense of personal identity."*

3. Personality includes everything about a person. It is all that a person has about him. It includes all the behaviour patterns, i.e., conative, cognitive and affective, and covers not only the conscious activities but goes deeper to semi-conscious and unconscious levels also.

4. It is not just a collection of many traits or characteristics that is known as personality. For instance by only counting the bricks how can we describe the wall of a house. It needs something more and actually personality is more than this: It is an organisation of some psycho-physical systems or some behaviour characteristics and functions as a unified whole. Like when describing an elephant, we cannot say that it is like a pillar only by examining its legs. Similarly by looking at one's physique or sociability, we cannot pass judgement about one's personality. It is only when we carefully study all the aspects — biological as well as social — that we can form an idea about his personality.

5. Personality is not static, it is dynamic and always in the process of change and modification. As mentioned earlier, personality is all that a person has about him. It gives him all that is needed for his unique adjustment in his environment. The process of making adjustment to the environment is continuous. One has to struggle with the environmental as well as the inner forces throughout one's life. As a result, one has to bring modifications and changes in one's personality patterns and it makes the nature of personality dynamic instead of static.

6. Every personality is the product of heredity and environment. Both contribute significantly towards the development of a child's personality.

7. Learning and acquisition of experiences contribute towards growth and development of one's personality. Every personality is the end product of this process of learning and acquisition.

8. Everyone's personality has more than one distinguishing feature that is aiming to an end or some specific goal. Adler, in his book 'Individual Psychology' opined that a man's personality can be judged through a study and interpretation of the goals he has set for himself to achieve and the approaches he makes to the problems in his life. In this way, he gives a very concise meaning to the personality of an individual by calling it 'lifestyle of an individual'.

Indeed this short and concise explanation of the term has a wide meaning. It draws a beautiful portrait of an individual's totality. It may be understood as the sum total of one's way of behaving towards oneself as well as others. It also predicts one's nature of behaviour as to how will one behave in a particular situation and one's pattern of adjustment to the ever-changing forces of environment.

Factors Influencing Development of Personality

The things and factors that are said to play a determining and decisive role in the development of personality can be categorised in two different ways outlined as follows:

1. One way of categorizing the factors or determinants of personality is to divide them into two broad categories — internal or personal and external or environmental.

   Internal or *personal factors* include the factors or things that lie internally within an individual and not externally in the environment. These may include factors like physical structure of the individual, (his physique, gender, nervous system, glands, etc.); his intelligence, motivation, emotional reactions, attitudes, interests, temperament, sentiments, etc.

   External or *environmental factors* are associated with the forces of the environment lying outside the individual. The influence of physical environment like climate and other physical facilities available to the individual as well as the impact of culture and social forces like home, family, school and society are included in this category.

2. Another way of classifying the factors or determinants of personality is based upon the viewpoints and angles from which personality is conceptualised. It includes biological, psychological and social and cultural perspectives. Accordingly the factors or determinants of personality may be classified as:

   (i) Biological factors,

   (ii) Psychological factors and

   (iii) Social and cultural factors.

   Let us now try to discuss the factors or determinants of personality by taking into account the latter mode of classification.

Biological Factors

The Biological factors or determinants of personality include factors such as:

   (i)   Hereditary influences

  (ii)   Nervous system

 (iii)   Ductless glands

 (iv)   Physique or somatic structure, and

  (v)   Body chemistry

Heredity Influences

Heredity influences transmitted at the time of child's conception through genes and chromosomes provide the base and structure for the future development of the personality. One's growth and development is in proportion with the contribution of the hereditary forces in the course of his personality development. In case he gets less from the hereditary stock, he has to work hard for attaining the desired level of personality development. The somatic structure one inherits, the nervous system he gets, the nature of intelligence and abilities he receives, all prove important in his future personality development.

Nervous System

Our behaviour, to a great extent, is controlled by our nervous system. How one behaves in a particular situation depends upon the judgement of one's brain. The sense impressions, which we receive through our sense organs, are meaningless unless they are given meaning by our nervous system. Therefore, our observation and perceptions are controlled by our nervous system. How intelligently we would react or make use of our mental power is again decided by our nervous system, particularly by the brain apparatus. The proper growth and development of nerve tissues and nervous system as a whole, helps in the task of proper intellectual development. Any defect in spinal cord or brain apparatus seriously affects the intellectual growth. Similarly, physical as well as emotional development is also influenced by our nervous system. Our autonomic nervous system plays a leading role in this direction. It controls the activity of involuntary processes like blood circulation, digestion, respiration and action of the glands.

These processes not only control the physical or emotional activity of an individual, but also exercise a great deal of influence over his physical and emotional development. Nerve tissues also cause the change in the secretion of hormones by some glands and consequently influence the emotional behaviour of an individual. Moreover, the nervous system acts as a coordinating agency for many operations going inside the body and harmonises the activities and functions of the body parts — internal as well as external. Hence, the nervous system should be considered as one of the important components of the human machine that plays a significant role in the growth and development of the personality of an individual.

Ductless Glands or Endocrine Glands

The ductless glands, with the secretion of their specific hormones, have a great influence in shaping the behaviour and personality of an individual. Let us try to discuss the location of these glands (Fig. 33.1) and their influence on the development of our personality.

Thyroid gland: It lies at the base of the neck in front of the wind pipe. It secretes a hormone called thyroxin, the main constituent of which is iodine. The thyroid plays a leading role in controlling the process of oxidation of food. It regulates the body's oxygen consumption and the rate of metabolism. Underdevelopment of this gland results in the undergrowth of the individual. The deficiency of thyroxin causes underactivity of the thyroid gland which not only retards the growth of the body but also causes mental retardation and disorders. Over-activity of this gland is equally harmful. It leads to unusual excitement, restlessness and irritability.

Parathyroid glands: These glands are located on the posterior of the thyroids and are generally four in number. The parathyroid hormone tries to counter-balance the exciting activity of the thyroid hormone. These glands remove toxic products from the body and restore the nervous system to relative calmness. Their underactivity produces muscular tension and overactivity produces lack of interest, fatigue and lethargic conditions.

The Pituitary gland: This gland is situated at the base of brain. It is called the 'master gland' because its hormones affect most of the other glands. This gland has two lobes — anterior and posterior.

The anterior lobe exercises great influence on the growth of bones. Its underactivity causes incomplete development and can lead to dwarfness, whereas an overactive anterior lobe results in gigantic growth of the human beings. The hormones produced by the lobe also supplement the activities of other glands like thyroid, adrenal and sex glands.

The posterior lobe also secretes valuable hormones. These hormones help in regulating blood pressure.

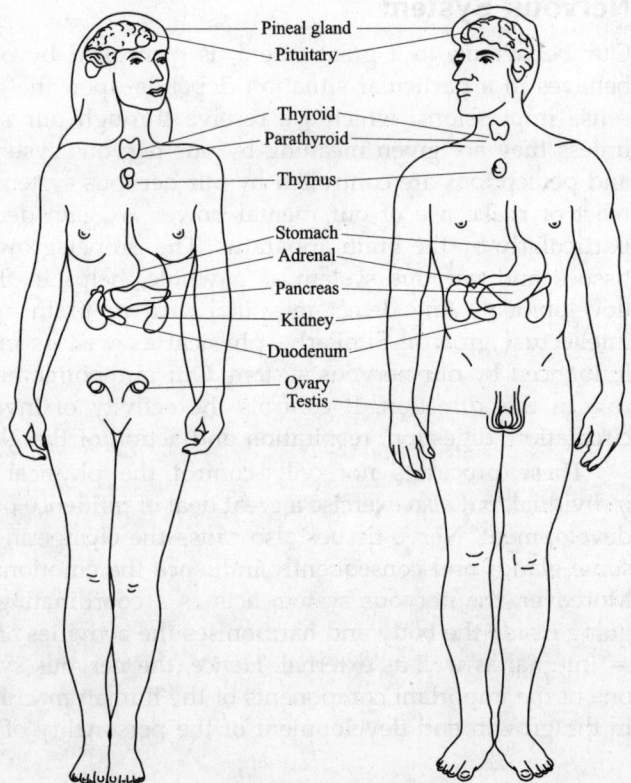

Pineal gland
Pituitary
Thyroid
Parathyroid
Thymus
Stomach
Adrenal
Pancreas
Kidney
Duodenum
Ovary
Testis

Fig. 21.1: Location of the major endocrine glands in the human body

Adrenal glands: These glands, two in number, surround the two kidneys separately. They are believed to secrete two separate hormones — cortin and adrenaline. The function of cortin is not definitely known. But adrenaline is known to exercise great influence over nervous, muscular and sexual functions. Adrenal glands are generally known as glands of survival as their underactivity makes an individual progressively weaker day-by-day.

During emotional current, the adrenal gland is known to perform a useful function. In such a situation more adrenaline is secreted that prepares an individual's organs for the particular emotional state. Their overactivity makes an individual highly active and energetic. It may also cause sexual maturity at an early age. A little girl or a boy may acquire secondary sex characteristics of a mature man or woman. In some case over-development of the adrenal glands results in increased masculine characteristics which in the case of women may produce extremely masculine characteristics like the growth of beard and moustache.

The sex glands or gonads: The sex glands or gonads are different in different sexes. Men possess male gonads and women have female gonads. The male sex glands or gonads are located in the testes. The hormones produced by the testes are known as androgens. The female sex glands are located in the ovaries. The hormones produced by the ovaries are known as estrogens.

The underactivity or overactivity of these glands caused by the deficiency or excess of hormones secreted by them as well as by the co-acting influence of other glands like thyroid, pituitary and adrenal, not only affects the sexual growth and development of an individual but also his entire behaviour and developmental process. A slight imbalance of these glands can cause restlessness, anxiety and weakness. Our physical strength, morale, thinking and reasoning power and decision-making ability — all depend upon the functioning of these glands. In short, these glands are found to play a dominant role in one's life. Without their proper functioning, a man or woman finds difficulty in leading a happy normal life.

All the endocrine or ductless glands discussed so far exercise a great influence on the various aspects of growth and development. These glands affect the behaviour of an individual by controlling his emotional behaviour and physiological activities. In this way, they have a direct bearing upon the entire personality of an individual. Actually, the hormones secreted by these glands are the ones responsible for developing the typical personality characteristics in an individual. These hormones are circulated throughout the body and influence all those tissues on which functioning of body system, emotional actions and even thoughts depend. As Gardner Murphy remarks:

> These hormones, ultimately, may be regarded as bathing the nervous system, including the brain and all the organs of the body in their own appropriate chemical juices. (1968, p.52)

Thus, the hormones secreted by different endocrine glands control the behaviour as well as the overall personality development of an individual.

Physique or Somatic Structure

Physique or somatic structure besides being one of the important components of one's personality affects the personality development in a significant way. The somatic structure and physical characteristics of an individual concerning his height, weight, physical appearance, physical strength or general health, physical deformities and abnormalities, etc., influence the development of the personality of an individual. This influence is exercised in two ways.

(i) The individual's gain or loss in these physical characteristics may influence his style of life — his modes of behaviour action, tendencies, goals of life and the ways of striving towards these goals, etc. Every person walks a sizable distance along a course according to his strength and stamina and so is the case with the process of personality development.

(ii) The physique itself does not directly contribute towards the development of personality but the self image formed by the individual through the reactions of his associates and other members of the society to his physical appearance play a significant role. It makes him conscious of his superiority or inferiority and develops such complexes as to affect his behaviour pattern.

Body Chemistry

The chemistry of one's body also exercises a great influence in determining one's behaviour and developing one's personality. Our body gets essential energy for its functioning on account of the chemical changes going inside our body. Sugar is converted into glucose, food is digested, oxidation takes place through the intake of oxygen and a number of similar chemical reactions take place continuously in our body. Our behaviour and functioning is largely governed by our body chemistry. In case there is some irregularity or malfunctioning in our body chemistry, it seriously affects our behaviour and personality make-up. For example a slight increase in the amount of nervous fluid in the body may cause nervousness in the individual. Similarly, the low or high level of sugar in the body may seriously affect the physical and mental state of an individual.

Psychological Factors

Psychological factors play a big role in the functioning of human behaviour and development of one's personality. A few important ones are discussed as follows:

Intelligence and Mental Functioning

One's intelligence and mental functioning play a significant role in the development of his personality. How one behaves is almost determined by his power of intellect and adjustment involving learning, acquisition of knowledge and skills, besides the way of taking decisions and dealing with people and situations. In this way, the behaviour pattern of an individual is effectively controlled by his intellect and his personality is shaped according to the functioning of his mental powers.

Interests and Attitudes

The pattern of one's interests and attitudes try to colour one's behaviour, ways of looking towards the things and people, his learning and striving for the goals in his life. He tries to move towards the things and people in which he has interests and favourable attitudes and it determines the development of his personality.

Level of Aspiration and Achievement Motivation

One can get success in a designed direction depending upon the level of his aspiration and achievement motivation. He, who does not aspire or desire for a thing, cannot be expected to attain satisfactory progress. Those who have high achievement motivation are found to struggle for their accomplishment, demonstrating distinct life style in comparison to those who have no aspiration or, low achievement motivation.

Will Power

One's will power determines his way of behaviour and personality make-up. Persons with strong will power are found to be credited with emotional stability, decision-making ability and persistence, etc., while those with weak will power are found to possess negative traits in their personality.

Emotional and Temperamental Make-up

The emotional and temperamental make-up of an individual casts a strong influence over his behaviour pattern and personality development. The presence of negative and positive emotions, the quality of emotional maturity, his temperament and the organisation of habits, sentiments, etc., colour his way of behaving and dealing with the things, ideas and people. He reacts according to his emotional, potential and temperamental make-up and his personality is fashioned accordingly.

Social and Culture Determinants of Personality

Most of our behaviour is learned and learning is controlled mostly by the environmental factors lying in one's society and cultural set-up. Consequently, the development of one's personality is largely carried out by the following social and cultural determinants:

Home and Family

No matter what the traits of the personality are, their development and fundamental pattern is always initiated and directed by the life at home. From the very birth of the child, the parents and the home and family atmosphere provide the foundation for the normal growth and development of his personality. If the child finds a healthy atmosphere at home, he has all the chances to develop his personality in the right direction. On the other hand, a poor and uncongenial atmosphere develops into maladjusted personality. Following are some important constituents of home and family environment that influence the development of one's personality:

(i) **Parents:** Their education, personality characteristics, their emotional and social behaviour, their mutual affection, love and quarrels, their interests and attitudes, general character, etc., all play a major role in the personality development of a child.

(ii) **Parental attitude:** How they behave with the child and their overprotective or rejecting attitude towards him.

(iii) **Size of the family and birth order:** How many sisters or brothers does the child have, the number of male and female children in the family, his own birth order, etc.

(iv) **Economic and social status of the family:** Besides parents, the behaviour and personality traits of other members of the family also cast a desirable impact on the personality development of children.

School Environment

School atmosphere also contributes a lot in the development of the personality of a child. The personality characteristics of the teachers, headmaster, classmates, the teaching methods, curriculum, opportunities for co-curricular activities, the values and ideals maintained by the institution and the general atmosphere of the class-room and school — all influence the personality development of a child. This is why there is a great demand and rush for admissions in good and reputed schools as they try to provide all that is desired for the balanced personality development of children.

Other Factors in the Social Environment

Besides one's home, family and school influences, there are many other social agencies and institutions that play a vital role in the growth and development of the personality of a child which are as follows:

Neighbourhood: Its proximity to a child and his family makes it a potent factor for casting its influence on the behaviour pattern and personality of the developing child. Whatever a child observes in his neighbourhood, he tries to imitate. The playmates chosen from his neighbourhood not only provide him company but also affect his behaviour and set the direction of his personality development.

Religious institution: Religious institutions like temple, church, gurdwara and their religious activities, fairs, ceremonies, etc., make a silent and sound appeal for the shaping of a child's personality according to their ideals.

Other social groups and institutions: There are other social groups agencies and institutions like clubs, means of entertainment and communications (radio, television films), advertisement material, newspapers, magazines, and other material and literature that is available in the social environment of a child that are capable of casting a strong impact on the personality of developing children. A child sees crime and fight scenes on the television screen and they may prove quite enough for his bullying and aggressive behaviour in school or with his brothers and sisters at home. Similarly, he or she may be greatly influenced by the role of a character he has read in a novel and may like to imitate personality traits of that character in his own behaviour. In this way, what is observed and experienced in the society by children plays a significant role in his personality development.

The cultural environment: The cultural environment of a child possesses a vital potential for shaping and determining his personality. This environment is characterised by the mode of living of people of the society, caste, and social group to which the child belongs. How do these people think, eat, dress, feel, behave with each other, deal with strangers, respect the members of other sex and observe rituals and ceremonies, their style of living and philosophy of life, etc., cast a strong influence on the behaviour of developing children and their personality is almost fashioned and tailored according to the pattern of their cultural environment. A cultural environment in which parents and elders are neglected by the younger generation and no responsibility is shared for their looking after, especially in the old age will definitely shape the behaviour and personality of the concerned individuals in the same way. On the other hand, in Indian society where old cultural values of respecting the old are present, the behaviour patterns and personality of the young and old generations will be tailored differently with a respect and a feeling of obligation towards each other in the environment of mutual love, cooperation and trust.

In this way, the development of the behaviour pattern and personality of children is influenced and determined by many factors, things and conditions broadly categorised as biological, psychological, social and cultural determinants. However, these can never be said to act independently for exercising their influence on the development of the personality of an individual. The determinants, in one way or the other way, have affiliation with one's heredity and environment in the task of personality development of an individual. It is easy to think that all these three factors or determinants of personality act and interact with each other for influencing and shaping one's personality.

Development of an Integrated or Well-balanced Personality

Meaning and Definition of an Integrated Personality

There are many aspects and dimensions of one's personality and therefore there is a need of its development in all these aspects and dimensions known as physical, mental. social, emotional, moral, linguistic and aesthetic. The process of growth and development in general thus proceeds in a unified and integrated way in all the aspects and dimensions of one's personality. The growth and development in one aspect influences the growth and development in the other areas or aspects of one's personality. At any point of one's growth and development, we have to take judgment about the personality and behaviour of an individual by taking in view a united picture of the growth and development going around the different areas and aspects of his personality. Such evaluative judgment may help us draw a picture of what we term his integrated personality. It helps us to know what a person is in his or her totality. It tells us the full story of his growth and development along with the various aspects and dimensions of personality, his way of behaving, his interest and attitude, his health and temperament, his aspirations and limitations and as well as making predictions about his relations and behaviour in a particular situation.

Development of an integrated personality, thus, represents a balanced harmonious growth and development of one's personality in relation to its various aspects and dimensions. The concept of integrated personality, thus, runs quite contrary to any lopsided development of one's personality at the cost or expense of his development in the other aspects or dimensions of his personality. In view of such a nature and characteristic of one's integrated personality, we may try to define it in a formal way in the following words:

The term integrated personality stands for a total complete picture of the person involving an all round balanced growth and development of the personality in all its various aspects and dimensions (e.g. physical, mental, emotional, social, moral, linguistic, aesthetic, etc.) contributing towards the proper welfare of a person and society.

Characteristics of an Integrated Personality

A person possessing an integrated personality may be found to be characterised with the following characteristics:

1. He demonstrates a balanced growth and development in the various aspects or dimensions of his personality quite contrary to the concept of lop-sided development in one aspect at the expense of the others.

2. In the process of such development of his personality in an integrated way, there seems to be a close coordination and partnership between/among the different aspects of personality (e.g., physical development contributing towards the development in mental, social, emotional, moral areas and likewise)

3. A person equipped with an integrated personality is found capable of making adjustment well with his self and the environment. In comparison to the people not equipped with integrated personality he has little chances of falling victim to maladjustment, failures and frustrations.

4. The development of his personality in an integrated, harmonious and balanced way may help the person in turning out to be a competent or whole being in his self.

5. The person characterised with an integrated personality is fully capable of attaining his personal and social goals by utilising well his abilities and strengths in proper coordination with the available opportunities and environmental conditions.

Development of an Integrated Personality

The following means and measures may be found quite effective in helping the task of the development of an integrated personality among children.

1. What is an integrated personality? What are the characteristics of an integrated personality? What is the role of a child's integrated personality in contributing towards personal and social welfare? The knowledge of these things is very necessary on the part of all — parents, elders, teachers and all those who are entrusted with the responsibility of developing the personality of children.

2. In providing education and caring for the bringing up of children, the parents, members of the family, teachers and the community all should try to make appropriate provisions of congenial environment, opportunities and facilities helpful for the balanced development of their personality.

3. The attempts made for helping children in their personality development should be controlled and coordinated in such a manner so as to allow them to get imbibed with an integrated personality. Care should be taken here as not to

allow the development in a particular aspect like physical, social, etc., to come in the way of developing other aspects or dimensions of their personality.

4. In case when a particular aspect or dimension of a child's personality gets developed in a substantial way, its development should be channelized as proving helpful rather than providing obstacles in the path of his development in other aspects or dimensions of personality. "His intellect is like a mouse and physical development is like an elephant;" such type of remarks tell the story of lop-sided development of one's personality. The occurrence of such lop-sided development in the personality of the children should be avoided.

5. The children should be properly told that they should always strive for attaining a well-balanced amount of integrated personality. They should also spend a required time and energy on their physical development and social/moral development in addition to that spent on their study and intellectual development. In fact, they should try to chalk out a wise plan for their development in all the dimensions of their personality by taking care of the principle of time and resource management in a proper way. They should always care that the developmental work should proceed in a well-coordinated, cooperative and integrated way resulting into a well-balanced personality.

6. In this way, the task of developing an integrated personality needs the well-coordinated efforts on the part of all stake holders such as teachers, parents, family members, community, etc., besides expecting the fully determined and motivated efforts on the part of children themselves. If tried in a properly united way, then it is quite possible to hope well for the development of integrated personality among children contributing towards their individual and social progress.

Summary

In associating with one's personality with his outward appearance or external behaviour, etc., we have developed certain wrong notions about the term 'personality'. It has resulted in evaluating one's personality exclusively in terms of his appearance, physical manners, character, temperament, etc. Although all these attributes of one's self need to be included in evaluating one's personality, yet it is wrong to equate personality with any of these attributes or even with the sum of all these attributes. Personality includes everything about a person. However, it is not just a collection of so many traits or characteristics that is known as personality. It may be defined as a complex blend of a relatively enduring but constantly changing pattern of a person's unique behaviour evolved as a result of his interaction with his environment.

Factors or determinants of personality refer to those things and factors that play a determining and decisive role in the development of one's personality. These can be broadly classified as internal and external factors or determinants of personality. Internal or personal factors refer to those things or factors that lie internally within the individual (like his physique, sex, interests, attitudes, etc). On the other hand, external or environmental factors are linked with the forces of environment lying outside the individual like impact of physical environment, social, cultural environment, etc.

All these internal and external factors or determinants of one's personality can be re-grouped or categorised in three distinct types — Biological, Psychological and Socio-cultural determinants of one's personality.

In the category of biological determinants of personality, we can include factors or things such as (i) hereditary influences transmitted at the time of child's conception through genes and chromosomes, (ii) the structure and functioning of one's nervous system, (iii) the nature of the secretion of specific hormones by ductless or endocrine glands, (iv) one's physique or somatic structure and (v) one's body chemistry.

In the category of psychological determinants, we can include factors or things such as one's intelligence and mental functioning, interests, attitudes, the level of aspiration and achievement motivation, will power and emotional as well as temperamental makeup.

In the category of socio-cultural determinants of one's personality, we may include all those factors lying in one's cultural and social environment which are responsible for influencing and shaping one's personality. The area of influence of these factors may start right from one's home and family. Here the parents, their personality characteristics, behaviour and attitude towards the child, size of the family and birth order and economic as well as social status of the family prove quite a potent factor in shaping one's personality. School environment linked with the personality characteristics and behaviour of teachers, classmates, school authorities and experiences encountered by the child in the shape of curricular and extra-curricular activities all prove quite effective in shaping the personality of a child. The other factors lying in one's socio-cultural environment like impact of neighbourhood, religious institutions, social groups, clubs, means of entertainment and communication, the cultural traditions, attitudes and mores prevailing in one's society all have a great potential in exercising control over the development of one's personality.

We should always keep in mind that all these types of factors or determinants of one's personality, categorised in whichever ways, can't work independently or mutually exclusive to each other. In one way or the other, these are associated with the hereditary and environmental influences to which we human beings are exposed since our conception till death. Therefore by all means we must regard the development of our personality as a coefficient of friction between ourselves and the environment.

In our all attempts of rearing and educating children we always aim to help them in the attainment of **an integrated personality,** i.e., seeking an all round balanced growth and development of their personality in relation to its various aspects and dimensions (e.g., physical, mental, emotional, social, moral, linguistic, aesthetic, etc). The concept of integrated personality, thus, runs quite contrary to any lop-sided development of one's personality at the cost or expense of development in the other aspects or dimensions of his personality.

An individual characterised with an integrated personality presents a total picture of his complete development in all the aspects and dimensions of his growth and development. He is fully capable of attaining his personal and social goals by (i) making his adjustment with the self and his environment and (ii) utilising well his abilities and strengths in proper coordination with the available opportunities and environmental conditions.

The task of developing an integrated personality needs the well-coordinated efforts on the part of all the stake holders such as teachers, parents, family members, community personnel, etc., besides the involvement of the fully determined and motivated efforts on the part of children themselves. For this purpose teachers, parents and elders first need to be well acquainted with the concept of an integrated personality and the methods and measures for the attainment of the same. The children in the form of self-education, as well as through the formal and informal educational and training procedures then should be well oriented, and helped for the attainment of an integrated personality under the guidance, and direction of well-intended adults, peers and other well wishers.

References and Suggested Readings

Adler, A., *Practice and Theory of Individual Psychology*, Harcourt Brace and World, New York, 1927.

Allport, G.W., *Personality – A Psychological Interpretation*, Holt, New York, 1948.

– – –, *Pattern and Growth in Personality*, Holt, New York, 1961.

Bhatia, H.R., *Elements of Educational Psychology*, 3rd ed., Orient Longman, Calcutta, 1968.

Cattell, R.B, quoted by C.S. Hail and G. Lindzey, *Theories of Personality*, (2nd ed.), John Wiley, New York, 1970.

Eysenck, H.J., *Dimensions of Personality*, Kegan Paul, London, 1947.

– – –, *The Structure of Human Personality*, 3rd ed., Methuen, New York, 1971.

Freud, S., *An Outline of Psychoanalysis*, Hogart, London, 1953.

Hall, C.S. and Nordby, V.J., *A Primer of Jungian Psychology*, New American Library, New York, 1973.

Hall, C.S. and Lindzey, G., *Theories of Personality*, 3rd ed., John Wiley, New York, 1978.

Janis, I.L., and Mahl, G.F. et al., *Personality Dynamics, Development and Assessment*, Harcourt Brace, New York, 1969.

Murphy, Gardner, *An Introduction to Psychology*, Oxford & IBH, New Delhi, 1968.

Prince, Motion, *The Unconscious*, Macmillan, New York, 1929.

Watson, J.B., *Behaviourism*, Kegan Paul, London, 1930.

– – –, *Behaviourism*, Norton, New York, 1970.

22

Parenting Styles or Child Rearing Practices

Meaning of the Term Parenting Styles or Child Rearing Practices

The term child rearing practices in its word meaning stands for the practices adopted for rearing or bringing up children by their parents. In its technical language, in psychology it is termed as parenting styles or practices of child rearing. The practices or styles adopted by the parents in rearing their children are quite unique in their nature and are largely determined by the factors like (i) influence of one's own parents and culture, i.e., they learn (copy or select) rearing practices from their own parents and culture in which they grow and develop; (ii) temperaments of children; (iii) their own temperaments; (iv) the circumstances and environment in which they have to rear their children.

The Types of Parenting Styles or Child Rearing Practices

Parents may be found to adopt one or the other type of rearing practices or parenting styles for rearing or bringing up their children to help and guide them in the needed tasks of their growth and development, adjustment and progress in their life. In view of Diana Baumrind (1967), the famous sociologist cum psychologist known for putting up an effective theory of parenting style, there are four basic elements — responsiveness v/s unresponsiveness and demanding v/s undemanding that may be seen involved in shaping one or the other practice or style adopted by the parents in rearing their children. These basic elements in their respective combination may give birth to four types of rearing practices or parenting styles such as: (i) Responsiveness and demanding, (ii) unresponsiveness and demanding, (iii) responsiveness and undemanding and (iv) unresponsiveness and undemanding.

Based on these combinations, Maccoby and Martin (1983) have emphasised the following four major practices or styles adopted by parents for rearing their children:

1. Authoritative parenting style or child rearing practice
2. Authoritarian parenting style or child rearing practice
3. Indulgent child parenting style or child rearing practice
4. Neglectful child parenting style or child rearing practice

Let us discuss these practices along with the influences they may carry on developing children.

Authoritative Parenting Style or Child Rearing Practice

In such practice or style there is proper positive integration of the elements' responsiveness and demanding, turning it into responsible and balanced parenting in a true sense. The main characteristics or features of such integration may be outlined as follows:

(a) **The element of responsiveness:** Parents exhibit responsiveness in rearing their children in terms of the following:

— They try to understand the feelings of their children and teach them how to regulate them.

— They help them in solving their problems by providing appropriate outlets and opportunities for doing so.

— They have desired interaction with their children by having communication channels open for verbal dialogues. Moreover in such communication they remain reasonably warm and caring.

— They do not believe in dictatorship and strict control, and thus allow their children to have freedom of exploration and make their own decisions based upon their own reasoning.

— Their approach in the rearing of their children remains mainly a child-centred approach instead of the parent-centred approach. They care for nurturing the needs, expectations, wishes and aspirations of their children instead of trying to fulfil their needs, expectations and desires.

(b) **The element of demanding:** On the other hand, parents remain quite watchful of the interests and welfare of their children by putting demands as follows:

— They set limits and expectations before their children for their growth and development in various dimensions of their personality.

— For the achievement of these limits and expectations, they set clear standards and milestones of progress before their children and monitor their progress regularly for keeping them necessarily attentive and alert towards the realisation of their goals.

— They expect and demand maturity in the behaviour of their children in accordance with their age and stages of development.

— However in meeting these demands, they remain quite reasonable and democratic. That is why the authoritative rearing practice or style is known as the assertive democratic practice (assertive as well as democratic in its nature). It can be demonstrated in their parenting behaviour in the following manner:

— They are attentive to their children's concern and typically adopt a practice of forgive and teach instead of punishing or pushing the child on his failure to reach the set limits and expectations.

— In case they punish their children, they resort to it with great concern and positive outlook, i.e., not punishing the child but his undesirable behaviour and lack of attention. Moreover, they are quite homogeneous, impartial and fair in their punishments whether one is a girl or boy child. The punishment mode is never harsh and arbitrary and the reason or motive of punishing the children is also made quite clear to them.

Influence on the Development

This type of authoritative rearing practice or parenting style is supposed to carry a number of positive and desirable effects on the proper development and progress of developing children on the following grounds:

— It provides due encouragement for the children to grow and develop their capacities by providing them proper freedom and opportunities but in doing so it does not allow them to get out of track, and still places needed limits and controls on their actions. Therefore, in the adoption of such rearing practice, there are few chances for developing children to get lost or de-railed on their path to development.

— The children reared so are found to be quite self-satisfied in terms of the fulfilment of their basic needs — physical, social and emotional. They know the ways of channelizing their instincts and emotions and developing their basic potentialities by their own independent efforts.

— They are found to be quite sincere in their duties and remain disciplined in life by observing self-restraint and are law-abiding by nature. They have been observed to feel obliged to their parents in providing them all that is needed for their proper growth and development with a proper check on their independent activities.

In this way this type of rearing practice, is expected to result in children having a higher self-esteem, seeking independent self-growth with higher achievement motivation. It can help in maximizing all round expected development of children in all the dimensions of their personality with no ill effects or painful memories in their mind and it is why this type of rearing practice or parenting styles is considered as the most recommended style of parenting by child rearing experts.

Authoritarian Parenting Style or Child Rearing Practice

In adopting such a rearing practice, parents are observed to be more demanding and less or least responsive to their children's needs capacities desires and ambitions. They do not give opportunities to their children for the expression of their needs, desires or ambitions but impose their own will and expectations by enforcing strict disciplines, code of ethics and their own authority. Some of the distinguished features and characteristics of such a rearing practice or parenting style may be outlined as follows:

• It is absolutely a totalitarian or authoritarian style of parenting and rearing one's children in contrast to the previously mentioned authoritative or assertive democratic style of parenting.

- It is a rigidly controlled strict disciplinary style in contrast to the authoritative balanced style and totally loose, unbridled or uncaring parenting styles.
- It is characterised by high expectations of conformity and compliance to the rules and directions framed by the parents and allows little or no scope for open dialogue between parents and children.
- It represents a quite rigid, non-flexible, restrictive and punitive style where the parents expect their children to follow their direction without raising any question and seeking reason behind the orders issued, rules prescribed or boundaries fixed for their movements.
- The parents are all set to see that children are observing the rules and respecting their work and efforts are directed towards goals and limits decided for them by their parents with the least care of their potential capabilities desires and ambitions.
- Here the parents are selfish and think always about their own ambitions and self-interests to be served through the outcomes or accomplishment of their children with the least care whether they are willing or capable of coming to their expectations or not. They wish and push their children forcefully to achieve all what has been denied to them in the past, i.e., the parents not fulfilling their own desire of becoming doctors/engineers/IAS officers may adopt an authoritarian parenting style for enforcing strict, restrictive and punitive style to their one or the other children to develop and progress on the lines and limits of their own dreams.
- Parents adopting this style are seen to shut their eyes and ears to the needs and desires of their children. They are not at all responsive and sensitive to their children's feelings, rather they cause the repression of their wishes and inner feelings by enforcing their authority rules and strict discipline. They always make their children follow instead of giving them any space for choosing their own path or course of self-development.

Influence on the Development

Authoritarian child rearing practice or style of parenting is said to influence the development of the children in some of the following ways.

- They may become incompetent in taking their own decisions and solving their problems or planning and executing the tasks of their life. This is because they have been reared in circumstances where they have been made to merely follow and not to take any initiative/decision on their own.
- Their intellectual, emotional and social development suffer a great set back on account of being denied the needed essential opportunities and independent facilities for doing so in their early life by their authoritarian parents.
- Their instinctive and emotional energies do not find the suitable expression and outlet for the desired channelization, sublimation or catharsis in the environment surcharged with authoritarian code of conduct prescribed by their parents. As expected, the repressed wishes, unfulfilled desires and the uneasiness felt by

children in such slave-like conditions that prevails in authoritarian rearing, may force the children to develop serious behavioural and conduct problems. If the demands and descriptions are pushed too forcefully upon the children, they may either make them withdraw from positive work and efforts for progress or burst into social deviant, rebellion or delinquents.

- This type of parenting does not help children acquire the social skills and competencies needed for leading their life in a proper way. They can't learn and live with democratic principles and ways of life. The qualities of democratic living and good citizenship can hardly be developed among children brought up in such an authoritarian parenting style.

Indulgent Parenting Style or Child Rearing Practice

This type of child rearing practice or parenting style is employed by those parents who are responsive but not demanding. In this way indulgent child rearing practice or parenting may be termed as a style of parenting in which parents may be found to be highly responsive, indulged or involved with the care and look after of their children by giving them over protection, warmth and affection at the cost of caring for placing any demand, expectations or control on them. The main features or characteristics of this style of parenting may be outlined as follows:

- The parents are too much attached and involved with their children. They show great concern and responsiveness to the needs and desires of their children by blindly accepting them genuinely for the joy and happiness of their children.
- The indulgent parents are observed to offer almost everything demanded by the children from time to time without placing any demand from the parental side and expecting the children to behave in a certain way or regulate and control themselves in term of showing desired behaviour appropriate to their age and stage of development.
- Indulgent child rearing practice is termed as most permissive, non-directive or lenient in the sense that here the parents are too lenient and non-directive so as to remain always playing on the terms of their children. They are unable to frame any rules or principles to be followed by their children for their good behaviour or learning desirable habits for their needed progress and development.
- Indulgent parents, although quite high on responsiveness, warmth and affection, are found quite low in terms of their accountability towards their children for their adequate age-related progress and development. The child rearing practice adopted by them is termed as free ranger parenting where a ranger or care taker allows all freedom without taking notice that such unbridled freedom may prove harmful and dangerous to their normal growth and progress in the years to come.

Influence on Development

Indulgent child rearing practice or parenting style may influence the development of the growing children in ways outlined as follows:

- The children brought up in this environment never learn to control their own behaviour and always expect to get their way.

- They grow up as impulsive, unreasonable and immature children and may be observed to demonstrate socially irresponsible deviant and morally deficient behaviour in their teen and adult life in the shape of drug addiction, heavy drinking, delinquency or other anti-social behaviour.
- Brought up under excessive care such children are hardly able to learn independent ways of leading their own life. They depend on others to solve their problems and arrange for the needs of their life.
- Children reared in such a setup may have all possibilities of de-figuring or spoiling their future prospectus. Most of them turn out to be 'spoilt brats' proving to be a red signal for the welfare of their self and society.

Neglectful Child Rearing Practice or Parenting Style

This type of child rearing practice or style is employed by the parents who are quite careless, negligent and irresponsible in exercising their roles as the parents towards their children. They may be found as quite uninvolved, detached, dismissive or hands-off in exercising their parental duties in the desired way. In going through their own easy and convenient style, they make themselves neither demanding nor responsible to the needs and desires of their children. The main features and characteristics of this style of parenting may be outlined as follows:

- Parents adopting this rearing practice do not show any indulgence or involvement in their children's life. They generally remain disengaged, indifferent or neglectful to the needs and desires of their children.
- They remain undemanding and do not convey any expectation as a parent from their children. They do not frame any rules or regulation for their children to behave in a certain way and set no limits, targets or boundaries for their expected development and progress.
- They are quite low in warmth and are generally not expected to show their parental love and affection towards their growing children. Either they do not intend to devote their time for doing so or may feel it useless or harmful to the independent growth of their children.
- Neglectful child rearing practice is characterised with the absence of necessary emotional touch, intimacy, interaction and verbal communication between the parents and their children. There is no place of children's opinions, emotional feelings, desires and wishes in the parent-child relationship as parents are in no mood or time to attend to them. In spite of getting support for the satisfaction of their basic needs like food, housing, clothes or pocket money, the children are hardly able to get necessary emotional support, attention and care from their parents. They can't open their heart before their parents and seek support/ guidance for their needed development and progress.
- Neglectful parents do not earn any respect or liking from their children. Such children soon may take note of their parent's indifference or negligence towards them. They may understand that other things in their parent's life are more important to them than they are. It may add to an increased distance and wide gulf in their relationship with their parents. While living under one roof, such parents and their children live their life in their own ways.

Influence on Development

Neglectful child rearing practice or parenting style may influence the development of growing children in the ways outlined as follows:

• This type of setup is unable to fulfil the children's social and psychological needs. As a result, they may remain emotionally starved and socially undeveloped throughout their life.

• They may be grasped with the feelings of insecurity or unsafety as an outcome of the neglectful or indifferent attitude shown by their parents in their upbringing and look-after. It may create quite undesirable complexes in their minds, and at times coupled with the feelings of anxiety, depression or rebellion attitude on the part of the growing children.

• The neglectful rearing environment may provide the children a defective model of social relationships and emotional bonds among the members of the family. It may take roots in their behaviour for being practiced in future life.

• The unbridled freedom, coupled with emotional insecurity and lack of support may push the children to adopt withdrawal or rebellion behaviour in their life style. As a result they may be found to suffer from shyness, social and emotional incompetency, delinquent and antisocial behaviour in their adolescence and adult life.

With the mention of these four child rearing practices or parenting styles, it should not be understood that parents generally stick to one or the other of these four styles in words and deeds. In their practical approach, they try to pick up their own style in a mixed aspect depending upon many factors, such as, the way they were reared or brought up, their own views and considerations about good parenting, the child's temperament and ways of behaving, prevailing environmental situations and cultural contexts, giving weightage to their own needs and desires or ready to strive for their children's future success. Whatever parental style or rearing practice they may adopt in a particular situation, it is absolutely true that it is going to cast a great impact on the nature of the development of their children. Where the positive factors or conditions inherent in one's rearing practice positively favours the direction and magnitude of their children's development, the negative one's bring quite adverse and negative effects to their adequate development and future progress. The rearing conditions where parents themselves are involved in bigger conflicts, show downs and mutual distrust, show partiality and favour to one child at the cost of other, engage in over protecting and appearing unfair to the child in any way, provide the child with harsh and cruel treatment through verbal abusing or corporal punishment or deprive them with the needed love, sympathy, support, praise, attention or encouragement, may prove quite detrimental to the normal development and progress of their children. In most cases, it may prove a great cause for arresting the normal development of the children and turning them into a quite maladjusted personality harmful to their self and to society.

Summary

From their birth onwards during the developing years, children are usually brought up or reared by their parents. On this account, parents all over the globe are found to adopt their own ways and means referred to as styles of parenting or child rearing practices for the bringing up and rearing of their children. In general, the styles or practices adopted for parenting or rearing the children may be classified into four major types such as, (i) authoritative (ii) authoritarian, (iii) indulgent and (iv) neglectful child parenting style or child rearing practice.

In adopting an **Authoritative Parenting Style**, parents try to make use of their authority quite judiciously by maintaining a proper balance between their own responsibilities to rear their children and expectations from the children in return. They exhibit a considerable amount of responsiveness to their children's needs, capacities, desires and ambitions and in turn expect their children to progress in tune with their capacities and developmental opportunities provided to them. This type of parenting style helps maximum all round expected development of the children in all the dimensions of their personality with no ill effects or painful memories in their mind, and that is why this type of rearing practice or parenting style is considered as the most recommend style of parenting by child rearing experts.

In adopting the **Authoritarian Parenting Style** parents are observed to be more demanding and less or least responsive to their children's needs, capacities, desires and ambitions. They do not give opportunities to the children for the expression of their needs, desires or ambitions but impose their own will and expectations by enforcing strict disciplines, code of ethics and their own authority. As a result, this style of parenting may yield quite negative effects or outcomes in the development and progress of the children in the shape of (i) becoming handicap in taking their own decisions in solving their problems or planning and executing the tasks of their life as well as demonstrating the qualities of democratic living and good citizenship (ii) developing serious behavioural and conduct problems on account of the repressed wishes and the uneasiness felt by the children in the slave-like conditions that prevail in authoritarian rearing.

In adopting the **Indulgent Parenting Style**, parents may be found to be highly responsive, indulged or involved with the care and look after of their children by giving them over protection, warmth and affection at the cost of caring for placing any demand, expectations or control on them. As a result the children brought up in such an environment (i) never learn to control their own behaviour and always expect to get their way, (ii) demonstrate socially irresponsible deviant and morally deficient behaviour in their teen and adult life, (iii) are hardly able to learn independent ways of leading their own life and (iv) most of them turn out to be 'spoilt brats' proving a red signal for the welfare of their self and society.

The **Neglectful Parenting Style** is employed by the parents who are quite careless, negligent and irresponsible in exercising their roles as parents towards their children. In going through their own easy and convenient style, they make themselves neither demanding nor responsible to the needs and desires of their children. Their rearing practice results in neglecting their children to the extent of non-fulfilment of the children's social, psychological and educational needs and it can then eventually lead such children (i) to remain emotionally starved and socially undeveloped throughout their life, (ii) to be grasped with feelings of anxiety, depression or undesirable complexes and (iii) to adopt a withdrawal or rebellion behaviour in their life style.

References and Suggested Readings

Alizadeh, S., Abu Talib, M. B., Abdullah, R., Mansor, M. (2011), "Relationship between Parenting Style and Children's Behavior Problems". *Asian Social Science*. 7 (12): 195–200.

Baumrind, D. (1967), 'Child care practices anteceding three patterns of pre-school behaviour,' *Genetic Psychology*, Monographs, 75 (1), 43-88.

Erickson, E., (1950) *Childhood and Society,* New York: Norton.

Kathleen, Stassen Berger, (2011). *The Developing Person through the Life Span,* New York: Worth Publishing.

Maccoby, EE and Martin, J A. (1983). "Socialization in the context of the family: Parent-child interaction". In P. Mussen and E.M. Hetherington, editors, *Handbook of Child Psychology,* Volume IV: Socialization, personality and social development, chapter 1, pages 1-101. New York: Wiley, 4th edition.

Rivers, J., Mullis, A. K., Fortner, L. A., Mullis, R. L. (2012). "Relationships between Parenting Styles and the Academic Performance of Adolescents", *Journal of Family Social Work*. 15 (3): 202–216

23

Schooling of Developing Children

Introduction

Schooling of developing children plays quite a key role in shaping the present and future of their adjustment, development and progress in life. There is no exaggeration in saying that a man can be identified and known through the type of schooling and name of institutions where he has received his education. It is also true that every school has its own impression or reputation for being relatively good or bad. These are labelled so on account of what is available there to the students for their desirable stimulation and learning helpful in providing needed direction and magnitude to their development and progress. There are two types of things that make one's schooling the reason to become their fortune maker. One belongs to the environment and type of schooling available for his education in a particular school and the other is related to his own as a learner and developing individual.

In the first category we may include things like (i) men, material, resources and their effective utilisation; (ii) school culture including the ideals and motto of the school, type of discipline and image in public; (iii) the type of curricular and co-curricular experiences available for the necessary development and progress; and (iv) the type of interaction and relationship prevailing between and among human elements such as teachers, students, support staff and administration personnel; and (v) the nature of school-community relationships.

In the second category we may include things of an individual and personal nature such as (i) the potential of the student for his learning and development; (ii) nature of his inclination, motivation and will to learn and progress; (iii) his age and maturity level; and (iv) the type of environment and facilities available to him for his development and progress outside the school. It is not possible for us to discuss all these factors or things making the schooling of a child a more purposeful and rewarding experience. At present here in this chapter we would be focusing our attention only on the following issues related to the schooling of the developing children: (a) peer influences, (b) school culture, (c) relationships with teachers, (d) teacher expectations and school achievement, (e) being out of school and (f) overage learner.

Peer Influences

Peers available in school to the developing children in the shape of classmates and school mates and the type of relationships existing among the peers exercise a great influence in the adjustment, education, development and progress of developing children studying in a school. In brief we can summarise the nature and impacts of peer influences in the following ways:

1. Peer influences exercise a big impact in the acquisition of desirable and undesirable behaviour on the part of developing children in the form of the acquisition of habits, interests, attitudes, learning styles, ways of working and behaving, cooperating and competing with each other, and engaging in the activities helpful or damaging to their progress and well-being.

2. On - positive side, the impact of peer influences may take quite a favourable turn to the developing children in the shape of (i) inspiring and motivating each other, (ii) helping one another in their respective advancement with the true spirit of cooperation and collaboration, (iii) working as a role model for learning and acquiring many things concerning the curricular and co-curricular areas, and (iv) imbibing a number of useful traits, habits, skills, interests, attitudes and ways of behaving that could be helpful in their wholesome personality development.

    In this concern, we should not forget that It has been strongly emphasised by humanists like Bandura and constructivist like Vygotsky and Bruner (and also confirmed through working experience in a number of situations) that a child learns and understands in a quite amazing manner in the company of an able peer even much better than the class and subject teacher or instructor.

3. On the negative side, we may see that a bad company of the peers comprising the incapable and inefficient, careless and aimless, failures and frustrated, timid and cowardice, spoiled and delinquents, problematic and maladjusted, truant and backbenchers, bullies and aggressive, rule breaker and bad reputed may push the developing children consciously and unconsciously into the behaviour and action patterns of their companion peers.

4. In the era of pre-adolescence and adolescence, the effect or influence of peer behaviour on the developing children is so intense and deep that they may be found to ignore the advice and warnings of their dearest and respected elders or teachers for the sake of maintaining their ego and showing their loyalty towards their peer groups. They want to think, feel and act as their companions in peer group think, feel and do.

School Culture

The term community or society culture, as we know, stands for the ways of living and behaving of the members of the community. How they eat, dress, walk, talk and communicate among themselves; what are their mores and traditions, values and ideals; how they marry and care for their children and aged; how women folk are treated by the male members in general; what is their standard of living, thinking and behaving with each other; what is their past, present or expected future in terms of material and spiritual progress, etc., all such things and many more like these are encircled in the definition of the term community or society culture. Since, school is also a miniature society inhabited by a number of people aimed to achieve its goals, the same criteria may also be properly applied for defining its culture named as school culture.

Accordingly, the term school-culture may solidly stand for a number of things representing a school's physical, socio cultural and educational environment including the ways of working and behaving of the school community (comprising of the students, teachers and other employees, and administrative personnel including head of the institution). It can be termed as good and favourable or bad and unfavourable for the development and welfare of the students depending on the nature of things comprising school culture. In a school carrying a good reputation in terms of the school culture we may witness that:

- There is quite a peaceful environment prevailing in the school campus including the status of pollution and hygienic conditions for working and behaving of the students, teachers and other school personnel.
- There is proper cooperation, collaboration and coordination visible in the functioning and working of teachers and school administration.
- Students have all opportunities for the appropriate interaction with their teachers as well as among themselves.
- There are appropriate provisions in the school campus for guidance and counselling services to students. Appropriate provision also exists there for seeking cooperation and involving the parents and community for the welfare of the students.
- The school enjoys a good reputation in terms of the nature of its constructive discipline, its democratic setup governed through well-defined rules, its ideals and values for which it stands and is known, its past practices, history and achievements, future plans, etc.
- In a school campus there is nothing like bad company and bad peer influences available to the students in general for derailing them on their development and path to progress.
- Proper opportunities and incentives are available to students for going ahead on their academic pursuits, wholesome personality development and brightening of their future.
- The school is wedded to democracy and desirable ideals and values like multiculturalism, secularism, peaceful co-existence, equity and equality, goodness of modernisation, globalisation, etc. It is almost free from the evils and deficiencies like discrimination, prejudices, stereotypes and marginalisation prevailing in society.

In schools carrying bad reputation in terms of the school culture we may usually witness the absence of the earlier-cited virtues and goodness helpful in the appropriate development and well-being of developing children. Contrarily, it may be found to be gripped with a number of problems and characterised with quite an unhealthy and unfavourable environment, and unpleasant and undesirable things going on in its campus and working places. There could be cases of disagreements, heated arguments, disharmony and leg-pulling among teachers, students and administrative personnel. Such a school stands for earning money and there is no place for ideals and moral values for the working and behaviour of the school personnel and students. The students have no respect for their teachers and school, and even feel guilty of being there in such a school. There is free entry of outsiders for spoiling the congenial environment of the school. It is quite usual scene to find students wandering aimlessly in the school campus, smoking, playing truant, coming late to the school and seeking late entry into running classes, or disturbing the peace of the institution by their problematic, unsocial and immoral behaviour.

The impact and influences of the healthy and unhealthy school cultures are also obvious. Where the schools having healthy culture are the most sought after and demanding by the parents for the admission of their children, those gripped with an unhealthy school culture remain the discarded ones and work as the last resort or only option for one or the other compulsion.

Relationships with Teachers

Teachers stand to be quite a potent factor in helping developing children in their desired learning in schools. The task of desired modification of the behaviour and wholesome development of their personality can only be performed with the active involvement and conscious efforts of the teachers in this connection. A teacher has to understand a student well in terms of his abilities, capacities, strengths and limitations for setting his learning path and guiding him on his learning path for the realisation of the set goals. For this purpose he needs to be in constant touch with his student and it can only be possible if the relationships between the teacher and student are mutually satisfying, cordial and respectful. The continuity of a teaching-learning act also can only be ensured on effective lines if there is no hurdle in the communication and exchange of opinion between teacher and student. Such effective communication can also be properly possible with the help of mutually satisfying cordial relationship between the teacher and student. In schools it is the learners whose interests are specifically watched by all. In fact all what stands in the schools in terms of men-material facilities and their organisation is essentially meant for looking after the interests of students and it can be effectively materialised with the active and satisfying relationships between teachers and students.

In case we try to visualise the significance of such healthy relationships from the view point of the students we may see that it is most essential for them to have quite satisfactory, cordial and trustworthy relationships with their teachers. The importance of having such healthy relationships can be realised on the grounds mentioned below:

1. Teachers are found to take much interest in classroom teaching and working with their students for guiding their learning path in cases where they find that their students pay due respect and listen to their advice and instructions in a proper way. In the absence of such a satisfactory relationship with their students they lose interest and begin to observe mere formalities with no real intention and absorption in their teaching and guiding assignments and this affects the learning outcomes of the students in quite an adverse way.

2. In the cases when a teacher is found to make negative opinion about a child related to some or the other negligence on the part of student regarding his

learning or about his misconduct and improper behaviour on one or the account, the same may be continued for a long time in the absence of a proper dialogue between them. The things can come on the right lines only when a satisfactory relationship exists between them for doing so at the right time in a right way. In its absence a vicious circle may start. The teacher may think that the student is wrong, he is careless and not serious at all about his learning or he is problematic, mischievous and spoiled and so he ignores or dislike him or punishes him in his own way. The child feels that it is not proper on the part of the teacher to behave with him in such a way; he is jealous of him or is prejudiced on account of his being a part of a different caste/gender/religion/region, etc. He shows his displeasure in one way or the other and his disrespectful or reactionary behaviour may further antagonise the teacher for taking further action against him and thus the gulf between the teacher and student gets increasingly wide. The ultimate sufferer is the student as he begins to lose his emotional balance and is distracted from his real goals.

3. In an environment where there prevails proper goodwill, mutual love and respect, and faith and trust in the intention and working of each other, teachers and students both find great opportunity for enjoying their efforts of teaching and learning. Students have the feeling that they are with their teacher for telling them about their fallacy, guiding them at the time of their needs, praising them at the time of their right step, and warning them about the inherent dangers and the same helps them much in their desired progress and career building. Nobody can match the magic of the teachers in guiding and enlightening the path of students in situations where a bond of the desired satisfactory relationships exist between the teacher and students. In its absence neither a teacher can teach well nor his students may learn well in the manner they are supposed to learn, for their proper development and well-being.

Teacher Expectations and School Achievement

Teachers who try to understand their students in a proper way are always in a position to have prediction about the success or failures of their students in one or the other ventures of their learning pursuits. Based upon their knowing about their students they may have certain expectations of one or the other nature from their students in relation to their progress and well-being. These expectations may range from quite a high level to a quite discouraging level of achievements expected from the students in one or the other learning pursuit at one or the other learning situation. These expectations made about their students by their teachers carry a wide significance in relation to the development and well-being of the developing children on account of their capability of exercising positive as well as negative influences on the achievements of the children in the way discussed and outlined below.

Positive Impacts and Outcomes

1. Expectations and aspirations of the teachers about their students are the first step for initiating and igniting the flame of determination and will power to do and perform one or the other tasks on the part of the students in such an

effective way as to turn their efforts into the real stories of their success much in line with the expectations and aspirations of their teachers.

2. It can be properly seen that the students who are high in the eyes of their teachers receives much attention, care and guidance on the part of their students in comparison to others. They are the favourable ones and thus receive more time to perform experiments in the laboratories, much time and facilities for carrying out their practice work and are helped more in learning the things in a more effective way and in a large amount with the expectations that they are going to bring name and fame to the teachers and the institution. Such special individual attention and extra facilities provided to them may help these students in excelling others in terms of their achievements and performances.

3. The expectations of the teachers from the students in a positive note may in still the favoured students with a new sense of motivation and expectation from their self. They are seen to have more self-confidence, self-efficacy and self-esteem in comparison to those who are estimated as incapable or inefficient in the eyes of the teachers and are thus consequently seen to surpass others in terms of good performances and high achievements.

Negative Impacts and Outcomes

1. A quite high expectation of the teacher from a developing child much above his underlying capacities and abilities may frustrate the teacher and students both in terms of the actual achievements and performances resulted through their efforts. It may adversely affect the self-confidence, self- esteem and self-efficacy of the developing children for their further learning and achievements.

2. The children with low expectations from their teachers begin to underestimate and see themselves through the eyes and expectations of their teachers in spite of the presence of required abilities and capacities for doing and performing in a better way than the teacher's expectations. It proves quite damaging to their progress and achievements in tune with their actual potential.

3. The mind-set of the teacher about the low expectation or discouraging outcomes from a student may naturally drift the teacher to pay less attention and ignore him at the time of usual classroom teaching and working in the laboratories. He may not encourage him to take initiative for the creative and constructive activities or engaging in useful projects and practice work with the assumption that it will not serve any useful purpose in developing their achievement and performance level. A negative attitude of the teacher and painting a student as a student of no hope or less expectation may thus push the student towards under-achievements and failures with no fault of him.

Being Out of School

It can be easily seen that a child spends a quite lot of time outside the school environment in proportion to the time spent by him in school. In a large proportion of his daily time schedule he thus lives and shares the experiences received by him at his home and family, neighbourhood, company of his peers, and community or society to which he belongs. The experiences received by him at these places for a considerable long period although seem to be quite unorganised and informal in nature in comparison to schooling, yet these are quite capable of providing their imprint on the adjustment, development and progress of the developing children in a considerable way. Let us try to see and analyse their impact.

1. The knowledge and understanding acquired and the skill learned about the various subjects and activities in school may get reinforced and intensified in proportion to the type of environment and facilities available to them outside the school for their enrichment, practice and application.

2. What is true for the fixation of cognitive and conative changes in children's behaviour is also true for the changes brought out in the affective domain (such as acquisition of habits, interests, attitudes, values and ideals) through the learning experiences received in school. These changes in their affective domain get fixation or diminish and vanish from their minds and hearts in proportion to the type of experiences or feedback received from the interaction with social agencies other than the school. As a counter influence and impact of these out of the school experiences, the child may be found to adopt or follow what is available for him or practiced in general by the people at his home, neighbourhood, community and other social agencies like temple, social clubs and propagated and communicated through newspapers, radio, television, and movies or websites and internet communications. As a practical individual he may choose to keep in his memory and practice what is more workable in practical life and more often it stands quite contrary to the school learning. He may then conclude that the school learning is merely meant for adding to his general knowledge, passing the examination and getting grades, receiving certificates and degrees. For example if a child learns that one should be truthful and honest in his behaviour and dealing but is bombarded by the experiences outside the school in quite contrary ways, he is more likely to be influenced and act according to what is ingrained in his mind through the experiences he receives during the period spent outside his school, which is much larger in proportion to the time spent in school.

3. The school learning as we see is totally cut off from what happens actually in the outside school environment. It is merely theoretical and does not match with the actual happenings in life. It cannot teach the child to acquire what is actually needed by him in leading his present and facing the actual necessities and problems of life. It is the practical outside experiences available in the out of the school environment that can help in supplementing what is learned in school for leading a successful life.

Overage Learner

In reference to a particular class or grade of the school, the term overage learners is referred to the learners who are much more in age then the average age ought to be for studying in that very class or grade. Let us make it clear by a simple analogy. A child is entitled to get entry into class I of an elementary school at the age of completion of 5 years. Accordingly, at the time of his studying in class VII he should be running in the age period of 11-12 years (in case he regularly passes out every class in one year). The average age of children thus studying in class VII should also lie approximately between 11 and 12 years. Now if the age of a child studying in class VII is considerably much more than the age period of 11-12 years, let's say 14 years or more, he is designated as overage learner — a learner who has passed away the average age of studying in that class. In this way, an overage child is generally older and more mature than other children studying with him in a class. In case if it is pointed out that how does one turn into an overage learner, the reasons for becoming an overage learner may be traced out as follows:

(i) One's getting entry in to class I of an elementary school relatively at a quite increased age.

(ii) His inability to pass out one or the other classes or grades in the prescribed time of one year.

(iii) His leaving out of school in between for one or more years for one or the other reasons.

Now the next question arises then after all what is the hitch of his being overage? Does it affect him or his classmates in any way and if so how? Let us think about it:

1. An overage learner may face difficulty in getting himself adjusted with the physical environment available in the classroom, laboratories and workshops planned and organised for the average age learners. For example, there may be small size chairs, desks and working tables, appliances and work instrument especially suited for younger and small children and certainly in this situation he may face a lot of difficulty in adjusting along with his classmates.

2. An overage child may face problems in terms of his academic adjustment while studying along with the children of the younger age in a particular class or grade. As we know, the teaching-learning task in any teaching-learning situation is always planned, organised and executed in view of the average age of the students studying in that class. Since the method of teaching-learning and execution of work activities does not match with his age and maturity level, the overage child has to face a lot of maladjustment on this account.

3. An overage child may also face a number of problems in relation to his socio-psychological adjustment and development such as:

(i) He has difficulty in establishing friendship and having useful interactions with his classmates on account of age difference and maturity level.

(ii) He faces rejection on the part of his classmates in play activities and games on account of his being much older than them.

(iii) He also faces much difficulty in getting along with his classmates in a number of co-curricular activities.

(iv) He feels a sort of guilt on account of his being overage. The same is also constantly reminded to him by his teachers and classmates on one or the other grounds.

    (v) He feels a sort of restlessness, anxiety and stress on account of lagging behind in the level of education and development needed for his age.

4.   The academic difficulties suffered by overage children coupled with their socio-psychological maladjustment may push them towards possessing a problematic and delinquent behaviour such as playing truant, bullying, becoming a drug addict, or falling in the company of socially undesirable individuals.

Summary

Schooling of developing children plays quite a key role in shaping the present and future of their adjustment, development and progress in life. However, such positive impacts of the schooling depend to a great extent on the congenial environment and appropriate facilities available in the schools. Some of the mentionable factors or elements associated with good schooling of developing children may be named as (a) peer influences, (b) school culture, (c) relationships with teachers, (d) teacher expectations and school achievement, (e) being out of school and (f) overage learner.

The term "peer influences" represents the influences or impact left over the adjustment, education, development and progress of the developing children studying in a school by peers in the shape of classmates and school mates and the type of relationships existing among peers. In this regard, peer influences are found to result in the acquisition of desirable and undesirable behaviour on the part of developing children in the form of the acquisition of habits, interests, attitudes, learning styles, ways of working and behaving, cooperating and competing with each other, and engaging in the activities helpful or damaging to their progress and well-being.

The term "school-culture" may solidly stand for a number of things, representing school's physical, socio cultural and educational environment including the ways of working, and behaving of the school community (comprising of the students, teachers and other employees, and administrative personnel including head of the institution). In the schools carrying commendable reputation in terms of the school culture we may usually witness the presence of all the appropriate virtues and goodness in terms of the proper behaving and working of human elements of the school helpful in the appropriate development and well-being of developing children.

"Relationship of the students with their teachers" in school and outside the school carry quite a strong impact over the adjustment, learning, and overall wholesome development of developing children. In fact, nobody can match the magic of the teachers in guiding and enlightening the path of the students in their learning and development. But it can be properly possible only when there is a cordial and healthy relationship between the teachers and students.

The term "teacher expectation and school achievement" stands for the type of expectations held by the teachers from their students in terms of their school performances or achievements. These expectations may range from a high level to a quite discouraging level of achievements expected from the students in one or the other learning pursuit at one or the other learning situation. These expectations made about their students by their teachers carry a wide significance in relation to the development and well-being of the developing children on account of their capability of exercising positive as well as negative influences on the achievements of the children.

The term "being out of school" stands for the time spent by school going children in the vicinity outside the school environment in the shape of living and sharing his daily time schedule and experiences at his home and family, neighbourhood, company of his peers, and community or society to which he belongs. The experiences received by him at these places for a considerable long period although seem to be quite unorganised and informal in nature in comparison to schooling, yet these are quite capable of providing their sizable imprint on the adjustment, development and progress of the developing children in a considerable way.

The term "overage learners", in reference to a particular class or grade of the school, stands for the learners who are much more in age then the average age ought to be for studying in that very class or grade. An overage learner is a misfit in the environment of the class, learning places and other experiences planned and designed for the learners of the normal age. As a result, he is bound (i) to experience difficulties with the physical environment and facilities, (ii) to face problems in terms of his academic adjustment while studying along with the children of the younger age, (iii) to experience a number of problems in relation to his socio-psychological adjustment and development such as establishing friendship and having useful interactions with his classmates on account of age difference and maturity level.

References and Suggested Readings

Bandura, A. & Walters, R.H., *Social Learning and Personality Development*, New York: Holt. 1963.

Biggie, M.L. and Hunt, M.P., (1968), *Psychological Foundations of Education*, New York: Harper and Row.

Brunner, J.S., *Culture of Education*, Cambridge MA: Harvard University Press, 1996.

Gates, A.I. and Jersild, A.T., *Educational Psychology*, New York: Macmillan 1970.

Hurlock, E.B. (1959), *Adolescent Development*, New York: McGraw Hill.

Vygotsky, L.S., *Mind and Society: The Development of Higher Mental Process*, Cambridge, M.A.: Harvard University Press, 1978.

Woolfolk, Anita, *Educational Psychology* (Ninth edition), First Indian Reprint, New York: Pearson, 2004.

24

Behavioural Problems of the Growing Children

Behavioural Problems of the Growing Children: Meaning and Types

Children are the real assets of a society or nation as the progress, welfare and future of a society is essentially linked with the development and progress of its children. It is the duty of parents and teachers for providing them all assistance that is needed for their proper growth and development. For this purpose, the children should be well understood in relation to their age-linked developmental needs. They may face difficulty in maintaining proper interaction and relationship with their peers, family members and teachers. It may cause them to fall victim to one or the other types of behavioural problems. In this regard, it is rightly said that as long as one feels satisfied or has hope for their satisfaction, he feels adjusted to his self and environment. Dissatisfaction or failure in this regard may drift him towards adjustment to his self and the environment making him a victim of one or the other types of behavioural problems. All such behavioural problems are quite common and universal existing at all stages of our life span ranging from infancy to old age. However, these are most common and usual with children and adolescents. The reason simply can be accounted in their lack of necessary maturity and understanding for coping with the needs of the environment. That is why they fall easy victims to the following behavioural problems:

(i) Bed wetting, (ii) nail biting, (iii) autism, (inability to relate socially), (iv) thumb sucking, (v) temper tantrums, (vi) lying, (vii) truancy, (viii) stealing, pick-pocketing and other types of juvenile delinquency, (ix) bullying or fighting, (x) hair plucking, (xi) phobic reaction against insects like cockroach, spiders, lizards, etc., (xii) speech disorders like stammering, (xiii) too much tearfulness and anxious, (xiv) copying, (xv) negativism, (xvi) sexually deviant behaviour, (xvii) substance or drug addiction.

These examples of children and adolescent behavioural problems may clearly reveal that their behaviour related with such problems is essentially far from the otherwise normal behaviour expected from them at their age level. It is noticed and takes into others cognition only because it is somewhat different from the expected or otherwise normal behaviour. It becomes a subject of serious consideration only when it is grown and committed in such a way that it becomes a problem for parents, classmates, neighbours, other elders or society as a whole. In this way a behaviour which is somewhat away from the normal is entitled to be included in the category of problematic behaviour only when it reaches a point of causing problems to the individual himself as well as to the members and resources of the society.

However such problems in a child or adult has abnormality only in terms of the problem-related behaviour or otherwise he is as normal as normal as others. It is not essential for him to demonstrate the signs of other types of abnormalities or mal-adaptation like mental retardation, physical or mental handicaps, immorality or criminal record, neurotic or psychotic disorders etc. In this way children or individuals affected with behavioural problems should never be confused with individuals suffering from developmental disorders and mental illness.

On the basis of what has been said earlier about the meaning and nature of the term behavioural problems, we are now in a position to define it in the following words:

The term behavioural problem or problematic behaviour stands for the type of behaviour of an individual which while causing a problem for his proper adjustment to self and the environment proves detrimental to his own well being along with the society.

In this chapter here however we would focus on the most challenging behavioural problems faced by the school going children such as aggression, bullying and substance- abuse or drug addiction.

Aggression

What is Aggressiveness?

Many times you must have come across with the people who try to demonstrate their dominance or assertion over other people bringing some sort of aggressiveness in their behaviour. Their behaviour may be seen to be coloured at this stage with a high intensity of emotion of anger, aggression and blind self-assertion. It may be their typical style of getting their way putting often down and thus seek their adjustment or fulfilment of their motive. Up to this point such behaviour may not cause much harm, because the victims of such aggression may find their own ways to deal with such excessive tone of assertiveness or aggression of cite aggressor. However, it becomes a problem in a situation when the individual begins to lose control over his emotions to the extent of causing harm to himself and others.

Children showing problematic aggressive behaviour may get engaged in the following behavioural activities:

- Pushing, kicking, biting, beating and hitting hard the victims especially the younger and weaker ones.
- Trying to throw and damage the articles, objects and immovable property.
- Using inappropriate language, expression and bad names while communicating with others.
- Forcing or thrusting their views or desires through their own ways like bullying, blackmailing, intimidation and manipulation.

- Providing a frightening or interning experience to others while letting them wondering what instigated such behaviour or what he or she has done to prompt aggression.
- Screaming and rolling on the floor in a threatening way.
- Beating the self including hitting the head with hard surfaces or objects.
- Disobeying and misbehaving with the elders in unsocial and uncivilised ways.
- Demonstrating a reactive behaviour, characterised with the feeling of insecurity and disturbed state of mind.
- Boasting braveness but proving their timidity before the stronger and more powerful children or adults.

Probable Causes of Aggressiveness

The following causes may be found to act behind the aggressive behaviour of the children:

1. Aggression is more likely to arise when a child is feeling hungry, thirsty, tired or sick. Children who want or need attention may also act aggressively to get it.
2. Children occasionally resort to aggression as a means of asserting themselves. You may notice a three year old who topples over a playmate's block tower. While this act may appear to an adult to be a sort of hostile takeover, it's more likely to be a declaration of independence, assertiveness or an attempt to initiate play, Nonetheless, children need to learn more appropriate vehicles of expression.
3. Children who witness violent behaviour either on television, in movies or at home are likely to imitate aggressive actions in their interactions with peers, teachers and family members, Likewise, children who are witness to or victims of abuse or violence at home or in school are likely to respond with temper tantrums in their play or any social situation.
4. Children who have not learned self-control often act aggressively. When the adults in their lives set clear and consistent limits, young children will eventually learn to set limits on their own behaviour. However, when children have limited or inconsistent guidance from parents and care takers, they have difficulty in recognising and monitoring their aggressive behaviours.
5. Children who have not learned more appropriate problem-solving techniques often resort to violence as a means to resolve conflict. When children become frustrated because their playmates don't share a favourite toy, a parent is busy talking on the phone or a sibling has got favour and recognition, they often respond with aggressive behaviour. Children need guidance in finding other strategies for solving these types of problems and venting their frustration.
6. Angry defiance may be associated with feelings of dependency and angry outbursts may be associated with sadness and depression. In childhood, anger and sadness are very close to one another and it is important to remember that much of an adult experiences as sadness is expressed by a child as aggression.

7. The uncongenial home and family environment may prove a germinating soil as well as nourishing agent for the aggressive behaviour of the child. When the child is unable to satisfy his basic physiological and socio-psychological needs, he begins to drift towards maladaptive styles of his behaviour including temper tantrum. In the environment, where a child feels, that he in unnecessary ridiculed, rebuffed and punished and is subjected to partial, prejudiced, cruel and unjustified behaviour at the hands of the elders he resorts to angry and aggressive behaviour for his self-defence to cover the feelings of insecurity or to take revenge.

8. Many times, the aggressive mode of the child's behaviour in the form of temper tantrums get linked with the reinforcement received by him through the satisfaction of his desires or needs through his temper outbursts. Once he realises his objectives through such means, he is habituated to repeat it whenever he needs so in future.

9. According to Adler, the famous psychologist belonging to analytical School of Psychology, the need to dominate or self-assertion is the prime motive or spring board of human behaviour. In some of the children, it is found in excess which may compel them for resorting to temper outbursts or uncontrolled rage in order to make others fearful and accept their dominance.

10. In some cases, biological factors may also play a decisive or side role for inciting or paving the way for sudden emotional outbursts and aggressive behaviour. The malfunctioning of the glands and nervous system may trigger off such situations in some or the other cases.

How to Deal with the Aggressive Behaviour Problem of the Children?

Handling children's aggression can be puzzling, draining and distressing for adults. In fact, one of the major problems in dealing with anger in children is the angry feelings that are often stirred up in us. It has been said that we as parents, teachers, counsellors and administrators need to remind ourselves that we were not always taught how to deal with anger as a fact of life during our own childhood. We were led to believe that to be angry was to be bad and we were often made to feel guilty for expressing anger.

It will be easier to deal with children's aggression if we get rid of this notion. Our goal is not to repress or destroy angry feelings in children — or in ourselves — but rather to accept the feelings and to help channel and direct them to constructive ends.

Parents and teachers must allow children to feel all their feelings. Adult skills can then be directed toward showing children acceptable ways of expressing their feelings. Strong feelings cannot be denied and angry outbursts should not always be viewed as a sign of serious problems; children should be recognised and treated with respect.

Although like other behavioural problems, aggression is to be handled as an individual case in itself. In general, the following points may prove quite helpful to parents, teachers and elders in dealing with aggression of their children:

1. **Try to anticipate a melt-down.** Being aware of when your child is feeling hungry, tired, sick or frustrated is your first line of defence against aggressive behaviour. If you know when aggressive behaviour is likely to strike, you can head it off with a diversion -food, a new activity or a break in the action.

2. **Encourage your child to use words for describing his feelings.** When your child seems out of control, help him talk about how he is feeling and let him know that you understand his feelings. I can see that you're feeling really angry right now because you want to stay at the playground. But it's time to go home now. Let your child know that it's okay to express his feelings in words. Help him to generate a list of words — angry, mad, sad, upset, grumpy, etc., for describing his feelings.

3. **Introduce acceptable strategies for dealing with aggression.** With younger children, it's sometimes helpful to offer an invigorating physical activity such as bouncing on a trampoline, running around the outside of the house three times or stamping their feet on the driveway to help them blow off steam.

   With older children (six and up), discuss appropriate times and places for handling anger. Teach children to count backward from 10 before acting out. If your child is on the verge of a breakdown in the middle of a shopping mall, remind her that a public place is not the appropriate spot, acknowledge her feelings and let her know that you'll discuss the situation with her as soon as you get home.

   Follow through with your commitment and be sure to give her plenty of time to vent her frustration. Children of all ages often find drawing a picture about a difficult moment or writing an apology letter to be a helpful cooling off technique.

4. **Set clear limits about aggressive behaviour.** Make sure your children understand the consequence of inappropriate actions and be consistent in following up on them. When your child initiates a loud tantrum during a play date, remove her from the situation immediately. Tell her, "It's not okay for you to behave that way. When you kick and scream, then we have to go home." Once you've established a rule, don't open it up to negotiation.

5. **Help your child develop appropriate problem-solving strategies.** With very young children, you'll have to initiate the technique. For example, with a two year old who's having difficulty sharing a favourite plaything set a timer so that each child has equal time.

   Encourage older children to work independently to develop solutions. Intervene only when necessary and limit your involvement. When siblings are arguing over the last cookie, state the problem and ask for solutions — "So, there's only one cookie left. What could you do so that all three of your could have a snack?" Then step back and let them negotiate with one another.

6. **Pay close attention to television viewing, video game playing and on-line surfing**. Set limits on the amount and type of television programming your children watch. Watch television along with your children and encourage discussion about program content.

   Don't be afraid to shut off an inappropriate program, prohibit violent computer games and closely monitor the on-line time.

7. **Choose books and movies that promote themes of kindness and assistance in finding appropriate books for children of all ages.** Reading aloud to children of all ages is a great way to promote conversations about values and appropriate behaviour. A family movie might provide an opportunity for similar conversations.

8. **Make a consistent effort to recognise kind behaviours**. Let children know that you value their kindness by pointing it out as often as possible. For example: "I noticed that you shared the last bit of Cheerio's with your sister this morning. That was very thoughtful." Making it clear that you expect good things and acknowledging positive acts will send a clear, motivational message to children.

9. **Hold male and female children to the same standards**. Many parents are tempted to follow the old "Boys will be boys" adage when it comes to managing aggressive behaviour. It's essential that both boys and girls learn to express their aggression appropriately. Make it clear that physical aggression will not be tolerated. At the same time, make sure that children of both genders are given ample opportunity to express their feelings.

10. **Be a supportive role model**. Above all, act kindly and compassionately toward your children and other family members as well as friends and strangers. Always use polite language toward your children and be sure to apologise for any unkind action. Avoid using sarcasm with children. Never respond to inappropriate behaviour with violent language or actions.

11. **Ease tension through humour**. Kidding the child out of aggression outburst offers the child an opportunity to "save face." However, it is important to distinguish between face-saving humour and sarcasm, teasing, or ridicule.

12. **Manipulate the surroundings.** Aggressive behaviour is mere likely to happen or reinforced by placing children in tough, tempting situations. We should try to plan the surroundings so that certain things are less apt to happen. Stop a "problem" activity and substitute, temporarily, a more desirable one. Sometimes rules and regulations, as well as physical space, may be too confining, Hence if you know what situations trigger temper tantrums in your child, try to avoid them.

13. **Use closeness and touching**: Move physically closer to the child to curb his or her angry impulses. Young children are often calmed by having an adult come close by and express interest in the child's activities. Children naturally try to involve adults in what they are doing and the adult is often annoyed at being bothered. Very young children (and children who are emotionally deprived) seem to need much more adult involvement in their interests. A child about to use a toy or tool in a destructive way is sometimes easily stopped by an adult who expresses interest in having it shown to him. An outburst from an older

child struggling with a difficult reading selection can be prevented by a caring adult who moves near the child to say, "Show me which words are giving you trouble."

14. **Use a time-out-briefly isolating the child immediately after the aggressive behaviour occurs**. Rather than scolding or physically punishing the child, place him in a quiet room or on a chair in the corner for a short period of time (many experts recommend one minute per year in age) in order to cool off.

15. **Try not to use physical punishment**. It may stop aggression temporarily, but there is evidence that in the long run such punishment may actually increase aggressive behaviour, probably because it conveys the idea that hitting is okay.

16. **Reinforce the non-aggressive and good behaviour** of the child immediately as and when it happens with your problem child.

17. **Reduce the time** your child spends with playmates who engage in aggressive behaviour.

A Five-Step Program to Reduce Aggression

1. Make a colourful chart with a space for each day of the week. If the child is young, divide each day into smaller intervals to accommodate a shorter attention span. Hang the chart on the wall.

2. For each time the child does not display aggression, give the child a sticker and help him place it on the chart. Say, "Good, you didn't hit" (or bite or kick, etc).

3. Supplement the sticker with a snack or treat or a few minutes of special attention.

4. After the child has gone a whole week without aggression (or a shorter time for a younger child), show him the stickers on the chart and say, "You haven't hit (or kicked, bitten, fought, etc.) for a whole week. Now, you've earned a special reward." This reward can be an outing with a parent, an extra period of time alone with mother, or anything you know your child would like. It should be unusual enough to motivate the child strongly.

5. When the child is aggressive, say, "no-hitting." At the end of the day of interval, show the child the chart and say "You didn't get a sticker this time because you hit."

Bullying

What is Bullying?

In its word meaning, bullying may be taken as a behaviour characterised well with the behaviour of a bull full of harassing and intimidating others especially the cow-like creatures of its own species. In the school context, it may be defined as an ongoing misuse of power and unwanted aggressive behaviour repeatedly demonstrated by a child (called bully) through his words and deeds to another child (called bullied) with the intention of causing him or her physical and/or psychological harm. It has real or perceived power imbalance in the sense that the bully seems to enjoy more physical strength, is relatively older and stronger in power and position than the bullied and is often assisted and encouraged by the members of his group. Bullying can involve an individual or a group misusing their power over one or more person It can happen in person or online, and may be obvious or hidden.

Types of Bullying

Bullying can happen anywhere at school, travelling to and from school, in sporting teams, or in a work place and activities going in and outside the school. In its occurrence, bullying behaviour may take a variety of forms as follows:

1. **Physical:** In this type of bullying a child is harmed physically, or economically through the bullying acts such as:
   - Slapping, hitting, pinching, punching, biting, kicking, pushing and shoving
   - Locking in a confined space
   - Making things to get one in trouble
   - Excluding from a group
   - Unwelcome touching.
   - Taking things, snatching or damaging belongings
   - Extortion

2. Verbal: In this type of bullying a child's feelings are hurt through the bullying acts like
   - Name-calling
   - Threatening and intimidating
   - Unwelcome teasing
   - Taunting
   - Spreading rumours, gossiping
   - racist or racial comments

3. Written or online bullying: In this type of bullying a child is threatened, harassed or intimidated by the bullying acts like
   - Threatening notes, and letters
   - Making silent or abusive phone calls
   - Sending insulting or threatening text messages,
   - Publishing someone's personal or embarrassing information online
   - Creating hate sites or starting social exclusion campaigns on social networking sites

Why do the Bullies Engage in Bullying?

- They think it's fun, or that it makes them popular or cool
- They want to impress or entertain their friends
- They feel more powerful or important, or they want to get their own way all the time
- They think that they will win or get what they want

- They feel insecure or lack confidence or are trying to fit in with a group
- They are fearful of other children's differences
- They are jealous of another child
- They are unhappy
- They do not even realise that they are hurting the other person
- They enjoy feeling power over someone because sometimes they are being bullied by someone else
- They are copying what they have seen others do before, or what has been done to them

The Role of Bystanders and Spectators in One's Bullying Behaviour

Most of the time bullying takes place with bystanders present. Bystanders are those who witness or know bullying is occurring. The way bystanders act has a major impact on bullying. Bystanders who are passive (take no action) or behave in ways that give silent approval (watching, nodding, walking away) encourage the behaviour to continue.

Why Don't Bystanders Step In?

- For fear of their own safety (now and later) or position in the group
- They think that someone else will help
- They are worried about making things worse
- They don't know what to do
- They think their actions won't make a difference
- They think it's none of their business
- They think the student being bullied deserved it
- They think it's fun to watch

The Impact of Bullying

Bullying has a negative impact on everyone involved; the target, the bully and the bystanders.

The impact over students who are bullied: Students being bullied are more likely to:

- Feel disconnected from school and not like school
- Have lower academic outcomes, including lower attendance and completion rates
- Lack quality friendships at school
- Display high levels of emotion that indicate vulnerability and low levels of resilience
- Be less well accepted by peers, avoid conflict and be socially withdrawn
- Have low self-esteem
- Have depression, anxiety, feelings of loneliness and isolation
- Have nightmares

- Feel wary or suspicious of others
- Have an increased risk of depression and substance abuse
- In extreme cases, have a higher risk of suicide, however, the reasons why a person may be at risk of suicide are extremely complicated

Impact on bullies: Students who frequently bully others are more likely to:

- Feel disconnected from school and dislike school
- Start doing poorly in school in matter of participation and achievements
- Come home with torn clothes, unexplained bruises, new clothes or other items, or money not accounted for
- Talk about responding to others in a way that may result in the school taking disciplinary action
- Demonstrate bullying behaviour to their siblings, neighbourhood and disrespect to their family members
- Get into fights, vandalise property and leave school early
- Be associated with an increased likelihood of theft, violent behaviour, delinquent acts and binge drinking

Impact on bystanders: Students who witness bullying may:

- Be reluctant to attend school
- Feel fearful or powerless to act and guilty for not acting
- Have increased mental health problems, including depression and anxiety
- Have increased use of tobacco, alcohol or other drugs

Impact on schools: When bullying continues and a school does not take action, the entire school climate and culture can be negatively affected. This affects student learning and engagement, staff retention and satisfaction and parental confidence in the school, which can lead to:

- The school developing an environment of fear and disrespect
- Students experiencing difficulty learning
- Students feeling insecure
- Students disliking school
- Students perceiving that teachers and staff have little control and don't care about them

The Remedial Measures for Controlling the Menace of Bullying

Bullying is a great menace and major problem in many of the schools. It affects badly the welfare and progress of the all connected and affected through this menace, i.e., the bullies, the bullied, the onlookers as well as the peace and progress of a school, family and society. The question that arises is how to get rid or put a reasonable restraint over the menace of bullying. The problem needs collaborative efforts form the part of all who are connected and affected through its consequences. Therefore we will be considering the role and contributions of each of the stake holders on this issue one by one. But let us first try to know why do some children turn to bullying. How and why do they pick up a bullying behaviour?

How Do the Children Imbibe the Skill and Habit of Bullying

Bullying is learned behaviour like other sorts of behaviour and habits acquired by the child in course of his upbringing and schooling. It is fashioned, designed and imbibed through the principles of classical and operant conditioning as well as social learning theory propagated by Albert Bandura. Let us see how do the children imbibe the skill and habit of bullying?

1. The children may learn bullying through direct experiences as well as indirect experiences. They may observe and witness the bullying behaviour of their elders at their home, neighbourhood, school, and other places of the social interaction and find it rewarding to those who resort to it as a habit of getting their way out. The bully may be his father, the elder sibling, or school mate or even a character of a movie or TV serial. Look at men who beat or intimidate their wives and scream at their kids. They've never learned to be effective spouses or parents. Instead, they're really bullies. And the other people in those families live in fear — fear that they're going to be yelled at, called names, or hit. Nothing has to be worked out, because the bully always gets his way. The chain of command has been established by force, and the whole mindset becomes, "If you'd only do what I say, there'd be peace around here." So the bully's attitude is, "Give me my way or face my aggression and be ready to face the consequences." When a child witnesses such behaviour of his elders, he may consciously and unconsciously adopt them as his role models, imitates their bullying acts and learns to imbibe the acts of bullying in his behaviour after finding the them as an easy way out for enjoying power, status and getting always his own ways without really trying to become capable of something worthwhile in his life.

2. The maladjustment felt by the children at their home, school and social company may also result in making them a bully. They are educationally and academically failed as well as emotionally and social starved souls in themselves who are grasped with the feelings of inferiority and fear of failing and social dejection. Their picked up bullying behaviour then works for them on temporary basis, a saviour of their lost honour and prestige before their peers. The varied reasons for their maladjustment and resorting to bullying behaviour may be summarised further as follows:

   • Some bully because they feel insecure. Picking on someone who seems emotionally or physically weaker provides a feeling of being more important, popular or in control.

   • In other cases, kids bully because they simply don't know that it's unacceptable to pick on kids who are different because of size, looks, race or religion.

   • In some cases bullying is a part of an ongoing pattern of defiant or aggressive behaviour.

- Some kids who bully at school and in settings with their peers are copying behaviour that they see at home. Kids who are exposed to aggressive and unkind interactions in the family often learn to treat others the same way. And kids who are on the receiving end of taunting learn that bullying can translate into control over children they perceive as weak.

3. In some cases the bullying behaviour of children may be the consequences of their learning helplessness, undiagnosed or diagnosed learning disability or educational and academic failure faced in the stream of our educational system. In such situations they may not get opportunities for learning the needed academic, social, emotional and problem solving skills for managing their strong emotions like anger, frustrations or insecurity and getting along well with their colleagues and expectations of their teachers and parents. As an easy way out then they try to practice the bullying behaviour and after finding them satisfying and rewarding imbibe them as a way of their usual behaving. Bullying behaviour may be satisfying to them as they don't have to learn problem solving, because they just threaten the other kids. They don't have to learn how to work things out because they just push their classmates or call them names. They don't have to learn how to get along with other people — they just control them. The way they're solving problems is through brute force and intimidation. So by the time that child reaches the adolescence, bullying is pretty ingrained — it has become their natural response to any situation where they feel socially awkward, insecure, frightened, bored or embarrassed.

Suggestions for Rectifying and Dealing With Bullying Behaviour

As already emphasised earlier, the problem needs to be solved with the cooperation of all who are connected and affected with the menace of bullying. Let us see what can be done by each of the stake holder.

The Role of Parents and School Authorities

Parents and school authorities are required to engage in the following activities for preventing as well as dealing with the incidence of bullying:

1. Producing own examples of good behaviour is the best thing that we elders can do for the welfare of our children. It is therefore needed on the part of parents, teachers and other members of the family not to indulge in unwanted aggressive and bullying behaviour among themselves and especially with the children.

2. As far as possible the children should be saved with any kind of emotional starvation and social isolation or getting maladjusted in any way at home or school. If noticed so, then suitable remedial steps should be taken without blaming and pushing them into acts of resentment and revolt.

3. It is advantageous to make children well aware about what a bully is and then set a standard that clearly warns them not to indulge in such behaviour in any way anywhere at home or school. It may help the children to remain conscious and alert to identify and stop the bullying behaviour, both in themselves and others.

4. There should be norms and rules for dealing with the cases of misbehaviour, indiscipline and bullying on the part of children at home and school and these should be strictly enforced. If anybody breaks the rule and indulges in bullying acts, he should be held accountable, and it's very important that we let him deal with the natural consequences and not try to shield or let him escape under one or the other excuses.

5. It is good on the part of the parents and school authorities to be vigilant and watchful for any undesirable activities, ragging and bullying going at home and school campus. The school may have CCTV camera fitted for noticing any unwanted activity going around the campus. Moreover, in your interactions whenever you notice any observable signs and symptoms of a bully or bullied in the child's behaviour, then necessary steps should be taken for probing further into the nature and causes of his or her peculiar behaviour for arriving at a necessary conclusion.

6. The bullies should be taught to learn how to solve social problems and deal with their emotions without acting out behaviourally. As a result, attempts should be made to make them learn (i) how to resolve conflicts and manage their impulses and emotions, (ii) how to share and make compromises and do sacrifices for the sake of unity, cooperation and getting along with others, (iii) how to stand with goodness and deal with injustice. A lot of benefits may be derived by making attempts for devising means for helping bullying to find socially desirable ways and outlets for letting out their unwanted aggression and overfilled impulses, instead of resorting to shortcuts of intimidation and harming the kids less powerful and junior to them.

7. The parents and school authorities should also necessary education and training to the children for facing the problem and menace of bullying to them as well as others. They should be made to learn the important things to be done on their part when they are made victims of bullying or they happen to watch some body being bullied.

The Role of the Child Who is Bullied

It is your duty to teach and train your children/students to do all what is necessary on their part for saving themselves from the sufferings at the hands of bullies. They can remind the children, the following:

*   Remember that it is you who has to take initiative in getting rid of your problem. If you are being bullied at school, tell a friend, tell a teacher and tell your parents. It won't stop unless you do. It can be hard to do this so if you don't feel you can do it in person it might be easier to write a note to your parents explaining how you feel, or perhaps confide in someone outside the immediate family, like a grandparent, aunt, uncle or cousin and ask them to help you tell your parents what's going on.

*   Your tutor needs to know what is going on so try to find a time to tell him or her when it won't be noticeable. You could stay behind on the pretext of needing help with some work. Don't be tempted to respond to any bullying or hit back because you could get hurt or get into trouble.

- In your first attempt, if the person you told cannot help you or does not do anything, find someone else! Never keep being bullied a secret!
- Try not to let the bully see you are upset. (Bullies are looking for signs that you are upset and they may do it more).
- Avoid areas where the bully feels comfortable picking on you (for example, places where teachers cannot see you - such as corners of the playground, lonely corridors, and behind large furniture in the classroom
- Try to surround yourself with friends and people who will stand up for you.

The Role of Bystanders and Spectators in Checking One's Bullying Behaviour

- Get friends together and talk to the bully. Let the bullies in your school know that bullying is not accepted at your school.
- Don't cheer the bully on or stand around to watch. (The bully might like the attention, and pick on the kid even more).
- If you see someone being bullied, find someone to help stop it. (Get another friend, a teacher, a playground safety, a principal).
- Be nice to, include, and get to know the people who are being bullied: You may find they are similar to you.
- Try to make friends with the bully too-show them other ways to interact with other. (They don't need to bully others to be accepted or cool).

Substance Abuse or Drug Addiction

Drag addiction is also considered as a major developmental disorder. In D.S.M II, the diagnostic and statistical manual of Mental Disorder-II, it has been put in the category of personality disorders after being named as "Drug dependence". Accordingly an individual suffering with such a disorder becomes too much dependent on certain types of drugs which not only proves fatal to his health but may turn him into a maladjusted, anti-social or criminal personality. Let us try to know in detail about this in the coming pages.

Meaning and Definition of Drug Addiction (as a personality disorder)

To know about such developmental linked personality disorder, let us first know the meaning of the term drug addiction. The term drug addiction carries with it the concepts of drug and addiction. Let us be first clear about these concepts.

Drugs: We generally make use of one or the other drugs for preserving our health and protecting as well as curing ourselves from illness or diseases. In this sense drugs are our best friends. However, this Is one side of the story. All drugs are not always so helpful to us. If taken in excess or in contradiction to the need of the body, they may prove fatal. It is more true with those drugs which are associated with intoxication. More while trying to know the meaning of the term "drug addiction", we must be specific that by the word drug we clearly mean drugs associated with intoxication. What arc these intoxicated drugs, bow do these affect one's body and mind? We will discuss these issues again later in this chapter.

Addiction: Physiological and psychological dependence on something may be referred to as our addiction for that thing. In this sense, we may have addiction for our breakfast, lunch or dinner. We may feel craving for morning or evening tea or taking milk before sleeping, etc. However, we don't take addiction in such a simple meaning when we try to integrate it with the habit of taking intoxicating drugs. Here we refer to it in the category of those harmful and relatively permanent bad habits and evils (like gambling, prostitution, alcoholism, stealing, pick-pocketing etc.) which are considered too fatal and detrimental to the affected individual and the society. Once adopted in one's behaviour, it becomes difficult to get rid of them in respect of their too damaging physical and social consequences. In the beginning one may make use of one or the other types of intoxicating drug casually for one or the other reason. However, its excessive and prolonged use may make him dependent on it physiologically and psychologically as well. Gradually, it becomes difficult for him to give up its use. The more he takes the intoxicating drug, the more he becomes all together dependent on it resulting into its such craving that one is compelled to take it on any cost irrespective of the consequences. In this way, starting from a casual intake and ordinary habit, drug addiction may take the shape of a dangerous personality disorder. In its developing stages this disorder may be seen to affect the individual gradually in the following way.

1. **The initial effects of drugs:** Intoxicating drugs are too powerful to exercise instant affect on the mind and the body of the individual. These drugs provide stimulating, sedative or mind blowing effects according to their own tendencies. One is attracted and begins to use them due to one or the other reason. He likes and use them again by saying that these help him in providing relief from the tension, stress, pains etc. or provides him opportunity to roam into his world of joy, happiness and with fulfilment.

2. **Conversion into a habit:** Whatever the reasons or circumstances may be for taking the first dose of an intoxicating drug, their initial instant effect is powerful in persuading or compelling the individual for taking the second or more subsequent doses in a chain reaction. Gradually, its use is turned into an essential routine and habit of one's day-to-day life so much so that one can't live without it.

3. **Tolerance for the heavy doses of the drugs:** You have seen the people who are not habitual to drink tea or coffee, employ it as a sort of medicine to get relief from a cold or headache. It works for them on account of the stimulation provided by the caffeine and cocaine, the main intoxicating elements present in their tea and coffee. However, the same is not true for people who are habitual to drinking tea and coffee. The prolonged and excessive use of tea and coffee makes one's body so accustomed and habitual that no such stimulation is provided now by the intoxicating caffeine and cocaine.

For generating the same stimulation, now there is either the need of the heavy doses or they may require some other more powerful drug for providing relief from cold and headache.

The same is true for all types of intoxicating drugs. Once used for any account or reason provides them such temptation and persuasion that they are habituated for their excessive and prolonged use. More they use a drug, more accustomed and habitual their mind and body become to bear its effect. As a consequence of such chain reactions, one has to take frequently more and more heavy doses of a drug for obtaining the same results and undergoing the same experiences as he used to experience with a relatively less frequency amount of the doses of a drug.

4. **Physiological and Psychological Dependence:** As said earlier the prolonged and excessive use of an intoxicating drug leads to increased tolerance. One now has to take more heavy doses of this drug with the increased frequency and amount for getting the similar relief and other intoxicating effects. Consequently the individual develops an increasing physiological and psychological dependence on them to the extent that he feels agitated, disturbed and miserable whenever a particular drug is not administered. By physiological dependence here we mean that his physical and physiological systems become so habituated for the use of the drug in such way that his physical or physiological activities can't be properly maintained or he can't get relief from the pains and other troubles of his body systems without the use of that drug. Similarly by psychological dependence on a drug, we mean that one is persuaded and compelled to think that his interest and welfare lie in the use of that drug. His mind is totally set for devising easy and means of getting that drug somehow without caring for any physical, physiological or social consequences. In this way his whole behaviour is now centred around the use and craving for that drug. In this way his mind and body-both become slaves in the hands of his drug addiction.

5. **Presence of withdrawal symptoms:** The increasing physiological and psychological dependence of the individual on the intoxicating drugs is clearly reflected through some or the other withdrawal (appearing in the case when someone is deprived of his intake of doses) symptoms like lack of appetite, loss of weight, constipation, restlessness, nervousness, nausea, vomiting, diarrheal, disinterest in sexual and social relationships and even epileptic seizures or acute brain syndrome in some cases. Besides, there is an intense craving for a particular drug. His actions and behaviour are directed for the gratification of the craving for the drug. He becomes restless, perturbed, uneasy, sad and tense. His pains and agonies get intensified with the denial of the drug and passage of the time.

In this way withdrawal symptoms may effectively reveal the intensity of one's physiological and psychological dependence on the intoxicating drugs.

6. **Developing into a personality disorder:** Too much physiological and psychological dependence on drugs makes an individual handicapped in terms of his proper physical, physiological and psychological functioning. All his actions and behaviour are centred around the satisfaction of his craving for the drugs. In case his needs in the shape of getting more and more doses of the drugs are not satisfied he demonstrates serious withdrawal symptoms. He tries his best to get the required dose of the drugs by fair or foul means regardless of the consequences. All such developments in his behaviour consequently lead him towards his total maladjustment to his self and the environment. He picks up

many abnormalities in his behaviour and ultimately get affected with a specific type of personality disorder associated with drug addiction.

After acquainting us with the meaning of the terms 'drug' and 'addiction', we may now proceed to define the term drug addiction in the following way.

The personality disorder associated with drug addiction .stands for that physiological and psychological state of an individual which is resulted through the prolonged and excessive use of an intoxicating drug and which may be characterised by (a) an intense craving or compulsion to obtain or consume it regardless of consequences; (b) a tendency to increase the dosage with time; (c) physiological and psychological dependence on the effects of the drug; (d) manifestation of particular withdrawal symptoms on abrupt discontinuation of the drug and (e) to live and work only for consuming the drug.

Drugs — Types and Effects

Depending upon the nature of their effects, drugs may be classified as stimulant, sedative and deliriant (mind blowing).

1. **Stimulant drugs:** These drugs stimulate the brain and sympathetic nervous system resulting in alertness and increase in response and motor activity. The major drugs of this category are nicotine, cocaine, caffeine, and amphetamines like Benzedrine, Dexedrine and Methedrine.

    The addiction to stimulant drugs makes an individual dependent, physiologically and psychologically, on its ever-increasing doses for the continuous stimulation of sense organs. In the long run it results in severe loss of appetite and weight, constipation, increased anxiety and irritability, sleep deprivation, gradual impairment of intellectual functioning and periodic episodes of delirium.

2. **Sedative drugs:** These drugs slow down the activities of an organism and diminish the response of the brain and nervous system. As a result they are used as pain relievers and sleep inducers and may be classified as narcotics and hypnotics. The major narcotic drugs are opium, morphine, heroin, codeine, Demerol and methadone and hypnotic drugs include barbiturates like amatol, Nembutal, seconal, and non-barbiturates like bromides, and paraldehyde chloral hydrate.

    The prolonged use of sedative drugs leads to increasing tolerance and physiological as well as psychological craving for them. The immediate effects are pleasant and there is relief from pain and lessening of voluntary movements followed by euphoria. But these effects are short-lived and are followed by a negative phase of craving for more of the drug and the consequent ill effects.

    The addiction to narcotics results in loss of appetite and weight, constipation, lack of sexual desire and social interests. Unlike narcotics, the addiction to barbiturates and other hypnotics primarily affects the brain resulting in intellectual impairment and disturbance of the motor functions dependent on the cerebellum.

    The sudden withdrawal of sedative drugs results in dangerous withdrawal symptoms like restlessness, nervousness, excessive perspiration, nausea, vomiting, diarrhoea, severe headache, marked tremors, cardio-vascular collapse and painful muscular cramps. In the case of hypnotics the withdrawal reactions may lead to epileptic seizures: and delirium. If not treated in time, the seizures can cause death. Tranquillisers like meprobamate also result in addiction and have the same results as with most of the sedatives.

3. **Deliriant or mind-blowing drugs:** These drugs produce transient states resembling psychoses resulting in marked confusion, distortion in thought processes, delirium, illusions and hallucinations. Marijuana produces an euphoric state involving increased self-confidence and a pleasant feeling of relaxation characterised by floating imagination. There is a considerable distortion of the sense of time and space. In some cases the individual becomes irritable. There is a marked impairment in the motor and intellectual functioning but the users usually think that their efficiency has increased. This false sense of adequacy gives rise to incidents of reckless driving and other antisocial episodes. In many individuals the intoxication of marijuana may produce acute psychotic reactions as found with hallucinogenic drugs.

The most popular mind blowing or hallucinogenic drug is LSD-25 or lysergic acid diethylamide. Other hard drugs of this category are mescaline (an alkaloid and the active ingredient of peyote), psilocybin (a crystalline power from the mushroom) and bufotenine. The outward symptoms of LSD and other hallucinogenic drugs addiction bear a strong resemblance to the behaviour of schizophrenic patients. There is marked confusion, muddling in one's thinking and development of visual and auditory hallucinations. There is a false sense of well-being and the patient gradually develops a high tolerance and dependence.

Another drug of this category which is most abused is methamphetamine (speed) taken in the form of intravenous injection. Prolonged use of this drug results in malnutrition, brain damage, disturbance of the heart rhythm, and a dangerous impulsive, paranoid unpredictable behaviour.

How do People Become Drugs Addicts?

Nobody is born a drug addict. He acquires this behaviour from his environment gradually by passing through the following main stages.

1. **Initial stage:** One may be initiated or persuaded to take first few-doses of an intoxicated drug under the circumstances given as follows:

   • One may take a particular intoxicating drug as a medicine prescribed by a medical practitioner or doctor or he may be advised by some friend or elderly person to do so for the cure and treatment of his illness.

   • One may be tempted for the use of a drug by imitating the behaviour of his parents, friends and other members of the society.

   • One may take it simply on account of his curiosity about the use of a new thing or for the sake of fun and pleasure or looking for new thrills, new kicks and possibility of mystic experience.

   • One may use it for showing no more a child now but has enough guts and courage for its use.

- One may resort to drugs simply for giving company and developing new relationships.
- One may use it on the plea of getting relief from anxiety, pressure and tensions.
- One may think of its use for seeking escape from boredom.
- One may be tempted to the use of drugs on the plea of generating necessary confidence, energy and initiative for committing a crime or anti-social act.
- One may be tempted, persuaded or forced to make use of drugs under the evil influences and underhand methods used by the anti-social or criminal personalities engaged in the drug trafficking business.

2. **Developing stage:** At this stage, the behaviour learned at the initial stage is reinforced and rewarded on account of (i) the assumption and false impression of adequacy and well being, (ii) temporary relief from anxiety, pain or stress or (iii) pleasant reverie, and short lived pleasing effects or state of euphoria created by the use of the drag. Reinforced by such instant effects of the first few doses, one is tempted and persuaded to repeat the intake of the similar drug and thus fall into the trap of using it again and again (with the increased frequency and amount) and thus developing it as a habit or characteristic of his personality.

3. **Final stage:** Up to reaching this stage one becomes habitual of taking the drug. The excessive use of the drug leads to increased tolerance resulting into the complete physiological and psychological dependence on them to the extent that he feels miserable, perturbed or tensed whenever this particular drug is not administered. In this way, what begins as an innocuous experiment at the initial stage, ends at the final stage in disaster. The individual now turns into a drug addict who has a strong compulsion and craving for the use of the drug. Neither he follows any norms nor he listens to any piece of advice but only cares and attempts for the required doses of his drug at any cost irrespective of the consequences. He now lives only for the sake of drugs intake and such intake becomes the only reason for running and taking away his life. His behaviour now becomes abnormal and maladaptive to the extent of being included in the category of personality disorders. He now reaches the point of no return. All the doors for his reforms are now closed. He himself realises that he himself can't give up the use of drugs but at one time or the other hopes for some miracle or somebody to come for his help in getting rid of the menace of drug addiction. In such an advanced stage although it is difficult to save him, there is still some hope for the correction of his behaviour through systematically planned and organised attempts which we will discuss in the causative measures mentioned ahead in this text.

Prevention and Treatment of Drug Addiction

Prevention: Prevention is said to be better than cure. Consequently it is always proper to think for the ways and means that may help the new generation for saving themselves from the clutches of this dreaded evil. The following measures may prove effective and fruitful in this direction:

- The beginning in this direction must be made through educating the public about the causes and consequences of drag addiction.

- There should be substantial provision in the schools for educating the children through various curricular and co curricular activities about the menace of the drug addiction.

- There is a need of restructurisation of unhealthy environment and reduction in the problems leading to frustration, tensions and anxieties among the youth. Job opportunities need to be increased and the education system should be so reshaped as to include job oriented and employment based courses.

- The energies of the children and youth should be channelized into constructive and creative projects like rural reconstruction, welfare of society and nation and helping the needy and the poor. This will provide them a sense of purpose and opportunity for adventure and new experiences, the things they try to seek through drugs.

- The intoxicating drugs which have a limited medical application should be banned. The parents and elders should not take such medicines which carry strong intoxicating effects. As far as possible, these should not be taken in the presence of children nor administered to them as medicine.

- Drug trafficking should be checked through strict social and legal means. The individuals who try to trap the children and youth, through temptation or coercion, into drug addiction should be carefully watched and strictly dealt through social and legal provisions.

- Parents and teachers should be vigilant about the company and living style of the children, especially during adolescence. They must try for the satisfaction of their basic needs and remaining on track with themselves and the environment. Any abnormality in their behaviour and day-to-day activities should be wisely attended and proper corrective measures should be taken for saving them from the danger of drug addiction.

Treatment of Drug Addiction

In case one becomes drug addictive, due to one or the other reason, then he needs proper attention, care and treatment for getting rid of himself from this compulsion. Truly speaking, drug addiction is not a law and order problem as imagined in certain circles. It is predominantly a social and psychological problem. Addicts should be distinguished from criminals who supply them with drugs and live off their misery. The irony of addicts is that they depend on drugs to the extent of pathological craving so powerful that they try and manage to get the drug regardless of legal or other obstacles. Keeping all these things in view, the following measures prove fruitful in the treatment of drug addicts.

1. **Compulsory hospitalisation:** Compulsory institutionalisation and hospitalisation is a major step in the treatment of drug addicts. If the doctor waits until the patient voluntarily seeks effective treatment, he may well wait until the patient dies. Drug addicts do not want treatment, they want drugs and in their surroundings

and environment they can't be deprived of drugs. The admission in hospitals may be able to cover the following major risks:

(*i*)   Rejection by family and society, (they can neither understand nor manage the patient), makes the patient depressed. This situation becomes worse when drugs are not available during the withdrawal phase.

(*ii*)   The tendency to go on to harder drugs or mixed drugs to get the desired effect may lead to disaster.

(*iii*)   There is a risk of killing himself by the patient on account of an accidental overdose or committing suicide when profoundly depressed or a misadventure under the intoxicating effects of drug.

(*iv*)   There is a danger of infection or other complications when the drug is injected in the body by the individual.

2.   **De-intoxicating or drying out the patient:** Attempts should be made to de-intoxicate or dry-out the patient. It may be achieved through (i) the 'cold turkey' procedure, that is, sudden total discontinuation of drugs; (ii) giving the patient progressively diminishing doses of drug leading towards complete cessation, and (iii) substituting a less addictive drug and later seeking gradual reduction of intake.

3.   **Medical measures:** With some patients, specially psychotic addicts, ECT or tranquillising drugs may prove helpful. Adequate care is to be taken for the provision of antibiotics as there is an inherent danger of possible infection. The withdrawal reactions should also be controlled as they lead to physical or mental disaster. Adequate dietary measures in the form of glucose and vitamins are to be ascertained for compensating the drug deficiency and also adequate feeding and fluids should be ensured.

4.   **Psychological treatment:** Psychological treatment of drug addicts needs patience and time. Long range psychotherapy and socio therapy are essential if the patient is to learn to face his problems and seek adjustment in the society without the use of the drug.

5.   **Long-term therapy and rehabilitation:** The long-term therapy is also essential. It may be achieved as follows:

   (i)   **Re-personalisation:** The drug addicts should be helped to form a proper relationship with therapists, doctors and nurses before they can re-establish any personal identity.

   (ii)   **Specific therapy:** Withdrawal reactions and complications should be well guarded against with the help of specific drugs. For example, epileptics may need anti-convulsants or schizophrenics may need phenothiazines.

   (iii)   **Re-socialisation:** The drug addicts must learn to socialise and adjust without the aid of drugs.

   (v)   **Re-occupation:** Once cured, the drug addicts should be helped in seeking employment and occupational adjustment. They need to be trained in the job skill and in persistence so that they may be accepted by their employers.

(v) **Re-housing:** They should be helped in getting adequate family adjustment and re-establish themselves by learning to accommodate and fend for themselves.

The duration and extent of long-term therapy depends upon the patient's potential, and the original level of maturity which the patient has reached. If adequately cared through therapy and rehabilitation, the patient should be able to lead a full life and to develop his potential.

Summary

The growing children should we well understood in relation to their age-linked developmental needs and behavioural problems. The term 'behavioural problem' refers to a type of serious abnormality in the behaviour of an individual resulting into his maladjustment with the self and the environment and proving detrimental to the welfare of his self and society. Examples of such behaviour are truancy, lying, stealing, aggression, bullying, drug addiction and juvenile delinquency.

Aggression refers to an intense uncontrollable outburst and expression of anger demonstrated through a number of undesirable physical acts like hitting, biting, calling bad names and fighting with others, destruction of property, etc. It may prove dangerous to those around as well as harmful to the functioning and welfare of the self and others. In all its way, aggression by its typical demonstration seems to be a pure attention-seeking and goal realising behaviour. A child may resort to such behaviour only to seek attention of others for making them agree or available for the satisfaction of his desirable as well as undesirable needs. This behaviour is totally acquired and not innate or inborn in any form. One learns this behaviour in order to realise his needs and objectives through the models and feedback available in one's environment. In seeking remedy for the aggression of the children, we must not resort to repressing or killing angry feelings or to punishing the child, but rather to accept him and his feelings in a natural way. Paying no attention and reinforcement of any kind (punishment is also a kind of reinforcement) may help the child in not repeating his aggression. By making the child realise the undesirability and ill consequences of his aggressive behaviour, employment of proper behaviour therapy and behaviour modification technique may help much in getting rid of such undesirable social behaviour of children.

Bullying refers to the behavioural problems of developing children in which a problematic child called bully is found to demonstrate an ongoing misuse of power and unwanted aggressive behaviour repeatedly through his words and deeds to another child (called bullied) with the intention of causing him or her physical, and/or psychological harm. The bullying behaviour may take its birth in bullies on account of so many social and psychological reasons chiefly involving the satisfaction of their ego, overshadowing the feelings of insecurity and inferiority and enjoying popularity and assertiveness among peers. However, in all its forms and dimensions, bullying is proving a great menace and major problem today in many of the schools. It is affecting badly the welfare and progress of all connected and affected through this menace, i.e., the bullies, the bullied, the onlookers as well as the peace and progress of a school, family and society. The remedy lies in fighting on all fronts. All those affected or connected with the problem need to join hands. Where on one front, the behavioural modification strategies need to be applied for the correction of problem behaviour among the bullies, the bullied and bystanders also have to play their defending roles in a proper way and the authorities have to make them alert and disciple minded for establishing a rule of law.

Drug addiction refers to the behavioural problem of our adolescents and youths in which they are found to getting addicted to harmful drugs associated with intoxication like LSD-25, methamphetamine or speed, marijuana, morphine, heroin, methadrene, Benzedrine, cocaine, etc. Drug addiction has no hereditary roots and is therefore a purely learned behaviour. At the initial stage, the first few doses of an intoxicated drug may be taken out of curiosity, for fun, getting relief from pressure, etc., under the influence of evil influences or by way of modelling of the behaviour of elders. The initiated behaviour then may get reinforced and rewarded on account of a false impression of adequacy and wellbeing — short-lived pleasure, effects created by the consumption of the drug and then it may result in total dependency (physiological as well as psychological) on the use of the drug. To save youngsters from the clutches of this behavioural problem, we must first think about the various preventive measures. However, in case one becomes a drug addict, then due attention should be paid to helping them get rid of this bad habit. Compulsory hospitalisation, de-intoxicating or 'drying out' of the addict, accompanied with special medical measures, psychological treatment including long-term therapy and rehabilitation, are some of the measures that can prove helpful in the care and treatment of children suffering from drug addiction.

References and Suggested Readings

Barton, Hall, *Psychiatric Examination of the School Child*, Edward Arnold, London, 1947.

Burt, C., *The young Delinquent*, (3rd ed.), University of London Press, London, 1938.

Carmichael, L. (Ed.), *Manual of Child Psychology*, John Wiley, New York, 1946.

Crow, L.D. and Crow, A., *Child Psychology*, Barney and Noble, New York, 1969 (reprint).

Hurlock, E.B., *Child Psychology*, McGraw-Hill, Tokyo, 1959, (Asian Students 3rd ed.)

Shanker, Uday, *Problem Children*, Atma Ram & Sons, New Delhi, 1958.

Verma, S.C., *The Young Delinquents*, Lucknow Pustak Kendra, Lucknow, 1970.

25

Counselling of Children in Specific Stressful Conditions

Introduction

Childhood as we all know is much remembered for the spontaneity of life, freedom to do and speak with no responsibilities on the shoulders. It is referred to as the most valuable and golden period of life where the child is found to lead an anxiety-free 'royal' life. However, whatever fine image we have built up for the childhood, it is not so universal and a bed of roses for everyone at every time. There are situations and circumstances where children may be found to bear the consequences of a lot of stress and adverse life conditions. In these adverse conditions many of the children may have to pass through a period of sadness, isolation, exploitation, oppression, cruelty and abuse of one or the other nature. At this time what is needed to them most is the availability of some type of proper guidance and counselling accompanied by measures to physically help them in their adjustment and living. In this chapter here we would like to focus upon discussion on the three more specific stressful conditions faced by many of the children in their life named as: (i) separation or divorce of parents, (ii) loss of parents in armed conflicts, etc., and (iii) victims or survivors of child abuse. Let us discuss them in reference to their nature, problems and its solution in the form of providing some appropriate counselling to the children.

Separation or Divorce of Parents

Meaning and Nature of the Problem

The social crisis named as separation or divorce of the parents is getting intensified day by day on account of various socio-psychological, economical and global cultural changes introduced in the structure and functioning of the family system. However, the most damaging effect of the separation or divorce among the married couple reflects is the problems faced by their children on this account. These problems in general may be of the following nature.

- Parents may engage in legal disputes to take custody of their children and these children may be forced to watch ugly scenes of disputes, quarrelling and fighting among their parents.

- The children may be forced to make their choices for remaining with their mother or father. It may put a child in a severe psychological conflict unable to decide what would be better for him or her.
- While forced to live with a single parent, mother or father, the child is deprived of most of the privileges, socio-psychological advantages and needs and satisfaction as enjoyed in the company of both. He or she may show a great hunger or need for having his / her mother or father in case he or she lives with a single parent.
- Many times, the divorced couple may make their child an orphan child as none of them opts for his / her brought up for one or the other reason such as getting re-married.
- The separation or divorce of parents may cause a great psychological damage resulting in intense grief, lack of security and fear, anger and frustration, depression, etc., to the suffering child. It may completely ruin his or her childhood and bring a shockwave to his / her mental health and overall well-being.
- These children may suffer from social exclusion and negative comments over the status of separation or divorce of their parents. Deprivation of any one of the parents costs them dearly in terms of their adjustment, development, rearing and wellbeing.

Counselling of Children Facing Separation or Divorce of Parents

The children facing one or the other types of these problems are in a great need of being counselled at the hands of the trained professionals and counsellors. As far as the meaning and purpose of counselling to problem ridden child is concerned, we can define it as a process carried out under the leadership of a counsellor to express care, understanding and concern towards the problems of the child on one hand and to make him understand his problems and develop the means to deal with them on the other. The purposes or goals of the process of counselling to a child thus may be laid down as follows:

- To help the child by creating an environment of trust expressing his / her emotions and feelings freely in a particular situation about his / her felt difficulty or problems arising out of parental separation or divorce.
- To offer proper opportunity to the suffering child for a direct and open relationship with the counsellor and create a proper environment for a useful dialogue between the child and counsellor with the hope of resolution of the child's problems.
- To help the child in understanding his problem / problems in a proper way resulting due to the separation of his parents and in the light of the circumstances being faced by him at the present moment.
- To help the child in developing means and measures for dealing with the problems or difficulties resulting through the separation of his parents.
- To help the child in building self-confidence and self-esteem by bringing out the feelings of shame or low self-esteem as a result of the separation of his parents and face the reality of life in a proper way.

Methods or Modes of Counselling

Methods or modes of counselling of the children who are the victims of separation or divorce of their parents may be broadly classified as group counselling and individual counselling.

Group counselling: In group counselling a group of children suffering on account of separation or divorce of their parents is subjected to counselling by special counsellors. In the group these children find valuable opportunities for getting along with peers passing through similar problems. They can easily open up to each other for the expression of their feelings and emotions and understand each other's problems for facing reality lying before them. In the group, these children may be made to learn how to deal with the hardships faced by them through group discussions, role playing and showing them videos or films related to dealing with crises.

Individual counselling: Here counselling is provided to suffering children on an individual basis. The counsellor tries to have support with the child for letting him / her express his / her feelings emotions and difficulties before him. The child is then gradually made to face the realities of his/her faced problems and learns to cope with them satisfactorily.

In addition to the counselling provided to the suffering children, efforts can also be made to provide needed counselling to the parents of the children. They must be made to realise that the innocent child should not suffer a heavy price due to their discord, separation or divorce. When a single parent, mother or father, feels a need of taking his or her child to a counsellor, he or she also shows a necessity for undergoing counselling for bringing needed behavioural changes for meeting the interests and welfare of their children.

Loss of Parents in Armed Conflicts

Meaning and Nature of the Problem

There may be a number of instances in the case of growing up children when they are found to suffer with the loss of their parents on one account or the other. These may be accidental death of their parents on account of meeting with some at the time of their road, train or air journey, trapped into a fire, drowning in river, etc. In addition to such accidental deaths, there may be instances where they may lose their parents on account of some armed conflicts such as a terrorist attack, robbery, attack of the enemy nation, armed turmoil in the region between rival groups, mutual clashes and armed conflicts among families and members of the communities for settling personal scores or becoming victims of caste and religion wars. The loss of parents on account of the latter reason, i.e., armed conflicts proves more costly and damaging to the suffering children than the loss of parents on account of the other reasons, i.e., accidental death as it provides more psychological setback to these children in the following ways:

- It becomes quite difficult for these children to forget the horrified experiences that they went through at the time of loss of their parents on account of armed conflicts.

- They can feel guilty for not saving or protecting their parents during the armed conflict.
- They may develop a strong feeling of revenge for those who are responsible for killing their parents in the armed conflicts and thus may indulge in acts of continuing rivalry and conflicts with the opposite camp.
- The experiences encountered on their part at the time of killing of their parents may result in affecting their mental health. They may fall victim to depression, fear, anxiety, low self-esteem, phobia and other neurotic / psychotic ailments.

What may happen in the real sense with the children losing parents in armed conflicts can now be properly witnessed in the stories and live scenes of the war torn or terrorism-ridden countries and regions of the globe. Whether it may be Syria, Iraq, Afghanistan or *naxalite* and terrorist-ridden parts of our own country, the miseries and agonies of children losing their parents in armed conflicts are quite sensitive and multi-dimensional. They are not only struggling in their day-to-day living but are also facing a number of problems for adjustment to their self and environment. Such children need properly planned and organised counselling services for coping with stress caused on account of the loss of their parents in such a way.

Counselling of Children Who Have Lost Parents in Armed Conflicts

Both group counselling and individual counselling may be carried out for helping the suffering children to cope with stress experienced by them on account of the loss of their parents in armed conflicts, etc. They can be helped in the following ways through counselling:

(i) To express their feelings, resentment and anger, fear and phobias related to their experience encountered at the time of loss of their parents in armed conflicts.

(ii) To help them in coming out of the shock and horrified experiences by resorting to therapies and techniques helpful in:
- De-conditioning of the fears and phobias related to the horrified experience.
- Providing them incidences for modelling of their behaviour and imbibe moral courage as well as self-confidence for dealing with the odds of their present circumstances with the help of stories and books, multimedia presentations, discussions and social interactions.
- Providing them mental peace and measures to seek adjustment with the self and environment by learning relaxation and conflict resolution techniques.
- Actualising their potentialities for becoming self-reliant and brave enough for finding out the solution of their difficulties and problems.

(iii) To help them in channelizing their resentment and anger towards constructive activities helpful to them and the society.

(iv) To help them in working as models for the others in coming out of similar difficulties faced on account of the loss of their parents.

Victims or Survivors of Child Abuse

Many of the children in the society worldwide may be found to pass through the horrified experiences of child abuse in one situation or the other. These children known as the survivors of child abuse grow up with the ill consequences and pains of the abuse lasting the rest of their life. Let us see what we mean by the term child abuse, its nature, types and consequence along with its prevention and cure.

What is Child Abuse?

Ill treatment and harm caused to children by adult members of the society in a physical, verbal or emotional form resulting in their pain and suffering in one or the other ways and affecting their life in a quite negative and adverse way is commonly known as child abuse.

Types of Child Abuse

Child abuse may be categorised into four distinct types depending on the nature of the harm or maltreatment caused to children by the adult members of the society:

1. *Physical abuse*: In such type of abuse, the child is subjected to maltreatment and assault on the part of adults in the physical form resulting in physical harm and agony accompanied with mental or psychological shock to the victim. The fact that a particular child has been subjected to physical assault and abuse is surfaced through the following physical indicators:

    (i) Unexplained bruises and welts on body parts suggesting the use of instruments like belt buckle, electric cord, hunters, sharp edged objects, etc.

    (ii) Unexplained burns in the shape of cigarette burns, utensils or kitchen appliance burns, rope burns on body parts.

    (iii) Infected burns or wounds indicating delay in treatment.

    In addition to such physical indicators, the survivors of physical abuse can also be identified through the following behavioural indicators:

    (i) Inappropriate or excessive fear of some particular adult such as caretaker, parent, teacher or a relative.

    (ii) Unusual shyness, withdrawal, depression, sadness and socially cut off behaviour.

    (iii) Anti-social behaviour such as drug addiction, truancy, running away from home, aggression and bullying, etc.

2. *Emotional / Psychological abuse:* In such type of abuse the child is subjected to maltreatment and misbehaviour on the part of adults in an emotional or psychological form inflicting mental / psychological pains, agonies and wounds on the mind and heart of the suffering child.

    In their actual happening, the emotional or psychological abuse may include a chronic pattern of criticism, coercion, humiliation, accusation or threat to one's physical and social safety.

In general, survivors or victims of such abuse may be found to exhibit the following types of physical and behavioural symptoms or signs:

- Exhibiting a number of maladaptive behaviour or disorders like eating disorders, including obesity or anorexia, speech disorders (suffering, stammering), anxiety or nervous disorders (rashes, facial ties, stomach aches), habit disorders (biting, rocking, head banging), aggression and cruelty (hurting others including animals), age in-appropriate behaviour (bedwetting, wetting, soiling), mood disorders, etc.
- Showing developmental delays in acquiring norms in terms of their physical, mental, social and emotional maturity.
- Exhibiting socially and emotionally deviant behaviour.

3. *Neglect abuse:* In such a type of abuse, the child is subjected to maltreatment and ill behaviour on the part of caring adults in the form of neglecting and showing indifference to the satisfaction of his or her basic needs — physical and socio-psychological. In such a situation parents and members of the family may be found to show negligence / indifference for maintaining proper hygienic conditions, providing food and eatables at the needed time in an appropriate way, caring for the proper clothing, living, vaccination and immunisation at the proper time, caring for their schooling and proper education, socialisation and culturalisation and emotional channelization in a proper way.

The negligence and indifference shown towards developing children on the part of parents, family members, teachers and care givers may prove quite costly to the developing children. They may be deprived from the satisfaction of their basic needs — physical and socio-psychological — and it can result in their under development and maladjustment with their self and environment making them hopeless and failures at one or the other situations in their life.

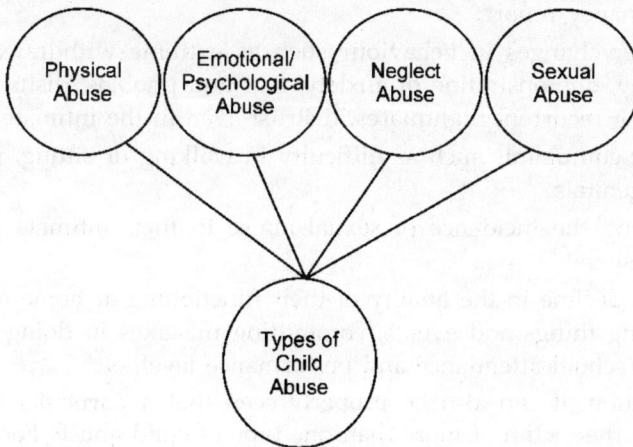

Fig. 25.1: Types of Child Abuse

4. *Sexual Abuse:* In such type of abuse, the child is subjected to maltreatment or assaults on the part of sex offenders (adults as well as peers) in the form of undesirable and unwanted sexual behaviour and harm or pain causing sexual

activities against the wishes and welfare of the victim. The range of sexual abuse committed to children is quite wide. The behaviour and activities like passing remarks or uttering indecent words, touching body parts especially the nipples, lips, buttocks, genitals of the female child with a motivated ill intention, engaging in oral and physical sex with the children (male or female) causing harm to their genitals and body parts, abuse of their bodies in the form of rape and coercion, etc., all fall in the domain of sexual abuse. Moreover, the range of people who may be found to commit such sexual abuses is also quite wide. Any person of any age, background and relationship having a developed sexual libido and more powerful than the victim, can be found to commit sexual abuses to the developing children.

The after effect and consequences of sexual abuse are quite bitter and hard hitting to the survivor or victims. In addition to suffering from physical damage, pain and agony, the victims are subjected to quite horrified experiences, distressing memories, anxiety and blockades to establish normal social relationship, intimacy and trust in their future life. The wounds inflicted in emotional and psychological forms are quite harder to be healed than the physical / bodily injuries inflicted on the sexually abused children.

Identification of the Victims or Survivors of Sexual Abuse

In general, the children subjected to sexual abuse may be found to exhibit symptoms and activities as follows in their physical examination, and day-to-day behaviour:

- Torn clothes and stained or bloody underclothes.
- Bruises and scratches on the body parts.
- Bleeding from external genitals, vagina or anal region.
- Detection of the attempts for sexual inter course through a medical examination or pregnancy report.
- Improper changes in behaviour such as extreme withdrawal from the social company, demonstration of anxiety, fear and phobias, disturbed sleep patterns including recurrent nightmares, distrust even in the intimate people, etc.
- Somatic complaints such as difficulty in walking or sitting, pain and irritation in the genitals.
- Disclosing the incidence of sexual abuse to their intimate parents and other well wishers.
- Sudden decline in the quality of their functioning at home and school such as forgetting things and events, committing mistakes in doing routine work, fall in their school attendance and performance level, etc.

In addition, it can also be properly seen that a particular child may also be found to be the victim of more than one type of child abuse. For example, a victim of sexual abuse may also be found to experience physical abuse and emotional abuse at his / her home and school. Similarly, a child experiencing physical abuse at his / her home may also be subjected to emotional abuse and neglect from one or the other corners of society. No matter, whether the child is subjected to one or the other types of abuses singly or in combination, it is quite certain that all types of abuse carry a long lasting influence and impact over the present and future life of the victimised children in physical, mental, social, emotional, moral and wholesome development and progress form.

How to deal with the problem of child abuse

The problem of child abuse is universal. It can happen with any developing child in any family and community all across the globe. As a parent, close family member, neighbour, acquaintance, friend, teacher or even stranger we can either play a substantial role in preventing or engaging in child abuse only because the child trusts us or he or she is more vulnerable for becoming a victim to one or the other type of abuses on our part. It is also quite difficult to detect the cases of child abuse that are taking place in quite silent and methodological ways at home, social places and the school by even the intimate one's unless they are reported by the children themselves or come into the notice of someone who dares to help the victim. However, the methods and strategies used for dealing with the problem of child abuse can be broadly categorised under three heads, namely:

(A) Educating the stakeholders,

(B) Creating awareness about Child Rights,

(C) Counselling the survivors of child abuse.

(A) Educating the stakeholders

The real issue and the thing that is coming in the way of preventing the problem of child abuse is lack of information and proper education in this matter to the many stakeholders such as parents, members of the community, teachers, media personnel and law enforcing agencies. This shortcoming needs to be properly handled by taking care of the availability of needed information and education to all the stakeholders in the following manner:

1. *Educating the parents and elders:* Parents as well as elders in the family are the real well wishers of their children. However, in search of the well being of their children they are many times misguided to resort to hard punitive measures like neglect or physical abusing of their loving children. Therefore, there is a need to teach alternative methods of disciplining the child in place of physical abusing. They should also be warned not to resort neglecting or depriving their children with the satisfaction of their basic needs – physical and socio-psychological as it may lead to the path of maladjustment and inadequate development that is harmful to them and the society. Emotionally, the children should not be felt starved and essential measures should be taken by the parents for the preservation and promotion of their mental health. Parents and elders need also to be educated properly for preventing the cases of sexual abuse. They must have a proper rapport with their developing children and try to get skilled in noting down any unwanted sudden changes in the behaviour of their children. By winning their confidence and trust, they should try to go in the deep of the crisis of physical, emotional and sexual abuse perplexing the mind and heart of their children. The physical symptoms regarding child abuse should be well noted and recognised by them for helping the children disclose any incidence

of abuse inflicted on them. In addition, the parents should also be helped in seeking remedy to the victimised child through a number of available legal provisions, community help centres and counselling services.

2. *Educating the teachers:* Like parents and elders, teachers also need to be properly educated in dealing with the issue of child abuse by learning and equipping them with the following things:

   - Awareness about the rights of the child including the legal provisions available for the enforcement of these rights.
   - Knowledge and skill related to the warning sign for child abuse.
   - The enforcement of constructive and self-imposed discipline in place of adopting hard punitive measures in the form of physical abusing or neglecting.
   - The ways and means of securing cooperation of the parents, community people, NGOs and Government agencies for the protection of child rights and prevention of child abuse.
   - The means and ways of establishing rapport and winning the confidence and trust of the children for knowing about their problems related to abusing or maltreatment by the elders or peers.
   - Providing needed guidance and counselling for children for the purpose of getting them aware of their rights, need and means of preventing abuses and maltreatment to them by the elders.

3. *Educating the children:* It is also essential for children to acquire needed information, knowledge and skills for getting them properly equipped for protecting themselves from the possible maltreatment and abuse on the part of their elders and peers. For this purpose the children should be helped by the parents, family members, NGOs, teachers and government agencies working for the education and welfare of the children to acquire knowledge and skills related to the following:

   - Awareness about their rights, known as Right of the children and agencies (Government as well as non government) helpful in securing these rights to them.
   - Way and means of securing needed help at the time of distress while subjected to physical or sexual abuse on the part of elders and peers.
   - Awareness of the type of touch, physical contact and behaviour shown towards them by the elders and peer that could be signalled as sexual abuse.
   - Ability to make use of self-defence methods or techniques for protecting themselves from physical and sexual abuse.
   - Providing cooperation to parents, teachers, guidance personnel and government agencies for the prevention as well as follow-up actions related to child abuse.

B. Creating awareness about the child rights

A proper awareness of the 'Child Rights' on the part of various stakeholders like parents, family members, care takers, community people, teachers and children themselves may help in the prevention of child abuse and follow up of the abuse survivors.

For this purpose, let us first understand the meaning and nature of these rights.

What are Child Rights?

By the term Child Rights we mean a category of those human rights that are universally available to all children, i.e., human beings below the age of 18. Worldwide, the Child Rights as a part of human rights have been defined by the United Nations and United Nations Convention on the Rights of the Child (UNCRC). According to the UNCRC, (United Nations, 1889), Child Rights (as a part of Human Rights) may be considered as those minimum entitlements and freedom that should be afforded to all persons below the age of 18 regardless of race, colour, gender, religion, opinions, wealth, birth status, disability or other characteristics and therefore apply universally to all children everywhere on the globe.

Types of child rights

By laying down rights for the children on the lines of establishing Human Rights for the human beings, UNCRC has tried to ensure children their required freedom and civil rights, appropriate family environment, necessary health care and welfare, education, leisure and cultural activities as well as special protection measures. For ensuring these to the children, the UNCRC has tried to classify the rights given to children with the four major types detailed as follows:

1. *Right to Survival:* A child's right to survival begins within the womb of the mother well before his or her actual birth. The right of survival ensured to the children includes the following: (i) Right to be born, (ii) Right to minimum standards of food, shelter and clothing, (iii) Right to live with dignity and (iv) Right to health care, to safe drinking water, nutritious food, a clear and safe environment and information to help them stay healthy.

2. *Right to Protection:* By providing this right to the children UNCRC tries to ensure the measure to be taken for the prevention of or responding to the incidence of child abuse, exploitation, violence and neglect of children. Accordingly, Right to Protection tries to ensure for the children: (i) Right to be protected from all sorts of violence, (ii) Right to be protected from neglect, (iii) Right to be protected from physical and sexual abuse and (iv) Right to be protected from dangerous drugs.

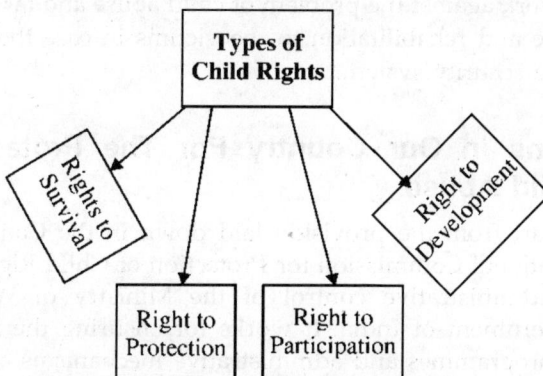

Fig. 25.2: Types of Child Rights

3. *Right to Participation:* The child as a human being has the right to participate and involve himself or herself freely to interact in any social situation. Accordingly, the right to participation given to the children includes the following:

   (i) Right to freedom of opinion, (ii) Right to freedom of expression, (iii) Right to freedom of association, (iv) Right to information and (v) Right to participate in any decision making that involves him / her directly or indirectly.

4. *Right to Development:* By laying down the right to the children, UNCRC has tried to ensure ways and means for the proper wholesome development of the developing children. Accordingly, the Right to Development given to the children includes the following:

   (i) Right to education, (ii) Right to learn, (iii) Right to relax and play, and (iv) Right to all forms of development — social emotional, mental and physical.

Although all these rights offered to the developing children cater to the satisfaction of their physical and socio-psychological needs, education and adjustment, leading to their proper progress and wholesome development, the Right to Protection is directly concerned to take care of the essential measures for the needed prevention and cure of one or the other types of child abuse inflicted on the children such as physical abuse, emotional or psychological abuse, neglect abuse and sexual abuse.

Right to protection ensures for the children the appropriate measures to be taken for the prevention of or responding to the incidences of all types of child abuse. In practice with regards to the prevention and responding to the cases of child abuse, it asks to employ ways and means for:

   (i) Providing sensitisation and awareness to the problem of child abuse in relation to the nature of its occurrence, its prevention and cure for the stakeholders — parents, teachers, community people and children themselves.

   (ii) Establishing appropriate laws and policies, mechanisms and systems for the prevention as well as responding to the cases of child abuse and taking care for their proper monitoring and implementation.

   (iii) Providing necessary access, assistance and relief for the victims of child abuse as promptly as possible.

   (iv) Seeking cooperation and assistance from all the stakeholders, support groups, non-government organisations and Government agencies to provide a proper safety network against the problem of child abuse and take proper measures for the cure and rehabilitation to the victims in case they fell through the holes in the security system.

Legal Provisions in Our Country For The Protection of Child Rights and Child Abuse

In our country, apart from the provision laid down in the Constitution, we have established the "National Commission for Protection of Child Rights" as a statutory body under the administrative control of the Ministry of Women and Child Development, Government of India. It works for ensuring the implementation of all laws, policies, programmes and administrative mechanisms as enshrined in the Constitution of India and also the UN Convention on the Rights of the Child.

In addition to dealing with the protection of child rights, the Commission enjoys the privilege of being armed with "The Protection of Children from Sexual Offences (POCSO) Act, 2012" specifically for helping children with sexual abuse.

The Act defines a child as any person below eighteen years of age, and regards the best interests and well-being of the child as being of paramount importance at every stage, to ensure the healthy physical, emotional, intellectual and social development of the child. It defines different forms of sexual abuse, including penetrative and non-penetrative assault, as well as sexual harassment and pornography, and deems a sexual assault to be "aggravated" under certain circumstances, such as when the abused child is mentally ill or when the abuse is committed by a person in a position of trust or authority vis-à-vis the child, like a family member, police officer, teacher, or doctor. People who traffic children for sexual purposes are also punishable under the provisions relating to abetment in the Act. The Act prescribes maximum term of rigorous imprisonment for life, and fine.

C. Counselling of the Survivors of Child Abuse

Consequences of child abuse are quite alarming and damaging to the victims of child abuse. They have to pass through a very difficult period filled with dreadful memories and horrified painful experiences after falling victims to physical and sexual abuse. The other types of abuses — emotional and neglect, are also quite powerful and act adversely on their mental health. Thus in all cases of abuse, the victims need the services of a good counsellor for helping them to come out from their inappropriate and damaging mental state.

Both individual and group therapies may be employed by counsellors for helping the abuse survivors depending upon the nature of their problem and the victims themselves. For example, in the cases where survivors need social support for coming out of their mental state and getting rid of the feelings of insecurity and vulnerability, group therapy may work well for them. But for those who fear the vulnerability and exposure, they may experience in a group setting, the individual therapy (working one-on-one with a therapist) can be more advantageous. Whatever mode one-on-one or group setting may be employed by the counsellor for helping the abuse survivors, it is bound to aim for the realisation of the following objectives:

1. To provide opportunities and environment for the victim to narrate and talk about his / her dreadful experiences related to one or the other types of abuse, open up his / her heart and mind to express his / her bottled emotion, feelings, anxieties, fears, phobias, and thinking on the various aspects of his / her problem.

2. To help the victim in understanding the true nature of his / her problem and feel necessity of finding and its situations with the search and adoption of some suitable means and alternatives.

3. To help the victims for coming out with the feelings of guilt and shame, self-condemnation and self-destruction and regain their self-confidence and feelings of self-respect and self-esteem.

4. To help them in giving up their inappropriate fears, anxieties, phobias and feelings of insecurity associated with the horrified experiences of their abuse with the application of suitable means and ways like aversive therapy, de-conditioning,

group support, narrative therapy, modelling, meditation and relaxation techniques, art and creative therapy, etc.

5.   To help them in regaining their trust in social relationships, company of others, elders and peers, and the environment conditions available to them at present for their proper adjustment and productivity at work.

Summary

Our children and adolescents may be found to face a number of quite stressful conditions in their living and working strong enough to create major obstacles in the path of their progress and development needing timely help, guidance and remedial steps from the elders. The most prominent ones for this purpose may be named as: (i) separation of parents, (ii) loss of parents in armed conflicts and (iii) victims or survivors of child abuse.

By the term **separation of parents** here we mean the parents of children who got separated or legally divorced for one or the other reasons. The worst sufferers on this account are their children who found them rootless for their further survival and proper nourishing. Separation of their parents may force them to be dependent on a single parent or sometimes on the mercy of others — relatives, owners of boarding houses or institutions, or the step father/ mother. This type of instability may induce a lot of stressful conditions among them needing timely help as well as proper guidance and counselling services.

By the term **loss of parents in armed conflicts** in relation to the suffering children we mean the children who are unfortunate enough to bear the losses of their parents in conflicts involving use of weapons,, i.e., victims of terrorist attacks, burglary, caste or community clashes, death in fighting or firing on the borders, etc. The loss is quite unbearable and stressful to the growing children and needs immediate care and appropriate counselling.

By the term **victims or survivors of child abuse** we mean the children who are bearing the brunt of child abuse at present or are experiencing the resultant physical agonies and mental torture on account of being abused in the past. The abuses inflicted on them by the adults in this direction may take various forms and ways like: (i) Physical abuse (assaulting the child in physical forms), (ii) Emotional/Psychological abuse (criticising, coercing, humiliating, accusing or threatening the child in order to harass or torturing him), (iii) Neglect abuse (neglecting and showing indifference to the needs of the developing children) and (iv) Sexual abuse (subjecting the child to sexual intimidation, i.e., undesirable and unwanted sexual behaviour).

The after effect and consequences of all these types of child abuses are quite bitter and painful to the survivor or victims. In addition to suffering from physical damage, pain and agony, the victims are subjected to quite horrified experiences, distressing memories, anxiety, and blockades to establish normal social relationship, intimacy and trust in their future life. They essentially need timely help, consolation and wise counselling on the part of the appropriate persons.

In dealing with the victims or survivors of child abuse, it remains useful to make use of the methods and strategies like: (i) Educating the stakeholders,(ii) Creating awareness about Child Rights, and (iii) Counselling the survivors of child abuse.

In all these three stressful conditions experienced by the victims or survivors one thing is quite obvious that all of them need timely help and organised counselling for their adequate adjustment and needed welfare.

Both individual and group therapies may be employed by the counsellors for helping the children passing through these painful stress conditions depending upon the nature of their problem and the suffering children themselves. For example, in the cases where there is a need of providing social support to a suffering child for coming out from the present painful mental state and getting rid of the feelings of insecurity and vulnerability, group therapy may work well. But for those who fear vulnerability and exposure that they may experience in a group setting, individual therapy sessions (working one-on-one with a therapist) can be more advantageous.

References and Suggested Readings

Biggie, M.L. and Hunt, M.P., (1968), *Psychological Foundations of Education*, New York: Harper and Row.

Gates, A.I. and Jersild, A.T., *Educational Psychology*, New York: Macmillan 1970.

Hurlock, E.B. (1959), *Adolescent Development*, New York: McGraw Hill.

Woolfolk, Anita, *Educational Psychology* (Ninth edition), First Indian Reprint, New York: Pearson, 2004.

26

Deprivation and Deprived Children

Meaning and Nature of Deprivation

The term 'deprivation', a noun has been derived from the word 'deprive', a verb. In any dictionary you may find the meanings of the word deprive as 'to take from', 'to debar', 'to dispose', 'to strip', etc. Accordingly, when we say that he has been deprived of something, we may mean either of the following:

- That very thing has been taken from him.
- He has been debarred from enjoying the privilege of that thing.
- The possession of a thing has been snatched from him and given to somebody else.
- He has been stripped of some rights or privileges.

In this way, whatever meaning we may take for the term deprive, it indicates a sort of deficiency or loss of a thing, an object or opportunity of doing and progressing or being debarred or denied by some rights or privileges. In case one does not get his due share, right or privilege, then he is named as being deprived of that share, right or privilege. In history you have read that the British rulers had deprived the Indian rulers of their rights to adopt somebody as the heir to their kingdoms by introducing the doctrine of lapse. The queen of Jhansi, Laxmibai was the victim of such deprivation. Many of the youngsters have to suffer severe deprivation, on account of the sudden demise of their parents. It deprives them of the needed parental love and affection, sense of security, encouragement, incentives, etc., for their proper development. In many cases, poverty becomes the sole reason for depriving individuals of the basic necessities of life and this deprivation may prove a hurdle or major deficiency for their normal progress and development. We may come across a number of instances and examples of such economic, social cultural, physical and psychological deprivation in our surroundings.

The people belonging to socially untouchable or scheduled castes may be deprived of taking water from a well, the only source of getting drinking water in the village. They may also feel deprived of the right of worship by not getting entry in temples or their children may be deprived of educational opportunities by not getting admission in a village school. Even a child belonging to the same family may also sometimes become a victim of some or the other type of deprivation, i.e., he may get less attention, love and affection, incentives and encouragement, opportunities of education, development and progress in comparison to his siblings or cousins. In this way there is no dearth of victims of the deprivation in our surroundings whether on the individual basis or as a group and community. Sometimes a whole community or all the inhabitants of a particular region may fall victim to severe deprivation on account of one or the other reason. The rural community feels deprived of many such facilities that are easily available to the urban people. Similar is the case with the people, living in remote, hilly, desert, coastal or forest areas who may feel deprived of the facilities enjoyed by the inhabitants of plain areas. Many of the districts or regions of a particular state may also suffer from such deprivation on account of political reasons or exploiting tendencies of the ruling party or Government. The people of Haryana remained victims of such deprivation in the hands of United Punjab, then rulers who showered undue favour to the progress of their region at the cost of the present Haryana region. The same sort of deprivation was faced by the people of India as a whole at the hands of the British rulers who deprived us many of our rights and privileges in the same way as faced by the oppressed and down trodden classes like women, scheduled castes and tribes, poor, have-nots, etc., in today's democratic and free India.

In this way the term deprivation stands for all those deficiencies, defects and ailments prevailing in one environment that may cause us to face disfavour, loss of deficit in respect of the desired facilities, opportunities, help and guidance for the proper development and adjustment in comparison to other people living in the same or other environment.

Types of Deprivation

In reference to the earlier discussed meaning and nature of the term deprivation, we may come across the following types of deprivation usually prevalent in Indian society:

1. Economic Deprivation
2. Social and Cultural Deprivation
3. Educational Deprivation
4. Emotional Deprivation.

Let us now discuss these types of deprivation, one by one:

1. **Economic Deprivation:** Proper economic conditions and well-being have greater value in today's materialised world. Every facility of life and opportunities for one's welfare and development is closely linked with one's prosperity in terms of wealth, money and sound means of earning livelihood. Poverty is taken as a great curse causing all types of deficiencies, deficits and obstacles in one's living, growing and adjusting to one's self and the environment. In this way, the term economic deprivation stands for all those deficiencies, deficits and obstacles suffered by an individual, on account of the paucity of economic resources, i.e., poverty, for the satisfaction of his basic needs, his proper growth and development and adjustment to his self and the environment.

In the circumstances of such economic deprivation, i.e., poverty, children and other members of the family can't get adequate means even for the satisfaction of their most essential basic needs like food, water, rest, sleep, etc. They don't get shelter for living and clothes for wearing. The youngsters are compelled to earn the livelihood or to help their elders in parental occupation. When they venture for schooling, they have no money for the school fees, books, dress or other educationally essential materials. In such a deprived condition, how, can we think about their all round development and adequate adjustment? All their efforts and energies are thereby concentrated on doing away with their economic deficiencies just to keep themselves alive and adjust in this world of high material values. In this way their whole behaviour and personality are ultimately shaped in the struggle for their economic existence and survival. In contrast to these poverty-ridden children and individuals there is an affluent layer of the society who has everything for the satisfaction of its basic needs and progress. The children belonging to this strata are born with a silver spoon in their mouth and as a result do not have to bear the wrath of economic deprivation. Therefore, it is but natural, that such inequalities and wide variation in the economic level of the different layers of the society will ultimately lead to widespread dissatisfaction, conflicts and tensions in the mind of those who suffer on account of such inequalities, deficiencies and deprivation.

2. **Social and Cultural Deprivation:** This sort of deprivation is directly linked with the deficiencies, deficits and obstacles faced by the individual family or the whole community in relation to the satisfaction of their socio-cultural needs. When a child is deprived of the company of other children for playing or utilising his leisure time, he is said to be a victim of social deprivation. In a single family many of the aged persons have to bear the wrath of social deprivation in the situations where they have no grand children for necessary company, their son and daughter-in-law are busy in their lives and there is no way to have neighbour's company on account of the multi-storied or bungalow living styles of the urban life. A family may fall victim of the socio-cultural deprivation in a colony, sector or village when all the other families residing there either belong to a separate religion, faith, region or linguistic groups or have a quite high or low socio-economic status.

The children studying in boarding schools or public schools far away from their homes and families may also suffer from the socio-cultural deprivation. They are uprooted from their own cultural traditions and social values and as a result may feel difficulty in adjustment afterwards in their family environment, society and local educational institutions. Similar deprivation is also suffered by the individuals and families which are forced to remain cut off from their own society and culture on account of the nature of employment, occupation and earning of livelihood. These deprivation effects become more severe in case when these are accompanied with poverty, backwardness and illiteracy. They and their children, then suffer from many deficiencies, deficits and obstacles in respect of the severe socio-cultural deprivation. This story is usually repeated with the minority status families or communities, especially Dalits and untouchables residing in the villages or small towns. Such socio-culturally deprived families are forced to lag behind in every sphere of human progress and their condition gets worsened from generation to generation.

The people and families belonging to the majority community also have to suffer on some other counts like illiteracy, ignorance, stereotypes and prejudices. They try to cut themselves off from the mainstream by adopting social evils, the rotten traditions, the habit of resisting, any new change, etc., in their behaviour and styles of living. This is what is happening with the tribal's and the communities residing in the far off hilly, coastal, desert and forest regions. They are still lost in their world of superstitions and make believe by completely remaining in the dark away from the world of the 21st century. Their own nature as well as the inattention paid to the progress of the essential transport, communication and educational facilities may be said to be responsible for their socio-cultural derailment from the national mainstream.

3. **Educational Deprivation:** The term educational deprivation stands for all those deficiencies, deficits and obstacles which are responsible for depriving the individuals, families or communities from the opportunities of getting education or having a feeling that some injustice or disfavour is being done to them in comparison to other individuals, families or communities residing in the same or other regions.

    Thinking in this way, there may be widespread varieties, shapes and dimensions of the educational deprivation. Some children get deprived of education on account of poverty, illiteracy, ignorance and socio-cultural backwardness of their parents, families and communities. Some become victims of such deprivation on account of lack of proper educational facilities and opportunities like absence of school, lack of the provision for girls' education, non-availability of the provision for higher, technical, vocational and professional education within the reach of their means. In other cases, they may have the educational provisions only for their own sake, in the paper or names only. This story is more often repeated in the villages and far off regions where they have schools with no teachers, buildings or other essential men and material facilities. Some may have material facilities, but are deprived of human resources. There are teachers, but they seldom visit schools or if they do so, they have no temperament or intention of teaching the children. Such deficiencies and deficits of the educational provisions ultimately bring in significant educational deprivation to the children studying in such ill-managed or neglected educational institutions. In many other cases, we may find a more differentiated and segregated type of educational deprivation when an individual, family or a particular community is subjected to one or the other type of educational deprivation on account of it being belonging to a particular caste, tribe, region, religion, linguistic group, gender, nationality, socio economic status, etc. The injustice done to the individuals or groups on account of such favouritism and unjustified inequalities brings them in collision with the mainstream of the society. As a result they may either have to suffer from generation to generation or have to revolt and adopt a revengeful attitude by becoming socially aggressive or anti-social personalities.

4. **Emotional Deprivation:** The term emotional deprivation stands for all those deficiencies, deficits and obstacles lying in one's environment that interferes with the normal process of the satisfaction of one's socio-psychological needs, more

particularly his emotional needs to the extent of being drifted towards severe emotional maladjustment. The following situations and factors present in one's family and school environment are generally responsible for such emotional deprivation:

- The conflicts and clashes between parents, to the extent of separation or divorce, the death of one or both the parents.
- The insulting, indifferent, partial, prejudiced and unjust behaviour of the parents to the child.
- The behaviour of the other members of the family, relatives, guardians or other members of the society in case of the non-existence of the parents either due to their death or of their in-competencies and indifference to the child.
- The conflicts, clashes, fighting and cold war among the members of the family leading to an uncongenial environment at the home.
- Non-attention or careless attitudes of the parents or members of the family towards proper rearing and bringing up of the child on account of ignorance, illiteracy, socio-cultural backwardness, selfish interests or other reasons.
- The unjust, insulting, partial or prejudiced behaviour of teachers or elder students of the class or school to the child.
- The non-essential restrictions, lack of reasonable freedom and autocratic, unreasonable disciplinary systems both at the school and home.
- Lack of self-expression and opportunities for self-actualisation at home and school.

The earlier mentioned and other likewise elements or situations present in one's family and school environment may have enough potentiality in vitiating and polluting all those sources that can work as a reservoir, means and sources for the satisfaction of the children's desired emotional needs. Imagine where a child can go? To whom he should approach for the satisfaction of his needs of love and affection, security and protection, assurances and encouragements, freedom to express and act, gaining respect and status etc.? Only parents, members of the family, teachers and elders are in a position to satisfy his emotional needs which are very essential for his proper development and adequate adjustment. But where it is not available, the children are bound to suffer in all aspects such as physical and mental health, physical, cognitive, social and emotional development, morality, language development, etc.

Deprived Children: Meaning and Concept

You have seen that children may have to suffer from so many types of disadvantages and deprivations prevalent in their environment. In this way, while on one hand there are children who are privileged to enjoy all the facilities needed for their education, development and progress, on the other there may be a number of children who are not no privileged and even suffer from a number of disadvantages and deprivation causing great obstacles in their proper upbringing, development, adjustment, education and progress. In general, the term deprived children may be referred to those children who suffer from one or the offer types of disadvantages or deprivation to the extent of proving a big obstacle in the path of their proper upbringing, development, adjustment, education and progress in life. These children may be further classified as economically deprived, socially and culturally deprived, educationally and emotionally deprived depending upon the type of deprivation or disadvantages coming in the way of their development and progress. There are many issues related to the deprivation, adjustment and development of these children which needs a careful attention and study on the part of teachers. In general we may list them as follows:

1. Poverty-ridden children
2. Children living in urban slums
3. Socially deprived girls
4. Children separated from parents
5. Issues related to schooling of children
6. Childhood in the context of Adult culture, Globalisation, Urbanisation and Economic changes
7. Children facing specific stressful conditions
8. Issues related to marginalisation and stereotyping in the society
9. Children with behavioural problems

We have already considered the issue related to behavioural problems of the children in the chapter sixteen of this text. Here in this chapter we would like to discuss about the first four issues. Other remaining issues will be discussed later on in the subsequent chapters of this text one by one. Let us first take up the issue concerning poverty-ridden children.

Poverty-Ridden Children

Poverty is a great sin and poverty-ridden children are the worst sufferers in terms of various types of deprivations and disadvantages suffered by them on one or the other accounts. The story of their sufferings and deprivations in this connection starts well from the time of their conception in the womb of their mothers and then gets continued throughout their developmental period affecting their growth and development, education and progress as well as interests and welfare in a variety of ways mentioned as follows:

1. The poverty-ridden children may inherit many of the hereditary diseases and ailments, inabilities and incapacities, weaknesses and limitations through defective genes and chromosomes transmitted to them by their immediate parents who are unfortunate enough to get inflicted by them on account of their poverty-ridden defective environment and humiliating conditions of living and working. This defective inheritance may prove them quite costly in terms of the poor base and weak structure for starting their journey of development and progress in their life.

2. In the womb of the mother these poverty-ridden children do not get adequate nourishment and care for their proper growth and development. The mothers are helpless in supplying them due nourishment as they themselves may be

found in passing through the state of starvation, malnutrition, unhygienic living, physical ailments and mental agony or stress.

3. At the time of birth also there may arise a number of problems and adversities to these new born children. There may be no proper facilities available for the delivery of these poverty-ridden children. The environmental and sanitary conditions are very poor and unhygienic and thus there are many chances of picking up a number of abnormalities and defects by these children at the time of their birth

4. Many times the birth of these children is not welcome on the part of their parents or other family members as they may think it as an extra burden on their poverty. They may thus have to bear the brunt of the negligence, indifference, apathy, antagonistic attitudes and ill feelings of their dears and nears with no fault on their part.

5. After birth onwards these children are deprived with what is needed to them in terms of their proper nourishment, care and satisfaction of their basic needs, availability of essential material facilities, education and progress in their developmental period. The poverty and poor socio economic status of their parents and family may stand firmly well against their progress and development in many ways and consequently they may have to face the brunt of so many disadvantages, discriminations, prejudices, stereotypes, marginalisation and deprivations of one or the other kind resulting in various negative outcomes to them as summarised:.

    •   On account of the poor and pathetic conditions the children of the poor families cannot dream of a balanced diet and nutritious food, clean water, hygienic living conditions and other physical and material facilities essential for their adequate physical development and healthy disease-free living.

    •   The poverty-ridden children being victims of malnutrition and unhealthy as well as unhygienic living conditions right from their conception do not have natural growth of their sensory nerves and brain cells. As a result there is every possibility of retardation in terms of their intellectual functioning.

    •   The poverty-ridden children do not get proper opportunity for their language development. Generally their parents and family members are uneducated and illiterate. They have neither the time for a proper dialogue with their children (on account of their struggling for earning livelihood) nor have the proper vocabulary and command over the language. In their poverty-ridden homes and neighbourhood there are no newspapers, magazines, books and library facilities, radio, television or internet services available to them so as to provide an adequate learning experience for the development of expressive and communicative skills.

    •   The deprivation suffered by the poverty-ridden children may cast quite an adverse and retrogressive impact up on the development of essential cognitive abilities, and attainment of essential social and emotional maturity and getting desired academic progress in their learning pursuits. One's thinking, feelings and actions are always influenced by what is going on with him as a living and social being. One's mental and emotional state at a particular time thus proves to be a great determinant of his mental, emotional, social and academic functioning. The disadvantaged poor children often remain tense, worried and emotionally maladjusted on account of the paucity of resources and humiliation suffered in meeting one or the other developmental and educational needs of theirs and it may cast an adverse effect on their mental, social, emotional and academic development and progress.

- The overall development, adjustment and progress of the poverty-ridden children may also suffer on account of the denial of proper educational facilities to them. Their parents do not send them schools on account of taking their help in their bread-earning pursuits, domestic assignments or getting engaged in child labour. In case they intend to send them to schools, then it becomes an uphill task for them to afford the expenses even for the state running institutions. The schooling of their children in the reputed good schools is entirely out of the question for the poverty-ridden parents. In case they get admission in some schools anyhow, they have to suffer from maladjustment on one or the other grounds. More often, here they are ridiculed, humiliated, discriminated, marginalised and victimised on account of the poverty or socio-economic status of their families. It gets them emotionally and mentally disturbed resulting in their under-achievement and backwardness in curricular and co-curricular pursuits.

- The hardships faced, discrimination and marginalisation suffered and obstacles faced in the developmental path cast a quite negative effect on the proper development of self-confidence, self-efficacy and self-esteem among the poverty-ridden children. More often these children are found to suffer from the feelings of insecurity, lack of self-confidence, guilty consciousness and inferiority complexes causing great harm to their adequate adjustment, development and progress in life.

In this way, it may be properly visualised that a child's poverty and low socio-economic status may prove quite costly to him or her in terms of his or her adjustment, development and progress in school, society and life. Such children, therefore needs adequate help, assistance and guidance for dealing with their problems and progressing to their maximum on the part of the government, nongovernment organisations, school authorities and teachers. The following suggestions may prove fruitful in this direction:

1. There should be well planned scheme on the part of government and non-government organisations for providing financial assistance and incentives to the poverty-ridden children for their schooling.

2. The schooling should be free to the poverty-ridden children. The community and government should take care of their dress and other reading material needed by them for their education.

3. There should be a fixed proportion of seats reserved for the poverty-ridden children in all types of schools (government-aided and private or public schools).

4. There should be proper arrangement of midday meal program especially suited to the poverty-ridden children.

5. Care should be taken to pay attention on the living conditions of the poverty-ridden families. They should be helped in improving their sanitary conditions and feeding them in a proper way. They should also be helped in having their *pakka* houses, electricity supply, kitchen gas and clean water to drink with a sufficient subsidy and concessional rates.

6. Provision of free essential medical facilities or on concessions should be made available to the poverty-ridden families and children.

7. The community services, games and entertainment facilities should be suitably made available to the poverty-ridden children at no cost.

8. They should be given all incentives to take part in co-curricular activities and programs helpful in the wholesome development of their personality.

9. They should be helped in knowing and learning that poverty does not stand in the progress and development of a person if he tries to proceed on his path with a firm determination. There should be arrangement of such motivational lectures, dialogues and workshops in the schools as well as in community centres.

10. Whenever, a poverty-ridden child is found to excel in one or the other field, he should be duly encouraged for his or her efforts and attempts should be made to produce him or her as a living example to others.

Children Living in Slum Areas

The rapid increase in the size and intensity of heavy industrialisation and urbanisation resulted through the process of globalisation in the modern era has given birth to a number of slum areas and localities as habitats for the labours and other people coming to the big towns and cities to earn their livelihood. These slum areas or localities may be seen to portrait the real hail or worst places for the living of human beings in the manner depicted as follows:

• They are often located in the unused and unauthorised or waste lands and places prohibited for living such as the land available on railway stations, area adjacent to dirty drainage or foul water collected in the low lying lands or nearby the pollution spreading factories.

• They do not possess the essentials of living such as proper pathways and roads, sewerage system and sanitation arrangement, water for drinking and other uses, electricity, gas supply, etc.

• The houses are most often built through temporary stuff such as tent house old clothing, plastic sheets, mud and thatches, and bamboo sticks, etc., unable to bear the brunt of summer, winter or rains.

• There is no provision of toilets and bathrooms, People have to bath in open and toilet in the areas adjacent to their localities causing hygienic problems to themselves and others.

• Since these are located in the unauthorised land and are not falling within the jurisdiction of the municipal committee or city boards, there exists nothing like parks, open places for the recreation and playing of their children, elementary schools and community centres.

- These are characterised with the heavy doses of air, water and noise pollutions.
- The inhabitants of these localities generally are the poverty-ridden masses, labourers serving in the nearby factories, rickshaw pullers, porters, domestic servants and low earning people. Most of them are illiterate or semi-literates with no social exposure of the globalised world.
- They are not much conscious about the sanitation, cleanliness and essential health measures being taken for the health and wellbeing of the pregnant mothers and developing children.

Impact on the Development, Adjustment and Education of the Developing Children

Children belonging to urban slums may be found to suffer from a host of deficiencies, deprivations and adversities affecting their adjustment, education and development in quite a detrimental way much in the ways as suffered by the poverty-ridden children. We have discussed all such ill impacts and negative influences on them already in this chapter. However, there is one thing more that needs to be mentioned in addition to what has already been said. It is concerned with the special damaging impact that it has on the developing children on account of the type of environment available to them for their adjustment and education and development. We can summarise it in the following manner:

1. They may be found to get inflicted with a number of diseases and ailments on account of poor sanitation and unhealthy living conditions and the adverse impacts of such unhealthy environment may cost them dearly in the impairment of their health and physical development.

2. They have nothing solid in their environment that can prove friendly, inspirational and helpful for their proper growth and development. In the form of peers and elderly models available for the observation, imitation and imbibing the habits and learning of the desirable behaviour their environment provides them quite a negative and undesirable models before them at their home, neighbourhood and locality. These may become school failures, drop outs, truants, problem children, alcoholics, drug addicts, gamblers, thieves, smugglers, delinquents and criminals. The company of such peers and elders may easily drift them along the path of antisocial, immoral, problematic or delinquent behaviour or they may be entrapped deliberately by the vested interests in the world of crimes and antisocial behaviour.

3. The slim locality stamp imprinted on them may prove costly to them in terms of their adequate adjustment and development. They may face a lot of discrimination, marginalisation and deprivation on this account. As a part of reactionary measure, it may drift them towards aggression, problematic, and delinquent behaviour. On the other hand there are more possibilities on their part for getting drifted into the state of failure, frustration, and depressions on account of lowering of their morale, self-confidence, self-esteem and self-efficacy in a considerable way. The children belonging to slum areas are thus usually found standing on the crossroads with no path available to them to lead towards

some satisfying development and progress. The frustration coupled with lack of confidence, initiative, pushes them towards unemployment or forcing them to seek employment as manual labour or other lower category jobs, which may further entrap them and their coming generation in the world of poverty and slums.

Measures to Bring Improvement in Their Status

Many of the measures adopted for helping the poverty-ridden children in their adequate adjustment, education and development may also work well for helping the children living in urban slum areas. We do not want to repeat them. However, the ill impacts and negative influences inflicted merely on account of their belonging to slums may need the employment of some extra measures for their welfare in the following manner:

1. Earnest attempts must be made for bringing improvement in the living conditions of slum dwellers. These colonies should be regularised and arrangement should be made for equipping them with the needed living amenities like toilets, pure drinking water, electric and kitchen gas supply, pakka houses, proper roads, food stuff on the subsidised rates, drainage system and sewerage, community centres, community parks, neighbourhood school and transport facilities.

2. The slum dwellers must be helped in making them literate and helping them to advance further in their learning pursuits.

3. They must be properly educated for being conscious about bringing improvement in their living and behaving. They should feel their responsibility of providing opportunities to their children for their education and development and realise that they should not do anything that may influence the behaviour and habits of the children in a negative and damaging way.

4. Attempts should be made to save the slum children from the company of the bad elements. In case they somehow entrapped in the net of the vested interests, they should be helped in coming out and lead their life in a new way.

Socially Deprived Girls

There has been prevailing a continuous trend and practice of hatred, indifference, prejudices, discrimination and marginalisation towards the girl child in the Indian families from the time immemorial on one or the other account. As a result, the girl child has been a clear cut object of social deprivation being witnessed in the following ways:

1. In most of the Indian families even in this age of so much technological progress and awareness, the birth of a girl child is not a subject of celebration. It is considered quite unfortunate to give birth to a girl child by the mothers and they are cursed and held responsible for bringing misfortune to the family.

2. There prevails a clear cut differentiation and discrimination in the upbringing of the girl and boy children on the part of parents and elders such as:

    •   Boys enjoy all privileges, care and attention in the satisfaction of their basic needs at the cost of their sisters.

- Girls are denied the opportunity of going to schools on the plea that they are made for household duties.
- They are denied a balanced and nutritious diet on the plea that boys require more energy and stamina for performing man-like responsibilities and they should be healthier and stronger than their female counter parts.
- The behaviour of the boy child is not condemned and decried even if it is undesirable and problem generating. On the other hand a simple natural slip in the behaviour of a girl child is punished and decried in every sort.
- Girls are denied opportunity to participate in outside activities, games and sports, driving and swimming, and any adventurism events on the plea that these task and activities are not feminine and fall predominantly in the task area of the boys.

3. There is a lot of discrimination and differentiation observed by the society in dealing with girls. They are always neglected in comparison to the boys in one or the other matters related to common welfare. In our society, women and girls are always treated just like commodities, the things of utilising in the service of manhood. The essentials like gender equality and respect for the fair sex are almost absent in our society. As a result there are more incidents of eve teasing, sex abuse, molestation, rape, and gender violence against the girls and they have to suffer a lot of humiliation, disrespect and agonies at the hands of the men and boys in social places including schools. It has caused in instilling among them a sense of insecurity and fear and lowering down their morale, self-confidence, self-esteem and self-efficacy in respect of their social movements and participation.

4. In schools also girls have to suffer from the menace of gender discrimination, differentiation and deprivation. They are not supposed to study mathematics, computer and engineering, the so-called study areas of boys. Similarly, they are deprived of the opportunities of activities promoting inventiveness, constructivism and discovery on their part. They are discouraged to have competition with boys in martial arts, sports and act of adventurism and take part in outdoor social and community activities thus snatching many valuable opportunities for their wholesome development and progress.

The picture portrayed regarding the discrimination and deprivation of the girls in our society is quite alarming. However, in this connection there is good news that things are changing fast on account of globalisation, urbanisation, modernisation, mass media, spread of literacy and development in ICT and computer applications. The girl child is no more considered a curse and burden on the family. People have started to provide all the needed facilities for the wholesome development of their daughters as they intend to arrange for their sons. In schools also necessary measures have now in progress for minimising the effect of marginalisation and deprivation on the girl children. A lot of more, needs to be done on the part of society and government for protecting the girl child from the humiliation and damage (physical, social and psychological) done to her on account of rising cases of sex abuse, molestation, rape and violence. On one hand, there is a need of awakening the conscious of the people and society as a whole to halt such cruelties to the girls and women and on the other there should be hard penalties with real intention of their enforcement prescribed by the legal authorities for dealing with the offences and crimes against girls and women.

Children Separated From Parents

It is a hard fact that there is no substitute to parents in the matter of rearing, nourishing and developing the children to their maximum. However, all children are not so fortunate as to enjoy protection, care, love and affection of their parents from their birth onwards. Many of them are found to get separated from their parents on a number of grounds such as:

- Stealing and kidnapping by some vested interests.
- Accidental separation from the parents and family in a crowded place and rail, motor or air accidents.
- Incidental or untimely death of mother, father, or both.
- The parental marital discord, separation or divorce.
- Time-bound separation from the parents for full day or few hours on account of their business or professional compulsion.
- Intentionally leaving the children in boarding houses or institutions on account of their abnormal emotional, physical or mental state.

Now the question that arises is what happens to these children who get separated from their parents on one or the other ground and are reared or guarded by somebody else. Let us think about them one by one according to their nature and reason lying behind their separation.

(i) Children reared in the hands of bad guys and criminals

You may well imagine the pathetic conditions and consequences suffered by the separated children at the hands of the vested interests. You may have witnessed on the TV and movie screen the scenes on how the body parts of the children (kidnapped or falling into the hands of the bad guys) are damaged for forcing them into begging; how they are left to die by extracting one or the other life organs of their body; how these innocent one's are pushed into the world of sex trade and crimes and how these are exploited in terms of bonded labour.

(ii) Children reared in boarding houses and institutions

For the children with special needs who are sent to boarding houses or day care special institutions by their parents, there is nothing bad. Such separation, rearing and educational practice may in fact may prove quite beneficial to them for their needed adjustment, education and progress well within their capacities and limitations.

(iii) Children reared by single parent (mother or father)

In the case of marital discord, the custody of the child is given to either to the parent, mother or father. The same responsibility of rearing a child all alone also falls on the shoulders of a mother or father when one of them dies. In such a situation we may see that every person has his or her own style of rearing. Depending up on one's capacity and resources in terms of time and facilities every single parent tries to provide appropriate caring to the child. However, the situation is altogether altered when separated parents are remarried. It all depends up on the circumstances and the sincerity of the step father or mother that the child may get favourable or unfavourable environment for his or her growth and development.

(iv) Children reared by relatives

In the situation where the children are so separated from their parents (on account of their marital discord or death) that neither of the parents is available for their rearing, the task may be left to their close relatives. Here the children may feel a lot of problems and difficulties in the way of their adequate adjustment, development and education. Depending up on the nature and behaviour of their keepers they may be fortunate or unfortunate for passing through their developmental years in a satisfactory or unsatisfactory way.

(v) Children reared in crèches

With an increasing pressure on the parents to earn money for their living and also for the sake of career building and self-satisfaction, both mother and father nowadays may be found to remain away from their infants. They have the compulsion for leaving the child under the care of the other members of the family such as grant parents or some relatives. However, such a facility is rarely available on account of the upsurge of the concept of nuclear family and the parents are forced to leave their infants for their rearing in crèches. The numbers of these crèches is increasing day by day in the urban localities of big towns and cities where we may find heavy concentration of the educated working mothers attending offices, schools and business establishments for a considerable length of the day. Let us think about the functioning and rearing practices adopted in these crèches:

- These crèches usually work in a dense locality of well-educated middle class. The parents are in practice of selecting a particular crèche on account of its nearness, coming in the route of their daily travelling to work places, or the reputation of their good rearing practices.

- They have full day as well as half day provision for leaving the children in their care and looking after depending up on the needs of parents and are capable of serving the rearing needs of the very small children such as four months old to the age of the two or three. For the little older children they work under the pattern of play schools where they perform the responsibilities of making the infants learn the rudiments of preliminary classes along with contributing their physical, social and emotional development.

- Usually, they hire girls and women for taking care of the infants and train them in accordance to their own methods or norms practiced for rearing besides providing dedicated services of their own (many times a whole family of the owner join hands for running a crèche).

- In rearing the infants, the individual needs and differences are strictly kept in view by the crèche runners. The success of a crèche depends up on the quality maintained in the rearing practices and the faith and trust of the parents earned by it for such rearing.

- The rearing responsibilities of the small children and infants are in fact a tedious and challenging job for the crèche runners. It needs on their part a lot of experience about the task of child rearing, infant psychology, patience and hardworking attitude, love and affection towards small children in a quite motherly fashion, and devotion and commitment to provide protection, emergency medical facilities, and best care in terms of their feeding, toilet and bath room-related activities, cloth changing, rest and sleep, play and recreation, sitting and walking, hygiene and health, and even transportation and picking and leaving them from their homes.

- The crèche rearing practice although, keeps the children of very tender age away for the care and protection of their own mothers for a considerable long duration, yet it is not found to exercise any adverse impact on the development and well-being of the children unless it is not doing its duty in a truly dedicated or professional way. Contrarily in many cases it may help them in acquiring best attention and timely caring for their individual needs and appropriate development.

(vi) Children reared in orphanages

A number of children separated from their parents are forced to take shelter in orphanages when (i) help from relatives are not available, (ii) when they are saved from the clutches of the kidnappers and bad guys, (iii) when they are deliberately abandoned by relatives and single parents in the orphanages (many children are left in temples, lonely places and the premises of orphanages by the unmarried mothers, widows, illegitimate relationship couples etc.)

These orphanages are regulated by one or the other social or religious organisations mostly on charitable basis. Initially the lead for the establishment of these orphanages is taken by some noble figures dedicated to community service and humanity but as the time passes, their management may be gripped up by the people who get engaged in the exploitation of the orphans along with the drying out the resources of the orphanage. We may witness such irony of the orphanages through the newspapers, magazines, radio and TV news or episodes and films shown on screens. Orphans have to face a number of sufferings and exploitation at the hands of management personnel, employees, politicians, and anti-social elements ranging from ill-treatment and starving to bonded labour and sexual exploitation.

In such an uncongenial environment it is quite natural for the children rearing in orphanages to suffer from one or the other deprivation or disadvantages such as:

(i) Deprivation suffered in terms of the satisfaction of their physical needs like availability of enough food for satisfying their hunger, lack of nutritious elements in their food stuff, clean water, cloths and other material for living.

(ii) Deprivation suffered in terms of satisfying their socio-cultural needs such as little or no opportunities for having company or interaction with the social and cultural life of the outside world.

(iii) Deprivation suffered in terms of satisfying their educational needs as no serious attempts are made for their proper education and schooling.

(iv) Deprivation suffered in terms of the satisfaction of their psychological needs such as need to get love and affection, empathy, cooperation, etc.

The earlier-cited deprivations suffered by the children rearing in orphanages are big enough to block all the ways and means for their adequate adjustment to self and environment. There is no hope for any worthwhile development and progress for these children rearing in the orphanages managed and run by the vested interests and bad guys.

However, as you know there is still good sense left on the part of good and noble people and these are those who are working sincerely for managing and providing the orphans what is essentially needed for their better living, behaving, adjustment and progress in life. One of such organisation is Manav Seva Sangh working in many regions of our country. It is providing the developing children rearing in its well-managed orphanages providing a quality life and opportunities for their wholesome growth and development by instilling necessary social and cultural values and confidence for achieving the targets of life.

Summary

The term **deprivation** stands for all those deficiencies, defects and ailments prevailing in an environment that may cause to face disfavour, loss of deficit in respect of the desired facilities, opportunities, help and guidance for a child's proper development and adjustment in comparison to other people living in the same or other environment.

In general, we may come across many **types of deprivation** prevalent in the Indian society such as (i) Economic Deprivation (deficiencies, deficits and obstacles suffered by an individual, on account of the paucity of economic resources, i.e., poverty), (ii) Social and Cultural Deprivation deficiencies (deficits and obstacles faced by the individual family or the whole community in relation to the satisfaction of their socio-cultural needs), (iii) Educational Deprivation (deficiencies, deficits and obstacles responsible for depriving individuals, families or communities from the opportunities of getting education or facing discrimination in the availability of education in a proper way in comparison to others, (iv) Emotional Deprivation (deficiencies, deficits and obstacles lying in one's environment that interfere with the normal process of the satisfaction of one's socio-psychological needs, more particularly his emotional needs to the extent of drifting towards severe emotional maladjustment).

In general, the term **deprived children** may be referred to those children who suffer from one or the offer types of disadvantages or deprivation to the extent of proving a big obstacle in the path of their proper upbringing, development, adjustment, education and progress in life. These children may be further classified as economically deprived, socially and culturally deprived, educationally and emotionally deprived depending upon the type of deprivation or disadvantages coming in the way of their development and progress. There are many issues related to the deprivation, adjustment and development of these deprived children which requires a careful attention and study on the part of teachers such as (i) Childhood in the context of poverty, (ii) Impact of Globalisation on the developing children, (iii) Children living in urban slums, (iv) Socially deprived girls and (v) Children separated from parents.

The emergence of the sections of **poverty-ridden families and communities** created by the ongoing rapid changes is responsible for affecting the development and well-being of the children right from the time of their conception in the womb of their mothers. They are found to experience severe type of set-backs in their developmental period affecting their growth and development, education and progress as well as interests and welfare in a variety of ways. Such children therefore need adequate help, assistance and guidance on the part of the government, non-government organisations, school authorities and teachers for dealing with their problems and progressing to the maximum.

The children who belong to **urban slums** may be found to suffer from a host of deficiencies, deprivations and adversities affecting their adjustment, education and development in quite a detrimental way. They are denied opportunities for their education and development and if somehow availed then are found to face a lot of discrimination and segregation in the schools and social interaction. The impoverished environment available in the slum area as well as poverty, lack of education and spoiled habits of their parents and slim dwellers may force these children into socially deviant and problematic behaviour.

The girl child in most of our communities in India is subjected to the prevailing practice of hatred, indifference, prejudices, discrimination and marginalisation in Indian families from time immemorial on one account or the other. As a result, the girl child has been a clear cut object of social deprivation being witnessed in the following ways and manners: (i) forced abortion in the womb of the mother; (ii) right from her birth showing indifference, hatred, and discrimination towards the girl child both in the family and community surroundings; (iii) depriving the girl child from availing needed educational and career advancement opportunity and (iv) showing discrimination towards the girls in work areas – educational and professional.

Children may get **separated from their parents** on one or the other grounds. Such separation may force them either to be on the mercy of (i) anti-social elements and criminals or (ii) the owners of boarding houses, institutions, crèches and orphanages or get reared by relatives and single parents. Where in the former case there lie all possibilities of getting them misused or maltreated at their hands, in the latter the suffering children may face deprivation and be handicapped in getting many essentials needed for their proper progress and development.

References and Suggested Readings

Baumrind, D. (1967), "Child care practices ante-ceding three patterns of pre-school behaviour,' *Genetic Psychology*, Monographs, 75 (1), 43-88.

Biggie, M.L. and Hunt, M.P., (1968), *Psychological Foundations of Education*, New York: Harper and Row.

Brine, J. (1919), *Under educating women: Globalization in equality*, Bukingham, U.K.: Open University Press.

Erickson, E., (1950) *Childhood and Society*, New York: Norton.

Giddens, Antony (1990), *The Consequences of Modernity*, Cambridge, U.K.: Polity Press.

Kuppuswamy, B. (1971), *An introduction to Social Psychology*, Bombay: Publishing House.

Marten Albrew and Elizabeth King (1990), *Globalization, Knowledge and Society* London: Sage.

Woolfolk, Anita, (2004), *Educational Psychology (9th ed.) First Indian Reprint*, New York: Pearson.

27

Marginalisation and Stereotyping in the Development of Children

Marginalisation: Meaning and Concept

Marginalisation in its simple meaning stands for the process or act of marginalising. In the available dictionaries (Merriam Webster, Oxford etc.,) the action verb "marginalise" has been defined as, "To put or keep (someone) in a powerless or unimportant position within a society or group." Accordingly, the term marginalisation may stand for the process or act of a majority community or group to put or keep an individual or a minority group in a deprived state, i.e., making them deprived of the power or privilege enjoyed by the members of the community in general. Agreeing with such meaning and concept of the term marginalisation, The Encyclopedia of Public Health (2002) has tried to define the term marginalisation as: "To be marginalised means to be placed in the margins and thus get excluded from the privilege and power found at the centre". All over the world, societies and nations suffer from this widespread problem known as marginalisation reflecting through the social exclusion of a particular minority group, locality, community and society from the mainstream of the society on one or the other accounts. In its practical application thus the term marginalisation and social exclusion are used interchangeably and thus both of them may stand for the process in which individuals or entire communities of people are systematically blocked from (or denied full access to) various rights, opportunities and resources that are normally available to members of the majority or ruling group.

Types or Forms of Marginalisation

Marginalisation suffered on the part of individuals in our societies may be visible in two main forms:
 (i) Individual marginalisation and
(ii) Community marginalisation

Individual marginalisation

It is concerned with the social exclusion of individuals at their personal or individual level. It results in an individual's exclusive marginalisation. As a result he or she may be (i) debarred from meaningful participation in society and (ii) denied access to a number of rights and privileges otherwise available to the members of the society.

As examples of such marginalisation or social exclusion we may name: marginalisation of widows, single mothers, poor, disabled persons, children, senior citizens and persons suffering from diseases like Aids, cancer, leprosy, etc. The state or conditions of the marginalisation suffered by these individuals may be well judged through the following instances:

- A girl child belonging to the same family may fall victim to marginalisation on account of her gender. She may get less attention, love and affection, incentives and encouragement, opportunities of education, development and progress in comparison to her male siblings or cousins.

- A senior citizen (male or female) may be subjected to seclusion and marginalisation at the hands of his own kith and kin. He may be given no attention and most often is denied the essentials of his proper living to the extent of facing social and emotional deprivation.

- A disabled child may not be allowed to make use of educational facilities available in his or her neighbourhood. He is debarred from taking part in the social functions of the family and community.

- A youth may fail to get employment despite his ability and performance shown in the interview on account of being marginalised and discriminated at the hands of the members of the board dominated by a particular community/caste.

Community marginalisation

In such marginalisation an entire community or a group having minority status may be found to face marginalisation at the hands of the majority group. The marginalisation of the blacks in European countries and women, untouchables, and scheduled caste people in India may be cited as examples of such marginalisation. The state or conditions of the marginalisation suffered by the groups or community as a whole may be visualised well through the following instances:

- The people belonging to a socially untouchable, scheduled caste or tribe may be denied or deprived of taking water from a well, the only source of drinking water in the village. They may also be denied the right of worship by not getting entry in temples and casting their franchise in a democratic way. Their children may also be deprived of educational opportunities by not getting admission in village schools since they are considered untouchables by the higher caste people. If admitted on a legal basis, they suffer from acute humiliation and discrimination on one or the other fronts.

- The rural community may feel deprived of many such facilities that are easily available to the urban people. Similarly a minority community may get victimised at the hands of majority and consequently may feel quite uncomfortable and unsafe even in their living and enjoying civic rights (e.g., Kashmiri Hindu population in the disturbed Kashmir regions).

- Many of the districts or regions of a particular state or nation may also suffer from seclusion and denied opportunities and facilities available to other citizens on account of political reasons or exploiting tendencies of the ruling part or government. The people of Bangladesh remained victims of acute discrimination and exploitation in the hands of the mighty Pakistan, then rulers who showered undue favour to the progress of the western Pakistan at the cost of the present Bangladesh.

• An acute impact of marginalisation was faced by us as a whole at the hands of the British rulers who deprived us of our rights and privileges in the same way as faced by oppressed and down trodden classes like women, scheduled castes and tribes (especially in rural India), poor etc., in today's democratic and free India.

The Factors or Contributors to Marginalisation

Marginalisation (visible on the individual or group/community basis) has resulted on account of the apathy shown and discriminatory attitude adopted for the individuals and minority groups by the majority, powerful and status enjoying section of the society. This apathy and discriminatory attitude germinated in the mind and behaviour of the majority group is based on the stereotypes prevailing in the society and negative attitude developed in their mind on one or the other account. The major contributors in this connection thus may include the following factors:

• Gender-linked factors like negative attitude towards girls and women, bisexuals, prostitutes, transsexuals, third genders, etc.

• Economy-linked factors like poverty, low socio- economic status and unemployment.

• Socio-culturally linked factors like belonging to different caste, race, colour, creed, religion, language, political affiliation, possessing radical views quite contrary to society and government, and migrants from other regions, states or countries.

• Exceptionality linked factors (being too much diverse from the norms) like being gifted or genius, backward or slow learner, suffering from one or the other disabilities or incapacities, etc.

The Consequences or Impacts of Marginalisation

The outcome or impact of marginalisation or social exclusion lies in the fact that affected individuals or communities are prevented from participating fully in the economic, social and political life of the society in which they live. Apart from being excluded, they often become victims of acute apathy, hate and discrimination on the part of majority and powerful segment of the society. They are deprived from taking part in the usual activities of the society and denied access to many essential amenities and privileges enjoyed by the majority group. Marginalised individuals or groups thus may have to suffer from a number of deprivations — socio-cultural, economical, psychological and educational so much so as to make them suffer badly in terms of their well-being and progress. Children and students are no exceptions. They also have to suffer badly on account of the ill consequences and damaging impact of the phenomenon of marginalisation.

We should also be quite clear in visualising that the developing children feel the heat of marginalisation on two fronts. One on account of the marginalisation faced by their parents and family, and the other on account of the marginalisation suffered by themselves in their home, school and society.

A. The Impact of Marginalisation Suffered by Parents and Family

The developing children depend on their parents and family for the support and facilities needed for their education, adjustment and development. In case where their parents and family get marginalised at the hands of the majority group or society, the ill consequences suffered by them on account of such marginalisation get automatically transferred to the developing children. In general, the marginalisation of parents and family members by the majority and powerful section of the society may lead family to the following disadvantages:

- Affecting the economy of the family in an adverse way to the extent of making it suffer from poverty and lack of essentials for living.
- Compelling the family to live in unhygienic conditions.
- Non-availability or denial of the essential medical and health facilities.
- Non-availability or denial of proper educational facilities to self and children.
- Getting psychological shocks on account of the ill treatment faced at the hands of the majority group.

A marginalised family deprived in such a manner then fails to contribute appropriately for the growth and development of its developing children. The children here (i) suffer from mal-nourishment right from their very conception in the womb of the mother, (ii) are forced to drink contaminated water, (iii) do not get health and medical assistance in time, (iv) suffer from ailments and diseases, (v) do not get due attention and caring from their parents on account of their struggling to earn a livelihood, (vi) do not get help from the parents and family members for the development of language and communication power on account of the helplessness and illiteracy of their parents and family members, (vii) do not get appropriate opportunity to imbibe healthy proper habits from the peers and neighbours on account of the poor neighbourhood and incapable playing mates and peers, (viii) fail to get appropriate educational opportunities in terms of admission in good schools and discrimination or marginalisation suffered in the school on account of the seclusion and socio-economic status of their families and (ix) remain deprived from the company, contacts and interactions with the members of the community and other social institutions and agencies helpful in their proper social, emotional and mental development. In this way, the physical and socio-cultural environment available in the marginalised and deprived families fails to provide the children what is needed for the satisfaction of their physical and socio-psychological needs and ag- related wholesome development. On the contrary it leads them to poor physical and mental health and ailments, social and emotional maladjustment, socially and morally undesirable habits, delinquent or socially deviant behaviour, drug addiction and alcoholism, communication and language problems, backwardness and learning difficulties, failures and drop outs, shutting up the doors of higher education, employment and proper settlement in life.

B. The Impact of Marginalisation Suffered by the Children Themselves

In addition to the ill consequences suffered by the children on account of the side effects and contributions of the marginalisation of their families, children are bound to suffer badly on account of their own marginalisation and victimisation in their families, schools and society. Let us try to think in this direction.

1. **Marginalisation in family:** It is quite possible for the children to suffer from acute marginalisation and discrimination at the hands of their own parents, step mother and father, care taker and family members in a number of ways. The apathy and antagonistic attitude of the family members towards, the girl child, widow child or children losing their mother/father or both, disabled, etc. in our society is well known. In such discriminatory and deprived physical and socio-psychological environment of the family, the children fail to get needed love and affection, attention and care, rearing and nourishing supplements, healthy interactions and timely guidance, incentives and reinforcement for their good behaviour and progress. As a result there arises a big gap in the physical and socio-psychological needs and their satisfaction. It leads them nowhere other than the path of painful maladjustment and failure in terms of achieving age-related milestones of their wholesome development and progress.

2. **Marginalisation in school:** The environment available in the school to the children for their education, adjustment and development may be quite defective, discriminatory and marginalised. The students may suffer from acute discrimination and marginalisation in the school on one or the other accounts like belonging to a particular gender, caste, colour, creed, religion, social status, region, language group and nationality, suffering from one or the other types of disabilities and incapacities, or may face the wrath of the personal disliking, negative attitude, jealousy and envy of the teachers and authorities developed towards them. In consequence, they may exclude and prevent a child from taking part in the regular activities of the school, ridicule or treat him badly in front of others, do injustice in evaluating their performance and achievements and thus harm him psychologically and educationally in a way as to put a lot of barriers in his adequate adjustment, development and progress. Such marginalised students then with no fault of theirs may be seen to be drifting towards backwardness, failure, truancy, delinquency, drug addiction and other types of antisocial and morally deviant behaviour.

3. **Marginalisation in society:** Members of the majority community and the environment also try to display a lot of marginalisation and discrimination towards the developing children by not allowing them to take part in the activities, festivals, rituals, worships and functions organised in the community venues from time to time. The discrimination and prohibition may be on any ground (such as being a women/girl, widow, disabled, lower caste or untouchable, poor, villager, following other sects, faiths or religion, black colour or disliked nationality) but in all its way it casts a quite negative and damaging influence on the adjustment and development of children by snatching the valuable opportunities of social interaction, community and social learning and outward self-expression.

Role of Teacher in a Marginalised Learning Environment Setting

A marginalised learning environment setting refers to a learning setting or the classroom situation where some students in a given learning setup are seen to get marginalised, secluded, discriminated or deprived of a number of rights, learning opportunities and resources while others may be seen to have full access to all of these. Such scenes may be witnessed in the learning environment of schools where a great deal of marginalisation is applied to students on the basis of gender, caste, colour, religion, rural or urban background, or socio economic status of their family. In all correctness schools are required to serve the interests and purposes of the society or community where they are functioning. It is therefore but natural for a school to run in tune with the ideals, traditions and mores of the society. In a society where an acute sense of marginalisation and discrimination is prevalent on the people on one or the other grounds, the same may naturally reflect in the school setup and attitudes of the school people, including teachers and students. Accordingly, there is no surprise to witness a vindictive and antagonistic environment against the girl child, widow girl child, the disabled children, the scheduled caste and scheduled tribes children, children belonging to poor and weaker sections, speaking other languages and belonging to other states or nations. But now the question that arises is what should be the role of a teacher in such a marginalised setting of the school? A teacher by the dignity of his profession has to be quite fair and impartial to all his disciples despite their being of a social group or characterised with any distinction or differences with respect to gender, colour, performance or abilities. He has to take necessary precautions in dealing with his students in the prevailing environment of marginalisation in the class and school. The things to be done on his part for this purpose may be broadly summarised as follows:

1. First of all he must try to imbibe a required level of sensitivity towards marginalisation, seclusion and discrimination prevalent in the society and field of teaching-learning in respect of its concept and ill consequences.

2. He should then try to get acquainted with the type and nature of the marginalisation practices prevalent in the school against one or the other types of students.

3. He should then take into confidence his higher ones and colleagues to put a halt to the practices and policies of marginalisation, seclusion and discrimination prevalent in the school. It should lead the teachers to remain cautious and vigilant in relation to:

   • Knowing the reasons of some students getting marginalised in the school along with the reasons of the marginalisation of their families in the society

   • Sorting out the ways and means of putting checks and control over the practice of marginalisation in the school.

   • Getting assured that no student should get discriminated and victimised on the basis of marginalisation in the classrooms and school.

   • Persuading the peers and classmates to have no apathy and antagonism with the student who differ from them in terms of gender, race, religion, cast colour or creed, socio-economic status, language, abilities and capacities, region or nationality.

4. He should build up necessary confidence in students belonging to marginalised group of society (such as girl students, widow students, scheduled castes and scheduled tribe students, minority status students, migrant students and foreigners) and provide them necessary help and guidance for helping them in their adequate adjustment, education and development.

5. He should work for the setting and successful working of an inclusive learning in the school so that the disadvantaged or deprived ones including the disabled may get an equal and conducive learning environment for their adjustment and holistic development well in tune with their abilities and capacities.

Stereotyping: Meaning and Concept

As its etymological derivation, the term stereotype has been derived from a combination of two Greek words: "stereos" (meaning as firm or solid) and "typos" (meaning impression or opinion). Therefore, it tends to stand for "solid impression" or "firm opinion".

The terms stereotype and stereotyping have been variedly defined in the available dictionaries and writings of scholars. Let us try to have a glimpse of these definitions.

Stereotype: Definition

1. **The American Heritage New Dictionary of Cultural Literacy (2005):** It defines the term stereotype in the following two ways: (i) A too-simple and therefore distorted image of a group, such as "Football players are stupid" or "The English are cold and unfriendly people." (ii) A generalisation usually exaggerated or oversimplified and often offensive, that is used to describe or distinguish a group.

2. **Webster's Seventh New Collegiate Dictionary (1970: 860):** Stereotype is "a standardised mental picture held in common by members of a group and representing an over simplified opinion, affective attitude or uncritical judgment (as of a person, a race, an issue, or an event)."

3. **McGarty, Craig, et.al (2002):** In social psychology, a stereotype is a thought that can be adopted about specific types of individuals or certain ways of doing things.

4. **Judd, C.M. and Park, B. (1993):** The thoughts and beliefs maintained about the people or issues. These thoughts or beliefs may or may not accurately reflect reality.

The definitions given above may help us in drawing following conclusions about the meaning and nature of the term stereotyping:

•   Stereotyping reflects the oversimplified attitudes and feelings of the people in general towards specific types of individuals, groups and communities.

•   It is the result of incomplete or distorted information accepted as fact without questions or putting into verification and critical judgment.

•   It is responsible for breeding an antagonistic attitude, ill feelings and prejudices against the persons who are subjected to stereotyping.

- Under the influence of stereotyping, the victims (individuals or groups) may be found to suffer from (i) prejudices, isolation, discrimination or marginalisation on a group or community level and (ii) anxiety of failure, inferiority complex and lack of confidence in terms of their adjustment and progress at the personal level.

Types or Forms of Stereotyping Behaviour

A stereotype is simply a widely held belief that an individual is a member of a certain group based on its characteristics. Due to the process of over generalisation within social perception, stereotyping leads to a great deal of inaccuracy in social perception. Sex, race, age, sexual orientation, religion and physical ability are various categories which exist in stereotyping.

Let us discuss common types of stereotypes existing in our society.

A. Sexual or gender stereotypes

- Girls like to remain dependent, protected and looked after than the boys.
- Parents hold an opinion that their daughters need nurturing of passivity and dependency and their sons to be aggressive and independent. (Therefore they punish independence in daughters and passivity in sons.)
- Females are more conforming and more concerned about displaying socially desirable behaviour than males are.
- "Boys don't cry" and "girls don't fight".
- Girls and females are most fit for doing household jobs and the boys and males for outdoor work.
- Girls and females are talkative and are not fit for serious and responsible assignments.
- Girls are not supposed to study mathematics, sciences, computer, commerce and technical subjects. They are suitable for the study of humanity and languages.
- In work-outputs girls and females are quite inferior and often lag behind their male counterparts.
- The girls are not supposed to take part in games and play activities involving adventure, muscle power and stamina like wrestling, boxing shooting, paragliding and trooping, rock climbing, weight lifting, etc.
- Girls always surpass boys in the demonstration of communication and social skills, musical and dancing abilities, aesthetic sense and artistic abilities.

B. Social class or racial stereotypes

- Children belonging to lower castes possess inferior cognitive, social and emotional intelligence than those belonging to higher castes.
- Children belonging to low socio class and communities and coloured population (in relation to Western countries) are better in athletics, games particularly in boxing, wrestling and the activities requiring toughness, physical stamina and adventurism.

- Children from urban backgrounds and urban culture are superior in intelligence but lag behind the rural children in the performances in sports.
- Children belonging to lower castes, low socio class, rural backgrounds and backward areas lag behind in their studies, create problems in class and school, and have more chances of becoming delinquents.

C. Poverty-related stereotypes

- The children belonging to poor families have a low level of aspiration and achievement motivation.
- The poverty-ridden children easily fall victim to problematic and delinquent behaviour.
- The poverty-ridden children usually suffer from maladjustment, as well as problems related to poor physical and mental health.
- The poverty-ridden children are poor in their school attendance, find little time and face difficulties in doing their home assignments and project activities.

Relationship of Stereotypes with Prejudices and Discrimination

Stereotypes, although having their separate identity and existence as the firm beliefs and attitudes of a person, are firmly attached with concepts like prejudices and discrimination. Stereotypes are regarded as the most cognitive component and often occur without conscious awareness, whereas prejudice is the affective component of stereotyping and discrimination is the behavioural component of prejudicial reactions. Thus, in this tripartite view of intergroup attitudes:

(*i*)   Stereotypes reflect expectations and beliefs about the characteristics of members of groups perceived as different from one's own, (cognitive behaviour exhibited by the person having stereotype).

(*ii*) Prejudice represents the emotional response exhibited by the person possessing the stereotype (affected behaviour exhibited by the person having stereotype).

(*iii*) Discrimination or marginalisation refers to actions (conative behaviour exhibited by the person having stereotype).

In this way, a stereotype (unfounded beliefs, expectations, opinions or attitude maintained about members of groups perceived as different from one's own) is first responsible for generating the prejudiced feelings and emotions against group members and then acting in a prejudiced way showing a lot of discrimination and marginalisation. As a result, a teacher who is under the influence of gender stereotype, "girls are talkative and non- serious" and the related prejudiced feelings will always be found automatically appointing boys as "group leader" and girls as "secretary" for the project or association activities.

Impacts of Stereotyping on the Development and Well-Being of Children

Stereotypes are a big problem for a society or nation as it creates great hurdles in their smooth and peaceful functioning as well as needed development and progress of its citizens. In the case of children, it hampers their welfare and development in an adverse way. Let us see how it affects the development and well-being of youngsters.

1. Stereotyping related to gender, race, social class and poverty etc., breeds prejudices in the children against the persons and groups. It can develop into hatred, enmity, rivalries among the peers and students of the same class and school. It can thus prove a big danger and obstacle in the cooperative and collaborative environment needed for the effectiveness of the teaching-learning process or attainment of school ideals and goals.

2. Stereotyping puts labels about how a person should act or live according to their sex, race, personality and other facts. This could affect the learning and working of the children who perhaps like different things or do different activities, but feel ashamed of doing so because of domain-related stereotypes (e.g., girls are poor in mathematical and scientific abilities). Consequently, a girl student may like to study and engage in the activities that are not meant for the girls according to the stereotypes prevalent in the society, but do not dare and come forward for doing them in spite of her abilities and capacities for learning and doing them.

3. Stereotypes create a misconception of how people are and how they live in other cultures, religions, or countries. This misconception may create distances in the minds and hearts of children studying in the same class and school. It can prove a big problem for a multi culture and democratic society or nation.

4. Stereotyping of any nature may result in the discrimination and marginalisation of victims. Children may face discrimination and marginalisation on account of stereotypes related to gender, caste, creed, colour, social class and poverty at their homes, neighbourhood, community, school and other social situations. It affects their adjustment, education, development and progress in an adverse and negative way.

5. The sufferings caused through a combined effect of prejudices, discrimination and denial of opportunities arising out of stereotypes may provide great harm to victimised children in the form of psychological set back. It may affect their physical and mental health and also affect their performance in learning and work performance. It has been noted that children get hurt and act more aggressively after they've faced prejudice and discrimination in a given situation. They are more likely to exhibit a lack of self-control and may feel difficulty in making good, rational decisions as a fall out of stereotyping.

6. Stereotyping may also be found quite harmful to children in terms of affecting their performance and outcomes in an adverse way. In this concern, it is quite interesting to note that both negative as well as positive stereotypes (e.g., members of some groups will perform more poorly or more appropriately than others) are found to carry equally adverse effects on the achievements and performances of children in testing and work performance situations. The reason that performance suffers under stereotype threat is still a matter of some debate. Research has shown that factors such as anxiety, physiological arousal and reduced cognitive capacity can all occur under stereotype threat and each

factor might contribute to a lowered performance. For example, a girl student may be found to be a victim of decreased performance in the tests and work situations related to mathematics, natural sciences and computer engineering with a psychological fear generated through the negative stereotyping against girls and females. But at the same his brother or class mate who is also appearing in that mechanical comprehension/mathematical or scientific ability test may also be found to perform poorly as a consequence of facing a lot of text anxiety simply for saving the reputation of his group by earning better scores than the female counterparts (justifying the positive stereotyping in favour of the boys/males).

7. Stereotypes are creating problems in children in many other ways. As an accepted ways of believing and behaving in the society they live, these stereotypes have taken a quite ideal shape in the minds and hearts of the children. They can't think beyond them. As a consequence, they are suffering from a number of negative effects in many areas not only in academics but also in sports, co-curricular areas, personality development and their overall progress and well-being. You can't imagine how the false images and ego built up by these stereotypes and discrimination or marginalisation suffered by the children on their account is making the children suffer in terms of their achievements, adjustment, development and progress.

Role of Media in Relation to Marginalisation and Stereotyping

Mass media has emerged as a very potent and effective source of moulding attitudes and shaping the behaviour pattern of the masses. In this age of its rapid revolutionalisation, it has surpassed all other means and methods of influencing opinion and attitudes of the people in an infinite number and locations simultaneously at a single time. As a result it has been found to cast an immense influence over constructing and deconstructing people's perceptions and ways of dealing with the issues of marginalisation and stereotyping in particular society or in a global way in general. In this connection, media may serve as a twin edged sword contributing on one hand towards the perpetuation of stereotyping and marginalisation in the society and providing a good evil vanishing weapon on the other. Let us try to analyse the role of media on these two fronts.

A. Role of Media in the Promotion or Perpetuation of Stereotyping and Marginalisation

Media may play a negative role by contributing in a variety of ways towards the promotion and perpetuation of the evils of stereotyping and marginalisation in the society. A few of its negative contributions may be cited as follows:

1. Media may expose the children to the world of stereotyping and marginalisation. As you know children are quite innocent by nature. They are away from the evils of prejudices, hatred, discriminations and separatism. Exposure to such evils may make them know, learn and practice these in their behaviour. No one can match the media in exposing the children to such evils associated with

stereotyping and marginalisation prevalent in a society. When a child reads from a printed media (newspaper, magazine or pamphlet) or listens and views from an AV media (radio, television, film, smart phone, computer devices etc.,) about the prevailing stereotypes and marginalisation, he can pick all about them in terms of their nature, occurrence, practice and impacts.

2. One's caste, race, gender, or social class is superior or inferior, good or bad, considerations and beliefs like such may be easily germinated and nourished with the magnificent influencing power of the media.

   When media exhibits and exposes that girls do not fare well in mathematics, sciences and computers, they are not fit for adventurism including adventure and stamina-related sports, serious tasks and professions, it is nothing but germination and perpetuation of the stereotypes prevalent in the society against girls and women. Discrimination and marginalisation against the girls and women may also get germinated and perpetuated through news items and exhibits in the media. A T.V. show may emphasise that how a particular individual or group belonging to a race, religion, caste or class is dangerous to the well-being of the society; it may work as a great reinforcement of the stereotype prevalent in the society about that race, religion, caste or class. As a result a person with an outward appearance of Bin Laden may always be as assumed to be a dreaded terrorist. The following that a particular religion or beard people are terrorists, this stereotype thus can take a deep root in the minds of children. It is not strange for the children, thus to keep distance from the children belonging to a particular religion, caste, race or social class simply for the reason that a negative stereotype about them has been circulated and repeated in media.

3. When children are exposed to the fact through media reporting and exhibits, that a certain type of marginalisation or stereotyping exists in the different regions of a country or globally in other countries, they may form the opinion in favour of the preservation and continuity of that marginalisation or stereotyping. The mass media quickly spreads this negative message to the masses existing on a global basis and its repetition on the media gets it reinforced and deep rooted in the minds and behaviour of the persons exposed to the media at a global level. The followers of a particular religion are terrorists, this stereotype and the related marginalisation of them on this account on a global basis, may be taken as a glaring example of the role and contribution of media in the promotion and perpetuation of stereotyping and marginalisation.

B. Role of Media In Saying Good Bye to Stereotyping and Marginalisation

Despite its, negative role as emphasised earlier, media can play a substantial role in getting rid of the evils of stereotyping and marginalisation in our society in the ways and means summarised as follows:

1. Instead of reporting, viewing and glorifying things concerning stereotyping and marginalisation, it can adopt a positive approach for addressing these issues in a constructive way. In adopting this role basically the media should try to say and exhibit that stereotyping and marginalisation are evils and vices and thus

need to be sidelined or abolished. It should provide news and stories, write ups and experiences, videos, serials and films that can contradict the notions and beliefs held about stereotypes and marginalisation present in the form of gender, race, caste, religion and social class bases and discriminations.

2. Media through its various platforms must try to portray the negative outcomes and devastating effects of marginalisation on individuals and groups subjected to such marginalisation. We should act as humans and not treat others in non-dignified and inhuman ways. The marginalisation of Dalits and untouchables on the caste-basis, girls and women on the gender ground and widows on marital status basis, minorities on religion, language and cultural basis, the differently abled or disabled on the basis of their disabilities or incapacities is not desirable. Their sufferings and difficulties on this account may be brought into the notice of the media users and viewers in such a way as to make them realise the necessity of stopping evil practices of discriminations and marginalisation. There should be a change in the attitudes, feelings and thinking of the people having negative stereotypes about people, group, communities and cultures.

3. Media should try to portray the positive image altogether contradicting the traditionally held stereotyped negative images of individuals and groups.

   For example it should report and exhibit that:

   (i) Girls are doing wonders and excelling in various areas and spheres of human life disproving and rejecting various stereotypes. They are surpassing boys in terms of winning merit positions, higher pass percentage in subjects like mathematics, sciences, engineering, management and computer applications supposed to be the areas meant for boys. They are excelling in the field of games and sports even in the areas specifically reserved for boys such as weightlifting, boxing, wrestling, adventure sports, rock climbing, mountaineering, navigating, etc. They are thus on the helm of affairs, and top of events in all walks and spheres of human life, fields and careers. Whether related to academics or politics, business, administration, literatures and arts, invention and discoveries, fashions and entertainment, etc.

   (ii) The other types of stereotypes and marginalisation related to caste, races, religion, poverty, social class and disabilities, etc., should also be properly addressed at the hands of media reporting and showing. It should always lean towards maintaining communal harmony, peace and brotherhood among the different social cultural and religious groups. It should leave no scope or incident to report and exhibit that how well a particular individual or group is excelling or contributing towards the welfare of the society, nation and humanity irrespective of the negative stereotype held by the public about it. How a person, belonging to a particular religion, caste race or extremist section has saved the lives of others by aborting a terrorist act and how it is unfair on our part to brand all the people belonging to a particular community race or caste as the villains, bad guys or terrorists. The things and events then should be highlighted and glorified. Similarly, the excelling of poverty-ridden deprived and disadvantaged children should also be highlighted for removing the notion that children belonging to lower caste, lower social or economic status can't excel in life.

(*iii*) How are government and non-government agencies trying to take measures of abolishing stereotypes and marginalisation on one or the other basis? What are our responsibilities in this regard? How are efforts in this direction bringing positive results? How are people contributing and cooperating for the success of these missions etc.?

In conclusion, thus we can say that it is true that many of the stereotypes, ways of behaving in a discriminating and marginalised fashion are imbibed among children with the courtesy of media. But media can also play a constructive and positive role by letting the perception of the children be altered in relation to the stereotypes and marginalisation prevailing in the society or resting in their minds. Through its continuous efforts it can teach children to value other people for what they are, and not what they appear to be. It can also teach the children to respect each other regardless of gender, sexual orientation, race, culture, religion, personality and more. It is important to teach them these values because children are the future of our society and nation.

The media can work well for bringing changes in the perception of prevailing stereotypes and marginalisation. It should portray the picture that all stereotypes are bad (regardless of their being labelled as positive or negative) because they give birth to pre-judgment without any valid rational behind them. The children should be made to respect and understand other cultures, religions, languages, regions and countries. This will help in resolving many issues selected to discriminations, prejudices and marginalisation.

Summary

Marginalisation as a term stands for a type of social exclusion in which individuals or entire communities of people are systematically blocked from (or denied full access to) various rights, opportunities and resources that are normally available to members of the majority or ruling group. In general, thus the marginalisation suffered on the part of individuals in our societies may be visible in two forms namely (*i*) Individual marginalisation and (*ii*) Community marginalisation.

Individual marginalisation is concerned with the social exclusion of the individuals at their personal or individual level. As examples of such marginalisation or social exclusion we may name: marginalisation of widows, single mothers, poor, disabled persons, children, senior citizens and persons suffering from Aids, Cancer and Leprosy etc.

In the case of **community marginalisation** an entire community or a group having minority status may be found to face marginalisation at the hands of the majority group. The marginalisation of the blacks in European countries, and women, untouchables, and scheduled caste people in India may be cited examples of such marginalisation.

The factors responsible or causes lying behind marginalisation-individual or community is resulted through the apathy shown and discriminatory attitude adopted for the individuals and minority groups by the majority, powerful and status enjoying section of the society. This apathy and discriminatory attitude germinated in the mind and behaviour of the majority group is based on the stereotypes prevailed in the society and negative attitude developed in their mind involving gender biases, poverty, differentiations based on caste, religion health conditions and disabilities.

As an **impact or outcomes of the marginalisation** suffered by the developing children on one or the other accounts, hurdles of every sort are placed in the path of the progress and development of the children. In fact, they are unfortunate enough to feel the heat of marginalisation on two fronts. One on account of the marginalisation faced by their parents and family and the other on account of the marginalisation suffered by themselves in their home, school and society. On one hand a marginalised family is found to fail badly in contributing appropriately for the growth and development of its developing children and on the other at individual level, they are made to suffer the heat of marginalisation with the denial of access to many opportunities and negative attitudes developed towards them on the part of school authorities, teachers and peers. In doing with such ill effects and outcomes of the marginalisation on the part of marginalised children, the teachers can play a quite constructive role. They can prove quite helpful in their proper progress and development by protecting them from the heat of marginalisation.

Stereotypes prevalent in the society are nothing but the firm beliefs and attitudes of a person or group of persons similar in nature as the prejudices and discriminating attitudes prevalent in the society. In general, a number of stereotypes may be seen to be prevalent in all most all the societies and communities all over the Globe. These stereotypes may be broadly classified as (i) sexual or gender stereotypes, (ii) Social class or racial stereotypes and (iii) poverty related stereotypes etc.

Stereotypes are a big problem for a society or nation as they are found to create great hurdles in their smooth and peaceful functioning as well as needed development and progress of its citizens. In the case of the children, they are found to hamper their welfare and development in an adverse way.

With regard to the role of multi- media or mass media (such as news papers, radio, television and modern social net working) it can be safely concluded that it can play it role quite effectively in terms of moulding attitudes and shaping the behaviour pattern of the masses in a particular direction-positive or negative. Therefore whatever opinions, feelings, attitudes exist in the society in terms of various types of marginalisation and stereotypes can be well circulated , enhanced and controlled with the help of one or the other means of mass or multi-media. Here it can work both ways (i) perpetuating the evils of marginalisation and stereotypes and (ii) bringing changes in the perception of prevailing stereotypes and marginalisation. Therefore it is the moral duty of the citizens and media persons for making the media to play its role in a quite constructive way, i.e., to do away with the evils and ill effects of marginalisation and stereotypes.

References and Suggested Readings

Eysenck, H.J. et. al (1972), *Encyclopaedia of Psychology*, New York: Phil. Lib.

Harriman, P.L. (Ed.), *Encyclopaedia of Psychology*, New York : Phil. Lib. 1946.

Judd, Charles M. and Park, Bernadette (1993), "Definition and Assessment of Accuracy in social stereotypes" *Psychological Review*, 100(1): 109-128.

Kagan, J. (1964), "Acquisition and significance of sex typing and sex role identity", In M.L. Hoffman and L.W. Hoffman (Eds.), *Review of Child Development Research*, New York: Sage.

Kuppuswamy, B. (1971); *An introduction to Social Psychology*, Bombay: Publishing House.

McGarty, Craig; Yzerbyt, Vincent Y.; Spears, Russel (2002:7). *Stereotypes as explanations: The formation of meaningful beliefs about social groups.* Cambridge: Cambridge University Press, pp. 1-15.

The American Heritage New Dictionary of Cultural Literacy (Third Edition), (2005), New York: Houghton Mifflin Company.

Webster's Seventh New Collegiate Dictionary (1970), Springfield, Massachusetts, G.C. Merriam Company, Publisher.

28

Child Development in the Context of Globalisation and Urbanisation

Introduction

Today we are passing through the era of 21st century. In this modern age we are witnessing a tremendous change in the pattern of growth and development of children and subsequent resultant changes in their behaviour and personality. The developments in the modern age have affected the development of the children in a variety of ways. However, the increasing gulf between the haves and haves not, rich and poor, educated and uneducated and cultural differences, etc., have resulted in a wide range of diversity and differences among the growing ups. Globalisation, and urbanisation. The question arises how these factors have affected the development of children? In this chapter here we would like to look at the childhood in the context of globalisation and urbanisation. However, let us first see what do we mean by childhood?

Child Development in the Context of Globalisation

Globalisation, a quite distinguished feature of modern era, has been responsible for influencing the development and behaviour of children in a variety of ways. Let us discuss it. However, before engaging into such a discussion let us first try to know about the meaning and concept of globalisation.

Globalisation: Meaning and Concept

Globalisation in its simple meaning stands for a sort of integrated and global view of the things and practices going on all over the globe in our world of living and behaving. It reflects a feeling that all what exists on the globe in the form of the contributions of nature or human beings may influence the life and work of all who belong to this globe. For its understanding and comprehension, the term globalisation has been defined in a variety of ways by many scholars and writers. Let us reproduce a few here in drawing conclusion about the meaning and concept of the term globalisation.

1. **Martin Albrow and Elizabeth King (1990: 8):** Globalisation represents all those processes by which the people of the world are incorporated into a single world society.

2. **Anthony Giddens (1990):** Globalisation can be defined as the intensification of worldwide social relations which link distant localities in such a way that local happenings are shaped by events occurring many miles away and vice versa.

3. **Thomas Larsson (2001: 9):** Globalisation is the process of world shrinkage, of distances getting shorter, things moving closer. It pertains to the increasing ease with which somebody on one side of the world can interact, to mutual benefit, with somebody on the other side of the world.

4. **Lechner and Boli (2012):** Globalisation means more people across large distances becoming connected in more and different ways.

5. **Brine, (1999):** Globalisation as a cultural process has been seen as an extension of mass media and the consequent universalisation of Western mores and culture.

6. **Gibson- Graham (1996):** Globalisation is a set of processes by which the world is rapidly being integrated into one economic space via increased international trade, the internationalisation of production and financial markets and the internationalisation of a commodity culture promoted by an increasingly networked global telecommunication system.

A close analysis of these definitions may help us reveal the following things about the meaning, nature and significance of globalisation:

- Globalisation stands for a process resulting in a number of productive outcomes influencing and affecting our living and behaving at the individual, group, community, national and international level in varieties of ways.

- It has helped in shrinking the boundaries and providing maximum opportunities as well as facilities for the mutual interaction and cooperation among individuals, communities and nations all over the globe by removing the barriers of space, distance and time.

- It is associated with the evolution and emergence of faith in industrialisation, commercialisation, barrier-free trading, banking and business promotion all over the globe between and among people and countries.

- It has provided scope and facilities for visiting places and seeking employment for people belonging to one area of the globe to other areas of the globe.

- It has resulted in the interactions and assimilation of different cultures on account of knowledge explosion and migration of the people belonging to different cultures from one area of the globe to another.

- It has helped in the establishment and maintenance of cross-border economic, political and socio-cultural relations between people, communities and nations of the world.

- It aims for sharing the knowledge and understanding, inventions and discoveries, ideologies and values, fashion and arts, means and programs of health, education and entertainment among the people and communities of the world.

- It owes its existence on the development and technological progress visible in the field of transportation, information and communication techniques, computer applications, space science and satellites technology.
- It has resulted in laying emphasis on material values and styles dominated by western philosophy and way of life.
- It has resulted in turning the people of the world into a single world society and feeling the jerk of the things and events happening in any corner of the globe.

In view of these meanings and features of globalisation we can refer to it as a process of interlinking and affecting the life and working of individuals and institutions of the world community, in a variety of means and ways such as economically, educationally, politically and socio-culturally by breaking the barriers of space and time.

Factors Behind Globalisation

What we see and witness as a process and outcome of globalisation may be found to be the handiwork of the following things and processes:

1. Services and facilities available through the development and progress in the means of transport.
2. Services and facilities available through the development and progress in the field of information and communication technology.
3. Services and facilities available through the development and progress in satellites and space technology.
4. Need of selling and purchasing one or the other commodities available on one or other side of the region or areas of the globe.
5. Heavy industrialisation, commercialisation and global capitalist economies emerging on the global scene.
6. Emergence of multiculturalism and transfusion and integration of various cultures.
7. Increase in migration of people from one region of the globe to another for seeking employment, enjoyment, comfort, asylum, etc.
8. The compulsion of natural sharing of the effects and happening on one side of the globe to the other (like natural disasters, global warming, rising level of pollution and radiation, stockpiling of nuclear arms, terrorist activities and political disturbances, border disputes, etc.).
9. Knowledge explosion and its transmission all over the globe.
10. Socio-cultural ties and religious affiliations between and among individuals and communities.
11. Exchange and organisation of socio-cultural events, games and sports and human welfare activities and programs all over the globe.
12. Cooperation, collaboration and competitions faced by individuals, communities and nations on the global scene at one or the other platforms.
13. Effect and outcomes of the various types of treaties, agreements, negotiations and pacts in political, economic, business and educational fields.

14. Emergence of the regional and international bodies and federations such as UNO and its functionary bodies, Confederation of Commonwealth Countries, EURO, BRICS, ASEAN countries, etc.

15. Impact of technologically developed modern means of social interactions like social media platforms or Facebook, Instagram, YouTube, and the emergence of smart phones and digital applications, films and television programs, etc.

Impact of Globalisation on the Development of Children

The changes affected on the economic, political, educational and socio-cultural fabrics of the global community on account of the globalisation process may be seen to cast quite mentionable impacts on the development of children and adolescents all over the world. As happens with the outcomes of any effort of introducing change or bringing modernisation, there is always a mixed trend of positive and negative influences. The same is also true with the impact of globalisation on the development of our children. We can summarise these impacts in the ways:

A. Positive and Favourable Impacts

Globalisation may be credited to offer a number of benefits, right opportunities and assistance contributing towards the proper progress and well-being of the children in the following ways:

1. Globalisation has resulted in the great exposure of the children to the world of multiculturalism. They have now more opportunities and facilities to get acquainted to with the living and behaviour of the people belonging to different cultures, religious faiths and ideologies. It has helped the children to develop respect and tolerance about the people and communities belonging to different religious faiths, cultures and ideologies.

2. Exposure to outside world coupled with knowledge explosion and scientific progress is helping children and adolescents in getting rid as well as protecting themselves from a number of social evils and disparities prevalent in our society in the name of superstitions, stereotypes, prejudices, marginalisation and deprivation.

3. The opportunities in abundance available to the children on account of the impact of globalisation for acquiring knowledge and skills of various sort are helping children in widening their horizon, seek proper development of their intellectual capacities and learning appropriate skills for their adjustment and progress in life.

4. Globalisation has been able to remove any type of hesitation and fear about going abroad. It has been responsible in developing the right attitude in children to utilise educational, business and employment opportunities available in different parts of the globe. The adolescents have started planning their careers and choosing subjects or courses that can help them in benefitting from the impacts of globalisation.

5. Globalisation has been responsible for the establishment and running of a number of world and regional bodies like UNESCO, UNICEF and WHO for rendering

necessary assistance to developing children, in their educational and cultural development, maintenance of health and hygiene and protection from diseases. These organisations have been doing commendable job in the task of helping children all over the globe in their proper development and progress. The efforts in the direction of the removal of deadly diseases like polio and measles, TB, etc., previously affecting the health and well-being of the children in a quite adverse way, may be cited as a glaring impact of global cooperation made possible through globalisation. Similarly we may witness a lot of cooperation and coordination among the communities and nations of the world on a global and regional basis for providing, assistance and help to the children in their educational and career building through the provision of scholarships; students and teachers exchange programs; and organizing educational seminars, workshops, conferences, etc.

B. Negative and Unfavourable Impacts

Besides, the positive and favourable impacts, globalisation may also be found to exercise quite a negative and adverse effect on the development of children in the following manner:

1. On account of providing a huge or say unlimited exposure to children to the outside world through its development in transport, ICT, electronic, mobile and computer technology, Globalisation has resulted in shaping and moulding life, working and behaviour of the children in a specific mode dominated by Western culture, ideals and values of life. Every culture or mode of life, adopted by the communities and races, has its strengths and weaknesses. Where its strengths or positivity provides inspiration and brings improvement in the life of the followers, the negativity and weaknesses takes them away from their right path. In imitation, as we know, it is the negative that attracts more and is picked up easily for one's living and behaving. Here the children and adolescents have been also attracted by the negativity and weaknesses present in the Western culture. It has been responsible in making many of our children and adolescents imbibe the habits, attitudes, interests, values and life style affecting their development in an adverse way. The same is the case with children who have been influenced and mesmerised with the ideas and doctrines spread over on the globe by many vested interests, religious extremists and terrorist organisations and have taken a wrong course for their living and behaving.

2. Globalisation is associated with the emergence of heavy industrialisation, urbanisation and centralisation of marketing, trading and commerce. It has resulted in the huge increase in the number of migration of people from one region to another region or one part of the globe to another for want of earning a livelihood or seeking better opportunities for living and earning. In some cases where the migrants have been fortunate enough to get better facilities, the cause of the development of their children in a better way has been satisfactorily served. But for quite a huge number of them their migration is proving quite detrimental to the development and well-being of their children. Many of them have to leave their families and children to their place of origin for taking time to get settled in their new employment or business. In the absence of the father,

the children do not get sufficient attention and care as needed for their adequate development. The case becomes more typical when mothers also have to serve or devote time in looking after the family occupation or source of earning.

3. Globalisation associated with the ideas or approaches of capitalism, materialism and a blind race of getting prosperous by hook and crook has been responsible for the loss of moral values all over the globe. The same has affected the ways of living and behaving of the world community and it has adversely affected the rearing and parenting styles, caring and education of the children responsible for the loss of moral, social and cultural values among children. The relations between parents and children, teachers and students and children as friends and peers have been centred round the narrow materialistic interests and self-defined goals and the same has been responsible for many drawbacks in the proper growth and development of children.

In this way, globalisation may be seen to influence the growth and development of children in both aspects of its positivity and negativity inherent in its nature and processing, However, globalisation, as a whole in its functioning and objectives stands for unity, cohesiveness, progress and well-being of the world community and as such it may be viewed and employed as a means of bringing a lot of improvement and hope in the activities and programs related to the development and well-being of children and adolescents.

Child Development in the Context of Urbanisation

Urbanisation: Meaning and Concept

We are quite familiar with the terms rural and urban areas or rural or urban people. While villages fall in our definition of rural areas, towns and cities are associated with urban areas. The people living in the villages are called rural people and those living in towns and cities are referred to as urban people. Now arises the next thing; what do we mean by the term urbanisation? Let us take the help of dictionary meanings for this purpose.

1. **Dictionary.com (2015):** The act or fact of urbanising or taking on the characteristics of a city.

2. **Webster's Seventh new Collegiate Dictionary (1970:976):** The quality or state of being or becoming urbanised (picking up an urban way of life).

The above dictionary meanings clearly emphasise that urbanisation is some sort of act or process of converting or transforming a thing into an urban way of life by picking up the quality or characteristics of a town or city. Here two things need to be answered.

(i) What is it which gets converted or transformed and (ii) what is the urban way of life or what is the quality or characteristics of a town or city?

In response to the former, we can say that it is nothing but all related to rural areas and ways of life that get converted into urban areas and ways of urban life. The rural people who migrate to towns and cities may be found to pick up the ways of urban life. The rural land that is transferred or merged into urban locality may pick up all the characteristics of the urban land. The rural culture and ideology gets transformed into urban culture and ideology, in the process of urbanisation of the rural people and rural land.

Now in response to the latter, we can summarise the quality and characteristics of a town or city or urban way of life as follows:

Quality or Characteristics of a City or Urban Way of Life

(i) The land known as urban land belonging to town or cities is non-agricultural land. It is used for residential, commercial, industrial educational and establishing or running of government and non-government offices and services.

(ii) There is continuous increase in the size and expansion characteristics of urban land due to increase in population and demand of the infrastructural facilities for residential, commercial and industrial purposes.

(iii) There is a continuous increase in the size of the population of urban areas chiefly on account of the migration from rural areas.

(iv) An urban area (town or city) is characterised with spatial concentration of people engaged in non-agricultural activities.

(v) There are more opportunities for the migrants to lead a better life in terms of getting more opportunities for employment and earning, living an independent and free life, enjoying the facilities and privileges of city's civic life, education and future of their children, etc.

(vi) Urban life can provide the privileges of a secular, multicultural and marginalisation free society.

(vii) Urban life is characterised with the presence and impacts of globalisation, industrialisation and modernisation.

(viii) It is also well characterised with the availability of proper living amenities and facilities in terms of drinking water, electricity, transportation, educational institutions, medical facilities, availability of things consumed in day-to-day living, means of entertainment, opportunities for leading luxurious life, having fun, pursuing the latest fashion trends and getting opportunity for the interaction with people belonging to different areas, cultures, religions, language groups, etc.

(ix) Urban life is also characterised with the evil influences of population increase industrialisation, modernisation and individualisation. There are frequent road jams on account of the increase in the number of vehicles, public transport is over-crowded. There are lots of problems in getting employment and means of earning livelihood in a better way. Slums are increasing and adequate living facilities in term of electricity, drinking water, education and medical facilities are creating problems for the urban people especially in poverty ridden slum areas.

Factors Responsible for Urbanisation

Why villages are going to vanish or becoming thinner and thinner in terms of population and land area? Why is the wind blowing in favour of the adoption of urban culture leaving behind the old rural ways of living and behaving? The reasons are many. Let us think about a few significant ones.

1. **Industrialisation:** The increasing demand of industrialisation has made it necessary to acquire lands for the establishment of industrial units and provision of adequate infrastructural facilities for running these units. It is also essential for attracting domestic and foreign investors to invest their money in the industrialisation of the country. The agricultural land is also frequently acquired as it may fall within the range of urbanised localities.

2. **Rising population of the city:** There is an increasing rising trend in the population of the city. It has made an increasing demand of more residential accommodation to the city dwellers. More and more property dealers and builders are coming into the field and they are purchasing agriculture lands for the purpose of constructing buildings. It is resulting in the increase in the size of urban land and decrease in the size of the rural land resulting in more and more urbanisation.

3. **Other push and pull factors:** Apart from the loss of agriculture land on account of rapid industrialisation, building of roads and other infrastructural facilities and residential accommodation, there are many other push and pull factors that may work not only for the migration of the rural people but also to adopt the ways of urban life for their living and behaving. These may be summarised as follows:

Push Factors: These factors are responsible for pushing and compelling rural people to seek migration to towns and cities and adapt modes and ways of urban living. Consider the following:

(i) There has been an increase in village population but the land area is either the same or it has reduced on account of its selling or acquiring by the government. The land holdings, however big they may be are divided among the several children and eventually their children. The earnings of this limited land is incapable of supporting the living needs of the families. Moreover there is always some adversity happening to the growth of crops and farm earning in the form of droughts, hail storms and other natural calamities or men made causes. It is forcing the rural people engaged in farming to migrate to the cities for their livelihood.

(ii) Other people engaged in vocations other than agriculture have also been forced to leave their villages. The rural crafts are declining so the craftsmen have been left with no alternative but to search for their living in cities. There are also rising cases of discrimination, marginalisation and injustice done to the minorities, lower caste people and youths having inter-caste and intra-*gotra* relationships and marital affairs. They have been forced to leave the villages in groups or individual basis for their safety and livelihood to settle in nearby cities.

Pull factors: These factors are responsible for attracting and luring village people to the life and privileges of the urban society. Such 'bright lights' and high expectations of the rural people may be named as follows:

- The expectation of getting employment and means of earning livelihood.
- Expectation of getting better facilities for their children's education and development.
- The attraction of enjoying urban facilities in terms of supply of electric light, pure drinking water, kitchen gas, transport facilities, medical facilities, social security and safety, means of entertainment, etc.
- Getting freedom from an oppressive life style, marginalisation, stereotypes, and discrimination on one or the other grounds may become a source of attraction for a number of people seeking migration from rural to urban society.
- The opportunity to assert individualism and lead life in one's own ways may also be a great attraction for many who seek migration from villages to cities.

Many times, the pull and push factors work in combination. People migrate and seek their adjustment in the life and living of the cities. In the process of their living and behaving, then gradually they begin to adopt urban culture and ways of living saying good bye to their previous mode of living.

Impact of Urbanisation on the Development of children

Urbanisation occurring in the structure and functioning of a country or society may produce positive as well as negative impacts or influences over the functioning and well-being of the nations, communities, families and individuals (including their children). Let us see how.

Urbanisation can work both ways in influencing and affecting the progress and well-being of the people affected through the process of urbanisation. The villagers who have migrated to cities may get proper employment, residential accommodation and many enjoy better living facilities for them and their children at their migrated places. On the other hand, the reverse may also happen for many of them. They may suffer from unemployment, get deprived from the essentials of living, forced to live in slums and suffer from a huge discrimination, injustice and marginalisation on one or the other grounds making 'hell' of their life and doom the future of their children. These positive and negative effects of urbanisation, in brief can be summarised in the following manner:

- Urbanisation, coupled with industrialisation, modernisation and globalisation may contribute towards a strong and developing economy for a country. The country may be able to spend more about providing better infrastructural facilities, civic amenities, education and other facilities for healthy and better living for its citizens and especially to the developing children. Contrary to this, urbanisation may also result in negative outcomes. On the one hand it may result in destroying rural economy and on the other no positive results are produced through unplanned industrialisation. We can't earn benefits through the export of manufactured articles that may become defaulters in terms of paying debts and dues and arranging for the needed facilities for the development and welfare of our citizens and children.

• On an individual level, the families and parents who get well settled in the urban life of their migrated places and are privileged in terms of positive changes in their economy may be able to provide good environment and better facilities for the development and well-being of their children. They can send their children to better schools, may look after well for their integrated wholesome development and provide them best exposure and experiences for their progress and well being in their life. Contrary to this, the individuals and families who have adverse effects on their economy and means of living on account of their migration, are compelled to live in slum areas, do not get the needed civic amenities, health care, social security, safety and educational provisions for their children. Their children do not get opportunities for healthy socialisation and emotional development and many times fall victims to the unhealthy and socially undesirable company of the evil elements of these slum areas.

In a nutshell whenever the process of urbanisation results into better and positive outcomes for the community, family or individuals in terms of arranging for them a better quality of living and behaving, they can afford in a better way for caring and helping children in their proper adjustment, education and progress. However, in case adverse conditions are available on account of the negative outcomes of urbanisation, then it can lead to exercise negative impacts in the form of great obstacles in the adjustment, education and development of children.

Summary

There have been tremendous changes in our social and cultural life on account of the ongoing rapid industrialisation, urbanisation and globalisation. It is affecting the development of the growing children from their early childhood in a variety of ways.

Globalisation, a quite distinguished feature of modern era, is influencing the development and behaviour of children in a variety of ways through it has its positive and negative impacts. On the positive side it can be credited to offer a number of benefits, right opportunities and assistance contributing to the proper progress and well-being of the children such as (i) great exposure to the world of multiculturalism and (ii) knowledge explosion and scientific progress for removing many of the social evils and getting rid of them in a variety of ways. On the negative side, it can be blamed for (i) polluting our cultural and social life by imbibing negativity and evils of multiculturalism on the part of developing children, (ii) bringing evils of heavy industrialisation and urbanisation, (ii) affecting adversely the very fabric of our moral values and ethics .

Urbanisation, a new trend and development of the modern age refers to the process of (i) heavy increase in the population of the cities and towns at the cost of decrease in the areas and populations of the villages, (ii) picking up of the urban way of life on the part of migrants from the villages to the urban areas. Urbanisation is affecting the childhood of our developing children in both a positive and negative ways. The villagers who migrated to cities may get proper employment, residential accommodation and many enjoy better living facilities for them and their children at their migrated places. On the other hand, the reverse may also happen for many of them. They may suffer from unemployment, get deprived from the essentials of living, forced to live in slums and suffer from a huge discrimination, injustice and marginalisation on one or the other grounds making 'hell' of their life and doom the future of their children.

References and Suggested Readings

Brine, J. (1919), *Under educating women: Globalization in equality*, Bunkingham, U.K.: Open University Press.

Dictionary. Com (2002), Retrieved from dictionary.reference.com/browse/permissive on 15/9/15.

Gibson-Graham, J.K. (1996), *The end of Capitalism (as we knew it): A feminist critique of political economy*, Cambridge, M.A.: Blackwell.

Giddens Antony (1990), *The Consequences of Modernity*, Cambridge, U.K.: Polity Press.

Lechner, F.J. and Boli, John (Eds.), (2011), *The Globalization* Reader, New Jersey: Willey Blackwell Publishers.

Larseen Thomas, (2001), *The Race of the Top: The Real Story of Globalization* Washington D.C.: Cato Institute.

Marten Albrew and Elizabeth King (1990), *Globalization, Knowledge and Society*, London: Sage.

Webster's Ninth Collegiate Dictionary (1969), Springfield Massachusetts HS, USA: Merriam Webster Publishers.

29

Impact of Media on Growing Children and Adolescents

The Meaning of the Term Media or Mass-Media

In its word meaning, the term mass-media stands for media (means and mode of communication) for the masses. It can thus represent all channels, means and modes that can be used for conveying information, messages or appeal simultaneously to a number of people breaking the barrier of location, places and timings. It can exist in audio, video or multi-sensory forms and thus may appeal a number of senses for producing lasting effects or impressions on the minds and hearts of an individual. The following means and modes may be properly included in the term mass-media:

1. Newspapers and magazines
2. Books (printed and e-form)
3. Advertisement
4. Radio broadcast
5. Telecasts
6. Films and movies
7. Internet and web material
8. The modern communication means like messages and audio-video material loaded on smart phones, Facebook, Blogs, Twitter, etc.

Impact of Mass Media on Growing Children and Adolescents

Mass media plays quite a dominant role in influencing behaviour and development of children and adolescents in a number of ways and forms. What they read, listen and watch through the mass media appeal to their senses and gets deeply embedded in the minds and hearts in a great way and as a result they may learn and imbibe so many things in their habits, ways of behaving and doing, that may go a long way to shape the events of their life in a particular way. Let us see how this happens.

1. When the children and adolescents read about things and events in newspapers, pamphlets, magazines, books etc., it may catch their attention and get them acquainted with so many things — positive as well as negative. It can add to broaden their mental horizon and learn so many new things. Learning as

you know can result in the desirable or undesirable developments of interests, attitudes, habits, temperament and so many other personality traits. It happens also in the case of children's exposure to reading material. They may not only get acquainted with the goods and evils, virtues and vices but also consciously and unconsciously try to imbibe them in their behaviour.

2. The audio-visual and multi-media means like radio and television, films and movies and what is available to them on their computer and mobiles screen, exercise much greater influences in shaping their behaviour and personality than their verbal comprehension of the material available in the newspapers, magazines and books. Here, the learning takes place in a more organised fashion. This multi-sensory and observational learning is much superior to the verbal. Which a child observes his most liked actor or actress to perform or do certain types of acts or behaviour, he can't resist the desire to copy it in his behaviour. It is nothing but hero worship that is most common among children, especially in adolescents. As a part of social learning, as advocated by Bandura (1977), all such observations on their part are imitated, practiced and assimilated in their behaviour by these children and adolescents who get exposed to such type of mass media experiences. The easy and unlimited availability of such multimedia exposure to youngsters through the development of electronic and computer means has almost revolutionised such type of social learning. As a result we may find tremendous changes in the interests, attitudes, ways of thinking, feeling and behaving of youngsters, affecting the task of shaping and developing their personality in a positive or negative way. The much observed and talked about influences of mass media (printed material and multimedia) as a whole may be summarised as follows:

(i) The exposure to available mass media resources has resulted in increasing awareness towards the things and events concerning one's environment. Children and adolescents of today have various opportunities to get exposed to their physical, social and cultural environment — local, regional, national and international in comparison to a few decades ago. Hence, much credit for the development in the cognitive behaviour of children goes to mass-media.

(ii) Mass media is also credited for bringing rapid changes in social, emotional, language, communication and aesthetic development of youngsters. Today children enjoy more opportunities for developing social relationships with each other and getting better connected in comparison to the olden days. Mass media has given them opportunities for getting acquainted with the social and cultural life of their own and others. They may know how people behave and live in their own country, or in other parts of the globe. It has thus contributed in understanding the many people living on this planet, developing global understanding, cooperation and collaboration.

(iii) Mass media also gets credit for removing a number of social barriers, stereotypes, social evils, discriminations, marginalisation and misunderstandings among the members of a community, region and nation. Children and the youth of today are proceeding towards a global society or community, having less rigidity and bondage of caste, colour, religion, language, nationality, etc. They are having inter-caste, inter-religion and international relationships, friendships and marriages. It is all happening due to the services of the developed mass media platforms and related technologies.

3. Though the exposure to available mass media has its valuable advantages and contributions it is also decried and criticised for a number of its negative influences on the behaviour and development of youngsters.

In this concern particularly we note that mass media is held responsible for exposing youngsters to the world of crime, hate, violence and sexual exploitation. There is too much violence, sex and other type of immoral, illegal and inhuman behaviour reported in newspapers, and shown in the news channels, television series and movies. The internet, web and other sources of social media are also loaded with such evil influencing material such as adult and child porn that is freely available on the internet.

There are more chances of children and adolescents drifting apart from their welfare path. Many of them waste their time, money, energy and mar their future by indulging in socially undesirable acts of violence and crime. They may also become victims at the hands of culprits, criminals, terrorist groups and sexual offenders since mass media many a times is used by notorious people for serving their own vested interests.

In this way, it can be observed that mass media has a powerful capacity to influence the development of children and adolescents in a positive as well as a negative way. In the case of adolescents, these influences may be cast in a selectively more forceful and devastating way since they are passing through a critical period of their life. Adolescents are characterised with too much self-consciousness, sex consciousness and emotional turmoil. In this age, children have relatively great chances of becoming attracted to unsocial and undesirable activities. Therefore, great care and precautions should be taken by the elders, parents and teachers for protecting them for the evil influences of mass media. Parents and teachers should join hands for helping adolescents to make best use of the opportunities available to them through mass media and provide them the needed direction for not getting victimised due to the evil influences and harms of mass media.

Deconstruction of Significant Events that Media Highlights and Creates

Media as we have seen above has a strong appeal to influence the behaviour and development of children and adolescents. However, more desirable benefits from the media can be earned in case necessary attention is paid over deconstructing the significant events highlighted or created by media. Let us see what is meant by the term deconstruction and deconstruction of media events.

The term deconstruction as a dictionary meaning stands for a process of analyzing or breaking down a thing into its components or elements in order to understand its nature and characteristics in a better way. In this way, when a news items, story or television episode appears before children, they must be helped in making its analysis for learning or picking up the inherent meanings. In our day to day language by the term deconstruction we mean a process of reconstructing a structure. It refers to a process of falling walls, only to build them again for sorting our requirements in a desirable way. Similarly here what is presented or portrayed by media should be so deconstructed as (i) to understand the inherent message delivered by it and (ii) interpreting this message in the interest and welfare of children.

Deconstruction provides one a way to have an objective assessment of the things conveyed through media. It helps in bringing and picking up positive messages from the things conveyed and displayed over media. Through deconstruction, we can replace or give more weightage to the things which leave more positive results and impressions on the minds and hearts of children in terms of their well being and progress. Similarly, deconstruction of the events portrayed by media should be made in such a way as to help in developing necessary social values, democratic virtues, ethical norms and humanity among developing children. They must be helped in getting rid of social evils, stereotypes and marginalisation practices prevalent in society. As illustration of such desirable deconstruction of media events we can cite the following:

1. In working over deconstructing the news or events related to communal riots occurring at some place in the country, the emphasis should be in highlighting the role of somebody (individual, group, organisation) who helped the victims of riots by risking his or her life with no consideration of caste or religion.

2. In the deconstruction of reporting and displaying terrorist activities by the media, while terrorism should be condemned as a most inhuman, uncivilised and cowardice act, due care should be taken not to brand and portrait all the people belonging to a particular community, race or caste as the villains, bad guys or terrorists.

3. The reports and displays in the newspaper, TV channels, movies or other electronic media should be presented before children in such a manner that children should be helped in deriving purposeful meaning and lessons from them so as to inculcate among them the habits and attitudes related to:

    (i) Love for animals and birds.

    (ii) Pollution-free environment.

    (iii) Cleanliness and tree plantation

    (iv) Freedom from superstitions, disbeliefs, prejudices and stereotypes.

    (v) Faith in democracy and democratic values including secularism, equity, equality, liberty, peaceful co-existence and universal brotherhood.

    (vi) Opposition to any type of discrimination injustice, oppression and marginalisation on one or the other accounts.

    (vii) Love for nature, adventurism, creativity and invention.

    (viii) Self-confidence, self-efficacy, self-learning and self-esteem.

    (ix) Striving for integrated wholesome development of their personality.

    (x) Loyalty and contribution towards the progress of the society and nation.

    (xi) Remaining away from socially and morally deviant behaviour, delinquent and criminal acts, anti-national or in-human activities.

4. In reporting and displaying of the media it should be so featured or deconstructed as to provide the masses including children a clear message that in a democratic society that is wedded to equity, equality, liberty and secularism, all have equal opportunities to get ahead on the path of their development and progress irrespective of their gender, caste, race, language or religion. Accordingly, on one hand, anything portraying negativity on this account should be sidelined, the positivity on the other hand of all sorts should be highlighted and presented before the public and children to get imbibed with the right attitudes, habits and action modes on this account. As examples here we may cite the following.

- Achievements of the girls and women in academic, sport, vocational, political and social field should be acknowledged and appreciated.
- Rise or progress of children from poverty-ridden environments, rural and tribal belts, socially and culturally deprived families to extraordinary positions.
- The incidence of providing due opportunities and encouragement for education and development of the girl child on the part of parents, families, societies and communities should be highlighted and produced as examples for being followed by others i.e., how a rural family belonging to Bhiwani district of Haryana, gave opportunities to all of its daughters (six in number) to rise as wrestles of international repute.

Summary

The term mass media stands for the type of media (means and modes) helpful in establishing communication links with the masses i.e., conveying information, messages or appealing simultaneously to a number of people breaking the barrier of location, place and timings. It can exist in audio, video or multi-sensory forms and may include means and modes like newspapers, radio, television, films and movies, internet and modern means of social networking.

Regarding the impact of mass media on the development of growing children, it can be well inferred that it has a wonderful capacity for influencing behaviour and development of children and adolescents in a number of ways and forms. What they read, listen and watch through mass media, appeals to their senses embeds deeply in their minds and hearts in a big way and as a result they may learn and imbibe so many things in their habits, behaviour and doing that may go to shape the events of their life in a particular way. However, here in their learning from the mass media presentations, there are also possibilities to learn undesirable and harmful things on their part. Therefore, great care and precaution needs to be taken by elders, parents and teachers in this concern for protecting the children from evil influences of mass media. In this direction, the deconstruction of significant events that media highlights and creates may prove quite helpful and beneficial to the children.

By the term deconstruction we mean a process of reconstructing a structure. In this sense what is presented or portrayed by media should be so deconstructed as to have an objective assessment of the things conveyed through media with the objective (i) to understand the inherent message delivered by it and (ii) to interpret this message in the interest and welfare of the children. Through deconstruction, we can replace or give more weightage to things which leave more positive results and impressions on the minds and hearts of children in terms of their well being and progress. Similarly, deconstruction of the events portrayed by media should be made in such a way as to help in developing necessary social values, democratic virtues, ethical norms and humanity among developing children. They must be helped in getting rid of social evils, stereotypes and marginalisation practices prevalent in the society.

References and Suggested Readings

Bandura A. (1977), *Social Learning Theory*, Englewood Cliffs, N.J: Prentice-Hall.

Eysenck, H.J. et. al (1972), *Encyclopaedia of Psychology*, New York: Phil. Lib.

Harriman, P.L. (Ed.), *Encyclopaedia of Psychology*, New York: Phil. Lib. 1946.

Kuppuswamy, B. (1971), *An Introduction to Social Psychology*, Bombay: Publishing House.

The American Heritage New Dictionary of Cultural Literacy (Third Edition), (2005), New York: Houghton Mifflin Company.

Webster's Seventh New Collegiate Dictionary (1970), Springfield, Massachusetts, G.C. Merriam Company, Publisher.

30

Protection of Child Rights

Introduction

On the line and pattern of Human Rights being prescribed for humans to live with dignity as human beings, Child Rights have also been prescribed and laid down on a global basis by world authorities like United Nations Organization (UNO) and United Nations International Children Emergency Fund (UNICEF). We have already initiated some discussion in Chapter 22 of this text regarding the meaning, nature and broad classification of Child Rights. The question here may further arise that what should be done for helping children in availing the benefits of these rights. In other words let us see, what should be done for the protection of the Rights prescribed or laid down for the children by the Global or Regional authorities and Agencies? In this chapter, we will discuss the role played by these various organisations and agencies for securing the protection of Child Rights in an appropriate way.

Role and Contribution of UNICEF

UNICEF having its headquarter in New York (USA) is one of the important UN agencies dedicated to helping the world realise the rights of the children.

It lays emphasis on developing community-level services to promote the health and overall well-being of children with the help of funds at its disposal created through the contribution from governments and private donors. According to its mission statement, "UNICEF is mandated by the United Nations General Assembly to advocate for the protection of child rights, to help meet their basic needs, and to expand their opportunities to reach their full potential."

Though the UNICEF headquarter is in New York, the organisation has its wide extension throughout the globe with its regional offices in its member countries. UNICEF's work can be grouped into five main strategic areas. They are all inter-related as progress in one leads to progress in the others. These are:

A. Young Child Survival and Development
B. Basic Education and Gender Equality
C. HIV / AIDS and Children
D. Child Protection
E. Policy Analysis, Advocacy and Partnerships for Children Rights

In this way, UNICEF may be found to work in all areas concerning the welfare of the children such as reducing gender bias to girl child, providing care for children and people affected with HIV / AIDS, immunisation of children, including helping in their proper nutrition and health maintenance, child protection in times of conflict and peace, assistance in times of disaster, and aim at improving the life of every child on the globe.

With regard to the protection of the Child Rights as defined by the United Nations and the United Nations conventions on the Rights of the Child (UNCRC), UNICEF is functioning at all its fronts by providing its multi-dimensional services for the protection of the civil, political, social, economic and cultural rights of every child, classified as: (i) Right to Survival, (ii) Right to Protection, (iii) Right to Participation and (iv) Right to Development.

For providing a shield and protection to these rights, UNICEF is actively engaged to provide its services and help (in the form of financial and technical support) to the children of the countries of the world in the following areas:

- Antenatal care of pregnant women and neonatal care in the first four weeks after birth.
- Providing vaccination services in developing countries, for protecting children from various diseases.
- Providing support to local programmes relating to nutritional diet to the poverty ridden children, and access to basic water and sanitation facilities.
- Promoting, funding and facilitating universal primary education and gender equality in developing countries.
- Support programs helping the prevention of mother-to-child transmission of HIV / AIDS, supporting children orphaned by HIV / AIDS and educating adolescents about the spread of these diseases.
- Providing support for creating needed protective environments to help prevent and respond to violence, exploitation abuse and discrimination, and for children made vulnerable by emergencies like separation of parents, survivors of child abuse and loss of parents in armed conflicts, etc.
- Strengthening national and local policies aimed to protect Child Rights to survive, protect, participate and develop in a proper way.

Role and Contribution of WHO

World Health Organization (WHO) is a specialised agency of United Nations (UN), working in the field of health. According to its mission statement, "WHO is mandated by United Nations General Assembly to support and improve Public Health System around the world by promoting health development, fostering health security, strengthening health systems, engaging in research, mediating partnerships and bring about reforms in health systems."

For the improvement of the health systems WHO also set out norms and standard of health and health services for being followed by respective stakeholders — the governments of the member nations. The WHO in this way is responsible for providing leadership on global health matters (including the health and well-being of developing children) by working in collaboration with its member nations usually through the Ministries of Health.

It has its headquarters in Geneva (Switzerland). The WHO country office for India is headquartered in Delhi. In collaboration with Ministry of Health, Government of India, WHO is engaged in carrying out the following six core functions:

(i) Providing leadership on matters critical to health and engaging in partnership where joint action is needed;

(ii) Shaping the research agenda and stimulating the generation, translation and dissemination of valuable knowledge;

(iii) Setting norms and standards and promoting and monitoring their implementation;

(iv) Articulating ethical and evidence-based policy option;

(v) Providing technical support, catalysing change and building sustainable institutional capacity; and

(vi) Monitoring the health situation and assessing health trends.

As a leading partner in securing good health to the world citizens, WHO is contributing substantially towards the child and adolescent health and development along with looking into the issues of their environmental health. Since one's health is a basic parameter of attaining success in developing one's full capacity and potential, it can help in ensuring a maximum number of things related to protection of human and Child Rights. WHO in collaboration with governments of the member states is constantly engaged in the activities related to the protection of a child's right to life, survival, maximum development, access to health and access to health services in a quite standardised form.

Role and Contribution of National Commission for Protection of Child Rights

The National Commission for Protection of Child Rights (NCPCR) is a statutory body working under the administration control of the Ministry of Women and Child Development, Government of India. It was set up in March 2007 under the Commission for Protection of Child Rights (CPCR) Act, 2005, an Act of Parliament. The Commission's Mandate is to ensure that all laws, policies, programs and administrative mechanisms are in consonance with the Child Rights perspective as enshrined in the constitution of India and also the UN convention on the Rights of the Child.

Composition

Besides the Chairperson, it has six members from the fields of child health, education, childcare and development; juvenile justice; children with disabilities; elimination of child labour; child psychology or sociology and laws relating to children.

Tasks and activities undertaken by NCPCR

In order to attain the commission's mandate of ensuring that each and every child has access to all entitlements and enjoys all his / her rights, the commission is engaged in carrying out the following activities:

- The first is to build public awareness and create a moral force in the country to stand by children and protect their rights. A national conscience has to be generated that captures the imagination of each citizen to take pride in the nation because it takes care of all its children.
- Armed with this kind of a mood the Commission's task is to look at the gaps in the policy framework and the legal framework and make recommendations to see that rights-based perspective is adhered to by the Government, while it makes its policies.
- Thirdly, the task of the Commission is to take up specific complaints that come up before it for redressal of grievances and also take up *suo moto* cases, summon the violators of child rights, get them presented before the Commission and recommend to the Government or the Judiciary, action based on an inquiry.
- Finally, the role of the Commission is in arming itself with proper research and documentation. The legitimacy and credibility to what the Commission says and does is based on solid research and data. Though everyone in the country knows that the predicament of the majority of children in our country is vulnerable and that children are not treated well, this has to be substantiated by information; it cannot just be an emotional argument.

The above tasks are to be rendered in a manner that the child is regarded as an individual with a character and mind of her own, not to be patronised in a relationship of benefactor and beneficiary. There is no favour to the child. It is the duty of the State to fulfil its obligations and the duty of society to create the environment where the child is in the centre of all decisions pertaining to the child. The Commission is of the opinion that in addressing the child, there is a focus on rendering dignity to the child, who is at the moment most vulnerable in society.

Role and Contribution of National Human Rights Commission

The National Human Rights Commission (NHRC) is an autonomous statutory body established in 1993 according to the provisions of the Protection of Human Rights Act, passed by the Parliament of India. *Composition*

It consists of a chairperson and six other members as follows:
- A chairperson should be the retired Chief Justice of India.
- One member who is, or has been, a judge of the Supreme Court of India.
- One member who is, or has been, the Chief Justice of a High Court.
- Two members to be appointed from among persons having knowledge of, or practical experience in, matters relating to human rights.
- One member who is the chairperson of National Commission for SC.
- One member who is the chairperson of National Commission for ST.

Functions and activities carried out by NHRC

Under the provision of the Protection of Human Rights Act, 1993 NHRC is required to carry out the following functions:

- Proactively or reactively inquire into violations of human rights or negligence in the prevention of such violation by a public servant.
- By leave of the court, to intervene in court proceeding relating to human rights.
- To visit any jail or other institution under the control of the State Government, where persons are detained or lodged for purposes of treatment, reformation or protection, for the study of the living conditions of the inmates and make recommendations.
- Review the safeguards provided by or under the Constitution or any law for the time beings in force for the protection of human rights and recommend measures for their effective implementation.
- Review the factors, including acts of terrorism that inhibit the enjoyment of human rights and recommend appropriate remedial measures.
- To study treaties and other international instruments on human rights and make recommendations for their effective implementation.
- Undertake and promote research in the field of human rights.
- Engage in human rights education among various sections of society and promote awareness of the safeguards available for the protection of these rights through publications, the media, seminars and other available means.
- Encourage the efforts of NGOs and institutions working in the field of human rights.
- Such other function as it may consider it necessary for the protection of human rights.
- Requisitioning any public record or copy thereof from any court or office.

In this way, National Human Rights Commission is responsible for the protection and promotion of human rights defined by the Act as "rights relating to life, liberty, equality and dignity of the individual guaranteed by the Constitution or embodied in the international covenants".

When any individual or institution finds that there is violation of human rights in its case, then a petition can be made directly to the commission in this concern by him / her or any NGO. After receiving such petition, NHRC is required to investigate the violation of human rights or the failures of the state or other to prevent a human rights violation.

The commission can visit state institutions and other places to examine the condition prevalent there for inquiring about the violation of human rights. It can also examine any law or constitutional provision, for ensuring the safeguards of human rights besides creating awareness among the people about their rights as human beings.

Role and Contribution of Child Helplines

Child helplines can play an effective role in safeguarding Child Rights especially in terms of their protection from child abuse and accidents and incidences of life.

What is a Child Helpline?

A child helpline is an emergency phone service responded by a friendly 'didi' or a sympathetic 'bhaiya' for helping the vulnerable children 24 hours of the day, 365 days of the year. It aims to respond to calls from children (or a concerned peer or adult) in distress offering immediate assistance and linking them to long term rehabilitation.

Child helplines exists as a uniform toll free number in a country. In our country it exists in the name of Childline 1098 Service. Immediate help is available to the child in distress by dialling this toll free number 1098 from any place in the country. The helpline known as Childline 1098 in our country works as a 24-hour free emergency phone outreach service for children in need of care and protection. It is supported by the ministry of Women and Child Development, Government of India, and run through the cooperation received from various sectors like Department of Telecommunication, Street and Community Youth, NGOs, academic institutions, the corporate sector, police system, health care, judiciary, transport, labour, media, elected representatives, individuals concerned and all of us. Some NGOs are providing quite commendable services on the account. For example, Childline India Foundation is providing toll free 1098 telephone service to children in distress. Its head office is in Worli, Mumbai and regional offices are in New Delhi, Kolkata and Chennai.

The Field of its Operation

The child helpline working in our country (1098 Tele Helpline) although stands for the welfare and protection of rights of all children in general, yet its main attention is focussed on helping children in distress, especially the more vulnerable sections, which include:

- Street children and youth living alone on the streets.
- Child labourers working in the unorganised and organised sectors.
- Domestic help, especially girl domestics.
- Children affected by physical / sexual / emotional abuse in family, schools or institutions.
- Children who need emotional support and guidance.
- Children of commercial sex workers.
- Child victims of the flesh trade.
- Victims of child trafficking.
- Children abandoned by parents or guardians.
- Missing children.
- Run away children.
- Children who are victims of substance abuse.
- Differently abled children.
- Children in conflict with the law.
- Children in institutions.
- Mentally challenged children.
- HIV / AIDS infected children.

- Children affected by conflict and disaster.
- Child political refugees.
- Children whose families are in crises.

Objectives Served by the Child Helpline

- To reach out to every child in need of care and protection by responding to emergencies on 1098.
- Creating awareness about Childline 1098 amongst every Indian child.
- To provide a platform of networking amongst organisations and to provide linkages to support systems that facilitate the rehabilitation of children in need of care and protection.
- To work together with the Allied Systems (Police, Health Care, Juvenile Justice, Transport, Legal, Education, Communication, Media, Political and the Community) to create child-friendly systems.
- To advocate services for children that are inaccessible or non- existent.
- To create a body of NGOs and Government organisations working within the national framework and policy for children.
- To be a nodal child protection agency in the country, providing child protection services to children in need of care and protection.
- To contribute and work towards strengthening and participating in a global movement that addresses issues related to child protection and ensures that children's voices are heard.

Functioning of a Child Helpline

A child helpline network may be found to be functioning in the following ways:

1. A call is received on the helpline toll free number 1098 at the help centre established for the purpose.
2. The staff working at the centre may respond in the following two ways:
   (i) It provides needed guidance and institutions for helping the child or well wishers of the child (who has dialled 1098) for coming out from his / her problem.
   (ii) It directs the call for the required intervention to the local intervention unit working in the neighbourhood of the child in distress.
3. The neighbourhood intervention unit then may get engaged in the help rendering tasks depending upon the nature of the emerging or distress reported through call which may be as follows:
   - Filing FIR and take the help of police personal if needed.
   - Providing immediate assistance in the form of food and water, medicines and doctors, temporary shelters, clothes and transport, etc.
   - Taking the help of experts and specialists for deciding what actions or help should be rendered to the child in distress.

- Linking the child in distress for getting benefit from the help and services of counsellors, health personnel and medical help centres, shelter homes, legal advisors and other individuals / institutions for providing help and assistance to come out from the period of his or her distress.

Role and Contribution of NGOs

What are NGOs?

Non-government organisations (NGOs) are organisations that are created by the community people for operating independently and differently from governmental organisations for rendering help and assistance to needy people and performing other works related to the service to humanity. These are essentially not a part of the government. In cases in which NGOs are totally or partially funded by governments, they maintain their non-governmental status by excluding government representatives from membership in the body of organisation or administration. NGOs are referred to as not-for-profit bodies, which means they do not have any commercial interest. NGOs are run on donations made by individuals, corporate houses and institutions. They engage in fundraising activities to raise money for carrying out the work they do. Ever since the time of providing a framework of goals for the vital activities of NGOs by the UN convention on the Rights of the Child (CRC), NGOs have played a crucial role in protection of Human Rights including the Child Rights in the developed and developing countries of the world.

The convention on the Rights of the Child (CRC) has issued guidelines for the NGOs to work on two lines simultaneously:

- To remind government of their obligation through approach to ministries, elected officials and media, and
- To undertake their own operational efforts.

Non-Governmental Organisations Operating at the International Level

Globally, NGOs are playing a significant role in championing the cause of Human Rights including the protection of Child Rights. For coordinating the functioning and operation of NGOs worldwide, there has been an attempt to establish a coordinating agency in the name of the NGO Group. It is a global network of a number of national and international NGOs committed to ensuring that all children fully enjoy their rights as defined by Convention on the Rights of the Child. The NGO Group provides a coordinated platform for NGO action and plays a central role in key child rights developments at the international level. The NGO Group works through its secretariat and thematic working groups to fulfil its mission to facilitate the promotion, implementation and monitoring of the Convention on the Rights of the Child (CRC).

Practically in a global scenario, there are a number of NGOs working on the international level for carrying out the mission of NGO Group of helping in the task of children's right protection. A few of these NGOs operating at the international level are as follows:

Amnesty International

Amnesty International is a worldwide movement of people who campaign for internationally recognised human rights for all. With more than seven million members and subscribers in more than 150 countries, they conduct research and generate action to prevent and end grave abuses of human rights and to demand justice for those whose rights have been violated. It has its headquarters in London, United Kingdom with the motto "It is better to light a candle than to curse the darkness". In India, it has its regional office in Bangaluru (Karnataka).

Children's Defense Fund

The Children's Defense Fund (CDF) is a child advocacy organisation that works to ensure a level playing field for all children. CDF champions policies and programs that lift children out of poverty, protects them from abuse and neglect, and ensures their right to equal care and education. Its headquarters are in Washington, D.C., USA.

Human Rights Action Center

The Human Rights Action Center is a non-profit organisation based in Washington, DC, headed by Jack Healey, world-renowned human rights activist and pioneer. The Center works on issues of the Universal Declaration of Human Rights and uses the arts and technologies to innovate, create and develop new strategies to stop human rights abuses. They also support growing human rights groups all over the world.

Human Rights Watch

Human Rights Watch is dedicated to protecting the human rights of people around the world. They investigate and expose human rights violations, hold abusers accountable and challenge governments and those who hold power to end abusive practices and respect international human rights. It has its headquarters in New York, USA.

Human Rights Without Frontiers

Human Rights Without Frontiers (HRWF) focuses on monitoring, research and analysis in the field of human rights, as well as promotion of democracy and the rule of law on a national and international level. It has its headquarters in Etterbeck, Belgium and is affiliated with European Union Agency for Fundamental Rights.

Non-Governmental Organisations Working at the National Level

There are a number of NGOs working in our country for the protection of human rights including child rights. The significant ones, in this regard are as follows:

1. *Sammaan Foundation* (established January 25, 2007): Originally established to link the poor to the mainstream through education, training and financial support, the current project of this NGO involves rickshaw pullers to help them earn a better livelihood. This NGO also has notable contribution in areas like children education, health services and welfare of women.

2. *Goonj:* A recipient of the "NGO of the Year" award in 2007 at the India NGO Awards, this NGO aims at solving the clothing problems of the downtrodden. Goonj also provided relief under the Rahat Floods Campaign during the devastating floods in West Bengal, Assam and Bihar.

3. *Akshaya Trust:* The sole aim of this NGO is to restore human dignity. Operating in Madurai., this NGO offers rehabilitation, healthy food and care to the street destitute.

4. *Smile Foundation:* The main aim of this NGO is the rehabilitation of the underprivileged by providing them education and healthcare services, thereby converting them into productive assets. It is run by a group of corporate professionals.

5. *Udaan Welfare Foundation:* The main aim of this NGO is to help the destitute, the main area of stress being women, children and senior citizens and also environmental welfare. One of their main projects is a cancer chemotherapy centre.

6. *Pratham:* The main aim of this NGO is to provide education to children living in huge slums of Mumbai and even providing education to those people who are unable to go to school. Their projects have increased enrolment of children in schools thus promising them a better tomorrow.

7. *Lepra Society:* This NGO aims at prevention and control of diseases like AIDS, leprosy and tuberculosis in poor communities.

8. *Deepalaya:* This NGO aims at providing education to children living in the slums of Delhi. Their projects also include providing healthcare, education, vocational training to the downtrodden and the physically disabled. They have contributed towards significant rural development in Haryana and Uttarakhand.

9. *Uday Foundation:* A New Delhi-based NGO, the Uday Foundation provides support to the parents and families of children suffering from congenital disorders and other syndromes. Their projects also include research to open new horizons of healthcare technologies. They also have health projects for common people. Their special stress is in the area of protecting child rights.

10. *Helpage India:* Established in 1978, the sole aim of this NGO is to provide resources to the elderly people of our country. Their objective is to make the senior citizens aware of their rights and to also protect the rights of the senior citizens of our country so that they can also play a key role in our society. They also work with the government (both local and national level) to implement policies that will be beneficial to the senior citizens of the country.

Summary

The term 'Child Rights' stands for the rights prescribed and laid down for the protection and welfare of the children on a global basis by world authorities like UNO and UNICEF. The enforcement of these rights, i.e., helping children to avail the privileges of these rights is a big challenge. Various organisations and agencies are working on a global, regional, national and local basis for meeting this challenge.

United Nations International Children Emergency Fund (UNICEF), an important Global Agency is known to be working with the mission of helping the world realise the rights of the children. It has been mandated by the United Nations General Assembly "to advocate for the protection of children's rights, to help meet their basic needs, and to expand their opportunities to reach their full potential". In its active assistance and working (in the form of financial and technical support) UNICEF is providing its multi dimensional services for the protection of all the prescribed rights to every child, classified as: (i) Right to Survival, (ii) Right to Protection, (iii) Right to Participation and (iv) Right to Development to the children of the countries of the world. In this connection, while assisting in the programs for the maintenance of health and caring for the education of the children, the UNICEF is assisting in the creation of needed protective environments to help prevent and respond to violence, exploitation abuse and discrimination, and for children made vulnerable by emergencies like separation of parents, survivors of child abuse and loss of parents in armed conflicts, etc.

World Health Organization (WHO) is a specialised agency of United Nations (UN), working in the field of health. Although it is true that its main work is rendering help and assistance in improving health of the children, yet it is playing its wonderful role in ensuring a maximum number of things related to protection of Human and Child Rights simply for the reason that one's health is a basic parameter for helping one to attain maximum help in his or her development and welfare. It is in this connection that we may have found WHO to get engaged in the activities in collaboration with governments of the member states related to the protection of a child's right to life, survival, maximum development, access to health and access to health services in a quite standardised form.

The National Commission for Protection of Child Rights (NCPCR) is a statutory body working under the administrative control of the Ministry of Women and Child Development, Government of India. It has been given a bigger responsibility of ensuring that all laws, policies, programs and administrative mechanisms are in consonance with the Child Rights perspective as enshrined in the Constitution of India and also the UN convention on the Rights of the Child.

The National Human Rights Commission (NHRC) is an autonomous statutory body established in 1993 according to the provisions of the Protection of Human Rights Act, passed by the Parliament of India. It is responsible for the protection and promotion of human rights in the country. Since, the protection of the rights of human being automatically involves the protection of the child rights, thereby NRHC may be found to play a quite substantial role in the protection of Child Rights in India. In its procedural functioning, when any individual or institution finds that there is violation of human rights (including the child rights) in its case, then a petition can be made directly to the commission in this concern by him / her or any NGO. After receiving such petition, NHRC is required to investigate and take suitable steps against the violation of rights or the failures of the state or others to prevent the rights violation.

Child helplines can play an effective role in safeguarding the Child Rights especially in terms of their protection from child abuse and accidents and incidences of life.

These helplines exist in the shape of a toll free emergency phone service responded by a friendly 'didi' or a sympathetic 'bhaiya' every time everywhere. It aims to respond to calls from children (or a concerned peer or adult) in distress offering immediate assistance and linking them to long term rehabilitation. In our country it exists in the name of Child line 1098 Service. It is supported by the ministry of Women and Child Development, Government of India, and run through the cooperation received from various government departments and private sectors.

Non-Government organisations (NGOs) working on the national and international levels can play a substantial role in championing the cause of Human Rights including the protection of Child Rights. These NGOs are almost seen to carry out two main functions namely, to remind government of their obligation and to undertake their own operational efforts in the areas and activities related to the protection of human and child rights. Some of the renowned NGOs working on the international levels are (i) Amnesty International (headquarters in London), (ii) Children's Defense Fund (headquarters in Washington), (iii) Human Rights Action Center (headquarters in Washington, (iv) Human Rights Watch (headquarters in New York), (v) Human Rights Without Frontiers (Headquarters in Belgium). In our country also a number of NGOs are functioning for this purpose in various parts of the country. The mentionable ones are (i) Sammaan Foundation, (ii) Goonj, (iii) Akshaya Trust, (iv) Smile Foundation, (v) Pratham, (vi) Deepalaya and (vii) Uday Foundation, etc.

References and Suggested Readings

Amnesty International, *Children's Rights*, http:www.amnetyyura.org/ou_Issues/Children/page, Retrieved on 2/23/17.

Franklin, B. (2001) *The new handbook of children's rights: comparative policy and practice,* London: Routledge

Lansdown, G. (1994). «Children›s rights,» in B. Mayall (ed.) *Children's childhood: Observed and experienced.* London: The Falmer Press.

UNICEF, *Convention on the Rights of the Child,* http:www.unicef.org/crc, Retrieved on 4/3/17.

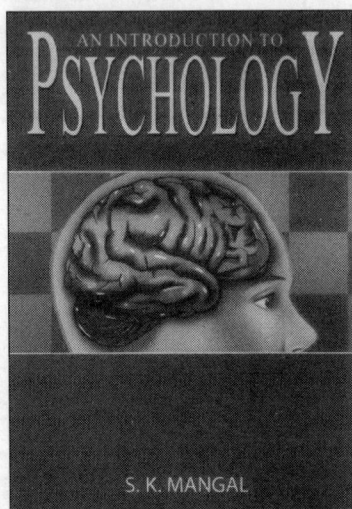